THE COMPLETE ILLUSTRATED HISTORY OF THE
INCA EMPIRE

THE COMPLETE ILLUSTRATED HISTORY OF THE
INCA EMPIRE

**A COMPREHENSIVE ENCYCLOPEDIA OF THE INCAS AND OTHER ANCIENT
PEOPLES OF SOUTH AMERICA WITH MORE THAN 1000 PHOTOGRAPHS**

DR DAVID M JONES

LORENZ BOOKS

CONTENTS

THE ANCIENT INCAS

When Francisco Pizarro and the Spanish conquistadors arrived in the Andes in 1532 they found a civilization of great sophistication and wealth. Well-planned cities with storehouses and complex ceremonial architecture, irrigated lands and an established system of agriculture, transport and communication routes, and an organized, hierarchical society were all signs of an intelligent and civilized people. Starting from the Cuzco Valley, the Incas had gradually expanded their power to form an empire, conquering and integrating land and settlements from the coastal plains inland to the rainforest. From its early roots it had developed from small farming villages to large cities with sophisticated forms of organization.

Below: A Middle Horizon bridge-spout effigy vessel from Tiwanaku with distinctive jaguar coat. Jaguars were revered by sierra cultures.

Yet despite these momentous achievements, the Incas' reign lasted less than 100 years. To understand how the Incas rose from around 40,000 people to form the largest empire in South America, we need to understand the land they lived in, their way of life, their conquests and spread of influence and, perhaps more than anything else, their religion and myths, for these lay behind so many aspects of Inca life and influenced everything from agriculture to temple building.

ANDEAN CIVILIZATION

South America comprises many dramatically different geological areas. From high Altiplanos to low coastal valleys, from lush, dense rainforest to dry, barren deserts, each landscape offers different rewards and challenges and shapes the lifestyles of its inhabitants. Such differences, and the geographical isolation of many settlements, led to different peoples in South America developing at different paces. At the same time, however, cultures in various large areas were aware of each other, and they developed links through trade, political alliance, conquest and the diffusion of ideas through direct or indirect contact.

Ancient South American cultures that can be described as 'civilizations' were confined to the Andes mountains and nearby western coastal valleys and deserts. Elsewhere, South American peoples did develop quite sophisticated societies and beliefs.

Above: Descending the Inca Trail from the Second Pass, the walker approaches the ridge-top ruins of the Sayaqmarka compound.

However, they did not build monumental ceremonial centres or cities, or develop technology of quite the same level of complexity as the Andean kingdoms and empires, and are therefore not defined as 'civilizations'.

This book concentrates on the 'Andean Area', where civilizations evolved in the sierras and adjacent foothills and coastal regions, north to south from the Colombian–Ecuadorian border to the northern half of Chile and east to west from the Amazonian Rainforest to the Pacific coast. City-states, kingdoms and empires evolved in this area, based on maize and potato agriculture and the herding of llamas, alpacas and vicuñas. The concentration of civilization in the Andean Area was due in part to the geography of the region. Within a relatively small area there is a range of contrasting landscapes, from Pacific ocean-bound coastal plains and deserts, to coastal and foothill valleys, to high mountain valleys and plateaus, to the eastern slopes running down to the edges of the rainforests and high pampas of Argentina.

A key factor in the development and endurance of these civilizations was access to and control of water, which became

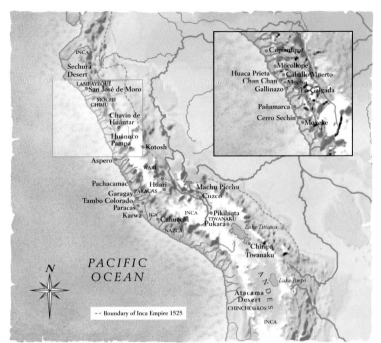

important not only functionally but also symbolically and religiously. Water was essential for agriculture, and people in naturally dry regions developed a sophisticated form of agriculture based on complex irrigation technologies, often combined with land terracing. As a result, a wide variety of crops was grown in both lowland and highland regions, which led to the development of trade between the two. The development of agriculture and trade led to different cultures specializing in different products – and not only essentials such as food but increasingly non-essential items such as ceramics and items with religious significance. As a result, these cultures developed into complex and orderly societies with sophisticated religious beliefs and structures. Thus empires are born.

SOURCES OF INFORMATION
Our knowledge of the Incas (and other South American peoples) comes from a variety of sources: from the Inca record-keepers themselves (both the *amautas* and

Below: Reed fishing boats and huts on Lake Titicaca, between Peru and Bolivia. Such vessels and materials are still used today.

the *quipucamayoqs*), from contemporary Spanish accounts and from archaeological investigations, both recent and in the past. All give us fascinating insights into a rich and colourful civilization with legendary rulers, a civil war, sacred places, mystical lines and images in the desert, imposing temples and evocative symbols, and a literal belief that the Incas will one day return to power.

REMAINS OF EMPIRES
The buildings constructed by the cult of Chávin de Huántar in the Early Horizon, the Wari and Tiwanaku empires in the Middle Horizon and the Incas in the Late Horizon can be seen and marvelled at today, along with other remains from the Andean Area. Such remains help us to understand the architectural and engineering skills of the various peoples, their social organization, their main forms of occupation and trade, and their religions.
    Chávin de Huántar was a pilgrimage centre, established *c*.900BC as a U-shaped centre (others include La Galgada and Sechín Alto, both built in the Preceramic Period). Its remains show a labyrinth of passages and galleries.

Above: General map of the Inca Empire and important sites, showing how the empire stretched the length of the Andes Mountains.

Other fantastic pre-Inca sites are the Gateway of the Sun at the Tiwanaku Akapana Temple; the Paracas Cavernas cemetery, known for its desiccated mummies; the Moche centre of Cerro Blanco, where two large ceremonial platforms – the Huacas del Sol and de la Luna – were built; and the Late Intermediate Period Chimú city of Chan Chan, which comprised a complex of compounds (*ciudadelas*) containing residences for the reigning king and earlier deceased kings.
    Famous remains from the Incas themselves include the city of Cuzco, the 'navel of the world', rebuilt in the plan of a crouching puma, and site of the Coricancha Temple; Huánuco Pampa, a seat of provincial admininstration; and the dramatically sited hilltop sacred city of Machu Picchu, a massive landmark on the Inca Trail. In addition, Inca engineers constructed an impressive array of roads and bridges, as well as enabling land to be developed for farming through the construction of terraces and irrigation canals.

PART ONE

CHRONICLE OF THE ANCIENT ANDES

The popular view of the Incas and other ancient peoples of South America is that theirs was a lurid story of bloodthirsty gods, terrifying rituals, human sacrifice and the lust for gold. It was in fact a rich and fascinating world, which saw the rise and fall of many cultures – the Moche, the Chimú, the Nazca and others. This history reveals the truth about the Inca sun kings, rulers of one of the largest-ever empires, and the countless other tribes and peoples of Peru and the Andes. It traces the development of the small city-state that eventually became the Inca empire of the sun, its marvellous expansion under the first great Inca leader, Pachacuti Inca Yupanqui, and the changes brought about by the Spanish conquest.

Above: Three views of a clay figurine from Huaca de los Idolos.
Left: Machu Picchu, high in the Andes mountains.

INTRODUCTION

The legends and myths of the Andean peoples, together with the remains found by archaeologists, constitute a record of ancient Andean religious belief.

Religious beliefs and deities were intimately linked with the forces of nature. Ancient South American peoples felt compelled to explain the important things in their universe, beginning with where they came from and their place in the larger scheme of things. To do this they developed accounts of what they could see in the sky and in the surrounding landscape to help them understand which things were important, and how and why this was so. Thus, the Inca god Inti belonged to the life-giving force of the sun, and Lake Titicaca, the most sacred of waters, was seen as the origin of life.

The explanatory accounts of these concepts provided a framework for living and for understanding and relating to the mysteries of the world.

COMMON BELIEFS AND IMAGERY

There were long sequences of traditional development among Andean and western coastal peoples and cultures, helped by trading and social relationships between the two. Many deities were almost universal, although given different names by different cultures, but some were individual and distinct, belonging to particular peoples and civilizations.

Left: Gold hammered sheet-metal sun figure from Tiwanaku. The rayed head is reminiscent of the Gateway of the Sun.

Above: Cotton-embroidered textile from the Early Horizon Paracas culture, with a figure reminiscent of the Chavin Staff Deity.

Nevertheless, long-standing places of ritual pilgrimage linked areas and regions and persisted despite the rise and fall of kingdoms and empires. The site and oracle of coastal Pachacamac, for example, had such potency and precedence that even the Incas recognized and revered it, although they felt compelled to establish their imperial authority by building a temple to the sun god Inti in its shadow.

Common threads run through the mythologies of Andean Area civilization and its cultures. Today's modern division of religion and politics was unknown then, at a time when the entire basis of political power was derived from divine development and designation. In Inca society, and probably in Chimú and Moche and other cultures before them, rulers and priests were often one and the same. The Inca ruler himself was regarded as the living divine representative of Inti. Although each had specific roles, rulers and priests were intimately entwined in ruling and regulating every aspect of daily life. Ruler worship was carried beyond death through continuing ritual with the mummies of past Incas.

The landscape itself was considered sacred. Numerous natural features were regarded as semi-divine; ceremonial centres were constructed to represent myth; and ritual pathways were made across long distances, such as Nazca geoglyphic or Inca *ceque* routes.

There were many common religious elements among ancient Andean cultures, some of them almost universal, some more regional. In most regions, for example, there was a named creator god. During the later stages of Andean civilization – the Late Intermediate Period and Late Horizon – Viracocha, with many variations, was the creator god, especially among the sierra cultures and many coastal cultures. Along the central and southern Peruvian coast there was also a certain confusion and/or rivalry with the supreme god Pachacamac.

Religious imagery throughout the Andean Area was profoundly influenced from the earliest times by rainforest animals (jaguars, serpents and other reptiles, monkeys, birds) and included composite humanoid beings. In particular, both Andean civilizations and Amazonian cultures share a fascination with the power and influence of jaguars and other large felines, such as pumas. Among symbolic motifs that persisted through the different cultures of the Andean Area, in addition to the jaguar, were feline-

Left: Nazca geoglyph forming a monkey in the desert of southern Peru. Such animals figure frequently in desert coastal cultures.

human hybrids, staff deities (often with a composite feline face and human body), winged beings, and falcon- or other bird-headed warriors.

ANDEAN THEMES

Several common themes pervade Andean Area religion. As well as the creator Viracocha, almost all ritual had a calendrical organization. There was a calendar based on the movements of heavenly bodies. Consultation of auguries was considered vital at momentous times of the year, including planting, the harvest and the start of the ocean fishing season.

Sacrifice, both human and animal, and a variety of offerings were other common practices. An important ancient theme was the assignment of sacredness to special places, called *huacas*, which could be either natural or man-made. Another widespread trait was the use of hallucinogenic and other drugs, especially coca and the buds of several cacti, in rituals connected to war and sacrifice. Yet another common practice was ancestor reverence and worship, charged with its own special ritual and governed by the cyclical calendar. The mummified remains of ancestors were kept carefully, and brought out on ritual occasions.

It is this diversity, imaginative invention and richness of expression and depiction, as well as its 'alien' appeal – at least to Western readers – that makes the religion/mythology of Andean civilization so fascinating.

Below: Chinchorros mummies, c.5000BC, in the Atacama Desert are the world's earliest known deliberate mummifications.

CHRONOLOGY OF ANDEAN AREA CIVILIZATION

The chronology of the Andean Area is complex. Archaeologists have developed a scheme based on technological achievements and on changing political organization through time, from the first arrival of humans in the area (15,000–3500BC) to the conquest of the Inca Empire by Francisco Pizarro in 1532. The pace of technological development varied in different regions within the Andean Area, especially during early periods in its history. The development of lasting and strong contact between regions, however,

Below: A wooden cup painted with an Inca warrior with shield and axe-spear.

spread both technology and ideas, and led to regions depending on each other to some degree. Sometimes this interdependence was due to large areas being under the control of one 'authority', while at other times the unifying link was religious or based on trade and technology.

The principal chronological scheme for the Andean Area comprises a sequence of eight time units: five Periods and three Horizons. Periods are defined as times when political unity across regions was less consolidated. Smaller areas were controlled by city-states, sometimes in loose groupings, perhaps sharing religious beliefs despite having different political organizations. The Horizons, by contrast, were times when much larger political units were formed. These units exercised political, economic and religious control over extended areas, usually including different types of terrain, rather than being confined to coastal valley groups or sierra city-states.

Different scholars give various dates for the beginnings and endings of the Periods and Horizons, and no two books on Andean civilization give exactly the same dates. The durations of Periods and

Above: The sacred Intihuatana (Hitching Post of the Sun) at Machu Picchu.

Horizons also vary from one region to another within the Andean Area, and charts increase in complexity as authors divide the Andean Area into coastal, sierra and Altiplano regions, or even into north, central and southern coastal regions and north, central and southern highland regions. The dates given here are a compilation from several sources, thus avoiding any anomalies among specific sources.

CHRONOLOGICAL PERIOD	DATES	PRINCIPAL CULTURES
Lithic / Archaic Period	15,000–3500BC	spread of peoples into the Andean Area hunter-gatherer cultures
Preceramic / Formative Period (Cotton Preceramic)	3500–1800BC	early agriculture and first ceremonial centres
Initial Period	1800–750BC	U-shaped ceremonial centres, platform mounds and sunken courts
Early Horizon	750–200BC	Chavín, Paracas, Pukará (Yaya-Mama) cults
Early Intermediate Period	200BC–AD600	Moche, Nazca and Titicaca Basin confederacies
Middle Horizon	AD600–1000	Wari and Tiwanaku empires
Late Intermediate Period	AD1000–1400	Chimú and Inca empires
Late Horizon	AD1400–1532	Inca Empire and Spanish Conquest

LITHIC / ARCHAIC PERIOD (40,000–3500 BC)

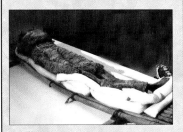

Above: This mummified body from the Chinchorros culture is 8,000 years old.

c.40,000 to c.20,000 years ago Ice-free corridors open up across the Bering Strait, but there is no evidence humans entered the New World until the late stages of this time period.

c.20,000 BC Migrating hunter-gatherers, using stone-, bone-, wood- and shell-tool technologies, probably enter the New World from north-east Asia.

from c.15,000 years ago Palaeoindians migrate south and east to populate the Americas, reaching Monte Verde in southern Chile c.14,850 years ago.

c.8500–5000 BC Hunter-gatherers occupy cave and rock shelter sites in the Andes (e.g. Pachamachay, Guitarrero, Tres Ventana and Toquepala caves). Evidence of tending of hemp-like fibre, medicinal plants, herbs and wild tubers.

c.5000 BC First mummified burials in the Atacama Desert, Chinchorros culture.

Below: Mountains high in the Andes proved a challenge to early settlers.

PRECERAMIC / FORMATIVE PERIOD (3500–1800 BC)

Above: Preceramic Period sculpture at the Temple of the Crossed Hands, Kotosh.

This period is sometimes also called the Cotton Preceramic.

c.3500–1800 BC True plant domestication accomplished – cotton, squashes and gourds, beans, maize, potatoes, sweet potatoes, beans, chilli peppers. Llamas and other camelids herded on the Altiplano.

c.3000 BC Coastal fishing villages such as Huaca Prieta flourish, using gourd containers but no ceramics, and produce early cotton textiles.

c.2800 BC Early northern coastal civic-ceremonial centres begin at Aspero – Huaca de los Idolos and Huaca de los Sacrificios.

c.2400–2000 BC Large, raised mound platforms are constructed at El Paraíso, La Galagada and Kotosh – Temple of the Crossed Hands. Spread of the Kotosh religious cult.

Below: Llamas and other camelids were first domesticated during this period.

INITIAL PERIOD (1800–750 BC)

Above: View of the Colca Canyon shows terracing that began in this period.

Spread of pottery, irrigation agriculture, monumental architecture; religious processions and ritual decapitation begin.

from c.1800 BC Sophisticated irrigation systems develop in coastal oases valleys, the highlands and Altiplano.

c.1800 BC Construction at Moxeke includes colossal adobe heads.

c.1750 BC Builders at La Florida bring the first pottery to this region.

c.1500 BC Cerro Sechín flourishes.

c.1400–1200 BC Sechín Alto becomes the largest U-shaped civic-ceremonial centre in the New World.

c.1300 BC Construction of the five platform mounds at Cardál.

c.900 BC U-shaped ceremonial complex at Chavín de Huántar begins.

Below: Garagay, central Peru, was a typical coastal U-shaped civic-ceremonial centre.

EARLY HORIZON (750–200BC)

Above: A stone severed head, with feline canines, from Chavín de Huántar.

Religious cults develop around Chavín de Huántar and Pukará. Decapitation, hallucinogenic drug use, spiritual trans-formation and ancestor worship become widespread.

from *c.*750BC The Old Temple at Chavín becomes established as a cult centre. Influence of the Lanzón deity and the Staff Deity spreads. The Paracas Peninsula serves as the necropolis site for several settlements, and the Oculate Being is shown on textiles and ceramics.

*c.*400–200BC The Old Temple at Chavín is enlarged to create the New Temple. The Chavín Cult spreads, especially at Kuntur Wasi and Karwa (Paracas).

*c.*400BC Rainfall fell in the Titicaca Basin. Pukará, northwest of the lake, is established, and becomes the centre of the Yaya-Mama cult.

*c.*200BC Chavín Cult influence waned.

Below: Vicuñas at Viscachani, now in Bolivia, were prized for their fine wool.

EARLY INTERMEDIATE PERIOD (200BC–AD600)

Above: The closely set stone blocks of the external walls of Sacsahuaman, Cusco.

The cohesion of Chavín disintegrates, and several regional chiefdoms develop in the coastal and mountain valleys.

from *c.*100BC Rise of the Nazca .

*c.*AD100 Burial of the Old Lord of Sipán in Lambayeque Valley.

*c.*AD100 to 500 The Nazca sacred cer-emonial centre of Cahuachi flourishes.

*c.*1st century AD The Moche dynasty is founded in the northern coastal valleys.

*c.*AD250 Rise of oracle of Pachacamac.

*c.*AD300 Burial of the Lord of Sipán in Lambayeque Valley.

*c.*AD500 The Moche ceremonial platforms of the Huacas del Sol and de la Luna are the largest in the area.

*c.*AD700 Moche/Nazca power wanes.

Below: This giant Nazca desert geoglyph of the spider is visible from space.

MIDDLE HORIZON (AD600–1000)

Above: The Staff Deity depicted on the Gateway of the Sun at Tiwanaku.

Much of the Andean Area is unified in two empires: Tiwanaku in the south and Wari in the north. They share common beliefs around the creator god Viracocha.

*c.*AD300 Major construction of the central ceremonial plaza at Tiwanaku begins.

*c.*AD400–750 Major phases of building of elite residential quarters at Tiwanaku.

*c.*AD500 The rise of Huari, capital of the Wari Empire.

by *c.*AD600 Huari is a flourishing capital city and rival to Tiwanaku.

*c.*AD650 Pikillacta, the southernmost Wari city, is founded.

*c.*AD750–1000 Third major phase of palace building at Tiwanaku.

*c.*AD900–950 Burial of the Sicán Lords at Lambayeque.

Below: The reed boats on Lake Titicaca have been made for thousands of years.

LATE INTERMEDIATE PERIOD
(AD1000–1400)

Above: The Late Intermediate Period Sicán Tucume pyramid, Lambayeque Valley.

An era of political break up is characterized by new city-states, including Lambayeque, Chimú and Pachacamac, the Colla and Lupaka kingdoms, and numerous city-states in the central and southern Andean valleys.

*c.*AD1000 Tiwannaku and Wari empires wane as regional political rivalry reasserts itself.

*c.*AD1000 Wari city-state is abandoned.

*c.*AD1000 Chan Chan, the Chimú capital, is founded in the Moche valley.

*c.*1100 The Incas under Manco Capac, migrate into the Cuzco Valley, found Cuzco and establish the Inca dynasty.

*c.*1250 City of Tiwanaku abandoned, perhaps because of changes in climate.

*c.*1300 Sinchi Roca becomes the first emperor to use the title Sapa Inca.

Below: The city of Cuzco was founded by Manco Capac, its legendary first ruler.

LATE HORIZON
(AD1400–1532)

Above: The Inca hillside site of Winay Wayna overlooks the Urubamba River.

In just over 130 years the Incas build a huge empire and establish an imperial cult centred on Inti, the sun god, whose representative on earth is the Sapa Inca.

*c.*1425 Viracocha begins the Inca conquest of the Cuzco Valley.

1438 Pachacuti Inca Yupanqui defeats the Chancas to dominate the Cuzco Valley.

1438–71 Pachacuti begins the rebuilding of Cuzco as the imperial capital to the plan of a crouching puma.

1471 Fall of the Kingdom of Chimú.

1471–93 Inca Tupac Yupanqui expands the empire west and south, doubling its size.

1493–1526 Huayna Capac consolidates the empire, building fortresses, road systems, storage redistribution and religious precincts throughout the provinces.

Below: The Spaniards built S Domingo on the foundations of the Inca Coricancha.

Above: Manco Capac, legendary founder of the Inca dynasty and 'son of the sun'.

1526 Huayna Capac dies of smallpox without an agreed successor.

1526–32 Huayna Capac's son Huáscar seizes the throne but is challenged by his brother Atahualpa. A six-year civil war ends in the capture of Huáscar.

1530 Inca Empire at its greatest extent.

1532 Francisco Pizarro lands with a small army on the north coast and marches to meet Atahualpa at Cajamarca.

1532 Battle of Cajamarca and capture of Atahualpa, who is held for ransom.

1533 Atahualpa is executed.

1535 Francisco Pizarro founds Lima as his capital in Spanish Peru.

1541 Pizarro assassinated in his palace at Lima by Almagro and his associates.

Below: The sacred site of Machu Picchu was rediscovered by Hiram Bingham in 1911.

DISCOVERING THE INCAS

Unlike many other ancient civilizations worldwide, none of the Andean peoples invented an alphabet or any other form of writing. As a result, the first accounts of any ancient Andean culture or history were written down by Spanish conquistadors, then later by 16th- and 17th-century Spanish chroniclers. These include the *Nueva Crónica y Buen Gobierno* by Felipe Guamnan de Ayala and the *Relación de Antiguedades deste Reyno del Pirú* by Juan de Santacruz Yamqui Salcamaygua.

The conquistadors related what they observed on discovering the Incas, while later chroniclers recorded accounts of the empire, its people and culture. They used two sources of information for their records: *quipucamayoqs* and *amautas*. The *quipucamayoqs* were people who devised the 'writing' system of knots known as *quipus*, which involved coloured cords tied into bundles with knots, while the second, or *amautas*, were court historians responsible for learning and relating details of their culture. Interpreting these accounts was not aided by the fact that many hundreds of languages and dialects existed at that time, although one language, Quechua, dominated.

During the 19th century, more was learned about Inca and pre-Inca civilizations from the studies and collections carried out by explorers and naturalists in the earliest excavations. Further additions to our knowledge come from the results and interpretations of 20th- and 21st-century archaeological discoveries, including that of the Inca sacred city of Machu Picchu.

Left: Shadows and light on the walls of the Sacsahuaman temple mimic the lighting on the sacred landscape that lies behind it.

THE SPANISH EXPLORATIONS

Europeans first discovered the New World ('Vinland') as early as AD986, although at that time they were unaware of the vastness of its lands. However, the settlement made there was all but forgotten by Europeans by the time Christopher Columbus and others began to explore across the Atlantic in the late 15th and early 16th centuries.

THE ARRIVAL OF THE SPANISH
After explorations from Hispaniola (modern Haiti and the Dominican Republic), during 1504–9, Spaniards established the first permanent occupation of Tierra Firme (the South American mainland) in Panama in 1509. From the isthmus, Francisco Pizarro and others explored and eventually conquered the vast Inca Empire of the Andes in 1533.

Their descriptions of the peoples and cultures they found formed the opinions of Europeans towards the new worlds they had 'discovered', and enhanced convictions already formed about the natives

Below: Atahualpa, the last Inca emperor, was engaged in a bitter civil war when Pizarro landed on the northern coast of the empire.

of the Caribbean islands. When Pizarro led his first expedition to Tierra Firme in 1524, the Aztec Empire had already been conquered by Hernán Cortés. (The reality that Columbus had not reached China but had found an unsuspected and unknown New World had become common knowledge.) Spaniards were sure that other vast empires and rich cities were there for the taking, and set out to conquer and exploit the wealth of these places for their own glory and enrichment.

With their belief that they were a superior race with a righteous duty to convert the 'heathens' they found to Christianity, to rule them and to exploit them, few Spaniards had any desire to engage with these civilizations.

A MAN WITH AMBITIONS
Pizarro made three expeditions: 1524–5, 1526–7 and 1531–3. In the first he only barely penetrated the coast of Colombia, but in the second he marched farther inland and sent his ship captain, Bartholomew Ruíz, down the coast.

Above: Early 16th-century Spanish caravels were the type of ships used by the explorers and conquistadors.

Pizarro met with a mixed reception but soon began to collect gold and silver objects, and to hear tales of vast cities and riches to the south. Ruíz brought back tales of many sightings of increasing population and civilization, and no apparent hostility or fear. Moreover, he encountered a balsa trading raft well out to sea laden with gold and silver objects, elaborate textiles and two traders from the Inca subject port of Tumbes, whom he brought to Pizarro along with the gold, silver and cloth. From these two men the Spaniards learned of fabulous Inca cities, palaces, llama flocks and endless stores of gold and silver objects.

Sufficient gold and silver was taken back to Spain to whet the appetite of the Spanish crown and to interest enough adventurers to raise funds to send a third expedition, this time into the Andes, with the purpose of conquest and conversion.

The Inca Empire discovered by Pizarro was at its greatest expansion, but had only recently itself conquered the kingdoms and peoples of the northern Andes and coasts of modern Ecuador and central Colombia. Nevertheless, Pizarro's chroniclers describe vast wealth in gold and silver objects, rich textiles, neatly laid-out cities and storehouses full of produce and other goods. There were masonry walls and fortresses of blocks so well fitted together that no mortar was needed, lands with irrigation systems and sophisticated agriculture and herds of 'sheep' (llamas). Balsa rafts traded up and down the coasts, while transport and communication were facilitated by a network of smooth roads and bridges along the coasts, across rivers and into the high mountains.

SMALLPOX AND CIVIL WAR
The Spaniards also found an empire in trouble, partly, although unknowingly, of their own doing. Ironically, smallpox, introduced into mainland America by the

Below: Francisco Pizarro and Diego de Almagro, his ambitious accomplice, as depicted by Guaman Poma de Ayala.

Above: Francisco Pizarro of Trujillo, of Estremadura, Spain (1475–1541), conqueror of the Incas.

Spaniards in their conquest of the Aztecs, spread rapidly south from Mesoamerica, infecting the last conquering Sapa Inca (emperor), Huayna Capac (1493–1526), along with his heir apparent. As he became ill, Huayna Capac received reports from traders from the northern reaches of his empire of bearded strangers who sailed in strange ships. These reports coincided with a series of ill omens, and his priests prophesied evil and disaster when they witnessed the death of an eagle, which fell out of the sky after being mobbed by buzzards, during ceremonies in honour of the sun god Inti.

When Capac died, his son Huáscar seized the throne but was challenged by another son, Atahualpa, who commanded the Inca armies and marched from the northernmost province of Quito. The Inca court split into two supporting factions and civil war raged for six years. At the time of Pizarro's arrival at Tumbes on the coast of Quito province in 1532, Atahualpa's generals had only recently defeated Huáscar's army at the Inca capital, Cuzco, and captured his brother to secure the throne. The disruption caused by the civil war had weakened the Inca Empire's cohesion. As in Cortés' conquest of the Aztecs, Pizarro was able to exploit the ill omens prophesied by the Inca priesthood, which had created misgivings among the Incas.

CHRONICLERS AND INFORMANTS

From the earliest explorations of Tierra Firme, chroniclers among the conquistadors left descriptions of the peoples they encountered. Later, historians in the 16th and 17th centuries wrote accounts of the Inca Empire and its past and descriptions of Inca culture and other peoples. Even so, the lack of a written language among any of the Andean Area civilizations before the Spanish conquest necessitates that these descriptions of Inca history and religion be complemented with archaeological, artistic and architectural images and evidence, particularly for pre-Inca cultures.

KNOT HISTORIES

Although no Andean culture developed a writing system, the recording device known as the *quipu*, a system of tied bundles of string with distinctive knotting and dyed colours, served as an *aide-mémoire* to designated *quipucamay-*

Above: The quipu, *a device of knotted and dyed cotton and wool string, was used by special court officials to keep records.*

Below: Felipe Guaman Poma de Ayala travelling in Peru. He chronicled the conquest of the Inca Empire and Inca life and culture.

oqs (literally 'knot makers'). Many of the first records of Inca culture transcribed by Spanish priests were based on the memories of *quipucamayoqs* and their recitals of Inca accounts and records, religious concepts and beliefs, and history.

For example, in the 1560s and 1570s the Spaniard Sarmiento de Gamboa, who was given the task of recording Inca history by the fourth Viceroy of Peru, Francisco de Toledo, claimed to have interviewed more than 100 *quipucamayoqs*, 42 of whom he actually names.

Colleagues of the *quipucamayoqs* were the *amautas* – officially appointed court philosophers and historians. They were responsible for memorizing, recounting, interpreting, reinterpreting, amplifying, reciting and passing on to successors the legends and history, family trees and special events of the Inca kings and queens. They therefore became another principal source of Inca history, legend, religious belief and social organization, and in this way were invaluable not only to the early Spanish chroniclers but also to colonial officials struggling to implement Spanish administration and to collect produce and

taxes. The *amautas'* detailed knowledge of the Inca *ayllu* (kinship), *mitamaes* (redistributed peoples) and *mit'a* (labour service) helped the Spaniards to take advantage of and adapt a system of obligations that was already in place.

INTERPRETING SOURCES

There was a danger, however, of taking such sources too literally, and of having to cope with the problems of conflicting accounts. Spanish chroniclers' and Catholic priests' transcriptions of the descriptions of Inca history and culture by *quipucamayoqs* and *amautas* were fraught with opportunities for misinterpretation. Deliberately or accidentally omitting some facts, embellishing others, and amending and reinterpreting what they had been told meant events could be retold to suit a particular bias. The resulting conflicting versions could be used to argue a particular legal claim or to justify a particular Spanish action or exploitative practice.

Nevertheless, the descriptions of Inca societies contained in these early records provide an invaluable source of information on Inca culture that can help make sense of archaeological evidence and vice versa.

SPANISH CHRONICLERS
About two dozen chroniclers' works provide information on the Incas and their contemporaries. Chief among them are the following writings. The mid-16th-century author Cieza de León's *Crónica del Peru* (1553 and 1554) contains much on Inca myth, while Juan de Betanzos' *Narrative of the Incas* (1557) recorded the subject from the point of view of the Inca nobility. Another record of Inca mythology is provided by Garcilasco de la Vega's (known as 'El Inca') *Comentarios Reales de los Incas* (1609–17), a comprehensive history of the Inca Empire.

The *Relación de los Quipucamayoqs* (written in Spain in 1608) comprises materials assembled to support the claims of a hopeful late pretender to the Inca throne, one Melchior Carlos Inca. He attempted to add depth and weight to his legitimacy by incorporating a version of the early foundation of Cuzco and the origin myth of the Incas, using as his source the manuscript of an inquest that had been held in 1542, the informants at which were four elderly *quipucamayoqs* who had served the Inca before the Spanish conquest.

Outside Cuzco, several sources provide accounts of myths from the regions of the empire. The exceptionally important Huarochirí manuscript, written in Quechua, *Dioses y Hombres de Huarochirí* (*c.*1610), records the myths of the central highlands of Peru. Two other sources relate accounts of the mythology of the peoples of the north Peruvian coast: Cabello de Balboa's *Miscelánea Antártica* (1586) and Antonio de la Calancha's *Crónica moralizada del Orden de San Augustinen el Perú* (1638).

THE CHRONICLERS
Accounts of mythology written by various Spanish-trained native Quechua-speaking authors include *Nueva Crónica y Buen Gobierno* by Felipe Guaman Poma de Ayala, written between 1583 and 1613, and *Relación de Antiguedades deste Reyno del Pirú*, which was written by Juan de Santacruz Yamqui Salcamaygua about 1613. Another set of documents, known as *idolatrías*, are records by Spanish priests and investigators who were attempting to stamp out idolatrous practices known to persist among the local populace under Spanish rule. These 17th-century documents are rich

Above: An early navigational map of the Spanish possessions in the Caribbean, New Spain, northern Peru and the Amazon.

in information on local myth based on interrogations of local authorities, native curers and 'witches' and other local diviners.

Lastly, the Jesuit priest Bernabé de Cobo, drawing principally from earlier chronicles, compiled the most balanced and comprehensive synthesis of Inca history and religion, in his monumental 20-year work *Historia del Nuevo Mundo*, books 13 and 14 of which, in particular, deal with Inca religion and customs.

LANGUAGES, DRAWINGS AND *QUIPU*

Hundreds of languages and dialects were spoken by the peoples throughout the Inca Empire, a fact even enshrined in Inca creation history. However, with no written language, the Incas relied on fine-line engraving and knot tying to keep records. Both these methods of recording data, events and customs provide modern scholars with valuable information with which to interpret the artefacts and structures from archaeological excavations. A combination of these finds and the information provided by the fine-line drawing and *quipus* enables us to discern the vast workings of the Inca Empire, and even pre-Inca times, and gives a greater understanding of Inca and other Andean cultures' beliefs about the universe.

Above: An Early Intermediate Period Moche pot with a 'narrative' scene, here showing weavers using backstrap looms.

QUECHUA, AYMARA, MOCHICA

The principal language of the Incas was Quechua (known to them as *Runa Simi*). This language was used throughout the empire for its administration and economic functions. Aymará, generally thought by linguists to be older than Quechua, was

Below: An Inca quipucamayoq *depicted by Guaman Poma de Ayala in his* Nueva Crónica y Buen Gobierno, *c.1613.*

spoken throughout the highland region around the basin of Lake Titicaca. Some scholars group the two languages together under the name Quechuamaran. In northern coastal Peru, Mochica was spoken, the language of the ancient Moche, their ancestors and descendants. Both Quechua and Aymará are widely spoken today in the Central Andes by some six million or more people. Mochica continued to be spoken in part of northern coastal Peru up to the beginning of the 20th century.

FINE-LINES IMAGES

Neither the Incas nor any of their Andean ancestors invented writing, and there are therefore no native historical records. However, fine-line drawings on pots reveal a great deal.

The graphic scenes they show provide records of a sort, depicting events. While such scenes are not specific historical events, many Moche fine-line drawings on ceramic vessels depict images representing commonly occurring episodes or practices in the culture. Such depictions provide invaluable information that contributes to the understanding of finds from archaeological excavations. For example, fine-line scenes of figures in

burial rituals show deities, or priests-shamans in the roles of deities, which explains the presence of masks on the faces of the dead in Moche elite burials.

RECORDING WITH KNOTS

The *quipu* (or *khipu*; Quechua for 'knot') was a unique Inca Andean recording device. It comprised a central cord to which were attached numerous subsidiary cords or strings, like a fringe. The subsidiary cords were of different colours and they were tied into different sorts of knots with differing meanings. *Quipus* were mostly made of cotton cord, but llama wool was also sometimes used. About 700 *quipus* have been found.

ACCOUNTS OF MANY COLOURS

According to 16th- and 17th-century sources, prominent among which are the 16th-century conquistador and governor of Cuzco, Garcilaso de la Vega's *Comentarios Reales de los Incas* and the 17th-century *Historia et Rudimenta Linguae Piruanorum*, quipus had several uses.

Right: An Inca quipu, *which is unusually attached to a wooden rod. Specific* quipus *held records for individual cities.*

They were account 'books', in which the different colours, knots and sequences served as tallies of goods in Inca store-houses throughout the empire, or censuses of labour groups and sources; and they were mnemonic aids for recall-ing oral traditions – historical-literary events, including what modern scholars would call myth and legend.

The Incas used the decimal system in counting and knew positional mathematics. Knots in different positions on the same string and different types of knot were used to record thousands, hundreds and single units. The Incas were also aware of the con-cept of zero, duly represented by a cord without any knots. The key to reading such numerical *quipu* knots and positions was discovered in 1912 by Leland L. Locke. Analysing a *quipu* in the American Museum of Natural History, New York, he compared its knots and their positions to descriptions by Garcilaso de la Vega.

Additional meaning was recorded in the *quipu* through the use of colours and their sequences and combinations. Colours used included white, blue, yellow, red, black, green, grey, light brown and dark brown. Colours and their combinations represented types of goods or produce. For example, yellow could represent gold or maize corn.

SUBTLETIES OF MEANING
Further sophistication in meaning is rep-resented by the orders of strings in series of the same colour. For example, in a counting of weapons stores, the most important ('noble') weapon was recorded at the left, and less noble weapons, in descending order, towards the right. The direction of the twisting of a cord itself added another layer of meaning: cords twisted to 'S' (clockwise) meant that the entire group referred to male categories

or subject matter, while cords twisted to 'Z' (anti-clockwise) meant that the entire group referred to female categories or subject matter. Even individual knots can be made clockwise or anti-clockwise.

So-called 'literary' *quipus* incorporated textile ideograms (symbols used to rep-resent whole words or concepts) among the strings. The same ideograms are found on Inca and pre-Inca textiles, pottery, sculpture and metalwork. The positions and numbers of knots below the ideograms indicate the syllables to be 'read'. The ideograms themselves relate to Inca (Andean) concepts of the universe, and to deities, man, animals and holy objects. An ideogram can also refer to a concept such as creation, the beginning of something, or to the elements and directions as represented by colours.

NAMING PLACES
The most recent breakthrough in *quipu* analysis has been made by Gary Urton and Carrie Brezine of Harvard University. Using a computer program designed to analyse the knot patterns in 21 *quipus* from a site in Puruchuco, an Inca administrative centre on the Peruvian coast, they discovered a recurring sequence of three figure-of-eight knots that appeared to rep-resent a place name. The placement of this sequence at the start of these *quipus* represents the name for Puruchuco, and the patterns of colour combinations and string lengths appear to rank three levels of authority among them. Thus, wherever these *quipus* went, they could be identi-fied with the Puruchuco administration and with Inca hierarchy, passing instruc-tions down from high-level officials.

EXPLORERS AND ARCHAEOLOGISTS

The Spanish conquistadors peppered their chronicles with descriptions that gave glimpses of the Inca way of life. The accounts and histories of colonial officials and priests attempted to provide a complete record of Inca history, society and religion, even if biased consciously or unconsciously. In the 18th and 19th centuries, these publications began to be re-examined by European and American scholars. Excavations, crude for the most part, had begun to be undertaken in Europe and America by antiquarians curious to understand their own and other's pasts and eager to make collections of antiquities for museums.

TRAVELLERS' TALES
Although most such early 'archaeological' activity in the Americas took place in North America, some scholars and travellers began to realize that there were also

Above: Alexander von Humboldt made the first attempts to collect Inca and pre-Inca antiquities and to understand their sequence.

ruins and remnants of ancient structures and artefacts throughout what had been the Inca Empire and elsewhere in South America. Paramount among these was Alexander von Humboldt (1769–1859).

Von Humboldt was the epitome of the late 18th/early 19th-century natural historian. As a gentleman traveller, scholar and popular lecturer, his travels were a combination of exploration, adventure and a pursuit of new knowledge, as he sought to uncover the continent's natural history, geography, geology and ancient history. In his two landmark publications – *Political Essay on the Kingdom of New Spain* (1811) and *Researches Concerning the Institutions and Monuments of the Ancient Inhabitants of America* (1814) – and in popular lectures he attempted to accumulate and record systematically as much data about the Americas as he could and to present it in a detailed but succinct manner. He attempted to remain unbiased in the way he recorded the data, trying to keep recorded fact and description separate from interpretation and speculation. Nevertheless, he was at

Below: Alexander von Humboldt travelled throughout South America gathering information for his treatise on the continent.

Right: Alphons Stübel at the Gateway of the Sun, Middle Horizon Tiwanaku. He published his notes with Max Uhle in 1892.

the same time a pioneer in his attempts to explain the presence of humans in the New World and their manner of coming and spreading throughout the two continents, as well as the apparent independent rise of sophisticated civilizations whose ruins were plain to see. His work and lectures brought international recognition to the antiquities of South America.

Following von Humboldt's example, and no doubt inspired by the explorations of John L. Stephens and Frederick Catherwood in Mesoamerica, books listing and describing sites and types of artefacts were published from the 1850s, and attempts were made to establish a historical framework for the bewildering amount of material that was being rediscovered about the ancient ruins of Peru and Bolivia especially. Frances de Castelnau published his *Expédition dans les Parties Centrales de l'Amérique du Sud, Troisuème Partie: Antiquités des Incas et Autre peuples Anciens* in 1854; Johann Tschudi his

Below: Ceramic kero *drinking vessels such as these were brought to private collectors and museums in the 18th and 19th centuries.*

five-volume *Reisen durch Süd Amerika* in 1869; Charles Wiener his *Pérou et Bolivie* in 1874; Ephraim G. Squier, echoing Stephens and Catherwood, his *Peru: Incidents of Travel and Exploration in the Land of the Incas* in 1877; and E. W. Middendorf his three-volume *Peru* in 1893–5, all primarily descriptive works.

DESCRIPTION AND EXCAVATION
Books and papers by Sir Clements Markham in 1856–1910, especially *A History of Peru* (1892) and *The Incas of Peru* (1910), were early attempts to synthesize and explain the data. A few scholars went one step further and actually undertook excavations: Alphons Stübel and Wilhelm Reiss excavated the Ancon cemetery on the Peruvian coast, an ancient burial place near Lima, and published their results in *The Necropolis of Ancón in Peru* (1880–7). Adolph Bandelier carried out excavations of Tiwanaku sites on islands in the Titicaca Basin, the results of which were published in 1910, and of Tiwanaku itself in 1911.

Bridging the development of archaeology between these early classifications and descriptions of Andean materials stands the all-important figure of Max Uhle (1856–1944), who was inspired by Alphons Stübel. In 1892 he collaborated with him to publish *Die Ruinenstaette von Tiahuanaco*, a study based on notes and photographs taken by Stübel at Tiwanaku. From 1892 to 1912, Uhle carried out

regular fieldwork in Peru and Bolivia. Armed with a thorough knowledge of Inca and Tiwanaku pottery types, his excavations at Pachacamac on the Peruvian coast enabled him to establish the first breakthrough in the modern construction of the chronology of Andean ancient history. He knew Inca pottery to be 15th and 16th century in date; likewise he knew that Tiwanaku pottery was pre-Inca and completely unlike Inca ceramics. Therefore, he reasoned that the pottery he excavated at Pachacamac, because it was unlike Tiwanaku ware but was sometimes associated in layers with Inca ceramics at Pachacamac, must come between the two in date.

Uhle's work was the beginning of the assessment of series of styles of artefacts in combination with their relative position in the earth to build a chronology of the ancient cultures of the Andes. During the next 30 years he carried out other excavations, including work in Ecuador and northern Chile. He synthesized his own and others' work into a Peruvian area-wide chronology, the first for the Andean region, because he also linked his Ecuadorian and Chilean finds to the sequence. While many other scholars – European, North American and South American – worked throughout South America into the early 20th century, most of their work was limited to collecting, describing and classifying museum pieces.

MODERN INVESTIGATIONS

Modern methods in archaeology began in the 20th century. Alongside increasingly sophisticated reasoning to establish chronological sequences and relationships among artefacts and site structures, more careful methods of excavation and recording and numerous new scientific methods brought greater understanding – but also more questions. Archaeologists were no longer content just to describe, classify, date and display the past: they wanted to interpret and explain it too.

SEEKING ANSWERS TO QUESTIONS
Recording of stratigraphy (distinctive earth layers or associations between architectural features) enabled archaeologists to understand and interpret the relationships between artefacts, structures and other features. Archaeologists throughout the Americas began to direct their fieldwork towards finding evidence to answer special questions and understanding a much wider and deeper picture of ancient history. Investigations

Below: Late 20th-century excavations near the Coricancha in modern Cuzco revealed Inca foundations and water channels.

Above: The Black and White Portal at the Early Horizon temple at Chavín de Huántar. Early 20th-century archaeologists realized this was one of the first pre-Inca civilizations.

sought evidence on all aspects and classes of ancient society, not just on the elite and the exquisite.

In addition to excavations at the ruins of individual ancient cities, area surveys began to establish the extent of ancient remains, the relationships between them and the varying importance of different regions. Work focused on specific questions and historical problems: When did people first arrive in the Andes?

When was the first pottery made? When did agriculture begin? How great was the influence of different cultures, kingdoms and empires?

Excavations yielded increasing amounts of metalwork and textiles and evidence of the artefacts and methods used to make them. Studies went beyond describing and classifying the art on ancient Andean pottery and stonework and explained the meaning of their depiction of scenes and religious events.

MAKING DATES
During the first 60 years of the 20th century, Alfred L. Kroeber and John H. Rowe refined and expanded the timescale of Andean prehistory. On the basis of which materials were found and where they lay within the site's stratigraphy, Rowe defined a 'master sequence' of alternating Periods and Horizons that broadly defined the course of Andean ancient history. In the late 1940s the discovery of radiocarbon dating began to provide absolute dates for these cultural periods.

The first native Peruvian archaeologist, Julio C. Tello, began a life-long career excavating sites of the earliest periods of Andean civilization, notably Paracas cemetery on Peru's southern coast, Sechín Alto in northern Peru and Chavín de Huántar in the central Andes. He defined these remote periods when Andean civilization began and distinctive socio-economic and religious traits were established. In 1939, Tello and Kroeber established the Institute of Andean Research. Similarly, Luis E. Valcarcel, Tello's successor at the Lima Museo Nacional, promoted the rich interchange between different fields of study to clarify Inca and pre-Inca society.

INTERNATIONAL EXPEDITIONS

After World War Two, large-scale, long-running projects were undertaken throughout the Andes, addressing every period, from the earliest inhabitants to the Incas. Principal among these was the Virú Valley Project, begun in 1946 by Wendell C. Bennett, William D. Strong, James A. Ford, Clifford Evans, Gordon R. Willey, Junius Bird and Donald Collier.

In the 1960s and 1970s, Edward Lanning, Thomas Patterson and Michael Moseley worked on the central Peruvian coast. Thomas Lynch, Richard MacNeish and others clarified the Palaeoindian period. Seiichi Izumi and Toshihiko Sono of Tokyo University investigated Kotosh and other early ceramic ceremonial sites. Luis G. Lumbreras and Hernán Amat renewed the study of Chavín de Huántar, as did Richard L. Burger of the Peabody Museum. Donald Lathrap and his students worked in the eastern Andes and adjacent lowlands.

In the 1960s to 1980s, John Rowe, John Murra, Tom Zuidema, Gary Urton and many others renewed the study of the Incas, including excavations at Huánuco Pampa by Craig Morris and Donald Thompson. Large-scale projects were undertaken by Michael Moseley and Carol Mackay at Chan Chan, by William Isbell at Huari, by Christopher Donnan and Izumi Shimada in the Moche Valley and by Alan Kolata in the Tiwanaku Basin.

No summary of 20th-century Andean archaeology can ignore three of its most spectacular discoveries. In 1911 the young explorer Hiram Bingham rediscovered the Inca fortress and ceremonial precinct of Machu Picchu in the remote Urubamba Valley north of Cuzco, bringing it to world fame. In the 1980s, Walter Alva and Susana Meneses made astounding discoveries and excavations of fabulous, unlooted elite Moche tombs at Sipán in the Lambeyeque Valley of northern Peru. And in 1995 Johan Reinhard and Miguel Zárate discovered rich child

Left: John H. Rowe recording findings at the Inca palace of Huyna Capac, at Quisphuanca, Peru.

Above: Late 20th-century excavations by Walter Alva of the rare unlooted tomb of an Early Intermediate Period Moche lord at Sipán in the Lambayeque Valley, Peru.

burials high on Mt Ampato in the southern Andes, explaining the Inca ritual of *capacocha* sacrifice.

RETURN TO SOURCES

Alongside 20th- and 21st-century excavations and analyses, archaeologists still return to the original texts: the chronicles and records of the conquistadors and colonial officials. However biased or conflicting these may sometimes be, they remain the only first-hand accounts of Inca society. Uhle knew that the ruins of Tiwanaku were pre-Inca because the Incas themselves told the Spaniards that the city lay in ruins when they subjugated the area. Similarly, when Morris and Thompson discovered 497 stone structures arranged in orderly rows along the hillside south of Huánuco Pamapa, the stacked pottery vessels of agricultural produce revealed these buildings to be none other than examples of Inca provincial storehouses in which, as described in the chronicles, they collected the wealth of the empire for redistribution.

In this way, the first Spanish accounts continue to help explain excavation finds and to provide a basis for interpreting aspects of pre-Inca civilization, whose material remains often demonstrate a link with Inca practices and social functions.

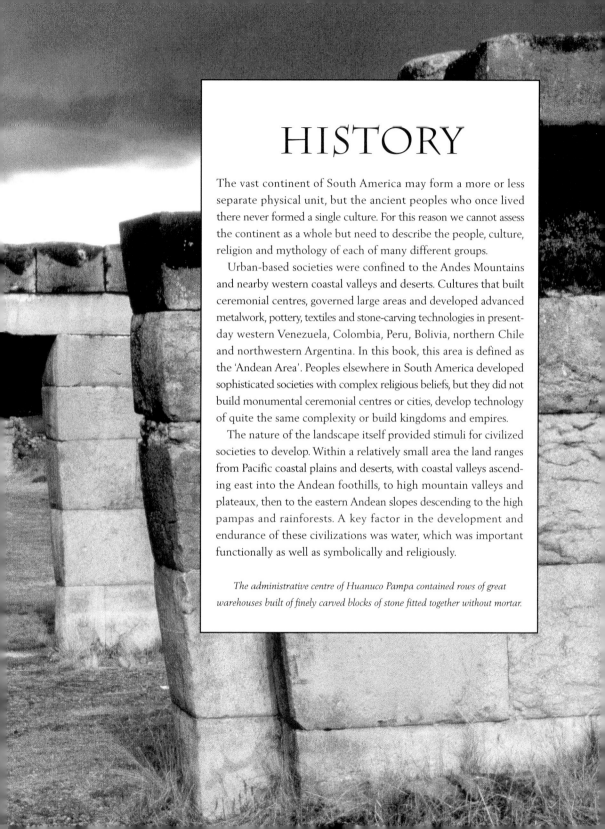

HISTORY

The vast continent of South America may form a more or less separate physical unit, but the ancient peoples who once lived there never formed a single culture. For this reason we cannot assess the continent as a whole but need to describe the people, culture, religion and mythology of each of many different groups.

Urban-based societies were confined to the Andes Mountains and nearby western coastal valleys and deserts. Cultures that built ceremonial centres, governed large areas and developed advanced metalwork, pottery, textiles and stone-carving technologies in present-day western Venezuela, Colombia, Peru, Bolivia, northern Chile and northwestern Argentina. In this book, this area is defined as the 'Andean Area'. Peoples elsewhere in South America developed sophisticated societies with complex religious beliefs, but they did not build monumental ceremonial centres or cities, develop technology of quite the same complexity or build kingdoms and empires.

The nature of the landscape itself provided stimuli for civilized societies to develop. Within a relatively small area the land ranges from Pacific coastal plains and deserts, with coastal valleys ascending east into the Andean foothills, to high mountain valleys and plateaux, then to the eastern Andean slopes descending to the high pampas and rainforests. A key factor in the development and endurance of these civilizations was water, which was important functionally as well as symbolically and religiously.

The administrative centre of Huanuco Pampa contained rows of great warehouses built of finely carved blocks of stone fitted together without mortar.

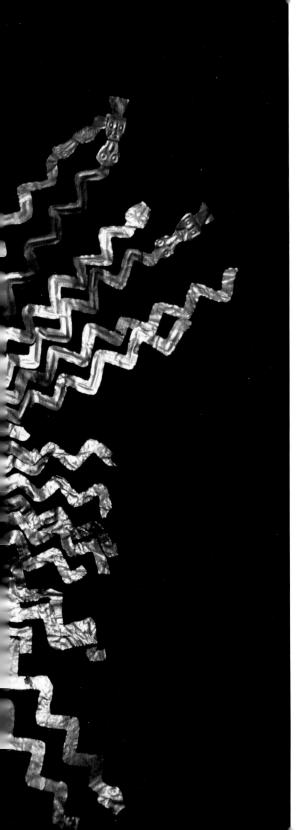

CHAPTER ONE

EMPIRE OF THE SUN

The Incas were a small group, or tribe, numbering perhaps 40,000 individuals or fewer in the Huantanay (Cuzco) Valley of modern central Peru. They were one group among many in the valley. Through conquest, first locally then beyond the valley, they built the largest empire that ever existed in the Americas. At its greatest extent, in AD1530, its northern border coincided roughly with the modern Ecuadorian–Colombian border, its southern extent stretched to modern central Chile, to the east it claimed regions into the lowlands bordering the Amazon Rainforest, and to the west it met the Pacific Ocean. Yet the Incas' rise to power lasted less than 100 years, and during the whole of this time they were engaged in wars of conquest or in the civil war at the end of this period.

Pachacuti Inca Yupanqui founded the imperial state of the Incas, and under his rule the Incas continued to dominate the Cuzco Valley. As the empire expanded, vast networks of roads were built to unite its far corners, coupled with impressive architectural and engineering feats that enabled planned towns and cities with great monuments to be built. Bridges were built and existing systems of terracing and irrigation expanded.

When the Spaniards under the leadership of Francisco Pizarro first arrived, the empire was still being expanded, but by the time of their third visit the empire was split by civil war. This war led eventually to the death of two rival sons of the Inca ruler, Huayna Capac, and the victory of Pizarro.

Left: The skilled metallurgists of the La Tolita culture were among many to depict the sun as a rayed golden mask.

LAND OF THE FOUR QUARTERS

The Incas called their world Tahuantin-suyu (or Tawantinsyu), literally meaning 'the land of the four united quarters'. Cuzco, the capital city, formed the focal point (although it was not the geographical centre) on which the four quarters were oriented and from which they emanated.

To the north-east of Cuzco was Antisuyu, the smallest quarter and the only one that did not border on the Pacific Ocean. To the north-west, stretching to the northernmost borders of the empire, was Chinchaysuyu. This quarter's northern extent had, in fact, only recently been extended into Quito province by the last conquering Sapa Inca, Huayna Capac (1493–1526), shortly before the arrival of the conquistador Francisco Pizarro in 1531. South and west of Cuzco was Cuntisuyu, second in size, and to the south-east was the largest of the four quarters, Collasuyu.

Below: Ephraim George Squier was the first to show a detailed plan of Inca Cuzco as a puma, its head formed by the fortress-temple of Sacsahuaman and its body and tail by the streets and water channels.

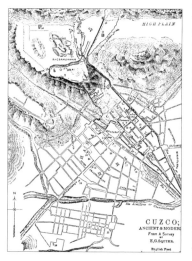

CUZCO;
ANCIENT & MODERN
From A Survey
by
E.G.SQUIER.

English Feet

Above: The Huacaypata Plaza, Cuzco, now the Plaza de Armas, was the site of ritual celebrations at solstices and festivals.

UNEQUAL QUARTERS

The four quarters were not only unequal in size but in population. They also differed extensively in the types of terrain they encompassed. Together they comprised a vast territory stretching from modern Ecuador to central Chile, north to south, and from the Pacific coast to the eastern flank of the Andes mountain chain, west to east. The empire was inhabited by a great variety of peoples and languages, each with long traditions of local development, masterfully united and socially co-ordinated and manipulated by their Inca masters. The Incas recognized this diversity as the deliberate actions of the creator god Viracocha, who, having formed the second world and its human inhabitants out of clay, dispersed them after giving them the clothing, skills and languages of the different tribes and nations.

Mention of the partition of the empire into four quarters was, as such, virtually ignored in most of Inca history. One legend, however, recounted in Garcilaso de la Vega's early 17th-century work, *Commentarios Reales de los Incas*, describes the division as the work of an 'Un-named Man' who appeared at Tiwanaku after the destruction of a previous world by great floods. This near lack of explanation is especially curious given the emphasis in Inca legendary history on the progress of the state creation from Lake Titicaca – near the geographical centre of the empire – towards the north and west, into the Huantanay (Cuzco) Valley.

This progress in one direction makes sense for Antisuyu, Chinchaysuyu and Cuntisuyu, but not for Collasuyu, which lies almost entirely to the south of Lake Titicaca. One explanation might lie in the fact that the Incas recast the origin mythology of the peoples of Collasuyu in order to bolster their own claims of origin from the Titicaca Basin, thus legitimizing their right to rule the region. The Incas were aware of the remains of Tiwanaku to the south and west of the lake, and no doubt of the relics of other previous great cities of the region, and must have recognized them as the centres

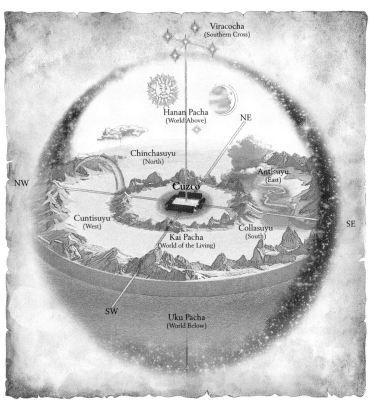

Right: A diagram of the land of the four quarters, based on a 1613 sketch by Juan de Santa Cruz Pachacuti Ymaqui Salcamaygua.

of former power bases. The Incas explained to the Spaniards that Tiwanaku lay in ruins when they invaded and conquered the Titicaca Basin.

THE FOUNDING OF CUZCO

The Incas regarded their capital at Cuzco as being at the centre of the world. Once again, Inca legendary history and heavenly associations formed the basis of their arrangments, for Cuzco equally reflected state and celestial organization. According to legend, Pachacuti Inca rebuilt the imperial city and the Coricancha (Sun Temple) in stone, being inspired by the ruined stone masonry of Tiwanaku. Indeed, archaeological excavations in the capital have shown that the Incas had no tradition of megalithic stone masonry before about AD1350–75, according to radiocarbon dating. The city was divided into upper (*hanan*) and lower (*hurin*) sections, respectively the quarters of the two social divisions of the populace believed to have been ordered by the first ruler, Manco Capac. Again according to legend,

Left: Inca surveyors linked the provinces of the entire empire with a masterly engineered road system.

Pachacuti named the renewed city 'lion's body' (by which the Spanish chronicler meant a puma), and, from above, the plan of the city indeed resembles a crouching puma with a head and tail.

HIGHWAYS AND LINES

From the central plaza, Huacaypata, four great imperial highways and four sacred cosmic lines radiated to the four quarters. From the nearby Coricancha emanated 41 sacred *ceque* lines: sightings lines to the horizons and beyond. They were grouped into upper and lower sets and further divided into four quarters. The upper set was associated with Hanan Cuzco and with the quarters of Antisuyu (north-east) and Chinchasuyu (north-west), while the lower set was associated with Hurin Cuzco and with the quarters of Collasuyu (south-east) and Cuntisuyu

(south-west). Together these highways, cosmic lines and *ceques* integrated the capital and the four quarters into the Inca state religion focused on Inti, the sun god, as a near equal to the creator Viracocha – perhaps another reason why they did not emphasize the history of the divisions.

ROADMAP OF THE STARS

A link with the heavens was further enhanced by the association of each of the four great highways along a route approximating (except when having to go around hills and mountains) a north–south/east–west axis of Mayu (literally 'celestial river'), commonly known as the Milky Way. In the course of 24 hours, ancient Andeans observed that Mayu crosses its zenith in the sky, and in so doing forms two intersecting axes oriented north-east/south-west and south-east/north-west. Thus, the divisions of the sky provided a celestial grid against which their world of Tahuantinsuyu was projected.

CUZCO AND BEYOND

The Inca Empire stretched more than 4,200km (2,600 miles) from north to south and east to west across the Andes, from the Amazon rainforests and Argentine plains to the Pacific coast. Throughout this vast area lived a variety of peoples whose earlier cultural evolution united them locally and regionally, especially at an economic and religious level. This was exploited by the Incas, who imposed imperial rule and economic stability on the empire.

ALL ROADS LEAD TO CUZCO

Imperial Cuzco, the capital city, was considered to be the navel of the Inca world. From it and to it led all roads, both physically and spiritually. This network linked peoples and cultures as varied as fishing communities, such as the Uru in the Lake Titicaca Basin, and the Kingdom of Chimú on the Peruvian north coast, a state whose sophistication might have rivalled the Incas. The empire reached its greatest extent beyond the Cuzco Valley in less than 100 years of conquests.

Below: Tambo Colorado, at the end of a major road running west, was one of many planned provincial administrative capitals.

SPREADING CIVILIZATION

A number of distinctive Inca cultural traits have been identified, which they spread to greater and lesser extents throughout the empire. These include: a corporate style of architecture, settlement planning, artefact styles, large-scale engineering works and terracing.

In the Cuzco area, most residential buildings (*kanchas*) were rectangular, single-room and single-storey affairs, arranged around courtyards. They were made of fieldstones or adobe bricks,

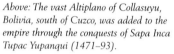
Above: The vast Altiplano of Collasuyu, Bolivia, south of Cuzco, was added to the empire through the conquests of Sapa Inca Tupac Yupanqui (1471–93).

gabled, with thatched roofs, and had doors, windows and internal niches usually of trapezoidal shape. A second basic form, the *kalanka*, was a rectangular hall used for several public functions. Structures for state purposes were mostly, but not always, made of finely cut and fitted stone. Most were in the capital and its immediate environs; fitted-stone architecture was rare in the provinces and restricted to special state buildings.

In settlement planning, the Incas practised a policy of relocating peoples away from their homelands for political and economic reasons. In such settlements, Inca engineers laid out *kancha* enclosures in blocks around Inca-style state administrative buildings where needed. Some provincial Inca settlements were established for specific purposes, perhaps one of the best known being Huánuco Pampa, an Inca imperial city about 675km (420 miles) north-west of Cuzco in the Chinchaysuyu quarter, which was established as a seat of provincial administration and also for the storage and redistribution of the products of the empire.

Above: Huánuco Pampa, a provincial administrative capital in Chinchasuyu, lay on the main northern trunk road up the spine of the empire, heading all the way to Quito.

In some provincial settlements, the Incas relied on local technology and adapted themselves to local political and social organization while retaining an over-arching control. In such cases any evidence of Inca presence, conquest and rule is found more in material culture, particularly pottery (but also textiles and metalwork), of distinctive Inca decorative design and techniques.

The vast majority of settlements were not Inca in origin and were, apart from the relocated populations in Inca-planned towns, left in their native styles and plans. Again, Huánuco Pampa provides an important example: the surrounding villages retained their local native character and Inca rule was exerted indirectly through local leaders.

Throughout the empire, Inca engineers were famous for their works. There were roads, bridges, agricultural terracing and accompanying systems of irrigation canals. Imperial highways linked Cuzco with the provincial capitals. Major imperial highways went north-west to Vilcashuaman, Huánuco Pampa, Cajamarca, Tumibamba and Quito and south-east to Chucuito, Paria, Tupiza, La Paya, Santiago and other cities. Westward-running highways branched off to major coastal cities – Tumbes, Pachacamac, Tambo Colorado, Nazca and others – and a parallel highway ran along the Peruvian coast as far as Atico. In many cases pre-existing roads were incorporated and it is often difficult to identify roads as specifically Inca-made unless there is also associated Inca architecture, or sometimes evidence of inhabitants. Similarly with bridges: it is often only the presence of stone foundations and Inca artefacts at river crossings that indicates where an Inca bridge stood.

Land terracing, especially throughout the Andes, was constructed to take advantage of every available opportunity to extend land for growing, especially maize. Again, it is not always possible to identify specifically Inca terracing from pre-Inca work without other associated Inca features, but it is certain that with the expansion of Inca domination the extent of terracing increased greatly.

KINSHIP AND TAXES

The Incas exploited and perhaps consolidated the economic and social arrangement called *ayllu*. This was a kinship charter based on actual or imagined descent between groups working the different environments between highlands and lowlands, especially farming and llama herding. Such a group of related people was an organization for both labour exchange and a common ownership of property, possessions and rights; it also established, monitored and regulated rules of social conduct, and solved social problems at various levels. In other words, it incorporated rights and responsibilities.

The Incas employed a state tax system of agricultural produce divided into three categories; land was divided accordingly to support each category. The first was for the support of the gods – in practical terms it went to the priests, other religious functionaries and shrine attendants. The second went to the emperor, to support the imperial household and into storage for redistribution in times of need. The third was for the communities themselves; it was collected, stored and distributed annually by local officials.

In addition to taxation there was a labour tax, or obligation, called *mit'a*. This was an annual draft of able-bodied males to undertake public work.

Although both *ayllu* and *mit'a* were established in pre-Inca times throughout much of the Andes, the Incas exploited and used them more extensively.

BUILDING AN EMPIRE

The Inca Empire began and ended in conflict. Its downfall was hastened by the Spanish invasion, yet, when the Spaniards arrived, the Incas were themselves engaged in civil war.

THE CUZCO VALLEY
The founding of the empire is obscured in elaborate legend and myth invented by the Incas. It began with a legendary figure and first ruler, Manco Capac, leader of the *ayars*, the legendary ancestors, and founder of the Inca dynasty. The founding involved mystical birth from the earth, the designation of Inca superiority and their destiny to rule.

There were four brothers, of whom Manco was senior, and four sisters/wives – providing consistency with the division of the empire into four quarters. It was Manco who ordered the division of the people into the *hurin* and *hanan* – the upper and the lower – and who formed 'the allies' into ten lineage groups: the ten *ayllus* of commoners at Cuzco to complement the ten royal *ayllus* of his and his brothers' descendants. After migration from Lake Titicaca and many

adventures, Manco, his sister/wife, and other sisters, and their son Sinchi Roca arrived in the Valley of Cuzco, where Manco organized the building of the city. Sinchi Roca duly inherited the throne and allegedly commanded the people of the valley to cultivate potatoes. He was followed by his son Lloque Yupanqui. We have no idea how long these rulers reigned, or if there were more than are named.

Archaeology provides only hints of the development of Inca power in the Cuzco Valley. We know little of what lies buried beneath modern Cuzco, and almost nothing of what lies beneath the 16th-century Inca city. It has been occupied continuously since Inca times, if not before, and many Inca structures were themselves used as foundations for Spanish colonial and later structures.

DEVELOPING POWER
Ceramic styles show us that the Incas were probably a local tribe, one of several in the valley, and that Cuzco began to emerge as a regional centre in the Late Intermediate Period from the early 13th

Above: Manco Capac allegedly founded Inca Cuzco and ruled in the 12th century, in the Late Intermediate Period.

century. No individual buildings, or any distinctive architectural style, can be identified with the Incas or with a specific Inca ruler until the reign of Pachacuti Inca Yupanqui (1438–71). We do not know whether the Incas ruled Cuzco from this early time, coexisted with their neighbours or actually lived elsewhere.

What is certain, however, is that they began to dominate the valley from at least about the beginning of the 15th century. A sort of defined style began to emerge in the late 14th and early 15th centuries and was strengthened by Pachacuti Inca Yupanqui. It was he who began the formation of the Inca imperial state; and the Late Horizon, which began *c.*1400, is defined by the beginning of his hegemony.

The intervening rulers between Lloque Yupanqui and Pachacuti are a mere name list: Mayta Capac, Capac Yupanqui, Inca

Left: Puca Pukara fort near Cuzco was used in wars against the neighbouring peoples in the Cuzco Valley and adjacent valleys.

Roca, Yahuar Huacac, Viracocha Inca and Inca Urco. We have little knowledge of their achievements other than that they inherited rulership of the Cuzco Valley, and continued to dominate their neighbours and strengthen their power within the valley. Mayta Capac defeated a local tribe called the Alcavicças, who were apparently dissatisfied with the Inca overlordship in the valley.

WAR AGAINST THE CHANCAS

Only Viracohca Inca and Urco emerge from legend as real people. During troubled times, undoubtedly the war with the Chancas (another valley tribe), Viracocha claimed that the god Viracocha came to him in a dream, calmed his fears and inspired him to rule. However, he and his son and named heir, Urco, fled Cuzco with much of the populace when the Chancas advanced on the city. Urco enjoyed the shortest reign – less than a year in 1438 – if he actually reigned at all.

Below: The tiered wall of Sacsahuaman, which forms the north-west quarter (Chinchasuyu) of Inca Cuzco.

His brother, Yupanqui, was more steadfast and stayed to defend the city. He too claimed divine inspiration, in an earlier incident giving him a vision of the future. In official Inca history, Yupanqui rallied his companions and repulsed the first two attacks. He called upon the gods for help and the very stones in the field allegedly became Inca warriors. The Chancas were defeated and, taking the name Pachacuti Inca ('Earth-shaker King'), he assumed the throne.

TO THE LIMITS OF THE EMPIRE

The date of 1438, which comes from the chronicler Miguel Cabello de Valboa, marked Pachacuti's defeat of the Chancas and his succession to the throne. He subdued the Cuzco Valley and declared all Quechua-speakers there to be honorary Inca citizens. He began Inca imperial aspirations by conquering the Lupaqa, Colla and other city-states to the south-east around Lake Titicaca. Then he turned his armies over to his son and chosen heir, Tupac Inca Yupanqui, to continue campaigning, while he returned to Cuzco and devoted his energies to consolidating the power of the Incas.

Above: Pachacuti Inca Yupanqui expanded the Inca Empire with conquests into Cuntisuyu, Chinchasuyu and Collasuyu.

Pachacuti is credited with developing Inca statecraft and with organizing the institutions and systems that were the hallmarks of Inca rule: national taxation and labour levies, roadways and an imperial communication network, and extensive warehousing of food and other commodities for redistribution throughout the empire. He also established the official Inca state religion based on worship of Inti – the sun – and commissioned much building in the city, including the temple-fortress of Sacsahuaman, which was dedicated to the worship of Inti.

Tupac (1471–93) extended the empire to its greatest extent with conquests to the north and south, especially of the powerful Chimú Kingdom on the north coast, defeating King Minchançaman. His successor, Huayna Capac (1493–1526), campaigned throughout the empire, largely consolidating earlier gains. He had recently subjugated the kingdom of Quito when he died suddenly of smallpox. In the turmoil that followed, two of his sons, half-brothers by different wives, claimed the succession: Huáscar, governor of Cuzco, and Atahualpa, who controlled the army in the north.

CIVIL WAR

Spanish sources leave some doubt as to whether Huayna Capac, the twelfth Inca ruler, had actually named his successor when he died suddenly. Some sources say there was an heir apparent, a young son Ninancuyuchi, others that Huayna Capac favoured his son Huáscar, or that he secretly hoped that another son, Atahualpa, would use his control of the army to supplant Huáscar. Still other sources indicate that he had planned to divide the empire among several sons, or even that the empire was so far extended that it was effectively dividing itself in 1526.

Needless to say, the various factions that still existed at the time of the Spanish conquest recited to Spanish chroniclers the versions of events and descendants that suited them. Nevertheless, upon Huayna Capac's death, the Spaniards had just arrived off the northern coast of the empire and the Incas plunged into a bloody civil war that itself threatened the demise of the empire and all it stood for.

Below: Soldiers of Atahualpa's army lead his brother Huáscar into captivity after his defeat at the Battle of Huánuco Pampa.

ONE THRONE: THREE HEIRS?

Huayna Capac had campaigned in the north of the empire for ten years. He had gone north, originally to quell a rebellion in Quito province, taking with him his sons Ninancuyuchi and Atahualpa. In Cuzco he left four governors, one of whom was Huáscar, another of his sons by his many wives. When an epidemic of smallpox broke out in the north and

Above: An Inca soldier painted on a wooden kero *drinking vessel, wearing traditional battle dress – a tunic and feather headdress.*

Huayna Capac contracted it, he anointed in formal ceremony his son Ninancuyuchi as his heir. But Ninancuyuchi also died of smallpox, and this situation left a dilemma and a plethora of possible claimants to the throne.

Huáscar seized the throne in Cuzco but was contested by Atahualpa, his younger half-brother. Atahualpa had been involved in the campaign against and subjugation of the Quito region in the far north of the empire. At his father's death he was left in command of the Inca armies of the north. At the death of Huayna Capac and Ninancuyuchi, he at first seemed to accept Huáscar's rise to power and ordered new palaces to be built for Huáscar in the northern city of Tumipampa. The local chief, Ullco Colla, however, resented Atahualpa and spread rumours of a plot against Huáscar. In the ensuing intrigue, Atahualpa and Huáscar became enemies and the former marched to confront his brother. The Inca court split into two supporting factions and civil war raged for six years.

BATTLE BETWEEN BROTHERS

Huáscar declared Atahualpa to be *auca* – a treasonous enemy of the state. He sent the army he commanded in Cuzco to attack Atahualpa and capture him in Quito.

Below: The imposing tiered walls of Sacsahuaman imply its use as a fortress as well as its main purpose as a temple to Inti.

But in a major battle Huáscar's forces were utterly defeated, and Atahualpa continued a relentless march south.

Huáscar sent larger armies against him. There were running battles and Huascar's forces were defeated but without conclusive results. Rivalry even broke out among Huáscar's generals. Huáscar sent even greater forces against Atahualpa, who again defeated them, until finally, in 1532, Huáscar himself marched with an army against him. Atahualpa's experience in the northern campaigns finally proved decisive, and this time Huáscar was taken prisoner. The final battle took place at Huánuco Pampa, north-west of Cuzco.

Atahualpa, whose forces were flushed with their victories, relied on speed. His generals marched immediately against Huáscar before further reinforcements could arrive from Cuzco. Given what had already transpired, Atahualpa offered no peace negotiations. The battle apparently lasted most of the day until Huáscar's troops broke and Huáscar was forced to flee with his immediate retinue of about 1,000 retainers and troops. Atahualpa's forces soon overtook him, however, seized Huáscar and put the remainder of his followers to death.

Above: Dressed in distinctive tunics and armed with axe-headed spears and shields, Inca armies subdued the empire.

ROYAL SACRILEGE

The ruthlessness of this prolonged war continued when Atahualpa marched on and captured Cuzco. He feigned a plan to return Huáscar to the throne as Sapa Inca and declared a day for the event. He commanded the attendance of the nobles and leaders of the empire, the provincial governors and chief administrators, many of whom were related to Huáscar, indeed to Atahualpa as well. Together they comprised the *panaca*, descendants of the royal household.

The provinces of the empire had been divided since the civil war had begun. Many cities had simply continued life as usual, while others in the most remote or recently conquered reaches of the empire rebelled or simply ignored Inca rule for the time being, awaiting the outcome of events. Now that Atahualpa was victorious, and apparently in control, however, they were being called upon to declare their loyalty.

Once everyone was gathered in Cuzco, Atahualpa had them all slain, so effectively ending further resistance by destroying the *panaca's* very existence.

Yet Atahualpa went further still in his aim to eliminate the royal family: he ordered the burning of the mummy of Tupac Yupanqui, the tenth Sapa Inca and ancestor of the *panaca*.

CONQUEST OF THE EMPIRE

Even before Francisco Pizarro (1475–1541) began his Andean explorations, an entire empire, that of the Aztecs, had been conquered in Mesoamerica by his countryman Hernán Cortés.

PIZARRO'S RETURN

A veteran of an expedition to Panama in 1509, Pizarro was eager to emulate Cortés. After two voyages from Panama to the South American mainland, he had returned with enough knowledge of the coast, stories of rich cities inland and to the south, and examples of gold and silver objects and textiles to convince him another civilization of great wealth lay to the south.

In 1526, had he attempted on his second expedition to invade the fringe of the Inca Empire, he would surely have been defeated. The empire was at its height under Sapa Inca Huayna Capac (1493–1526), with provincial garrisons and a strong army able to move quickly from centre to province along an efficient road system. In 1531, however, an attack

Below: The walls and defensive gateway of the fortress city of Rumicolca, about 35km (21 miles) southeast of Cuzco.

and pillaging of the coastal, provincial port of Tumbes by the inhabitants of Puná Island went unavenged, for Capac's successor, Huáscar, was otherwise engaged.

Pizarro visited Tumbes in 1526. When he returned in 1532, he still had the two native interpreters from the town, whom he had taken with him to Spain to raise royal permission and funds for his third expedition. Now the Inca Empire was in a state of turmoil. Huáscar's army had recently been defeated by his half-brother, Atahualpa, Huáscar had been captured, and Atahualpa had seized the throne.

IMPERIAL OMENS

Even before this civil war, Huayna Capac told his sons that Inti, the sun god, had informed him that his reign was the last of the twelve Sapas. Inca rule would end with the arrival of powerful strangers, whom he believed to be the foreigners recently reported arriving by sea on the north coast. Their coming was foretold by ill omens: during ceremonies honouring Inti, an eagle was mobbed and killed by buzzards and the priests prophesied disaster; and one night the new moon had three halos – one red, one black, one smoky.

Above: Francisco Pizarro, who was born illegitimate in Trujillo, Estremadura, turned from swineherd into soldier of fortune.

The priests said the red ring foretold war between the Sapa's descendants, the black ring the demise of Inti and the smoke the vanishing of the empire. These were weaknesses that Pizarro could exploit.

Huayna Capac ordered his sons to obey the strangers, for they were in every way superior. Written after the fact, the Spanish-Inca historian Garcilaso de la Vega's account appears to be a combination of political expediency and rationalization for the collapse of the empire, which the Incas believed to be perfect. In reality, weaknesses in the Inca hierarchy, civil war, the size of the empire and the shear audacity of Pizarro better explain the subsequent events.

THE MARCH TO CAJAMARCA

The arrival of reinforcements from Panama brought Pizarro's grand army to 260 men (198 foot soldiers and 62 cavalry). Tumbes had supported Huáscar in the civil war, providing a ready-made ally. Leaving a garrison in Tumbes, Pizarro marched inland with his best troops.

Left: A fanciful depiction of Atahualpa before his capture by Pizarro. Inca soldiers did not march and fight naked.

20 cavalrymen, then Hernando Pizarro with another 20, were sent to seek Atahualpa, who waited for them at his quarters, together with his court and some 400 warriors.

The Spaniards had to push their way through the Inca ranks. Accounts of the exchange vary: de Soto impressed the Incas with a display of horsemanship, then invited Atahualpa to the Spanish camp. Hernando arrived. Atahualpa declared that he was fasting and would visit on the next day. He claimed that one of his chiefs had killed three Spaniards and a horse back on the march. Hernando denied that any Inca could overcome a Spaniard. Atahualpa complained that one of his provincial chiefs had disobeyed him and Hernando bragged that ten horsemen could put down the revolt. *Chicha* was brought in large gold vessels. Etiquette was served; macho was displayed. It was left at that.

Below: Hernando Pizarro and Hernando de Soto were sent by Francisco Pizarro as envoys to Atahualpa at Cajamarca.

To win more allies, he adopted a pacific approach. He forbade looting, and encouraged his Dominican friars to convert the heathens; but opposition, where met, was put down brutally – opposing provincial chiefs were burned as examples. His campaign became a crusade.

Atahualpa marched his army – reportedly 40–50,000 warriors – nearly 1,600km (1,000 miles) to Cajamarca to await Pizarro, who was himself travelling on a litter. With 110 foot soldiers and 67 cavalrymen, Pizarro camped near Tambo Grande and sent his lieutenant, Hernando de Soto, to reconnoitre. De Soto returned with an Inca official bearing gifts and an invitation to Cajamarca. Pizarro accepted the gifts, sent the official back with gifts of his own and a message that he represented the most powerful emperor in the world, offering service against the Sapa's enemies, and continued his slow march south and east towards the 4,000m (13,000ft) pass to Cajamarca.

Atahualpa sent a gift of ten llamas. The messenger gave an account of the war with Huáscar, and Pizarro allegedly delivered a speech declaring peaceful intentions, but was prepared for war if challenged. Another day's march involved being greeted by an Inca official with *chicha* (maize liquor) in gold cups – he was to lead the Spaniards to Cajamarca.

An allied chief whom Pizarro had sent to Atahualpa returned. He attacked Atahualpa's official, calling him a liar, and claimed that the Sapa had refused to receive him. He said that Cajamarca was deserted and Atahualpa had deployed his army on the plain ready for war. Atahualpa's ambassador retorted that Cajamarca had been vacated to make it ready for Pizarro – that it was the Sapa's custom to camp with this army on campaign (meaning the civil war). These exchanges must have left Pizarro more confused than ever.

Finally Pizarro, his men suffering from altitude sickness and exhaustion, climbed the hills into Cajamarca Valley. At any time Atahualpa could have destroyed him, yet he did nothing.

ETIQUETTE OBSERVED

Pizarro marched into Cajamarca's main courtyard on 15 November 1532, passing the vastly larger Inca army, his men arranged in three divisions to make the most of his comparatively meagre force. No envoy awaited or arrived. De Soto and

CAPTURE AND REGICIDE

Atahualpa arrived at the Spanish camp late on 16 November. There had been debate among his advisers and he had decided to visit with an armed entourage. Inca warriors lined the route and surrounding grasslands. Atahualpa, carried by his chiefs on a litter adorned with gold and silver plates, was preceded by elite warriors in colourful chequered livery, singing, dancing and sweeping the roadway before him. Atahualpa himself was bedecked with gold and turquoise jewellery, and the entire retinue displayed his wealth and majesty.

The journey was less than 6km (4 miles), yet Atahualpa hesitated, sent a messenger that he would come the next day, then changed his mind and resumed progress, now with only 6,000 unarmed followers. Atahualpa's indecision revealed a lack of human confidence despite his obsession with displaying his dignity and status as a living god. He simply could not understand the nature of the men he was dealing with.

SLAUGHTER AND CAPTURE

Entering the empty courtyard, Atahualpa was greeted by Pizarro's friar, Valverde, brandishing a Bible and a crucifix. He delivered a discourse on Christianity.

Left: In early meetings with Atahualpa's noble ambassadors, Francisco Pizarro and Hernando De Soto professed peace.

Historians will forever remain unsure of the ensuing events. Despite the message having to pass through an interpreter, it seems clear that Atahualpa understood what was being demanded of him: renunciation of everything he believed in, of his entire world. Allegedly, Valverde handed him the Bible; allegedly he threw it down, pointing at the sun and declaring 'My God still lives.'

Valverde retrieved the Bible and retreated. Pizarro gave the signal to attack: a cannon was fired into the crowd, followed by arquebuses (long-barrelled guns); then his men charged. Atahualpa's chiefs fought with bare hands to save their emperor, and were butchered in the attempt. A wall collapsed in the frenzy of retreating natives. Those trapped in the courtyard were slaughtered until night fell and Atahualpa was taken captive. Thus treachery was accomplished. It must have seemed to Pizarro that this was the only way to succeed against clearly overwhelming odds. The chronicler Zárete records that the whole plot had been discussed and decided the night before. Pizarro had indeed emulated Cortés by taking the emperor hostage.

GREED AND BETRAYAL

The passivity of Atahualpa's people and army is astounding. They simply melted away, leaving their possessions in camp. The Spaniards looted Cajamarca and the chiefs' tents, seized the army's llama herds and raped the women abandoned in the royal baths.

The remainder of the story is equally sordid. Realizing Pizarro's lust for gold and silver, Atahualpa offered to fill the 5.5 by 7m (18 by 23ft) room in which he was held, as high as he could reach, with gold. Pizarro demanded that, in addition, the adjoining smaller room be filled twice

Above: Having captured Atahualpa at Cajamarca, Pizarro imprisoned him in a palace room while a ransom was negotiated.

with silver. Atahualpa agreed to these demands, asked for two months, and ordered the collection of gold and silver objects from all over the empire.

At Atahualpa's request, three Spaniards, including de Soto, were sent to Cuzco to hasten the collections. They found the captive Huáscar, who offered to treble his half-brother's ransom. Learning this, Atahualpa gave secret orders for Huáscar to be murdered.

In January 1533, Hernando was sent on an expedition to Pachacamac. In April, Diego de Almagro and reinforcements arrived from Panama. Pizarro bided his time, while his soldiers grew restless – they had come for conquest and spoils.

There remained the problem of Atahualpa. Despite incomplete fulfilment of his agreement, Pizarro absolved him of further obligation, but still held him – 'for security'. He was now an encumbrance; Pizarro wanted power and Atahualpa, now only a rallying point for native rebellion, stood in his way. De Almagro and his men wanted action and plunder. Rumours of native insurrection, the 'demands' of his men and the Spanish Inquisition provided Pizarro with justification for a 'trial'. He and de Almagro were the judges. Atahualpa was accused of usurpation of the Inca throne and the murder of Huáscar the true heir, of inciting insurrection, of distributing gold and silver that should have been used to fulfil his ransom agreement and of adultery – as Sapas had numerous wives – and idolatry. He was convicted and condemned to be burned at the stake.

THE END OF INCA RULE

The final shameless act in these procedures followed. Twelve captains called the affair a travesty of justice, but were persuaded of its political expediency. When Atahualpa realized that he was to be burned, he agreed to be baptized a

Right: Despite this image, Atahualpa was strangled to death, after becoming a Christian to avoid being burned at the stake.

Christian for the favour of strangulation, for if he were burned, in Inca belief he would be condemned in afterlife, unable to be mummified and to continue to participate in life.

Pizarro finally marched to Cuzco and established Spanish government – a year after the events in Cajamarca. Alleged plans for insurrection by Challcuchima, one of Atahualpa's own generals, 'justified' his execution. A puppet Sapa, Manco, another of Huayna Capac's sons, was crowned. The last of Atahualpa's generals, Quizquiz, was defeated and fled to Quito, where he was killed by his own men.

The first years of Spanish rule were fraught with embittered rivalry between Pizarro, de Almagro and others. Pizarro enjoyed power for a mere eight years before being assassinated by rivals.

Below: The alleged 'ransom room' in Inca Cajamarca in which Atahualpa was imprisoned after being captured.

CHAPTER TWO

THE LAND

The continent of South America has a geography of extremes. Its mountains are some of the highest in the world – up to 7,000m (23,000ft); its deserts are some of the driest; its rainforests some of the wettest and densest; and its western offshore seas – the Humboldt Current – teem with some of the most abundant fisheries. Climates range from damp, steaming jungles to cold, dry deserts, and from cool, high plains to lofty, oxygen-rare summits. Rainfall can range from near zero to as much as 8,000mm (315in) a year.

Within this continent lies the Andean Area, which includes the two Cordilleras of the Andes, bordering the Amazon Rainforest on one side and the Atacama and other deserts on the other. Here humans have had to adapt to life at high altitudes. South of the Cordillera lies the Altiplano, where much of the area's farming is carried out. Here potatoes and other root crops were grown, and large herds of llamas kept for their wool. To the west lie coastal valleys and oases within the desert, where a variety of crops were grown.

East of the Andes is another world. The eastern mountain flanks descend more gradually through forested slopes, known as *montaña,* to the low, hot tropical forests, known as the *selva.* Here human settlement was more dispersed, yet products of the rainforest remained prominent in Andean and western coastal cultures throughout history.

Despite such extremes and a land of independent settlements, the Incas did not live in isolation: rather trade and social contact linked the settlements in both highlands and lowlands.

Left: The Callejon de Huaylas in north-central Peru epitomizes the sweeping slopes and high sierra valleys of the Andes.

PEAKS AND MOUNTAIN VALLEYS

The Andean Cordillera has been shaped in two distinct ways: by the movement of tectonic plates and by the weather.

FORMATION OF THE ANDES
Nearly two million years ago, the westward-moving South American continental plate met the eastward-moving Nazca ocean plate along the Pacific coast, moving at up to 15cm (6in) a year. The ocean plate, which has a heavier stone composition, was pushed beneath the lighter and less dense continental plate. Friction and drag where the two plates met caused folding, which created the Andean mountain chain. Where the ocean plate melted from the friction, the sedimentary rocks cracked, hurling molten rocks to the surface as volcanoes.

Below: Llamas, alpacas and vicuñas helped Andean civilizations to develop and survive in the Altiplano and high mountains.

Along their widest stretch, the spine of the Andes comprises two parallel ridges. On the east, the higher Cordillera Blanca borders the Amazon Rainforest. On the west, the Cordillera Negra fronts the Atacama Desert. South of this broad range the ridges diverge to flank, east and west, the broad Altiplano; to the north the mountains split into several ridges running parallel to the main ranges, and are cross-cut by shorter ridges to frame numerous sierra basins and valleys known as *puna*.

EFFECTS OF THE WEATHER
The distant Atlantic Ocean is the source of most of South America's precipitation. Westward-moving rain and snow meet the high Andes and fall on the eastern escarpments. West of the Andes, which lies in the rain shadow, a more arid Pacific weather pattern predominates. The Andes become drier as they become higher, and the Altiplano around the drainage of the

Above: In the challenging terrain of the sierra valleys and basins, rivers provided the vital water needed for agriculture.

Lake Titicaca basin forms a huge region of uninterrupted agricultural flatlands. Ninety per cent of Andean drainage runs east, ultimately to the Atlantic. Ten per cent drains into the Pacific, in numerous short, east–west-running river valleys from the western Andean flank.

The Andes also deflect prevailing ocean winds to blow north, causing the Pacific to flow northwards along the coast. Upwelling water from the deep tectonic trench brings cold, nutrient-rich and therefore seafood-rich currents, but also chills the air, so causing sparse rainfall.

A CHALLENGING ENVIRONMENT
The mountainous and highland regions of the Andes provide one of the most challenging environments on earth to their inhabitants. High mountain ecosystems are characteristically of low productivity, yet the majority of people in the central Andes live above 2,500m (8,200ft). Such altitudes comprise steep-sided valleys and basins, rugged terrains and a generally fragile landscape. Limited flat agricultural land, poor soils and a short growing season make production difficult. In addition, low oxygen levels, infrequent rainfall, high winds, high solar radiation and prevailing cold temperatures make survival tenuous.

Above: Mt Ausangate, in the central Peruvian Cordillera, was a typical abode of apu *spirits: sacred deities who inhabited the peaks.*

ADAPTING TO ALTITUDE

The high altitude causes stress on all life forms, and in humans, in particular, it decreases blood oxygen saturation by up to 30 per cent, which means breathing can be difficult for the unaccustomed. Andean peoples' bodies have, of course, become adapted to these conditions, with large chest cavities and lung capacity. Their cellular metabolism has modified to sustain higher red blood cell numbers. Nevertheless, strenuous work demands more energy to sustain the raised breathing, circulation and metabolic rates needed to maintain body temperature. As a result, highland peoples need to eat more to maintain a high basic metabolic rate, yet ironically they live in an environment where it is difficult to produce and obtain the necessary food for this diet.

The peopling of the Andes was thus a slow process, with generations at one altitude gradually becoming adapted to life at that level before their descendants could move into the next, higher zone, where the adaptive process took place again. Europeans, for the most part from comparatively lowland environments, have still been adapting through the generations since colonization began.

Unfortunately, we have no records of how lowland South Americans fared or coped with the high altitudes. Comparisons of the skeletons from lowland and highland burials, however, show that the two populations were more related within than between their respective groups.

POTATOES AND LLAMAS

In these highlands, agriculture consisted of a combination of root crops and herding. Because there are relatively few sizeable valleys – the valleys around Cuzco being exceptions – the steep slopes of valley and basin sides had to be adapted to provide flat areas for cultivation. Considerable labour and expertise were devoted to building millions of hillside terraces (*andenes*) and networks of irrigation canals.

The staple highland crop was the potato. Beans, squashes, peppers and peanuts were also important food crops. Maize can be grown at altitudes of up to 3,300m (11,000ft), but is at great risk from frost and hail at such heights.

The only domesticated animals were camelids (llamas, alpacas and vicuñas), dogs, guinea pigs and ducks. Llamas were herded in great flocks and provided the only pack animals for transport. They were also used for their wool (as were alpacas), meat and medicine. Dogs were raised as hunting companions and for food. Guinea pigs and ducks were raised for food, and also eggs in the case of the latter.

Below: Geographic map of the Andean Area, showing coastal plains, the Andes and the eastern rainforest.

ABUNDANT PLAINS – THE ALTIPLANO

The vast Altiplano (high plain) south of the central Peruvian Andes is formed where the principal Cordillera Blanca and Cordillera Negra diverge. Centred towards Lake Titicaca at the present Peruvian–Bolivian border, it lies at nearly 4,000m (13,000ft) above sea level. It forms a long trough, 800km (500 miles) north-west to south-east and drains north to south through a chain of lakes from Lake Azangaro in Peru through Titicaca to Lake Poopó in Bolivia. It is the largest expanse of agricultural flatlands in the Andean Area. The depth (up to 200m/650ft) and expanse (8,600 sq km/3,320 sq miles) of Lake Titicaca provides, as do the other lakes, a moderating influence on local temperatures.

In much of this region there was less need for labour-intensive terracing. Instead, pre-Hispanic peoples developed several methods for intensifying agricultural

Below: The high plains of the southern Andean plateaux are punctuated by volcanic cones, such as El Misti, believed to be the homes of gods whose destructive powers were feared.

Above: The sparser, bleaker high plains of the southern Altiplano provide little scope for agriculture, but they were widely used for llama herding.

production. Rivers were tapped by canals dug to channel their waters into the fields and to regulate ground water levels. In addition, check dams were constructed to collect and store run-off water, and aqueducts and dikes were made to divert and distribute it among the fields to water the crops.

CLAIMING THE LAND

During periods of high precipitation, the large region of low land, relatively speaking, around Lake Titicaca and the other lakes was reclaimed for agriculture by creating long, wide, ridged fields of mounded soils. They were separated by channels of slow-moving water, which provided protection from frost by releasing overnight the heat they had absorbed from the sun during the day. Nevertheless, to help maintain dense population levels, the steep slopes of the surrounding hills were also terraced to provide extra agricultural fields.

In drought years, when the lake level could drop by as much as 12m (39ft), some 50,000ha (124,000 acres) of formerly

Above: Alpacas were a species closely related to the llama. They provided a finer grade of wool than the llama.

cultivated land were left without the usual water channels and were simply abandoned temporarily.

As in the *puna*, the principal crops of the Altiplano were root vegetables. There were multiple varieties of potato, various tubers, legumes and grains such as quinoa domesticated from regional native species. In addition, the lakes, and especially Titicaca, provided a rich variety of aquatic resources. The deep, cold waters of the lakes supported abundant fish stocks, which had been exploited from early times. Migrating waterfowl (ducks and flamingos) provided plenty of seasonal meat and eggs. The shallow lakeshores harboured edible reeds – also used for roof thatching, clothing and for making fishing boats, and various water plants provided animal forage and were gathered as fodder for domesticated llama herds and guinea pigs.

GREAT HERDS OF LLAMAS

The llama and alpaca were both cornerstones of the Altiplano economy. Great herds of them were especially kept in the southern and northern Altiplano to sustain a pastoral way of life. From being the hunting grounds of the earliest inhabitants, these grasslands became the focus of llama and alpaca domestication from as early as 5000BC. Throughout the Andean

Area they were bred carefully for multiple purposes. The primary reason was for their wool, providing woven textiles for clothing, hats, bags and slings, as well as for exchange with lowland settlements for their produce. Textiles were also used to fulfil social taxation obligations.

As well as wool, several by-products were also of value. Llama meat and fat were important sources of protein and energy. Their bones were made into many tools, from scrapers, knives, needles and awls to musical instruments. The hides were made into clothing and other articles. Their dung was used as fuel and provided a source of fertilizer to re-enrich fields left fallow between growing seasons. Whole llamas were frequently sacrificed in religious ceremonies, and figured prominently in Andean cosmology. Finally, they were the pick-up trucks of pre-Hispanic Andeans, used to transport commodities over long distances.

Below: Vicuñas were prized for their fine wool and have adapted to high altitudes, where drought and freezing nights are the rule.

Above: Llamas were valuable, sure-footed pack animals for transporting goods between highlands and lowlands.

LIFE AT THE EDGE

Beyond the Altiplano lake basins, and especially towards the southern extreme of the great trough that forms the Altiplano, the landscape becomes increasingly arid. It would have been unsuitable for agriculture, or even llama herding, except in various isolated areas where a tenuous growing season could have been exploited with careful irrigation.

WESTERN DESERTS AND COASTAL VALLEYS

The western descent to the coastal strip of the Andean Area was an important and rich area of isolated cultural oases, at least in earliest pre-Hispanic times.

The region's climate is controlled by the Humboldt Current, which brings cold water northwards along the coast and creates cool, arid conditions inland. While the coastal air remains humid, causing coastal fog, temperature inversion (whereby air decreases in temperature less quickly than usual as it climbs) over the land inhibits rainfall and creates deserts inland – chiefly the Sechura in the north and the Atacama in the south of the Andean Area.

There is more arable land in the northern coastal valleys than in the southern coastal area. From north to south. there are three climate zones: semi-tropical in the north, sub-tropical in the middle and sub-tropical to desert in the south. The principal pre-Hispanic products of the coastal valleys and desert oases were maize, beans, squashes, peanuts, manioc, avocado and other semi-tropical fruits, and cotton.

Above: Eroding salt deposits of ancient raised shorelines are seen here at San Pedro de Atacama in Chile, the driest desert environment in the world.

IRRIGATION SYSTEMS

Along the Pacific watershed of the coastal strip virtually all desert farming and 85 per cent of sierra–coastal valley agriculture is reliant on run-off irrigation. More than 60 short rivers, rising in the steep western Andean slopes, descend through rugged then quickly levelling terrain to the Pacific Ocean. Tapping them for their water involved elaborate, labour-intensive projects to dig canals and channels to bring water from distant rivers to terraced fields. The very nature and sophistication of such works encouraged different regions to work together to establish and maintain them.

In the southern region of the coastal strip large expanses of desert provided a different challenge. Here people needed to bring water from the nearby sierra and from more widely spaced rivers. The Nazca and other rivers in this region flow on the surface in the upper

Left: Off-shore islands, such as Ballesta Island, Peru, were valuable sources of guano, used as fertilizer and a valuable trade item.

valleys only; down-valley they disappear into subterranean channels. In response to this condition, and perhaps enhanced in times of drought, the peoples of the area built elaborate underground irrigation systems of aqueducts to bring water from the underground rivers and to gather the water table through an arrangement of trenches and tunnels into catchment cisterns that could be tapped when needed.

HARVESTING THE SEA

In addition to agriculture, especially in the northern valleys (and largely independently from the southern desert valley agricultural societies), coastal cultures exploited the extremely rich maritime resources of the Pacific. Molluscs and crustaceans were collected on the foreshore; large and small fish were taken in nets and by hook (anchovies and sardines were harvested throughout the year and seasonally, respectively); sea mammals were hunted with harpoons; and sea birds were regularly taken. Offshore

islands, havens for vast seabird colonies, provided a regular source of guano for fertilizing the fields. Even edible kelp leaves were collected as a food source.

One commodity sought from farther north was the bivalve *Spondylus princeps* – the spiny or thorny oyster. Native in the coastal waters from Ecuador north to Baja California, it was exploited by coastal peoples from as early as 3000BC. Its collection is not easy, because its habitat is

Above: Vast deserts along the coasts of Peru and northern Chile contained scores of river valleys, providing oases for early agriculture.

18–50m (60–160ft) deep. Nevertheless, divers regularly collected it, and throughout pre-Hispanic times it provided a rich source of coastal and inland trade to both the north and south. It was sought as a ritual object and provides evidence of long-distance trade and contact between different cultures.

OASES CULTURES

In times of drought, oases cultures were stretched severely and it required, besides their religious beliefs, fortitude and ingenuity to sustain their cultural ways. Each river supplying an oasis valley, desert oasis or western sierra basin was otherwise isolated. Such isolation enabled several nearly self-governing populations to arise and maintain their independence. At the same time, however, there was a need for contact and the trading of goods from one region to another. Such links between desert oases, and indeed valleys, were spiritual and military enterprises whose strengths waxed and waned throughout Andean Area history.

Left: Ancient peoples of the desert coastlands relied on the rich harvest of the sea, and traded exotic shells with highland cultures.

THE *MONTAÑA* AND EASTERN RAINFORESTS

The geography of the eastern flank of the Altiplano and Cordillera provides a complete contrast to the western Cordillera. Here there are high, bleak plateaux called the *montaña* or Ceja de Selva, where the terrain and vegetation make agriculture difficult and careful terracing and water management are necessary. Llama herding is widespread here. Starting at about 4,000m (13,000ft) above sea level, the *montañas*, known as cloud forests, drop towards the east until they merge with true tropical forest. Rainfall averages 2,000–4,000mm (80–160in) a year.

RAINFOREST PRODUCTS
In addition to llama products, the hard and soft woods of the slopes provided the only major source of timber and wood for everyday and religious objects in the Andean Area. Agriculture on the middle slopes included maize, beans, squash, peanuts, peppers and cotton, all of which were transported by llama caravans specially commissioned by the rulers and elite of the Altiplano.

Most importantly, the *montaña* was the source of coca *(Erythroxylon coca)*, used for both practical and spiritual purposes. The alkaloid compounds derived from

Below: The stealth and power of the jaguar was revered by Andean peoples. It was a common 'form' for shape-changing shamans.

the dried leaves of the coca plant or shrub provided (and continue to provide today) stimulation to relieve the fatigue of strenuous labour at high altitudes. It was also a ritual commodity of symbolic and real importance from very early times. Its importance and limited availability also encouraged political arrangements and even wars over its control. The true tropical rainforest lies mostly outside the Andean Area. Here precipitation can be

Above: The dense rainforests of Antisuyu were the source of many products, including hallucinogenic mushrooms.

in excess of 8,000mm (315in) per year, and it flows into rivers destined for the Atlantic Ocean. However, both the eastern *montaña* descending from the Altiplano and the north-eastern slopes from the northern Andes meet the Amazon Rainforest.

This closeness of *montaña* and rainforest encouraged cultural links, trade for rainforest products and a reverence for its creatures. The red, blue and yellow feathers of rainforest parrots, kingfishers and macaws were coveted by highland peoples. Harpy eagle feathers were also sought, and the bird's predatory nature admired. Cayman and serpent representations featured in much highland art and religious iconography, starting with the Chavín culture. Gold collected in placer mines, hallucinogenic plants (especially mushrooms and tobacco), resinous woods and various tropical fruits and medicinal plants all made their way to Andean cities. Jaguar pelts and monkeys were sought as both were revered animals whose cunning, courage, fierceness and cleverness was to be emulated.

THE LIMITS OF CIVILIZATION

The eastern boundaries of the Inca Empire extended to the edges of the Amazon. To the Incas this was the land of the Antisuyu quarter and the eastern edge of Collasuyu quarter, the place where civilization ended and savagery began. It was Inca Roca, the sixth Inca ruler, who defeated the Chunchos of Antisuyu only by adopting their savage tropical forest methods of fighting – he 'became' a jaguar and wore a green cloak. Viracocha, the eighth Sapa Inca, established the boundary between civilized highlands and savage Antisuyu when he destroyed the town of Calca 'with a fireball', 'propelling' it to the other side of the River Vilcanota. Manco Capac, the founding Inca – who was defined in legend as carrying maize, the highland, civilized crop – defeated the Hualla Indians in the Cuzco Valley. They were described as growers of rainforest crops such as peppers and coca.

The Incas made several attempts to conquer parts of the rainforest, but the environment proved too alien. Once within the forest, Inca generals lacked familiar points of reference on a visible horizon and their disorientated armies thrashed about in the dense, unfamiliar terrain. Pachacuti Inca Yupanqui, Tupac Yupanqui and Huayna Capac all sent campaigns into the jungles, and all were defeated. Despite this, bowmen from the *montaña* and tropical forest borders were recruited into the Inca army.

Above: Exotic rainforest birds provided the colourful feathers for ritual capes, tunics and headdresses made by skilled craftsmen.

A PLACE APART

To the Inca, the rainforest was *hurin*, feminine and subservient, despite their failure to conquer any of it or coerce any of its inhabitants into taxable submission. Ollantaytambo and Machu Picchu in Antisuyu defined the edge of Inca civilization, and one of their purposes in their border positions was to attempt to control coca production.

The trading relationship between highland cultures and tropical forest peoples was mostly one-way: from the tropical forest to the highlands. Although trade, both in commodities and ideas, was brisk at the borders, no serious attempts were made by highland peoples to colonize the rainforest or to establish large trading settlements at the borders. The rainforests remained in this passive role throughout pre-Hispanic history, providing precious raw materials, imagery and inspiration, but otherwise remaining a separate world.

Left: Winding rivers in the rainforest were home to the cayman, the South American crocodile, which inspired religious images.

LAND OF EXTREMES

The Andean Cordillera occupied by the Incas and their predecessors is an area of extremes, both environmental and ecological. They include the full global range of geographic landscapes and seascapes, from dense rainforests to teaming oceans. The Cordillera's inhabitants would have had to cope with fundamental contrasts in terrain, soil, water resources, sea, weather and temperature, depending on where they settled. Characteristically, though frustratingly for farmers, where there is adequate level land for cultivation there is often little water, and vice versa. Equally, seasonal and cyclical weather patterns mean that periods of regular rainfall, producing fertile growing conditions, are interspersed with periods of drought sometimes lasting years, decades or even centuries.

IRREGULAR RAINFALL

The mountainous landscape of the Cordillera means that rainfall is irregularly distributed. It is seasonal, starting about late October and November, climaxing between December and March and virtually disappearing from June to September. This annual cycle is decidedly irregular, however, swinging between values above and below the median, which occurs only about once every four years. This irregularity introduces another paradox in Andean survival. Rainfall for higher-altitude agriculture, where farmers devised methods to make more cultivatable land available, but where there is less water, generally fluctuates less. Yet run-off agriculture, which is generally more productive, is possible mostly where the rainfall fluctuates the most.

Highland farming is most successful when rainfall is heavy enough to cause sufficient run-off for crop production. (The run-off is stored in a structure of suitable size and construction and used to water the land during dry periods.) But arid mountain soils absorb fixed amounts of moisture, and so run-off occurs only when this absorption level is exceeded. Rainfall exceeding this capacity generally occurs only between about 3,900m (12,800ft) and 4,900m (16,100ft). Above about 5,000m (16,400ft) most available water is locked-up in glaciers and ice fields. Therefore, severe fluctuations in rainfall in this crucial altitudinal zone have a severe effect on the amount of

Above: The Incas conquered the parched, desiccated surface of the Atacama and other western coastal deserts.

run-off water available down-slope in the most important agricultural basins and valleys. This unbalanced relationship between rainfall and run-off also explains the dramatic variation of the rivers of the Pacific coastal valleys.

STRESSFUL CONDITIONS

The effects of living at high altitude and coping with low blood oxygen saturation made life stressful for early Andeans. They needed to eat more than lowlanders to maintain their metabolic rate, yet changeable weather patterns and scarce foodstuffs made life precarious. Supporting and sustaining civilization in highland regions was thus measurably more costly in many ways than it was in lowland areas.

Alongside the daily stresses of living, earth movements and weather cycles caused problems. Tectonic activity, both small and large scale, brings disastrous consequences. Relentless tectonic creep exacerbates erosional patterns and affects canals and water collection methods by altering slopes, damaging canals and affecting their performance.

Left: The lush, well-watered Amazonian rainforest proved to be too alien and disorientating to the Inca armies.

Sudden disaster also came from earthquakes and volcanoes. Shifts from the plates that formed the Andes brought an earthquake of magnitude 7 or greater on the Richter Scale about once a decade. The immediate effects and consequent landslides caused fatalities as well as damage to buildings, canals and other structures. Volcanic activity persisted throughout ancient times, and into the present, especially in the northern Andean Area in Ecuador, southern Colombia and the Vicanota region of southern Peru.

Unable to explain these events scientifically, peoples of the Andes developed their own spiritual explanations involving cosmic battles and angry gods. Even into modern times they believed in mountain gods. When Mount Huaynaputina in southern Peru erupted in AD1600, the power of the explosion blew the entire crown of the mountain away, leaving a huge crater. Natives believed the event to be a rebellion of the ancient deities against the victory of the Christian gods.

Below: The sierra valleys were well watered but challenging. Raised fields and terracing maximized the amount of level ground for crops.

THE DREADED EL NIÑO

The phenomenon known as El Niño disrupted even what could be regarded as the 'regular' rainfall cycles described above, introducing perennial episodes of hostsile weather conditions. El Niños occur about every four to ten years. They are caused by the warming of the eastern tropical Pacific, changing atmospheric conditions, and altering weather cycles in the far and central Pacific. The conditions

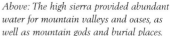

Above: The high sierra provided abundant water for mountain valleys and oases, as well as mountain gods and burial places.

also act to magnify the effects of changes in solar radiation. Usually lasting about 18 months, El Niños generate torrential storms accompanied by cataclysmic floods along the western coasts. Simultaneously, because the weather patterns have been reversed, the mountains and Altiplano become subject to prolonged periods of drought.

Along the desert western coasts, tonnes of debris deposited by earthquake-induced landslides, having lain loose for years, are flushed into the sea in the floods. Ground into fine sands by wave action, it is redeposited along the beaches. Strong offshore winds then collect it into huge dunes that can choke the life out of cities and settlements far inland.

Even longer-term droughts and wet periods affected Cordillera civilization. Evidence from glacier ice shows a substantial increase in atmospheric dust caused by drought between c.2200 and 1900BC; other extended droughts occurred in 900–800BC, 400–200BC, AD1–300, 562–95 and 1100–1450. Wetter periods occurred in AD400–500, 900–100 and 1500–1700.

LIVING WITHIN THE LANDSCAPE

Andean cultures faced great challenges, many of which were presented by the landscape around them. With its high mountains, dense rainforests and arid deserts, much of the Andean Area was not suitable for habitation, but, even so, communities developed wherever they could.

ESTABLISHING LINKS
Most early Andean communities developed in isolated situations in the western coastal valleys, the desert oases and the basins that lay between the mountains. Surrounding terrain made such settlements, by their very nature, independent and self-sufficient for the essentials of life.

Despite their isolation, however, such communities began to make contact with peoples in other regions and from other cultures. This may have been instigated as much by curiosity as by a desire to foster trade in order to supplement limited foodstuffs and other goods. As these links became established, social contact and trade took place across long distances. Inca civilization, as the empire was expanded, developed and exploited long-established patterns of long-distance trade.

Below: Maize was grown on the north coast of South America and throughout the Andean Area at 2,000–3,000m (6,600–9,800ft).

Above: This burial mantle displays a religious motif of mountain pumas or rainforest jaguars, from whose tails dangle trophy heads.

CONTRADICTORY CONDITIONS
Successful agriculture in the Cordillera and the development of civilization relied upon adequate sunshine, favourable temperatures, fertile soil, arable land and sufficient water – and also on the presence/availability of domesticated plants and animals.

In the *punas*, where agricultural settlements were carefully managed, the ruggedness and steepness of the land, along with poor weather conditions, increase with altitude, making the lower slopes the obvious places to develop. Yet in times of drought, mountain precipitation and soil moisture shift up-slope by 100–400m

(320–1,300ft) above normal distribution, leaving these lower slopes arid. Claiming and maintaining drought-tolerant ground for agricultural purposes required massive investments in materials and labour to check the erosion of thin mountain soils on steep slopes and to direct water to fields and terraces, and considerable will and co-operation to accomplish it.

The dramatically different environmental conditions between highlands and lowlands described earlier in this chapter

clearly reinforced the economic and cultural differences among the mountain, maritime-oasis, and *montaña* and rainforest peoples.

Each region in the Andean Area had strengths and weaknesses to encourage, challenge or inhibit its inhabitants. During periods of regional settlements, these varying strengths encouraged cultural variety. Yet, at the same time, the most important river valleys were centres for the spread of cultural developments that unified different regions. Prominent examples include the Chavín culture from its mountain valley, the Moche people in the Lambayeque and adjacent northern coastal valleys, the Nazca culture from its southern coastal desert oasis, the Wari and Tiwanaku 'empires', respectively in the high Cordillera and the Altiplano, and the Incas from their central Andean mountain valley.

Sierra basins and east–west-running river valleys of the western coast form self-sufficient oases for settlements. Steep mountain gorges, high passes and dry deserts make access between regions difficult and inhibit contact between their

Below: The potato provided a staple of the Andean diet. It was cultivated at elevations of 2,000 to nearly 4,000m (6,600–13,100ft).

inhabitants, separating and segregating rather than uniting them. Vast amounts of effort would have been needed to incorporate large areas into states and kingdoms, as occurred throughout Andean prehistory.

The periods of drought described above affected farming reliant on run-off water much more than agriculture reliant on direct rainfall. This was because arid, absorbent mountain soils better retained the moisture available. Alternating wetter periods brought greater benefit to run-off agriculture and coastal irrigation schemes because of the reversals of the 'normal' distributions of weather patterns and precipitation.

REDISTRIBUTION OF ASSETS

Cultivation reliant on run-off water normally provides higher yields than rain-fall farming. Thus, the vast plains of the Altiplano were exploited with raised fields, and the western coastal valley and desert oases with re-channelled water from the rivers. Both areas developed joint labour schemes to build the necessary structures. Such methods secured more arable land at high altitudes than in the lowlands, but, frustratingly, only about 20 per cent of Andean cultivated crops grow well above 3,000m (9,800ft), while 90 per cent grow best below 1,000m (3,300ft), so there is a limit on how much production increases.

Above: The transport of goods by llama caravans enabled trading between lowland and highland regions to take place.

These differences in the distribution of productive land, crops and resources led to the development of relations between regions to the point that they were dependent upon each other. Raw materials and products were exchanged through trade from very early times, but also through conquest and coercion. During periods of unity, not only were produce and rare commodities traded between coast and mountain, and between mountain and *montaña* and rainforest, but also the ruling elite actually redistributed groups of people to moderate the effects of adverse seasonal weather patterns. These practices are well documented for the Inca, and archaeological evidence from earlier cultures, kingdoms and empires indicates that such practices were developed much earlier.

The redistribution of both goods and labour enabled rulers to maintain control by making sure that everyone under their rule had sufficient resources to live on. To such an end, the Incas used llama caravans to take produce and manufactured goods between highlands and lowlands. Potatoes, maize, peanuts, chilli peppers, coca leaves and much else were transported in woollen and cotton sacks in llama caravans.

CHAPTER THREE

SACRED LANDSCAPES, SACRED SKIES

The ancient Andean cultures revered every aspect of their environment: the landscape and seascape, and the very skies above them. Unable to explain their universe scientifically, ancient Andeans, like other ancient peoples, explained their surroundings with reconstruction stories that were rooted in their view of the world.

The Milky Way, known as Mayu, was thought to be *the* celestial river, and thus the source of all moisture – a vital part of Andean life. Mayu also had important influences on daily life, and the Incas formed links between the stars in the sky and myths. They also formed a view of a cyclical world.

Nature was considered a living, breathing being. It was something to engage with rather than to conquer, to co-operate with rather than to dominate. The landscape and skies were animate and charged with interactive, reciprocal forces.

There were many sacred places called *huacas* within the Andean Area. Most *huacas* were natural places, but others were man-made or were human modifications of natural work. Mountain tops, known as *apus*, were also venerated, although volcanoes and earthquakes were more feared for their destructive powers – the anger of the gods.

Further elements of mystery are added to the Andean landscape by Nazca lines, forming natural figures and shapes in the desert, and *ceque* lines – sacred pathways radiating from Cuzco.

Left: Mt Illimani, in the Cordillera Real, and other peaks were believed to be the source of water and the homes of the gods.

PLACES OF WORSHIP

To the Incas, and no doubt to their Andean Area ancestors, their entire surroundings were sacred. Throughout the landscape, special places that had been revered for generation after generation, and where offerings were made or special rituals performed, were known as *huacas*. As well as the powerful central deities of the Inca pantheon, whose presences were manifested in individual temples in the Coricancha in Cuzco, Andean peoples recognized a host of lesser nature gods, spirits and oracles that existed throughout the land. *Huacas* were places where such lesser figures could also be revered and, if necessary, placated.

INCA *HUACAS*
Huacas were hallowed places where significant mythological events had taken place and/or where offerings were made to local deities. It is thought that all Andean cultures had *huacas* that were special to them, and thus most *huacas* were of ancient origin. The majority were natural

Below: The sacred Intihuatana (Hitching Post of the Sun) at Machu Picchu typifies natural outcrops carved as sacred huacas.

features of the landscape, such as mountaintops (*apus*), caves, springs and especially stones or boulders, but they could also be man-made objects, or natural objects or landscape features modified by human workmanship. An Inca *huaca* could also be a location along a sacred *ceque* line (a sacred route), such as the pillars erected on the western horizon above Cuzco for viewing the sunset from the Capac Usnu for special astronomical observations.

In and around Cuzco there were more than 300 *huacas*. Other Inca sacred places were concentrated wherever there was an association with a ruler. For example, Huayna Capac, the twelfth Sapa Inca, undertook a special pilgrimage to visit the favourite places of his father, Tupac Yupanqui, in Cajamarca, as did Atahualpa those of Huayna Capac in the northern provinces before marching against his brother Huáscar. Ironically, it was in Cajamarca that Atahualpa met defeat at the hands of Pizarro.

Ceque lines themselves, by their very nature as sacred or ritual pathways, were also *huacas*, and, equally, they incorporated *huacas* as points along the sacred routes they provided.

Above: The outcrop of Qenqo, north of Cuzco, was one of the Inca's most sacred huacas. *It resembles a seated puma.*

ANCESTRAL *HUACAS*
Royal and elite mausoleums, where the mummified remains of ancestors were kept, were also regarded as *huacas*. Spanish colonial sources identify many Inca royal *huacas*; and Chan Chan, the capital of the rulers of Chimú, surrounded their royal mausoleum compounds. These records reveal what appear to be the two basic classifications of such man-made *huacas*: the *huacas adatorios* – the sanctuaries and temples where gods and goddesses were worshipped; and the *huacas sepulturas* – the burial places of the most important members of the deceased.

A characteristic *huaca* is the collection of stones known as the Pururaucas around Cuzco. These were revered as the re-petrified ancient stones that had allegedly risen up and become Inca warriors to help Pachacuti Inca Yupanqui defend Cuzco against the Chancas in the early 15th century. Other examples include Qenqo, just north of Cuzco, where one large

Above: Stone cairns on mountain passes were a special type of huaca *called an* apacheta. *They were thought to hold local deities' spirits.*

upright boulder was left untouched, presumably because its silhouette resembled that of a seated puma, and the sacred shrines and statues of Viracocha at Cacha and Urcos. In some cases a *huaca* was a combination of the natural and the miraculous. Once again the stones of Pururaucas are a prime example. Another is the stone of the ancestor brother Ayar Uchu atop Huanacauri Mountain, which is believed to be the petrified body of that ancestor. Yet another example is Pariacaca, which/who seems to have been simultaneously a mountain and a mobile deity or culture hero.

PROVINCIAL *HUACAS*
The movements and final resting places of important rulers strengthened attachments to the natural symbolism of *huacas* as ancestral or 'parental'. The hill called Huanacauri above Cuzco, for example, was regarded as the father of three of the founding Inca ancestors, each turned to stone as a prominent rock or crag. Other Andean

peoples regarded the local mountains as being 'like parents' who gave birth to the local community. Indeed, such beliefs are enshrined in the story of the creation of peoples by the god Viracocha, who assigned each people their region as a sacred act.

Most tribes, 'nations' and towns undoubtedly had a particular place that was recognized as their group's *huaca*. Equally, most kinship groups, the *ayllus*, also had their own *huacas*. It was believed that the spirit of the *huaca* exerted a special influence over the lives and destinies of the members of the group. *Huacas* continue to be recognized by local peoples in the Andes today in a mixture of pre-Christian and Catholic belief.

LINKS FROM PAST TO PRESENT
Reverence at *huacas* and the following of *ceque* lines represented a strengthening of the past, a reassurance of the present and an insuring of the future. Indeed, the myth-history attached to Inca sacred places infused the very landscape.

The stories attached to individual *huacas* have survived mostly in fragments. Many are recoverable, however, from traditions transcribed in the longer narratives

of Inca history. Although the sacred *huaca* system is well known in and around Cuzco, there is less surviving direct evidence of other local shrines; but much may still be discovered through further research.

Below: All rivers and lakes were held sacred by ancient Andeans because water was universally recognized as the source of life.

SACRED WATERS

Water was vital to the Incas and their predecessors, and as such was revered almost as a god. They believed the cosmos itself to include a celestial ocean upon which the Earth floated.

CELESTIAL RIVER
The Milky Way, Mayu, was *the* celestial river, counterpart to all earthly rivers and the source of all moisture. Water from the sea was collected into Mayu, flowed into and across the sky and was released as rain and snow on the mountains to fill the streams, rivers and lakes, flow into the sea, and form as dew, frost, mist and fog on the land and over the ocean. From small runnels developed the mountain streams and rivers that watered the landscape. Humans then exercised the utmost ingenuity to make the most of the collection of water and use it to water crops.

Inca records transcribed in the Spanish sources describe how Andean farmers followed Mayu's movements carefully, for the solstices of the Milky Way coincide with the beginnings of the wet and dry seasons. Weather patterns, however, were

Below: The River Urubamba was a major source of irrigation in the central Andes and one of the most sacred rivers.

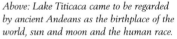

periodically disrupted by El Niño events, causing long periods of drought in areas where regular seasonal rain had made the land fertile. Such times were very difficult for people in the western sierra, valley and desert oases, mountain basins and the Altiplano.

Such careful observation and the invention of an explanation of the seasonal associations demonstrates the seamless link in the pre-Hispanic Andean mind between the practical necessity of water and the sacred origin of it. In addition to its strictly practical uses, water played an

Above: Lake Titicaca came to be regarded by ancient Andeans as the birthplace of the world, sun and moon and the human race.

important role in religious ritual. Andean peoples reliant on rainwater for their agricultural survival made offerings to the natural forces through the deities that controlled them. By 'feeding' the gods in this way, they created a reciprocal obligation, which, it was hoped, would secure a reliable supply of water.

HIDDEN WATERS
This sacred and practical association began with the earliest Andean civilizations. In religious ceremonial centres, water clearly played an important part and was used to complement ritual. U-shaped temples were oriented towards mountain sources of water. At Chavín de Huántar, an intriguing aspect of the galleries and passages within its temples is the apparent acoustic use of water within its hidden interior. The system of conduits to the chambers could literally be made to roar when water was flushed rapidly through the drains and the sound vented around the chambers. What this sounded like and what feelings it evoked in the hearts and minds of worshippers in the courtyards outside can only be imagined.

In the Early Intermediate Period, the Nazca culture inhabiting the dry desert landscape of the southern Peruvian coast naturally found the capture, collection and use of water paramount to their survival. One of the functions of their geoglyphs was the promotion and maintenance of communication with distant mountain deities who controlled the flow of water. For geological reasons, the Nazca River (and others in this drainage system) disappears into subterranean channels at mid-valley. The site of the ceremonial centre of Cahuachi in the mid-Nazca River drainage area appears to have been deliberately placed between the two zones of surface water flow. Residential settlements up and down the valley apparently used Cahuachi as their sacred gathering place for worship. Underground cisterns connected by aqueducts and reached by stone-cobbled spiral paths formed a system of water supply and control.

Below: The sacredness of water was encapsulated in channels and fountains in Inca cities, as here at Machu Picchu.

THE PUMA'S TAIL

Given the earlier Andean preoccupation with the importance of water, it is no coincidence that one-third of the sacred *ceque* pathways around Cuzco led to or were otherwise oriented by the major springs and other sources of water in the region. When Pachacuti Inca Yupanqui rebuilt Cuzco after securing Inca supremacy in the valley, the Huatanay and Tullumayu rivers were partly re-routed to conform to the new plan of the city – that of a crouching puma. At the south-east end of the city, where the two rivers converge, the triangular patch of land thus created forms the puma's tail.

Above: The zigzag water channel cut into the natural outcrop at Qenqo branches, then rejoins. It was used for ritual libations.

SACRED TITICACA

The sacredness of water in pre-Hispanic Andean civilization is most fundamentally shown in the singular reverence for Lake Titicaca as the place of origin. The focus of the Tiwanaku Empire in the Early Intermediate Period and Middle Horizon, Titicaca was regarded as the legendary place of the origin of the cosmos. Peoples throughout the Andes created myths and legendary historical links to establish their origin at Titicaca/Tiwanaku.

MOUNTAINS OF THE GODS

In a land dominated by dramatic landscapes, it was inevitable that mountains and their features and characteristics became the focus of awe and were imbued with divine powers. Mountains were regarded as the dwelling places of the gods or even as the gods themselves. They were associated with weather patterns and recognized as the ultimate source of water.

SACRED MOUNTAIN LOCATIONS
Among the mountains there were several special types of *huacas*. A stone or stones regarded as the petrified ancestor of a people or *ayllu* was known as a *huanca*. Especially prominent or large boulders in the landscape, which were believed to incorporate the essence of an ancestor of one or more local kinship groups, were typical examples of *huancas*. Such *huancas* were (and still are) to be found in town centres or placed upright in the middle of a field. As the physical

Below: The primeval Moche mountain god, also associated with the creator god Ai Apaec, is depicted at the Huaca de la Luna.

manifestation or representation of an ancestor, they were thought to act as a guard on the interests of the local community.

The *apacheta* comprised a pile of stones at the top of a mountain pass or at a crossroads. *Apachetas* were believed to hold the spirits of local deities, and travellers would seek the favour of these gods by leaving offerings of coca leaves (*Erythroxylon coca*, the source of cocaine) or clothing, or by adding a stone to the heap before continuing their journeys. In a practical way, such features also no doubt acted as way-markers for travellers unsure of the route ahead.

With virtually every mountainscape dominated by volcanic peaks, they were only too evident as sources of mysterious power. Such special *huacas* were venerated as *apu* (literally 'lord') and were believed to have a direct influence on animal and crop fertility for those who lived in their vicinity. Sacred pilgrimages to such mountaintops to seek the favour of the spirit of the *apu* were a regular feature of Andean traditional religion – a long-standing practice that continues to the present day.

Above: The Late Intermediate Period Sicán Tucume pyramid in the Lambayeque Valley mimicked the shape of a mountain.

THE PRIMEVAL MOUNTAIN GOD
The concept of a god of the mountains was one of the most ancient aspects of Andean civilization. In one of his earlier manifestations, as the mountain god of the Moche, he was recognized as both a creator and sky god, but was believed to have played only a remote part in human affairs. He thus remained nameless but was represented frequently on Moche pottery and textiles with feline features. The depiction of images of fanged beings on Chavín pottery of much earlier date might have been his prototype, and thus the concept of a divine mountain power was spread far and wide.

The obvious association of mountains and the weather was reflected in the close association of the mountain god and Ai Apaec, sky god or perhaps son. The mountain god's throne was usually placed on a mountaintop, beneath which his manifestation as Ai Apaec was more active in association with terrestrial affairs. Moche military conquest and/or ritual combat was partly undertaken for the purpose of taking prisoners for sacrifice to these deities. According to some authorities, Ai Apaec was also the principal god of the Chimú of the Late Intermediate Period, derived from the Moche culture. Others argue that Ai Apaec simply means 'to make', and was therefore an invisible creator comparable to later Inca Viracocha.

Above: Volcanoes were recognized as the homes of the gods, whose anger with humans was also shown by destructive earthquakes.

VOLCANOES AND EARTHQUAKES

Volcanic eruptions, although not frequent occurrences, were seen as the wrath of the gods, not necessarily as punishment for wrong-doing in a retributional sense, but rather simply as demonstrations of how much the fate of humankind was in the hands of the gods. Earthquakes were even more prominent in this role and were perhaps equal in importance only to water and the sun in influencing Andean civilization.

Earthquakes disrupted the very framework of civilization, wreaking great physical damage and affecting the fabric of society and its organization. Reliance on water and its careful redirection and distribution from mountains to agricultural terraces paradoxically left the dependants knowingly vulnerable to the destruction of the terraces by the very deities who provided the water and who dwelled at its source.

Cyclopean architecture and the close-fitting blocks of Inca architecture also reflect the influence of earthquakes. Built to withstand seismic shocks, Inca architecture is often more stable than the Spanish colonial and later structures that replaced it or were built on Inca foundations. Perhaps even the fact that so many *huacas* are stones was influenced by earthquakes: such natural formations, as part of the landscape often not destroyed in earthquakes, may have been perceived to be one of the immutable elements of cosmic structure.

A principal god of earthquakes was Pachacamac, synonymous with and worshipped at one of the most ancient sites of Andean civilization. The site and the god rivalled the Island of the Sun in Lake Titicaca for supremacy as the most sacred location of the Andean Area. Pachacamac was the Earth-shaker – even the most minor tremor was a reminder of his presence and power. In recognition and reverence, Pachacuti Inca Yupanqui assumed the name of Earth-shaker after his defeat of the Chancas and domination of the Cuzco Valley.

THE INFLUENCE OF MOUNTAINS

The divinity of mountains also influenced the architecture of ancient Andean civilizations. From earliest times, U-shaped temple structures were oriented to the mountains, perhaps opening their arms to the divine powers and pleading for the water they provided. Pyramidal temple structures seemed to mimic in miniature the mountains around them, and yet themselves still dwarfed the humans who built them, seemingly reminding them of their powerlessness in the hands of the gods. The fabric of many pyramidal mounds, which were built of millions of adobe (mud) bricks, is the result of the mixing and moulding together of both earth and water – the two fundamental mountain elements.

The sacredness of mountains and their power over the survival of civilization remained a feature throughout Inca times. Llibiac, a god of thunder and lightning, was the principal deity of the Llacuaz Ayllu of Cajatambo – showing the continuity of belief and its interconnection with Andean social organization.

A final and rather poignant reminder of mountain-top sacredness is the use of remote mountain peaks as the place of child sacrifice in Inca times. In recent years the discovery of the freeze-dried mummies of some of these sacrifices has provided some of the most spectacular and informative evidence of pre-Hispanic religious practices.

Below: Mt Ausangate in the Cordillera Central was the personification of the apu *sacred mountain spirit.*

LINES IN THE DESERT

The coastal desert *pampa* of southern Peru was the home of the Nazca culture, which flourished from about 200BC to AD500. All aspects of Nazca culture were dominated by ritual. Perhaps the most dramatic evidence of this was the making of lines and images in the desert in the form of geoglyphs. Many people have investigated the lines and their meaning over decades, including Paul Kosok, Maria Reiche and Anthony Aveni.

Other line figures were made in the Pacific coastal valleys from Lambayeque to northern Chile.

SHAPES IN THE DESERT

The Nazca desert lines are the most famous examples of pre-Inca sacred routes. The lines, which can be best seen and most appreciated from the air, were made by scraping the patinated desert surface gravel and stones to one side to reveal the lighter coloured, unpatinated under-surface. The lines are formed by

Below: The sacred route at Cantalloc on the Nazca Desert plain of southern Peru typifies a geometric geoglyph in its spiral pathway.

the combination of light sand and aligned gravel and stones. The region's natural aridity has helped to preserve them.

More than 640 sq km (425 sq miles) of the desert are covered with these lines, figures and shapes. They comprise recognizable figures, geometrical shapes and seemingly random lines and cleared areas. Recognizable figures are of animals revered in the Nazca religious concept of the world – spiders, monkeys and birds – plus flowers and human-like supernatural figures. Some lines run perfectly straight

Above: The Giant of Atacama at Cerro Unitas, northern Chile, is the world's largest hill figure at 86m (280ft) high.

for great distances across the desert. Others spiral, or converge on a single point. Altogether there are some 1,300km (800 miles) of such lines.

FIGURES AND PATTERNS

There are two principal types or groups. Figures on low slopes or hillsides seem to be placed such that they are obvious to travellers on the plains below, even though seen obliquely. Patterns of lines, both straight and curving, form 'enclosed' or designated areas, geometric shapes and large cleared patches.

Sets of lines form geometric patterns, and clusters of straight lines converge on common nodes, or, conversely, radiate from 'ray centres' on hills. In his researches, the archaeo-astronomer Anthony Aveni has identified and mapped 62 such nodes and radiations. Some of the lines lead to irrigated oases, or link sites, such as the line between the settlement of Ventilla and the ritual centre of Cahuachi. Individual straight lines of various widths are more than 20km (12½ miles) long. One famous set of lines, which forms a huge arrow of 490m (roughly 1,600ft), pointing towards the Pacific Ocean, is thought to be a symbol to invoke rain.

Each animal or plant figure comprises a single continuous line, with different beginning and ending points. The line never crosses itself. There is a hummingbird, a duckling, a spider, a killer whale, a monkey, a llama, several plants and human-like beings, as well as trapezoids and triangles of cleared areas, zigzags and spirals. Altogether there are some 300 such figures, and, combined with the lines, about 3.6 million sq m (10.8 million sq ft) of *pampa* floor have been scraped away to create them.

MYSTERIOUS LINES?

The Nazca figures are difficult to conceive, and certainly impossible to see as whole figures from the ground, except obliquely. Their presence has prompted a variety of speculation regarding their meaning, and argument has raged for more than 60 years over the meanings of these and other geoglyphs. Proposals range from their having been made by beings from outer space – for which there is categorically no evidence – to their use for astronomical observation – which seems plausible but has not yet been conclusively demonstrated.

There is no evidence that the lines were made by anyone other than the Nazca themselves. Although we will never know the exact meaning of each line or figure, they are clearly ritual lines,

Below: The great hummingbird geoglyph on the Nazca Desert plain represents a messenger from the gods.

shapes and figures that reflect Nazca religious concepts. Their similarity to patterns on pottery and textiles, associations with Nazca burials and mummification, and with Nazca settlements and water sources reflects Nazca cosmology.

Creating the lines was a simple matter of proportional geometry. There is no difficulty in tracing an envisioned figure in the sand, and then translating the shape into a giant figure on the ground: only multiplication and proportional ratios are necessary to replicate a drawing using strings and pegs to trace and pace out the positions of the lines and patterns. Straight lines that cross the desert are easily produced by aiming at fixed positions on the horizon. Practical experiments to make neo-Nazca lines have proved the ease with which they can be created and the relatively small number of people and time needed to do so.

WHAT WERE THEY USED FOR?

The most plausible, and indeed obvious, explanation of the meaning of the Nazca lines is linked to the landscape, climate and accompanying features of Nazca settlement and material culture. The lines were associated with the Nazcas' necessary preoccupation with water and the fertility of their crops, together with the worship of mountains – the ultimate source of irrigation waters – and a pantheon of deities

Above: The geoglyph at Paracas, southern Peru, might have been a symbol of desert fertility and an orienteering aid to fishermen.

or supernatural beings who were believed to be responsible for bringing or withholding the rains.

Some lines may be related to astronomical observations – especially the positions of the sun through the year – that reflect times for planting and harvesting. Geometric patterns are ritual pathways, created and owned by groups within Nazca social organization for ceremonial processions. Ceremony, praying to the gods for the elements of life itself, is part of the 'mystery' of the lines. The axes of most lines run parallel to watercourses. Other lines are just as clearly the paths between settlements and the ceremonial centres themselves.

The number of lines, and their creation over a period of 700–800 years, over-marking each other in great profusion, shows that they were not conceived as a grand overall plan. The lines and figures appear to have been made by and for small groups – perhaps even individuals. Some may have been created for a single ceremony; others were used repeatedly. 'Solid' cleared areas might have been for congregations, while figures probably formed ritual pathways to be walked by people for specific ritual purposes.

CEQUE PATHWAYS

The *ceque* system of sacred routes was a uniquely Inca theoretical and practical concept interwoven with myth, astronomical observation, architectural alignment, and the social and geographical divisions of the empire. Sacred routes, however, were vital parts of pre-Inca cultures as well, and in this light the Inca *ceque* lines can be seen as integral with a long tradition of systems of sacred routes and pathways dating from pre-Hispanic Andean culture.

Ceques were straight, sacred 'lines' radiating from the Coricancha sacred precinct in Cuzco. Each line linked numerous *huacas* along its length. There were 41 such lines uniting 328 *huacas* and survey points within and around Cuzco. It is perhaps significant that the 328 *huacas* and stations correspond to

Below: Map showing the ceque *system of sacred or ritual routes linking the shrines and their locations.*

the number of days in the 12 sidereal lunar months (328/12 – the 27.3-day period of the rotation of the moon around the Earth–moon centre of mass). They were grouped according to 'upper' (*hanan*) and 'lower' (*hurin*) Cuzco and thus to the four quarters of the empire. Although theoretically straight, for practical purposes *ceques* sometimes had to obey the restrictions of the actual terrain through which they ran.

MULTIPLE PURPOSES

Points along the lines also served to regulate land holdings, water distribution, labour divisions, and ritual and ceremonial activities. *Ceques* were used as processional routes followed by *capacocha* (sacrificial individuals) at the beginnings of their journeys to the place of sacrifice. Combinations of *ceques* and their associated *huacas* distinguished the different *panaca* kin-group land-holdings within Inca society.

Above: Inca roads followed valley routes between cities, crossing mountain passes and river gorges using grass-fibre bridges.

For example, sunset on 26 April and the observation of the setting of the Pleiades on or about 15 April were made from the same place in the Capac Usnu plaza in central Cuzco. The settings were viewed between two stone pillars, together regarded as a *huaca*, which had been erected on the skyline west of the city. Farther on, beyond the horizon, another *huaca* was the spring named Catachillay, another name for the Pleiades.

The movements of Mayu, the Milky Way, were linked to the *ceque* system by a division separating the four quarters along the inter-cardinal (between-the-compass-points) axis of Mayu, and the southernmost point of Mayu's movement in the night sky.

The 16th-century Spanish chronicler Juan de Betanzos describes the sixth *ceque* of Antisuyu quarter, on which lay the sixth *huaca*, as 'the house of the puma'. Here the mummified body of the wife of the emperor Pachacuti Inca Yupanqui was kept, to whom child sacrifices were offered.

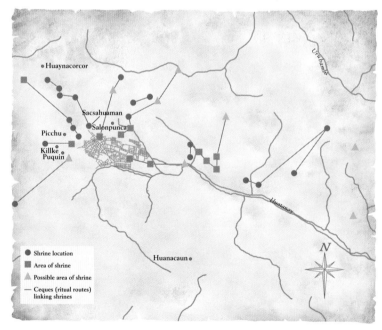

Huaynacorcor

Sacsahuaman

Picchu

Salonpunca

Killke
Puquin

Huancaun

Urubamba

Huatanay

N

- ● Shrine location
- ■ Area of shrine
- ▲ Possible area of shrine
- — Ceques (ritual routes) linking shrines

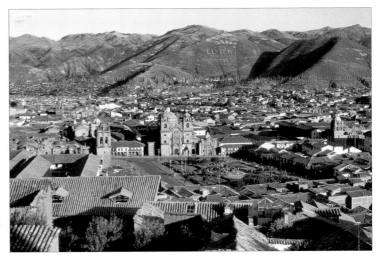

CEQUES AND SOCIAL STRUCTURE

Once again it was the vital importance of water in Andean life that formed an important part in the creation and use of the *ceque* ritual routes. The four *suyus* (quarters) of the Inca Empire, represented in the four divisions of Cuzco, were demarcated by the organization of the flow of water through the city. In turn, the radiating *ceque* lines organized the kinship *ayllu* groups into a hierarchy of positions either up or down river. This hierarchy itself reflected the nature of Inca society, in which different *ceque* lines were associated with the different bloodlines, particularly with the royal *panacas*, each of which was the origin of one of the primary descendants of the Inca ruler.

Thus, each *ceque* was created by and held information about irrigation, the Inca calendar and religious worship. Each *ceque* and its functions were maintained and tended by the appropriate kinship group

and social rank – aristocratic, mixed-blood or common – in a rotational system as the *ceque* lines were marked off around the horizon surrounding Cuzco.

In his *Historia del Nuevo Mundo*, Bernabé de Cobo describes the eighth *ceque* in the Chinchaysuyu (north-west quadrant). At its seventh *huaca*, a hill called Sucanca, a channel brought water from Chinchero. Two towers erected on the hill marked the position of the rising sun on the day when maize planting had to begin. Consequently, sacrifices at the *huaca* were directed to the sun, soliciting him to appear and shine through the towers at the appropriate time.

The system of *ceque* lines also regulated the Inca organization of annual labour, especially seasonal labour to do with agriculture and the maintenance of irrigation systems. Once a year, in the central plaza of upper (*hurin*) Cuzco, a ritual ploughing took place. Chosen representatives from 40 families selected from the four quarters dug up as if for planting a designated portion of the plaza field. Such a system of shared civic responsibilities and duties in prearranged patterns and rituals, and at determined times through the seasons of the year, appear to be a culmination of such systematic practices in pre-Inca cultures.

Left: The modern Inca Trail near Intipunku, Peru, follows the route of an ancient Inca road from Cuzco.

Above: The modern Plaza de Armas, Cuzco, was the ancient Huacaypata Plaza, centre of the Inca capital.

WHERE ARE THEY NOW?

The Dutch anthropologist Tom Zuidema devoted more than 40 years to the study of *ceques* and the sources of their organization and meaning. The *ceque* routes are described in considerable detail in Cobo's chronicle and other Inca colonial sources. However, the structures, such as towers at *huacas*, have long since been dismantled.

In the late 1970s Zuidema and archaeo-astronomer Anthony Aveni devoted four seasons of fieldwork to careful interpretations of the chronicles and surveyed the likely routes of *ceques* and locations of the *huacas* in Cobo's descriptions, using their knowledge of the terrain and landscape around Cuzco. Their efforts proved the validity of the system. In addition to mapping the locations of numerous *huacas*, they located three original places where astronomical *huacas* were used for measurements. One was a pair of towers to mark sunset at the June solstice, situated on a hill called Lacco, north of Cuzco. The second, another pair of towers, marked the December solstice from the Coricancha. The third was four pillars on Cerro Picchu, in western Cuzco, marking planting time; sighted from the *ushnu* stone in the Coricancha, they were used to track the sun on its mid-August passage through its lowest point.

RELIGION AND TRADE

The agricultural staples of Andean civilization were maize corn, the potato and various squashes and legumes. Pastoralism – llama herding – in upland regions and the exploitation of rich marine fauna were practised. In the Andean Area, variety and diversity of crops decreases with altitude. Consequently, people in upland regions were characteristically both farmers and herders because the combination of activities was more productive than either was singly.

In contrast, in lowland areas ancient Andeans tended to be specialists, engaging primarily in agriculture in the coastal desert valleys or in marine fishing. Here, by contrast to the uplands, the pursuit of one activity or the other as a full-time occupation was more productive than practising a combination of the two. In tropical forest areas, people needed to combine several sources of living – farming small cleared forest plots, hunting and fishing the rivers.

EARLY TRADE

Yet, even from the earliest times, although the bulk of the population was engaged in producing food through agriculture or marine fishing, there was contact between different regions for the exchange of the products of different areas. These contrasting activity zones, spaced across the land but with very different farming activities at varying altitudes, required different solutions to the problems of supply and demand, and fostered the classic highland–lowland reciprocal trade of the Andean Area.

In upland regions, communities of farmers tended to be self-sufficient in producing

Left: The importance of maize to northern coastal oasis valley cultures is shown in this Early Intermediate Period effigy vessel of maize cobs.

Above: From the most ancient times, the peoples of valleys and basins used terracing and irrigation channels to maximize land use.

their own essentials through a combination of hill farming and herding. In the lowland valleys and marine fishing areas, however, communities of specialists bartered for each other's produce. The variety of activities for making a living and the practice of exchange between regions naturally led to the movement of people and ideas, as well as of goods, between areas.

The physical nature of water preservation, its distribution in elaborate irrigation systems, the making of raised fields and extensive hill terracing have been described elsewhere. Maximum exploitation was made of physical resources and modifications of the natural landscape to increase production, presumably partly as the solution to rising population. Yet soon, living at mere subsistence level would not be enough for most people.

Above: Inca farmers harvesting a potato crop, depicted by Guaman Poma de Ayala in his Nueva Crónica y Buen Gobierno, *c.1613.*

GROWTH IN RELIGION

Natural processes were in control of the seasons and thus of the water supply and of agricultural success or failure. Ancient Andeans modified their landscape as much as they could to alleviate the seeming unpredictability of nature. However, lacking scientific explanations for the seasons, their direct observations led to the creation of supernatural explanations, or in other words, religion.

They also began to understand the connections between seasonal changes and recurring natural occurrences in their different regions, for example that drought on the coasts corresponded with greater rainfall in the mountains. All Andeans lived under the same sky, and their observations of the heavens also enabled them to invent explanations for the world around them and to exchange these explanations with each other.

Having moved beyond existing at mere survival level, Andean peoples now related their day-to-day experiences to cosmological ideas that explained them. To appease and solicit the gods who controlled human fate, significant numbers of people in society were devoted to the production of objects that produced no immediate physical subsistence, but did aid spiritual well-being. By the time of the Late Intermediate Period and Late Horizon urban civilizations of the Chimú and the

Inca, large numbers of specialist craftspeople were state-sponsored producers of non-essential goods (non-essential only in the sense of not being necessary for survival, but nevertheless considered essential for the well-being of society).

Potters, metallurgists, textile and feather workers were employed by the state to make huge amounts of specialized objects solely for burial and royal tombs. In addition, priests and dedicated royal historians and record-keepers were employed to continue and sustain state religion and history. Furthermore, regional administrators were required to regulate the collection, storage and redistribution of produce to ensure that all citizens of the state had enough to live on, and to support those not actually engaged in agriculture, herding, marine fishing or trading.

TRADE IN RITUAL OBJECTS

For each community to practise its religious beliefs, it needed the objects and images that it perceived to be significant. Finding these items, however, often meant looking outside the settlements, thus expanding trading relationships that had hitherto dealt purely with essential goods.

As urban and ritual sites became more complex and relationships between settlements more elaborate, the exchange of both types of goods grew more organized and sophisticated. The images on pottery, textiles and architecture, and the artefacts found in archaeological sites and burials in the earliest settlements and ritual centres in uplands, lowlands and tropical forests show that each sought the produce and exotic materials of the other.

Marine products such as the thorny oyster, shark teeth, stingray spines and shells were important ritual objects that became essential in ceremony in both upland and lowland religious centres. Likewise, mountain deities, ocean gods and sky gods were considered the explanations or the controllers of human fate. The attributes of tropical animals – particularly jaguars, serpents and monkeys – were revered among mountain and forest dwellers alike. Hallucinogenic products such as mushrooms, coca and cactus buds, essential in shamanism and religious ritual, were traded over great distances.

With trade, direct or indirect, came ideas. Although regions of Andean society worshipped special local deities, there soon developed a core of features that can be called pan-Andean religious concepts.

Below: Coastal valley peoples' reliance on the sea is represented by this Moche stirrup-spout vessel of a fisherman and his totora *craft.*

COSMOS AND GALAXY

Throughout the world, agricultural societies and others living close to the elements recognized the relationships between the seasons and the cycle of their farming, herding and fishing activities. They also learned to make connections between the movements of the stars and planets and the sequence of their yearly tasks. Ancient Andeans were no exception in this.

We know most about the cosmological beliefs of the Incas in particular because they were partially recorded and preserved by Spanish priests and administrators. General themes through the evolution of Andean civilization show that it is unlikely that Inca beliefs were unique to them, except in certain details. Rather, it seems more likely that Inca cosmology represents, generally, the product of beliefs common throughout the Andean Area. The unusual and specific features of the Andean environment, such as the dramatic mountains, led to responses and explanations that fitted the ancient Andeans' own view of life.

WORLDS ABOVE AND BELOW

Andean cosmology saw the universe as a series of layers. The terrestrial layer – Kai Pacha or Hurin Pacha, the Lower World – is punctuated and represented in numerous sacred places and phenomena called *huacas*, as described earlier. Nature was thought of as a dynamic, living being, composed of interactive forces and perceived in dual and reciprocal form: everything was part male and part female, dark and light, hot and cold, positive and negative. Deep reverence was held for Pacha Mama, the earth mother, and for Viracocha, the creator god (also known by various other names).

Below the terrestrial layer was an inner-terrestrial sphere, Uku Pacha, the World Below, while above the outer, celestial sphere, Hanan Pacha, the World Above. The underlying primeval belief envisaged a remote past when giant beings and superhumans 'emerged' from the earth to battle for its domination. A great flood then engulfed the world, sweeping away these beings and

Above: The Torréon temple at Machu Picchu was used as an astronomical observatory for sightings of the night sky.

transforming them into the landscape. Thus, they became the mountains and plains, the rivers and valleys, the oceans and rocky shores.

The first humans ascended from Uku Pacha in various versions, coming from caves, from the earth itself and from springs and other earth cavities. Directed by the sky god or creator god, different people chose their homes and occupations in life according to the god's directions. The world before humans became a text of sacred places from the earliest times, representing the story of time and the changing landscape, from super beings to the present human beings. In this way, all life represented a continuous cycle and nourished the reverence for people's

Left: The Milky Way, known to the Incas as Mayu, the celestial river. Here seen with a meteorite streak running through it.

ancestors, who were perceived as beings in another state but still interactive with the present.

CYCLICAL WORLD

These cosmological beliefs fostered a relationship with the earth that strove to work with it rather than to master it. Knowing that elemental forces were beyond their control, and to some extent unpredictable, ancient Andeans believed that there were always balancing forces to maintain the equilibrium over time, and sought the permission of the gods to use the landscape and enjoy its largesse. In this universe, human beings were only one part, and they were considered of less importance than the plants, animals, landscape and celestial bodies who personified the deities.

It was believed that the gods were all-powerful, and could instantly bring about the end of humankind if not worshipped and appeased. Humans could not survive if the sun suddenly ceased to shine, or if the rains stopped for ever.

The world was believed to have evolved and to operate in cycles known as *pachacuti* (literally a 'revolution': from Quechua *cuti*, 'turning over', and *pacha*, 'time and space'). The annual seasons, the revolutions of the stars and planets in the sky, and human life itself were all cyclical, and so incorporated both time and space. The Incas thought of themselves as the final creation in a succession of creations, destructions and re-creations of the world and its inhabitants by the gods in an effort to create the most perfect form of beings to honour them.

THE INCA CALENDAR

Most prominent and observable in Hanan Pacha was Mayu, the Milky Way, the celestial river. Mayu's movements across the night sky were observed keenly by the Incas and their predecessors. Observation of Mayu was the starting point for correlations between the

Above: The Intihuatana (Hitching Post of the Sun), at Qenqo, north of Cuzco, was formed by natural outcrop pillars.

calendar and the natural changes of earthly conditions and seasons. This Andean concept of Mayu as the starting point is in marked contrast to the calculations of most other cultures, which proceed from observations of the movements of the closest single celestial bodies – the sun and the moon. By contrast, their observations of the Milky Way are of a vast galactic rotation.

DIVIDED UNIVERSE

The Incas also partitioned the universe horizontally according to the points of the compass, forming an imaginary cross corresponding to the axis of the Milky Way, which lies between the compass points. This is Mayu's southernmost point of movement in the night sky as it crosses its highest point through a 24-hour period. A vertical axis passed through Hanan Pacha, Hurin Pacha and Uku Pacha, intersecting the centre of the quartered cross and holding the cosmos together as an interacting organic whole.

HEAVENLY CONSTELLATIONS

Observation of the Milky Way as the starting point for formulating a calendar and as the axis of the universe provided an all-encompassing scheme by the Incas to chart the correlations between the positions of the stars and changes on Earth, and to organize daily, seasonal and annual labour and ritual on this basis. The movements of all the celestial bodies were used by the Incas to regulate and predict zoological and botanical cycles, both wild and domestic, and to organize the care of their crops and llama flocks. Theses celestial beings were held responsible for procreation on Earth.

DIVISIONS OF MAYU

The plane of the Milky Way's rotation inclines noticeably from that of the Earth by 26–30 degrees. Mayu's movements follow a sequence that rocks it slowly through the course of the year such that during half the year it tilts from right to left and then changes during the other half of the year to tilt from left to right. When Mayu's movements are plotted from the southern hemisphere, the broad band

of the 'river' forms another tripartite division, this time of the sky into three sections: above, below, and Mayu.

These divisions of the sky provided a celestial grid against which all other astronomical observations could be plotted, including not only the obvious luminated planets, stars and constellations but also immense stellar voids, or 'dark cloud' constellations. The Incas devoted considerable effort to tracking and calculating the paths of celestial bodies and constellations. Careful records were kept of the first appearances (heliacal risings) and last settings (heliacal settings) of stars and planets.

DARK MATTERS

Most of the named constellations and prominent individual stars are within or very close to the axial plane of the Milky Way. In Andean astronomy, individual stars or constellations were named as architectural structures or as agricultural implements. Seemingly in contradiction, Andean so-called 'constellations' are the dark spaces, the interstellar dark matter, between the stars.

Above: An Inca astrologer as depicted in Guaman Poma de Ayala's Nueva Crónica y Buen Gobierno, c.1613, complete with sighting stick and quipu records.

To the Incas, these voids were named animal constellations: an adult llama, a baby llama, a fox, a condor, a vulture, a falcon, a tinamou (a partridge-like bird), a toad and a serpent. The luminary bodies included Collca (literally 'the granary'), which is the Pleiades; Orqoi-Cilay (literally 'the multicoloured llama'), another star group, and Chaska-Qoylor (literally 'the shaggy star'), which is also known as Venus or the morning 'star'.

CONSTELLATIONS AND MYTHS

Practical observations and applications were interwoven with myth. For example, the toad constellation, although he creeps across the night sky, always wins the nocturnal race against the tinamou, for the tinamou, or *yutu*, is slow and stupid and flies around aimlessly when stirred.

Left: The dark spaces between the stars represented various constellations to the Incas, including the condor and the fox.

Right: The Horca del Inca, Bolivia, is one of many ridge-line sets of stone pillars for astronomical sightings.

The solstices of Mayu coincide with the Andean wet and dry seasons, and thus the celestial river was used to predict seasonal water cycles. Yacana, the 'dark cloud' llama disappears at midnight, when it was believed to have descended to Earth to drink water and thus prevent flooding. In contrast, black llamas were starved during October, in the dry season, in order to make them weep, seen as a supplication to the gods for rain.

Collca, the Pleiades, disappears from the night sky in mid-April, at the beginning of harvest. It reappears in the sky in early June, after the harvest has been gathered, and is thus associated throughout the Andes with these activities and called 'The Storehouse'.

One *ceque* route from Cuzco also associates myth with the Pleiades. A female coronation gift made from a provincial chief to Huáscar was Cori Qoyllur, 'Golden Star'. She proceeded along the *ceque*, stopping at *huacas* on the route for banquets and to make sacrificial offerings to the gods. The *ceque* itself is aligned with the disappearance of the Pleiades in mid-April. Another *huaca* marks the sun's lowest point on 18 August, the beginning of maize-sowing. Cori Qoyllur thus represents wives who walk the *ceque* at night and are transformed into *huaca* stones. Cori Qoyllur was herself turned to stone as a *huaca*, marking the point where the Pleiades disappear, and she is held responsible for fecundity in the Inca universe.

CELESTIAL MOVEMENTS
The movements of the sun were used to calculate the two most important ritual dates in the year – the winter and summer solstices, Capac Raymi and Inti Raymi.

In like manner, the first appearance of the Pleiades just before sunrise was correlated with the regular sidereal lunar months (the 27.3-day period of the rotation of the moon around the Earth– moon centre of mass), beginning on 8–9 June and ending on 3–4 May. In Ayrihua (the month of April), as this lunar-plotted year ended, there were ceremonies in Cuzco honouring the royal insignia, and a pure white llama was dressed in a red tunic and fed coca (*Erythroxylon coca*) and *chicha* (maize beer) to symbolize the first llama to appear on Earth after the great flood that destroyed the previous world.

AXIS OF THE MILKY WAY
Mayu's movements were reflected in the organization of the Inca Empire into its four quarters, and also regulated the routes of the four principal highways emanating from Cuzco to these quarters. For, except for a certain necessity to respect the physical demands of the landscape, these routes approximated the axis of the Milky Way, which lies between the compass points. Mayu's axes were also associated with sacred *ceque* ritual alignments, at least one of which correlated to the southernmost point in the Milky Way's movements.

CHAPTER FOUR

EARLY SETTLERS TO EMPIRE BUILDERS

The sweep of human history in the New World started at least 15,000 years ago, when humans migrated into the New World from the Old World, though the exact timing and detail of how long this journey took are obscured in the distant past.

During the Lithic, or Archaic, Period, humans began to live a more sedentary lifestyle. As with early human culture in the Old World, the existence and nature of the beliefs of these earliest South Americans can only be deduced from the very few facts available, combined with speculation.

In the earliest settlements, South Americans developed a more stable source of food in the beginnings of domestication of both plants and animals. Hunting and gathering and the exploitation of sea resources were never abandoned, however.

Later, the development of ceramics and, later still, metallurgy brought greater and greater divisions of labour within Andean societies, and consequently greater complexity. Sophisticated architecture, including U-shaped complexes, and masonry and adobe building techniques also developed.

Social hierarchies, elitism and rulership evolved alongside technological advances, as did religious belief and the explanation of human existence. In the absence of written records, archaeologists and historians seeking to understand the nature of the earliest Andean societies can only project what they know of later societies into the past.

Left: A marching, club-wielding warrior of the procession carved on stone monoliths at Cerro Sechin.

THE FIRST ARRIVALS

The story of the human colonization of the North and South American continents began at least 15,000 years ago. The earliest dating for human occupation comes from Monte Verde, southern Chile – about 14,850 years ago. Following herds of migratory land animals, and possibly sea animals as well, intrepid colonizers, the Palaeo-Indians, crossed the Bering Strait when world climatic change created a land bridge there at the end of the last great glacial period.

The new continent was occupied by an abundance of fauna and flora, most of which had evolved indigenously, independent of Old World animals and plants, for millions of years. Some of the large game animals or their immediate ancestors, such as the Columbian mammoth, or American mastodon, had probably migrated from Asia during earlier breaks, known as interstadials, in world glacial periods long before the human migration, when climatic fluctuations had opened and closed earlier Bering land bridges.

The Lithic culture of this period persisted for about 10,000 years, to about 5,000 years ago, when post-Ice Age (Pleistocene) sea

Below: Migrants used stemmed chert spear points with the atl-atl (spear thrower).

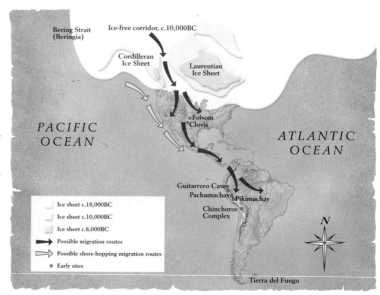

Above: Map of the early settlements of South America showing possible migration routes and the shrinking of the ice sheet.

Ice sheet c.18,000BC
Ice sheet c.10,000BC
Ice sheet c.6,000BC
Possible migration routes
Possible shore-hopping migration routes
Early sites

levels became stable at about where they are today. During this time definitive changes occurred in climate and environment: glaciers retreated from huge sheets of ice to mountain isolation; global ocean levels rose by about 100m (330ft); ecological zones shifted as climate changed and animals, plants and humans migrated to higher altitudes; meteorological patterns and marine currents shifted. The results were the climatic and environmental conditions of the present.

MIGRATION ROUTES
Evidence for the very earliest human occupants in North America is sparse. Only the records for the later millennia of the Lithic Period are more abundant. Several claims for much earlier human occupation, from several sites in South America – for example Pikimachay Cave, Peru, 20,000 years ago – are not universally accepted. Nevertheless, the long journey from northernmost North America into and throughout South America must have taken place over many generations,

indicating that migration probably began significantly earlier than the earliest dates for occupation in Chile.

The geologically traced pattern of glaciation in North America reveals an ice-free corridor between the great glacial sheets of Canada, through mid-continent, at this migration period. It has long been assumed that this was the most logical route into the interior. It has also been argued that an equally viable route would have been along the western coasts. Any evidence for coastal migration, if it exists, lies beneath the present ocean. Nevertheless, radiocarbon dates from Peruvian and Chilean coastal sites prove that occupation along the shoreline began at least 11,500 years ago, from the time when evidence for occupation in the New World in general is more abundant. Another recent theory suggests that a smaller and earlier migration possibly

Above: Large, fluted spear points, such as this chert Palaeo-Indian Folsom point, were used to hunt big game.

came from Europe across the ice floes of the North Atlantic into north-eastern North America. This argument is based on conclusions about similarities between the Solutrian lithic culture of south-western France, which flourished about 22,000 to 16,500 years ago, and the Clovis stone point tradition of North America, though this theory is rigorously disputed.

PALAEO-INDIAN SITES

The pace of migration is impossible to calculate and can be based only on a set of assumptions and speculations about population numbers, available game and other living resources, and the need to continue moving south. Thus, the precise time of the beginning and the exact nature of the migration cannot be known.

The evidence of molecular biology and DNA in contemporary Native Americans proves descent from three or four biologically distinct populations. There were, therefore, several incidents of original migration by different groups into North America. The biology and blood-group evidence shows that descendants from only one of these groups crossed the Isthmus of Panama into South America.

The earliest confirmed, substantially occupied Palaeo-Indian site is Monte Verde, Chile. Here were found round sling stones, grooved stones for use in a bolas, and chipped stone artefacts, including long projectile points, scrapers mounted on wooden handles and possibly a drill. Other wooden finds include a lance, digging sticks and mortars. Dwelling remains were of pole-and-animal-skin-framed huts, joined at their sides and forming two rows. Separate was an isolated, open-sided, wishbone-shaped structure with a small platform at the back. Its packed sand and gravel floor had remains of burnt medicinal plants and chewed leaves, and around the structure were hearths, medicinal plants and mastodon bones.

Other Palaeo-Indian sites with several traditions of fluted projectile-point shapes, including harpoon points for maritime hunting, have been found; they generally date from about 11,500 years ago and later.

PLANTS AND BELIEFS

The earliest-known domesticated plants come from this early period, from Guitarrero Cave, northern Peru. Although fibre plants dominated the findings, specimens of domesticated beans and chilli peppers were found, both *not* native to the region and thus cultivated there.

Representations of the earliest Andean beliefs are partly actual and partly speculative. There are suggestions of some form of shamanism and perhaps a belief in a multi-layered world with the Earth layered between celestial and inner spheres. The remains at Monte Verde show special use of plants and animal bones at a specialized structure, supporting shamanism. Concrete evidence of belief in an afterlife, or at least the honouring of selected deceased, comes from fishing settlements at Chinchorros and La Paloma on the central Peruvian coast. From the former come the earliest mummified remains in Andean culture (*c.*5000BC). From the latter come the first bodies buried in an articulated, decorated state.

Below: The coastal peoples of the Chinchorros culture (c.6000–1600BC) mummified chosen individuals after death.

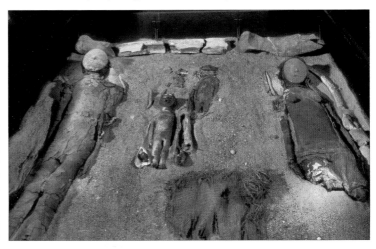

DEVELOPING COMMUNITIES

The Lithic Period did not end abruptly. An increasingly sedentary lifestyle developed towards the end of the period in some areas of South America, while in others a hunter-gatherer economy continued to form most or a significant part of people's lifestyles. In the Andean Area, village life became more important as an adaptation to developments in climate and habitat in the post-Ice Age environment. Sedentism, or the shift of people from living in non-permanent settlements to permanent settlements, was not at first accompanied by the development of pot-making in Andean South America, and so archaeologists call the period the Preceramic, or Formative, Period, or sometimes the Cotton Preceramic.

EARLY DOMESTICATION
Recognition of the usefulness of particular plants and animals fostered the special observation of these species and gradual greater attendance to their care and proliferation. The process of domestication was an evolutionary one, helped wittingly by humans but with practical rather than specific scientific understanding. In the archaeological record, the end result is

recognizable only when genetic changes render the plants and animals biologically distinguishable from their wild progenitors. Thus, the beginning of the process cannot be pinpointed in time.

The results, however, show anatomical changes that are unmistakable. Equally, the regular cultivation of species in areas outside their normal wild distributions shows human mastery over their use. The earliest known domesticated plants date to about 10,000 years ago in the Andean Area, from Guitarrero Cave in northern Peru. Fibre plants dominate most assemblages of Lithic Period sites. Numerous wild hemp-like plants were used to make a wide range of artefacts, from tools and clothing to bedding. Many other kinds of plant were apparently of medicinal importance – and perhaps also of religious importance.

At Guitarrero Cave, locally native tubers, rhizomes, fruits, chillies and beans were found; from Tres Ventanas Cave, central Peru, at an altitude of 3,900m (12,800ft), also come tubers – ulluco and the potato; and from several cave deposits in the Ayacucho region come gourds.

THE FIRST CIVILIZATION?
As sedentary lifestyles increased from the time of these earliest domesticated plants to about 5,000 years ago, communities derived greater proportions of their nutrition from this source, alongside intensive tending and gathering of wild food sources. Andean Preceramic communities cultivated mostly self-watering regions, relying on rainfall and river run-off, and developed agro-pastoralism with llama herding. Coastal peoples pursued lifestyles exploiting the rich marine resources and cultivated cotton in seasonally watered valley bottoms. Such diversity was the beginning of the highland–lowland (or coastal) division.

The variety of environments within the Andean Area, both in different regions and at different heights, discouraged integration between communities, although it was forged within them. Nevertheless, the products of different regions were sought after and traded over long distances with increasing regularity, and with this trade the exchange of ideas was inevitable.

There is little evidence for powerful regional political leadership, but there *is* evidence of integrated communal effort in the form of the first monumental architecture between about 3000 and 2000BC. Inter-regional contact and trade also began the long Andean tradition of textile use – cotton cultivated in the lowlands and llama wool from herding in the highlands continued the earlier Andean Area focus on fibre technology, including the earliest weaving.

ARCHITECTURE AND TEXTILES
Increasing reliance on cultivation drew sierra populations to lower altitudes, into well-watered highland valleys and basins. Shared religious beliefs, manifested in architecture and on textiles, is known as

Left: The Preceramic Period adobe mud sculpture at the Temple of the Crossed Hands, at Kotosh (c.3000BC).

the Kotosh Religious Tradition in the highlands, after Kotosh, a site in highland central Peru at about 2,000m (6,600ft). Farther north, La Galgada was another highland valley community. Along the western coast more than a score of early sites are known, including Huaca Prieta, Salinas de Chao, Aspero and El Paraíso in north-central coastal Peru. Here architectural traditions called Supe, Aspero and El Paraíso developed.

The architecture at these sites varies in detail. For example, Supe Tradition communal structures are smaller and are associated with domestic buildings and artefacts, indicating they were constructed by their local communities. The much larger structures at sites of other traditions indicate more regional communal efforts, as centres for several communities. What is common, however, is the beginning of Andean central worship and a long generic tradition of ceremonial mounds and sunken courts or plazas. Both oval and rectangular examples

Below: Cotton, domesticated by at least 3000BC in the northern Peruvian coastal valleys, was a valuable commodity to trade.

of sunken plazas are known. The two elements were made adjacent to each other and, in general, the plazas were smaller in area than the adjacent mounds.

These combined civic-ceremonial constructions are the earliest manifestations of Andean universal belief. They show both vertical and horizontal divisions of space for ceremonial purposes, and the special making and use of such space for communal worship drawing several communities together.

Alongside these architectural developments, textile design and decoration began to predominate among other media, such as stone, bone, shell, gourds, wood and basketry. Cotton was twined with spaced wefts and exposed warps; looping, knotting and simple weaving were also developed. The geometric nature of lattice-like fabric lent itself to

Above: Cotton was typically woven into open-work fabrics, such as this Chancay textile from the Late Intermediate Period.

angular decoration in different colours and to symmetry. Stripes, diamonds, squares and chevrons were used individually, in patterns, and to depict humanlike beings and animals that were important locally in an economic sense and universally as revered beings. Crabs, fish, raptors and serpents predominate.

Although the specifics of belief systems of such an early period can only be surmised, such detailed imagery, through its universality and repetition, reveals underlying religious belief. Coastal animals and motifs were copied in the highland traditions and vice versa. It seems that religion was, even at this early period, at the foundations of Andean civilization.

NEW AGRICULTURE AND ARCHITECTURE

The environmental diversity within the Andean Area meant that communities had to adapt in varying ways to suit conditions. The increasingly sedentary lifestyles of ancient Andeans reveals their increasing ability to manipulate the environment to increase domesticated production. However, progress was uneven. The wild progenitors of the classic cultigens that provided the bulk of carbohydrate and protein nutrition of ancient Andeans – maize, potatoes, beans and squashes – were native to different altitudes and regions, as were llamas and the other camelid species.

Following the Preceramic Period, the pre-eminent technological developments were pottery and irrigation agriculture. Archaeologists call it the Initial Period.

FARMING AND CERAMICS

In South America, pottery-making was discovered outside the Andean Area. The earliest ceramics were made in coastal Ecuador by the end of the 6th millennium BC, and the well-watered tropical areas of Colombia and Ecuador were the first areas where the 'civilization-defining' combination of intensive agriculture and pot-making became the predominant lifestyle by about 3000BC. The spread of intensive farming and ceramics followed a path of least resistance, from low self-watered environments to higher self-watered regions, to the more arid high Andes and western coasts.

By about 1800BC the combination was well established in northern and central highland Peru and in the fertile valleys of the north-central coast; by 1600BC, communities in the Titicaca Basin in the southern Andes were making pottery; and another few hundred years later ceramics had diffused to the dry coasts of southern Peru and northern Chile. In Altiplano regions, however, agriculture was combined with llama herding, while in coastal valleys agriculture was teamed with fishing.

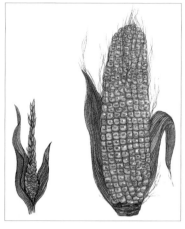

*Above: From its diminutive wild ancestor, maize (*Zea mays*) spread into the Andean Area from Mesoamerica.*

PAN-ANDEAN FOUNDATIONS

The increased security of grown food and rich sea resources, together with plentiful supplies of cotton and wool, made increases in population inevitable. With the ability to irrigate and terrace the valleys and basins and thereby increase the yields and available land for agriculture, new areas could be opened. The practice of exchange of coastal and highland products continued the flow of contact among otherwise independent regions and communities. At the same time, the architectural and religious practices begun in Preceramic days continued.

The intensified concern with stable agriculture deepened the reverence for 'mother earth', setting the stage for the veneration of Pacha Mama (as she was known to the Inca). The need to regulate agricultural, herding and fishing activities throughout the year encouraged careful observation of heavenly bodies, the stars

Left: The people of Garagay decorated their ceremonial centres with sculpted and painted adobe walls.

Above: Garagay in the Rimac-Chillon Valley, central Peru, was a typical coastal U-shaped civic-ceremonial centre in the Initial Period.

and constellations, and of Mayu (the Milky Way) as a whole. These two facets were the fundamental elements of ancient Andean religion. The strengthening and consolidation of these foundations in the Initial Period secured their prevalence throughout the remainder of Andean ancient history.

U-SHAPED COMPLEXES
The Preceramic Period tradition of monumental architecture continued. It was a great age of civic-ceremonial construction. Hundreds of sites are known but relatively few have been excavated extensively.

Ceremonial mounds and platforms were built up using soil-filled mesh bags for interior bulk and adobe brick exteriors. Clearing the silt that built up in irrigation canals provided an abundance of suitable fine clays for bricks to build bigger and more elaborate structures. Sunken courts became larger, presumably to accommodate growing congregations. Subterranean temple complexes became more extensive and façades were decorated with relief sculpture and painted in bright colours.

The Paraíso Tradition that started in the Preceramic Period developed the enduring form of civic-ceremonial architecture in the northern Andean Area – the U-shaped complex. Regional details varied, as ever, but the classic elements were the same everywhere. A large central platform-mound formed the base of the U. In front of it, flanking a large central plaza, were two lower, elongated platforms. Variations included rectangular or circular sunken courts, wings extending from the central platform, walled vestibules and multiple temples on the platforms.

The builders of ancient ceremonial complexes seemed consciously to vie with one another in ostentation and display. Visual impact was important. Themes for enduring Andean architectural religious advertisement are exemplified by Cerro Sechín, where at least 27 megalithic slabs were erected along the front of the temple mound, carved in low relief. They depict dead individuals, many of them dismembered, and individual heads in a gruesome afterlife procession. At Garagay and Moxeke, human–animal transformation is depicted in adobe friezes of insects with human heads, fanged heads in spider webs, humans with

fangs and condor features. At Huaca de los Reyes there is an adobe head sculpture with a fanged mouth.

The largest U-shaped complexes were in the coastal valleys: Sechín Alto, Sechín Bajo, Cerro Sechín, Huaca de los Reyes, El Paraíso, Cardal, Garagay, La Florida and Moxeke-Pampa de los Llamas. A prominent highland example is La Galgada.

In the Titicaca Basin, a separate architectural tradition began at Chiripa, featuring a large mound with a central sunken court at the top surrounded by rectangular temples.

EXPANSION HALTED
Communal practices of civic-ceremonial construction begun in Preceramic times increased with the communal activities of canal building and shared land use. The intensification of farming, herding and fishing, expansion into new areas and increased growth to support a great labour force were self-propelling processes. Their only limitations were the availability of land and the unpredictabililty of climate.

And so it was. For beginning about 900BC, towards the end of the Initial Period, the pattern of El Niño and related climatic events brought severe drought that prevailed for centuries.

ORACLE AND SHRINE: CHAVÍN DE HUÁNTAR

Generalized themes permeated Andean cultures during the Initial Period. Although the valleys, mountain basins and coastal oases were largely independent, each was dominated by one or a few civic-ceremonial centres, and religion was developing across communities as a unifying theme. This process culminated in the first great period of region-wide unification: the Early Horizon.

DROUGHT AND DISASTER

The prolonged drought that began and defined the end of the Initial Period was a phenomenon not previously experienced by Andean farmers. Disaster ensued as crops failed year upon year. The new irrigation systems could not cope, and the extra land brought into cultivation as village farming became more efficient and sophisticated was useless when drought prevented farmers from watering it.

Before they abandoned many of the sites, the ancient builders of the U-shaped civic-ceremonial complexes must have devoted considerable time in pondering why the gods had forsaken them.

Below: The mysterious Lanzón Stone was erected in the dark oracular chamber within the Old Temple at Chavín de Huántar.

Above: Sharp-toothed images of stylized caymans were a common symbolic Chavín motif in stone carvings on walls.

A UNIFYING CENTRE

The regularity and the quantity of rainfall began to increase again from about 800BC. By now, northern sierra and coastal Andean communities that had weathered the drought through several generations were very subdued. However, religious themes that had begun in the Initial Period did not disappear; instead they re-emerged within two extensive regional spheres of influence – the northern and southern Andean Area – under the newly encouraging conditions.

The more widespread unifying sphere was centred in the northern Andean Area at Chavín de Huántar, sited on the eastern slopes of the Cordillera Blanca in the Mosna Valley, more than 3,000m (9,800ft) above sea level.

Chavín de Huántar was established about 900BC or shortly after, at the beginning of the drought, as a new U-shaped civic-ceremonial centre joining La Galgada as an extension of the U-shaped Tradition that had developed in the coastal valleys. It went through several phases of development, initially mainly confined within its immediate valley as it persisted through the drought years. Chavín de Huántar appears to have been deliberately and strategically located in the Andes

roughly midway between the coast to the west and the tropical lowlands to the east. From its position it controlled several passes running between mountains. In a time of scarcity, but with an entrenched tradition of inter-regional exchange, such a strategic position must have given Chavín special status and importance among declining civic-ceremonial sites. Its location appears to cater to both the mountain deities, believed to control the weather and rainfall, and the coastal deities, where the revered Pacha Mama (earth mother) of valleys that were once productive was apparently now forsaking her people.

As climatic conditions and agricultural production improved, Chavín's artistic influence began to spread. With its distinctive symbolic art, it became the source and focus of a pan-Andean religion. Principal themes focused on feline and serpentine attributes, on fish and other aquatic animals, on human-like raptors, and on a pervasive Staff Deity. These images appeared on the architecture of Chavín de Huántar itself, and on Chavín

Below: Tenoned, stone severed heads, with feline canines, were typical wall 'decorations' at Chavín de Huántar.

Above: The façade of the New Temple at Chavín de Huántar, which incorporated and enlarged the Old Temple from c.500BC.

ceramics, textiles and metalwork. The spread of Chavín symbolic art went hand-in-hand with its equally crucial role in the spreading of emerging technology.

BIRTH OF A CULT

Chavín was not the largest ceremonial centre of the Early Horizon, but it was certainly one of the most elaborate. It does not seem to have been a centre of political power or unity, except perhaps within its valley, but it was a unifying centre for religions. Although not truly urban in layout and proportions, it must have accommodated a resident population of priests, officials, artisans, servants and pilgrims to support and serve the cult. Its deliberate establishment at the beginning of the drought period and persistence through it must have made it seem a particularly blessed ceremonial centre to ancient Andeans. It therefore became the focus of pilgrimage for peoples throughout the northern Andes.

The centre of the site was a classic U-shaped complex, which went through several phases of temple development, both inside and out. Within its base ceremonial platform, called the Castillo, was a multi-galleried temple. The original (Old) temple housed the cult object of the Lanzón, an obelisk-like, lance-shaped stone

carved with human, feline and serpent attributes and the snarling mouth of the Chavín supreme deity. The gallery holding it has an upper oracular chamber.

The New Temple, which combined and enlarged the Old, was entered through an elaborate doorway: the Black and White Portal. Its two columns – dark (male) and light (female) – were carved with human-like raptor figures. The New Temple housed the cult figure known as the Raimundi Stela, an elaborately carved slab depicting the Staff Deity.

In the courtyard outside the temple complex stood the Tello Obelisk, a huge stone carved with two jungle caymans, and other animal and plant symbols.

The temple galleries included an elaborate system of water channels. When water was flushed through the system, accompanying acoustic properties literally made the temple roar.

Chavín's importance lasted for some 700 years, into the 3rd century BC. The power of its cult continued to spread through a second period of drought, roughly 400–200BC, the persistence of which perhaps precipitated its eventual decline.

STAFF DEITY AND TROPHY HEADS

One of the most prominent Chavín deities was the Staff Deity. This was a figure with feline, raptor and serpentine attributes, holding a staff in each hand with outstretched arms on either side of the body. Sometimes the staves were serpents. The Staff Deity could be male or female, identifiable by distinctive characteristics.

Another distinctive Chavín Cult theme was the trophy head. Appearing on all media, these were disembodied human heads, often with feline or serpentine attributes, thought to portray shamanistic transformation.

Below: The dual-columned stone Black and White Portal of the New Temple at Chavín de Huántar.

SOUTHERN CULTS: PARACAS AND PUKARÁ

Environmental decline occurred in the southern Andean Area, along the coast and in the Altiplano in the late Initial Period. In the Peruvian southern coastal desert, the natural aridity, exacerbated by drought in the inland mountains, presented a considerable challenge to the ingenuity of the coastal fishing village inhabitants. In the Titicaca Basin, the lake level fell dramatically and fields were abandoned all along the southern shores, as farmers could no longer raise crops or feed animals there.

PARACAS MUMMY BURIALS

The Paracas Peninsula was the site of a necropolis of elite burials. Apart from the Chinchorros mummy burials in northern Chile, the Paracas desiccated mummies are the earliest in the Andean Area, beginning a long tradition of mummification in Andean civilization. The elaborately wrapped, multilayered burial bundles demonstrate a preoccupation with the continued life, or participation in the present, of physically deceased important individuals. The richest ceramic and textile products, and exotic goods from afar, were saved for the burials; indeed, some goods were produced specifically for this purpose. Their existence begins the equally long Andean tradition of ancestor worship.

While the peninsula is the site of the Cavernas cemetery, the inhabitants who created it lived in the adjacent area inland around Cerro Colorado, where some 54ha (137 acres) of scattered domestic architecture has been found. The economy was based on local fishing.

The cemetery was a specially dedicated site. The dead were placed in their mummy bundles into large subterranean crypts, which were either bell-shaped pits or masonry-lined rectangular mausoleums. These were used through several generations, and the individuals appear to be kin. As the numbers of burials appear to exceed the requirements of the immediate adjacent settlements, it is

Above: The flying Oculate Being of the Paracas and Nazca southern coastal cultures, depicted on a woollen burial shroud.

thought that the necropolis was also a pilgrimage or cult centre serving communities through a wider region.

The stages for the preparation for these burials were inland in the Chincha Valley. These comprised low rectangular mounds aligned at the front and back of a high-walled central court, sunk to near ground level, such as the one found at Huaca Soto. The court walls are so thick that the complex is reminiscent of a single mound with a sunken summit courtyard. Huaca Soto comprised two interior courts, plus a thick-walled frontal entry court. The whole structure was 70m (230ft) by 200m (650ft) and stood 15m (49) high.

IMPORTANCE OF PUKARÁ

In the Altiplano around Lake Titicaca, emphasis on mother earth (Pacha Mama) and father sky (Yama Mama) continued as people remained close to the land and struggled to cope with drought. The importance of the regional centre at Chiripa waned and the site was eventually left to decline. The replacement for Chiripa as the focus of religion became the ceremonial centre of Pukará, some 75km (47 miles) north-west of the lake. Pukará arose around 400BC and exerted its influence over the Titicaca Basin for four centuries.

Unlike U-shaped complexes, Pukará comprised monumental masonry-clad structures terraced against the hillside. The principal terrace had a monumental staircase and was topped by a

rectangular sunken court with one-room buildings around three sides, reminiscent of the Chiripa complex.

The hallmark of Pukará cult symbolic art was the depiction of *yaya* (male) and *mama* (female) figures on opposite sides of slab monoliths erected at Pukará and other sites. Other Pukará stone carving, pottery and textiles displayed ubiquitous Andean images, including felines, serpents, lizards and fish.

Like the Chavín Cult, Pukará art images featured disembodied human heads. Some of these were trophy heads accompanying realistically depicted humans; others accompanied super-natural beings with feline or serpentine attributes, as in the Chavín Cult, and are thought to represent shamans in trans-formational states. Many Pukará temple sites were rebuilt and used over several centuries. The assemblages of structures around Pukará sunken courts show considerable variety.

Below: Early Horizon Paracas mummified bodies were buried in multiple layers of cloth, the richness of which reflected their status.

Above: Nested geometric patterns in the Pukará culture included the multi-stepped 'Andean Cross'.

PARACAS AND PUKARÁ LINKS

There are generic artistic links between the Paracas and Pukará art styles and symbols used. Both styles feature monochrome and polychrome pottery with multicoloured motifs framed with incised lines. Some of the earliest phase styles, especially at Paracas, are attributed to Chavín influence because they represent a change from the local pottery that preceded it. There is an emphasis on non-human faces adorned with fangs and feline whiskers, especially on pottery. As Paracas pottery developed, it showed a more naturalistic style akin to Pukará ceramics. Local coastal subjects such as falcons, swallows, owls and foxes later predominated. The images and patterns painted on Paracas pottery were also used in their textiles.

In this way, Paracas, Pukará and Chavín styles, although distinct, show themselves to have a pan-Andean combination of features, including, especially, the Chavín emphasis on feline, serpentine and raptor attributes. The combination of cotton textiles and the importation of alpaca and llama wool for use by Paracas weavers shows another highland influence.

THE OCULATE BEING

One supernatural being or deity that stands out as distinctly Paracas, and which carries on in the succeeding Nazca civilization, is known as the Oculate Being. Depicted on textiles, the being was portrayed horizontally – as if flying upside-down – as if looking down on humankind, and crouching. His/her frontal face has characteristic large, circular, staring eyes, and long, streaming appendages originate from various parts of the body and end in trophy heads or small figures.

Below: The bodies of Paracas mummies were tightly constricted into compact bundles and held by cords.

NAZCA CONFEDERACY AND MOCHE STATE

Cult foci such as Chavín, Paracas and Pukará represent distinct local political entities that were united between their regions predominantly by religion. The following Early Intermediate Period saw the break up of Chavín's religious unity, but also the rise of at least one regional state political unity.

COASTAL POWER BASES
As in the Early Horizon, there were two principal regional bases: one north, one south – both coast-based. Centres between mountains and on the Altiplano persisted, but by about 200BC Chavín de Huántar had begun to wane and its importance as a pilgrimage centre was languishing. The construction of new monumental architecture became restrained in central and northern Peruvian valleys that lay between mountains. The decline of Chavín influence is attributed to it lacking the political attributes necessary to maintain long-term stability.

Below: Exposed Nazca group burial in the southern coastal desert. Tombs were often reopened to insert new mummy bundles.

In the Titicaca Basin, Pukará was eclipsed by its contemporary and power inheritor, Tiwanaku. The real political ascendancy of Tiwanaku in the southern Altiplano, however, was yet to dominate the region, although the monumental architecture that was to become its hallmark had begun.

A NEW CULT CENTRE
Nazca civilization flourished in the southern Peruvian coast and adjacent inland valleys from c.100BC to c.AD700. It continued the Andean tradition of religious cult practices by remaining a focus of regional worship and pilgrimage.

The dominance of daily life by ritual was emphasized across the desert floor by the Nazca geoglyphs, whose nature and importance in ritual have been described earlier. Perhaps like the Paracas necropolis, the sheer number of lines and ritual pathways, and the apparent short-term use of many of them, meant that they served a much wider community than just the settlements immediately nearest them.

Above: Nazca woven and dyed woollen tunic, exemplifying the exchange of highland llama wool for coastal craftsmanship.

THE NAZCA CONFEDERACY
Two of the most important Nazca settlements were Cahuachi and Ventilla, the first a ritual 'city', the second an urban 'capital'. Ventilla, the largest Nazca site recorded, covered at least 200ha (495 acres) with terraced housing, walled courts and mounds. It was linked to its ceremonial and ritual counterpart by a Nazca line across the desert.

Through the centuries, increasing drought in the highlands to the east caused growing aridity in the coastal plains. Such was the pressure for water that the Nazca invented an ingenious system of underground aqueducts and galleries to collect and channel underground waters around Cahuachi to minimize evaporation and to provide water in the dry season.

On pottery and textiles the Nazca continued to develop themes begun by people in the Paracas culture. Preoccupied

Above: The strong facial features on this Moche effigy-jar indicate it may have been a portrait of a real person, who seems to be male.

with and motivated by religious symbolic art and ceremonial ritual, they used mythical beings and deities to decorate effigy vessels and cloth with serpent beings, monkeys and other animals, and trophy heads. A cult practice collected caches of trepanned, severed trophy skulls of sacrificial victims in Nazca cemeteries.

Nazca settlements appear to be in part a continuation of Paracas, since Paracas layers are found beneath some Nazca settlements. The cooperative nature of Nazca culture for control of water and for making geoglyphs shows strong ties with other regions but no centralized political power. It was more like a confederate state of independent but highly interacting cities.

THE MOCHE STATE

In the northern Peruvian coastal valleys, the roughly contemporary Moche created the Andean Area's first true state. Here a Moche elite embarked on military domination of the northern valleys between the Sechura Desert and the Casma Valley. They ruled from their capital at Cerro Blanco in the Moche Valley, where by AD450 two huge pyramidal structures of adobe bricks had become the focus of political and religious power. The Huaca del Sol was a four-tiered, cross-shaped platform with a ramp on the north side; the Huaca de la Luna, at the foot of Cerro Blanco, was a three-tiered structure with walls that were richly decorated by friezes depicting mythological scenes and deities. The two ceremonial platforms sat within a sprawling metropolis, which at its maximum size occupied about 3 sq km (740 acres).

Roughly 100 years later, a sand sheet choked the canal system and stifled agriculture, causing abandonment. The focus of Moche politics and religion shifted north to the Lambayeque Valley, to the sites of Pampa Grande and Sipán. The rise of the Wari State, to the south-east out of the Andes, also appears to have been an influence.

The large city of Pampa Grande covered some 6 sq km (1,485 acres) and flourished for about 150 years. Its most imposing structure, Huaca Fortaleza, had a similar function to Huaca del Sol and was the focus of the elite residents of the city. Like Cerro Blanco, Pampa Grande was abandoned abruptly, owing to a combination of agricultural disaster caused by an El Niño weather event and the continued expansion of the Wari State. Internal unrest may also have been a factor.

Left: A pattern of crabs sculpted in adobe mud on a wall frieze at the Huaca de la Luna, Moche, shows its coastal heritage.

Above: In all Pacific coastal cultures, seafood formed an important part of the local cuisine, such as this crayfish on a Nazca pot.

A DERIVED CULT

Moche imagery became a potent religion, with distinctive art symbols and a pantheon of gods much derived from the Chavín Cult. It was characterized by humans and humanized animal figures, serpents, frogs, birds (owls in particular) and sea animals (crabs and fishes), and by standardized groups and ceremonial scenes, including a coca ritual recognizable by distinctive clothing and ritual combat.

Murals, friezes and decorative designs on pottery depict the capture and sacrifice of 'enemies', drinks offered by subordinates to lords and gods, and persons passing through the night sky in moon-shaped boats. Richly furnished burials at Sipán, which are some of the few unlooted tombs of the Andes, reflect scenes that confirm the images on walls, ceramics, textiles and metalwork excavated from other Moche sites.

Although the names of the Moche deities ae not known, the later Chimú Ai Apaec and Si (sky/creator god and moon goddess) may have derived from Moche deities. Especially prominent on ceramics and textiles is the ritual depiction and rich ceremony of the Decapitator God. A Moche mountain god has been identified in an oft-depicted feline-featured being.

MOUNTAIN EMPIRES: WARI AND TIWANAKU

In the Middle Horizon, ancient Andeans began to consolidate large areas of land into political states for the first time. Politics and religion became a corporate whole in official state cults that were imposed with military and economic conquest. Local religious deities were assimilated, easing the imposition of official state religion.

Two dominating empires arose: Wari in the north and Tiwanaku in the south. Despite political and military rivalry, both cultures shared a use of religious iconography and symbols, which arose as a result of their collection and consolidation of the local deities, cults and similarities in religious imagery in the regions they conquered.

Below: Sculptured stone severed heads are tenoned into the walls of the Kalasasaya sunken court at Tiwanku.

DOMINATING THE HIGHLANDS

The city of Huari, which had been established in the preceding Early Intermediate Period, began rapid expansion within the central Andean Huamanga and Huanta basins from about AD600. For the next 200 years its armies conquered and dominated the highlands and coastal valleys of central and northern Peru almost to the present Ecuadorian border.

The capital city occupied a plateau among mountains, 2,800m (9,200ft) above sea level. As a civic, residential and religious centre, it grew rapidly to cover more than 300ha (740 acres), with peripheral residential suburbs occupying a further 250ha (620 acres). Alongside military expansion, the Wari spread a religious hegemony characterized by a distinctive use of symbolic art, much of which shows continuity with ancient

Chavín traditions, which survived the political fragmentation of the Early Intermediate Period. Shortly before AD800, however, a political crisis caused building within the capital to abate rapidly and cease. At the same time, Pachacamac, a political centre and religious shrine on the central Peruvian coast that had flourished as a cult centre since the later Early Intermediate Period, and which had only recently been occupied by the Wari, began to reassert itself and possibly even to rival Wari power. Wari expansion ended abruptly, and the capital was abandoned by AD800.

DOMINATING THE ALTIPLANO

The Tiwanaku power base emanated from the Titicaca Basin of southern Peru–northern Bolivia, at 3,850m (12,600ft) above sea level. Like Huari, the city was founded in the Early Intermediate Period and became the capital of a unified state established through conquest and economic domination. In its heyday it occupied 4.5 sq km (1,100 acres).

The earliest major constructions at the site were begun by AD200, and by AD500 Tiwanaku was the capital of a considerable empire within and beyond the Titicaca Basin, stretching east and west to the Bolivian lowlands, west and northwest to the Peruvian coast, and south into northern Chile. Its cultural and religious influence extended even farther. Its chief rival to the north was the Wari Empire, and the two empires 'met' at the La Raya pass south of Cuzco, which became a sort of buffer zone between them. Curiously, the prosperity of Tiwanaku endured for roughly a millennium, fortuitously matching the 1,000-year periods of ages in Andean cosmology.

Tiwanaku's core comprised ceremonial-religious-civic structures, including monumental buildings, gateways and stone sculptures exhibiting religious motifs and gods whose depiction shows obvious affinities to Chavín images.

This core, aligned east–west, was confined within a moat and was surrounded by residential compounds built of adobe bricks.

Tiwanku belief was a culmination of the religious antecedents that appear to have united the peoples of the Titicaca Basin from as early as 1000BC. Ceremonial architecture at Chiripa and Pukará, for example, heralds that at Tiwanku.

The location of the city appears to have been chosen deliberately both for its position in the midst of fertile land and for the perceived sacredness of the landscape. The surrounding natural features constituted every element regarded as sacred within Andean Area religion: the sacred waters of Lake Titicaca to the west, the snow-capped peaks of the sacred mountains to the east, and in the middle of the lake the sacred Island of the Sun and Island of the Moon.

A SHARED RELIGION

Much of the religious and mythological imagery of Wari and Tiwanaku was virtually identical and originated in much earlier times. Derivation from Chavín demonstrates the continuity of pan-Andean religious belief. Despite the two capitals' obvious military opposition, scholars have entertained the possibility that religious missionaries from one city visited the other. It might have been that the priests were willing to set politics aside and let religious beliefs transcend such matters.

Shared religious imagery included in particular the Staff Deity image, winged beings in profile (sometimes with falcon and condor heads) and severed trophy heads. Winged beings appear both accompanying the Staff Deity and independently, and seem to be running, floating, flying or kneeling. The frontal Staff Deity, with mask-like face, radiating head rays (sometimes ending in serpent heads), and dressed in tunic, belt and kilt,

Left: The so-called 'monk' monolith at Tiwanaku. Such large stone statues were believed by the Incas to represent a former race of giants from an earlier age.

Above: The ruins of Pikillaqta, the largest and southernmost Middle Horizon Wari highland city, which guarded the border between the Wari and Tiwanaku empires.

appears on pottery and architecture and might have been the prototype for the creator god Viracocha.

Despite this apparent religious unity, the focus of the religious imagery at Huari differed from that at Tiwanaku. At Huari it was applied primarily to portable objects, particularly to ceramics; at Tiwanaku it was applied to monumental stone architecture, but rarely appeared on pottery. Thus, while Wari ceramics spread the word far and wide, Tiwanaku imagery was more confined to standing monuments in the capital and a few other sites. Similarly, religious ceremony at Huari appears to have been more private and confined to smaller groups, judging by its architecture, while at Tiwanaku it seems to have been more public and to have taken place inside large compounds designed for the purpose. Tiwanaku's bold pyramidal platforms and huge sunken courts contrast starkly with the repetitive, incremental, unit-like constructions at Huari.

KINGDOMS AND SHRINES

The Late Intermediate Period is defined by the break-up of the Wari and Tiwanaku empires. Once again political fragmentation prevailed in the Andean Area while, as in earlier periods, a certain pan-Andean religious unity persisted.

BREAK-UP AND RIVALRY
In the Altiplano, the Tiwanaku state succumbed to a multitude of smaller city-states collectively known as the Aymara Kingdoms: Colla, Lupaka, Cana, Canchi, Umasuyo and Pacaje. Rivalry was stirred up, and this was perpetuated by repeated droughts from about AD1100 through the next 400 years as El Niño weather events and consequent adverse environmental conditions affected Lake Titicaca's water level and the productivity of the surrounding land.

In the central and northern sierra the first glimmerings of what would become the Inca culture began to manifest themselves in distinctive art styles in the Cuzco Valley. People in these regions abandoned many of the cities and towns

Below: The great ramp to the summit of the temple to Pachacamc and one of its numerous surrounding courts.

in the valleys and moved to higher, moister locations, and towards the wetter eastern Cordillera. Competing centres protected the resources of their immediate areas: Pikillaqta (a southern Wari survival), Chokepukio (Wari's nearest inheritor), and clusters of settlements of ethnic groups known as Lucre, Killke, Wanka (whose capital was Wari Wanka) and Campa, and the Gran Pajaten city in Chachapoyas. Petty rivalry and temporary alliances were typical.

Along the central and southern Andean Area coasts the periods of drought affecting the highlands were even more severe. It was precarious enough in such desert coasts, but stress increased when irrigation systems failed as run-off from the mountains was further reduced. Mountain cities, by contrast, were able to survive on rainfall agriculture. The stress and decline of coastal centres incited local rivalry and the establishment of numerous small polities fighting for survival: Chiribaya, Ica and Chancay.

THE KINGDOM OF CHIMÚ
Two of the most prominent centres that stand out and perhaps typify this period were Chimú – or the Kingdom of Chimú

Above: For this Chimú wooden and mother-of-pearl jaguar figurine, a Pacific shell was used to create the coat of a rainforest animal living thousands of kilometres (miles) away.

– and Pachacamac. As in the Early Intermediate Period, these centres of power were coast-based.

The Chimú were the inheritors of Early Intermediate Period Moche power in the Moche and Lambayeque valleys. Duplicating the Moche pattern, the Chimú conquered to north and south, invading and subduing the northern Peruvian coastal valleys from the sea. Through later Inca records, historians of Chimú encounter legends of early kings of Chimú and the earlier dynasty founded by the legendary ruler Naymlap and ending with the disastrous reign of Fempellec.

The Kingdom of Chimú was the largest Andean Area state up to its time. At its height it controlled two-thirds of all irrigated land on the desert coasts, while elsewhere states were more localized.

Some scholars believe that the term 'Kingdoms' of Chimú is more appropriate, as the nature of the valley politics indicates that there may have been dual or multiple rulership among them. Inca records gleaned by the Spanish conquistadors describe two dynasties: Taycanamu at Chan Chan in the Moche Valley and Naymlap in the Lambayeque Valley. In the latter, it is tempting to equate the rich burials of the Sicán Lords with the descendants of Naymlap.

CHAN CHAN OF THE CHIMÚ
The fantastic site of Chan Chan, capital of the Taycanamu rulers, was founded around AD 1000. It comprised a massive complex of individual compounds covering an area of 6 sq km (1,480 acres), around which domestic and workshop suburbs spread to cover 20 sq km (4,940 acres) in total. Each walled compound (known as a *ciudadela*) of the central core was rectangular in plan, its long axis oriented north–south, and made of thick walls up to 9m (29½ft) high of poured adobe mud. Most had only one entrance, on the north side, guarded by painted wooden human figures set in niches on either side. Each court contained the residences of the reigning Chimú king, his retainers and officials. Around other courtyards

within the compounds were store rooms, U-shaped structures called *audiencias*, and burial platforms. Adjacent wings contained rooms for service and maintenance retainers, as well as walled-in wells.

From the historical records we know the names of at least three Chimú deities: the creator god Ai Apaec, the moon

Below: The Tschudi complex: even the walls of smaller enclosures within the ciudadelas *of the Chimú capital at Chan Chan were carefully moulded with geometric decoration.*

Above: The great temple-platform at Pachacamac – a huge pyramid of adobe bricks that grew to the size of a hill.

goddess Si and the sea god Ni. Chimú religious imagery merges Moche and Wari styles, and continues the long Chavín traditions of fanged beings, jaguars and serpentine images.

THE CULT OF PACHACAMAC
The site of Pachacamac on the central Peruvian coast was established in the Early Intermediate Period. In the wake of Chavín decline, it rose to prominence as a cult and pilgrimage site in the later half of the period, from about AD 250. It was at this time that the first phases of the pyramid-platform to the sun and adjoining Temple to Pachacamac were built and presumably when the cult statues were installed. The name itself, in Quechua, means 'earth-maker'.

As a centre of local political power in the Middle Horizon, Pachacamac succumbed to Wari conquest, but as a religious cult centre it weathered the period of subjugation to persist as a cult and pilgrimage centre for more than 1,000 years through the Late Intermediate Period into Inca times. As a creator god, Pachacamac was the only serious rival to Viracocha, supreme god of the Inca, for that title.

CONQUEST AND EMPIRE: THE INCAS

The final chronological period of ancient Andean Area history is the Late Horizon, which began about AD1400. It is marked by the rise of the Inca and their domination of the Andean Area, forming the largest empire ever known in the New World. Inca hegemony lasted a mere 132 years, however, until it met its match in cunning and military guile in the person of Francisco Pizarro.

EARLY BEGINNINGS

Inca beginnings were in the early Late Intermediate Period. During the political fragmentation of that period, the Inca were one of several local tribes or ethnic groups competing for survival within the Cuzco region and among numerous city-states scattered throughout the sierra. From the founding of the Inca ruling dynasty by the legendary Manco Capac in the mid-13th century, the Inca began to conquer the sierra and coastal regions and to unify them into a state in which central control was paramount. As with earlier Andean states, military conquest

Below: A carved wooden face on a post from the Inca coastal regions, c.1400.

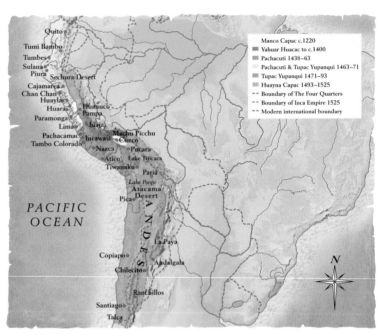

brought economic regulation and compulsory state religion. Both impositions on the losing parties were made more palatable through long-surviving traditional pan-Andean religious concepts, and by the incorporation of local deities, cults and religious practices into existing versions and the inclusion of local rulers in Inca government.

Manco Capac and his successors first defeated local rivals within the Cuzco Valley. The threat of their arch-enemy, the Chancas, nearly ended this early progress when they marched on Cuzco in 1438. The crushing of the Chancas by Pachacuti Inca Yupanqui, steeped in legend and the source of some of the most sacred *huaca* sites around the city, secured Inca domination of their immediate territory.

It was from this date that the Incas began their rapid expansion throughout the Andean Area. The date highlights the

Above: Map showing extent of the Inca Empire and the Four Quarters from the time of the legendary founder Manco Capac to the rule of Huayna Capac in the 16th century.

fact that the empire endured less than 100 years as the pre-eminent power in Andean America.

DOUBLING THE EMPIRE

Pachacuti ruled until 1471. His first campaigns subdued the city-states of the central Andes north to Huánuco and south to the northern and western shores of Lake Titicaca. The biggest prize of all was the conquest of the Kingdom of Chimú, which occurred in 1470–1. Together with his son and principal heir, Tupac Yupanqui (The Unforgettable One), Pachacuti doubled the size of the Inca Empire in less than ten years, incorporating Chimú and beyond into what is now Ecuador.

Upon his succession, Tupac Yupanqui more than doubled the size of the empire again, in 22 years of long and ruthless campaigns – to the coast west of Cuzco and to the farthest southern reaches, into modern Chile and Argentina. Upon his death, the throne was briefly disputed. Once secured by Huayna Capac, one of Tupac's sons, his reign (1493–1525) was occupied principally with campaigns to fill in corners in the northern provinces, mainly in the eastern Andean foothills and selva, with consolidation of Pachacuti's and Tupac's conquests, and with putting down local rebellions. Huayna Capac's attempts to conquer the selva had limited success.

KEYS TO SUCCESS

The success of Inca rapid expansion and domination lies in what had been established and entrenched in Andean political, social and economic structures before then. The Middle Horizon Wari and Tiwanaku empires, the former including the Cuzco region, had consolidated (as did the Late Intermediate Period Chimú) principles of centralized political control, organized through a network of administrative centres, roads and rapid communication. The practice of labour tax used levies of workers to co-ordinate labour distribution; it was an annual obligation to the central government. Such structures enabled the gathering, storage and redistribution of goods and the exchange of commodities between highland and lowland regions, ensuring the prosperity of all.

The Incas reconstituted these systems where their remnants remained and imported them into

Right: On this Moche pot, two warriors probably engage in ritual combat while one of them holds a decapitated head.

regions where they had not formerly existed. They maintained political power through the control of resources and the practice of resettling large groups of people around the provinces, and by using existing local chiefs to administer their command and removing to Cuzco the sons of local rulers, to hold hostage.

The nature of pan-Andean religious belief reinforced the Inca's 'right to rule' through the incorporation of local deities and icons into the state religion. At the same time it imposed the official state cult of Inti – the sun – personified by the Sapa Inca himself. In addition to hostages, the Incas took regional sacred objects to the capital; and craftsmen from the provinces were removed to Cuzco to construct buildings and produce imperial goods for the royal household.

Above: Inca warriors attacking a fortress during their many campaigns of conquest, shown in Nueva Crónica y Buen Gobierno.

ELEMENTS OF COLLAPSE

Perhaps inevitably, strains and tensions within such a vast and diverse empire brought successional rivalry. It had happened when Tupac died, and when Huayna Capac died, a bitter civil war broke out between his two sons Huáscar and Atahualpa. This was the situation in which Francisco Pizarro arrived on his third visit, in 1532.

Manipulating this disruption, Pizarro was able to bring the empire to its knees with a few hundred Spaniards. He exploited resentment in the recently conquered provinces to gain native allies, he played one royal faction against the other in the dispute over succession and used the assassination of one brother, Huáscar, by the other, Atahualpa, to imprison the latter and demand a huge ransom that bankrupted the empire. By such methods the Spaniards kept the Incas off balance. As the empire's cohesion crumbled, the alliances, social organization and economic structure of the empire were reconfigured to suit Spanish greed and rule. Feeble revolts attempting to reinstate Inca power were quickly crushed by increasing Spanish might in the new colony.

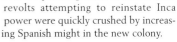

CHAPTER FIVE

THEMES AND PEOPLES

The earliest sites of human habitation in the Andean Area date to about 11,500 years ago. It has been biologically demonstrated that the inhabitants of the New World descend from three or four distinct populations and several incidents of migration into North America, but that migrants into the South American continent all descend from only one of these groups.

The diverse landscape and regional variety of the Andean Area encouraged technological, social and economic innovation. As the hunter-gatherer lifestyle of the earliest Lithic Period evolved into an era of farming and permanent settlement, people adapted differently to the challenges provided by the coastal and mountain environments, and many different cultures developed throughout the Andes from the late Initial Period onwards.

Different languages also developed, and linguists have identified major language groups within this area. Indeed, throughout South America they estimate as many as 2,000 languages were once spoken, though only about 600 have been attested.

Recognition of the existence of different peoples among ancient Andeans is revealed in their many stories of the origins of humankind. In one story, the creator god Viracocha shaped men and women from clay then painted them in different colours, wearing different styles of clothing, and gave them their languages, cultural practices, songs, arts and crafts, and the knowledge of agriculture to distinguish between the different tribes and nations.

Left: The eastern façade and entrance to the Temple of the Cult of Chavín, the first great ancient Andean pilgrimage centre.

CIVIC-CEREMONIAL CENTRES

Two principal themes characterized pre-Hispanic Andean civilization: a general unity through shared religious beliefs across the Andean Area, and a settlement pattern of independent yet linked communities. From the earliest farming villages, through the construction of monumental civic-ceremonial centres of increasing complexity, to the establishment and growth of cities, universal patterns developed in cross-regional trade, shared methods of craftsmanship and organized political and social systems of labour. This was for growing crops and for the production of pottery, textiles, metalwork and other artefacts. With detailed variation, these universal patterns gave developmental impetus to the process and progress of Andean civilization.

ARCHITECTURAL 'TRADITIONS'

Different 'traditions' of civic-ceremonial architecture developed in tropical, desert coastal and sierra settings. Within varied lifestyles, regional cultures centralized religious belief and integrated labour to build special places for communal worship. These special places held sacred objects that represented the gods, and some places became sites of pilgrimage serving large regions. Eventually, a select few became the most important pilgrimage centres, some of them enduring for long periods.

In the forested north (now in Ecuador), Valdivia Tradition settlements were characterized by central oval or circular plazas, with domed oval communal structures surrounded by houses. Sometimes the

communal buildings were on top of low earthen mounds. One type, known as a 'charnel house', was for mortuary ritual, to prepare corpses for burial elsewhere; a second type, called a 'fiesta house', was for feasting and drinking.

In the coastal valleys of northern and central Peru the establishment of civic-ceremonial centres became a mainstay of Andean civilization from about 2850BC. Known as the Supe-Aspero Tradition and the El Paraíso Tradition, they take their names from the 17-mound centres in the Río Supe Valley and the site of Aspero, and from El Paraíso. Both traditions featured raised mounds that provided flat, open spaces on top for congregational ritual and to support complex multi-chambered structures. Ceremony seems to have emphasized public-oriented activity, the flat top providing a stage for the ritual to be viewed by a large congregation assembled in front of the mound. Within this cohesive theme there was considerable variation in the sizes and shapes of coastal platforms and in the building complexes on top. Ceremony involved burnt offerings, but the locations and contexts of these varied.

REGIONAL CENTRES

The extensive platforms at Salinas de Chao, Los Morteros and Piedra Parada lack surrounding domestic remains, indicating that they were built as venues for communal ritual by the peoples of surrounding settlements. The extensive 17-mound complex of the Supe Valley also suggests regional worship, and perhaps influence beyond. If true, the extended 'site' was the earliest in a long Andean tradition of pilgrimage sites. In contrast, at Río Seco, Bandurria, Culebras, Huaynuna and Huaca Prieta the modest sizes of the ceremonial structures

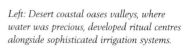
Left: Desert coastal oases valleys, where water was precious, developed ritual centres alongside sophisticated irrigation systems.

Right: Reconstruction of the circular sunken court and the terraced platforms built against the hill slope at Salinas de Chao.

and associated domestic buildings and refuse indicates that they were built by and largely for their local communities.

Many chambers in the complexes on top of Supe-Aspero platforms included rectangular niches, possibly for sacred objects. At Caral, the ceremonial complex includes an element of exclusion where it enclosed a large walled plaza with a 'fire altar' in one corner; another chamber housed a sacred obelisk. At Huaynuna, Piedra Parada and Caral there is evidence of contact with sierra ritual in the construction of oval ceremonial chambers and sunken courtyards. Room complexes of later building phases at some sites feature bilateral symmetry.

ASPERO

The largest of the Supe sites, Aspero, comprises an extensive mound complex: six major flat platforms and 11 lower (1–2m/3–6½ft) mounds surrounded by 15ha (37 acres) of public and domestic remains. The larger mounds rise up to 4m (12ft) above the valley floor, or 10m (32ft) where banked against the side or top of a hill. Two of these, Huaca de los Idolos and Huaca de los Sacrificios, produced radio-carbon dates as early as 3055 and 2850BC respectively. Both platforms underwent several phases of covering and later enlargement.

Right: A figurine of unbaked clay, which was deliberately broken and buried at Huaca de los Idolos. The fragmentary figure is shown in the first two drawings; the drawing on the right shows a projected reconstruction.

The free-standing platform at Huaca de los Sacrificios included an elite, textile-wrapped ritual infant burial, apparently accompanied by an adult sacrifice, showing that social hierarchy had clearly become established. At Huaca de los Idolos, one ritual chamber on top of the platform included a buried cache of 13 or more deliberately broken clay figurines.

EL PARAISO

The largest Preceramic Period stone-built civic-ceremonial centre was El Paraíso. Radiocarbon dates of 2000BC and later indicate that its civic-ceremonial complex represents a transitional stage from the Preceramic traditions and the Initial Period U-shaped complexes described earlier. It comprised two long parallel raised platforms (250 x 50m/820 x 140ft) forming the sides of a U framing a 7ha (17 acre) plaza. The base of the U comprises several smaller ruins rather than a central platform. Other masonry complexes were built near by as El Paraíso expanded. Evidence of fire ritual and an absence of domestic debris around the ceremonial complexes indicate that El Paraíso was built as a ritual centre for people living throughout a larger region.

COMMUNAL RITUAL: KOTOSH

Farming community peoples in the mountain valleys of central and northern Peru also cultivated communal ritual by building large communal structures. While the environment of isolated valleys was conducive to social division and variation between valleys, the development of similar corporate constructions demonstrates social union and amalgamation, reveals contact among valleys and reveals underlying common religious belief here as well. To build such structures required political control and the mobilization of communal labour. The buildings must also have served civic and administrative purposes.

THE KOTOSH TRADITION

Ritual and special-purpose architecture in the sierra is known as the Kotosh Tradition, after the type-site, Kotosh, situated at about 2,000m (6,600ft) above sea level, in a region of temperate climate and limited seasonal rainfall in the eastern Andes. Its location typifies lower sierra village settlement and offered access to the natural resources of both higher and lower ecological zones. The early Kotosh economy was mainly hunting and gathering – there are many chipped stone tools and debris, and charred seeds, but at first no evidence of cultivated plants. Anatomical changes on the animal bones found at Kotosh show that guinea pigs and llamas were domesticated, or at least kept and herded. Deer bones show that hunting remained an important source of meat.

Like coastal architectural traditions, Kotosh sites featured platform mounds. These mounds, however, were more standardized in shape and size, and served as platforms for structures of a more excluding nature. A characteristic of the Kotosh tradition was the raising of a large twin ceremonial mound complex, indicating the early establishment of social division into two kin-related groups.

Excavations at Kotosh reveal long periods of use, perhaps

Above: As a staple of life, maize and other crops exemplified Pacha Mama (Mother Earth), from which all life sprang.

through generations, comprising ten superimposed constructions. Early mounds were built by people who made no pottery, and the later mounds were made by their pottery-making Initial Period and Early Horizon descendants.

A second Kotosh form was the sunken court or plaza (*plazas hundidas*). Every platform mound and plaza was a place of protocol and designed behaviour. People participated in the construction of these non-subsistence buildings and in prescribed ritual activity, presumably led by religious specialists.

The contemporary site of La Galgada, in the central sierra north of Kotosh, demonstrates similar characteristics. At about 1,100m (3,600ft) above sea level and located roughly equidistantly between the Pacific coast and the semi-tropical eastern selva, it too exploited both zones for ornamental products. La Galgada burials

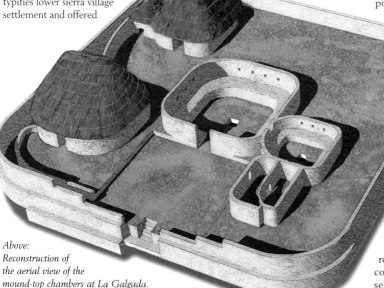

*Above:
Reconstruction of
the aerial view of the
mound-top chambers at La Galgada.
It is not known if such temples were roofed.*

contain shell beads and discs from the coast and Amazonian tropical bird feathers from the east. The La Galgada economy was demonstrably based on farming. There are remains of domesticated beans, squashes, fruits, chilli peppers, gourds, cotton and a single maize cob. Remains of ancient irrigation canals are consistent with the necessity of irrigation to grow these plants.

POSITIVE AND NEGATIVE SPACES
Platforms and sunken courts organize space in two distinct ways. Platforms are positive structures – exterior and elevated. They divide space vertically and support hierarchical buildings for special purposes. The mounds themselves, and more especially their buildings, hide ritual from the general populace and render them exclusive to specialists. Sunken courts, on the other hand, constitute negative space – interior and secluded. Their walls restrict space and confine activities within them. At most sites both platforms and sunken courts were built, though at a few sites only a sunken court was built.

SOCIAL DIVISIONS
The ceremonial constructions at La Galgada, as at Kotosh, comprise twin mounds surrounded by dwellings, again indicating a two-part social division. Each mound has a main central platform and subsidiary buildings. Each comprises a series of superimposed mounds and buildings, and the larger platform produced radiocarbon dates ranging between 2200 and 1200BC.

Both Kotosh and La Galgada were clearly sites of regional importance. The presence of exotic commodities at both sites implies the beginnings of exchange between coast and sierra and between sierra and tropics – a tradition so characteristic of later Andean civilization. Their inhabitants had succeeded in achieving an economy and lifestyle that afforded them the time to

Above: The ritual honouring of important ancestors began perhaps with mummification among the Chinchorros of northern Chile.

marshal their labour for the purely non-subsistence activity of special architecture, religiously focused sites and special burials. These constructions, to their builders' minds, were vital to the continuity of their existence and were the earliest such sites in an Andean tradition of meeting such existential or religious needs in this way.

THE CHINCHORROS
Much farther south of the coastal and sierra traditions, sites on the desert coast of Peru and northern Chile reveal a singular economy based on the riches of the sea. Chemical analysis of the bones of the inhabitants of the culture shows a diet of 90 per cent marine foods. So rich were

the marine resources that large towns could be supported with little or no farming of edible cultigens. Coastal floodplain plants were gathered and later cultivated for fuel, clothing fibre, shelter, water craft, nets, fishing line and floats, basketry and other tools for marine exploitation.

Chinchorros domestic structures include burials of the earliest mummified bodies, preserved with salt and reed-mat wrappings, presaging the Andean traditions of both mummification and burial among the living to keep the deceased as part of the present.

EXCHANGE OF GOODS AND IDEAS

The architectural traditions of Kotosh, Supe-Aspero and El Paraíso reveal the beginnings of an exchange that became characteristically Andean. It involved the interchange of both commodities and religious ideas within and between geographical zones: among respective regions at similar heights (horizontal exchange) and between highland and lowland communities, such as sierra and coast and sierra and selva (vertical exchange).

DISTRIBUTION AND EXCHANGE
The exchange of goods became a necessity in Andean civilization for the trading and obtaining of either key products that could not be grown in one zone or another or exotic materials that were native to one zone or another.

Adaptation within Andean civilization was shaped by the distribution of natural resources and by the limits within which various domesticated plants and animals could be grown, reared and herded. For example, food staples such as maize can be grown at altitudes up to about 3,000m

Above: Highland staples, particularly the potato, also became lowland staples through trade between the two areas.

(9,800ft), but are at risk from frost and hail; crops frequently fail. Maize domestication and cultivation thus spread from coast to highlands. In contrast, the potato, originally a highland crop, was eventually cultivated throughout a range from nearly sea level to 3,800m (12,500ft). A similar division into zones applies to growing cotton and herding llamas and alpacas for meat and wool. Tropical fruits and lowland products such as peanuts, avocados, manioc, chillies and squashes were redistributed among zones through trade as they became part of Andean Area culture.

In coastal desert oases, resources were similar despite the

Left: Exotic objects, such as this Pacific spiny or thorny oyster, were traded from the far northern coasts to the highlands.

long coastline. The same is true of vast tropical lowlands. Environmental similarities are reinforced by limited annual temperature fluctuation. These factors contribute to exchange within and between valleys or selva regions. At increasing elevation, however, seasonal variation increases and growing periods shorten. In highland areas, zones of cultivation are compressed and stacked within the environment. Highland peoples consequently practise greater vertical movement within these zones to pursue cultivation in basins and valleys and herding in the Altiplano. These factors contribute to exchange between communities at different altitudes within the highlands and also between highlands and lowlands.

AVAILABILITY AND DEMAND
It is frequently the case in the Andean Area that where abundant flatlands (potentially useful for crop-growing) occur, there is less rainfall, a threat of drought and a need to irrigate. In contrast,

Above: The decorations on many Moche pots depict scenes of daily life. Here a fisherman sets out in a balsa boat.

highland zones have greater rainfall and are less affected by drought, but flat lands suitable for agriculture are more restricted and there is a need to increase growing space by terracing. For these different reasons both zones required the input of organized labour as populations increased. However, fewer than 20 per cent of major Andean cultivated plants grow above 3,000m (9,800ft), while 90 per cent thrive best below 1,000m (3,300ft). This inversion of available land and crop diversity created a perennial strain on supply and demand, and it is this tension that underlays exchange between peoples at different elevations in ancient Andean civilization.

MOVEMENT OF PEOPLE

Exchange was not only of goods but also of peoples, adapting to different land zones to exploit cultivation possibilities. Andean highland peoples regularly exploited irrigated farmlands for maize, cotton, peppers, gourds and squashes in a lowland zone, in middle-zone potato lands and in Altiplano herding pastures. Furthermore, evidence in Inca times shows that the peoples in these zones were kin-related groups with a regularized system of obligations and duties to the whole group.

Among coastal valley and plain cultures the sea provided a natural highway for the movement of goods and peoples up and down the coast. The Moche kingdom,

for example, was a seafaring nation that pursued conquest from one valley to another by sea invasion.

As regions came under the control of larger political entities, the redistribution of products required greater regulation and intricate administration. To maintain economic balance, both products and labour needed control and regulation. Later imperial cultures, and ultimately the Incas, practised active transportation of peoples within the empire and colonization of regions to obtain materials from distant areas or exotic locations.

RITUAL GOODS AND IDEAS

To maintain religious integrity and appease the gods, and so secure the well-being of humans, rulers needed to obtain exotic raw materials considered essential for ritual. Thus, tropical products such as tobacco, coca and forest mushrooms required not only secured sources but also organization and security in transport. The use of cotton and llama wool textiles at coastal and highland sites, and of coastal shells (including *Spondylus princeps* – the spiny or thorny oyster from Ecuador and farther north) in highland ceremonial contexts confirms the early beginnings of both horizontal and vertical exchange. As weaving became an entrenched part of Andean cultural expression and part of state control, the redistribution of cotton and wool became heavily regulated in Inca times and was no doubt equally regulated in earlier kingdoms.

The exchange of exotic products across such distant regions implies the exchange of ideas associated with the items and their suppliers. The nature of both highland and coastal ceremonial architecture from the earliest Preceramic times shows recognition of mountain, earth and sea gods throughout Andean cultures, and the association of them in ritual structures.

Below: From ancient times, coastal valley oases probably consisted of numerous small growing fields sharing an irrigation system.

CONFLICT AND CO-OPERATION

Coastal El Paraíso was the first example of the U-shaped ceremonial complex that became the hallmark of Initial Period civic-ceremonial architecture. This period showed both the start of a widespread similarity in civic-ceremonial construction and signs of conflict between political units. These are manifestations of the two alternating themes of political cohesion and fragmentation in Andean civilization.

The combination of platform mounds and sunken courts in the late Preceramic Period at Kotosh, La Galgada and coastal sites may have constituted a Kotosh Religious Tradition, perhaps the first widespread Andean 'religion'. Scholars speculate that to agricultural people the sunken court was the focus for veneration of the Pacha Mama (Mother Earth), or even for the ritual re-enactment of creation or birth in a descent into the court and re-emergence from it. Where both structures were built, the sunken court was situated before the ascending staircase of the platform, its own staircase aligned to it. This combination – the elevated and

Above: When peoples gather to trade their produce, ideas are also exchanged and bonds developed between different regions.

the subterranean – suggests rituals that proceeded from a descent into Mother Earth followed by an ascent into the sky to the father Apu (or vice versa perhaps).

FARMING AND RITUAL

In the early centuries of the third millennium BC, climatic improvement and increased rainfall fostered the spread of intensive agriculture throughout the Andean Area. Intensive agriculture with irrigation works at coastal sites was added to maritime exploitation.

Agriculture and pastoralism spread into the higher sierra and Altiplano, including the Titicaca Basin. Increasing population and agricultural production, and the exploitation of new lands, brought economic prosperity. Easier living created time for increased sophistication of political structure and for concern with religious concepts.

Left: Conflict between city-states is evident from at least the Initial Period in stone sculptures of warriors, as at Cerro Sechín.

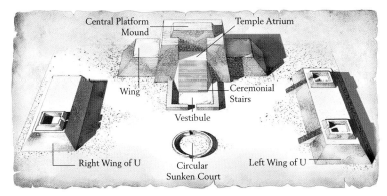

Above: A U-shaped temple showing the large central platform mound flanked by left and right wings and a circular sunken court.

Intensive agriculture, manifested by irrigation works and concern for rain and run-off water, may have fostered increased veneration of Mother Earth, Pacha Mama, and of mountain deities represented by Apu. Increased concern with the Milky Way (Mayu) accompanied the need to track the movements of stars and planets for agricultural scheduling.

These concerns brought an unprecedented spate of civic-ceremonial complex-building throughout the Andean Area. As in the Preceramic Period, Initial Period coastal complexes were small and local and also vast, presumably to serve a wide region. There were scores of complexes throughout the valleys. New phases of building at Kotosh, La Galgada and El Paraíso created U-shaped complexes at the last two sites about 1900 and 2000BC respectively. Sunken courts changed from circular to rectangular.

The largest Initial Period civic-ceremonial complex was at Sechín Alto in the coastal Casma Valley. Begun around 1400BC, the huge platform forming the base of its U-shaped complex was 300m (980ft) long and 250m (820ft) wide and still stands 40m (130ft) above the plain. Platforms forming the arms of the U flank a succession of plazas, including two circular sunken courts, in an area 400m (1,300ft) wide by 1,100m (3,600ft) long.

Right: Co-operation within and between cities enabled people to build and maintain extensive field terraces and irrigation systems.

Surrounding this complex was 10.5 sq km (2,600 acres) of buildings and smaller platforms. Other classic coastal U-shaped centres included Huaca de los Reyes, Cardal, La Florida, San Jacinto and Garagay.

SIGNS OF CONFLICT

Accompanying this unity in architectural form were signs of conflict between the political units associated with different civic-ceremonial centres, or perhaps between valleys. Cladding their ceremonial mounds with hand-made mud bricks, the builders of different sites vied with each other to decorate them with enormous adobe friezes, often painting them in rich colours. Two smaller, yet imposing, sites exemplify theses developments, both in the Sechín–Casma Valley.

Cerro Sechín was a multi-roomed sanctuary adorned with adobe friezes painted with felines and fish. About 1200BC, this complex was filled to make a

large rectangular platform surrounded by a facing of incised megaliths. Two processions of armed warriors carry axe-like clubs and march from the sides around the front of the building to converge on the main entrance. On either side of the entrance, monoliths depict fluttering banners.

A few kilometres (miles) away, Llamas-Moxeke is dominated by two huge rectangular platforms about 1km (½ mile) apart and equidistant from a square court. The Moxeke platform, 25m (82ft) high and 165m (540ft) on each side, had a façade decorated with huge niches framing high-relief friezes painted red, blue, white and black. Figures depicted include two human faces, two richly dressed individuals and a person with his back turned out and arms bound behind him as if a prisoner.

The coastal flowering lasted until about 900BC, from which time a period of drought took severe effect and almost all coastal ceremonial complexes were abandoned within a century or two. Sierra ceremonial complexes faired better, many remaining functional into the last few centuries BC, into the Early Horizon. The rise of a new highland U-shaped ceremonial centre, Chavín de Huántar, hailed the beginning of an ecumenical Andean religion that was widespread and enduring.

RELIGIOUS COHESION

The common use of platforms, U-shaped complexes and the association of sunken courts suggests religious ecumenicalism, and use both for ritual and civic functions – even that the two activities were functionally intertwined. A Kotosh Religious Tradition has earlier been suggested.

In the succeeding Early Horizon, while coastal centres remained modest after centuries of drought began to abate, one sierra centre arose that without question became a cult and pilgrimage centre. It was the 'cathedral' of Andean religion and included all the classic features that had been developed in earlier periods in coastal and sierra traditions. This was Chavín de Huántar.

THE RISE OF CHAVÍN DE HUÁNTAR
From about 900BC, as coastal ceremonial centres were abandoned, Chavín de Huántar rose to prominence. It was not urban in size or layout and lacked a surrounding domestic district. Instead it comprised a modest complex to accommodate a small population of priests, officials, artisans, servants and pilgrims to support and serve its cult. Its influence stretched throughout the central and northern Andes, and west and east to the coast and tropical lowlands. Further, it played a crucial role in the dissemination of technology. Its central location appears to have established and perpetuated its importance.

At its largest, the Chavín de Huántar ceremonial centre covered about 42ha (104 acres), with 2,000–3,000 inhabitants. The Old Temple framed a circular sunken courtyard. Scores of sculpted heads project from its four-storey stone walls. The temple interior comprises a labyrinth of interconnecting narrow passages and chambers, the southern wing of which was later doubled in size as the site flourished, and is known as the New Temple, although both temples were used simultaneously after the expansion.

MONOLITHIC SCULPTURE
In one interior gallery stands the stone idol called the Lanzón (after its lance-like shape) or Great Image, probably the earliest pan-Andean oracle: a carved granite monolith 4.5m (15ft) high. The Lanzón faces east and portrays a humanoid form, but overall depicts a monster visage. Its right hand is raised and its left lowered by its side; its feet and hands end in claws. Its mouth is thick-lipped, drawn in a hideous snarl and punctuated by long, outward-curving canines. Its eyebrows and hair end in serpent heads; its earlobes hang heavy with pendants. It wears a tunic and headdress, both of which are decorated with feline heads. Its notched top protrudes through the ceiling into an upper gallery in which priests probably sat in secrecy, projecting their voices as that of the god.

Left: Plan of Chavín de Huántar, one of the most elaborate ceremonial centres of its period, with its U-shaped temples.

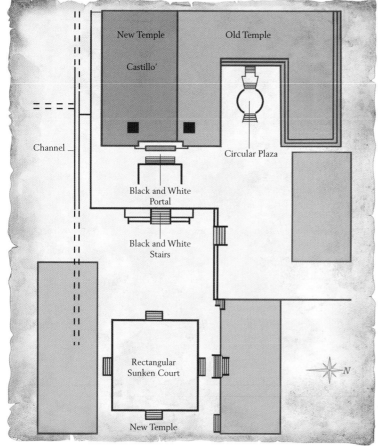

New Temple

Old Temple

Castillo'

Channel

Circular Plaza

Black and White Portal

Black and White Stairs

Rectangular Sunken Court

New Temple

N

CULT CENTRE

That Chavín de Huántar was the site of a cult seems indisputable. In a gallery next to the sunken plaza, excavators found 800 broken ceramic vessels decorated in styles from cultures as far apart as the northern coast to the central highlands. Scattered among bowls and containers were llama, deer, guinea pig and fish bones – thought to have been either offerings or a store of ritual trappings for ceremonies.

Chavín iconography drew its inspiration from both the natural world – animals, plants and aquatic life – and a variety of ecological zones – the ocean, coast, the mountains and tropical lowlands. The Tello Obelisk is a low-relief carved granite monolith 2.5m (8ft) high, in the shape of a supernatural cayman. Notched at the top like the Lanzón, it probably also stood upright in a gallery or courtyard. Additional carvings on and around the cayman depict plants and animals, including peanuts and manioc from the tropical lowlands and *Strombus* and *Spondylus* shells of species native to the Ecuadorian coast, attesting to the wide influence of the Chavín Cult. Other carvings depict jaguars, serpents, and harpy or crested eagles.

As the cult's fame spread and the site was enlarged, ceramic styles and other exotic foods, plants and animals continued to inspire its artistic imagery. Evidence from the domestic buildings shows the development of social hierarchy in the unequal distribution of goods and of craft specialization. The cult supported artisans applying its symbolism to portable artefacts and spreading it through exchange, thereby expanding and entrenching the cult.

With the expansion of the south wing of the temple, the imagery became more elaborate. The relief of a new supreme deity was erected in the patio of the New Temple. Like the Lanzón, this is a humanoid figure with a fanged mouth, multiple bracelets, anklets and ear pendants. It holds a *Strombus* shell in its right hand and a *Spondylus* shell in its left hand.

THE STAFF DEITY

Another huge carved stone slab, the Raimondi Stela (2m/6½ft long), depicts a deity who in some ways epitomizes the cult: the Staff God/Goddess. Ubiquitous

Left: The Raimondi Stela at Chavín de Huántar is the ultimate representation of the Staff Deity. It can be read either way up.

Above: The ray-encircled Staff Deity is the central figure on the Gateway of the Sun in the Kalasasaya enclosure at Tiwanaku.

in Chavín iconography, this figure was portrayed with male or female attributes. The full-frontal, standing figure is a composite of animal and human characteristics. Like those of other Chavín deities, the hands and feet of this figure end in claws, the mouth displays huge curved fangs and the ears are bedecked with ornaments. The arms are outstretched and clutch staffs in one form or another, themselves elaborately festooned with spikes and plume-like decorations.

The exact significance and meaning of the Staff Deity is unknown. That he/she was a powerful deity is attested by the application of the image all over Chavín de Huántar on stones and walls, and throughout the central Andes and coast on portable objects, including ceramics and textiles. The potency of the Staff Deity is likewise demonstrated by the fact that the imagery of a frontal, staff-bearing deity endured from the Early Horizon until Inca times. Given this exceptional importance, it seems certain that the Staff Deity was a supernatural being with a distinct 'personality', possibly a primeval creator god.

PEOPLES OF THE EMPIRE

Spanish administrative and judicial archives contain chronicles and records of the Inca conquest of numerous ethnic groups, chiefdoms and political units called *señorios*. From these sources we have a veritable roster of the peoples of the empire.

RIVALS OF THE INCAS

Guaman Poma de Ayala's history refers to the chiefdom of the Ayarmacas, one of the many politico-ethnic divisions of the Acamama region around Cuzco. As the first powerful Inca rivals, the Ayarmacas played an instrumental role in the founding of Cuzco. Poma de Ayala identifies 'some first Incas' called Tocay Capac and Pinahua Capac, whom other sources call 'kings', or identify as generic

Below: One of the greatest Inca conquests involved capturing the Chimú fortresses, such as that of coastal Paramonga.

titles for the rulers of two allied chiefdoms – Ayarmaca and Pinahua – comprising 18 towns south of Cuzco.

Prolonged Ayarmaca campaigns against the Incas of Cuzco resulted in stalemate. However, as the Incas subdued other neighbours and expanded within the valley, the Ayarmaca lords were relegated to the status of local chiefs within the Inca hierarchy. As the Incas wrestled for control, their new arch-rivals became the Chancas, whose defeat in 1438 was a defining point in the rise of the Inca state, and the traditional date for the beginning of the empire, along with Pachacuti Inca Yupanqui's ascent to the throne.

PEOPLES OF THE INCA EMPIRE

Pachacuti turned his attention to the Altiplano chiefdoms. His predecessor Viracocha had formed an alliance with the Lupaqas of Chucuito against the Hatun Colla, but

Above: Huayna Capac, 12th of the Inca dynasty and the last great conquering emperor, ruled from 1493 until 1526.

success against the Chancas changed Pachacuti's perspective on domination. The Collas were utterly defeated in battle, and the peace scene frequently depicted on *kero* drinking vessels shows the Collas wearing especially tall headdresses, emphasizing the cultural variety and distinction between ethnic groups. At the victory celebration in Cuzco, Pachacuti ordered the beheading of the Colla leaders, warning others who might resist.

The effect was immediate and the remaining Altiplano lords accepted Inca overlordship without further resistance. This Cuntisuyu quarter formed the core of the empire, incorporating the chiefdoms of the Soras, Lucanas, Andahuaylas, Canas, Canchis, Paucarcollas, Pacajes and Azángaros, and exposing the western coastal *señorio* of Collao.

The Chinchas of Collao submitted peacefully at the intimidating approach of Inca armies led by Tupac Yupanqui. Pachacuti and Tupac next expanded north, creating Chinchaysuyu quarter, valley chiefdoms falling one after another: the

Below: In less than 100 years, the Incas subdued peoples from Ecuador to Chile and from the Pacific to the Amazon Rainforest.

Guarco and Lunahuaná chiefdoms in the central Andes; the Collec *señorio*, including the Chuquitanta, Carabayllo, Zapan, Macas, Guaraui, Guancayo and Quivi chiefdoms; and the Ychsma *señorio*.

THE KINGDOM OF THE CHIMÚ

The Inca armies marched on the vast, ancient northern Kingdom of Chimú. Garcilasco de la Vega's *Comentarios Reales de los Incas* describes the confrontation:

The brave Chimú [Minchançaman], his arrogance and pride now tamed, appeared before the prince [Tupac Inca Yupanqui] with as much submission and humility, and grovelled on the ground before him, worshipping him and repeating the same request [for pardon] as he had made through his ambassadors. The prince received him affectionately in order to relieve [his] grief … [and] bade two of the captains raise him from the ground. After hearing him, [Tupac] told him that all that was past was forgiven. … The Inca had not come to deprive him of his estates and authority, but to improve his idolatrous religion, his laws, and his customs.

Unlike the treatment of Colla leaders, Tupac set a new precedent, incorporating new states and recognizing their integrity under Inca overlordship. Perhaps the size and importance of Chimú prompted special treatment.

Farther north, the coastal chiefdoms of the Quito, Cañaris, Huancavilcas, Manta and Puná were conquered; then the Huarochirí, Yauyos, and the *señorio* of Guzmango. These northern chiefdoms fell so rapidly that there was hardly time

Above: The centre of the empire was Cuzco, here seen from the fortress-temple of Sacsahuaman overlooking the city.

for incorporation and consolidation; archaeology and the chronicles, however, attest to the rapid imposition of Inca rule, installation of local elites as provincial governors and collection of tax produce into large centres for redistribution.

OUTSIDERS AND REBELS

The Incas also recognized peoples beyond imperial borders, against whom their campaigns were less successful. The chronicles of Tupac Yupanqui's incursions into the selva of Antisuyu quarter mention the Opataris, Manosuyu, Mañaris, Yanaximes, Chunchos and Paititi.

Many chiefdoms accepted diminution of their authority reluctantly. Tupac's son Huayna Capac campaigned against the Chiriguanas of Collasuyu quarter, and, in the far north, the Chachapoyas of Chinchaysuyu, the Caranquis, Otavalos, Cayambis, Cochasquis and Pifos, all of whom had rebelled. The Huanca of Chinchaysuyu allied themselves to Pizarro in a final bid to throw off Inca domination.

The Incas strove for political unity by utilizing local rulers and incorporating them into the Inca hierarchy, giving local elites and subjects a sense of belonging. Nevertheless, local independence had lasted for generations, so there was considerable resentment of Inca impositions, particularly among more far-flung peoples. This potential instability, especially at the death of Huayna Capac in 1526, played into Spanish hands.

111

CHAPTER SIX

POWER AND WARFARE

By the end of the Initial Period, civilization in the Andean Area had established an underlying unity in religious concepts and some basic civic-ceremonial architectural forms, culminating in the cohesion in the Chavín Cult in the Early Horizon. Subsequent periods continued the alternation of less-unified periods and more politically unified horizons, although in every period there were some kingdoms or empires.

Patterns established in earlier periods continued to focus on three areas: the central and northern Peruvian coastal valleys, the central and southern Peruvian/Bolivian sierras and Altiplano, and the southern Peruvian and northern Chilean coastal deserts. Within each of these areas powerful social hierarchies developed and elite individuals ruled alongside a specialized priesthood or state shamans. Elite individuals were buried elaborately in rich tombs, sumptuously adorned and often accompanied by sacrificial victims. State cults of the dead flourished, establishing the principle of a continuously revolving cycle of life and death and the perpetuation of the dead in the living world.

The principles of state control over ordinary citizens became stronger and more elaborate, culminating in one of the two greatest empires ever established in the Americas: the Inca Empire. The chronicles and histories preserved by Spanish priests and administrators, together with archaeological discoveries, make it possible to gain a detailed picture of the way of life and beliefs of the Incas.

Left: This painted Chimú textile depicts a shaman in a trance, surrounded by snarling felines, serpents and birds.

THE NAZCA CONFEDERACY

Early Horizon Chavín was not a state religion. It brought religious unity throughout the central and northern Peruvian Andes and coast, but it was not a centralized state.

The number and variation in size and architecture of civic-ceremonial centres, and the large domestic populations of many, indicate both local rule and social organization. Specialist artisans spread and perpetuated the cult by making large quantities of portable objects adorned with Chavín symbolic art, constantly reminding the inhabitants of the towns and cities of their over-arching religion. Chavín de Huántar remained the premier pilgrimage centre, and constant trade among coastal and mountain valleys re-enforced shared beliefs.

Contemporary with later Chavín was the Paracas culture on the southern Peruvian coast. Like Chavín, Paracas was

Below: Nazca effigy jar suggesting a severed head. Ritual decapitation, widespread in Andean civilization, was a Nazca speciality.

Above: Nazca burials include collections of trophy heads and were often wrapped in textiles fringed with pictures of woven heads.

not a centralized state. The most famous Paracas feature – its Cavernas cemetery of richly adorned, carefully mummified burials – was a distinct locale serving, but physically separated from, the living town of Cerro Colorado. Close spiritual association between Paracas living and dead, demonstrated by the lavish treatment of the latter by the former, shows a cult-like relationship between religion and a loose socio-political organization. With some early Chavín influence, Paracas religion soon developed its own character, which was particularly represented by a prominent figure known as the Oculate Being.

NAZCA CITY-STATES

In the same desert coastal area as the Nazca were the Early Intermediate Period inheritors of the Paracas legacy, *c.*100BC–AD700. As with Paracas, no strong central Nazca political unity prevailed; rather there was a loose confederation of city-states in the river valleys. Ventilla, the largest Nazca site known, covered at least 200ha (495 acres) with terraced housing, walled courts and small mounds, and is thought to have been a Nazca 'capital' of one such city-state.

Ventilla was linked to its ritual counterpart, Cahuachi, by a line or 'road' across the desert. Cahuachi comprised a profusion of ceremonial kin-group mounds and associated plazas scattered over 150ha (370 acres). The mounds were built of adobe bricks modifying the tops of about 40 natural hills in mid-valley. The largest mound, known as the Great Temple, was a 30m (98ft) high modified hillock comprising six or seven terraces with adobe-brick retaining walls.

Cahuachi's location was chosen deliberately at mid-valley where, for geological reasons, the Nazca River disappears underground and re-emerges down-valley. Increasing drought in the sierra to the east intensified desert aridity and pressure for water conservation. The Ventillana-Cahuachi people constructed an elaborate system of subterranean channels to direct water into cisterns, which were reached by spiral ramps on terraces faced with river cobbles, and from which water could be drawn for irrigation.

A CITY FOR RITUAL

Cahuachi was a sacred 'city', where the citizens performed religious ceremonies and where the dead were prepared and then buried. The burials and artefacts associated with the mounds show that the entire site was a pilgrimage centre and ritual burial ground of family plots, each kin-group constructing its own mound. The focus was on ancestor worship and a pantheon of gods now nameless.

Some burials were of elite or favoured dead, while others appear to be sacrificial victims. Honoured burials were mummified and accompanied by exquisitely decorated, multicoloured woven burial coats and pottery, and sometimes by animal sacrifices. Others – men, women or children – had excrement inserted in the mouth, the skull perforated and threaded on a cord, the eyes blocked, the mouth pinned by cactus spines or the tongue removed and placed in a pouch. The meanings of such ritual practices are unknown, but the relationship between Ventilla and Cahuachi resembles and perpetuates the affiliation between the living and dead at Cerro Colorado and Cavernas.

NAZCA CRAFTS

Nazca textiles and pottery continued many Paracas traditions. They were adorned with images of the gods: half-human, half-animal – felines with long, ratcheted tails, spiders with human faces, birds, monkeys and lizards. Fringes on some textiles display rows of dangling heads or mummified

Left: A Nazca warrior or masked shaman with spear and atl-atl *(spear thrower), in a stance reminiscent of the Chavín Staff Deity.*

skulls with staring eyes, or lines of figures wearing short tunics, dancing above round-eyed deities who seem to be flying, continuing the Oculate Being tradition.

Caches of severed and trepanned skulls and dangling heads on textiles represent a Nazca trophy-head cult of sacrificial victims. Like the severed heads so prominent at Chavín de Huántar and other northern sierra and coastal sites, they demonstrate the strength of severed-head symbolism in ancient Andean religion.

RITUAL PATHWAYS

Ritual dominance of daily life was further emphasized across the desert floor by geoglyphs – the famous Nazca lines. Desert figures and patterns, resembling those on Nazca ceramics and textiles, began to be made as early as the settlements at Cahuachi, Ventilla and other sites, but increased in number and complexity as Cahuachi was abandoned. Hundreds of geometric patterns, clusters of straight lines and recognizable figures frequently cross, but individual patterns or figures are each made of a single, continuous line. Animal and other figures each comprise a single line with different beginning and end points.

Nazca geoglyphs were ritual pathways, walked for reasons no longer fully understood, but which presumably involved religious cycles. Each figure or pattern appears to have been made by and for a small group – or perhaps even an individual – each for a separate, but jointly agreed purpose and small group's use. Experiments have shown that a few people can make a geoglyph in a short time. Their number and interference with each other indicates that geoglyph-making endured over a long time period, and that individual patterns may have been for short or even a single use.

Increasing aridity of the region and disastrous earthquakes appear to have caused the Nazca to abandon Ventilla, Cahuachi and other sites. At the same time, an increase in the number and elaboration of geoglyphs seems to indicate increasing ritual, perhaps asking the gods for help.

Below: In the Nazca desert, water was channelled from underground rivers to subterranean cisterns with terraced entrances.

THE MOCHE STATE

In contrast to the loose confederacy of the Nazca, the Early Intermediate Period in the northern Peruvian coastal valleys saw the emergence of Moche state-builders.

THE FIRST TRUE STATE

Moche is arguably the first true ancient Andean state or kingdom. For about the first 600 years AD it dominated the northern coastal valleys from the Piura Valley in the north to the Harmey Valley in the south. The Lambayeque and Moche valleys are roughly in the middle of the area, a few valleys apart.

The Moche state comprised two neighbouring spheres, northern and southern, in which two related languages were spoken: Muchic from the Lambayeque Valley northwards and Quingan in the south.

Of an energetic military temperament, Moche rulers established a powerful kingdom over several hundred years through conquest and domination of the valleys

Below: The invading warrior on this Moche stirrup-spout vessel stands on a fanged-beast-prowed boat.

Above: This fierce, grimacing, half-human, half-jaguar face is that of the Moche Decapitator God at the Huaca de la Luna.

north and south of the southern sphere 'capital' at Moche in the valley of the same name. From the 4th century, Moche rulers mounted campaigns from valley to valley by sea, and many Moche pots depict narrative battle scenes of armies and pairs of warriors. A developing strong social hierarchy was reflected in burial practices.

Quingan speakers remained dominant, and Moche was the capital city for several hundred years.

HUACAS DEL SOL AND DE LA LUNA

The focuses of political and religious power in the capital were the two huge pyramidal structures known as the Huaca del Sol and the Huaca de la Luna, which reached their full sizes around AD450. Each required a massive amount of labour and was built of millions of hand-made adobe bricks. Distinctive marks on the bricks record the different labour gangs who built the platforms. The sudden appearance of similar platforms in the valleys indicates Moche conquest of the local populations.

Huaca del Sol, the seat of the Moche dynasty, comprised a four-tiered platform in the plan of a huge, stubby-armed cross

of unequal parts. Its 40m (130ft) high summit was reached by a north-side ramp. Just 500m (1,640ft) away stood the Huaca de la Luna at the foot of Cerro Blanco. La Luna was a three-tiered structure whose walls were richly decorated with friezes depicting mythological scenes and deities. The area between the two platforms, occupied by dwellings and workshops, is believed to have been the elite residential area of the city. Around this core a sprawling urban setting covered as much as 3 sq km (740 acres).

NEW CAPITALS

In the 6th century Moche power shifted north and the new 'capitals' became Sipán and, later, Pampa Grande, both in the Lambayeque Valley. Moche the capital was eventually eclipsed altogether when climatic change brought drought and the formation of a huge sand sheet that clogged the city's canal system, stifling agriculture and causing the inhabitants to emigrate. Some of Moche's inhabitants were

Above: Huaca del Sol at Moche was the largest solid, adobe-brick pyramid platform ever built in the New World.

probably responsible for the settlement of Galindo farther up the valley. Early encroachment on Moche territory by the nascent Wari state from the south-east might also have played a role in the northern power shift.

The late phase of Moche culture (Moche V) blends into the Middle Horizon, in which the Wari Empire dominated across the northern Andean Area. Nevertheless, this final, 150-year flowering of Moche culture is reflected in the rich ruler burials at Sipán, some of the few unlooted tombs of pre-Hispanic Andean civilization. They contain sumptuous burials, richly furnished with the exquisite ceramics, metalwork and textiles of Moche state artisans. These artefacts depicted scenes or represent themes similar to those on the walls, ceramics, textiles and metalwork found at Moche and other sites.

MOCHE RELIGION

Like Chavín, Moche imagery represented a potent religion, with distinctive symbols and a pantheon, albeit much derived from Chavín. It was characterized by humans and humanlike animal figures, serpents and frogs, birds (owls in particular) and sea animals (crabs and fish), and also by standardized groups and ceremonial scenes, including a coca ritual recognizable by distinctive clothing and ritual combat. Murals, friezes and vignettes on pottery depict the capture and sacrifice of 'enemies' being led with ropes around their necks, the drink offerings by subordinates to lords and gods, and persons passing through the night sky in moon-shaped boats.

Such narrative scenes offer scholars some of the earliest 'historical' sources to corroborate archaeological interpretation. Some of the characters depicted have been discovered in elite burials, being represented by their regalia. For the first time, pre-Hispanic Andean personages, if not known individuals, can be recognized.

No Moche deities are known by name. However, when the Moche state declined, the inheritors of their legacy, the Chimú, worshipped Ai Apaec, a sky/creator god, and Si, the moon goddess. They may represent religious continuity from Moche times, and were perhaps represented on the murals of the Huaca del Sol and Huaca de la Luna pyramids. The coastal region also revered a mountain god, represented by images of a feline-featured being on Moche ceramics and textiles, and on wall friezes. Even more prominent were fanged deities and a deity known as the Decapitator God, who appears frequently in the rich ceremony and ritual depicted on pots and textiles. Later Moche imagery shows a mingling with Wari style, and subtle changes in the depiction of eyes and headdress ornaments suggest the beginnings of the influence of Chimú imagery.

Left: A helmeted, kneeling Moche warrior or shaman, painted for combat, with a socketed hand, perhaps to hold a spear or war club.

THE EMPIRE OF TIWANAKU

At the same time as Chavín influence was waning in the northern sierra and coast, the peoples of the Titicaca Basin shifted their own religious fervour from the early ceremonial complex at Chiripa to several sites north of the lake. The principal site was Pukará, and the religious tradition is known as Yaya-Mama. The imagery of Yaya-Mama included universal Andean subjects – felines, serpents, lizards, birds and fish, and severed heads – but was focused especially on stone monoliths with carved male (*yaya*) and female (*mama*) figures on opposite sides.

TIWANAKU CITY
In the 1st–2nd centuries AD, however, the focus of the Titicaca Basin's political power and religious influence shifted south of the lake again as the city of Tiwanaku grew.

Below: The great Gateway of the Sun at Tiwanaku depicts a central Sun God or Staff Deity, flanked by rows of running 'angels'.

Above: The great semi-subterranean court of the Kalasasaya Temple, Tiwanaku, was one of the main ceremonial courts of the capital.

At 3,850m (12,600ft) above sea level, Tiwanaku expanded between AD200 and 500 to cover 4.5 sq km (1,100 acres) as the capital of a considerable empire within and beyond the Titicaca Basin, stretching east and west to the Bolivian lowlands, west and north-west to the Peruvian coast, and south into northern Chile. Its cultural and religious influence

extended even farther, but its north-western frontiers were established where it met its chief Middle Horizon rival, the Wari Empire, at the La Raya pass south of Cuzco and in the upper reaches of the Moquegua drainage area west of Titicaca.

The core of the city formed a ceremonial-religious-civic centre, including several monumental buildings, gateways, and stone sculptures exhibiting religious motifs and gods, whose artistic symbols show particular affinities to those of Chavín, and whose influence shows the continuity of ancient religious beliefs. The civic centre was aligned east–west, confined within a moat, and surrounded by residential compounds of adobe bricks.

Tiwanaku religion was a culmination of beliefs that united the peoples of the Titicaca Basin from the Initial Period through civic-ceremonial complexes at Chiripa and Pukará. Surrounding the capital were the natural features long regarded as sacred: the waters of Lake Titicaca to the west and the snow-capped mountain peaks to the east. Tiwanaku was located in the midst of fertile land, enhanced by a sophisticated system of dikes, canals, causeways and aquaducts to irrigate crops.

The ceremonial centre was planned on a grid pattern and its structures oriented on the points of the compass. The moat around the religious precinct segregated it from the residential sections of the city, making it an artificial island, a representation of the sacred Islands of the Sun and Moon in the lake.

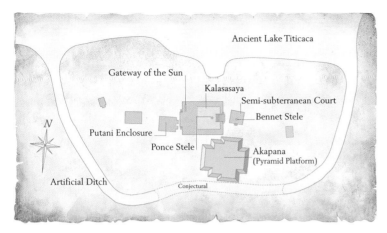

Left: Site map of Tiwanaku showing the Gateway of the Sun, the Akapana Temple, the Kalasasaya and other monuments.

A TRULY IMPERIAL CAPITAL

Construction of the major elements had begun by AD300. Stone temples, sunken courts, gateways and architraves were carved with religious imagery. Some of the buildings were probably residential palaces, but the gateways and gargantuan monumental sculptures were the focuses of public open spaces meant for civic participation in ritual and ceremony. Traces of gold pins within the stone blocks and remains of paint show that the sculptures were decorated and/or clothed in textiles.

The core of the artificial island was the Akapana Temple, a mound raised 17m (56ft) high in seven sandstone-clad tiers. Lake Titicaca and Mt Illimani are visible from the summit. Roughly T-shaped, a quadrate cruciform sunken court of andesite and sandstone slabs occupies the 50 sq m (540 sq ft) summit. Staircases climb the east and west terraces, and two staircases enter the court near rooms that might once have been priests' quarters. Subterranean stone channels drained water from the sunken court to the Tiwanaku River.

South-east of Akapana, the Pumapunku Temple T-shaped mound comprised three sandstone-slab-covered tiers, rising 5m (16ft) high and covering 150 sq m (1,615 sq ft). Its sunken summit courtyard has carved stone doorways and lintels and might have been the original location of the Gateway of the Sun.

Right: The monumental stairway of the Kalasasaya sunken court leads through a dressed-stone portal framing the Ponce Stela.

North of Akapana is the Semi-Subterranean Temple, a sunken court 28.5 x 26m (94 x 85ft), entered by a staircase on its south side. Its interior walls are adorned with carved stone heads, and at its centre stand several carved stone stelae, originally including the 'Bennett Stela' (now in La Paz). Standing 7.3m (24ft) high, it portrays a richly dressed human thought to be one of Tiwanaku's rulers or the divine ruler. He/she holds a *kero* beaker and a staff-like object, perhaps a snuff tablet.

KALASASAYA

The Kalasasaya – north of Akapana, west of the Semi-Subterranean Temple – is a low-lying rectangular platform 130 x 120m (427 x 394ft). It forms a large ceremonial precinct for public ritual, with walls made up of sandstone pillars alternating with smaller ashlar blocks. Its stairway is carved from stones set between two gigantic stone pillars.

The famous Gateway of the Sun stands at its north-west corner. It appears to comprise two monolithic stone slabs supporting a third, carved, slab across their tops, but is in fact a single huge andesite block. The crossing top face is completely carved: the central figure portrays the 'Gateway God' – a humanlike figure standing on a stepped platform resembling the tiered mounds of the sacred precinct itself. Holding staffs with its outstretched arms, it bears an obvious resemblance to the Chavín Staff Deity. It is flanked by three rows of winged figures in profile.

Within the Kalasasaya stands the giant stone Ponce Stela, 3.5m (11ft 6in) tall and visible from within the Semi-Subterranean Temple framed by the main gateway. Like the Bennett Stela, it portrays a ruler or deity, richly clothed/carved and holding a *kero* beaker and staff/snuff tablet.

Tiwanaku endured until about AD1000, waning between 900 and 1000 as climatic change brought repercussions throughout the Andean Area.

THE WARI EMPIRE

Huari was the capital city of the Wari Empire and the northern rival of Tiwanaku. Together the two empires represent the political cohesion that united the Middle Horizon for more than 500 years.

BIRTH OF AN IMPERIAL STATE
Wari dominated the central Andes and coastal valleys, and expanded into the regions of the north almost to the Ecuadorian border. One of its northern-most outposts was the city of Cajamarca in northern Peru; its southernmost was Pikillaqta near Cuzco. It met Tiwanaku expansion at the Pass of La Raya, south of Cuzco, and openly confronted Tiwanaku in the upper reaches of the Moquegua drainage area west of Titicaca, where it established a colony on the defensive summit of Cerro Baúl. This region, split between Tiwanaku in the north-west and Wari in the south-east, constituted a buffer zone between the two empires.

Below: The need for the hilltop fortress of Carangas is an example of the tense rivalry between the Wari and Tiwanaku empires.

From humble beginnings in the 3rd century AD, major constructions at Huari from the 5th century reflect the city's growing power. Its main period of imperial expansion lasted from about AD600 to 800.

The capital occupied the plateau of a mountain valley at about 2,800m (9,180ft) above sea level between the Huamanga and Huanta basins. Serving as a civic, residential and religious centre, it grew rapidly to cover more than 100ha (247 acres), then 200ha (495 acres), then 300ha (740 acres), with an additional periphery of residential suburbs occupy-ing a further 250ha (620 acres). Its population has been variously estimated at 10,000–35,000 inhabitants.

From about 600 the Wari state spread a dominant religion, characterized by a distinctive symbolic art, through military expansion in much the same way that its coastal rival, the Moche, had expanded earlier in the northern coastal region.

Shortly before 800 there appears to have been a political crisis that caused building within the capital to slacken and cease. Simultaneously, the political

Above: The city of Huari was gradually expanded through regular additions of angular walled precincts and dressed-stone sectors.

centre and religious shrine of Pachacamac, on the central Peruvian coast, began to reassert itself and possibly even to rival Wari power. Pachacamac had flourished since later Early Intermediate Period times and had only recently been occupied by the Wari. Similarly, in its north-west provinces, the rising local power of the Sicán lords of the Lambayeque Valley challenged Wari overlordship in the late 7th century. Wari expansion ended abruptly and the capital was abandoned by AD800.

RUINS OF THE CAPITAL
The architecture of the site of Huari, although megalithic, has not survived well. Some of it approximates the grandeur of the ceremonial architecture at Tiwanaku, although more crudely. Numerous walls remain as high as

Above: The rigidly planned border fortress of Pikillaqta, the southernmost Wari town, included an extensive defensive wall.

6–12m (20–40ft). There were several rectangular compounds, and some buildings had projecting walls that supported multiple storeys.

In contrast to Tiwanaku, however, Huari's rapid expansion appears to have occurred at random, without the deliberate and preconceived planning of its competitor. The huge enclosure of Cheqo Wasi (or Huasi) included dressed stone-slab chambers. Two important temple complexes were Vegachayoq Moqo and Moraduchayoq, the latter a semi-subterranean compound resembling the one at Tiwanaku. In keeping with the comparatively frenetic pace of Huari's development, the Moraduchayoq Temple was dismantled around AD650.

SHARED RELIGION

Wari and Tiwanaku's political ambitions and military aims made them political rivals, yet they also shared symbolic religious imagery and mythology.

Much of the religious and mythological art imagery of Tiwanaku and Wari was virtually identical, which demonstrates religious continuity from the Early Horizon through the Early Intermediate Period. Despite military opposition, scholars entertain the possibility that religious missionaries from one city visited the other. It might have been that the priests were willing to set politics aside and let religious beliefs transcend such matters.

Continuity and similarities of religious symbols used in art include, in particular, the Staff Deity image, but also winged and running falcon- and condor-headed creatures – often wielding clubs – and severed trophy heads. It is reasoned that similarities in imagery show similarities in religious and cosmological belief. It seems that the gods of Chavín endured as the Staff Deity of Tiwanaku and Wari, and were responsible for human origins and for the fertility of crops and flocks. Winged beings appear both accompanying the Staff Deity and independently, and were depicted running, floating, flying or kneeling. The Staff Deity – with mask-like face, radiating head rays (sometimes ending in serpent heads), and tunic, belt and kilt – appears on pottery and architecture and might have been the prototype for the creator god Viracocha.

Despite such apparent religious unity, the focus of religious imagery in Wari differed from that in Tiwanaku. In Wari it was applied primarily to portable objects, particularly to ceramics; in Tiwanaku, however, it was concentrated on monumental stone architecture, and appeared less frequently on pottery or textiles. Thus, while Wari ceramics and textiles spread the word far and wide, Tiawanaku imagery was more confined to standing monuments at the capital and a few other sites. The ceremonial core at Tiwanaku was designed and developed as a preconceived plan, and was therefore one of public ceremony and, apparently, participation. The Wari capital of Huari, by contrast, appears to have developed more haphazardly, and religious structures were smaller and more private, implying that they were the focus of ritual of a more personal and intimate nature.

RIVALS OR ALLIES?

Given these similarities and differences, the exact nature of the relationship between the two kingdoms or empires remains enigmatic. The two empires seemed to keep each other at arms' length, but they may have exchanged political and religious ambassadors to each other's capital city. Nevertheless, it is clear that religious concepts and imagery prevailed through the politically fragmented Early Intermediate Period as well as within the more unified imperial Middle Horizon.

Below: Although political rivals, Wari and Tiwanaku shared a religion, here represented by a kero *drinking cup with a serpentine motif.*

THE KINGDOM OF CHIMÚ

Adverse climate change and early Wari incursions in the early Middle Horizon pushed late Moche power north to the Lambayeque Valley. A new capital was established at Pampa Grande, which endured for about 150 years. Moche religious belief also changed, dropping much of the old pantheon and focusing on maritime imagery – a precursor to the Chimú symbols that followed in the Late Intermediate Period.

PAMPA GRANDE

This new capital covered some 6 sq km (1,485 acres). Its most imposing structure, Huaca Fortaleza, appears to have served a function similar to the Huaca del Sol at Moche. Rising 38m (125ft) above the valley floor, its summit was reached by a 290m (950ft) ramp. At the top, columns supported the roofs of a complex of rooms, one containing a mural

Below: The founders of the Chimú dynasty arrived from the sea, as demonstrated by this Chimú stirrup-spouted burnished pot.

showing feline beings. Huaca Fortaleza was probably the elite sector of the city, with lower-class residences spread around it.

Like Moche, Pampa Grande was abandoned abruptly, owing to agricultural disaster caused by an El Niño weather event and the continued expansion of the Wari Empire from the south. Fierce internal unrest may also have occurred, for archaeological evidence has revealed intense destructive fires in the centre of the city, so hot that adobe mud bricks of the Huaca Fortaleza were fired.

THE SICÁN LORDS

The inheritors of the late Moche flourishing in the Lambayeque Valley were the Sicán Lords. For centuries overshadowed by the power of the Wari Empire, they emerged as a local power and made rich burials from the 9th to the 14th centuries at Batán Grande as Wari power waned.

The Sicán Lords were one of many local resurgences repulsing Wari and Tiwanaku power.

Above: Detail of a painted cotton Chimú textile of a shaman or chieftain flanked by two felines and wielding an axe.

After Pampa Grande and Batán Grande, northern coastal power shifted again, back south to the Moche Valley, where the rise of the Kingdom of Chimú (or Chimor) eclipsed Sicán power.

THE RISE OF THE CHIMÚ

The Chimú established their capital across the Moche River at Chan Chan, in the shadows of Moche Huacas del Sol and de la Luna.

Chimú was the largest Andean Area empire before the Incas. Over 400 years, Chimú lords subdued the northern coastal and inland valleys, eventually controlling two-thirds of the irrigated land along the desert coast. With Chimú begin obscure historical accounts, although these are filtered through Inca interpretations.

The Chimú came from outside the valley and their history seems to hark back to a legendary conqueror called Naymlap, possibly the Moche king who invaded the Lambayeque Valley. Naymlap's eldest son, Cium, established a dynasty of 12 rulers, each of whom kept the green stone statue-idol of Yampallec set up by Naymlap. The final ruler, Fempellec, wanted to remove the

idol but was thwarted by 'the devil', and the priests, who abducted Fempellec, threw him into the ocean and ended the dynasty.

Two sources describe the foundation of Chimú by a conqueror from the sea (possibly from Lambayeque), variously called Chimu Capac or Taycanamu. A dynasty of 12 rulers might correspond to the Chimú compounds at Chan Chan, although the Chimú king list recorded by the Incas names only ten kings.

CITY OF THE LIVING AND DEAD

Chan Chan was founded about AD1000 and was conquered by Inca Tupac Yupanqui in the 1470s. Its core was an inner city of the living and the dead, a complex of individual compounds (called *ciudadelas*) covering 6 sq km (1,480 acres). Surrounding residential and industrial suburbs covered another 14 sq km (3,460 acres). There are ten compounds (although different interpreters propose

Below: A wooden figure with a mud-plaster face mask. This would have stood in a niche at the entrance to a ciudadela *compound.*

between nine and twelve). Nine compounds have a truncated pyramid in the south-east corner, entered from above through a court to a suite of cells and a larger room thought to have housed the mummified body of a king.

Each *ciudadela*, a rectangle oriented north–south, comprised a miniature city enclosed within thick poured-adobe mud walls up to 9m (30ft) high, most with a single, northern entrance. Niches on either side of the entrances held painted wooden human figures as guards. Established as the court of the ruler, each *ciudadela* formed the residence of the reigning king, his officials and retainers, and became a sealed city of the dead after his death. Inner walls divided the compounds into courtyards surrounded by houses, storerooms, U-shaped structures (*audiencias*) and walled-in wells. Resident retainers perpetuated a cult of each deceased king. Along the south walls of the compounds ramps led up to burial platforms for each royal family.

The U-shaped structures appear to reflect recognition of and reverence for ancient U-shaped ceremonial complexes of the area. Burials were placed in and near them and their shape may represent a 'cosmic niche'. Association with store rooms suggests that they were also for redistribution, part of a tightly controlled

Above: The core of the Chimú capital at Chan Chan comprised ciudadela *compounds, each devoted to the cult of a deceased king.*

system for the collection and distribution of wealth, foods and commodities among the nobility and general populace, according to social rank.

Five monumental adobe mounds at Chan Chan might have been temple platforms, although they have been so damaged by treasure seekers that it is not possible to be sure of their function. One platform, however, contained more than 200 bodies, including young women who might have been sacrificed to accompany a Chimú king into the afterlife.

Generally, Chimú imagery found at Chan Chan and elsewhere was a merging of Moche and Wari styles. Chimú ritual architecture reveals Wari influence in fanged deities, jaguars, jaguar-humans and serpents alongside marine imagery. The *ciudadela* walls were carved with repetitious friezes of geometric patterns, images of birds and marine animals, and of the double-headed rainbow-serpent being, the last apparently associated with Si, the moon goddess, one of the few Chimú deities that we know by name. Ai Apaec was the sky/creator god who was very ancient to this region, and Ni, the sea god, reflects northern coastal marine importance.

THE INCA EMPIRE

The Inca Empire was the largest political unity ever created in the New World. It was as large and powerful as many contemporary states in Europe.

DESTINED TO RULE

The foundation of the empire, or the early stages of the Inca state, is steeped in the legendary journey of a band of brothers and sisters. Modern scholars regard the tale as a mythical hero-legend, especially in its mystical implications of underground journeys and re-emergence from the earth. The archaeological and historical evidence shows that the Incas arose in the Cuzco Valley as one among many local 'tribes' or nations – town- or city-states – all of which were of long-standing native origin.

The arrival of influential individuals from outside, however, may have some basis in fact as a group of assertive individuals who were able to persuade the Incas of their rulership abilities and legitimacy, and to lead them on a path towards domination of their rivals in the valley. Once the Incas had overcome their neighbours, their rulers embarked on a dedicated programme of conquest beyond the valley. From Pachacuti Inca Yupanqui, who overcame the Incas' principal rivals, the Chancas, in 1438, the conquest of vast territories in all directions from Cuzco was what drove the empire.

The Incas believed in their destiny, and therefore in their right, to rule. They considered themselves to be the pinnacle of cyclical development in the world – politically, religiously and socially. They and their systems were not the culmination of, but the final solution to a predetermined course of history that would end sometime in the future by the empire's descent into chaos and by the beginning of, or more accurately, the 'turning over', of the cycle and the start of a new 'Sun' or age.

Above: In addition to the axe-spear, a favourite Inca weapon was the stone- or iron-headed war club.

RECORDING HISTORY

The Incas recorded their history orally and through the use of bundles of knotted string called *quipus*. State history was kept by imperial officials called *amautas* (court historians) and *quipucamayoqs* (knot-makers). Using *quipus* as an *aide-mémoire*, they were responsible for keeping the state histories alive through detailed oral history and regular recital. They kept, and on official state occasions reminded the populace of, the official history of the foundation and growth of Cuzco and of the Inca conquests. The early history was grounded in the story of the founder brother-sister pairs and their legendary journey, and of the exploits of early leaders and state heroes. The *amautas* also memorized and recited the royal genealogy, a formidable task, as Inca rulers had several wives and many children, and the royal household grew to include hundreds of members.

As the empire was expanded through conquest, the *amautas* were tasked with adding to the official history of the state, and with reconciling the events and situation 'on the ground' with Inca concepts and their perception of the cycle. To do this, much of their new subjects'

Below: Map of Cuzco with an inset map showing how the city plan was in the shape of a crouching puma.

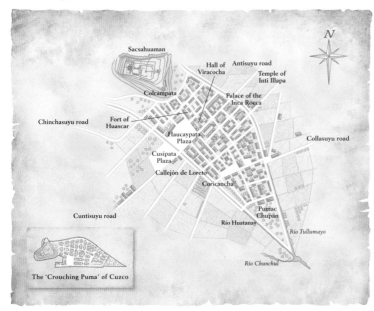

Sacsahuaman

Hall of Viracocha

Antisuyu road

Temple of Inti Illapa

Colcampata

Palace of the Inca Rocca

Chinchasuyu road

Fort of Huascar

Haucaypata Plaza

Collasuyu road

Cusipata Plaza

Callejón de Loreto

Coricancha

Cuntisuyu road

Pumac Chupan

Río Huatanay

Río Tullumayo

Río Chunchul

The 'Crouching Puma' of Cuzco

N

Above: The circular tower and surrounding walls of Sacsahuaman at Cuzco may represent the sun as the central temple to Inti.

myths, legends, histories, dynastic ties and religious tenets were recast and/or incorporated into the Inca story, as if they had been part of the history in the first place. This official version was particularly important in the establishment of Inti the sun as the supreme being and object of official state worship, which had to be construed in such a manner that it was acceptable to conquered peoples who harboured their own local deities, most of whom were long-standing and entrenched.

Paralleling the obscurity of the early stages of the Inca version of history, the archaeological record leaves scholars with little evidence of pre-Inca Cuzco. The capital has been continuously occupied since Inca times, especially since being substantially rebuilt by Pachacuti Inca Yupanqui and his successors through the 15th and early 16th centuries. As a result, many Inca structures form the foundations for Spanish Colonial and later buildings, and therefore it is not known what lies beneath. No recognizably distinct Inca

architectural style can be identified with any of the pre-Pachacuti Inca emperors. It is not certain if the earliest Inca rulers ruled from Cuzco, co-existed with other local rulers or even lived in Cuzco.

SUBJUGATION PROBLEMS

Inca subjugation was through armed conquest, but such was the success and perceived inevitability of Inca rule that many tribes gave them little resistance. Nevertheless, resentment among peoples at the extremes of the empire led to frequent truculence, even open revolt, and peoples beyond the imperial borders raided into the fringes, sometimes with local collusion.

Tribes of the eastern tropical forests were the only group that successfully resisted conquest. The Incas, a mountain people, were psychologically attuned to distance vistas and lines of sight, and to a landscape of rugged variation. In attempting conquest into the rainforests flanking the eastern Cordillera, therefore, they were simply out of their element. Their commanders were lost; their points of reference were lost. They were up against an illusive foe that fought not *en masse* in open warfare but by stealth from

protected cover. Yet the Incas admired tropical forest warriors and used their bowmen in the imperial army. Similarly, animals of the rainforest, especially the jaguar, were revered for their power, strength and cunning.

Below: A kero or painted wooden drinking cup showing an Inca warrior in a feather headdress and holding a spear.

POLITICS OF EMPIRE

The Inca Empire was divided into four unequal quarters, radiating from Cuzco. The quarters were known as *suyus* and formed Tahuantinsuyu – the 'four united parts' or 'four parts together'. The word itself is recorded only in later Spanish colonial sources, and it is not known if the Incas actually used the word themselves in this context. The term might have been first used around 1570 by Titu Cusi Yupanqui, the leader in Vilcabamba of an Inca revolt against Spanish rule. Alternatively, use of the term might have been an inflation of a more restricted use for the organization of the *ceque* shrines around Cuzco, first located by the Spanish magistrate Polo de Ondegardo.

Antisuyu, the smallest part, comprised the eastern Andean slopes and tropical forests north-east of Cuzco; Collasuyu, the largest part, stretched south-east from Cuzco, comprising southern Peru, the Titicaca Basin, western Bolivia, north-western Argentina and northern Chile; Chinchasuyu comprised the north-west

Above: A collca *(storehouse) built in traditional Inca vernacular style at Ollantatamba in the Urubamba Valley.*

region of western Peru and Ecuador; and Cuntisuyu comprised south-western Peru to the coast. The common point of the four *suyus* was the Coricancha Temple, the most sacred precinct in Cuzco. From this point radiated real and sighted sacred lines and routes known as *ceques*.

INCA STATE ORGANIZATION

The Inca state was rooted in the past, following a long line of political and social arrangements that had developed in the Andean Area from early times. Much of Inca state organization owed a debt to the Middle Horizon and Late Intermediate Period empires of the Wari, Tiwanaku and Chimú.

The foundation of Inca strength, and often the basis of others' capitulation, was the ancient Andean practice of the formalized exchange of goods and ideas between highlands and lowlands –

between mountain and coast, Altiplano and desert. The Wari and Tiwanaki states had established regional administrative centres, formalized systems of exchange, roads and way-stations, and a sponsored state cult. In the farther-flung regions of the Inca Empire, administrative centres often had to be created from scratch if nothing lingered there from earlier times.

KEEPING CONTROL

The Inca appointed provincial governors (*tocoyrikoqs*) over conquered nations and city-states. Local chiefs (*curakas*) were incorporated into the system by being retained alongside the *tocoyrikoqs*, and together the pair administered the regional *mit'a*, or labour tax. Inca state tax was of

Below: Inca accountants keep records on a quipu *of the collection of produce into storehouses for distribution among subject peoples.*

three types: agricultural, *mit'a* and a textile tax. Agricultural taxes were extracted from the produce of *ayllu* kinship-owned land, imperial land and general communal land regulated by the *curakas*; it involved the labour of men and women. The *mit'a* tax was extracted only from able-bodied men. The textile tax was paid mainly as cloth woven by women, but also included fibre cordage and rope made by men.

Inca state control was maintained in a number of ways. In addition to military force, they practised various forms of removal and hostage holding.

One form was the deliberate transfer of whole or portions of populations within the empire. Known as *mitamaqs*, the practice was used to exercise demographic and social control, and to sustain an even economy. Local *curakas* were removed with their people. By shifting large groups of people around within the empire, the Incas could redistribute labour and the commodities grown and produced by different groups and mix peoples' ideas of geographic identity and religious/mythological concepts. One prominent example was Inca Tupac Yupanqui's relocation of thousands of individuals from several ethnic groups to the Cochabamba Valley (Bolivia) in Collasuyu, where the Inca wanted to increase coca production.

Relocating loyal peoples to frontier provinces helped to secure the imperial borders against hostile outsiders. Conversely, relocating rebellious groups served to break up and disperse potential seditious peoples within the empire. An example was the relocation of the Cañari people of Chinchasuyu, after defeating them in battle, to the Yucay Valley near Cuzco. The Cañari became such loyal servants that the Inca granted them the status of Incas-by-privilege. The practice undoubtedly had a significant impact in creating a state religion, and the result authorized the Incas to rule as a chosen people, whose semi-divine ruler was sanctioned by the creator god Viracocha.

FRAGILE EMPIRE

Rapid expansion of the Inca Empire in the 15th century brought together a multitude of local ethnic groups, large and small city-states and regional political confederations, and many languages, customs and local religious practices. The rapidity and incompleteness of expansion, as well as the disruption caused by the Spaniards, who first arrived in 1502, probably undermined state stability and contributed to a lack of cohesion. The variety of ethnic groups

Above: Communications in the empire were maintained by a system of trunk roads from Cuzco and linking roads to provincial towns.

contributed to local loyalty, and Inca political practices were designed more for securing state revenue and begrudging state loyalty by one form of coercion or another than for genuine national unity. Even the Inca practice of relocation kept people within their ethnic units rather than integrating nationalities.

SOCIAL ORGANIZATION

The general populace of the empire was known as the *hatun-runa* ('great populace'), the bulk of which were farmers or herders. Within the empire, however, the people were subdivided into units by age, occupation and kinship groups.

INCA SOCIAL UNITS

The Inca administration organized the empire into a hierarchy of units comprising up to 10,000 individuals. The smallest unit was ten individuals, which was overseen by a foreman. Ten such units were overseen by a 'chief of 100'. A regular census was taken and monitored, and any necessary reorganization carried out accordingly.

The populace was classified into a number of age groups according to the types of work each was expected to do. For example, many males, especially single males, between the ages of 25 and 50 were expected to serve in the army. Others were expected to work the land,

Below: On the Altiplano *of Collasuyu the Incas used raised and irrigated fields to feed the growing population of the empire.*

including work on imperial lands to fulfil the labour tax. Census records were kept on *quipus* by special officials who were known as *runaquipu-camayoc* ('people-*quipu*-specialists').

Family lineages or kinship groups were organized into *ayllus*. An *ayllu* comprised the group of related individuals, their property, and a social charter of recognized mutual and collective obligation among the members.

THE SAPA INCA AND *PANACAS*

The Inca ruler was known as Sapa Inca – 'sole' or 'unique' Inca. Each Sapa Inca was regarded as the direct descendant of the founder-brother Manco Capac, and simultaneously the manifestation of the sun – Inti – on Earth. His presence brought light and warmth to make the world habitable. Such belief perpetuated the early Andean melding of politics and religion: the Sapa Inca was not only the supreme ruler, but also the supreme god on Earth, presented in human manifestation.

The ruling Sapa Inca had many wives, one of whom was his principal wife. Maternal descent was of equal, if not

Above: Inca potato and quinoa planting, depicted by Guaman Poma de Ayala in his Nueva Crónica y Buen Gobierno, *c.1613.*

dominant, importance in Inca succession to the throne. The royal household comprised several *ayllus*, called *panacas*. Each *panaca* was divided into two halves – termed *hanan* (upper) and *hurin* (lower). A principal responsibility of the *panaca* was the care of the mummy of the deceased Sapa Inca. Thus, in theory, a new *panaca* was formed at the death of each emperor. Within the Cuzco Valley, peoples conquered in the early expansion of the empire were given special benefits and called 'Incas-by-privilege'.

SECURING GOODS AND LOYALTY

Each *ayllu* owed *mit'a* service to the royal household, and the produce of their labour belonged to the state or, ultimately, to the Sapa Inca. *Mit'a* labour could take the form of working royal agricultural lands, tending royal llama flocks or producing quotas of goods such as ceramics, metalwork or textiles in state installations. It could even involve working as keepers and clerks in the *collcas* (royal warehouses) into which the produce provided by *mit'a* labour was collected.

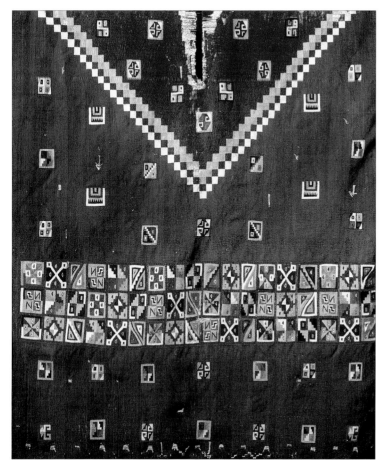

Above: The production of exquisite textiles for the rulers and nobles, and for the army, was an Inca state-sponsored industry.

bureaucracy, thus encouraging through them the loyalty of subject peoples. So impressed were the Incas with the Chimú that they took their lords back to Cuzco along with an entourage of their best gold- and silversmiths.

CHOSEN WOMEN

Another detached group within Inca society comprised the *acllas* (literally 'to choose'): 'chosen women' picked to serve in the state cults, particularly those of the sun and of the moon. Usually chosen when they were prepubescent girls so that they could be trained for the position, *acllas* also often became secondary wives and were used in imperial marriage alliances. *Acllas* were housed in special buildings called *acllahuasi*. The principal one was in Cuzco, but *acllahuasi* were also located in many provincial administrative centres. The fact that these chosen women were removed permanently from their homelands at an early age meant that they became so incorporated into the Inca system that they retained little attachment to their provincial roots and were therefore loyal to the empire.

Collca storehouses were distributed throughout the provinces. In them were stored agricultural produce, especially maize, and industrial products – surpluses of food, ceramics and other manufactured goods, and textiles for redistribution. In return for organizing and providing *mit'a* labour, the *curakas* received payment in luxury items from the Sapa Inca: fine textiles, metalwork and *chicha*, the beer made from fermented maize. It has been suggested that one reason behind continued Inca expansion was the need to secure more *mit'a* labour to meet the state's pact with the *curakas*, clearly a system that perpetuated itself.

The Sapa Inca's court also included selected retainers known as *yanacona*. These individuals were given various positions within the empire, including appointments at local-level governorships, whose loyalty to court could be relied on because they had no direct ties to the native population.

Members of the local elite, or the sons and daughters thereof, were taken to Cuzco as hostages. They were treated well, but were nonetheless held under house arrest. Likewise, the sacred objects of conquered peoples were removed to Cuzco to be held for safe-keeping as a means of ensuring loyalty – a practice used by the Wari and the Tiwanaku and continued by the Incas. Another practice was to train the sons of local chiefs to fill positions in the lower ranks of Inca

Below: This Inca storehouse is within walled compounds among terraced fields, making maximum use of available growing surfaces.

MYTH AND RELIGION

The peoples of the ancient Andean civilizations regarded their entire surroundings as sacred. Maintaining a balanced relationship with the landscape, seascape and skyscape was considered essential to their well-being in the land of the living. Shamans were responsible for maintaining a dialogue with the past and, theoretically, with things to come in an endless cycle of history. Sacred powers were everywhere, and were both revered and feared. Ritual offerings, sacrifices and the maintenance of a link between the living and the dead were a necessary part of everyday life. Although we call it 'myth' today, Andean peoples' beliefs and their perception of the universe was their religion.

This part of the book concentrates on the deities and their stories as recorded mostly by Spanish chroniclers and by native record-keepers who were converted by Spanish priests. Although there were elements of regionalism, many deities were universally accepted throughout the Andean Area, sometimes under different names. Ancient Andean beliefs tended to be widespread, both at a given time and through time. The narrative of Andean belief in a cyclical history even incorporated their eventual defeat by outsiders, but continues today in the belief that time will turn again, reversing their defeat in perpetual revolution.

The Paracas–Nazca Oculate Being is shown flying across the sky on this woollen burial shroud.

CHAPTER SEVEN

A PANTHEON OF GODS

Sanctity permeated the ancient Andean world. Sacred powers were everywhere, in all living things. Survival in this world, the land of the living, was dependent not only on producing enough to eat, but also on revering the gods and appeasing them through rituals, sacrifices and offerings. At the same time, there was a fatalism in the belief in the great cycle of being, of life and death, which gave rise to the reverence of ancestors.

The peoples of the Andean Area held a range of beliefs and appear to have worshipped a pantheon of deities with control over different aspects of nature. Their religious beliefs developed from the earliest times, and they can be detected in the architecture and art of the earliest Andean civilizations. Many deities were universally accepted throughout the Andean Area, sometimes called by different names but having the same essential attributes, powers and roles.

A linking factor throughout Andean life was that of continuity, of how all things are connected and so part of a cycle, and this was demonstrated through the concepts of mutual exchange, duality and collectivity, which were all vital parts of spiritual and daily life for ancient Andeans. Continuity was intensely developed in Andean civilization through the pilgrimage centres, such as Chavín de Huántar and Pachacamac, that persisted over centuries and endured despite political rivalry and changing political developments.

Left: The central figure of the Gateway of the Sun, at Tiwanaku, is a ray-encircled face in the pose of the Chavín Staff Deity.

THEMES AND BELIEFS

The long sequence of development among Andean highland and lowland peoples fostered mutually beneficial relationships between cultures. Constant contact between regions brought the exchange of ideas as well as produce and commodities.

ANDEAN THEMES

Through Andean history, common themes were expressed in art and architecture. Coastal animals and motifs were copied in highland traditions and vice versa.

The early combination of temple platforms and sunken courts shows this exchange of ideas in the architectural elements of the ceremonial centre. Platforms mimic mountain peaks and plateaux, while sunken courts mimic valleys and coastal desert oases. It can be argued that ritual progression through such ceremonial complexes reflects the symbiotic relationship between highland

Right: An Early Intermediate Period Nazca bridge-spouted pot depicts the Oculate Being accompanied by trophy heads.

Below: Part of the outcrop of the sacred Inca huaca *at Qenqo, north of Cuzco, was believed to be a giant seated puma turned to stone.*

and lowland cultures and between mountain and coastal deities.

This architectural combination also shows the early appearance of the Andean concept of duality. The late Preceramic Period union of platform mound and sunken court, both in highland and lowland sites, constituted the first widespread Andean 'religion'. To agricultural peoples, the sunken court was probably the focus for the worship of 'mother earth' – for the ritual re-enactment of birth or creation represented by spring crops. The ascent of the platform may have been the recognition of the upper world in which the god of creation dwelled, or from which came the waters that made agriculture possible.

The highland site of Chavín de Huántar not only combined the elements of platform and sunken court, but also introduced the idea of a sacred location

widely accepted as the focus of worship for peoples throughout the central Andes and coast. The Chavín Cult developed the labyrinthine temple complex within which cult statuary was secreted, with all its obscure meaning, perhaps interpretable only by shamans.

With the development of the Chavín cult also came religious art expressing duality and a prototype supreme creator god, forerunner to representations of Viracocha in later Andean civilizations. The Staff Deity, significantly represented both as male and female, was an undisguised representation of duality. In varying forms, a deity holding staffs with outstretched arms was an artistic motif from Chavín to Inca times. In the courtyard of Chavín de Huántar's New Temple stood the 0.5m (1½ft) stone sculpture of the supreme deity. Holding a *Strombus* shell in one hand and a *Spondylus* shell in the other, the deity also manifested duality, as a metaphor for the balancing of male and female forces in the universe, and the union of opposing forces, providing completion through unity.

COMMON BELIEFS

Thus, despite variations in regional and cultural detail, the earliest ceremonial centres reflect common elements of belief.

The continuing highland–lowland interchange was cemented in the recognition of certain ceremonial centres as places of pilgrimage, Chavín de Huántar being the first. Platforms with sunken courtyards and pilgrimage centres were elements of Andean civilization for 2,500 years. Pilgrimage centres were recognized by both highland and coastal states, linking regions and persisting through political change. The cult centre of Chavín de Huántar endured for more than 500 years, while the site and oracle of coastal Pachacamac, beginning in the 1st century AD, lasted more than a millennium.

The Incas had a complex calendar of worship based on the movements of heavenly bodies, including solar solstices

Below: A Late Intermediate Period Chimú mummy bundle with a copper burial mask, painted red, feather headdress and two flutes.

Above: An Early Intermediate Period Nazca sheet-gold burial mask. A burial with such a mask indicates high-status.

and equinoxes, lunar phases, the synodic cycle of Venus, the rising and setting of the Pleiades, the rotational inclinations of the Milky Way, and the presence within the Milky Way of 'dark cloud constellations' (stellar voids). Consultation of auguries concerning these movements was vital at momentous times of the year, such as planting time, harvest time and the beginning of the ocean fishing season. Inca practices represent the final stage of the development of such beliefs.

Sacrifice, both human and animal, and a variety of offerings were common. Ritual strangulation and beheading are well attested in burials and art such as ceramic painting, murals, architectural sculpture, textiles and metalwork.

As well as pilgrimage sites, tens of thousands of places – *huacas* – were held sacred. Like pilgrimage centres, their importance could endure for centuries. *Huacas* could be springs (emphasizing the importance of water), caves (prominent in human origin mythology), mountains, rocks or stones, fields or towns where important events had taken place, lakes or islands in them, or man-made objects

such as stone pillars erected at specific locations. Shrines and temples were sometimes built at *huacas*, but just as often the object/place was left in its natural state.

The ritual use of hallucinogenic drugs was widespread. Coca (*Erythroxylon coca*) leaves were chewed in a complex and multi-stage ritual connected with war and sacrifice. Cactus buds and hallucinogenic mushrooms were also used.

The reverence for ancestors is evident in the special treatment of mummified burials in the Chinchorros culture of northern coastal Chile. Such practice developed into ancestor worship and became charged with special ritual, governed by the cyclical calendar by Inca times. Mummified remains of ancestors were carefully kept in special buildings, rooms or chambers, or in caves, and were themselves considered *huacas*. They were brought out on ritual occasions to participate in the festivals and to be offered delicacies of food and drink, as well as objects and prayers.

Preoccupation with death included the underworld. Skeletal figures, depictions of priests imitating the dead to visit the underworld, and skeletal figures with sexual organs or the dead embracing women were associated with fertility beliefs and the source of life in the underworld.

PACHACUTI – THE ENDLESS CYCLE

To the ancient Andeans everything around them, in all directions, was sacred. They believed themselves to be in a universe that was forever in cycle, *pachacuti*, in an endless revolution of time and history. The concept of *pachacuti* is further revealed in the Andean belief that humankind went through several phases of creation, destruction and re-creation. This progression was held to reflect the gods' desire to create an increasingly perfected form of humans. Honour and worship of the gods was so important that it took several efforts to create beings of proper humility. This veneration was essential because it was 'known' that at the slightest provocation they were capable of destroying the world.

A DIVIDED UNIVERSE

The ancient Andeans' universe comprised three levels: the world of the living, which the Incas called Kai Pacha, the world below, called Uku Pacha, and the world of the heavens, called Hanan Pacha. Kai Pacha comprised the relatively flat surface of the earth and lay between the other two. As the world of humans, Kai Pacha was also called Hurin Pacha – lower world. As well as this vertical arrangement, the

Inca universe was divided by two horizontal axes running through the points of the compass. The centre of both realms ran through Cuzco, where the vertical axis of the three realms and the horizontal axes intersected.

Pervading the entire universe was the creator god – the all-powerful, "formless" one – Viracocha (as the Inca and many others knew him).

Above: Warrior figures on this Paracas burial textile, c.500BC, are shown in the symbolic pose of the Chavin Staff Deity.

AN ECOLOGICAL RELATIONSHIP

The relationship maintained between ancient Andeans and their universe can be characterized as 'ecological'. Because they perceived their environment as sacred, they believed that they were on earth not to exploit it but rather to enjoy its benefits through the grace of the gods. The relationship was one of deity power and human supplication. Humans considered themselves to be not the centre or focus of the world but only one group among all living things – including animals, plants and the stars. Thus humans appealed to the gods for their permission to make use of the various other elements of the world. Indeed, the animals, plants and stars were rather more important than humans, for it was in them that the gods were personified.

Left: Long-distance trade contacts also spread imagery. Here a rainforest monkey decorates a coastal desert Nazca ceramic vessel.

Right: An Inca textile showing a deity or a shaman, impersonating a god with sky-snake image and the stance of the Staff Deity.

AN EVOLVING RELIGION

More is known about Inca beliefs than other beliefs of the Andean Area because they were formed into an official state religion and cult of the emperor, Inti, as the earthly representative of the sun. Inca religion itself was the final stage in a long sequence of development from primitive beliefs. Inca conquest brought their people into contact with many other cultures and regions, each of which also had its own religious development.

Upon conquest, Spanish clergy and administrators recorded Inca beliefs and concepts in their attempts to under-stand more about the peoples of the empire. Archaeologists believed that the concepts and physical remains of Inca religion can be projected into the pre-Inca past. They also detect many common themes in ancient Andean development because the archaeological evidence indicates that pre-Inca deities, whose names are mostly unknown, nevertheless represented the same or very similar concepts to those of Inca deities.

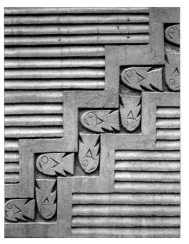

FUNDAMENTAL DUALITY

Following the fundamental Andean belief in duality, the universe and everything in it comprised two parts in opposition, but striving for completion through unity, thus male/female, light/dark, hot/cold, good/evil, the sun/the moon.

To civilizations based primarily on agriculture for their day-to-day existence, the natural world and its physical forces represented essential elements of survival. The natural elements were considered divine and ruled human existence as evidence of the gods' powers. Ancient Andeans naturally sought to give the

Left: Fish, perhaps in a river channel, decorate the sculpted compound mud walls at the Chimú capital of Chan Chan.

deities and their powers 'forms' in representational art and architecture, and common themes can be detected from at least the Initial Period in its ceremonial architecture. A pantheon of deities and beliefs is evident from at least Chavín times in the Early Horizon.

The Andean pantheon in its entirety was extremely complex and varied throughout the regions. Almost universal, however, was the belief in a creator god, known as Viracocha in the highland and inland regions and Pachacmac among Pacific coastal cultures. In addition, the sun and the moon were deities called by numerous names in different cultures and through time. Usually, but not always, the sun was regarded as male and the moon as female.

EVERYTHING IS CONNECTED

Mutual duality, or reciprocity, was a major feature of the ancient Andean worldview. It comprises the viewpoint that for every idea or object there is a reciprocal part or counterpart. Through reciprocity, therefore, all things in the world are connected.

FORMS OF RECIPROCITY
The concept of reciprocity is not unique to Andean culture, but it is heavily emphasized in the civilization and permeates every aspect of culture – from the physical exchange of goods between highlands and lowlands to its mental realization in religion, daily life and material culture. This reciprocity need not be symmetrical.

The economic face of reciprocity was demonstrated in vertically organized exchange. Traders in the products of different altitude zones such as the highlands and lowlands exchanged basic commodities including maize and potatoes, and also such exotic materials as *Spondylus* shells, available only from the far north-western coasts, or coca or hallucinogenic mushrooms from tropical regions. It occurred in political form in state organization to redistribute wealth. It was the state's recognition of its obligation to provide for all of its members.

At the same time, all members of the government recognized their duty to contribute to the continuing existence of the state and thus serve their role, whether it was rulership or the contribution of labour.

Above: The colours of the Black and White Portal at Chavín de Huántar and the carved male hawk and female eagle symbolize duality.

Socially, kinship divisions within the state also reflected reciprocity, with the dual social units of *hanan* and *hurin* (upper and lower) providing balance and cohesion. At the individual level, male and female represent reciprocals, and perhaps they were essential to understanding the concept in Andean culture, since they were the fundamental arrangement formed by the gods in creation.

The physical divisions of the Inca Empire and its products reflected groups of dual regions or opposed areas, such as mountain valleys and coastal valleys, dry deserts and rainy mountains, hot plains and cold sierra, lush tropics and sparse deserts.

Left: Frequent use of sheet gold, the 'sweat of the sun', reflects its use as the representative of the sun.

DUALITY IN RELIGION
Humankind and the deities themselves were a perfect manifestation of dualism and counterpoint, both in their existence and in their hierarchical positions – the one to worship and obey, the other to be worshipped and to rule. Life and death itself were perhaps the ultimate dualism. The parts were intimately linked, as the concept demanded, through the intermediary of shamanism, keeping the dead among the living and including the dead in ritual ceremony.

Philosophically and cosmologically every idea had its opposite or counterpart: light/dark, dry/wet, high/low, happy/sad, courage/cowardice – all fundamental and observable qualities evident in everyday life. Even the divisions of the universe reflected reciprocity, with the earth and the world of the living between reciprocal worlds above and below.

Right: This jaguar, revered for its power and cunning, on a Chavin stele represents contact between mountain and rainforest cultures.

Reciprocal or dualistic thinking might have been inspired and indeed validated by the appearance of the sky in the Southern Hemisphere. The familiar individual stars and star-to-star constellations were seen as architectural structures or agricultural implements – physical things. Countering these both in type and visual appearance were the dark constellations, the spaces or dark voids between the stars, which were seen as animals – living things. Further, the animals themselves represented the conceptual counterparts of the living animals on earth because they were regarded as responsible for procreation on earth. For example, the Incas (and presumably their predecessors) saw a balance between the dark-star llama (*Yacana*) in the Milky Way, with stars for its eyes, and the living llamas in their herds. *Yacana* drank nightly from the ocean to prevent it from flooding the earth.

DUALITY IN ART

Throughout Andean art there is an emphasis on duality, on interlocking parts or pairs, and contrasts between light and dark or complementary colours. These features can be seen in ceramics and their shapes, in textiles and their colours, and in the beings shown on both. There is doubling and mirror-imaging of all kinds. Textiles and their interlocking images show dovetailed creatures, mirrored at each side, for example as two identical crabs or birds, or as double-headed creatures facing in opposite directions. The Staff Being from the Chavin Cult of the Early

Left: This Nazca ceramic effigy vessel depicts perhaps the most universal symbols of reciprocity – man and woman.

Horizon represents a perfect example. Holding two staffs, one on each side, and represented as either male or female, it is the ultimate example of dualism and is shown in textiles, on pottery and in architectural sculpture, persisting from the Early Horizon to Inca times.

Architecturally, Andean structures are counterparts to natural earth shapes. In some cases, naturally shaped stones were modified by sculptors and became locations for ritual as *huacas* – linkages of the natural and man-made and of the ordinary world and religion. Structures sculpt the world in light and shadow, space and solid. The dual nature of many Andean ceremonial centres in the Initial Period and Early Horizon reflected a worldview of dualistic nature. Pyramidal platforms and sunken courts demonstrate the organization of space into solid and void, positive and negative spaces, elevated and subterranean areas, upper world and lower world, and even into concepts of descent, birth and the Earth Mother, and ascent to the Sky Father.

COLLECTIVE THINKING

Reciprocity within society was complemented by another concept, collectivity,
which permeated life at all levels.

A COLLECTIVE SOCIETY

Collectivity was the overriding mode of
operation in Inca (and their predecessors')
society. Corporate thinking demanded
that the group always took precedence over
the individual, since the individual was part
of the whole and could not function
effectively except as part of the whole.
Collectivity complements reciprocity in
the idea that all things are connected and
therefore part of a whole and of the cycle
of the universe. As a supreme example,
the Inca Inti shows reciprocity and
collectivity at the same time. As the earthly
representative of Inti the sun, he was an
intermediary between the people and the
gods – and thus part of the collectivity that
was necessary for the whole to function
effectively. In contradiction of this,
however, he was individual and supreme
above all other Incas.

The varied and often harsh environments of the Andean Area favour, perhaps
even demand, a need to adapt in order to
achieve group organization in most activities. Like reciprocity, collectivity does
not necessarily render all individuals
within the group as equals. Most aspects of
Andean cultures are hierarchical, showing
an uneven distribution of power and
wealth. Most obvious are differences in

*Above: A less elaborate burial textile from
Nazca shows a stylized human figure
within a simple, repetitive pattern.*

burials, from royal and rich elite tombs
to common graves, and from elaborate
'natural' interment to ritual sacrifice.

The concept can be traced to the
earliest Andean civilizations. Architecture,
from these times, demonstrates such
hierarchy in quality of construction,
decoration and apparent function.
Common dwellings surrounded great
ceremonial centres that were the hubs of
the cities. Such architecture, however,
represents the ultimate in corporate
thinking in the marshalling and command
of the labour to build ceremonial structures
to serve the community. The Incas

Left: A mass-produced Inca chicha *jug and*
kero *drinking cup represent state-controlled
industry and the redistribution of goods.*

Above: The Incas collected agricultural produce into state-controlled warehouses for redistribution according to need and rank.

ingeniously incorporated subject peoples into the empire, embracing myriad cultures and nuances of belief and local political, social and economic arrangements. Yet, they also represent the extreme of inequality within collectivity – the few ruling the many in the pyramid of power; the Incas, who numbered about 100,000, ruled more than ten million people.

The social fission that might result from challenging environments and from such inequality was mediated by ritual, to re-emphasize social collectivity or corporateness. The Inca Quechua term for such ritual was *tinku*, referring to the joining of two to form one.

THE IMPORTANCE OF ROLE

Andean artistic collectivity is shown by a general sparsity of portraiture, historical detail and narrative. The details of special features, physical location or the actions of specific people are usually unimportant: it is the person's role that is important to show, and religious art overridingly features supernatural imagery. The deities have aspects by which they can be recognized, and it is these aspects that must be shown accurately. Artistic decoration emphasizes continuous and repetitious patterning, itself an obvious manifestation of 'corporateness'. As early as the Initial Period, the architectural monolithic mosaic at Cerro Sechin shows this

concept, forming converging processions of figures and banners. Rather than representing individuals, the figures are stylized representations of warriors and captives in a procession of conquest, triumph and sacrifice – a *tinku* ritual and convergence of duality in ceremonial temple architecture.

Moche art is a notable exception to these concepts. Recent research and discoveries show portraiture and narrative, especially in Moche ceramics and in the scenes painted on them, and historical details, in which the entombed in elite burials represent the deities or priests and priestesses depicted on pots and murals.

ARTISTIC ANONYMITY

The extensive use of moulds in ceramic production and repetitious dual- and mirror-imagery also show collectivity. Although the names of individual artists are unknown, scholars recognize their particular styles. The distinctive 'makers' marks' on the millions of adobe bricks used in the construction of the pyramid platforms of the Moche capital are another demonstration of corporate thinking. The idea was not to distinguish the brick-makers but rather to account for the labour or quota required of collective work units.

Right: Llama effigy figures. Llama herding for wool and other products was also state-controlled.

The seemingly intentional anonymity of ancient Andean artists, craftsmen and labourers does not render their art generic. Individual sculptures, pots, murals and metalwork are idiosyncratic, dynamic and distinctive. They can be recognized by archaeologists today and therefore must have been identifiable when made. The specific styles of ancient Andean cultures and regions are certainly distinctive. However, within these there are styles of imagery, some of which lasted for more than 1,000 years, even though some details changed over time.

Nevertheless, it is the image and concept of a piece that are important, not its maker. The religious message was paramount, and that subsumed the whole. This combination of collectivity and stressing the abstract in art rendered ancient Andean culture highly sophisticated yet unconcerned with specific or individual conspicuousness or eminence.

TRANSFORMATION

Ancient Americans throughout the North and South American continents believed that the universe existed on multiple levels. The Inca tripartite realms of the living world, a world above and a world below were the culmination of developments from the beginning of Andean religion. The realms were not held to be exclusive, nor were they necessarily separated in time. Rather, they existed in parallel, and each was vital to the existence of the other two.

Communication between these worlds was achieved through transformation. Birth, living and death were therefore considered states of existence in an endlessly continuing cycle of time, rather than as mutually exclusive states. Each realm could influence the others, and actions in the realm of the living could influence the effects of the other realms on it. Thus, it was important to maintain communications between the realms by worshipping the gods and by honouring one's ancestors, who were believed to be 'living' in the realm of the dead. Shamanism provided the medium that enabled communication between worlds, and it was through shamans or 'priests' that instructive and corrective messages could be obtained in the world of the living.

A BALANCED ORDER
The world was ordered according to specific rules that governed how things should be and how they should work. Social and economic order had to be upheld in order to maintain the balance between the worlds.

Right: This Sipán sheet-gold burial mask represents various Andean themes: the sun and the shamanic transformation or human representation of a deity.

As with reciprocity and collectivity, equal power among individuals was not required, only that all were included within the scheme and received sufficient necessities. In this way, social and economic functions can be seen as constant factors within the different political systems that evolved over time in the Andean Area. For example, the architecture of ceremonial centres, from the early U-shaped structures and sunken courts of the Initial Period, through to Chavín temples in the Early Horizon to Late Horizon Inca state religion, continued the theme of dualism, as did the practice of the collection and redistribution of goods and divisions of labour, despite the rise and fall of kingdoms and empires.

STATES OF CHANGE
The universe was considered to be in a state of flux, but its changes were cyclical and orderly. The seasons changed in regular succession, the climate altered between wet to dry seasons. Moisture was collected into and channelled by earthly rivers, taken up into the celestial river, and fell back to earth as rain and snow in a never-ending redistributive cycle. Planting, harvest, storage and redistribution formed an endless cycle. The movements of the sun, moon, planets and stars were observed to be regular, as was the progression of the Milky Way through the night sky. Thus, orderly regularity governed all realms.

Likewise, individual lives were in states of flux, from birth to youth to old age, and continued in death as the next plane of existence.

Such cyclical thinking was (and continues to be) the key to the Andean worldview. Human history progresses but is perceived to repeat itself constantly. For example, the Incas saw in the ruins of Tiwanaku a former earthly kingdom that preceded their own and thought of themselves as the inheritors of Tiwanaku power in the Altiplano.

HUMAN TO SUPERNATURAL
Andean art served to reflect these planes of existence and to unite them. It captured transformations such as the metamorphosis of shamans into supernatural beings. Artists strove to develop methods and media to depict the world as dynamic and to show two things as one, or the existence of a shaman beyond terrestrial space. Transformational examples can be seen in the statuary of Initial

impersonating and transforming into animals – subjects of this world as representations of the superhuman world. Likewise, the importance of communication between realms is clearly shown in numerous Moche ceramics depicting shamanistc acts, and in the inclusion of Inca mummies in the annual ritual cycle.

Finally, Inca religious narrative abounds in examples of transformations: ancestors to stone, animals to stone, humans /deities to stone, humans to animals, and stones to supernatural warriors. Early Cuzco itself owes its survival to 'stones transformed into warriors'.

Above: The transfixed stare of this effigy figurine represents a shaman under the influence of hallucinogenic drugs, a frequent theme in Moche ceramic art.

Right: A deer-headed human-like ceramic figurine, representing the completed transformation of a shaman into a revered animal. His headdress bears a knife for ritual sacrifice.

Period sites such as Huaca de los Reyes, in the fibre human effigies at Mina Perdida and in the painted adobe sculptures at Moxeke. The composite features of these beings, which were represented by non-human eyes with pendent irises, feline noses, fangs, drawn-back lips and facial scarifications, and condor markings on the Mina Perdida fibre effigy, are all indicative of human transformation. Such elements heavily influenced the Chavín style of the Early Horizon in jaguar and serpentine animal–human transformers. The Staff Being him/herself carries all these elements, as do the various monumental

stone sculptures of Chavín, especially the more than 40 sculptures, stone heads and relief panels on the walls of the New Temple, showing a time-lapse sequence of human to supernatural transformation from shaman to feline.

The care with which Paracas and Nazca burials were wrapped and preserved, the sumptuous burials of Moche and Sicán lords and the ritual preservation of Chimú and Inca rulers are all indicative of the importance of transformation between states of being. Many Paracas and Nazca textiles depict humans ritually

A UNITED WORLDVIEW

Essence is a fourth fundamental concept or theme in ancient Andean belief and artistic expression. Essence united the Andean peoples' worldview, incorporating reciprocity/duality, collectivity and transformation. It expressed their belief that the core element or underlying substance was more important than appearance.

REALITY AND MEANING

The symbol of an object represented its reality, even if it was hidden by its outward appearance. It was not important for an image to be visible, or for the material of an object to be pure, for its essence was still present and governed belief. Objects were created for their own sakes and in this sense de-humanized. Such lack of emphasis on the importance

Above: Beneath the stonework of the Machu Picchu Observatorio lies a ritual room made with minimal sculpting of the natural rock.

Below: The essence of gold is conveyed through the gilding of less precious copper and silver in this Moche Sipán funeral mask.

of the human audience underscores Andean regard for humans as only one part of the universe in their worldview. Even the depiction of humans in ancient Andean art was not necessarily the most important component. With the exception of Moche art, there was little individualism or recognition of people. Individuals normally played a part in the whole and are subservient to the theme of the work.

Symbolism was far more important. It was used to convey the idea and to represent the thought or the character of a deity or of a scene. The idea was to characterize someone or something through the use of recognizable traits commonly known and spread with the movement of religious cults.

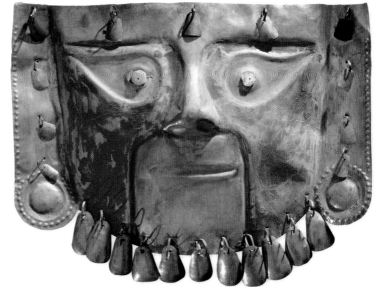

ESSENCE IN ART

A large part of artistic production was not created for daily use but was made for its own sake by craftworkers, and by artists who were subsidized by the political elite. Thus, Andean potters used moulds to make hundreds, if not thousands, of identical pieces representing aspects of Andean life and religion. Metallurgists would mask a base or less precious core with a more precious metal, or gild objects made of alloys. Architectural sculpture emphasized interior decoration and symbolic representation of deities and sacred acts. Elaborate, rich burials were filled with products made solely to be included in the burial. Textile weavers executed such elaborate patterns that the subject often became illegible but was still true to the supernatural subject.

Left: Moche red-on-white 'story' vessels depicted common activities as well as ritual: here a fisherman uses a pelican to fish.

Essence explains why it was not necessary for the Nazca geoglyphs and other ground drawings to be seen in their entirety: it was quite acceptable that the ritual pathways they prescribed could be followed and that the lines fulfilled their function in religious devotion. Thus, their essence was conveyed in the doing rather than in the seeing.

Similar reasoning may explain the use of openwork weaving in Late Intermediate Period Chancay textiles. The designs could be seen as the weaver worked them on the loom, creating interlocking animals and birds, but once removed from the loom the threads contracted and their symbolic imagery became illegible when the garment was worn. Only when spread out against a dark background could the imagery be appreciated – an example of the value of essence over appearance.

Likewise, sacred images were often placed in obscure or hidden locations within temples. The meaning and essence was conveyed to the people by shamans, sometimes personifying the deity concerned, sometimes rep-

Above: Traces of red paint on this sheet-gold Chimú funerary mask show that its essence (pure gold) was hidden in a reverse of the idea represented by gilding (see opposite).

resenting the deity through transformation. Similarly, the symbolic images could be so complex, or arranged so strangely over a stone or a pot, as to render them accessible only to an elite few. For it was what the images stood for that was important rather than that all should be able to stand before them and 'read' their intimate meaning.

Most artistic production was created for its own sake, for the afterlife, for its ritual efficacy or for use within the realm of the supernatural.

RHYTHM AND ENERGY

Reciprocity, collectivity, transformation and essence facilitated the rhythms of ancient Andean life. Their interconnections guided the flow of the world and manifested the Inca concept of *ayni*, the principle that governed cyclicity. In the words of one scholar, reciprocity was 'like a pump at the heart of Andean life'. Together these concepts represent the energy that bound the cycle of the universe, the *ayni* and *mink'a* – the positive and negative, the give and take that made the Andean universe work.

MULTIPLE MEANINGS IN ART

Art often elicits dual meanings, inviting opposite or multiple interpretations. Such double readings are common in Andean art. Textiles from the earliest times right through to Chancay and Inca weaving in the Late Horizon dovetail mirror images of birds and animals. Two-headed supernatural creatures are shown in textiles, painted decoration and sculpture. Inca architecture plays with opposites, 'sculpting' natural stone to display light and shadow. Beings, real and supernatural, with double meanings, portrayed as a single motif with multiple identities abound in Early Horizon Chavin and Paracas art and continue through the ages in the art of later highland and coastal cultures.

Below: The shape of this Nazca effigy vessel makes it difficult to interpret. The mythological themes on its faces may be individual or may comprise a narrative.

EARLY SYMBOLIC ART
The idea that essential meaning could be depicted visually, and that a representation could contain multiple meanings and show a composite being was present in some of the earliest Andean art. Cotton textiles from Huaca Prieta employed a relatively simple twining technique. More than 9,000 cloth fragments were excavated. The most famous piece, only known as a photographic reproduction, shows a clearly recognizable raptor with a hooked beak and outstretched wings. Closer inspection shows a coiled snake within its stomach. The subject's basic symmetry, broken by its left-facing beak, is balanced by the right-facing slant of the snake.

The embedded serpent reveals a multi-layered meaning. Here is a raptor and its prey. The obvious victory of raptor over snake, however, may represent a religious belief or hierarchy. The zigzag contours of the piece indicate that it was held sideways as it was twined, revealing that the weaver was able to visualize the final design during execution. The use of this method may also have been so that the visual impact of the zigzag was of beating wings. Thus, complexity of meaning and mode of manufacture reveal how essence of meaning was paramount and more important than both simple imagery and method.

Another example of multiple meaning and of the early portrayal of a composite being also comes from Huaca Prieta. A twined cotton fragment shows the symmetrical figure of two crabs in a rhomboidal composition. One crab occupies the lower left and the other the upper right. Outstretched legs indicate that they are scuttling. Curiously, one has eight legs while the other has six. However,

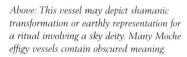

Above: This vessel may depict shamanic transformation or earthly representation for a ritual involving a sky deity. Many Moche effigy vessels contain obscured meaning.

they are not just crabs. The bases of the crabs are united by one pair of their claws across the centre of the composition. Each of the other claws, however, bends in an acute angle back towards the head of the twin crab and turns into a snake's head. The angular representation hints at the nature of the animal. Not only is there double meaning in this piece in the representation of a land and a sea animal, but also the multi-layered meaning of one animal turning into the other. Perhaps the wearer was meant to become infused with the character of the animals.

MEANING WITHIN ARCHITECTURE
At the other end of the Andean chrono-logical scale, the Inca *huaca* of Qenqo, just north of Cuzco, shows the same concepts rendered in architecture and stone sculpture. The natural outcrop has been heavily modified, its protruding surfaces

carved extensively with steps, shelves, indentations and niches. There is also a zigzag channel that branches and rejoins, which may have been for libations. Such heavy alteration rivals the outcrops' natural irregularity. It is difficult to decide whether the modifications are meant to mimic, oppose or balance the natural irregularities. The play on light and shadow is carried to the extreme, yet some flat surfaces reflect the sun's rays so fiercely that the 'play' becomes one-sided.

Beneath the huge boulder lies hidden meaning. A large natural cleft has been carved into a small chamber. The natural 'heart' of such a stone was a quintessential Andean place of sacredness, and the modification of it recognized this and rendered it available for ritual purposes. It is the essence of the outcrop that is important; its modification by humans emphasizes and enhances its sacredness. Its use recognizes its vitality.

To ancient Andeans, Qenqo and other such sites were not inanimate objects but living beings, part of the universe. The hidden heart at Qenqo's base isolates it from the secular world; its alteration and use bring it into the spiritual world.

A separate, protruding monolith to one side of the main outcrop is naturally triangular and has been left uncarved.

Above: Eagle and hawk carvings on the columns of the Black and White Portal of the New Temple at Chavín de Huántar.

When viewed from a certain angle, its shape resembles that of a seated puma. It is framed by a small square wall and by an enclosing curved courtyard wall. Once again, the recognition of its shape and use as a place of ritual draws it into the Inca universe. A rainforest creature in this mountain setting unifies the realms of the world.

Left: Rolled-out reconstruction drawings of the female eagle (left) and male hawk (right) carved on the columns at Chavín.

HIDDEN RITUAL AND MEANING

Every form of ancient Andean art contains layers of meaning. Obscuring this meaning within many possible interpretations and in a complex design became fully developed in Early Horizon times at Chavín de Huántar, like so many features of ancient Andean religion. Earlier elements of Chavín religion can be seen in the preceding Preceramic and Initial Periods.

PLATFORM MOUNDS

The architectural tradition of Preceramic platform mound sites began the practice of building small courtyards and chambers or groups of chambers on top of platforms. It is not possible to describe in detail what rituals took place in them, but they were clearly meant to hide whatever activity they enclosed. The platforms' location at the centres of ceremonial complexes and above domestic buildings isolated them, and their relatively small size made them accessible to only a chosen few. The steps leading up to such platforms presumably provided the venue for ritual display to multitudes. In this way, what different groups within society witnessed could be selected and controlled.

The deliberately broken and buried figurines at Huaca de los Idolos at Aspero represent one of the earliest examples of such hidden, selective ritual, as do the infant and adult burial at its companion mound of Huaca de los Sacrificios.

Above: The high, thick compound walls of the Huaca el Dragón, near Chan Chan, enclose the people performing the rituals within them.

The tradition was elaborated in the Initial Period at sites such as La Galgada, Kotosh, Caral and Chiripa. Twinned and multiple mounds were built at many sites, and chambers were either detached but grouped, a tradition that continued through to Inca times, or became combined in complexes divided into rooms. Larger halls were subdivided into separate chambers or divided partially to hide one part within another. Parts of complexes were made difficult to enter through long galleries leading around behind a main complex.

Kotosh, La Galgada, Aspero, Piedra Parada, El Paraíso, Sechín Alto, Cerro Sechín, Huaca de los Reyes, Garagay and numerous other sites went through such transitions. In the Titiucaca Basin, Chiripa shows the emphasis on symmetrically grouped detached chambers built on top of a platform.

HIDDEN PLAZAS

The tradition of hidden plazas (*plazas hundidas*) established an opposing organization of space by enclosing and isolating ritual within negative space. Hidden plazas

Left: The Semi-subterranean Court beyond the Kalasasaya portal at Tiwanaku is an example of a sunken ritual courtyard.

may have been venues for ritual re-enactments of creation and earth veneration. The combination of the two traditions became common at sites in the late Initial Period and Early Horizon and is most elaborately represented at Chavín de Huántar. Hidden plazas were initially circular at northern Andean sites. The transition from circular to rectangular took place at Chavín de Huántar in the 1st millennium BC. Within the arms of the U-shaped platform housing the Old Temple stood the circular sunken court, while the plaza of the New Temple incorporated a square sunken court, and heralded the persistence of the rectangular form in the Altiplano until the demise of Tiwanaku at the end of the 10th century AD.

The objects of worship and the chambers that housed them also became more complicated, hidden and controlled. The labyrinthine chambers of the Old and New Temples at Chavín de Huántar are the classic example. Deep within its galleries and corridors, a dimly lit room in the Old Temple held the Lanzón Stone monolith and in the New Temple stood the Raimondi Stela. A third monolith, the Tello Obelisk, stood in the sunken court of the New Temple.

ORACLES AND IMAGES
The use of oracles at Chavín de Huántar and at Pachacamac represents another aspect of ritual obscurity. Only specialists could interpret the oracles' pronouncements. The supplicant required shamanistic intervention and interpretation. At Chavín de Huántar, the base of the Lanzón Stone stood in the lower chamber, while an upper chamber, into which its top protruded, provided a hidden chamber for the voice of the oracle. The principal idol at Pachacamac was a wooden statue kept in a windowless room at the summit of the main terraced platform.

Above: Detailed scenes or mythical events painted on Nazca pottery must be read carefully to obtain their full meaning.

The symbolic images of the Chavín monoliths and of the Black and White Portal of the New Temple show multiple meaning and obscurity in several ways. All three sculptures depict supernatural beings and include snarling faces. They are three representations of the supreme being, and the features on them are repeated in modified form in Chavín portable art found throughout the central Andes and coast regions in Early Horizon settlements.

The positioning of the images enhances the obscurity of their meaning. They are not only extremely intricate and complex but are also wrapped around the monoliths or columns of the portal and thus cannot be seen all at the same time or in total without walking around the sculpture. The location of the Lanzón Stone makes this impossible. In the Titicaca Basin the Yaya-Mama tradition on monolithic slabs at Pukará and other sites, showing a male (*yaya*) and a female (*mama*) figure on opposite faces, demonstrates a similar principle.

These traditions of isolating and secluding ritual continued to the Late Horizon. The Late Intermediate Chimú capital at Chan Chan comprised a huge complex of individual rectangular complexes. The Inca Coricancha in Cuzco enclosed a group of chambers dedicated to individual deities and secluded ritual for specialized priests, who thus controlled the rare display of venerated objects.

Below: The Circular Sunken Court at Chavín de Huántar brought a coastal ritual feature to the mountain cult.

SYMBOLS OF DIVINITY

The integrated nature of the ancient Andean worldview regarded natural objects as sacred. Mountains, water and caves were universal divine symbols. Within ancient Andean belief there was an intentional melding of what modern Western cultures regard as natural and cultural; both were regarded as 'living'.

SUN AND MOON
Tracking the cycles of the sun and moon is important to agricultural peoples, and the ancient Andeans were no exception. The sun, Ai Apaec (Moche and Chimú) or Inti (Inca), and the moon, Si (Moche and Chimú) or Quilla (Inca), were universal symbols of reverence and were believed to exercise enormous influence on human life. They were associated with precious metals: gold with the sun, silver with the moon. The association became a physical metaphor to the Incas: sweat of the sun

Below: The cult of Inti, the Inca sun god, centred on Intihuatana (Hitching Post of the Sun) sites, such as this one at Machu Picchu.

and tears of the moon. Most cultures considered the moon to be the consort of the sun. They symbolized opposing forces, and their intermingled cycles achieved the unity necessary to the world's balance. Their controlled cycles gave stability to the pre-Hispanic world.

The Incas epitomized the importance of the sun in their state cult, in which the emperor was the sun's earthly representative – son of the sun. The Incas regarded themselves as the children of the sun and moon, and in the creation myth Viracocha, the creator god, is also described as the sun.

The sun is not easily identified in pre-Hispanic art. Gold generally symbolizes it, but a specific solar deity is not obvious. Inca gold-rayed masks clearly represent the sun, and the god in the centre of the lintel of the stone portal at Tiwanaku may represent the sun, hence its name Gateway of the Sun.

The moon was intimately related to earthly matters. Images of a crescent moon feature especially in pre-Inca Moche and Chimú art.

JAGUARS AND OTHER CREATURES
The religious imagery of Andean and Pacific coastal cultures was influenced from the earliest times by rainforest animals – jaguars, serpents and other reptiles, monkeys and birds. Aquatic animals, both oceanic and fresh water, and birds were also widespread outside their natural habitats. Such common imagery undoubtedly reflects a basic animism and naturalism in Andean belief. It is also reasoned that the widespread occurrence and repetition of themes infers an underlying universality in the beliefs of Andean cultures.

In particular, both highland and lowland civilizations shared a fascination with the jaguar. The jaguar face inspired the imagery

Right: A sky deity is shown on this Paracas textile with the Oculate Being, complete with serpent tongue, feline whiskers, slithering snakes and streaming trophy heads.

Right: Spiders feature frequently in Andean art, from tiny golden figures on Moche jewellery to this giant Nazca desert geoglyph.

of fanged deities from the earliest times to the Inca Empire. Jaguars were depicted frequently on stationary and portable artefacts –wall paintings, stone carvings, ceramics, textiles and metalwork. Before the prominence of Chavín de Huántar, numerous U-shaped ceremonial centres in the coastal valleys of Peru show an apparently widespread religious coherence, with carvings and paintings of fanged beings at Cardál, Garagay, Sechín Alto, Cerro Sechín, Cabello Muerto, Moxeke and other sites. The plan of Cuzco itself was a feline profile (the shape of a crouching puma), and even the rock at Qenqo, a 'natural' object, was regarded as the profile of a seated puma.

COMPOSITE BEINGS

Composite creatures, combining the features and characteristics of several animals, and human-like beings were also common. Feline-human hybrids, the staff deities (with composite feline face and human body), winged beings, and falcon-headed or other bird-headed warriors all symbolized divinity and were painted and sculpted on ceremonial architecture. The variety of fanged beings implies a wealth of imagination in conjuring up fearful deities to strike awe in the intended worshippers.

In addition, creatures were often shown in cultures that were alien to them. For example, the Tello Obelisk

Right: On this Nazca effigy vessel a bird shape is combined with a human face, feline masks and an Oculate Being-like face on the breast.

at Chavín de Huántar shows the creation myth and features the cayman (a jungle creature) in a sierra culture. Mountain raptors appear frequently on coastal textiles. Pacific shells, especially *Strombus* and *Spondylus*, are found as grave goods and are depicted on pottery

and architecture throughout the Andean Area. Finally, the ritual pathways of the Nazca trace the outlines of creatures that were alien to the desert, for example a monkey and a whale. Their sacredness was incorporated in the act of following the ritual route. Such representations of 'misplaced' creatures show links between highland and lowland cultures and demonstrate universal reverence.

The Staff Deity of Chavín became a persistent symbol for 1,500 years, with full-frontal beings in various forms featuring widely in Andean art. Its portrayal on the Raimondi Stela epitomizes the Chavín Cult. The full-frontal, standing figure is a composite of animal and human characteristics. Symbols of the Staff Deity, ubiquitous in Chavín imagery, were spread throughout the central and northern Andes and coast on portable art.

Serpents, like felines, were also pan-Andean and were used often in all media: wall paintings, stone carvings, ceramic decoration, textiles and metalwork.

CHAPTER EIGHT

HONOURING
THE GODS

In his *Historia del Nuevo Mundo*, the 17th-century Spanish chronicler and historian Father Bernabe Cobo names 317 different shrines in Inca Cuzco alone. From this, there is no doubt that religion permeated Inca society.

From the earliest times, it is evident that ancient Andean cultures honoured their gods. The treatment shown in special burials and in the construction of special architecture in the midst of domestic dwellings in towns and cities reveals a deep reverence for things beyond day-to-day survival. Whatever their nature, religious considerations were intermixed.

Political arrangements came and went. Rulers were seen to participate in religious ritual, and to be representatives of the gods on Earth. Yet when kingdoms fell and regions were broken up into smaller political entities, the gods remained. In this sense, religion was both integral to and independent of politics in ancient Andean civilization.

The gods and goddesses were depicted on all media: ceramics, textiles and metalwork, and on small and monumental stone, clay and wooden sculpture. They were both portrayed directly, as men and women dressed to represent them, and symbolized in architectural complexes. Features of the landscape were held to be imbued with their presence and therefore representative of them.

Left: Supernatural beings, including a figure reminiscent of the Staff Deity, on a Moche dyed and finely woven cotton textile.

RELIGIOUS CONQUEST

It is not certain, especially in the earliest Andean civilizations, if religion was spread through military conquest. The evidence of the distribution of the art styles and supernatural imagery of different cultures might be interpreted as having been spread through conquest, and the Moche, Wari, Tiwanaku, Chimú and Inca were certainly warlike states engaged in the acquisition of territory through military conquest. The image of the severed head or trophy head was common from the Initial Period onward in virtually every culture. The close association of rule, Inca conquest and the spread of the state cult in the Late Horizon might have been the culmination of a widespread practice.

RELIGION AND ADMINISTRATION
Archaeologists argue that sunken courts and raised platforms, found in both lowland and highland cultures, represent earthly and heavenly deities and themes as well as reflecting the landscapes of the two regions. The central locations of ceremonial complexes among domestic sprawl, or in other cases the isolation of them among surrounding domestic settlements, shows that architectural ceremonial complexes were places for the gathering of people for special rituals. The increasing complexity of elements of ceremonial complexes – divisions into rooms, labyrinthine temples, multiple groupings of platforms, and intricate images of supernatural beings – demonstrates the development of a specialized priesthood to hold the truths of belief and to perform the rituals associated with them.

These centres must also have been places for carrying out civil duties. The sacredness of vital elements – sunshine, water, the well-being of the crops and herds – may have been under the control of the gods, and soliciting the gods' favour may have been the responsibility of the shamans on the peoples' behalf. However, once the crops had been gathered it was the responsibility of a civil structure that had had no direct physical input into their production to administer their distribution.

Thus, the distinction between religion and politics can never have been very clear-cut in ancient Andean cultures.

THE ROLE OF CERRO SECHÍN
The ceremonial complex at Cerro Sechín was built, used and modified over a period of several hundred years. It eventually covered 5ha (12 acres) and must have served as a political and religious centre for a considerable region. Its principal pyramidal structure formed a quadrangle with rounded corners, 53m (174ft) on a side, and its outer wall was adorned with some 400 stone sculptures. The sculptures of the late platform portray humans marching towards a central entrance. They are clearly warriors, and among them are dismembered bodies, severed heads and naked captives. One warrior has severed heads hanging from his waist as trophies.

Below: The cult of Inti was spread throughout the empire through the establishment of Inti-huatana (Hitching Post of the Sun) temples.

Left: Map showing early religious cults and traditions, including the Kotosh Religious Tradition, the Chavín Cult and Yaya-Mama.

A CONQUERING CULT?

Legends recorded by Spanish chroniclers describe how northern coastal dynasties had been established through invasions from the south. They may be the hazy records of the establishment of the dynasty of Moche lords. Among the Moche, narrative scene painting on pottery and textiles depicts ritual combat and ceremony, including ritual sacrifice. Blood offerings are made to deities impersonated by men and women, presumably priests and priest-esses. Burials have been found with elite corpses wearing the costumes depicted in the scenes. This sequence and the scenes might represent the spread of religious ideas with territorial conquest.

The scene seems to show the successful return of an army and can be interpreted as endemic of regional warfare. Yet, this scene is of a late renovation of the Cerro Sechín complex. Was it a war memorial? A stone pilaster of much earlier date depicts essentially the same scene. Or does such repetition over time represent a mythical or legendary battle and victory rather than a specific event? Is it, rather, symbolic of religious conversion combined with territorial claims?

A PEACEFUL CULT?

Archaeologically, the distribution of the symbolic imagery of the Chavín Cult demonstrates it was spread across a large region and that the gods of Chavín were revered among both highland and coastal peoples. Architecturally, Chavín de Huántar was both the inheritor of and participating member in the elements of the ceremonial complex that had developed through the Initial Period and Early Horizon. Yet much of the spread of Chavín religious imagery, especially through portable art, appears to have been achieved alongside the spread of technological innovation.

Like all religious missionaries, those spreading the Chavín Cult would have been faced with explaining complex concepts and evoking other-worldly experiences through objects and representations of them based ultimately on analogy and metaphor.

Chavín artists, either instructed by or acting as shamans, made these themes central to their art. The complexity of Chavín imagery conveys 'otherness'. New techniques in textiles and metallurgy seem to appear suddenly and spread rapidly, conveying the Chavín Cult. This appears to be not military conquest, but rather the perpetuation of regional links already established for economic reasons.

Right: An elaborately decorated Inca wooden kero or drinking vessel in the shape of a head, decorated with figures carrying keros.

ANIMAL AND SUPERNATURAL SYMBOLISM

The fantastic imagery on ancient Andean pottery, textiles, metalwork and stone sculpture is clearly highly symbolic, and it conveyed important meaning to those who knew how to interpret it. Its complexity increased with time to the point where specialized individuals were needed to act as intermediaries between the deities and powers the symbolism represented on the one hand and the general populace on the other.

SHAMANS AND NARRATIVES

The feline and serpentine features that adorned the faces of supernatural beings and humans representing, or being transformed into, them constitute perhaps the most notable imagery used through time and throughout the civilizations of the Andean Area. Close seconds are the uses of birds of all kinds, and of spiders and crabs, particularly in coastal cultures, and the use of double-headed imagery. The general image of the Chavín Staff Deity, by repetition over a widespread area and through time, is a familiar symbol of sacredness and representative of a god and goddess.

More generally, there are several themes that can be identified. Shamanic expression is one that seems easy to recognize. The staring eyes, deep incisions and transfixed expressions on many painted, woven and sculptured faces depict shamans in the state of trance experiencing visions under the influence of hallucinogenic drugs. The contexts of their portrayal, for example a shamman administering to a 'patient' or in a state of transformation into an animal or into a supernatural being, makes this clear.

Another theme is the narrative. Many scenes show a ritual in the process of being performed. This is the case on much Nazca and Moche pottery, on which sacrifices and ritual combat are depicted. Series of images, such as those of shamans and jaguars on the walls

at Chavín de Huántar, give a still-photo-like sequence of transformation. Other scenes imply movement and a 'story', as they depict a hunting or a fishing scene. A sense of perspective is given by overlapping limbs and other elements. Some other scenes show what appear to be obvious themes, such as hunting or fishing, or the harvest on Nazca pots, or battle scenes on Moche and Wari pottery, but these pictures can also carry more complex, extended or additional meanings.

Above: Detail on an early Nazca burial shroud of the sun god, symbolically shown in human form with main and fine rays.

ADDITIONAL MEANINGS

The Nazca 'harvest festival' textile, at face value, shows the produce of the harvest. In detail, however, the Staff Deity-like stance of the figures, their masked or supernatural faces, their complex interlocking pattern and the fact that some are upright and others upside down all contribute to an appearance of hidden or

Right: Regional deities incorporated symbolic themes, as in this Paracas embroidered burial mantle depicting a feline with eyes reminiscent of the staring Oculate Being.

less obvious meanings connected with the ritual significance of the harvest in Nazca religious belief.

Similarly, in the Moche mural (now destroyed) called *The Revolt of the Objects*, everyday objects employ weapons to attack humans. For every human depiction, there is a reciprocal object, such as a warrior with a fox head or a boat with legs, representing duality.

MYSTERIOUS SYMBOLISM

The Moche culture had waned by about the end of the 8th century AD, yet in the 16th century a story about the revolt of 'inanimate' things was told to the Spaniards, seemingly as a general folk story or myth. The survival of the legend for nearly a millennium reveals its apparent common acceptance.

Knowledge that the Inca (and presumably pre-Inca cultures) viewed their world differently from Europeans by regarding virtually everything, including the actual landscape, as living parts in the universe gives a symbolic meaning to a story that Westerners find difficult to interpret. Other themes are equally complex and difficult to interpret, if they can be interpreted now at all. The symbolism of the Lanzón monolith at Chavín is easier to identify than to interpret. There are two caymans. But why is a river creature featured as the primary deity in a sierra culture? And why, in a culture that existed more than a millennium and a half before the Incas, with their belief in the upper and lower world spheres, are the caymans pointing in celestial and earthly directions?

Left: Detail of three supernatural beings on a Moche cotton textile, one with a staff and, perhaps, a representation of the cratered moon, Si, the northern coastal moon goddess.

SYMBOLIC MEANING

The complexity of Andean Area religion and its different worldview have led scholars to conclude that ancient Andeans infused all their art with potential double meaning. There are images that are real, others that are unreal, and yet others that are purely symbolic. Even real images may operate on a higher symbolic level as well as simply depicting, for example, a man leading a llama or a woman weaving. Does a Moche scene of a man hunting simply portray the act of hunting, or are we meant to be reminded of male characteristics, man's role in society or, perhaps, of a symbolic hunt? Does a female figurine represent a woman, or should it indicate fertility, or, higher still, the mother of humans?

The frequent repetition of such 'scenes' indicates that they are not to be taken at face value. It seems that on one level the essence of appearance is operative and on another level that a hidden, double or reciprocal meaning is operating.

Below: Agricultural abundance is symbolized in this Nazca bridge-spouted vessel, showing a man grasping a maize plant with bulbous roots and laden with ripening cobs.

Many Moche faces painted on pottery, as ceramic effigies or in precious metal, show what appear to be laughing faces but could be snarling or shamanic hysteria.

Some ritual practices are plainly depicted on pots, especially on Moche fine-line red-on-white narrative scenes. Some show blood sacrifices and offerings to deities, or to humans representing deities. Others show individuals engaged in combat. However a closer examination is necessary to see that the combat scenes, for example, show Moche fighting Moche, not a war against Moche enemies. A Nazca stepped-bridged double-spouted vessel painted with a battle scene of interlocking warriors in brilliantly coloured regalia appears equally straightforward. But is this a war of conquest or a depiction of a mythical battle, a symbolic representation of some universal religious 'event' to remind viewers of how the world began and how it operates?

COMPOSITE IMAGERY

Humans with animal heads and other features, a conflated man and peanut or an owl with a trumpet are clearly unreal but may be deeply symbolic of something that we cannot now fully understand. Male and female effigies are clearly shamans by their contexts and visages, but we are unable to understand the full symbolism of the imagery within its own cultural context. The conclusion that the scenes on Moche pots were mythologically symbolic of general religious belief, however, is strengthened by the elite burials of individuals dressed in the identical regalia shown in the narrative scenes.

SYMBOLIC ORGANIZATION

The manner of the organized production of ceramics is itself symbolic. In the Moche and later states, if not earlier, specialists were employed to make thousands of highly crafted pieces as a state-supported enterprise. Many are from burials and seem to have been produced

Above: The meaning of this Moche prisoner effigy vessel is unmistakable: bound wrists and a rope around his head and penis show capitulation, defeat and domination.

specifically for the burial rite. Such a set-up was representative of the power of the state – to command and control ceramic manufacture – and of social organization – part of the populace producing essentials and sharing them with another part through state redistribution of wealth. They are symbolic of the ancient Andean belief that such an arrangement was necessary because not having it would neglect religious belief. Similar arrangements prevailed for the manufacture of precious metal objects, textiles, featherwork and other materials.

For example, there were ceramic workshops at the Moche towns of Galindo and Cerro Mayal. The Cerro Mayal workshop occupied 29,000 sq ft (9,000 sq m). These towns were the western equivalent, perhaps, of a town with a car factory, wherein much of the local economy was focused on the factory employment.

LOCAL HEROES

The sacrificial scenes on Moche red-on-white painted narratives show not just ordinary citizens, but also combatants who were elites. If not actually of the ruling class, they were at least specialists in their role in ritual combat. Just as potters were state specialists, they also were chosen and trained into the role that they are shown performing. Recent research on Moche effigy pots by Christopher Donnan has produced convincing arguments that the Moche, seemingly unique among pre-Hispanic Andean cultures, actually produced portraiture. More than 900

Below: Detail of a Nazca embroidered textile showing a priest in a tunic displaying the ray-headed Staff Deity, and himself in a similar pose, holding a staff and a trophy head.

Above: Drawings of the Revolt of the Objects, *an Andean mythological theme that survived to Inca times. The original was at the Moche Huaca de la Luna.*

examples are known to show individuals with such distinctive facial features that they cannot be anything other than true likenesses. If they had other meaning as well, this may have been in combination with the use to which they were put, rather than what they depicted.

Their symbolism is revealed by the fact that they were not just one-off portraits, but that groups of them were portraits of the same individual as he grew up. One group, for example, portrays just such an individual who was chosen, trained for ritual combat, was successful in his youth, but was eventually defeated and submitted to sacrifice. His body was dismembered and his blood offered to the gods. The entire sequence of his life, including the manufacture of the effigy vessels to record it, represents a sort of legend and symbolic example. This is symbolism on the order of commemorative event ceramics, coronation crockery, and modern celebrity memorabilia.

REPETITIVE ADDITIONS

Such symbolism and theme-related 'decoration' continued to be the practice in later periods, with certain modifications. Much Wari decoration is geometric and

reflects systematic divisions of space similar to their architecture. Late Intermediate Period art shows a tendency to be additive and non-individualistic, to represent an assembly of elements in repetitive patterns. Yet, among the repetition there is often an anomaly – a singular shape and/or colour that contrasts with the rest of the pattern. Does this represent individual expression in an otherwise rigid society? Or perhaps some understood, and necessary, break in perfection?

Royal and elite cult practice became even stronger, particularly in the Chimú state, in which a huge area of the capital was devoted to enclosed compounds as the palaces of deceased royals, their relations, and their living entourages and dedicated caretaker priests. The entire arrangement was state supported, like the manufacture of pottery and other artefacts, as part of the cult. Once again, the organization symbolized and reinforced the rigid social framework, state power and territorialism.

RITUAL SYMBOLISM IN ARCHITECTURE

Ancient Andean architecture, like portable artefacts, incorporated multiple meanings. From the earliest ceremonial complexes of the Initial Period, once special architecture became the focus of settlement ritual, the architecture and its decoration symbolized religious belief.

CLASSIFICATIONS OF SPACES

Ritual space comprised positive volume, negative volume and neutral areas. Platforms and stepped pyramids were positive structures that mimicked the surrounding landscape of hills and mountains. Negative spaces – sunken courtyards, temple interiors and walled compounds – mimicked natural voids such as caves, valleys and gullies. Walled compounds divided space into territories to confine people, things and activities within the compound, and to restrict some people from the space. Neutral space can be conceived in the more open areas of ceremonial complexes, such as larger courts at ground level, or particularly large walled areas, in which the general public could be accommodated to witness and participate in part in ritual ceremonies.

Above: The double-headed rainbow deity in sculpted mud plaster decorates the platform walls at Huaca el Dragón, near Chan Chan.

Below: Stone heads at Tiwanaku perpetuated a long tradition of decapitation and trophy-head cults, also prominent in the Chavín Cult.

Within neutral space the public could be included as far as they were allowed by the specialists. Their activities could thus be controlled by the ruling elite and specialist religious leaders.

Architectural spaces thus represented specialized areas where ritual enactment could proceed in a controlled manner. The spaces themselves symbolized part of the ritual.

COLOURS AND SOUNDS

Decoration on architecture also symbolized religious concepts. The bright colours painted on sculptural adornment were signals, although their meanings are only generally understood by reference to Inca records from the Spanish chroniclers. The effort to produce the pigments and the use of such bright and numerous shades indicates an early significance, even if their exact meanings are unknown. Apart from anything else, the colours drew attention to the sculpture and architecture, enforcing the presence of the deities portrayed and invoking awe within the beholder. For example, the gaze of the fearsome-looking supernatural face

Above: Even minor detail was symbolic. Here two shaped white stones represent the sacred condor's bill at a fountain at Machu Picchu.

of the Decapitator God on the platform walls and Great Plaza of the Huaca de la Luna at Moche cannot be escaped.

Similarly, there is some evidence for the use of sound. Various shell and pottery trumpets, and drums, must have been used in ritual, and their full effect would have been best appreciated from the heights of platforms by a congregation below. The ritual use of water, channelled through temples and compounds, is notable at Chavín de Huánta (where it is linked to sound), at Tiwanaku and in Cuzco, showing that the practice was a long tradition from the Early to the Late Horizon. It can only reflect the importance of water in ancient Andean survival and agriculture, as benign and life-giving rains filled the lakes and rivers, but also as the power of the weather gods and the forces of storms and thunder. It has been argued that the intricate channelling of water within the temple interiors at Chavín de Huántar was deliberately used to replicate the roar of the elements, from the temple to a presumably awestruck congregation in the courtyard outside.

PATHWAYS AND PROCESSIONS

The ritual pathways of the Nazca lines and of the Inca *ceque* lines represent architectural extensions. 'Owned' by selective groups, they represented symbolic procedures and procession routes. As well as geometric designs similar to those used on pottery and textiles, the Nazca lines and other geoglyphs form the shapes of animals and plants that were held sacred. Such animals were

recognized as representative of religious concepts and powers. Large cleared rectangular areas among the Nazca geoglyphs presumably also served as arenas for group ceremonies.

The *ceque* routes of the Incas were both physical and theoretical. They were actual roads followed by intended victims, leading up to their ritual sacrifice, and also lines of sight for astronomical observation and priestly divination. *Ceque* lines divided up the space between them into sacred parcels. Along them, architectural elements were encountered (natural rock outcrops, sometimes modified, caves and springs) and man-made temples.

Moche murals display ritual processions, again in bright colours. They hark back to the single-colour procession of warriors around the platform at Cerro Sechín, one of Moche's predecessors in the north coast valleys. These murals, along with similar scenes on ceramics and elite burials with the costumes of the scenes' participants, are known to depict ritual combat, sacrifices and blood-offerings dedicated to powerful and demanding gods and goddesses.

PAN-ANDEAN SYMBOLISM

Such careful organization of space and the use of prescribed ritual routes were incorporated into Andean religious thought from the first ceremonial complexes. They are recognizable in the U-shaped complexes of the northern coastal valleys and sierra; in the Nazca platforms and plazas of Cahuachi; in the carefully laid-out courts and temples of Chavín de Huántar; in the great mound complexes of 'mountains' on the coast built by the Moche; in the temple-topped pyramid and open plazas of Pachacamac; in the multiple platforms and walled courts of Tiwanaku; in the rigidly organized architecture of Wari central sierra cities; in the sacred royal compounds of Chan Chan of the Chimú; and in the ritual layout of puma-shaped Cuzco and the Sacsahuaman angular-walled Temple to the Sun. The repeated use of the same fundamental forms reveals the underlying essence of the most ancient Andean creation beliefs.

Below: A procession of naked slaves or war captives decorates the Moche pyramid-platform of El Brujo.

COLOURS AS SYMBOLS

The use of bright colours to decorate ceramics, textiles, and adobe and stone sculpture in ancient Andean cultures was universal. From the earliest times, ceramics were painted, textiles featured a variety of dyed colours and were painted on, and murals and sculptures were painted. Stone and metal were often chosen for their colours to create contrast and symbolic statements.

Black, white, green, blue, yellow and shades of red were the primary colours used. Although such deliberate use of colour must reflect metaphorical meaning, its specifics cannot be known with certainty.

EARLY COLOURING
The Initial Period adobe sculptures at Moxeke and Huaca de los Reyes/Caballo Muerto, and the Cerro Sechín sculptured stone slabs were all originally painted in reds, blue and white. The use of black limestone and white granite on the Black

Below: Vivid use of red on an Inca wooden kero *drinking cup symbolizes domination and perhaps blood in a llama-herding scene.*

Above: Black llamas, much rarer than white and grey ones, were especially sacred and valuable for sacrifices as well as their wool.

and White Portal of the New Temple at Chavín de Huántar was a deliberate choice, and must have been meant to convey a statement: juxtaposing two opposites, and reflecting duality and the opposing forces of nature. As well as the choice of stone colours, the two columns were carved with a male hawk and a female eagle, reinforcing the message.

On Chavín textiles, the background colour was laid out first, then design lines filled in with blue, gold and green threads. Nazca potters perfected no fewer than 13 ceramic slip colours, and such deliberate craftsmanship and choice reflects the importance that colours had in the culture.

The juxtaposition of contrasting colours was a universal practice, presumably a visual symbol of duality and opposition. In Wari art the use of one contrasting colour within a general scheme of harmonious colours must have conveyed some meaning to those who knew how to interpret it. Metallurgists' choice of metals frequently contrasted gold and silver, presumably for the same purpose.

BLUE
Spanish chroniclers recorded some colour meanings among the Inca. How far this can be projected into pre-Inca times is unknown.

The *Huarochirí Manuscript* describes Huatya Curi, son of the sky god Paria Caca. In one of his many contests with his hostile brother-in-law, he danced in a blue feather tunic and white cotton breechcloths, the colours of the sky and clouds, worn, presumably, to honour his father. The Inca rarely used blue, but this colour became more common in clothing in colonial times.

RED
This colour was favoured in Moche ceramics and textiles. Red-on-white fine-line narrative drawings were a Moche speciality. Many narrative scenes show ritual sacrifice, and it is assumed that red is therefore symbolic of blood. It might also be representative of the dawn and dusk skies, when sacrifices might have been performed, also of mud-laden rivers during the rainy season in north coast valleys.

The Incas associated red with conquest and rulership, as blood and perhaps symbolizing conspicuousness. The Inca state insignia, Mascaypacha, comprised a crimson tassel hung from a braid tied around the head. The chronicler Murúa says that each woollen red thread represented a conquered people and the blood of an enemy's severed head. Red seems to have become symbolic of the long tradition of severed heads that began as early as the stone panels at Initial Period Cerro Sechín.

The Inca founder Manco Capac wore a bright red tunic when he stood on the hill of Huanacauri to impress the populace. His 15th-century successor Pachacuti wore a long red robe when he confronted the giant storm god who came down the River Urubamba wreaking destruction.

Inca ritual face-painting featured a red stripe from ear to ear across the bridge of the nose. Sometimes pigment was used,

Below: This Moche scene shows a sacred sky serpent across the stirrup spout and a fishing boat representing the abundance of the sea.

but at other times the blood of a sacrificed llama or the blood of a child *capacocha* sacrifice was used. The blood was smeared across the face of the deceased Inca's mummy to emphasize and enforce the bond of conquered peoples to the living emperor.

Coloured threads and combinations of threads in *quipu* recording devices were also used to represent commodities and perhaps directions, places and numbers.

GREEN
In contrast to red, the Incas associated green with tropical peoples and lands. When Inca Roca, sixth emperor, marched against the rainforest Chunchos of Antisuyu, he went in the guise of a jaguar, donned a green mantle and adopted tropical habits such as chewing coca and tobacco, both green.

The significance of the green stone idol, Yampallec, brought by the legendary conqueror and dynasty founder Naymlap to the north coast, is unknown. The dynasty must have associated green stone with ritual and rule.

Green was also associated with the rainy season, a somewhat obvious link with plant growth and, by extension, with sorcery, drugs and love. Finally, the chronicler Betanzos describes the association of green with ancestors: Pachacuti Inca's kin group washed and dyed themselves with a green herbal plant.

BLACK
Black was fundamentally a metaphor for creation and origins. The Incas, and presumably pre-Inca cultures, associated black with death. In the Camay Quilla ceremony (January/ February) to officially end the rainy season, celebrants dressed in black clothing and blackened their faces with soot. They held a long rope wrapped around the emperor, and newly initiated teenage boys held a mock battle in black tunics. A year after the death of an emperor, his kin group

Above: An Inca noble painted on a wooden kero *drinking cup is dressed in symbolic red, representing conquest and rulership.*

painted their faces black and held a ceremony with his mummified body. Four men with blackened faces concluded the ceremony at the time that it was believed the spirit of the dead Inca arrived at its destination.

Black llamas were sacrificed in the same month, to signify reciprocal ties between the Inca ruler and his subjects. Men dressed in black performed the Mayucati ritual – throwing the ashes of the year's sacrifices into the River Ollantaytambo and following it out of Cuzco by night. The ashes were carried though conquered lands and ultimately to sea as offerings to Viracocha, the supreme deity.

The black-cloud constellations of Inca cosmology, comprising the spaces between stars, were believed to be sources of life and fecundity. They were linked to the colours of the rainbow by association with the deep purple stripe, which the Incas considered the first colour, representing Mama. The remaining colours, called 'lower thing' and 'next thing' descending in colour intensity, were held to descend from Mama.

PILGRIMAGE AND ORACLE SITES

The difficulties inherent in explaining supernatural concepts through images difficult to produce with the existing technology may have fostered the growth of pilgrimage centres. Their symbolic art, meant to show the complexities of supernatural belief, could be combined with complex architecture and mystery in a central place. The spread of religious ideas could be accomplished by bringing converts to a place held most sacred and then dispersing them again, convinced of or reinforced in their belief in the cult. Portable art decorated with the symbolic images of the religious concepts would help remind those living at distance from the cult centre of the tenets of the cult.

Similarly, the sacredness of a cult centre, where the truth was held and expounded by its priests, would become a focus for other-worldly experience. The architecture of the centre could provoke and enhance such an experience.

Below: The Semi-subterranean Court enclosed formal ritual space at Tiwanaku, capital city of the Titicaca Basin.

Above: The city of Pachacamac endured as a powerful centre of religious devotion to the supreme being for more than a millennium.

A WESTERN VIEW?
These general concepts seem self-evident, yet they are overlain with concepts of conversion and missionary work as documented in Western European and North American historical experience. This experience may be different from, and so not directly applicable to, ancient Andean religious experience, for which there is essentially no archaeological evidence.

The growth in the importance of special sites as religious cult centres is not unique to Andean civilization. It is, however, a centrally important part of ancient Andean belief from at least the Early Horizon. The central location of ceremonial complexes either within a domestic settlement or among surrounding domestic settlements began in the preceding Initial Period. Many sites are identified by scholars as pilgrimage sites: Chavín de Huántar, Cahuachi, Pukará, Tiwanaku, Pachacamac and Inca Cuzco itself.

THE PACHACAMAC MODEL
It is the Spanish colonial records describing the cult and oracle at Pachacamac that provide the basis for the model of ancient Andean pilgrimage and oracle sites. Essential elements of the Pachacamac model were a special chamber housing a cult idol, access to which was restricted to specialist priests; oracular predictions; public plazas for general ritual; and the establishment of a network of affiliated shrines in other communities.

CHAVÍN DE HUÁNTAR
The earliest widely recognized cult centre in ancient Andean civilization was Chavín de Huántar, for it appears to fulfil at least some of these criteria. Its complex architecture deliberately instilled a sense of mystery, supernatural presence and exclusiveness. First the Old Temple, then

the much larger New Temple, comprised numerous interconnected chambers holding a cult monolith carved with the symbolic image of a supernatural being. Its isolation within the temple clearly restricted access to it and made it more awesome and powerful. Its complex symbolic imagery made it necessary for specialists to interpret it.

The Old Temple contained the Lanzón, or Great Image, monolith and the New Temple held the Raimondi Stela. The curious position of the former, piercing through the roof of one chamber to a hidden upper chamber, implies an oracular room. The acoustics of the water channels of the temples also implies the mysterious use of echoing and mimicry of the elements.

Both the Old Temple and the New Temple were accompanied by open plazas. These were wide, flat spaces between the arms of the U-shaped platform mounds, and within each was a sunken ceremonial courtyard: round in the Old Temple, square in the New Temple.

The imagery of several Chavín deities became widespread: the Staff Deity and feline and serpent imagery in particular. Yet, felines and serpents were common

elements in earlier cultures throughout an even wider area. Several sites, however, show imagery, though locally produced, that is identical to that from Chavín.

At Huaricoto, north-west of Chavín, the Early Horizon ritual precinct contained a carved stone 'spatula' depicting the deity of the Lanzón. There is also decorated pottery of Chavín design. Other sites in adjacent highlands also have portable artefacts of Chavín style. It may be, however, that the Chavín Cult was adopted in addition to established local patron deities.

More revealing is Karwa on the southern coast, near the Paracas necropolis site. Textiles from the Karwa tomb are

Above: The Inca trail has become a modern 'pilgrimage' route. This is the sentry post of Runkuaqay on the way to Machu Picchu.

decorated not in the local Paracas style but in the bright colours and images of the Chavín Cult, including their composition, bilateral symmetry and double profiling. The Chavín Staff Deity, here in female form and sometimes called the Karwa Goddess, is unmistakable. Such faithful adherence to the Chavín orthodoxy seems to betray Chavín presence or a shrine in a network of Chavín shrines.

In the northern highlands, Chavín stone sculpture from Kuntur Wasi and Pacopampa clearly displays Chavín imagery. In the upper Lambayeque river drainage, two matching carved stone columns were found, reminiscent of the Black and White Portal columns at Chavín de Huántar. Further, in the Chicama Valley there were painted adobe columns (now destroyed), one of which was painted with a winged creature like those on the Black and White Portal.

The distribution of these sites across cultural spheres and production zones indicates the establishment of Chavín shrines and may imply the integration of the cult into local community structures.

Left: Chavín de Huántar became the earliest widely recognized pilgrimage and oracular site in the Early Horizon.

TEMPLES AND SUNKEN COURTS

The earliest ceremonial complexes in the northern coastal valleys and adjacent northern Peruvian sierra organized both positive and negative space in the forms of platforms and sunken courts. The forming of a U-shape, comprising a tiered platform at the base and two elongated platform wings enclosing a sunken court and a level, open plaza around it, was clearly symbolic. The form was repeated at numerous coastal valley and northern and central Peruvian high-land sites. Its mere repetition underlies a core of common religious belief.

U-SHAPE ORIGINS

The U-shaped ceremonial structure was the culmination of the development of two elements: platforms and subterranean courts. The U-shaped temple established at Chavín de Huántar as the centre of a reli-gious cult had representations as far afield as the southern coastal valleys. But the form began much earlier, in the Initial Period.

The building of platform mounds began at least as early as 3000BC. The earliest were those at Aspero in the Supe Valley: the Huaca de los Idolos and the Huaca de los Sacrificios, among a ceremonial complex of as many as 17 platforms. Within the next few centuries

Above: The great temple pyramid platform of Huaca Larga incorporated La Ray Mountain in the centre of the Moche city Tucume Viejo.

smaller complexes of mounds had been built at Piedra Parada, also in the Supe Valley, El Paraíso in the Chillón Valley, Río Seco in the Chancay Valley, Bandurria in the Huaura Valley, Salinas de Chao and Los Morteros in the Chao Valley, and at Kotosh, a highland site in the Río Huallaga-Higueras Valley.

Ancient Andeans were thus building ceremonial architecture as early as the first royal pyramids in Egypt and temple platforms, called ziggurats, in ancient Mesopotamia; and Andean ceremonial platforms are the earliest in the New World, predating the first Olmec earthen pyramids in Mesoamerica by at least 1,000 years.

Two 'traditions' of raised platforms developed, both based on ritual on top of the platform and open ceremonial space at the base for an attendant congregation: the Supe-Aspero Tradition and the El Paraíso Tradition. Chambers and niches to house ritual objects were built on top as the traditions evolved.

The practice of building circular sunken courts (*plazas hundidas*) also began in northern Peru during the 2nd millennium BC. Most often they were built in association with a platform at its base and aligned with the platform's staircase. Early examples include Salinas de Chao, Piedra Parada and highland La Galgada.

Only occasionally was a sunken court built as the sole ceremonial element, for example at Alto Salavery.

By about 2000BC the stone-built civic-ceremonial centre at El Paraíso was the largest Preceramic Period civic-ceremonial centre on the coast. With a group of small temples forming a base and two elongated parallel platforms, it was a configuration transitional to the classic U-shaped struc-tures of the Initial Period.

Below: The mud-plaster walls of the Middle Temple at Garagay feature a fanged being with spider attributes and water symbolism.

Below: Huaca de la Luna, mimicking the hill behind it, another Moche mud-brick temple of the Early Intermediate Period.

SECHÍN ALTO

By 1200BC the U-shaped ceremonial complex at Sechín Alto was the largest civic-ceremonial complex in the New World. At its fullest development it included all the elements of the classic U-shaped ritual centre. Construction began in about 1400BC (although one radiocarbon date from the site is as early as 1721BC). Its principal platform ruin still stands some 44m (144ft) above the plain and covers an area 300 × 250m (985 × 820ft). The huge U-shape is formed by sets of parallel platform mounds extending from the base corners of the pyramid, and forming part of a ritual area 400 × 1,400m (1,310 × 4,600ft). Running north-east from the principal pyramid is a succession of plazas and sunken courts.

The principal wings enclose a plaza with an early, small sunken court. Beyond the ends of these mounds there is a larger circular sunken court, then another open area formed by two long, thin parallel platforms flanking a plaza approximately 375m (1,230ft) square. Forming the end of the complex, 1km (½ mile) north-east of the principal platform, an H-shaped platform faces the main pyramid and flanks the largest circular sunken court, 80m (262ft) in diameter. The principal pyramidal platform is faced with enormous granite blocks set in clay mortar. Some of the blocks are up to 1.4m (4.5ft) on each side and weigh up to 2 tonnes (tons).

Surrounding the Sechín Alto complex there was 10.5 sq km (2,560 acres) of buildings and smaller platforms.

Above: The high stone walls of the rectangular Semi-subterranean court at Tiwanaku were decorated with stone trophy heads.

Like other U-shaped complexes, the site must have been a religious centre that served its surrounding area. Judging by its size, it may have served a considerable region as well.

RITUAL MEANINGS

The practical aspects of the arrangements of the U-shaped complex seem obvious: a raised platform from which to address a crowd, an open area for the crowd to stand in and a sunken court for exclusive ritual. There is an element of implied control in the arrangement: the congregation was partly confined between the arms of the U-shape, and their attention could be monitored from the height of the platform or focused on the sunken court.

Perhaps the two elements symbolize the concepts of a sky deity and an earth deity. Ritual may have involved procession from one to the other. Assuming strong naturalism in early Andean religious thought, the gods were believed to inhabit or infuse the natural landscape. Thus platforms were representative mountains and sunken courtyards representative valleys or caves. Further, their shapes might have represented the sky father and the earth mother, the womb and the symbolic shapes of man and woman. In seeming recognition of the source of life-giving water as the mountain thunder and rainstorms, the open ends of U-shaped complexes were oriented towards the mountains, their U-shapes imitating the collecting valleys.

Below: The ultimate sacred circular court of the great Sacsahuaman Temple of Cuzco formed the puma's head of the Inca capital.

SACRED CEMETERIES

Honouring the gods in the southern coastal desert cultures was focused on cemetery rites and ancestor worship. The dry climate has been instrumental in preserving the buried bodies and artefacts in the tombs.

SHARED TRADITIONS
The Paracas and Nazca cultures developed in continuous succession through the Early Horizon and Early Intermediate Period in the southern valleys and deserts of Peru, focusing their settlement and economy around sea fishing and shellfish collecting, and later on maize and cotton agriculture. Early Paracas ceramics and textile decoration shows much influence from Chavín de Huántar. At Karwa, near the early Paracas necropolis, textiles from an elite tomb are decorated with one of the best representations of the Staff Deity. Here she is the Staff Goddess, thought to honour a local goddess while at the same time acting as a 'wife' or 'sister' shrine to the Chavín Cult in the north.

Below: Stone slab circles at the Sillustani necropolis of the Colla people possibly served as the sites of burial ceremonies before bodies were taken to their kinship chullpa tower.

The Paracas and Nazca developed their own distinct style and deities. Quintessential was the Oculate Being, a wide-eyed distinctively local deity depicted in brightly painted ceramic masks and portrayed, flying, on pottery and textiles.

THE CAVERNAS CEMETERY
Paracas settlements covered an area of some 54ha (133 acres) around a core area of about 4ha (10 acres) on the low slopes of the Cerro Colorado on the Paracas Peninsula. Among the sprawling habitation remains, special areas were used as cemeteries for hundreds of burials, possibly the foci of family cults for nearby and more distant settlements.

Great care was taken in the burial of the dead in the Cavernas cemetery area. The naked corpse was tied with a cord into a flexed seated position. The body was wrapped in several layers of richly coloured textiles, both cotton and wool, revealing trade contact with highland cultures for llama wool. Placed in a basket and accompanied by plain and richly decorated ceramics, and sheet-metal jewellery, the whole was finally wrapped in plain cotton cloth. Such 'bundles' were

Above: Cahuachi, a sacred 'city' of about 40 temple mounds, served as a funerary and pilgrimage centre for Nazca religion.

then enshrined in large subterranean crypts, which were reopened and used repeatedly over generations, presumably by kin groups as family mausoleums.

PARACAS INFLUENCE
A prominent element in Paracas and Nazca religious ritual was decapitation. Trophy heads adorn pottery and stream from the waists of Oculate Beings on textiles. In addition, the skulls of many Paracas burials show evidence of ritual surgery, with small sections of the cranium being removed by incision and drilling. The exact purpose of this operation is unknown – it may have been ritual or medical. The Nazca inherited veneration of the Oculate Being from the Paracas culture.

Highland drought had caused increasing aridity in the coastal plains. It seems likely, therefore, that the Oculate Being was

associated with water and precipitation. Flying Oculate Beings perhaps betray a fixation with the sky. As a practical measure, the Nazca developed an elaborate system of underground aqueducts to collect and channel the maximum amount of water around Cahuachi. Great stepped spiral galleries, cobbled with smooth river stones, gave access to the wells.

Two of the most important Nazca settlements were Cahuachi and Ventilla, the first a ritual 'city', the second an urban 'capital'. Ventilla covered an area of at least 200ha (495 acres) with terraced housing, walled courts and small mounds. It was linked to Cahuachi by a Nazca line across the intervening desert.

Revealing their wide Andean contacts, Nazca ceramics and textiles are also decorated with a multitude of supernatural, clearly symbolic images. As well as sea creatures, crabs, insects and serpents that would have been familiar local sights, images of monkeys, felines and tropical birds from the rainforests were also used.

Below: In the Nazca cemetery (and Paracas, shown above) of the southern desert coast cultures, the desiccated conditions preserved the hair, fibres and textiles of the deceased.

The trophy-head cult extended to caches of trepanned, severed skulls of sacrificial victims being found among the remains in Nazca cemeteries.

LINES AND CEREMONIAL MOUNDS
Nazca religion is defined by two elements. Cahuachi was a ritual complex concerned with spiritual matters rather than daily life. Covering an area of 150ha (370 acres), it comprised a complex of 40 ceremonial mounds made by shaping natural hillocks into terracing and associated plazas. It was used from about AD100 to 550, and thereafter continued in use as a mortuary ground and place of votive offering. The entire site appears to have been devoted to mortuary practices, probably as family vaults following the Paracas tradition.

The largest mound was 30m (98ft) high, modified into six or seven terraces with adobe-brick retaining walls. Most of the tombs have been looted, but the few unlooted tombs excavated yielded mummified burials accompanied by exquisitely decorated, multicoloured woven burial coats and ceramics. Some contained animal sacrifices and ritual human sacrifices of Nazca men, women and children. Some skulls had excrement inserted into the mouths; some had been perforated and a

Above: The Paracas cemetery (and Nazca, shown below left) of the Early Horizon and Early Intermediate Period served numerous cities as kinship burial mausoleums.

carrying cord inserted; some had blocked eyes, cactus spines pinning the mouth shut, and tongues removed and put in pouches.

The second element was the Nazca lines, the geoglyphs forming geometric patterns, clusters of straight lines and recognizable animal and plant figures. There are some 1,300km (808 miles) of such lines, including 300 figures. A huge 490m-long (1,600ft) arrow, pointing towards the Pacific Ocean, is thought to be a symbol to invoke rains. The lines were undoubtedly associated with the Nazca preoccupation with water and crop fertility, together with worship of mountain deities – the ultimate source of water.

Cahuachi was abandoned as the coastal valleys became more arid. Simultaneously, there was an increase in the number and elaboration of Nazca lines. Regarded as ritual pathways, perhaps like the family vaults dedicated to kin groups, the increase in their use represents desperate efforts to placate the gods who had forsaken them. As Cahuachi was abandoned, people covered the mounds with layers of sand.

CEREMONIAL COMPOUNDS

Platforms and U-shaped complexes continued to form the core elements of ceremonial centres in the northern coastal valleys and highlands through the Early Horizon. In time, Moche platforms of the Early Intermediate Period achieved both the shape and proportions of hills, as if the people were building their own mountains on the coast. The Huaca del Sol and Huaca de la Luna at Moche are the largest adobe-built pyramidal platforms ever constructed in the Americas.

ALTIPLANO TRADITIONS

In the southern highlands of the Titicaca Basin architectural symbolism also mirrored the landscape. Here there developed a tradition comprising a central platform mound with a central, square sunken court at the top surrounded by rectangular temples arranged symmetrically around the court. This 'tradition' of a sacred compound flourished in the late 2nd and 1st millennia BC and is named after its principal example, Chiripa, near the southern end of Lake Titicaca. Compared to the huge mounds built at U-shaped complexes, Altiplano mounds were relatively modest in scale. The final height of the Chiripa mound, reached late in the 1st millennium BC when the site was used by people from Tiwanaku, was a mere 6m (19½ft).

Below: The ciudadelas of Chimú and Chan Chan comprised courtyards and chambers for ritual and ceremony as 'cities' of the dead.

THE PUKARÁ TRADITION

In the Early Horizon, religious and political focus shifted north of the lake during the latter half of the 1st millennium BC and became centred at the site of Pukará, northwest of Lake Titicaca. Unlike U-shaped complexes, the Pukará Tradition comprised monumental masonry-clad structures terraced against hillsides. The principal terrace had a monumental staircase and was topped by a rectangular sunken court with one-room buildings around three sides – a style that was reminiscent of Chiripa.

The Pukará Tradition's religious focus was on the Yaya-Mama cult of male and female symbolism, although it also shared the feline and serpentine imagery prevalent throughout contemporary Andean civilization. This emphasis on father sky and mother earth is reflected not only in the carved images of Yaya and Mama monoliths, but also in the combination of platforms and sunken courts in association with ritual architecture.

These developments were not isolated, however. The economy of the Altiplano was largely based on llama pastoralism and the wool was traded with the southern coastal cultures of Paracas and Nazca and farther

Above: The mud walls and rooms at the Tchudi ciudadela at Chan Chan were sculpted with attention to detail throughout.

afield. Thus, religious ideas must have been encountered from northern regions through the Chavín Cult and its aftermath.

THE TIWANAKU COMPOUND

Pukará dominated the Titicaca Basin Altiplano for about four centuries. Its inheritor in the later Early Intermediate Period and the Middle Horizon was Tiwanaku, a ceremonial city of proportions and complexity to rival the waning Chavín de Huántar and any northern and southern coastal valley contemporaries of the Moche and Nazca.

Two rival empires eventually dominated the Middle Horizon: the highland peoples of Tiwanaku and Wari. Although they shared religious concepts, they conquered respective areas and reached an uneasy settlement with each other at a highland boundary in the La Raya Pass south of Cuzco.

Ceremonial buildings at Chiripa and Pukará herald those at Tiwanaku. The tradition of the enclosed courtyard was continued and expanded into large public, walled ceremonial areas and semi-subterranean courts. Platforms remained relatively low and sunken courts stayed rectangular in shape.

From Tiwanaku, Mt Illimani dominates the view and is perhaps replicated in the platform mound of the Akapana pyramid. In nearby Lake Titicaca sit the Island of the Sun and the Island of the Moon, believed to be the birthplaces of the sun and moon. The moat around the Akapana and Kalasasaya structures renders the complex a symbolic island, although it can be argued that in the flat compound the water in a moat would flood the structural footings and drains. Nevertheless, the essence of the symbolic island is there.

AKAPANA AND THE PUMA PRIEST
The Akapana temple comprised a six-stepped mound in the shape of half a stepped diamond, known as the Andean Cross. The top was occupied by either a palace/temple or by a sunken court in the shape of a full-stepped diamond cross.

Above: Wari's southernmost provincial centre, Pikilacta, was laid out as repetitive, adjoining, symmetrical stone-walled compounds.

Excavations revealed that ritual eating and burials took place there, including the primary burial of a man seated and holding a puma effigy incense burner. There was also a cache of sacrificed llama bones, and most of the skeletons found buried on the first terrace and under its foundations were headless. The upper terraced walls of the platform were decorated with tenoned stone puma heads, and at the base of the western staircase a black basalt image of a seated, puma-headed person (*chachapuma*) holding a severed head in his lap was found. Another *chachapuma* sculpture is a standing figure holding dangling severed heads.

Such symbolism – severed heads, pumas, the western location indicative of the setting sun and night – implies shamanic ritual, puma transformation and death.

On the huge Sun Gate at Tiwanaku, the central figure has often been associated with the sun, owing to his rayed head. The frontal stance and arms holding staffs equally associate the figure with the Staff Deity of Chavín. Another interpretation, however, can be based on the stepped dais on which the figure stands. It is identical to the half-stepped diamond court of the Akapana and could imply association with the *chachapuma*.

Such complex, composite, enigmatic imagery is typical of the tradition of multiple meanings and hidden or obscure meaning in Andean religious symbolism. Specialists are needed to interpret the imagery, perhaps according to the ceremony and occasion.

Left: In its remote mountain location, Machu Picchu was a sacred Inca city and religious retreat at the heart of the empire.

THE PACHACAMAC NETWORK

The religious network of Pachacamac was organized in sympathy with Andean concepts of community, mutual exchange, taxation and kinship.

THE ORACLE SITE

The cult centre was the city of Pachacamac at the mouth of the River Lurín, south of modern Lima. It comprised a complex of adobe platforms and plazas. An isolated chamber at the summit of the principal platform housed an oracle. There were open plazas in which pilgrims could fast and participate in public ceremony. Access to the oracle chamber was strictly limited to cult specialists. Oracular messages were given by these specialists concerning life and the future: predictions about the weather, favourable interventions of the gods with the elements, protection

Below: Pachacamac, established in the 3rd century AD, soon became a cult centre for the supreme deity, Pachacamac.

against diseases, specialized knowledge about the best times for planting and the harvest. Earthquakes, crop failure and other disasters were believed to be the result of antagonizing the god Pachacamac.

Much of what is known of the Pachacamac oracle site is from descriptions from Inca and early Spanish colonial sources. The elements of the central coastal ceremonial city incorporated the full range of Andean religious architecture: platform mounds, sacred compounds and plazas for congregational worship, and exclusive chambers for restrictive ritual performed by specialists.

Distant communities solicited the priests for permission to establish branch shrines to Pachacamac. If deemed to have the ability to support cult activities, a priest from Pachacamac was assigned to the new shrine and the community supplied labour on and produce from assigned lands to support him and the shrine. Part was kept for the shrine and

the rest sent to the Pachacamac oracle site. Such branches were thought of as the wives, children or brothers and sisters of the main cult complex.

THE CULT

Pachacamac – 'earth/time maker' – was the creator deity of the peoples of central coastal Peru and the adjacent Andes. The Pachacamac cult and shrine began to become important in the latter half of the Early Intermediate Period. By the 16th century a network of shrines spanned the range of Andean Area production zones from the coast into the highlands, as well as north and south along the coast.

The cult itself spread from the coast, first north and south, then inland into the highlands, where worship of Pachacamac rivalled the highland creator deity Viracocha. Its spread inland is associated with the inland spread of the Andean Area Quechua language.

In the Middle Horizon and Late Intermediate Period the cult and oracle site overtook the importance of local deities to the north and south coasts – those of the Nazca and Moche. Even when the mountain empire of Wari rose and its armies threatened the coast, ultimately to conquer Pachacamac and incorporate the city into its empire, Pachacamac remained independently important as an oracle site. In fact, despite being politically demoted to an outpost of Wari power, Pachacamac remained religiously important throughout the Late Intermediate Period.

When the Incas arrived in the Late Horizon they immediately recognized the importance of the oracle, not only locally but also throughout the region and beyond. They recognized Pachacamac's importance in relation to Viracocha and sought to accommodate the religious concepts that both gods embodied.

The cult thus endured for more than a millennium. In addition to its primary religious purpose, it became entrenched in

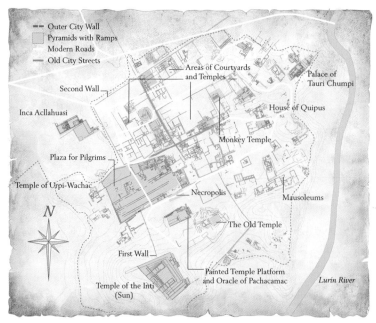

Outer City Wall
Pyramids with Ramps
Modern Roads
Old City Streets

Areas of Courtyards and Temples

Second Wall

Inca Acllahuasi

Palace of Tauri Chumpi

House of Quipus

Monkey Temple

Plaza for Pilgrims

Temple of Urpi-Wachac

N

Necropolis

Mausoleums

The Old Temple

First Wall

Painted Temple Platform and Oracle of Pachacamac

Lurín River

Temple of the Inti (Sun)

the community and its social structure, in its agricultural production and in the redistribution of wealth. There is, however, no recorded evidence of the use of missionaries to spread the cult's ideology.

EARLY ORIGINS

The site of Pachacamac became important locally from the latter half of the Early Intermediate Period, when the first phases of the pyramid platform to the sun and adjoining Temple to Pachacamac were built. It became an important political power during the Middle Horizon, and may have been partly responsible for the northern shift of Moche power in the late Early Intermediate Period/Middle Horizon.

Wari presence is attested by the architecture and a Wari cemetery, and the continuance of the site's religious importance is implied by a wooden post carved with figures of Wari-like divinities, as well as stone figurines. The upper part of the post depicts a man holding a bola and wearing a chest ornament; the lower part is carved with double-headed serpents, jaguars and a figure with attributes like those of the 'angels' on the Gateway to the Sun at Tiwanaku.

LATE HORIZON PACHACAMAC

The 16th-century chronicler Cieza de León noted the importance of the shrine and Inca reverence for it, while the 17th-century writer Father Bernabe Cobo devoted an entire chapter to a detailed description of the ancient site.

Cobo describes how devotees of the Pachacamac Cult visited the centre specifically to petition the priests there to establish satellite shrines in the cities of their homelands, and to permit them to erect 'wife', 'son' or 'daughter' shrines of their local deities, to Pachacamac. Prophecy from the oracle was sought for everything from health, fortune, the well-being of

Below: The Incas recognized Pachacamac's importance, but also built a temple to Inti, the sun god, here.

Above: The main pyramid platform at Pachacamac was surrounded by a vast complex of courtyards and platforms.

crops and flocks, the weather and even the prognosis of Inca battle plans. Defying or neglecting Pachacamac was believed to provoke earthquakes. Offerings in solicitation of oracles included cotton, maize, coca leaves, dried fish, llamas, guinea pigs, fine textiles, ceramic drinking vessels and gold and silver – no doubt useful to the priests.

The arrival of aliens – the Spaniards – caused the oracle to fall silent, although worshippers still visit Pachacamac today to make offerings.

STATE RELIGION

Although the Incas embraced the cults of all those they conquered, and worshipped a pantheon of deities, they insisted on the supremacy of a state religion or cult centred on their own two principal deities: Viracocha and Inti.

Viracocha was more of an all-embracing entity than a specific god or idol. He was not exclusively Inca, rather a long-standing highland creator god. The Inca traced the origin of their right to rule the Andean Area to Viracocha.

Inti, the sun god, was increasingly favoured in day-to-day worship in the late 15th and early 16th centuries, as the empire grew. The importance of the person of the emperor himself was emphasized more, in an attempt to focus the various peoples of the empire on a state cult, not in replacement of long-held beliefs, but to empower the state and enhance the importance of the new regime the Incas brought.

In keeping with Andean pantheism, other major Inca deities were Quilla (moon goddess), Chaska-Qoylor (goddess of Venus), Illapa (weather god: thunder, lightning, rain) and Cuichu (god of the rainbow). The two principal temple complexes in Cuzco were the sacred Coricancha precinct and the imposing Sacsahuaman edifices.

Below: The carved stone walls of the Temple to Inti at the fortress of Ollantatambo – one of many temples spreading the state cult.

Above: This La Tolita (Ecuador) sheet-gold mask of the sun god is similar to the golden image of Inti in the Coricancha Temple.

THE CULT OF INTI

The universality of the sun notwithstanding, the Inca cult of Inti was in many respects unique. The emperor's person became regarded as the earthly embodiment of the sun. His presence and well-being were vital to the life of every subject, and to the prosperity of the land in general. Although the emperor's power was absolute, Inti was believed to be benevolent and generous. Solar eclipses were regarded as signs of his anger and required sacrifice and the solicitation of the return of his favour. As the power of the state cult grew, Inti came to be regarded as Viracocha's intermediary.

By the 16th century Inti/the emperor was so central to the state's well-being that an incident witnessed by priests during ceremonies in his honour appeared to foretell the empire's end. In the reign of Huayna Capac, priests witnessed the fall of an eagle from the sky mobbed by buzzards. The event coincided with reports of the spread of an unknown deadly disease – now known to have been smallpox brought by the Spaniards and spreading from Mesoamerica.

The Coricancha was the centre of the state cult dedicated to Inti's worship. A great mask of sheet gold, moulded into a human face, wide-eyed and grinning, and with rays of zigzag sheet gold ending in miniature masks was housed in its own chamber within the temple.

Rituals and offerings to Inti served constantly to reinforce his power and to confirm the acceptance among the people of the emperor as representing Inti himself. The dead emperor's mummified remains were brought out on ritual occasions, and offered food and drink, and sacrifices, in the belief in the ultimate immortality of Inti.

THE RIGHT TO RULE

Inca right to rule was integral in the state cult. The Incas were painstaking in their efforts to establish, and to alter as necessary, an elaborate mythology to support this close association of Inti, the emperor and power. The Incas demonstrated their right to rule, and unified the empire, by proving that all peoples were descended from the same ancestors, namely the Inca ancestors. The beliefs and cosmologies of those they conquered had to be incorporated into the state religion. To do this alongside continuous acquisition of territories and peoples required an unremitting effort to add to and alter the state mythology. It was important to extend this continuity right back to the first ruler of Cuzco, Manco Capac, and to link the state foundation myth with creation mythology itself.

Official mythology describing the wanderings of the ancestors after their emergence from Tambo Toco cave included the sun's sanction of the founder Manco Capac to rule in his name. In another version Manco Capac is said to have bedecked himself in gold plates to give credulity to his divine appearance when he presented himself at dawn to the people of Cuzco. As the myth was developed, Pachacuti Inca Yupanqui

Below: Machu Picchu was an imperial retreat and sacred city devoted to Inti. This stone-walled chamber was possibly a royal tomb.

(AD 1438–71) added his dream visit and discovery at the spring of Susurpuquio of a crystal tablet bearing the image of Viracocha, who sanctioned his right to rule.

Pachacuti and his son Tupac Inca Yupanqui (1471–93) rebuilt much of Cuzco to accommodate the state cult, including the rebuilding of the Coricancha to enhance the importance of Inti. Thus, the creator, the sun and the emperor were united in one stroke.

ONLY ONE RIVAL

Viracocha's, and therefore Inti's, only serious rival was the cult and oracle of Pachacamac. The site was duly included in the wanderings of Viracocha. The Incas recognized Pachacamac's ancient importance, but to establish the state's

Above: The Observatorio at Machu Picchu was the focus of the cult of Inti. Its central window is placed to align with the rising of the sun on the winter solstice (21 June).

supremacy they built a temple to Inti alongside that of the Pachacamac oracle. Pachacamac's importance was noted, but the temple to Inti in the city was more than a reciprocal shrine dedicated to a regional deity.

The peoples of the empire were also continually reminded of their bond with Inti by *capacocha* sacrifices. Annually, chosen victims were brought from the provinces to Cuzco, then marched back out to their respective provinces again for ritual sacrifice in the name of both Inti and the emperor.

THE SACRED CORICANCHA

The Coricancha or Golden Enclosure of imperial Cuzco, was the centre of the Inca cosmos. It was the supreme ceremonial precinct of the capital, the most sacred *huaca*. It housed the images of Viracocha, the creator, and Inti, god of the sun, and other principal Inca deities. From it emanated the sacred *ceque* lines, both physical roads and cosmic routes of sacred meaning. Forty-one *ceques* led to 328 sacred locations: *huacas* such as caves, springs, stone pillars and points on the surrounding horizon, and important locations such as critical junctions of the city's irrigation canals. One Spanish chronicler, Bernabe Cobo, listed 317 shrines.

These lines bound the Inca world, physical and religious, to the Coricancha 'navel' of the world. From points within the precinct, priests plotted the movements of Mayu (the Milky Way) across the night sky – for example from the Ushnua Pillar, from which sightings of Mayu were taken between two pillars on the distant horizon.

The complex was in the tail of the puma image profile that formed the plan of Cuzco, at the confluence of the rivers Huantanay and Tullamayo, emphasizing the importance of water in the Andean psyche. The second most sacred shrine of the city, Sacsahuaman, formed the puma's head at the prominence above the rivers.

THE SACRED WASI
The complex is sometimes referred to as the Temple of the Sun (Inti), but in fact, the temple to Inti was one of several temples forming the precinct. It was built of stone blocks so carefully fitted together that there was no need for mortar. Its walls were covered with sheet gold – referred to as 'the sweat of the sun' – while another of the temples, to Quilla, was covered in silver ('tears of the moon').

Above: The entrance to the Golden Enclosure of the Coricancha in Cuzco, centre of the state cult of Inti (the sun god).

The precinct comprised six *wasi*, or covered chambers, arranged around a square courtyard. Each *wasi* was dedicated to one of the six principal Inca state deities: Viracocha, Inti, Quilla, Chaska-Qoylor (Venus as morning and evening star), Illapa (weather, thunder, lightning) and Cuichu (rainbow), ranged hierarchically in that order, although Viracocha and Inti were near equivalents.

Each temple housed an image of the deity and the paraphernalia of ritual and worship. A special room was reserved for the storage and care of the mummies of deceased emperors (*mallquis*). On ritual days – for example the winter and summer solstices of Inti Raymi and Capac Raymi – the *mallquis* were brought out in their rich vestments, carried on royal litters in procession around the capital and offered food and drink while court historians recited their deeds. The temple courtyard was also the venue for incantations to and the sanctification of *capacochas* – specially selected sacrificial victims. From the Coricancha they set out

Below: The sacred Coricancha included separate chambers dedicated to and housing the idols of the principal Inca deities.

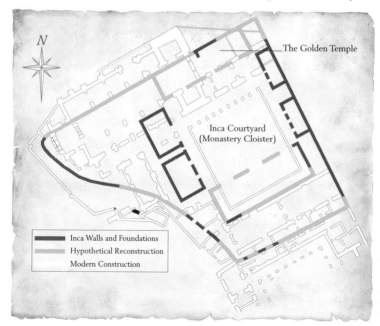

N

The Golden Temple

Inca Courtyard
(Monastery Cloister)

Inca Walls and Foundations
Hypothetical Reconstruction
Modern Construction

Above: Exterior of the Temple of the Moon in the Coricancha, Cuzco, showing the closely fitted blocks without mortar.

on their ritual journey following *ceque* lines back to their provinces, where they were sacrificed.

Other rooms were used to store the sacred objects taken from conquered provinces, including a *huaca* from each subjugated population. These *huacas* were kept in perpetual residence as hostages, and nobles from each subject population were forced to live in the capital for several months each year.

A GOLDEN GARDEN

The intimate mythological connection between Inti and gold was manifested in the temple garden. Here were gold and silver sculptures of a man, a woman, animals and plants representing creation. There were not only jaguars, llamas, guinea pigs and monkeys, but also birds, butterflies and other insects.

The arrangement of the Coricancha was established by the tenth emperor, Pachacuti Inca Yupanqui, in the 15th century, along with his rebuilding of much of the capital.

Something of its splendour was captured in the words of the conquistador Pedro de Cieza de León, as recorded in his *Crónica del Peru*, published in Seville between 1550 and 1553:

'[The temple was] more than 400 paces in circuit…[and the finely hewn masonry was] a dusky or black colour… [with] many openings and doorways… very well carved. Around the wall, half way up, there was a band of gold, two *palmos* wide and four *dedos* in thickness. The doorways and doors were covered with plates of the same metal. Within [there] were four houses, not very large, but with walls of the same kind and covered with plates of gold within and without…. In one of these houses…there was the figure of the Sun, very large and made of gold…enriched with many precious stones.

They also had a garden, the clods of which were made of pieces of gold; and it was artificially sown with golden maize, the stalks, as well as the leaves and cobs, being of that metal … . Besides all this, they had more than 20 golden sheep [llamas] with their lambs, and the shepherds with their slings and crooks to watch them, all made of the same metal. There was [also] a great quantity of jars of gold and silver, set with emeralds; vases, pots, and all sorts of utensils, all of fine gold.'

It was with this golden wealth of the Coricancha that Atahualpa attempted to secure his freedom when he was captured and imprisoned by Francisco Pizarro at Cajamarca in 1532.

Below: Each of the six deity chambers of the Coricancha temples was made with finely dressed stone masonry.

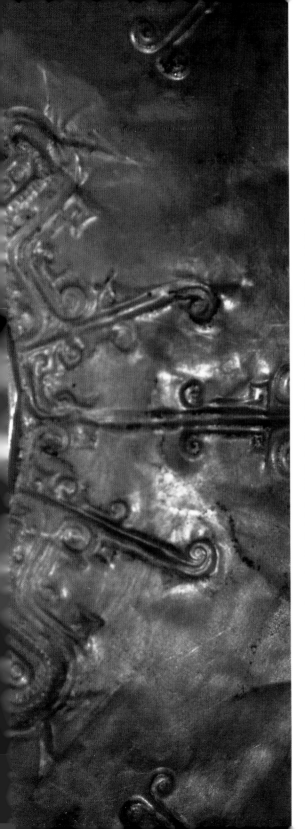

TALES OF THE GODS

Andean religious beliefs are replete with tales and stories of the deities and their representatives on Earth. However, it is not until the final stages of Andean history that we have this literature, and it is only because the stories were recorded by Spanish chroniclers, priests and administrators from their Inca informants.

These stories concentrate on Inca belief, creation and the rise of the Inca state. Some of the tales hark back to earlier cultures – those collected by the Inca in their conquests. For most of the pre-Inca cultures, however, we have only the archaeological evidence. For the Moche culture in particular, there is a rich 'narrative' of painted scenes on pottery, but most other imagery is of a more static than narrative nature. Nevertheless, an event in progress can be detected in the series of marching figures at Initial Period Cerro Sechín and in the tenoned stone heads on the walls of the temple court at Chavín de Huántar, showing the transformation of a shaman into a jaguar.

The use of creatures from distant, alien environments in the art reveals the contact of cultures across widely dispersed regions. By comparing the images with Inca history and mythological tales, it may be possible to find the origins of belief in pre-Inca cultures. Common imagery, modified through time, inevitably reflects continuity in belief.

Left: The face of the sun god on a gold dish made by a Manteño craftsman (Ecuador) at the far north of the Inca Empire.

SUN GOD AND MOON GODDESS

Ancient Andean traditions link the sun and moon as consorts, the sun being male and the moon female. Both were created and set into motion in the sky by Viracocha, the creator. His association with the sun in particular is made in the east–west orientation of his wanderings. The Islands of the Sun and of the Moon in Lake Titicaca were believed to be their birth places.

There is no doubt that the regular cycles of the sun and moon established recurrent, cyclical ritual calendars in ancient Andean cultures. The association of the sun with celestial matters and the moon with earthly cycles was probably reflected in the first ceremonial architecture – raised platforms symbolizing proximity to the sun and sunken courts providing links to the Earth.

Below: Silver and gold, 'tears of the moon' and 'sweat of the sun', represented an essential Andean duality.

The sun and moon were the epitomy of the Andean concept of duality. As opposites they represented light and dark, warmth and cold. However their importance to life and its everyday cycle was balanced, and thus they achieved oneness through the unity of their cycles.

Neither the Incas nor more ancient Andeans made obvious images of the sun or moon. Faces with radiating appendages are common but cannot be categorically identified as the sun. Images of a crescent moon, however, are found among the pre-Inca northern coastal Moche and Chimú cultures, hinting at a complex mythological tradition now obscure. It may be that the Inca suppressed the Chimú's closer association with the moon by their advocacy of the state cult of Inti, the sun.

AI APAEC AND SI
Among the Moche and Chimú the sky god Ai Apaec was perhaps combined with the sun. He was a somewhat remote and

Above: Niches in the interior of the walls of the Temple of the Moon at Pisac resemble those in the Coricancha in Cuzco.

mysterious creator god who, like Viracocha, paid little attention to the daily affairs of humans. Pictured in art as a fanged deity, his throne was regarded as being the mountaintops. His perception as a sky god appears to be implied by his association with a tableau of two scenes separated by a two-headed serpent. In the upper part appear gods, demonic beings and stars; in the lower part are musicians, lords, or slaves, and rain falling from the serpent's body, implying a celestial and terrestrial division.

Si was the Moche and Chimú moon goddess or god, sometimes regarded as the head of the Moche and Chimú pantheon. He/she was a supreme deity, omnipresent, who held sway over the gods and humankind, and controlled the seasons, natural elements, storms and therefore agricultural fertility. His/her origins can be traced to an un-named radiant and armoured war deity who rivalled or even replaced Ai Apaec in importance among the Chimú. One source refers to a Temple of Si-an dedicated to Si, interpreted as the Huaca Singan in the Jequetepeque Valley, possibly the structure known today as the Huaca del Dragón.

The Moche and Chimú realized that the tides and other motions of the sea, and the arrival of the annual rains, were

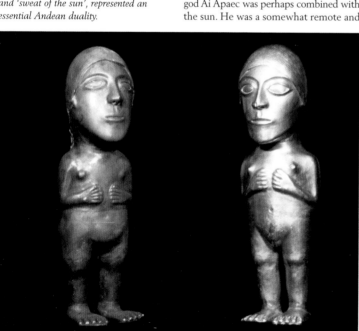

*Above: The sacred Intihuatana Temple to
Inti the sun god at Pisac, a palace city of
Pachacuti Inca Yupanqui, north-east of Cuzco.*

linked to the phases of the moon, and
thus allocated great power to Si because
the food supply and well-being of flocks
depended upon his/her beneficence.
In contrast, the sun was considered to be
a relatively minor deity. Si was regarded
as more powerful than the sun because
he/she could be seen by both night and
day, and eclipses were believed to be
battles between the moon and sun.
An eclipse of the moon was considered a
disastrous augury and regarded with fear;
an eclipse of the sun, however, was
treated as a joyful occasion.

INTI AND QUILLA

The Incas specifically claimed descent
from the sun, but refer less frequently to
the moon as their mother, and her role in
Inca creation myth is less obvious.

Nevertheless, the chronicler Garcilaso de
la Vega describes the moon as sister and
wife of the sun, and thus mother of the
ancestral Incas.

The Incas worshipped Inti, the sun, but
did not frequently portray him. The
emperor was regarded as the 'son of the sun'
and therefore Inti's embodiment on Earth.
They associated the sun with gold, calling
it the 'sweat of the sun', and the moon
with silver, calling it the 'tears of the
moon'. The sun and moon had separate
chambers in the Coricancha Temple. The
sun was represented by a sheet-gold mask
with radiating gold appendages; the moon
by a silver image in the shape of a woman.

The solstice days of Capac Raymi (sum-
mer/ December) and Inti Raymi (winter/
June) were auspicious days in the Inca
ritual calendar.

The Inca empress was regarded as the
earthly embodiment of the moon, Quilla,
and in her role regulated lunar worship
in the capital at Cuzco. A spring moon

festival was held in October. An eclipse
of the moon was believed by the Incas to
be an attempt by a huge celestial serpent
or mountain lion to eat Quilla. During
such events they would gather in force in
their sacred precincts and make as much
noise as possible to scare off the creature.

*Below: The Temple of the Moon at Machu
Picchu was formed from fine masonry and
built within a natural rock overhang.*

FELINES AND SERPENTS

Feline, serpentine and reptilian imagery pervades Andean religion. Religious animism took the characteristics of such creatures and revered their power, guile and cunning. This was indicative of underlying religious ceremony. Shamans were frequently shown transformed, or transforming, into jaguars or snakes. The cayman was also prominent from early times. The use of feline and reptile imagery also reveals the widespread contacts between cultures that characterized Andean civilization.

Fangs are the most common feature, and they are sometimes indistinct; with claws and a cat-like face, or with a writhing body, the meaning becomes clear. Both images are frequently used in the same compositions.

JAGUARS AND OTHER FELINES
Jaguars and jaguar-humans are universal in the mythology of peoples throughout South America. Among Andean and Pacific coastal cultures the jaguar's face clearly inspired much of the 'fanged god' imagery from the earliest times to the Inca Empire. Its presence confirms the importance of the jungle and of jungle products from the earliest times. Feline creatures were frequently depicted in wall paintings and stone sculpture, and on ceramics, textiles and

Below: A complex row of cayman-like teeth on the cornice at the entrance to the sunken court of the New Temple at Chavín de Huántar.

metalwork. Feline features, especially prominent curved canines, were used on humanoid beings representing shamans and inspired the monster gods of pre-Chavín, Chavín, Moche and Chimú art.

An early example comes from the Initial Period Caballo Muerto Complex in the Moche Valley. The façade of the Huaca de los Reyes two-tiered platform is adorned with six huge, high-relief feline heads, each 2m (6½ft) high, framed within niches. Sculpted in adobe, they have wide feline noses, fangs protruding from drawn-back lips, pendant irises and deep facial

Left: A Late Intermediate Period Chimú wooden jaguar figure, inlaid with bone and mother of pearl, supporting a decorated gourd container.

scarifications – features that influenced later Chavín imagery. They were probably painted.

Jaguar imagery at Chavín de Huántar shows classic shamanic transformation. The Circular Sunken Courtyard within the wings of the U-shaped complex of the Old Temple had two sets of steps descending into it, aligned with the entrance to the central passageway of the temple. The stone-lined walls are made with two strata of large, flat rectangular (lower) and square (upper) slabs, separated by smaller rectangular blocks.

SHAMANIC TRANSFORMATION
The panels are carved in low relief. The upper panels show a parade of composite beings, depicted in profile and many carrying San Pedro hallucinogenic cactus stems. Their stance is human-like but their feet and hands have claws and their grimacing mouths with interlocking fangs show them to be transforming into jaguars. From their headdresses and waists hang snakes, the symbol of spiritual vision. The lower panels form a line of prowling jaguars. Upper and lower panels form

Below: Intertwined desert serpents decorating an Early Intermediate Period Nazca painted bowl.

human-like and animal pairs around the walls. Revealingly, the felines have coat markings that distinguish them as jaguars rather than as highland pumas, with their monochrome coats, and so confirms the mountain–jungle liaison.

The more than 40 tenoned stone heads adorning the New Temple walls of Chavín de Huántar give an equally graphic display of shamanic transformation. They were placed high up, spaced every few metres (yards). Although only one remains *in situ*, reconstruction based on the logic of changes in their features shows them to be a sequence of human to supernatural transformation, from shaman to feline.

Fanged beings remained prominent in the art of later cultures. The Moche Decapitator God has distinctive protruding fangs and double ear-ornaments and the Moche-Chimú sky or creator god Ai Apaec also has a distinctive feline mouth.

SNAKES

Serpentine imagery was as early as feline and, like fanged beasts, was pan-Andean and used in all media: wall paintings, stone carving, ceramic decoration, textiles and metalwork. Snakes feature on the earliest textiles from coastal Preceramic Huaca Prieta, shown in a typical double-meaning composition of snakes and crabs. The combination of a feline head with a serpentine body is also not infrequent.

Initial Period Moxeke has three high-relief, painted adobe sculptures on a 4m (13ft) wide panel on its principal platform. The left and central figures are headless torsos, probably deliberately decapitated; the right-hand sculpture is a colossal head, also probably a decapitation. The two torsos are caped figures, and the central figure has four snakes writhing down its front. The identities are uncertain, but the snakes on the central figure highlight its spiritual role, probably that of a shaman. The composite imagery and presence of snakes are indicative of transformation and spiritual vision. Similar adobe sculptures at Huaca

de los Reyes show human-like figures with snakes hanging from their waists, as do figures in the circular sunken courtyard at Chavín de Huántar described above.

LANZÓN CAYMANS

The Lanzón monolith in the Old Temple at Chavín de Huántar displays many of the features described for later Chavín imagery, but is less specific. It portrays a fantastic beast with a tusked mouth and

Below: A snarling jaguar-faced, bridge-spouted effigy vessel from the Early Intermediate Period Lima culture.

Above: A feline head tops the sinuous serpentine body of an Early Intermediate Period Recuay effigy vessel.

thick, up-turned lips and clawed hands and feet, but is not distinctively feline or reptilian. With only upper fangs, rather than the crossed canines of the jaguars of the circular sunken courtyard, its fanged mouth could have been inspired by several animals. More important is its association with snakes: they adorn its eyebrows, form its hair and dangle from its waistband. Its headdress comprises stacked feline heads, and its waistband is a row of similar feline faces. Significantly, one hand gestures up, the other down, indicating a supreme being whose ruler-ship embraces the universe.

The New Temple Tello Obelisk depicts the creation myth and features two almost identical caymans, identifiable because a cayman's upper row of teeth shows even when its mouth is closed. Additionally, 'flame eyebrows' resemble the heavy brow-ridges, and the form of the legs and feet resemble those of crocodilians. Snakes' heads and other fanged faces also adorn the stone. The dual cayman image represents an early manifestation of duality. The arching figures of 'dragons' at Chimú Huaca del Dragón appear to combine feline, serpentine and celestial elements in a single rainbow-like image.

THE STAFF DEITY

The Staff Deity was the earliest widespread pan-Andean deity. The image originated in the Early Horizon with the Chavín Cult and endured to the Late Intermediate Period. The Staff Deity was portrayed frontally with outstretched arms holding staffs, and could be either male or female. He/she epitomizes the Chavín Cult and the early development of pan-Andean religious belief.

COMPOSITE BEING

Much Chavín imagery was inspired by the natural world. The Staff Deity was a composite human-like being, with male, female or non-distinct genitals. Like other Chavín imagery, the hands and feet end in claws, the mouth displays curved feline fangs, pendant irises hang from the curve of the eyes and the ears are bedecked with all kinds of ornaments. Outstretched arms clutch staffs in one form or another,

and they are themselves often festooned with spikes and plume-like decorations. In many cases the staffs held by the Staff Deity are writhing snakes.

THE RAIMONDI STELA

At Chavín de Huántar, the pilgrimage centre of the cult, the most distinctive portrayal of the Staff Deity is undoubtedly the Raimondi Stela (1.98m/6½ft h). Its stylistic similarity to the human-like creatures on the columns of the Black and White Portal of the New Temple suggest that it once stood within one of the New Temple's chambers.

The image on the Raimondi Stela is an incised composition on a highly polished granite-ashlar slab. It has all the hallmarks of the Staff Deity: clawed feet, taloned hands, down-turned, snarling, fanged mouth and pendant irises. Curiously, its genitalia are non-specific. Perhaps, as the most important cult deity at the central cult city, it was meant to represent the unity of opposites (male and female) in order to achieve balance in the Andean worldview.

DUAL MEANING

The Raimondi Stela is not simply a portrait of the Staff Deity. It is an early example of complex, multiple meanings within one image. When viewed as a standing figure, the stela is clearly a Staff Deity wearing an elaborate headdress. The staffs are made up of faces, snakes, vegetation and curved embellishments. Viewed more closely, the headdress comprises similar vegetation, feather-like projections and what appear to be two stacked faces or miniature-bodied standing figures.

This is not all: if the entire image is inverted it shows a different figure. The same principal incised lines of the

Left: A bizarre Staff Deity-like warrior figure on a shallow dish of the Middle Horizon Cajamarca culture of northern Peru.

Above: Andean representations of the Staff Deity in art would be either male or female. This version is male.

The celestial orientation of one image and the earthly orientation of the other reveal two deities within one composition. The very viewing point for each of the images points to its respective realm. In context with a platform mound and sunken court at Chavín de Huántar, the

Above: The Raimondi Stela, depicting the supreme deity of the Chavín Cult, can be viewed with meaning either way up.

Staff Deity face form a new face. What were the irises become nostrils above an upturned, toothy and be-tusked mouth; what were the nostrils of a pug nose become upraised irises; and what were apparent chin dimples beneath the down-turned mouth become the eyes of a grinning face on the forehead of the new face. Finally, the elements that made up the headdress of the Staff Deity image become three sinister-looking faces in which the pendant irises of the headdress faces become nostrils and the new dark areas become widely spaced squinting sets of eyes.

The Staff Deity image appears to be rising, and its various sets of eyes appear to gaze skyward. The inverted features, however, appear to plunge from the sky.

WHO WAS THE STAFF DEITY?
The exact significance and meaning of the Staff Deity is uncertain. His/her power is attested by the number images at Chavín de Huántar on stones and walls, and throughout the central Andes and coast on portable objects. He/she appears to be predominantly associated with agricultural fertility, which is incorporated in the composite features.

The Raimondi Stela image, however, clearly demonstrates aspects of the earliest universals in Andean religion. The profound complexity of the image gives an equally profound religious message of duality within unity.

Above: A female representation of the Staff Deity, showing outstretched arms clasping staffs festooned with decorations.

theme of dual divinity – sky god and earth goddess – was disclosed. Further, the deep recesses of the New Temple secreted meaning and divided worshippers into inclusive and exclusive groups.

AN ENDURING DEITY
The Staff Deity's potency is likewise demonstrated by endurance. The imagery is interrupted in the Late Intermediate Period, but early colonial depictions of the Inca kings show them holding a staff in each hand. Such exceptional importance through longevity imbues the Staff Deity with a distinct 'personality' and the supernatural power of an early creator god.

Chavín Staff Deity images were found everywhere throughout central Andean and Pacific coastal sites in the Early Horizon, on stone sculptures, ceramics and textiles. Of particular note are the Staff Deity images painted on cotton textiles from the Karwa culture of the Paracas Peninsula. There are more than 25 of them, all clearly female. Appendages of cotton growing from the staffs and headdress symbolize the principal agriculture of the coast, and perhaps reveal her to be wife or consort of the Chavín deity, in a locally focused cult.

The most prominent Middle Horizon representation of the Staff Deity is the central figure on the monumental portal at Tiwanaku. Staff Deity images are frequent in both Tiwankau and Wari art.

MUMMIFICATION AND THE OCULATE BEING

The Paracas culture of southern coastal Peru was one of the first Andean cultures to practise mummification. Great reverence is shown by the elaborate preparation of the bodies. The mummies were 'bundled' in tight, foetal positions, placed in baskets and wrapped in layers of high-quality cotton and llama-wool textiles displaying a wealth of natural imagery and supernatural iconography – a rich mythology associated with ritual practices. The burials were accompanied by decorated and plain pottery, many in the shapes of animal effigies, and by sheet-gold ornaments. The freshness of the textiles indicates they were made specifically for burial. Some pieces were even unfinished before needed!

Above: In this woven example, a human-like Oculate Being has whiskers, eyes with pupils, a golden diadem headpiece, and trophy heads.

Among and between sprawling areas of habitation, special necropolis sites had been chosen for hundreds of burials. These might have been the foci of family cults. As the numbers of burials appear to exceed the needs of the immediately adjacent settlements, it is thought that the Paracas necropolises might also have been pilgrimage centres for a regional cult, with honoured individuals being brought from more distant settlements for burial.

A LOCAL DEITY

The Paracas style was heavily influenced by the Chavin style of the north-central Andes, but had soon developed its own regional flavour. Without written records we can only surmise the names and details of Paracas deities and ceremonial practices. Fanged creatures – highly stylized feline faces – feature frequently on textiles and ceramics, but among them one is especially prominent: the Oculate Being.

Left: The Nazca inherited the Paracas Oculate Being. In this rather stylized version, the Oculate Being is shown with his essential feature: blank, staring eyes.

The Oculate Being was most often portrayed horizontally on textiles and ceramics, as if flying, often upside-down (perhaps looking down on humankind), and crouching. With no distinctively female attributes, 'he' is assumed to be male. He has a characteristic, frontal face with large, circular, staring eyes – hence the name. Long, streaming appendages originate from various parts of his body and end in trophy heads or small figures.

He is depicted on textiles and pots, and in the form of distinctive ceramic masks brightly painted with his countenance. Significantly, the Oculate Being is the only image shown on these masks, a fact, it is argued, that emphasizes his importance as a regional deity. His face is often heart-shaped on pottery and in textiles, and sometimes sprouts a smaller head from its top. On other figures, he wears a headband identical to sheet-gold headbands found in some Paracas burials.

SHAMANS AND SERPENTS

Dilated eyes are characteristic of shamanic vision, perhaps inspired by the perceived powers of the round, reflective eyes of nocturnal animals. Numerous birds are depicted in Paracas and Nazca art, in all media, and it is not surprising that the owl was known in later Andean religion as an alter-ego of the shaman.

Despite his regional ownership, the Oculate Being employs the universal Andean iconography of the serpent. Flying Oculate Beings often have long, trailing serpentine tongues; on one textile, two images share a tongue, forming a duality. They often wear writhing belts of snakes trailing behind their legs, demonstrating a sense of artistic perspective. Oculate Being masks have undulating double-headed snakes across the face; on some such masks the forehead snake forms the arms of the miniature figure on the brow, and the figure itself also has a serpent across its forehead.

Above: Here the Oculate Being is shown several times inside a ceramic bowl with typical feline attributes, serpentine tongue, snakes and sky symbols.

DECAPITATION

There are also indications of ritual decapitation. One textile shows a group of flying Oculate Beings each carrying a crescent-shaped knife typical of the *tumi* shape known to be used for decapitation, especially among the Moche, Lambayeque (Sicán) and Chimú cultures of the Early Intermediate to Late Intermediate Periods. Other images of the Oculate Being show him holding a staff, not in a frontal stance with two staffs, like the Staff Deity of the Chavín Cult, but still possibly inspired by Chavín iconography. Later Paracas textiles show the Oculate Being more stylistically, owing partly to the use of a new weaving technique known as discontinuous warp and weft.

In the Early Intermediate Period, the Oculate Being cult continued to form an important part of the art images of the succeeding Nazca culture in the same region. One Nazca painted textile shows figures facing forwards and holding agricultural products. Their visages appear bespectacled and they have strange flaring moustaches and beards. One holds a mask. Another painted textile, known as the 'Harvest Festival', shows a crowded scene of little figures, facing front, with outstretched arms holding agricultural produce. Their stances resemble the Staff Deity, while their faces have the wide-eyed stare characteristic of the Oculate Being or of shamanic trance.

THE MEANING OF THE BEING

The role of the Oculate Being is difficult to determine. His round visage, association with flying and burial, and depiction with decapitation knives all indicate attributes of a god of the sun, sky, death or sacrifice. With such combined characteristics, perhaps he was an early manifestation of the supreme deity. The relationship between the Oculate Being and the Chavín Staff Deity is equally unknown, despite the appearance of unmistakeable Chavín influence at Karwa, just south of the Paracas cemeteries.

THE DECAPITATOR GOD

In a diamond frame, the grimacing face of a fearsome-looking half-human, half-jaguar peers from the walls of Platform I and the Great Plaza of the Huaca de la Luna at Moche. Stylized, stepped supernatural faces surround it, linked by a common 'thread' as if woven in textile. The face is outlined in red. Black hair and a beard curl from the head and chin. A sausage-shaped, down-turned mouth snarls, displaying human-like rows of white teeth and interlocked feline canines. His ears appear to be pierced and decorated with double ear-ornaments. Huge white eyes underlined in black and with heavy red brows stare menacingly with large black pupils. Curious, alien-looking miniature faces surround the head. This mural depicts the Decapitator God. What fear and reverence might he have struck in citizens as they stood beneath his gaze watching priests perform ritual sacrifice?

Below: Murals at the Huaca de la Luna depict a wide-eyed shamanic face with pierced ears, human teeth and feline canines.

RITUAL BLOOD-LETTING

The Decapitator God so graphically dominating the Moche capital was depicted in friezes and murals in temples and tombs, and on ceramics and metalwork at Moche and other north coastal valley sites, including Sipán in the Lambayeque Valley. He has several guises: as an overpowering face that grips one's attention, or full-figured, holding a crescent-shaped *tumi* ceremonial knife in one hand and a severed human head in the other. The elaborate plaster friezes at the Huaca de la Luna of Early Intermediate Period Moche are the most renowned, but the development of his imagery can be traced back to the Early Horizon in the preceding Cupisnique culture of the same region.

The Decapitator God is portrayed in an elaborate blood-letting rite painted on pottery and on temple and tomb walls. His role, acted out by priests, embodied

Above: There is no mistaking this sheet-metal and shell inlay depiction of the Decapitator God, with his grinning sinister expression, tumi *sacrificial knife and his latest victim's head.*

a gruesome sacrificial ritual. Although once thought to be merely representational of a mythical event, archaeological evidence discovered in the 1980s attests to its reality. An enclosure behind the Huaca de la Luna platform contained the buried remains of 40 men, aged 15 to 30. They appear to have been pushed off a stone outcrop after having been mutilated and killed. The structure, outcrop and enclosure seem to mirror the nearby Cerro Blanco and valley. Some skeletons were splayed out as if tied to stakes; some had their femurs torn from the pelvis joints; skulls, ribs, fingerbones, armbones and legbones have cut marks. Several severed heads had their jaws torn away.

A thick layer of sediment, deposited during heavy rains, covered the gruesome scene, and it is suggested that the sacrifice was performed in response to an El Niño event that might have disrupted the economic stability of the realm.

RITUAL COMBAT

The Decapitator God and sacrificial ritual are put into context by scenes painted on Moche ceramics and walls. Friezes show warriors in paired combat, almost always both wearing Moche armour and bearing Moche arms. The combatants are shown in narrative sequences: instead of killing a vanquished foe, the loser is next shown stripped and tied by the neck with a rope, being marched off for their arraignment. The final scenes show the captives naked, having their throats slit. Their blood is given in goblets to four presiding figures.

The most elaborate of these is the Warrior Priest. He wears a crescent-shaped metal plate to protect his back, and rattles hang from his belt. To his right sits the Bird Priest, wearing a conical helmet bearing the image of an owl and a long beak-like nose-ornament. Next to him is a priestess, identified by her long, plaited tresses, dress-like costume and plumed and tasselled headdress. The final figure, with a feline face, wears a headdress with serrated border and long streamers.

THE REAL THING

These scenes show ritual warfare in fields near Moche cities for the purpose of 'capturing' victims for sacrifices to the gods. Excavations in the 1980s of unlooted Sipán tombs in the Lambayeque Valley dated c.AD300 corroborate their actual occurrence. The elite citizens buried in the tombs, accompanied by sacrificial victims, were richly adorned and surrounded by the artefacts of sacrifice and ritual; the bodies were decorated with gold, silver, turquoise and other jewellery, and textiles. They wore

Right: A Chimú gold sacrificial knife handle, representing the legendary leader and conqueror Naymlap.

costumes identical to those of the four figures in the sacrificial ceremonies.

The principal body personifies the Warrior Priest. He wore a crescent-shaped back-flap and belt rattles, just as in the scene. The Decapitator God image decorates both back-flap and rattles – in this case the face is symbolized by a spider with a human face, perched on a golden web. The spider imagery is thought to reflect the parallel of the blood-letting and sucking the life juices of its prey. Offerings included three pairs of gold and turquoise ear-spools – one of which shows a Moche warrior in full armour – a gold, crescent-shaped headdress, a crescent-shaped nose-ornament, and one gold and one silver *tumi* knife. At the Warrior Priest's side lay a box-like gold sceptre, embossed with combat scenes, and a spatula-like handle of silver studded with military trappings.

Near by, another tomb, less rich, contained the body of a noble with a gilded copper headdress decorated with an owl with outspread wings – clearly the Bird Priest. Sealed rectangular rooms near the tombs contained more offerings, including the bones of severed human hands and feet.

Two tombs dated c.AD 500–600 at San José de Moro in the Jequetepeque Valley contained the skeletons of women. Their silver-alloyed copper headdresses had tassels and other accoutrements of the priestess figure. Finally, at El Brujo in the Chicama Valley, a terrace frieze shows a life-size warrior leading a procession of ten nude prisoners by a rope placed around their necks. On a terrace above (later destroyed by looters) was a huge spider or crab with a fanged mouth and double ear-ornaments, one leg brandishing a *tumi* knife – the 'arachnoid decapitator'.

189

CON THE CREATOR

Con created and shaped the natural world, made the first generation of humans and gave life to the animals and plants. He is central in a generic creation myth, but is not always benevolent. His name forms part of other Andean creator deities such as Con Tici (or Titi) Viracocha Pachayachachic, Coniraya Viracocha of the early 17th-century *Huarochiri Manuscript*, and Wakon. The word 'con' is indicative of heat, energy and creation.

CON VERSUS PACHACAMAC
Con was a formless figure, without bones or joints, who came from the north and was a child of the sun and the moon. After walking up and down the coast, shaping the land and creating all things in it, he disappeared into the sea and ascended into the sky.

The central Andean Colloas believed that Con created the sun, then made stone figures of the various Andean peoples, whom he placed throughout the valleys before bringing them to life and instructing them in his worship.

Con's rival or opposite was Pachacamac. Because he had left the world's inhabitants without a leader or protector, Pachacamac, who came from the south, transformed these first humans into pumas/jaguars, foxes, monkeys and parrots.

WAKON AND THE SPIDER
In a later tradition, Wakon was a malevolent being opposed to Pachacamac, who, with his consort Pacha Mama, were sky and earth deities respectively. Their union produced twins, a boy and a girl, after which Pachacamac died and disappeared into the sea, leaving Pacha Mama and the twins alone.

Wakon, who lived in a cave, appeared semi-naked to the twins. He asked them to fetch some water and while they were away seduced Pacha Mama. He ate part of her and threw the rest of her body into a cooking pot. When the twins returned and learned of her fate, they fled. Wakon asked

Above: A puma-headed reed boat on Lake Titicaca on whose shore the survivors from the flood landed.

the animals and birds where the twins were hiding. Spider suggested that he go to a mountaintop and call to the twins, imitating Pacha Mama's voice. Spider, however, had prepared a trap, a chasm on the mountain, into which Wakon fell and was destroyed, causing a violent earthquake. Pachacamac then returned, apologized to the twins and transformed his son into the

sun and his daughter into the moon. Pacha Mama 'survived' as the snow-capped mountain La Viuda (the widow).

In later myths, Con became blended with Viracocha. The central Andean Cachas, for example, called him Con Tici Viracocha Pachayachachic, literally 'god, creator of the world'.

CON TICI OF THE TIWANAKU
In one version of the Inca creation myth, related by the 16th-century chronicler Cristobal de Molina, the world was already

peopled when a great flood destroyed all except one man and one woman. They were cast up on land at Tiwanaku, where Con Tici Viracocha appeared to them and created a second race of humans of clay and stone in the Titicaca Basin, including the Inca ancestors. He also made birds and animals, two of each, and spread them among their habitats, designated their foods, and gave each bird its song.

He named two of his creations (sometimes said to be his sons) Imaymana Viracocha and Tocapo Viracocha, the inclusion of 'Viracocha' imbuing them with divinity and supernatural power. With them he travelled throughout the land giving life to the peoples, animals and plants that he had created. Imaymana Viracocha went north-westwards along the forest and mountain borders, Tocapo Viracocha went northwards along the coasts, and Con Tici Viracocha went along a route between them,

Below: Con/Viracocha, the bodiless or formless deity, is appropriately represented in this blocky, rather abstract form.

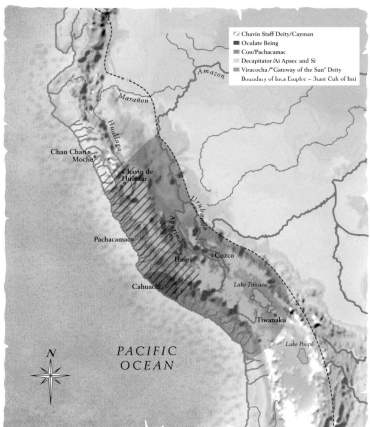

through the mountains. They continued to what became the north-westernmost edge of the Inca Empire, to the coastal site of Manta, where they walked out across the sea until they disappeared.

Coniraya Viracocha of central Andean Huarochiri mythology, like Con, was a coastal creator deity who wandered throughout the world, reshaping the landscape before disappearing across the western sea. Like Wakon, Coniraya sought Pachacamac's children by asking the animals and birds about them.

HISTORY BEHIND A MYTH?
The conflict between Con and Pachacamac might represent the later mythologizing of historical consciousness, a shared general memory of past events in a culture without written records. In the versions related above, Con comes from either north or south, and travels up and down the coasts,

Above: Map showing the distribution of the major creator deities, from the Decapitator in the north to the Oculate Being in the south.

mountains and forests. From the north, he would have represented a Moche or earlier deity of the northern coastal valleys. It has also been suggested that the shapeless Con is represented by the flying human-like sky deities on the textiles and pottery of the Paracas and Nazca peoples of the southern coasts, and continued as the winged attendants associated with the Staff Deity at Tiwanaku. Together, these cultures span the Early Horizon, Early Intermediate Period and Middle Horizon.

The conflict between them and the replacement of Con by Pachacamac would thus reflect the decline of southern cults and the rise of the importance of middle coastal Pachacamc as a deity, and of his associated temple and pilgrimage cult.

THE YAYA-MAMA RELIGIOUS TRADITION

A tall stone post from Taraco on the northern shore of Lake Titicaca is carved on all four faces. Two opposite faces have a male and a female figure, giving the name Yaya-Mama – father and mother – to a regional cult. Below each figure, and on the other two faces, there are writhing serpents. Three of the four serpents on the faces adjacent to the figured faces are double-headed.

A REGIONAL CULT

Pukará, another Yaya-Mama site north of the lake, flourished as a regional cult centre in the late Early Horizon and Early Intermediate Period, before the rise of the Wari and Tiwanaku states to the north and south. Yaya-Mama developed independently of the Chavín Cult to the north, and provided the template for later south-central Andean civilization. Tiwanaku people revered the Yaya-Mama tradition, as evidenced by their incorporation of Yaya-Mama sculptures in their own ceremonial complexes. For example, Yaya-Mama Stela 15 (2m/6½ft high) was erected beside the much taller Bennett Monolith (7.4m/24ft high) in the Semi-subterranean Temple at Tiwanaku; and the lower part of the Arapa-Thunderbolt Stela was taken from Arapa, at the north end of the lake, and placed in the Putuni Palace at Tiwanku. Altogether there are a total of seven Pukará sculptures at the city of Tiwanaku.

Above: At Lake Titicaca the cult of Yaya-Mama/Pukará was established at ceremonial centres around the lake.

Pukará stone sculpture is blocky and columnar. Its imagery features flat, squared-oval eyes. Movement is indicated in the poses and limbs of figures, and ribs show prominently. Hands sometimes hold objects. Heads are frequently rayed with feathers and animal images emanating from the main heads. As well as monumental stone sculpture, there were roofless temples and sunken courts, complex supernatural artistic symbols and ritual paraphernalia.

Dozens of Pukará temple sites are distributed more or less equidistantly around Lake Titicaca, located on hill summits, on artificial platforms and at the bases of cliffs. Yaya-Mama temples typically comprise a rectangular sunken court, which is surrounded by individual, multi-chambered structures arranged symmetrically around the court.

Left: Pukará ceramics shared features that resemble later Tiwanaku styles in the use of incised decoration and colours.

The courts are stone lined, either plain or carved with heads that have appendages radiating from them. Sometimes there are burials around the court.

A TWO-PHASED TRADITION

Most Yaya-Mama stone sculptures have not been found *in situ*. Some are still objects of local veneration. Lasting about a millennium, the style comprises two phases, characterized by examples from Chiripa (earlier) and Pukará (later). Earlier pieces are mostly pecked designs of geometric symbols, animals and humans on stone slabs or four-sided posts. Later examples are incised and carved in the round, showing greater finishing. Generally, human figures are carved in the round while animals and geometric motifs are in low relief.

Early Yaya-Mama stone imagery shows pairs of figures, male and female, with arms raised to their chests. Human heads have appendages radiating from them that often end in triangular serpent heads. There are also severed human heads.

Above: The characteristic Pukará-style Yaya-Mama features a life-size or larger stone head with a turban-like headdress.

Animals include felines, birds with outstretched wings, frogs and/or toads, snakes, or supernatural serpentine creatures with flared ears and zigzag bodies. Geometric designs include checkered and Maltese-like crosses, chevrons and rings.

The most common animal on pottery is the spotted feline – the spotted coat indicating the jaguar rather than the monochrome mountain lion. There are also trophy heads and dismembered sacrificial victims, birds, coiled snakes and camalids. The characteristic vertical division of eyes into black and white halves of Tiwanaku and Wari imagery is first seen in Pukará art, as are tears below the eyes.

Later Pukará stone sculptures feature large slabs carved with felines, coiled snakes, frogs and/or toads, steps, volutes and zigzags. Humans are carved in the round. There are seated and standing males figures, one wearing a serpent-head decorated hat. The Pukará Decapitator depicts a seated male figure,

holding an axe in his right hand and a severed head in his left. His cap is decorated with supernatural faces. He is either a supernatural composite being, or a man wearing a representative mask with a fanged mouth. The round, staring eyes are indicative of shamanic trance or transformation.

RITUAL PARAPHERNALIA

Yaya-Mama ritual paraphernalia includes ceremonial burners, ceramic and *Strombus* shell trumpets, miniature pottery vessels, including painted and effigy-shaped pieces, and architectural models. Pottery vessels are invariably found in pieces and contexts that indicate deliberate breakage.

Two prominent ceramic themes are the 'feline man' and the 'woman with alpaca'. The first depicts pairs of fanged men lunging forward or running, facing each other or one chasing the other. Each figure carries a severed head and a staff. Some figures wear feline pelts. The 'woman with alpaca' shows a single, skirted, frontal-standing figure leading an alpaca by a rope. She carries a bag and holds

a distinctive staff with an I-shaped head, and she wears a plumed cap. She is associated with plants and sometimes a rayed-head motif.

From the Pukará temple come rectangular stone boxes, subdivided and externally decorated on six equal panels with stylized faces, each with 16 appendages ending in a variety of serpent or circular heads. Ceramic models are of miniature temples, complete with the details of their windows and doors.

These objects and images imply ritual combat, agricultural and pastoral themes, and fertility. Ritual clearly included incense burning, feasting and music-making. Images of severed heads – a feature of religious symbolism throughout the Andean Area – and dismembered bodies, and a cache of human mandibles found at Pukará, indicate ritual sacrifice and/or warfare, either in the real world or in the world of mythological concept.

Below: Accurate, individual and natural features are complemented by ringed/lidded eyes, but without pupils.

VIRACOCHA: THE SUPREME ANDEAN DEITY

Viracocha was the supreme deity, almost universally regarded throughout the Andean Area as the creator of the universe, the human race and all living things. He became a rather remote and inaccessible deity, although regarded as omnipresent and inescapable.

In Cuzco he was represented in his own shrine by a golden statue slightly smaller than life. He was white, bearded and wore a long tunic, as described by the Spaniards who first saw him there. In Inca legend, he travelled south to Cacha, c.100km (60 miles) south of Cuzco, where another temple and statue were dedicated to his worship. Another shrine and statue were at Urcos.

THE PRIMORDIAL CREATOR
To the Incas, Viracocha was primordial. He remained nameless, and instead was referred to by descriptive terms befitting his role in the various permutations of the creation myth. He was Illya ('light'), Tici ('the beginning of things'), Atun Viracocha ('great creator), or Viracocha Pachayachachic ('lord, instructor of the world'). The earliest Spanish chroniclers to describe him, Cieza de León and Juan de Betanzos around 1550, personify him, but to ancient Andeans 'he' represented a concept – the force of creative energy. The Quechua elements of his name, *vira* ('fat, grease, foam') and *cocha* ('lake, sea, reservoir'), can be rendered as 'sea fat', 'sea foam', or 'the lake of creation'.

As supreme deity, Viracocha's name has been used for the creator god in the pantheons of many pre-Inca cultures. Much of his history and legend therefore owes to the Inca's adoption of him from their conquered subjects. For example, his portrayal with weeping eyes was a characteristic almost certainly adopted from the weeping god imagery of Tiwanaku. In Inca legend he bestowed a special headdress and stone battle-axe on Manco Capac, the first Inca ruler, and prophesied that the Incas would become

great lords and would conquer many other nations. Viracocha Inca, the 15th-century eighth Inca ruler, took his name, presumably as representing strength and creative energy. As a concept, he could also be regarded as "shapeless" or "boneless".

CREATION AND LAKE TITICACA
Many Andean cultures believed that Lake Titicaca was where the sun, moon and stars were created, and that the lake waters were the tears of Viracocha acknowledging the sufferings of his creations.

Viracocha first created a world of darkness, then populated it with humans fashioned from stone. But he was disobeyed, so he destroyed them with a flood or by transforming them back into stones. These beings could be seen, it was

Above: Viracocha came to be associated with other sky symbols such as the double-headed rainbow serpent found in Chimú art.

thought, at ruined cities such as Tiwanaku and Pukará. Only one man and one woman survived, and were magically transported to Tiwanaku, where the gods dwelled.

Viracocha next created a new race of humans, and animals, of clay. He painted distinctive clothes on the humans and gave them customs, languages, songs, arts and crafts, and the gift of agriculture to distinguish the different peoples and nations. Breathing life into them, he instructed them to descend into the earth and disperse, then to re-emerge through caves, and from lakes and hills. These places became sacred, and shrines were established at them in honour of the gods.

The world was still dark, so Viracocha ordered the sun, moon and stars to rise into the sky from the islands in Lake Titicaca.

SPREADING CIVILIZATION

After his creations, Viracocha set out from the Titicaca Basin to spread civilization, but he did so as a beggar, bearded, dressed in rags, and under many names, and dependant on others for his sustenance. In other accounts he was described as a tall white man wearing a sun crown. Many of those he encountered reviled him. He was assisted by two of his creations, variously called his sons or brothers: Imaymana Viracocha and Tocapo Viracocha. The inclusion of the name 'Viracocha' imbued them with divinity and supernatural power.

He commanded Imaymana Viracocha to travel north-westward along a route bordering the forests and mountains and Tocapo Viracocha to journey northward along a coastal route. He himself followed a route between them, north-westward through the mountains. As they passed

Below: Temples were dedicated to Viracocha throughout the Inca Empire, as here at Rachi in the Vilcanota Valley.

through the land, they called out the people, named the trees and plants, established the times when each would flower and bear fruit, and instructed the people about which were edible and which medicinal. They taught humankind the arts and crafts, agriculture and the ways of civilization, and worked miracles among them, until they reached Manta on the Ecuadorian coast (the most north-

Above: A portrayal of Viracocha's face in sheet gold features typical Tiwanaku sun rays around the head, and weeping eyes.

western edge of the Inca Empire), where they continued across the sea, walking on the water until they disappeared.

Another version, recorded by Cristobal de Molina, begins with the world already peopled. A great flood destroyed all except one man and one woman, who were cast up on land at Tiwanaku. Con Tici Viracocha appeared to them and ordered them to remain there as *mitimaes* (people resettled by the Incas), then repopulated the land by making the Inca ancestors out of clay, and as before, giving them customs, languages and clothing.

This active role on Earth likens Viracocha to the preacher heroes in much pre-Inca legend. To the Incas, Viracocha remained remote, interacting with humans through other gods, particularly Inti, the sun god, and Illapa, god of weather. His purposeful travels relate to ancient Andean pilgrimage traditions. The trinity implied by the three Viracochas suggests a strong element of Christian interpretation in the descriptions of the Spanish chroniclers.

PACHACAMAC THE CREATOR

Pachacamac, 'earth/time maker', was the creator deity of the peoples of the central Peruvian coast. His Quechua root words, *pacha* ('time/space', 'universe/earth', 'state of being') and *camac* ('creator', 'animator') render him as potent as Viracocha and reveal lowland–highland association through the spread of Quechua from coastal regions to the Andes.

AN ANCIENT ORACLE

The centre of Pachacamac's worship was the pilgrimage city and oracle of the same name near modern Lima. The 16th-century chronicler Cieza de León noted Inca reverence for the shrine, and the 17th-century writer Father Bernabe Cobo describes it in detail. The Earth Maker was represented by a wooden staff (destroyed by Hernando Pizarro, brother of the conquistador) carved with a human face on both sides and housed in an oracular chamber, epitomizing the Andean concept of duality. Other carved wooden idols, which were scattered about the city, survive from other parts of the site.

Below: For more than a millennium, complexes of courtyards at Pachacamac accommodated pilgrims.

Pachacamac's following was ancient and widespread among central coastal civilizations, enduring from the Early Intermediate Period for more than a millennium. The oracle, like Early Horizon Chavín de Huántar, drew visitors from throughout the lowland plains and valleys, and the adjacent Andes. The principal temple platform was surrounded by a vast complex of courtyards and subsidiary platforms for the accommodation of pilgrims. Like Lake Titicaca and the Coricancha in Cuzco, it was one of the most sacred sites in the Inca Empire.

THE CREATION MYTH

There are many threads to Pachacamac's mythology. He was a serious rival to Viracocha. His cult developed independently and much earlier than that of Inca Inti, but the predominance of ancient contact between the coastal lowlands and the Andean highlands inevitably brought the two creator gods into 'contact' at an early date, long before the Inca compulsion to incorporate all their subjects' myths and pantheons of gods.

Mythology shows the two deities to have distinct identities, yet many similar traits: they created the world; they held control over the creation and destruction of the

Above: Guaman Poma de Ayala's depiction of a child sacrifice to Pachacamac in his Nueva Crónica y Buen Gobierno, c.1613.

first people; they travelled throughout the lands and taught, often in the guise of a beggar, and punished those who mocked them for this; they met, named, and gave their characters to the animals and plants.

In the principal myth, Pachacamac was the son of the sun and moon. An earlier deity, Con, had created the first people, but Pachacamac overcame him, and transformed the first people into monkeys and other animals.

Pachacamac then created man and woman, but, because he did not provide them with food, the man died. The woman solicited the sun's help, or in another version accused the sun of neglecting his duty, and in return was impregnated by the sun's rays. When she bore a son, she taught him to survive by eating wild plants. Pachacamac, jealous of his father (the sun) and angered by this independence and apparent defiance, killed the boy and cut him into pieces. He sowed the boy's teeth, which grew into maize; planted the ribs and bones, which became yucca, or manioc, tubers; and planted the flesh, which grew

into vegetables and fruits. The story appears to be a mythical précis of the discovery of cultivation among coastal peoples.

Not to be outdone, the sun took the boy's penis (or umbilical cord) and navel and created another son, whom he named Vichama or Villama. Pachacamac wanted to kill this child too, but could not catch him, for Vichama had set off on his travels. Pachacamac slew the woman instead and fed her body to the vultures and condors.

Next, Pachacamac created another man and woman, who began to repopulate the world. Pachacamac appointed some of these people *curacas* (leaders) to rule.

In the mean time, Vichama returned, found his mother's remains and reassembled her. Pachacamac feared Vichama's reprisal as the pursued became the pursuer, and he was driven, or fled, into the sea, where he sank in front of the temple of Pachacamac/Vichama. Wreaking further revenge, Vichama transformed Pachacamac's second people into stone, but later repented and changed the ordinary stone of the *curacas* into sacred *huacas*.

Below: The Incas established a temple to Inti (the sun god) alongside the ancient platform at Pachacamac.

SOCIAL ARRANGEMENTS

The second part of the tale explains the creation of social order among humans. Vichama asked his father, the sun, to create another race of people. The sun sent three eggs, one gold, one silver and one copper. The gold egg became *curacas* and nobles, the silver became women, and the copper egg became commoners. Thus, the world was populated. A variation describes how Pachacamac did the final deed by sending four stars to earth. Two of these were male, and generated kings and nobles; the other two were female, and generated commoners.

Other variations combine Con and Viracocha, emphasizing the latter's opposition to Pachacamac. The Huarochirí, between coast and sierra, incorporate Pachacamac's shrine, wife and daughters (including the seduction and attempted seduction of Pachacamac's daughters) into the itinerary of Coniriya Viracocha.

Such variations reflect lowland–highland and inter-coastal exchange and political tension. In the interests of empire, the Incas sought to alleviate any potential conflict by amalgamating the deities and by presenting variations as different names for the same events, as if it had always been so.

Above: Pachacamac was principally a coastal creator god who was ultimately combined with Viracocha, the highland creator deity.

INTI THE SUN GOD

The solstices were crucial days in the Inca ritual calendar. At Capac Raymi (summer/December), there was an imperial feast and initiation rites for noble boys; Inti Raymi (winter/June) honoured Inti, the sun, with feasting and the taking of important auguries. Plotting and confirming their dates was based on observations from the sacred Coricancha Temple in Cuzco.

THE CULT OF INTI

In Inca belief the sun was set in the sky by Viracocha, creator being of indistinct substance. The founding Inca ancestor, Manoc Capac, was believed to have been descended from the sun – the son of the sun – and this belief began the special relationship between the Incas and Inti. The adoption of the cult of Inti was associated especially with the ninth ruler, Pachacuti. Inca imperial expansion probably introduced a solar element into the mythologies of coastal peoples, as the father of Con and Pachacuti. Thus began the combining of creation myths with Inti, the sun.

Inti's image was most frequently a great sheet-gold mask, moulded as a human-like face, wide-eyed and showing a toothy grin. Sheet-gold rays, cut in zig-zags and ending in miniature human-like masks or figures, surrounded the face. Rayed faces were a common feature of pre-Inca

Below: The Christian Church of Santo Domingo, superimposed on the Coricancha Temple, dedicated in part to Inti.

Above: Llamas were frequently sacrificed to honour Inti, as depicted in this colonial painting of a sacrificial ceremony.

imagery, but their identification as the sun is not always tenable.

The sacred Coricancha precinct in Cuzco was the centre of the official state cult dedicated to Inti's worship. By the 16th century, the cult of Inti was so important that an incident witnessed by the priests during ceremonies in his honour appeared to foretell the fall of the empire. An eagle, mobbed by buzzards, was seen falling from the sky in the reign of Huayna Capac about 1526, coinciding with reports of the spread of an unknown, deadly disease from the north, now known to have been smallpox.

CAPTURING THE SUN

The emperor was seen as Inti's embodiment on Earth. Although regarded with awe because of his power, Inti was believed to be benevolent and generous. The sun was symbolically captured at special locations called *intihuatanas* ('hitching posts of the sun'), for example at Machu Picchu – carved stone outcrops probably used for astronomical observations. Together with set stone pillars,

priests used the shadows cast by them to observe and record regular movements of the sun in order to understand it and to predict the future. Solar eclipses were regarded as signs of Inti's anger.

INTERMEDIARIES

By the second half of the 15th century, as the empire reached the limits of expansion, Viracocha had become a remote deity, and Inti came to be regarded as his intermediary. Inca rulers emphasized this relationship carefully, and it became the basis for cultivating their intimate association with Inti. They became intermediaries between the sun and the people, and their presence was regarded as essential to assure light and warmth to make the world habitable. Elaboration and adoption of regional mythologies and combining them with Inca myth created an association between Inti, the emperor and power. Ceremonies and ritual offerings to Inti served constantly to reinforce this link.

Above: Perhaps the most celebrated
intihuatana *is the one located at the highest*
point of the sacred city of Machu Picchu.

THE RIGHT TO RULE

Historical and archaeological evidence shows that the expansion of the Inca empire beyond the Cuzco Valley began in earnest with Pachacuti Inca Yupanqui (1438–71) and with his son Tupac Yupanqui (1471–93). To unify the empire and convince their subjects of the Inca right to rule it became necessary to demonstrate a mythical common ancestry – namely the Inca ancestors. Thus, the first ruler, Manco Capac (at first called Ayar Manco), after emerging from the cave of Tambo Toco, acquired divine sanction when his brother Ayar Uchu flew up and spoke to the sun. Ayar Uchu returned with the message that Manco should thenceforth rule Cuzco as Manco Capac in the name of the sun.

Other versions of the creation myth name Inti as the father of Ayar Manco Capac and Mama Coya (also Mama Ocllo), and the other brother/sister/partners collectively known as the ancestors. Manco Capac and Mama Ocllo were sent to Earth to bring the gifts of maize and potato cultivation, establishing the Inca right to rule on the basis of their benevolence.

Below: The Intihuatana *or Hitching Post*
of the Sun at Machu Picchu was probably
used for astronomical observations.

A somewhat more sinister variation says that 'son of the sun' (Inti) was the nickname given to Manco Capac by his father to trick the populace of Cuzco into handing over power. Manco Capac wore gold plates to lend credulity to his divine dawn appearance to the people of Cuzco.

The emperor Pachacuti Inca Yupanqui's discovery of the crystal tablet in the spring of Susurpuquio, with its image of Viracocha, was followed by renewed construction and rearrangement of the sacred Coricancha, giving greater prominence to Inti. It was Pachacuti, too, who visited the Island of the Sun in Lake Titicaca, where ancient Andeans believed the sun to have been born. The construction of Sacsahuaman, at the north-west end of the capital, was probably also begun by Pachacuti. It became a sacred precinct and place of sacrifice to Inti, and probably also a site for cosmological observations. All these legendary events enhanced the importance of Inti and therefore the Incas.

CHAPTER TEN

CREATION AND THE FIRST PEOPLES

The creation story of the Ancient Andean peoples involved a layered world that revolved in endless cycles of creation and rebirth. They linked these concepts to their intimate association with their landscape to explain both its bounty and the difficulties and trials it sometimes presented.

The Spaniards recorded a wealth of rival, even seemingly contradictory, tales of creation among the peoples of the Inca Empire – and indeed throughout their New World colonies. However, as among the cultures of Mesoamerica, Andean cultural accounts of cosmic origin and the creation of humankind had common elements that arose from a long and common inheritance, strengthened by millennia of trading and social contact between highland and lowland peoples.

First was the belief that humanity originated at Lake Titicaca, and that Viracocha was the creator god. Second was the concept that, wherever they lived, a tribal group identified a particular place or feature in their landscape as the place from which they emerged. Third was a dual relationship between local people and a group of outsiders, which, whether it was portrayed as one of co-operation or conflict, defined the nature of how the groups interrelated. Finally, there was the conviction that there was a correct ordering of society and place in terms of rank and hierarchy.

Left: Lake Titicaca, with its sacred waters, came to be regarded by Andean peoples as the birthplace of the world.

CAVES, TUNNELS AND ISLANDS

The Earth, the Lower World of Hurin Pacha, lay between the worlds of Hanan Pacha (the World Above) and Uku Pacha (the World Below). Also known as Kai Pacha, it was the physical world in which humans lived, and was, theoretically speaking, flat. Completing the cycle of the universe, it was connected to the worlds above and below.

The celestial river of Mayu, the Milky Way, channelled water across the heavens, having collected it from earthly sources – a perfect representation of the endless cycle, *pachacuti*. In theory, all living things on Earth had celestial counterparts in stellar and dark cloud constellations (the spaces between the stars). Connection to the underworld was through caves, underground tunnels and springs.

MOTHER EARTH

Crucial in Andean and coastal peoples' belief was worship of mother earth, or Pacha Mama, as she was known to the Incas. To peoples so closely involved with agriculture and the harvesting of the sea for their living, and thus exposed to the periodic extremes of nature, it was natural to develop belief in an all-embracing mother goddess whose whim reflected and was responsible for their environment.

The earth goddess was a primeval deity responsible for the well-being of plants and animals. Worship of her was at least as early as the first U-shaped platform groups and sunken courts, and continues to the present day in the form of offerings of coca (*Erythroxylon coca*) leaves, *chicha* maize beer, and prayers on all major agricultural occasions. She is sometimes identified with the Virgin Mary of Christianity. In one myth, the Inca founders sacrificed and offered a llama to Pacha Mama before they entered Cuzco to take it over. One of the sister/wives, Mama Huaco, sliced open the animal's chest, extracted the lungs and inflated them with her own breath, then carried them into the city alongside Manco Capac, who carried the gold emblem of the sun god Inti.

Above: The first age in Inca creation was inevitably interpreted by author Guaman Poma de Ayala as Adam and Eve.

CAVES

These were believed to be the openings from which people emerged to inhabit the Earth. In the story of the creator god Viracocha, he created the second race of human beings from clay – the Earth. Having painted his creations with distinctive clothes and given them the different languages and customs that would distinguish them, he breathed life into them and caused them to descend into the earth and disperse. In his wandering he called them forth, to re-emerge through caves, and from lakes and hills.

The cave also features in the battle between the coastal creator god, Pachacamac, and the malevolent deity, Wakon, a classic duel between good and evil. Wakon lurked in a cave, enticed the twin son and daughter of Pachacamac and Pacha Mama and sent them to fetch water so he could seduce their mother.

Left: The massive gateway entrance to the Kalasasaya compound at Tiwanaku, which was surrounded by a moat.

Having done so and then destroyed her, it was the humble spider, servant of the Earth, who tricked Wakon in his search for the twins by laying a mountain chasm trap, into which Wakon fell and was destroyed.

SACRED LINKS
Caves were linked by tunnels running beneath the earth. Using these tunnels, the peoples created by Viracocha were thus redistributed throughout the known world. In one of the many versions of the Inca creation myth, it was held that the ancestors were born on the Island of the Sun, in Lake Titicaca. The senior ancestor, Manco Capac, led them from there, underground, to Capac Toco cave at Pacaritambo, south-west of Cuzco, from which they emerged to take over the valley.

The original inhabitants of the Cajatambo region, in highland central Peru, were the Guaris. Their patron god was a giant called Huari, who lived among the caves. Another important Guari deity was the 'night-time sun' – the sun after sunset, which it was believed passed through a hidden, underground watery passage until the next day's sunrise.

Left: The first Inca 'coat of arms' showed elements of their origin: Inti, Quilla and the cave from which the Inca ancestors emerged.

Above: Inca ancestors would have approached Cuzco across the southern mountains, including sacred Mt Ausangate (centre left).

These sacred links between Mother Earth, the sky deities and the underworld were symbolized in ceremonial architecture from earliest times. U-shaped structures and sunken courts feature from the Initial Period to the Late Horizon. The inner labyrinths of temples, particularly at Chavín de Huántar, mimic cave-like mystery. Paracas and Nazca tombs were cave-like structures in which descendants could inter ancestors and re-enter to place more burials within them. They were places of symbolic rebirth through mummification, as well as of burial. The underground water channels of Cahuachi can also be regarded as links. Life-giving waters that had disappeared into the earth on their course from the mountains was tapped underground and brought to the surface for the rebirth of the crops in an endless cycle. Ritual processions through ceremonial complexes descended into the sunken court – a symbolic cave of creation

– before being reborn to ascend the celestial heights of the platform to complete the link with the upper world.

ISLANDS
These were also significant in the mythology of creation. The Island of the Sun and the Island of the Moon in Lake Titicaca were believed to be the birthplaces of the celestial bodies, created by Viracocha, and from which they were caused to rise into the heavens. The sacred Akapana and Kalasasaya compound at Tiwanaku were surrounded by a moat, effectively making it an island, whether or not the moat was actually filled with water.

The Incas recognized the ancient sacredness of Tiwanaku not only because of the significance of the Islands of the Sun and the Moon, but also as the birthplace of an earlier race of beings – giants who preceded the Incas and were represented by the great stone statues at the site.

AGES OF MAN

The most important ancient Andean religious theme is continuity, progressing in cycles of events through time. Despite changes to the landscape, climatic change and the ebb and flow of political change, generations of Andean peoples developed beliefs in a sequence of ages that led through a series of creation efforts to their own times. The final expression of this theme was recorded as the Incas told it to Spanish chroniclers.

THE AGE OF GIANTS

The creator god was, to name him fully, Con Tici Viracocha Pachayachachic – 'creator of all things'. He rose from the deep waters of Lake Titicaca and created the first world, a world without light. There was no sun, moon or stars. Viracocha made giant models of beings in his own likeness, which he painted. He wanted to see if it would be a good thing to have a race of people who were that large. They lived in darkness and were unable to worship him.

Below: Lake Titicaca, the most sacred place in the Andean world, where Viracocha made the world and all its forms and living beings.

Viracocha ordered these giants to live without conflict and to obey and worship him. But they did not obey him, and in retribution he turned them into stone and other features of the landscape. The Incas regarded the great stone statues among the ruins of Tiwanaku as a record of this first age.

It began to rain and continued to do so for 60 days and 60 nights. A great flood known as *unu pachacuti* – 'water that overturns the land' – engulfed the land. Some giants, who had not been turned into stone, were destroyed by the waters and swallowed into the earth. Some people believed that all living things were drowned in the flood, but it seems that one man and one woman of normal size survived by hiding in a box or drum, which floated on the flood waters and came to land at Tiwanaku.

THE SUN, MOON AND STARS

Con Tici Viracocha next went to the Island of the Sun, in Lake Titicaca, near Tiwanaku. There he made the sun, moon and stars and ordered them to ascend into the heavens to give light to the world. He set them in motion to create the cycle

Above: The Incas regarded such great stone statues as the Ponce Stela at Tiwanaku to be a record of the first age of giants.

of day and night, the waxing and waning of the moon and the progression of the seasons. The moon shone more brightly than the sun, and the sun became jealous. In rage, he threw ashes into the moon's face, diminishing its glow and causing the shades of grey on its surface.

A SECOND AGE OF HUMANS

Viracocha then returned to Tiwanaku and created a second race of humans. This time he wanted his creation to be more perfect, so he created men and women of a stature similar to his own. He sculpted these beings from 'the pliable stones' of the lakeshore – meaning clay. He painted the men and women of different nations and tribes with their characteristic costumes, hairstyles and jewellery. He gave each

designated group its own language, special songs and the precious gift of agriculture in the form of seeds to sow.

Viracocha then dispersed these peoples throughout the land by causing them to descend into Mother Earth and to migrate

Below: Viracocha was represented in many stone images at Tiwanaku, usually in Staff Deity pose, recalling the ancient Chavín god.

to their 'places of origin' (*pacarinas*). They were instructed to wait there as *mitimaes* (the name given to communities forcibly resettled by the Incas) until called forth to inhabit the land. (This arrangement clearly fitted Inca notions that they were the chosen people with a right to rule others, for Viracocha seems to anticipate what would happen when the Incas began to create their empire.)

Two men, called his sons or brothers, were kept aside as his helpers. Viracocha taught them the names of the various peoples and told them to memorize their designated valleys and provinces of origin. He said, 'just as I have made them they must come out of the springs and rivers and caves and mountains'. He instructed each helper on his route, directing each to start by heading towards the sunset. Lastly, Viracocha made a sacred idol on the Island of the Sun to commemorate what had been accomplished.

CALLING FORTH THE NATIONS
The brother-son Imaymana Viracocha travelled north-west along the border of the mountains and jungles. Tocapu Viracocha went to the coast and travelled north along the ocean provinces. Con Tici

Above: The Incas recognized the Island of the Sun, in Lake Titicaca, as the birth place of the sun and moon, and built a temple there.

himself went between them, following the highlands, towards Cuzco along the River Vilcanota. As they passed through the land, they called forth the nations, telling the people to obey the orders of Con Tici – to spread across the valleys, settle the land and multiply.

A third helper (in one variation), Taguapaca, refused to follow Viracocha's commands. Viracocha ordered Imaymana and Tocapu to seize Taguapaca, bind his hands and feet and throw him into the river. Cursing and vowing to return to take vengeance, Taguapaca was carried by the river into Lake Titicaca and disappeared. Much later he reappeared and travelled to preach, saying that he was Viracocha, but people were suspicious and most ridiculed him.

The three Viracochas taught the people and performed many miracles in their travels, finally reaching the end of their journey on the north-west coast. Viracocha (or, in one version, all three) continued out to sea, walking on the water (or in a boat made from his cloak).

TALES OF HEROES

Heroes and rulers of the most ancient times are unknown because there are no written sources to name them. It is not until the Later Intermediate Period and the Late Horizon that there are accounts of legendary kings and their dynasties, and several legendary heroes who stand out among the ancient Andean cultures. Apart from obvious figures in the Inca state creation myth – Manco Capac and his brothers and sisters – there are a few founders of dynasties in pre-Inca cultures whose legends have survived because they were important in some way to Inca imperial claims to rulership and territory. They have survived in turn through the Spanish chroniclers.

The ancient Moche deities are, for the most part, unnamed except by epithets created by archaeologists – for example the Decapitator God and the bird deities depicted in painted ritual scenes. If the

Right: The Naymlap dynasty afforded noble burials filled with exquisitely crafted burial gear, such as this gold hip plate.

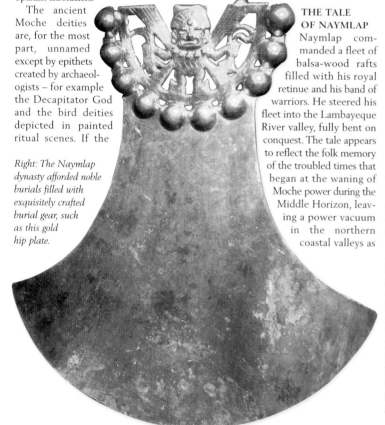

priests impersonating these deities were also rulers, their names are likewise unknown, even though their reality is confirmed in the rich burials of the Moche Lords of Sipán, burials with all the rich trappings of rulership and a style of dress identical to the figures in the painted scenes. Royal dynasties are again attested by the rich burials of the later Sicán Lords of the Lambayeque Valley farther north.

The story of the founding of a dynasty of kings, so clearly attested by these archaeological discoveries in the northern coastal valleys, however, emerges in the legend of Naymlap, a founder hero.

THE TALE OF NAYMLAP

Naymlap commanded a fleet of balsa-wood rafts filled with his royal retinue and his band of warriors. He steered his fleet into the Lambayeque River valley, fully bent on conquest. The tale appears to reflect the folk memory of the troubled times that began at the waning of Moche power during the Middle Horizon, leaving a power vacuum in the northern coastal valleys as

Above: This pair of Moche turquoise and gold earrings from Sipán, c.AD 400, shows warriors carrying spears and ropes and reflects the richness of Naymlap's 'noble company'.

Wari and Tiwanaku rulers built powerful sierra empires farther south. It seems that Naymlap, even if only one among several powerful war leaders, stepped into the breach and may be one of the first real people of ancient Andean civilization known today. The Lambayeque (or Sicán) culture that succeeded the Moche appears to have been a loose confederation of petty states in these northern coastal valleys, possibly linked through dynastic inheritance and royal descent as the sons of kings founded sister cities in the adjacent valleys.

A BRAVE AND NOBLE COMPANY

Naymlap led a 'brave and noble company' of men and women. Accompanying him were his wife, Ceterni, his harem and 40 followers. There were Pitz Zofi, Preparer of the Way; Fonga Sigde, Blower of the Conch Trumpet; Ninacola, Master of the Royal Litter and Throne; Ninagintue, the Royal Cellerer (presumably for *chicha* beer); Llapchillulli, Provider of Feather Garments; Xam Muchec, Steward of the Face-paint; Occhocalo, the Royal Cook; and Ollopcopoc, Master of the Bath.

Naymlap also brought his symbol of royal power, the greenstone idol called Yampallec, from which the Lambayeque Valley takes its name. The idol's visage, stature and figure was a double of the king himself.

NAYMLAP'S DYNASTY

With his men, Naymlap invaded the valley and built a palace at the place called Chot, which archaeologists have identified as the site of Huaca Chotuna in the Lambayeque Valley. The conquest of the local peoples was successful, and together the invaders and invaded settled down in peace. After a long life, Naymlap died and was buried in the palace. He had

Below: Detail of a gold and jade kero, *or cup, from Lambeyeque, which may show the legendary dynasty founder Naymlap.*

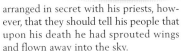

Left: Like the earlier Naymlap dynasty, founders of the Chimú dynasty in the Moche and other northern coastal valleys came from the south by sea in balsa boats, represented in this Chimú ceramic vessel.

arranged in secret with his priests, however, that they should tell his people that upon his death he had sprouted wings and flown away into the sky.

Naymlap was succeeded by his eldest son, Cium, and thereafter by ten other kings in his dynasty, until the last ruler, Fempellec. Cium married a local woman named Zolzoloñi. The Spanish text refers to Zolzoloñi by the word *moza*, 'commoner' or 'outsider', making it clear that she was not one of Naymlap's people or descendants. Cium and Zolzoloñi had 12 sons, each of whom married and also produced large families. As the population of the valley grew, each son left the capital and founded a new city within the valley.

A DYNASTY BETRAYED

Fempellec was the 12th ruler of the dynasty. Unlike its founder, however, he is noteworthy for having brought dishonour and disaster to the kingdom. He was insistent upon a plan to remove

the stone idol of Yampallec from Chot to another city, an act of which his priests heartily disapproved. Before he could accomplish this sacrilege, however, a demon appeared to him in the form of a beautiful woman. She seduced him, and after his betrayal it began to rain heavily, an event all too rare in the region. It rained for 30 days, and then was followed by a year of drought and, inevitably, hunger, as the crops failed.

By this time the priests had tired of their scheming ruler. They seized Fempellec and tied his hands and feet; carried him to the sea, threw him in, and left him to his fate, thus ending the dynasty of Naymlap and his successors.

The legend of Naymlap is so lost in time that it is impossible to be certain whether his tale is to be associated with the founding of the Early Intermediate Period Moche, or one of its dynasties, or with the Late Intermediate Period Kingdom of Chimú, or indeed with the intervening Lambayeque (Sicán) civilization.

THE KINGDOM OF THE CHIMÚ

The Late Intermediate Period kingdom of Chimú (or Chimor) occupied the northern coastal valleys the Moche had previously occupied, filling the power vacuum apparently left by the collapse of the Moche and Lambayeque-Sicán dynasties. Chimú was centred in the Moche Valley, south of Lambayeque. Again there are stories of legendary rulers; early accounts were handed down through the generations before being recorded by the later kings of Chimú and the Incas, then passed on through Spanish chroniclers.

A NEW DYNASTY

Taycanamu was the first of a new Chimú dynasty established in the 14th century. Like so many pre-Inca rulers in the kingdoms subjugated by them, knowledge of the dynasty is obscured in legend. Taycanamu was said to have arrived at Moche on a balsa-wood raft, 'sent' from afar with the express mission of governing the peoples of the valley. Was he a late descendant of the northern dynasties? Several unnamed and little-known kings succeeded him until the conquest of the valley by the Inca prince Tupac Yupanqui in the mid-15th century. The *ciudadella* compounds at the capital, Chan Chan, appear to be the dedicated sacred compounds of the succeeding kings of Chimú.

Chimo Capac, literally 'Lord Chimú', was undoubtedly one of these kings. In the late 14th or early 15th century he invaded the Lambayeque Valley from Moche, possibly after the death of Fempellec and his contemporaries. Like Naymlap, he came by sea. He appointed a man named Pongmassa to rule the valley as the local *curaca* (official), then returned to Chan Chan. Pongmassa was succeeded by his son and grandson. During the grandson's time, the Incas invaded and subjugated Chimú. As was characteristic Inca policy, they

Above: The administrative sector of Chan Chan, capital of Chimú and South America's largest pre-Hispanic mud-brick settlement.

continued to rule the valley through its local *curaca*, five more of whom succeeded before the Spanish Conquest.

THE SUBJUGATION OF CHIMÚ

Minchançaman (or Minchancamon) was the last of the independent rulers of the Taycanamu dynasty, the sixth or seventh ruler in that line. The account of Tupac Yupanqui's invasion demonstrates the Incas' method of incorporating new kingdoms into the fabric of the empire, firmly establishing their overlordship while at the same time recognizing the integrity and power of the ruling dynasty:

'The brave Chimú [Minchançaman], his arrogance and pride now tamed, appeared before the prince [Tupac Yupanqui] with as much submission and humility, and grovelled on the ground before him, worshipping him and repeating the same request [for pardon] as he had made through his ambassadors. The prince received him affectionately in order to relieve [his] grief ... [and] bade two of the captains raise him from the ground. After hearing him [Tupac Yupanqui] told him that all that was past was forgiven.... The Inca had not come to deprive him of his estates and authority, but to improve his idolatrous religion, his laws, and his customs.'

TALES FROM THE SOUTH

The abandonment of the ceremonial city of Tiwanaku on the southern shores of Lake Titicaca occurred at the end of the Middle Horizon. Archaeological evidence indicates that the withdrawal from use of the various monumental structures and ceremonial courts was quite abrupt, even violent. We can only speculate as to why the rulers of the city abandoned it or were overthrown. However, one tale from Inca

Below: A drawing by Guaman Poma de Ayala showing humans from the first age cultivating the crops and tilling the land.

records that may be relevant tells of the legendary rulers of two city-states in the Titicaca Basin, Cari and Zapana.

Cari sought the help of the Incas of Cuzco against his rival Zapana. The Incas, however, saw this as an opportunity (or an invitation) to invade the region and to subjugate both cities. Although the story dates from long after the civilization of Tiwanaku had collapsed, the still visible ruins were revered by the Incas. They recognized that the city was ancient and had been powerful. The ruins inspired them to use these invasions to claim descent from the ancient rulers or deities of the region. Perhaps the story is a long folk memory of the break-up of Tiwanaku, recording how rival factions within the Titicaca Basin sought the help of the Incas as the rising power in the Cuzco Valley to the north-west.

THE UNNAMED MAN

A mysterious figure features in the story of Inca beginnings – the Unnamed Man. The Incas divided their empire into four parts and referred to it as Tahuantinsuyu – land of the four quarters – which were named Chinchaysuyu, Antisuyu, Cuntisuyu and Collasuyu. The story of the Unnamed Man is the only substantial account of this division and of the appointment and naming of the *suyu* (quarter) rulers.

Above: From the Titicaca Basin, backdrop to the ancient city of Tiwanaku, the Unnamed Man appeared after the great flood.

After the waters of the great world flood receded, a powerful, but unnamed, man appeared at the ancient city of Tiwanaku in the Titicaca Basin. The Unnamed Man used his powers to designate the four quarters and to appoint rulers for each of them. To Chinchaysuyu (the north) he named Manco Capac; to Collasuyu (the south) he named Colla; to Antisuyu (the east) he named Tocay; to Cuntisuyu (the west) he named Pinahua. He commanded each king to conquer his allotted quarter and to govern his people.

The brief story is recounted in Garcilaso de la Vega's *Commentarios Reales de los Incas*. The dearth of further explanation is curious, given Inca emphasis on their origins at Lake Titicaca in one version of the official state creation myth. Recognizing Tiwanaku as an ancient seat of power, they wished to bolster their claimed right to rule. Tiwanaku was, in fact, much closer to the actual centre of the empire than was Cuzco.

The rich lands of the Lupaqa Kingdoms – the late inheritors of Tiwanaku power – were important acquisitions to the Inca, as were the vast llama lands of the Altiplano.

EL DORADO AND CHIBCHA HEROES

Although the Chibcha area of present-day Colombia is not technically in the Andean Area as defined here, no book on ancient Andean mythology would seem complete without a description of the legend of El Dorado.

THE GILDED MAN
El Dorado, literally the 'Gilded Man' in Spanish, was the legendary king of the chiefdom of the Chibcha, or Muisca, of the far northern Andes in Colombia. El Dorado was a person, a city, an entire kingdom and, in time, a myth. In their lust for gold, once tales of untold wealth from that quarter had reached their ears, the Spaniards generally associated the legend with the entire region of

Below: The myth of El Dorado was represented in a multi-necklace- and earring-wearing man from the Calima culture.

central Colombia. In reality, the quest for gold and riches beyond belief turned out to be a chimera: El Dorado was always just one more range of mountains away, but was never found.

The most reliable sources of the legend focus on the Chibcha/Muisca and their chiefdom around Lake Guatavita in central Colombia, north of Bogotá. Gold was extremely important to all the chiefdoms of the far northern Andes, and several distinctive gold-working styles developed throughout the region from the first century BC/AD; the Muisca style itself dates from the 8th century AD. The Spaniards learned the story of the Gilded Man from many sources, including the Chibcha, who had actually witnessed the ceremony before the Spaniards arrived. Every conquistador and chronicler of this northern area makes mention of the Gilded Man, but the most complete account is that of the mid-17th-century chronicler Rodríguez Freyle, who was told the legend by his friend Don Juan, the nephew of the last independent lord of Guatavita.

THE ANOINTING OF A KING
The ritual that gave rise to the legend was performed at the inauguration of a new king. The heir to the throne spent the days before the ceremony secluded in a cave. During this time, he was required to abstain from sexual relations with women and was forbidden to eat chilli peppers or salt. On the appointed day, he made his first official journey to Lake Guatavita, there to make offerings to the gods. At the lakeside, a raft of rushes was made and bedecked with precious decorations and treasures. Four lighted braziers were placed on the raft, in which *moque* incense and other resins were burned. Braziers of incense were also lit along the

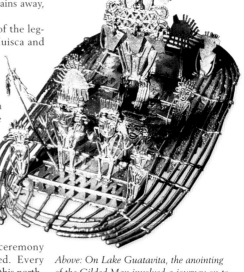

Above: On Lake Guatavita, the anointing of the Gilded Man involved a journey on to the lake and the deposition of golden gifts.

shoreline, and such a quantity of smoke was produced by them that the light of the sun was said to be obscured.

The king-to-be was stripped naked and his body smeared with a sticky clay or resin. Over this he was covered with glittering gold dust, shown being blown from a tube in an engraving of 1599. He then boarded the raft, accompanied by four principal subject chiefs, all of whom were richly attired in 'plumes, crowns, bracelets, pendants, and ear rings all of gold', but also otherwise naked. The king remained motionless on the raft and at his feet was placed a great heap of gold and precious stones (called 'emeralds' by Freyle).

The raft was pushed off across the lake, whereupon musicians on shore struck up a fanfare of trumpets, flutes and other instruments, and the assembled crowd began to sing loudly. When the raft reached the centre of the lake, a banner

was raised as a signal for silence. The gilded king then made his offering to the gods: all of the treasures on the raft were thrown into the lake, one by one, by the king and his attendants. Then the flag was lowered again, and the raft paddled towards shore to the accompaniment of loud music and singing, and wild dancing.

Upon reaching the shore, the new king was accepted as the lord and master of the realm.

CHIBCHA LEGENDS

A few Chibcha heroes are known. Bochica was their legendary founder hero. He arrived among them from the east, travelling as a bearded sage, and taught them civilization, moral laws and the craft

Below: Guatavita, the 'El Dorado' lake in Colombia where Chibcha chiefs dived covered in clay and powdered gold.

of metalworking. Not all accepted his teaching, however. A woman named Chie challenged him by urging the Chibcha to ignore him and make merry, whereupon Bochica transformed her into an owl.

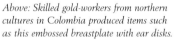

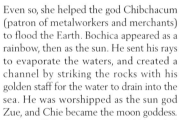

Above: Skilled gold-workers from northern cultures in Colombia produced items such as this embossed breastplate with ear disks.

Even so, she helped the god Chibchacum (patron of metalworkers and merchants) to flood the Earth. Bochica appeared as a rainbow, then as the sun. He sent his rays to evaporate the waters, and created a channel by striking the rocks with his golden staff for the water to drain into the sea. He was worshipped as the sun god Zue, and Chie became the moon goddess.

A parallel tale concerns an old bearded man called Nemterequeteba, who came to the Muisca from a distant land. He, too, taught the Chibcha the art of weaving and civilized behaviour. His rival was Huitaca, goddess of evil and patroness of misbehaviour and drunkenness. She challenged Nemterequeteba and in one version of the legend she was transformed into the moon by him. She is therefore sometimes confused with the Muisca moon goddess Chie.

The obscurity of these tales might reflect troubles on the distant northern borders of the Inca or earlier kingdoms. Chie/Huitaca, clearly a local deity, resented the appearance of an outsider from afar, who came essentially in a guise similar to the wandering creator god Viracocha.

EMPIRE OF THE SUN

Manco Capac was the legendary first Inca ruler and founder of the Inca dynasty Hurin Cuzco. He was the principal character in Inca mythology surrounding the origins of the state and Inca power.

THE STATE CREATION MYTH
Various permutations of the Inca state creation myth prevailed simultaneously, a fact that caused the Spanish chroniclers considerable consternation. The most prominent version described how four brothers and four sisters came forth from the central one of three 'windows', or caves, in the mountain called Tambo Toco ('window mountain'). These were 'the ancestors', led by the eldest brother, Manco Capac (originally Ayar Manco), who, with his brothers (Ayar Auca, Ayar Cachi and Ayar Uchu) and sisters (Mama Ocllo, Mama Huaco, Mama Ipacura/Cura and Mama Raua), led the people of Tambo Toco in search of a new land to settle, where a capital city could be built.

Below: The endurance of Inca culture is exemplified by this characteristic Inca trapezoidal doorway in Cuzco, still in use.

Above: Manco Capac, legendary founder of the Inca dynasty and 'son of the sun'.

After much wandering they came to a hill overlooking the Cuzco Valley. Miraculous signs informed them that they should settle there, so they came down from the mountain, overcame local resistance and took possession of the land.

EMERGENCE FROM CAPAC TOCO
The standard version comes from Sarmiento de Gamboa, in his *Historia de los Incas* (1572), an early source that relied heavily on interviews with keepers of the Inca state records, the *quipucamayoqs*.

Pacaritambo, overlooking which was Tambo Toco, was the 'house of dawn', the 'place of origin'. According to the chroniclers it was six leagues (about 33km/20 miles) south of Cuzco; in fact, it is closer to 26km (16 miles) south of Cuzco. In the beginning, the mountain there, Tambo Toco, had three windows, the central one of which was called Capac Toco – 'rich window'. From this window emerged the four ancestral couples, the brother/sister–husband/wife pairs: Capac with Ocllo, Auca with Huaco, Cachi with Ipacura/ Cura, and Uchu with Raua. From the flanking windows, Maras Toco and Sutic Toco, came

the peoples called the Maras and the Tambos, both Inca allies. A divine link was immediately established in the promotion of the myth when it was claimed that the ancestors and allies were called out of the caves by Con Tici Viracocha.

Ayar Manco declared that he would lead his brothers and sisters, and the allies, in search of a fertile land, where the local inhabitants would be conquered. He promised to make the allies rich. Before setting out, the allies were formed into ten *ayllus* (lineage groups) – the origin of the ten *ayllus* of Cuzco commoners. The ten royal *ayllus* (called *panacas*) were the descendants of the first ten Inca emperors.

THE JOURNEY BEGINS
Ayar Manco led his followers north, towards the Cuzco Valley. He carried a golden bar, brought from Tambo Toco. With this he tested the ground for fertility by thrusting it periodically into the soil.

Progress was slow and there were several stops. At the first stop Ayar Manco and Mama Ocllo conceived a child. At the second stop a boy was born, whom they named Sinchi Roca. They stopped a third time at a place called Palluta, where they lived for several years; but eventually the

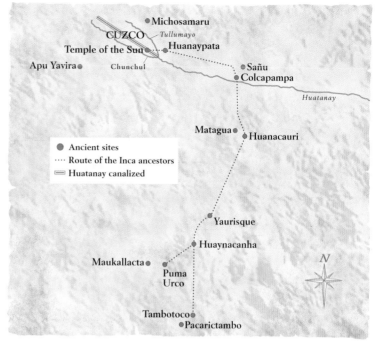

land proved unfertile, so they moved on to a place called Haysquisrro. Here the company began to break up.

BREAKING UP OF THE COMPANY

Ayar Cachi was unruly and sometimes cruel. He always caused trouble with the local inhabitants through his tricks and rowdiness wherever the ancestors passed through or stopped. He was a powerful slinger, and could hurl stones so hard that he could split open mountains, causing dust and rocks to fly up and obscure the sun. The other ancestors began to consider him a liability, so they formed a plan to dispense with him. Manco told Cachi that several important objects that should have accompanied the golden rod had been left in Pacaritambo: a golden cup (*topacusi*), a miniature llama figurine (*napa*) and some seeds. Ayar Cachi at first refused to return to Capac Toco, but agreed to do so when his elder sister, Mama Huaco, herself forceful in character, chided him and accused him of laziness and cowardice.

Below: A fanciful Spanish genealogy of Inca emperors, from Manco Capac onward.

Cachi journeyed back to Capac Toco with a Tambo companion called Tambochacay ('the Tambo entrance-bearer'). He was unaware, however, that Manco and the others had convinced Tambochacay to get rid of him. When Ayar Cachi entered the cave to retrieve the forgotten items, Tambochacay quickly

Above: After their underground migration from Lake Titicaca and emergence from a cave, the Inca ancestor pairs went to Cuzco.

sealed off the entrance, trapping Cachi inside forever. The site, later known as Mauqallaqta ('ancient town'), became an important Inca sacred *huaca*.

The ancestors' next stop was Quirirmanta, at the foot of a mountain called Huanacauri. They climbed the mountain, and from the top saw the Cuzco Valley for the first time. From the summit, Manco threw the golden rod into the valley to test the soil. To the ancestors' amazement the rod disappeared into the Earth and a rainbow appeared over the valley. They took these signs to mean that this should be their homeland.

Before they could descend the mountain, Ayar Uchu sprouted wings and flew up to the sun. The sun told him that, thenceforth, Ayar Manco should be called Manco Capac, the 'supreme rich one', and that they should go to Cuzco, where the ruler, Alcavicça, would welcome them. Uchu returned to his brothers and sisters, told them this news, and was transformed into stone, becoming a second *huaca*.

213

Inca Cuzco (the plaza called Huanay-pata), the remaining brother-ancestor, Ayar Auca, was turned into a stone pillar, which, like Mauqallaqta and Uchu, became a sacred *huaca*.

This left Manco Capac, his sisters and his son Sinchi Roca, a convenient outcome, which was in keeping with later Inca imperial practice of sister/wives, and a chosen descendant to the rulership. They began the building of Cuzco.

INCA AMBITIONS

This 'standard' version contains all the necessary elements of Inca legend, including in mythical form the wandering, conquering, alliances and divine intervention needed to telescope what must have been the folk memory of their long and complex history.

Left: A fanciful 18th-century Spanish colonial depiction of an Inca prince sporting a sun pendant, indicating his imperial status.

Below: Regarded as the 'sons of the sun', Inca emperors were carried about in stately fashion on a litter, shown here on a wooden kero *cup.*

THE FINAL ROAD TO CUZCO

However, the remaining ancestors did not proceed straight to Cuzco. They stopped first at nearby Matao, where they stayed for two years, and where another strange event occurred. Mama Huaco, an expert slinger, hurled a stone at a man in Matao and killed him. She split open his chest, removed his heart and lungs and blew into the lungs to inflate them. The watching people of the town fled in terror.

Finally, Manco Capac led the ancestors to Cuzco. They met Alcavicça and declared that they had been sent by their father, the sun, which convinced Alcavicça to allow them to take over. In return the ancestors 'domesticated' the inhabitants of the valley by teaching them to plant maize. (In one version it was Manco Capac who planted the first field; in another it was Mama Huaco.) At the place that would become the centre of

Above: The large oval eyes, feline grin, snake, trophy head and other symbols of this sheet-gold Inca sun disk seem to be a composite of sacred ancient Andean iconography.

The Incas were ambitious, however. They felt a need to link their personal creation to world creation, and thus legitimize their right to rule through divine sanction. They vigorously promoted their own political agenda, and were particularly keen to establish their origins as special and to convince others that *their* place of origin was universal – that is, the same as that of the Incas. The 17th-century Jesuit priest Bernabé Cobo describes this official state line as 'caused by the ambition of the Incas. They were the first to worship [at] the cave of Pacaritambo as the [place of the] beginning of their lineage. They claimed that all people came from there, and that for this reason all people were their vassals and obliged to serve them'.

VARIATIONS ON A THEME
In other variations of the story, the Incas were more devious – they rewrote and reshaped their story to justify their actions and to incorporate long-held beliefs of the peoples they subjugated. Thus, in one version the ancestors deliberately tricked the inhabitants of the Cuzco Valley into believing them to be the descendants of the sun, not just his ambassadors. Manco Capac made, or had made, two golden discs – one for his front, one for his back. He climbed Mt Huanacauri before dawn so that at sunrise he appeared to be a golden, god-like being. The populace of Cuzco was so awed that he had no trouble in assuming rulership.

Another version, given by four elderly *quipucamayoqs*, contains an undercurrent of the resentment that must have been harboured by local inhabitants at the outsiders' invasion. The story suggests that the whole fabric of Inca rule was illegitimate.

In this variation, Manco Capac was the son of a local *curaca* in Pacaritambo, whose mother had died giving birth to him. His father gave him the nickname 'son of the sun', but also died, when Manco Capac was 10 or 12, never having

explained that it was just a nickname. What is more, the commoners of the town were convinced that Manco was actually the son of the sun, and the two old priests of his father's household gods encouraged this belief. As Manco Capac reached early manhood, the priests promoted Manco's conviction, telling him that it gave him the right to rule. Filled with this idea, he set off for Cuzco with several relatives and the priests, taking his

father's idol, Huanacauri. He arrived on Mt Huanacauri at dawn, bedecked in gold, thus dazzling the people and convincing them of his divine descent Yet another version of the state origin myth associates the ancestors with the Island of the Sun in Lake Titicaca, from which Manco Capac led them underground to Pacaritambo. This was a deception meant to justify Inca conquest. Being born on the Island of the Sun made Manco Capac 'son of the sun'. Local myth described a great deluge that destroyed the previous world and claimed that the sun of the present world first shone on the island. He placed his son and daughter on the island to teach the locals how to live civilized lives. The Incas believed that these were Manco Capac and Mama Ocllo, and that the creator, Viracocha, bestowed a special headdress and stone battle-axe upon Manco Capac, prophesying that the Incas would become great lords and conquer many other nations.

Below: In a 20th-century revival of the Inti Raymi (June/winter solstice festival) women are dressed to represent aclla *virgins.*

ISLANDS OF THE SUN AND MOON

The Island of the Sun and the Island of the Moon were sacred places in the southern half of Lake Titicaca, just off-shore north of the Copacabana Peninsula. Sitting almost at the centre of the lake, the Island of the Sun was a dramatic location from which to observe the passage of the sun across the high, clear mountain sky. The Incas believed that the islands were the birthplaces of the sun and the moon, or that the sun, moon and stars were created and set in motion from the Island of the Sun by the god Con Tici Viracocha Pachayachachic – 'creator of all things'.

A MOST SACRED PLACE

The Incas identified and named the Island of the Sun and built a shrine there dedicated to Viracocha. The shrine was the focus of an annual pilgrimage by the Inca emperor and nobility. Alongside the sacred Coricancha in Cuzco, and the much more ancient shrine and oracle to Pachacamac in the central coastal city of the same name, this shrine was one of the most sacred sites in the Inca realm until

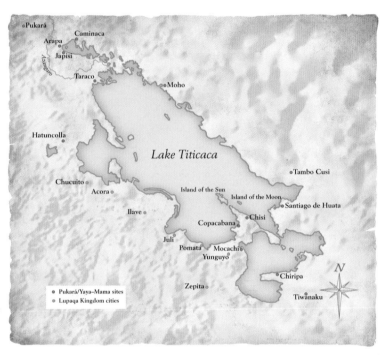

Above: This map shows Lake Titicaca, with the sacred Islands of the Sun and Moon, and ancient sites of religious importance.

Below: The sacred Island of the Sun, Lake Titicaca, rising steeply from the lake, where Viracocha created the sun and the moon.

sacked by the Spaniards in their lust for gold. A sacred stone – the Rock of the Sun, a partially modified natural boulder – set up in an open space, and from which the sun was believed to have risen, still stands on the island overlooking the lake.

In one version of the Inca state creation story Manco Capac and his sister/wife Mama Ocllo (and in some variations their siblings as well) were associated with the Island of the Sun in a deception meant to justify Inca conquest of the local peoples. They were said to have led their brothers and sisters from the Island of the Sun, either through the earth or overland to the caves at Pacaritambo.

A PRE-INCA CULT

When the Inca emperor Pachacuti subjugated the Titicaca Basin in the mid-15th century, part of his task was made easier by entering into alliances with some of

Above: The Incas revered the site of Tiwanaku on the southern lakeshore. They built temples to Viracocha and Inti on the Island of the Sun.

the city-states there, such as the Lupaca. The Incas no doubt played on local rivalries to conquer those who resisted their incursions. Pachacuti soon realized the ancient importance of the lake and islands in local religious belief, and with characteristic Inca policy, recognized and honoured the local ruins still visible at Tiwanaku on the southern lakeshore.

Hard evidence of the pre-Inca sacredness of both islands is given by archaeological finds. Hammered sheet-gold and silver objects in the forms of cut-out llamas and the image of Tiwanaku's principal deity – the god with large round eyes and a rounded square face depicted on the Gateway of the Sun, so-called for the sunlike rays surrounding the god's face – have been found on both islands and on the mainland at Tiwanaku itself. A gold disc depicting the god, along with a gold cup and ceramic vessels, were found in the lake off Koa Island, just off the north end of the Island of the Sun. The llama features frequently in Tiwanaku and later sacrificial ritual, and clearly these objects were sacred offerings to the sun by priests or pilgrims.

AN INCA PILGRIMAGE SITE

It was Pachacuti, the great builder, who began the Inca temple and shrine on the Island of the Sun. According to Inca records the temple was administered by 2,000 cult retainers. The temple complex included a *tambo* (a way-station to accommodate pilgrims) and an *acllahuasi* (a 'house of the chosen women' known as *acllas* – hand-picked Inca girls trained to serve the cult of Inti, the sun god, who was ultimately regarded as the Inca emperor himself). In addition to the *tambo* and *acllahuasi*, storehouses were built near Copacabana to provide provisions, clothes and other supplies to the temple attendants and pilgrims.

It seems likely that the Incas adopted a much older cult of the sun established by the people of Tiwanaku, or earlier peoples, on the island. The association of the island as the birthplace of the Inca ancestors would certainly have been an advantageous link in Inca efforts to justify their belief in the right to rule others. One Spanish chronicler, the Augustinian Alonso Ramos Gavilán, claims that the local inhabitants had sent a priest to Cuzco to seek patronage from Pachacuti.

Father Bernabé Cobo devotes an entire chapter of his book on Inca religion to 'the famous temple of Copacabana'. He calls the two islands Titicaca (Sun) and Coata (Moon) and says that there were in fact 'two magnificent temples', one on each island. It is Cobo who claims that the islands were regarded as sacred before the Incas arrived in the region and declares that 'they took charge of enhancing the shrine'. Cobo describes how Tupac Yupanqui, Pachacuti's successor, undertook to enhance the shrine, first by fasting there for several days to show his devotion, and then by establishing an annual pilgrimage to the temple. To reach the Rock of the Sun, pilgrims were obliged to undergo a long ritual route including many stops for observances and offerings, both at mainland *huacas* and on the island.

Below: The extensive ruins of an acllahuasi *on the Island of the Moon bear witness to the importance of these sites of annual pilgrimage.*

CHAPTER ELEVEN

LEAVING THIS EARTH

The Incas regarded life and death as two of many stages in the cycle of being in which all living things took part. From birth through life and into death, there was a rhythm and sense of renewal. In a sense, in Andean belief one never 'left' the earth, for it was from the earth that people came (as described in the creation myth, when Viracocha created humans from clay, and also when they emerged from the earth into which he had dispersed them) and to it that they returned, becoming part of it at burial or remaining on it as a mummy preserved for ritual occasions.

Death did not always occur naturally, of course, and there is wide evidence of ritual sacrifice in an endless attempt to placate the gods. Once dead, rich and powerful ancient Andeans could expect an elite burial with all the trappings, possibly including mummification. Their bodies might be stored in family *chullpas* (burial towers) or buried.

The Lower World (the earth), or Hurin Pacha, was intimately linked to the World Above (Honan Pacha) and the World Below (Uku Pacha), the worlds of the gods, supernatural beings and spirits. Trained individuals, the shamans, could leave Hurin Pacha temporarily through the use of hallucinogenic drugs. They could travel in their altered mental state to converse with and seek help from the gods on behalf of individuals and the nation in general. In order to do so they could also transform into another being, for example a jaguar or an owl, taking on that being's perceived supernatural powers.

Left: Inca agricultural terracing on the steeply rising slopes above Bahia Kona on the Island of the Sun, in Lake Titicaca.

THE CYCLE OF LIFE AND DEATH

Andean belief held that the cycle of being for all living things was a procession through states of being. It began as a general vegetative state, passed through a tender, juicy young state (babies, young shoots) into a progressively drier, firmer more resistant state (adulthood, mature plant), then became a desiccated, preserved state (mummies, dried and stored crops). But this was not the end. When a person died, his or her desiccated remains were like dried pods from which seeds dropped to begin the cycle anew, as their spirit proceeded to its final resting place.

Such basic concepts seem logical in societies that were ultimately reliant on agricultural and pastoral ways of life. Birth, growth and seeding were metaphors taken from the plant world; stages of life were like those observed so closely while tending herds of llamas. The origin of each new generation from the seeds of the last was essentially an exchange of the old for the new.

Below: This Moche painted ceramic piece depicting young maize cobs on the stalk reminded the Andeans of birth and growth.

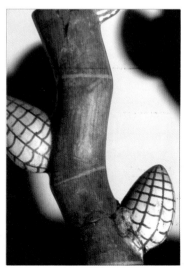

A CARING SOCIETY

During life on earth, the individual was bound into a web of mutual caring. Adults cared for babies and children just as the young cared for the aged. Each individual had their personal role in society and exchanged produce and commodities, depending on their occupation. Shamans cared for the people, while priests, who looked after the welfare of the state and were intermediaries to the gods, were supported by the people and made offerings and sacrifices to the gods on their behalf. Finally, rulers governed and redistributed the wealth of society according to each person's needs within fixed, accepted roles and stations. On a larger scale, different regions were engaged in exchange networks, both socially and for trade. Such networks of exchange were mimicked by the belief that death represented an exchange of old for new.

The Inca sources from which the Spaniards recorded these beliefs must be the culmination of beliefs from the earliest agriculturalists, refined and elaborated through millennia.

METAPHORICAL IMAGES

The cult of the founding ancestors reflects these themes. The Quechua word *mallqui* (tree) can be glossed as 'ancestor'. The three caves or windows at Tambo Toco were depicted with a tree. From the middle window, Capac Toco, came Manco Capac and the other Inca

Above: Ancient Andeans were reminded of the cycle of life by objects around them, such as this effigy bottle representing old age.

brother/sister–husband/wife ancestors. In it was a golden tree whose branches and roots connected it to the left-hand window, Maras Toco, occupied by Manco Capac's paternal ancestors. Next to the golden tree was a silver tree, connected to the right-hand window, Sutic Toco, occupied by his maternal ancestors.

Above: Ancient Andeans learned to maximize crop production through the use of natural fertilizer, such as guano from off-shore islands.

Another metaphorical depiction of regeneration and reproduction showed the *mallqui* next to the *collca*, the store-house in which the year's harvest was kept.

Reflecting an animal metaphor, the rotting of the dead body was conceived as a process that lasted a year after the living body ceased to breathe, during which time the bodily fluids and flesh became desiccated. As this happened, the spirit of the individual emerged, just as a living seed escapes from a dried plant pod, to go to its rest.

PACARINA: RETURN TO ORIGINS

The concept of *pacarina* incorporates rebirth or regeneration. *Pacarina* was the place of origin, the place from which one's ancestors (one's tribe, nation or *ayllu* kinship group) emerged. It could be a tree, rock, cave, spring or lake, and it was a magical shelter from the ravages of the world. Andean tradition held that, after death, the spirit returned to its *pacarina* – the essence of being finally returning to its birthplace.

THE DYING PROCESS: A JOURNEY

Ancient Andeans thought of death as a gradual process, one that continued beyond the time when the body actually ceased functioning on earth, and during which the dead continued to inhabit the living world. Temporary states of being during life were regarded as near-death conditions, such as deep sleep, fainting, drunkenness and drug-induced states.

The journey ultimately began at birth. However, with the cessation of breathing and earth-life functions, the body began its death journey towards fulfilling its purpose of reunion with its ancestors and regeneration. The human spirit was the 'vital force' (Quechua *upani* or *camaquen*; Aymara *amaya* or *ch'iwu*; and in Latin/Spanish translation *alma* and *anima*).

Different sources name the spirit's final destination. Inhabitants of Collasuyu and Cuntisuyu called it Puquina Pampa and Coropuna. Cajatsmbo documents name Uma Pacha, and documents of the Lima region name Upaymarca. Coastal peoples called the final resting place the Island of Guano. More generally, the final resting place was perceived to be a land of farms, where the dead sowed their seeds. The spirit continues to tend the fields and crops, and to experience thirst and hunger as the body does on Earth, and is fed by the living with offerings of food and drink.

The spirits of the deceased were regarded as dangerous, and it was necessary to help them reach the end of their journey, lest they wander among the living, causing violence, sickness and accidents. To reach the Island of Guano, the *anima* was carried by sea lions. To reach Upaymarca, the spirit had to cross a broad river on a narrow bridge made of human hair, known as Achachaca (Bridge of Hairs). In one variation of the cycle, the spirit must encounter a pack of black dogs. Thus, the link is maintained between 'living' and 'dead'.

Right: This Moche stirrup-spouted vessel is a portrait of a living, healthy, laughing man, enjoying life to the full.

BURIAL PRACTICES

Burials of the earliest periods are rare. Few are known from the Preceramic Period, suggesting that bodies were exposed to the elements or otherwise unceremoniously disposed of. Those burials that have been found within Preceramic cave sites were mostly in a flexed position, often on one side. Food, stone tools, beds and pigment fragments were the usual grave goods. As belief in an afterlife or life cycle developed, more care was taken of the deceased, leading to the elaborate preparation and burying of bodies.

Like Paracas, the long-lived pilgrimage and oracle site of Pachacamac was a prime burial place for both rich and poor. The desire was obviously to be buried at the sacred site, and Pachacamac served a large region for more than a millennium.

BODY PRESERVATION
The Chinchorros culture of northernmost Chile provides some of the earliest mixes of ordinary and distinguished burials. Between about 8,000 and 3,600 years

Below: Inca burials were accompanied by ceremonial drinking of chicha beer from kero cups to help the deceased into the next life.

ago, most bodies were buried without special treatment. On about 250 bodies, however, a tradition of deliberate preservation is evident: bodies were de-fleshed and disarticulated, then reassembled and buried inside cane or wooden shafts. About 6,000 years ago, at La Paloma on the central Peruvian coast, corpses were salted to arrest deterioration before being placed in burial pits. These two cultures introduced the long-held practice of preservation of at least chosen individuals, and the belief that the body must be intact in order to enter the afterlife.

Burials in the late Preceramic and Initial Period onward, whether especially elaborate or not, were commonly in the shape of some type of crypt. At Preceramic Kotosh, for example, stone-built chambers were used for ritual and then as burial crypts.

SUBTERRANEAN CHAMBERS
The Early Horizon necropolis on the Paracas Peninsula has many more burials than would have been needed by the nearby surrounding settlements. It can, therefore, be concluded that it was a dedicated cemetery for communities within a large region stretching inland. The burial chambers are intermixed and show obvious social differentiation, indicated by the sizes of the burial bundles, the sizes of chambers, and the grave goods that accompanied the bodies on their final journey.

The burial chambers were large, subterranean, bottle-shaped tombs. They often contained multiple burials, indicating that they were reopened repeatedly through generations. One tomb contained 37 burial bundles. The bundles were piled on top of each other, and in some cases the largest bundle, of the most important person, was placed in the centre of the chambers and surrounded by 'his people'.

The nature of Paracas burial shows the early development of kin-group association in ancient Andean civilization. In life, kin-groups worked together within agreed

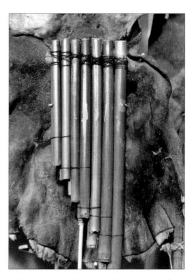

Above: Mummification techniques, together with the extreme desiccation of the Atacama Desert, preserved both human bodies and other organic matter, such as these reed pipes.

reciprocal obligations; in death, the kin-groups were buried together in their group associations over generations.

BURIAL BUNDLES
All bundles were elaborately wrapped in layers of textiles. Commoner bodies were wrapped in plain and fewer layers of cotton textiles and accompanied by plain ceramics and perhaps a few 'special' pieces. The richest burials were wrapped in much more elaborate textiles and accompanied by the richest ceramics, metalwork and exotic products from afar. Low mounds inland from the cemetery were apparently stages for the preparation of the bodies into mummy bundles.

The association of burial and rich textiles established in the Paracas and succeeding Nazca cultures was an association that continued right through to Inca society. The importance of textiles is attested by industries that produced

Above: The dry Nazca desert preserves the remains of thousands of burials, but, when exposed, the elements soon destroyed any textiles and artefacts that were not looted.

cloth exclusively for burial wrappings – which was a substantial demand on the state economy and human labour.

SUPPLIES FOR THE JOURNEY

Burial rites among most Andean peoples included gifts of clothing, food and *chicha* beer for their journey in the cycle of being.

Middle Horizon Wari tombs were often equipped with a hole in the top or side of the crypt, plus a channel to facilitate offerings of food and drink long after the individual had been laid to rest. Such feeding maintained the vital link between a people and their deceased ancestors. In Inca society, mummies were brought out on ceremonial occasions and offered food and drink.

SPECIAL PRACTICES

Burial in the Middle Horizon, Late Intermediate Period and Late Horizon was commonly in a subterranean chamber

in a seated position. Burials were often in shaft-like chambers, with later burials placed on top of earlier ones, maintaining the tradition of reopening kin-group mausoleums. Besides crypts and subterranean chambers of various sorts, several special types of burials have been discovered. For example, elongated hall-like rooms around the patios of Wari dwellings sometimes had human burials beneath their plastered floors, sometimes with small caches of valuables. The Akapana temple at Tiwanaku included ritual eating and burial, the primary burial being a man seated holding a puma effigy incense burner. In the Late Intermediate Period in the Titicaca Basin seated, subterranean chamber burials endured, but more important individuals developed the practice of burial in raised towers called *chullpas*.

One special Inca ritual practice was deliberate exposure to lightning, although it was recognized as potentially fatal.

Right: Inca funerary rites as depicted by Guaman Poma de Ayala c.1613. Note the mummified body in a chullpa *burial tower.*

A *qhaqha* (person or animals killed by lightning) was buried at the place where they were killed.

As the body was taken to its burial place, the Incas would make a mourning sound for the dead like the cooing of a dove. It was invented upon the death of the founder ancestor Ayar Uchu, according to the state creation myth.

ELITE BURIALS

Archaeological evidence from elite burials is abundant. Unfortunately, though, many rich tombs have long since been looted by treasure seekers.

ELITE INCA BURIALS
Father Bernabé Cobo, in his 17th-century *Historia del Nuevo Mundo*, describes Inca burial customs as he observed them. He declares that there was greater concern for one's place of burial than for one's dwelling when alive. Although graves and rituals varied, each province having their own practices, it was common for the elite dead to be buried lavishly. The body was dressed in all its finery – the deceased's best clothing and jewellry. Depending on the person being buried, the body would be accompanied by weapons or a person's tools of trade. Food and drink were placed on top of the dead body.

Important local men were often buried with servants and favourite wives, who would be ritually strangled before being placed in the grave, or made drunk before being buried alive with the corpse. The funeral was conducted by relatives and friends, who escorted the body to a

cemetery with mourning and chanting, dancing and heavy drinking. The ceremony lasted for a longer or shorter time according to rank. Chants recalled the most memorable deeds of the dead person, told where he or she had lived, and good deeds done by the deceased to or for the chanter.

Extremely important, legendary Inca individuals were often not 'buried' but recognized as special sacred *huacas*.

Left: Elite members of society were wrapped in numerous rich textile mantles and other garments.

Above: The Late Intermediate Period and Late Horizon Colla of the Titicaca Basin buried generations of mummified bodies in chullpas – as at the Sillustani necropolis.

According to legend, Manco Capac was turned into stone when he died. The stone was located by the Polo de Ondegardo, a Spanish magistrate, in 1559 in Membilla, now a suburb of Cuzco. A *quipu* found in an Inca burial mound indicated that the individual was an important local leader or governor.

ELITE BURIAL PARACAS STYLE
Elaborate burial accompanied by rich grave goods began in the Early Horizon Paracas culture of the southern Peruvian coast. The status of the burials in the Cavernas Paracas cemetery is revealed by the number and sumptuousness of the accompanying burial goods, since the most important individuals were sent on their journey into the afterlife with splendid riches. Less wealthy individuals were buried in plain bundles, and some bundles contained more than one body.

Some desiccated mummy bundles were 2m (6½ft) high. Offerings included gold, feathers, animal skins and imported goods, such as shells from distant shores. Paracas bodies were tightly flexed and held together with cords. Their skulls sometimes show trepanation: pieces of skull drilled and removed by incision with an instrument or by scraping.

PREPARING A MUMMY BUNDLE

Each elite Paracas mummy bundle is unique, but its preparation and basic configuration followed important shared 'rules' or procedures.

One representative bundle was 1.7m (5½ft) high and 1.4m (4½ft) across the base. The entire bundle comprises no fewer than 25 plain cotton wraps and 44 richly decorated wraps. The body was placed on a deerskin within a large basket. Offerings of maize, yuca tuber and peanuts, and of unspun llama fibre, a *Spondylus* shell from the distant northern coast, a cloth pouch probably containing body paint, and a human skull were grouped around the body.

This assemblage was wrapped within multiple layers of cloth. Most of the pieces were wound around the body, rather than 'dressing' it. First, there are 15 embroidered garment sets, many of them unfinished, indicating that they were burial 'gifts' prepared specifically for entombment. Their decorations include common symbolic images and themes: felines, serpents, sea creatures, birds and supernatural beings.

Around these, and including the basket, were several layers of plain cotton cloth, some pieces up to 10m (33ft) long. This made the person 'larger than life' and thus emphasized their importance, as it would have been emphasized in life by the wearing of layers of loincloths,

skirts, tunics, shoulder mantles, ponchos, headbands and turban-like headgear. These outer bundles enclosed two staffs, a third staff with a feather top and an animal skeleton; six shoulder mantles; a leather cape; a bright yellow, tropical, Amazonian bird-feather tunic; and a headband. Finally, the entire mummy bundle was encased in a huge plain cloth sewn up with long stitches. It is estimated that the manufacture of the textiles and the preparation of such a bundle required anything from 5,000 to 29,000 hours.

Such elaborate ritual burial practices continued in the succeeding Nazca culture in the same region.

COLLA *CHULLPAS*

Special burials were accorded to important individuals in the Late Intermediate Period and Late Horizon Colla of the Titicaca Basin in unique *chullpa* tower stone burial chambers among the Collas people – as at the Sillustani necropolis. *Chullpas* are fitted stone volcanic masonry structures of one to three storeys, round or square in base plan. They were erected near towns or in separated groups, functioning as family mausoleums. Most *chullpas* contained generations of burials, with bodies wrapped in rich textiles, and they continued to be built into Inca times.

The richest elite burials ever found in the Americas were discovered in the Lambayeque Valley, where the Moche flourished in the Early Intermediate Period and early Middle Horizon, followed by the Lambayeque-Sicán culture of the later Middle Horizon and Early Intermediate Period. Neither used mummification.

ELITE BURIAL, MOCHE STYLE
The rich, unlooted tombs of the Moche Lords of Sipán were discovered by Walter Alva and Susana Meneses in the 1980s. The Sipán tombs reveal the riches and the exquisite craftsmanship of Moche metallurgy and ceramics. Yet Sipán was neither the capital nor the main focus of much Moche power during c.AD100–800. It is hard to imagine what riches have been lost that must have come from looted tombs, or that lie as yet undiscovered in unfound Moche tombs.

At Sipán, altogether twelve tombs were found in six levels of generations of burial. In the lowest level was the 'Old

Below: Ritual burials have been found beneath many Andean pyramid platforms, as here at Moche El Brujo.

Above: Early Intermediate Period Moche lords were elaborately buried in richly furnished tombs, only a few of which remain unlooted.

Lord of Sipán' and in the topmost level were the tombs of the 'Lord of Sipán' and of the Owl Priest. The levels of tombs contain burials, artefacts and depicted scenes that confirm the ritual scene images on the walls, ceramics, textiles and metalwork excavated at other Moche sites, especially the ritual sacrificial scenes painted on red-on-white ceramics and on murals. The Sipán tombs date from c.AD100–300. The offerings in the tombs and the costumes worn by the deceased are identical to those worn by the priests depicted in the sacrificial ceremonies.

LORDS OF SIPÁN AND OWL PRIEST
The principal body in Tomb 1, of the 'Lord of Sipán' – undoubtedly that of a local noble or regional ruler of the Lambayeque Valley – personified the Warrior Priest. He wore a crescent-shaped back-flap and

Right: Moche elite deceased were richly dressed and their faces covered with sheet-gold masks. This example has copper inlaid eyes and traces of red paint.

rattles suspended from his belt. Both back-flap and rattles are decorated with the image of the Decapitator God, in this case a human-like spider with a characteristic Decapitator fanged mouth and double ear-ornaments, perched on a golden web. The spider imagery is thought to reflect the parallel of the blood-letting of sacrificial victims and the spider's sucking of the life juices of its prey.

Offerings consisted of three pairs of gold and turquoise ear-spools (one of which shows a Moche warrior in full armour); a gold, crescent-shaped head-dress; a crescent-shaped nose-ornament; and one gold and one silver *tumi* knife. At the Warrior Priest's side lay a box-like sceptre of gold, embossed with combat scenes, with a spatula-like handle of silver studded with military trappings.

Near Tomb 1, Tomb 2 contained offerings not quite so rich, but significantly including the body of a noble with a gilded copper headdress decorated with

an owl with outspread wings – clearly the Owl or Bird Priest of Moche friezes. Sealed rectangular rooms near the two tombs contained other rich offerings – ceramic vessels and miniature war gear, a headdress, copper goblets – and, even more tellingly, the skeletal remains of severed human hands and feet, probably those of sacrificed victims.

In the lowest levels, Tomb 3 contained the body of the 'Old Lord of Sipán', who lived about five generations earlier. His burial goods included two sceptres – one gold, one silver – and he wore six necklaces – three of gold and three of silver.

PRIESTESS FIGURES

Futher rich tombs confirming the accuracy of the Moche friezes and ceramic scenes come from San José de Moro in the Jequetepeque Valley. Here Christopher Donnan excavated the tombs of two women, which contained silver-alloyed copper headdresses with plume-like tassels, and other trappings of the priestess figure. These tombs have been dated to *c.*AD500–600.

Left: Repoussé-decorated sheet-gold kero *drinking cups from a rich Chimú burial. The one on the right shows warriors or possibly the ancient Chavin Staff Deity.*

ELITE BURIAL, SICÁN STYLE

The Sicán culture, which succeeded the Moche in the Lambayeque Valley, has produced equally rich tomb burials at Batán Grande, a few kilometres (miles) across the valley. Batán Grande was the largest Middle Horizon–Early Intermediate Period religious centre of the Sicán culture in the Lambayeque Valley. The ceremonial precinct comprised 17 adobe brick temple mounds, surrounded by shaft tombs and multi-roomed enclosures, with rich burials and rich furnishings reminiscent of the Moche Sipán lords' burial.

In the 1980s Izumi Shimada excavated the tomb of a Sicán lord at Huca Loro, one of the Batán Grande temple mounds, dated *c.*AD1000. The burial was of a man about 40–50 years old, accompanied by two young women and two children who had probably been sacrificed to accompany him. The lord was buried seated and his head was detached and turned 180 degrees, and tilted back to face upwards. He wore a gold mask and his body was painted with cinnabar. The grave contained vast numbers of objects – most of them gold, silver, or amalgamated precious metals (*tumbaga*) – arranged in caches and containers. The lord's mantle alone was sewn with nearly 2,000 gold foil squares. Other objects included a wooden staff with gold decoration, a gold ceremonial *tumi* knife, a gold headdress, gold shin covers, *tumbaga* gloves, gold ear-spools and a large pile of beads.

RITUAL SACRIFICE

Human and animal sacrifice was a common practice throughout ancient Andean civilization. It became a part of ritual from the Preceramic Period and continued into Inca times. Llama sacrifice was especially important in Tiwanaku, Wari and Inca ritual. The latter is an important scene in the Inca state creation myth. The founders sacrificed a llama to Pacha Mama before entering Cuzco. Mama Huaco sliced open the animal's chest, extracting and inflating the lungs with her breath, and carried them into the city alongside Manco Capac and the gold emblem of Inti.

SEVERED HEADS
These are perhaps the most powerful image of ancient Andean human sacrifice, and are a common theme in textile and pottery decoration, murals and architectural sculpture. Severed heads can be seen dangling from the waists of humans and supernatural beings in all ancient Andean cultures. As well as heads, other severed human body parts feature pictorially and in actuality in tombs.

The marching band of warriors on the monumental slabs at the ceremonial complex of Cerro Sechín is interspersed with dismembered bodies, severed heads – singly and in stacks – and naked captives. One warrior has trophy heads hanging from his waistband. One of the three adobe images at Moxeke is thought to represent a giant-sized severed head.

Severed heads form an important theme in the Chavín Cult, used both as trophy heads and as portrayals of shamanic transformation.

In Paracas and Nazca culture the Oculate Being has streaming trophy heads floating from its body at the ends of cords. Trophy heads feature frequently on Paracas and Nazca textiles and pottery. Real severed human heads were placed in Paracas and Nazca burials. There was

Above: A Nazca warrior or priest displaying a fresh trophy head – an integral part of ancient Andean religion.

a Nazca cult that collected caches of the severed and trepanned trophy skulls of sacrificial victims, and many human skulls have been modified to facilitate stringing them on to a cord.

DECAPITATORS
Titicaca Basin Pukará imagery also featured disembodied human heads. Some were trophy heads carried by realistically depicted humans; others accompanied supernatural beings with feline or serpentine attributes, thought, as in the Chavín Cult, to represent shamans undergoing transformation. The Pukará Decapitator sculpture is a seated male figure holding an axe and severed head, and the Pukará ceramic theme known as 'feline man' depicts pairs of fanged men lunging or running, facing one another or one chasing the other, each carrying a

Left: Nazca cemeteries included caches of skulls, many of which show trepanation and perforations for threading on to a cord.

Above: The Moche Pañamarca mural (restoration drawing) depicts the sacrifice ceremony, presided over by a priestess.

severed head and a staff. A cache of human lower jawbones found at Pukará indicates ritual sacrifice and/or warfare, either in the real or mythological world.

Images of the Decapitator God dominated temple and tomb friezes and murals in the Moche capital and are found at Sipán in the Lambayeque Valley, where the tomb of the Lord of Sipán was found. The nearby tomb of the Owl Priest contained boxes of offerings that included the bones of severed human hands and feet. Similar to the Pukará Decapitator, the Moche god holds a crescent-shaped *tumi* ceremonial knife in one hand and a severed human head in the other.

Tiwanaku and Wari craftsmen continued the severed-head theme in all media. The Akapana Temple at Tiwanaku incorporated a buried cache of sacrificed llama bones. Most of the human skeletons found buried on the first terrace and under its foundations were headless, and at the base of the western staircase a black basalt image of a seated, puma-headed

person (*chachapuma*) holding a severed head in his lap was found. Another Tiwanaku *chachapuma* sculpture is a standing figure holding a severed head.

The ultimate severed head is perhaps that of Atahualpa/Inkarrí, who was killed by the Spaniards. His body parts were buried in different parts of the kingdom, with his head in Lima. It is said that one day a new body will grow from his head, and the Inca emperor will return to revive the people's former glory.

SACRIFICIAL BURIALS

Human sacrifice became not only a part of religious ceremonies necessary to honour the gods, but also a ritual associated with elite burial, emphasizing the power and importance of the individual.

The earliest evidence indicative of human sacrifice comes from two burials at Late Preceramic Huaca de los Sacrificios at Aspero. The first was of an adult, tightly flexed with the joints cut to force the unnatural position and to fit the body into a small pit, wrapped only in plain cloth. The second was of a two-month-old infant placed on its right side. It wore a cloth cap and was wrapped in

cotton textile. Accompanying it were a gourd bowl and 500 clay, shell and plant beads. This bundle was placed in a basket, the whole wrapped in another layer of cloth, then rolled in a cane mat and tied with white cotton strips, and finally laid on two cotton wads. The assemblage was covered with an inverted, finely sculptured stone basin. The pair appears to commemorate the premature death of an infant of important lineage and a sacrificial victim to accompany its burial.

The Paracas Cavernas and Nazca Cahuachi cemeteries show numerous signs of ritual human sacrifice. Caches of skulls and trepanning have been mentioned. At Cahuachi it is obvious that some individuals were sacrificial victims. While honoured burials were mummified and accompanied by exquisitely decorated, multicoloured woven burial coats and pottery, sometimes with animal sacrifices, the sacrificial victims – men, women and children – had excrement inserted into the mouth, their skull perforated for threading on to a cord, their eyes blocked, and their mouth pinned by cactus spines or the tongue removed and placed in a pouch.

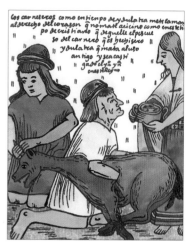

COMMEMORATIVE SACRIFICES

The roughly contemporary Moche culture of the northern coastal valleys practised a ritual of elite burial through generations as the huge Huaca del Sol pyramid was built in the capital, Cerro Blanco. A burial oriented north–south, as was the pyramid platform, was made near the base of the first phase of construction. Later burials were incorporated in successive phases as the platform was enlarged. There were several burials with mats and textiles within the adobe brick layers of the third phase, some of them of adolescents. Lastly, on top of the final construction stage of the fourth phase was an interment of a man and a woman, extended on their backs, accompanied by 31 globular vessels. The exact meanings of such burials cannot be known, but their association within construction phases of the huge platform was probably as sacrificial offerings for the well-being of the Moche people and their rulers.

Such a conclusion is strengthened by what can only have been a mass sacrifice behind the twin pyramids of Huaca de la Luna, also at Cerro Blanco. An enclosure at the base of the platform contained the mass grave of 40 men, aged 15 to 30, many of them deliberately mutilated. They may have been sacrificed to the gods during a time of

Above: As well as human sacrifice, animal offerings to the gods were a regular ancient Andean religious practice, performed at designated times of the year.

heavy rain caused by an El Niño event to solicit the return of good weather, for the sacrificial victims were covered in a thick layer of water-deposited sediments and the bones showed signs of cutting and of deliberate fracturing. As El Niño events occurred regularly in cycles, there may be other such mass sacrifices yet to be discovered.

The sacrificial scenes on Moche ceramics were actually performed by Moche lords such as the elite individuals known as the Lord of Sipán and the Owl Priest at Sipán. Judging by the frequency with which the scenes are shown on ceramics and murals, the ritual was a regular event, perhaps re-enacting a mythical story. The tradition of sacrifice appears to have survived the collapse of Moche power, even within the Lambayeque Valley, as illustrated in the sacrifice of two women and two children at later Lambayeque-Sicán Huaca Loro (Batán Grande).

CAPACOCHA SACRIFICE

The Incas associated red with conquest and blood. The chronicler Murúa says that each red woollen thread of the Inca

Left: Ritual sacrifice was performed by priests, perhaps impersonating gods or in shamanic 'transformation', as here, wearing a jaguar or puma mask.

state insignia, the Mascaypacha – a crimson tassel hung from a braid tied around the head – represented a conquered people and also the blood of an enemy's severed head.

The Inca practice of *capacocha* sacrifice was a ritual that continued these ancient traditions. As well as honouring the gods, it emphasized the power of the Inca rulers and maintained control over subjugated peoples. Specially selected individuals, usually children, from among the high-ranking *ayllu* kinship lineages of the provinces of the empire were brought to Cuzco to be prepared for the ritual. The selection was made annually and those chosen were destined to be sacrificial victims after ritual ceremonies in the capital. *Capacocha* sacrifices

Right: A Chimú ritual gold tumi *sacrificial knife, for slitting the throat of the victim, decorated with possibly feline heads.*

were offerings to either the sun god Inti or the creator god Viracocha, or to both of the gods. Momentous events such as war, pestilence, famine or other natural disasters could also provoke *capacocha* sacrifices.

In Cuzco, the chosen ones were sanctified by the priests in the Coricancha precinct, who offered the victims to Viracocha, and then marched back to their home provinces along sacred *ceque* routes that linked the provinces to the capital. The victims were sacrificed by being clubbed to death, strangled with a cord, having the throat slit before burial, or by being buried alive in a specially constructed shaft-tomb.

Capacocha sacrifices renewed or reconfirmed the bond between the Inca state and the provincial peoples of the empire, reasserted Inca overlordship and reaffirmed the hierarchy between the Inca centre and the provincial *ayllus*.

CAPACOCHA CHILDREN
Children were sometimes drugged with *chicha* (maize beer) before being sacrificed. Votive offerings usually accompanied the victim in death, such as elaborate clothing, male or female figures of gold, silver, bronze or shell dressed in miniature garments, llama figurines and miniature sets of ceramic containers.

The victims were sometimes carried up and left on high mountaintops regarded as sacred *huacas*, where their bodies

Left: A deer sacrifice performed by Death as a skeleton, displayed on a Moche ceramic stirrup-spouted ceremonial vessel.

would sometimes become preserved in the cold dry conditions that prevailed at such high altitudes. Famous examples include those at Cerro el Plomo in the Chilean Andes, Mount Aconcagua on the Argentinian–Chilean border, Puná Island off the coast of Ecuador, the 'ice maiden' at Mount Ampato and the two girls and a boy sacrificed and buried on Mount Llullaillaco.

MUMMIES AND MUMMIFICATION

This preservative treatment of the human body before burial, or even as a state precluding burial, was the ultimate ancient Andean expression of ancestor reverence. It was not an attempt to cheat death on Earth, nor a denial of the cycle of life, but rather an act of recognition of the next stage in the cycle. It was a preparation for the journey and a method of preservation that maintained the contact between those living in this world and those who had moved on to the next stage. In fact, mummification was not necessarily always achieved deliberately, but could also be the result of climatic conditions, since the desiccating conditions of the desert would preserve exposed bodies. In the same way, desiccation and freeze-drying methods used to preserve stored foodstuffs had been discovered by the ancient Andeans probably accidentally originally, and then deliberately applied.

Above: Cinchorros mummifiction in northern coastal Chile predates Egyptian burials by some 500 years.

THE CHINCHORROS MUMMIES

The earliest mummification in the world was practised by the people of the Chinchorros culture in the Chilean Atacama Desert, starting about 5000BC. The Atacama is one of the bleakest places on Earth and officially recognized as the driest.

Mummification by the Chinchorros predates the earliest Egyptian mummification by about 500 years. It also demonstrates the beginnings of differentiation in burial practices within their community by the special treatment of chosen individuals. Most Chinchorros dead were buried in earthen graves without special treatment. About 250 individuals, however, had been preserved. Curiously these earliest mummies were not of revered elderly members of society; rather the majority of them are of newborns, children or adolescents.

Chinchorros 'morticians' perfected a high degree of skill. The deceased body was left exposed to decompose then completely de-fleshed. Cerebral and visceral matter were extracted and the

Left: Removal of the soft material, salting and careful wrapping helped to preserve organic materials in Paracas burials.

skin treated with salt to help preserve it. The bones were then reassembled as in life and secured in their positions with cords and cane supports. The form of the body was then replaced with fibre, feather and clay stuffing, held inside the skin, which was stitched in sections at the tops of the arms, wrists, torso, abdomen, groin, knees and shins as necessary. A clay death mask was applied to the skull, complete with sculpted and painted facial features, and a coating of clay applied to the body to delineate fingers and toes, with painted finger- and toenails. A wig of human hair was often attached as well. The result was a stiffened, statue-like form.

There is variation in treatment, presumably owing to individual skill and developments in preservation methods over generations.

The mummy was kept above ground as a continuing family member. Some mummies show surface damage, which in some cases was repaired. The preserved cadavers were clearly kept accessible for some time before finally being buried. Some burials were in family groups of adults and children. One such interment spanned three generations from infants and children to mature adults and a few very aged adults.

The inclusion of infants and children, especially separately or in group burials of the young, seems to rule out specific ancestor worship. However, the development of social hierarchy and perhaps lineage privilege is shown by the selection. Presumably special treatment and inclusion above ground within the community continued until the lineage no longer merited a distinct social position, at which time the mummy was then buried in an earthen grave.

LA PALOMA

The Chinchorros mummies were not the only ancient Andean attempts to preserve the body after death. The Preceramic site of La Paloma on the central Peruvian

coast in the Mala Valley was short-lived, but comprised three superimposed settlements with some 4,000 to 5,000 circular huts in total. Abandoned huts later served as graves in which, from as early as about 4000BC, corpses were treated with salt to deter putrefaction. In combination with the dry coastal desert climate, the bodies were desiccated and stiffened as whole forms. At the time, such treatment contrasted sharply with the burial of disarticulated bodies in tropical and other areas.

THE ESSENCE OF PRESERVATION

Even these earliest methods of mummification seem to recognize the concept of essence. The methods do not attempt to halt decomposition of the flesh. Rather

Above: A richly coloured Paracas woollen burial wrap, decorated with felines and perhaps the face of the Oculate Being, reveals the high status of a burial.

they preserve the essence of the earthly form, presumably in order to provide a 'vessel' for the journey of the spirit, or 'vital force', that ancient Andeans believed to be the next stage in the cycle of life. In Inca times, mummies were the preferred symbol of corporate identity and kinship solidarity. The Chinchorros and La Paloma peoples' early efforts at mummification reveal the antiquity of Andean belief that an intact body vessel was critical for the spirit to be able to enter the afterlife and join the world of the ancestors.

Above: An Inca mummy bundle borne on a litter for deposit in a mausoleum, from which it could be brought out on ritual occasions.

The elite burials of the north-coast Moche Sipán lords and later Sicán lords in the Lambayeque Valley were not deliberately mummified. The tradition of elaborate trappings certainly prevailed, but there was no deliberate mummification of the bodies. Their exquisite garments and tomb furniture did not, in the long term, preserve the bodies of the deceased lords, but their dress and grave goods certainly reveal a desire to prepare them and supply them for their journeys into the afterlife.

THE PARACAS/NAZCA MUMMIES

The traditions and concepts established at Chinchorros and La Paloma continued at Early Horizon Paracas and Early Intermediate Period Nazca, about halfway along the coast between the two Preceramic sites. The elaborate mummy bundles interred in the three Paracas

Below: Richly dyed multiple layers of cotton and woollen burial textiles and a feathered headdress emphasize the importance of this Paracas individual.

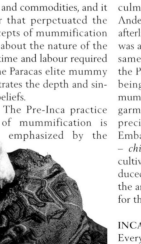

cemeteries – Cavernas, Cabeza Larga and Necropolis – and the Nazca Cahuachi cemetery show a multi-layered established social hierarchy, clearly defined by the levels of treatment in burial. The dry desert climate was a significant element in preservation, while the elaborate treatment of Paracas and Nazca corpses in multiple layers of burial textiles protected the mummies from deterioration. Social position was indicated by the size and elaboration of the mummy bundle. Once again, the treatment was to provide a vessel for the journey into the afterlife.

The attention to detail in procedures and the multiple layers of textiles and other trappings in Paracas and Nazca burials have been described above. The importation of foreign objects and materials in Paracas and Nazca graves – including exotic shells and llama wool garments, as well as the native-grown cotton textiles – reveals the extent of contact and trade between the coast and other regions, both sierra and tropical. It is significant that with such long-distance communication must have come ideas as well as objects and commodities, and it is this factor that perpetuated the Andean concepts of mummification and concepts about the nature of the afterlife. The time and labour required to produce one Paracas elite mummy bundle demonstrates the depth and sincerity of these beliefs.

The Pre-Inca practice of mummification is emphasized by the discovery of a row of mummy bundles in the burial of the puma-headed priest (*chachapuma*) beneath the summit structures of the Akapana platform at Tiwanaku. The priestly mummy's importance was accentuated by a row of mummies facing him in the tomb.

CHIMÚ/INCA MUMMIFICATION

Late Intermediate Period Chimú and Late Horizon Inca mummification was the culmination of the long tradition of Andean preservation of the body for the afterlife. Chimú and Inca mummification was achieved in a manner essentially the same as the methods developed by the Paracas people, the critical elements being desiccation and an elaborate mummy bundle of textiles and elaborate garments and jewellery, including precious metals and exotic items. Embalming included the use of alcohol – *chicha* beer made from the maize cultivated in a field near Cuzco was produced expressly to embalm the body of the ancestor Mama Huaco and was used for the succeeding Inca Qoya empresses.

INCA *MALLQUIS* MUMMIES

Every Inca community would have had its special *mallqui* (as it was called in the central and northern Andes) or *munao* (as it was called along the central coast).

The *mallqui* mummy was the community-level founding ancestor, the protohuman descendant of the deities – the great *huacas* such as Inti (the sun) or Illapa (thunder and lightning). In time, the term was applied to more recent ancestors of the kin group. Alongside *mallquis*, ancestors could also be 'mummified' in a transformed state: ancestors who had been petrified and who stood in sacred locations around the landscape. These were known as *huancas*, *chacrayocs* and *marcayocs*. Like the *mallquis*, these stone ancestors represented the first occupation of the region and the first *ayllu* kinship group called out by Con Tici, Imaymana or Tocapo Viracocha at the time of creation.

Inca *mallquis* were commonly kept in caves or in special rooms near the community. Some caves were reported by Spanish priests to hold hundreds of mummified ancestors. The Inca royal mummies – both the Sapa Inca (Inti) and the empress Qoya (Quilla) – were housed in special rooms in the Coricancha Temple in Cuzco, to be brought out on auspicious occasions and festivals and included as 'living' members of the royal household. After the Spanish Conquest they survived, hidden by Incas reluctant to relinquish ancient beliefs, until the late 16th century, when Spanish priests and administrators finally tracked them down and burned them as heretical.

CHIMÚ ROYAL MUMMIES

The immense Chimú capital at Chan Chan in the Moche Valley had at its core the walled city of *ciudadellas*, which housed the living and dead royal households of the Chimú kings. Each *ciudadella* compound comprised a 'city within the city' to accommodate the mummified remains of the king and both dead and living retainers. They 'lived' in rooms on special platforms, including labyrinthine divisions and thousands of storerooms and niches, and even miniature U-shaped ceremonial structures harking back to the most ancient cultures of the north coast.

FREEZE-DRIED MUMMIES

Another type of mummification occurred, perhaps intentionally, in the desiccated climatic condition of remote mountaintops. These were the *capacocha* child and young adult victims of the Inca ritual sacrifice of chosen representatives from the provinces of the empire. Cold storage of sierra agricultural production was a long-standing practice, complementing the

Above: A Middle Horizon Wari mummy bundle. They were preserved and brought out on special occasions by most Andean cultures from the Early Horizon onward.

hot, dry conditions used to dry foods by desert cultures. In the remote, dry, cold high-sierra locations of *capacocha* sacrifice and burial, the combination of elaborate bundling in textiles and the climatic conditions naturally preserved the bodies. The locations and the intent to revisit the *huacas* thus created by the sacrifice indicates that preservation through mummification was counted upon.

ANCESTOR WORSHIP

Reverence for one's *ayllu* kinship ancestors was integral in Inca society regardless of social rank. Special veneration was given to nobles and supreme respect to the royal pair. The enshrined mummies of the Incas and their Qoya wives were carefully tended. Even today the skull of an ancestor is kept in some Andean households to 'watch over' it and its occupants.

Signs of pre-Inca ancestor reverence are evident in the elaborate preparation and care of bodies in Paracas and Nazca cemeteries; especially revealing is the continued reopening of tombs to inter new family members or the maintenance of access to *chullpa* towers for the same purpose. Like so many practices in Andean civilization, the intensity of

ancestor worship reached its most vivid and demonstrative phase among the Incas, who, with the Chimú, developed substantial industries around ancestor worship.

THE ROLE OF *MALLQUIS*
The mummified remains (*mallquis*) of Chimú and Inca rulers and their queens were cared for by dedicated cults. At Chan Chan they were housed in the *ciudadella* compounds. The cults of Inti and Quilla were housed in the Coricancha precinct in Cuzco. The *acllas* (chosen women) of Inti not only tended the *mallquis* of former Sapa Incas but were also the concubines of the reigning Sapa, thus forming a worldly link between the ancestors and the living Inti.

Every *ayllu* maintained mummified ancestor bundles and housed them carefully in special buildings or in nearby caves. *Mallquis* were believed to be the repositories of supernatural powers. As founding ancestors they were regarded as revered divinities, or representatives of the gods, and infused with *camaquen* – the vital force of all living things. They were able to transfer *camaquen* to crops to make them grow and to llama herds to make them multiply. Legendary exploits of *mallquis* were told about their ability to sustain agricultural production. They were responsible for the introduction of the different regional crops and for maintaining the fertility of the land. They had taught the people the different methods of agriculture such as irrigation and terracing to increase production.

Such beliefs maintained established land rights and the mutual obligations within and between *ayllu* kinship groups. They helped to co-ordinate labour between groups, communities and regions.

CONSULTING THE FOREBEARS
Inca ancestor mummies were consulted for numerous reasons, both for everyday concerns and on ceremonial occasions on issues of vital importance. They were consulted before undertaking a journey outside the community, for naming and marriage ceremonies in the life cycle, and on auspicious dates in the agricultural calendar such as sowing and harvesting.

On these occasions they were brought out to participate in the ceremony. They were dressed in fresh clothing, offered food and drink, and generally treated as living, active members of the community. Songs and dances were performed before them and the stories of their exploits told.

Left: An Inca carved wooden head with shell inlay eyes, dressed in dyed textiles – probably from a mummy bundle or more probably a huauque *double.*

Right: Ancestor worship began as early as the Nazca, who placed generations of the deceased in mausoleams and had kinship areas at ritual sites such as Cahuachi.

Spanish attempts to eradicate what they regarded as idolatrous beliefs were fiercely and secretively resisted. Local-level ancestors were considered crucial to community coherence, and most survived well into the 17th century.

HUAUQUES

The Quechua word *huauque* means 'brother'. The term was especially applied to man-made doubles – statues made in the images of the ruling Sapa Incas and other chiefs and nobles during their lifetimes. In his *Historia del Nuevo Mundo*, Bernabé Cobo describes these effigies as well dressed and of various sizes, and says that they were held equivalent to the imperial and noble *mallquis*. They included hollows wherein parts of the reigning emperor were placed when he

Below: As the Incas were so attached to their mummies and ancestor worship, here depicted by an ancestor mummy on a litter, it took the Spaniards over a century to stamp it out.

was alive, such as trimmings from his hair or fingernails. Upon his death the ashes of his burned viscera were usually put into the hollow. Many such duplicates were hunted down by the Spaniards and destroyed along with the actual mummies.

Huauques were made of different materials and had more refined characteristics according to rank. The *huauque* of the upper division of an *ayllu* would have proper facial and other human-like features. That of the lower division would have amorphous or animal features. The *huauques* of earlier Sapa Incas were made of stone while those of the later rulers were made of gold.

After the Sapa Inca's death his royal *panaca* corporation undertook the care of his *mallqui* and *huauque*. During another emperor's lifetime such statues could be used as *mallqui* substitutes, especially on occasions when the real

mummy might be at risk of damage, such as on a long journey or when the living emperor was on a campaign of conquest. The loss of such an idol would be less serious than the actual destruction of a *mallqui*, for loss of the latter would amount to a state disaster: it would mean the loss of the *panaca's* identity.

A *huauque* could also represent a mythical ancestor. In this case invented descent could be confirmed by the effigy for political expediency. Once again, Inca practice appears to follow ancient Andean traditions. The greenstone idol Yampallec of the Sicán ruler Naymlap accompanied him in his conquest of the Lambayeque Valley, and the attempt of his descendant Fempellec to remove the idol was fiercely and successfully resisted by the priests who constituted the royal *panaca*. Nevertheless, the dynasty ended with Fempellec when the priests disposed of him.

TRANCES AND TRANSFORMATION

The ancient Andean cycle of life included trances and transformations during which life on earth was left and other worlds or states of being were entered.

TRANSFORMATIONAL STATES

Some temporary states of being could be experienced by everyone: for example near-death conditions, deep sleep, fainting and drunkenness. More profound states, such as transformation in order to commune with the spirit world, however, were usually drug-induced and were the realm of the shamans and high priests.

Below: This Moche effigy vessel depicts a jaguar-attired shaman with a jaguar emerging from his head.

That such beliefs, like most Andean religious concepts, were ancient is shown in the series of transformation sculptures at Chavín de Huántar in the circular sunken court of the New Temple. These portray a classic trip – the transformation of a human shaman into a revered jaguar. During such a transformation the shaman acquired the powers and wisdom of the animal into which he or she was changed.

Other states of transformation included the conversion of animals and of human heroes or deities into stone, to become sacred regional *huacas*. The reverse could also happen: stones or other features of the landscape could temporarily transform into living beings. The classic example is the calling upon the gods by Pachacuti Inca Yupanqui for help against the Chanca assault on Cuzco, traditionally in 1438. The gods transformed the stones of Pururaucas field into warriors. After the defeat of the Chancas, Pachacuti ordered that the stones should be gathered and distributed among the capital's shrines.

The Moche mural known as the 'Revolt of the Objects' represents another transformational theme – that of everyday objects sprouting limbs and humans with animal heads. This mythical story of the world gone mad and then returned to order was still told in Inca times and recorded by the Spaniards.

SHAMANSIM

This is the term used to describe a person who has special powers, usually aided by hallucinatory plant drugs, to gain access to the spirit world. In ancient Andean cultures the role of the shaman was crucial in everyday life. Priests of the most important temples, including the retainers of the most important oracles and shrines, such as Chavín de Huántar, Pachacamac and the

Above: On a stirrup-spouted vessel, a shaman wearing a jaguar headband and mushroom cap treats a woman with his healing touch.

Island of the Sun, were supreme shamans, but every local community would have had their local shaman as well. While the high priests served as intermediaries between the community and the lofty world of the gods, local shamans were consulted for everyday issues such as sickness and fortune.

Shamans in transformational states or in drug-induced states of being have been depicted in Andean cultures from the time of the building of the earliest dedicated ceremonial precincts. Such duality

*Above: The San Pedro cactus (*Trichocereus pachanoi*) was, and is, a rich source of vision-producing mescaline.*

in being is perhaps expressed in the symbolic crossed-hands friezes of the temple walls at Preceramic Period Kotosh. At the Initial Period coastal sites of Garagay, human–animal transformation is depicted in images of insects with human heads, and at Moxeke the earliest representation of shamanic trance may be represented by the adobe sculptures. Spiders with human heads, frequently depicted in the Moche and other cultures, were symbolic as predictors of the future, especially on climatic matters. Moche effigy pots even depict scenes of shamans at work, bent over their patients lying prone before them.

Below: A northern Moche ceramic figurine from the Vicus region shows a shaman clearly in a trance, sporting enhanced feline canines.

The role-taking of humans as deities in scenes of ritual is most famously depicted in the sacrificial scenes on Moche pottery and murals showing the Warrior Priest, Owl Priest and a priestess re-enacting the blood-letting ritual after symbolic combat.

HALLUCINOGENS

Shamanic transformation and trance for curative or special powers was normally induced through the use of hallucinatory plant drugs. The most common hallucinogens were coca leaves (*Erythroxylon coca*), coca incense, the San Pedro cactus (*Trichocereus pachanoi*) (the source of vision-producing mescaline), tobacco and various tropical mushrooms.

Classic characteristics of a hallucinogenic trance are shown in the adobe sculptures of Moxeke and Huaca de los Reyes: jawless lower mouth and/or fangs, flared nostrils and wide eyes with pendent irises. Such symbolic imagery is prolific in Chavín art and widely distributed in the northern and central Andean and coastal regions, and farther south at Karwa (Paracas). Drug-induced stares were woven into the faces of Paracas and Nazca fabrics and on pottery decoration. The faces of countless Moche cera   mic effigy vessels and figures in ceramic and mural story scenes reveal other-worldly states of being.

In addition to depictions of various hallucinogenic states, there was a variety of drug   paraphernalia, including snuff trays, tubes, pipes and small knives for chopping. Coca leaves were chewed in a complex, many-staged ritual connected to war and sacrifice. Coca was also frequently used, along with *chicha* beer, to drug sacrificial victims before dispatching them.

Drug paraphernalia has frequently been found among grave goods, but a unique cave burial of a local medicine man, herbalist or shaman of the Callahuaya people, dated to the latter half of the 5th century AD, was found near Huari. He was accompanied by the tools of his practice: a wooden snuff tablet decorated with a Tiwanaku 'attendant angel' figure with a trophy head on its chest; a basket with multi-coloured front-facing deity figures; and various herbal plants that would have been used in his trade.

Left: The Moche often displayed shamanic healing rituals in their ceramics. Here a shaman wearing a feline headband prays, probably to the gods, on behalf of a sick or dead person.

CHAPTER TWELVE

A NEW GOD

Conversion of the peoples of Mesoamerica and South America began shortly after Columbus landed on the islands of the Caribbean Sea. Once it was realized that he had not sailed west and reached the Orient, the Christian kings and queens of Spain and Portugal and their clergy saw a ripe new world for conversion to the path of Christ.

Many concepts in Christianity – in this case Spanish Catholicism – were ideas not unfamiliar, superficially, to ancient Andean beliefs. Similarly, Christian priests interpreted various elements in the mythical stories related to them by their converts as aspects of or vague references to Judeo-Christian truth.

Native Andeans were selective in their adoption of Spanish customs and tried to maintain as many of their cherished beliefs as they could. They were accustomed to having foreign gods forced upon them and to incorporating them into their pantheon, for the Incas had been as energetic as the Spaniards in this practice.

Andeans interpreted Christianity in their own way, blending it into their own beliefs, and adapting to incorporate the new 'faith'. The outcome was an 'Andean Catholicism' that persists to the present day. In this way Andeans are 'dual citizens' in the worlds of the past and the present.

Despite great changes in Andean culture during the 500 years after the Spanish Conquest, much of Andean life remains inspired by the ancient concepts of exchange, collectivity, transformation and essence.

Left: An eighteenth-century Spanish colonial Corpus Christi procession. The bearing of the figure on a litter may be a vestige of Inca ancestor worship.

THE MEETING OF TWO GREAT FAITHS

When the Incas were expanding their empire, they had insisted that the state cult of Inti become part of the religion of their subjects. However, ancient Andean religious belief had always had many gods, not just one: there was an overarching creator god (with several regional names), but also many local gods. Belief in the entire landscape as sacred could not deny the relevance of local gods in the development of pre-Inca cultures. So the Incas tried to incorporate all these gods into their cult rather than to exclude them, and to show that the ancient ways and legends were, in fact, part of their own inheritance, and that they were merely the final arbiters.

When their fortunes changed with the arrival of Francisco Pizarro, however, it was the turn of the Incas to be converted. Attempts to convert them and their subject peoples began with Father Valverde, the friar who accompanied Francisco Pizarro

Below: This engraving fancifully depicts an offering to Inti, the Inca sun god. The kneeling man may represent a Catholic priest.

on his expedition against Atahualpa. Feigning peace, Pizarro had instructed Valverde to approach Atahualpa brandishing a crucifix and a Bible as they entered the main courtyard of Cajamarca on 15 November 1532. Valverde delivered a speech on Christianity. His words, translated by an interpreter, were said to be understood by Atahualpa, though we can never be sure. Atahualpa certainly understood what he was being asked to do – forsake his own god for another – for when Valverde handed him the Bible he threw it to the ground and replied, pointing at the sun, 'My god still lives.' This declaration refers to the cult of the Sapa Inca, who, as representative and son of Inti, the sun, was worshipped as a deity.

THE CULT OF VIRACOCHA

Before the Inca state cult transferred its focus to the sun god Inti, Viracocha had been the centre of attention and worship. Yet the antiquity and history of the cult of Viracocha is open to debate. What seems clear is that the Inca Viracocha was a combination of elements. The legend of

Above: Father Valverde, presumably appalled, had his Bible defiled when Atahualpa allegedly threw it to the ground.

his wanderings gives him the full names of Con Tici (Ticci, Titi or Ticsi) Viracocha Pachayachachic, or Coniraya Viracocha, sometimes including Illya. *Con* was the name of a central coastal creator deity. *Tici* is foundation, beginning or cause. *Ticsi* refers to crystal, *illya* to light. *Pacha* is an element in another coastal creator god, Pachacamac, meaning the universe, time and space. Finally, *yachachic* means teacher.

Viracocha's temple in Cuzco was at Quishuarcancha. Father Bernabé Cobo records that it contained a golden statue of him in human form about the size of a 10-year-old boy. Another Viracocha image was made of textiles and kept in the Temple of the Sun in the Coricancha.

The rise to dominance of Inti over Viracocha occurred during the 15th century, when there was a power struggle in Cuzco. The dispute was between the Inca

Above: The Spaniards symbolically built the Church of Santo Domingo on the foundations of the Inca sacred Coricancha.

ruler Viracocha (and his chosen heir Inca Urco) and Inca Pachacuti, another of his sons. The history was about 100 years old when Pizarro arrived, and details were obscured by time and by the Incas' obsession with having an official version for the new ruler. However, it cannot be coincidental that Viracocha had the name of the deity ultimately to be displac ed and that his supplanter's name was the Quechua word for the revolution of the cycle of time! It was Pachacuti Inca Yupanqui who initiated the installation of the sun cult of Inti and began the rebuilding of Cuzco, the Coricancha Temple and the great Sun Temple of Sacsahuaman.

Among ordinary people the cult of Viracocha was not nearly so prominent as the worship of local deities, especially mountain deities and the earth deity Pacha Mama. The original derivation of *vira* and *cocha* can be traced to Aymara in the Titicaca Basin. In fact, Viracocha became a term used to refer to Spaniards and Christians in general and today is an honorific name for Westerners.

JESUS THE SUN

The Andean equation of Jesus Christ with the sun began in the early colonial period, an association that conformed to their 'former' belief that the Sapa Inca was the son of the sun and their association of Viracocha, creator of the sun and the moon, with Inti. The Christian god and the sun were both celestial deities and their conceptualization was similar.

The sun cult was revived in the 20th century. Today the sun is addressed as Huayna Capac (Young Lord), Hesu Kristu (Jesus Christ), Inti Tayta (Father Sun) and Taytacha (also Jesus Christ), a perfect combination of celestial deity, sun, and father and son.

The equation of the Virgin Mary with Pacha Mama is also colonial. Mary is linked to the moon through the moon's intimate association with the earth and its annual cycles through the agricultural year. The association is most prominent in August, at crop planting. In September the ritual of Coya Raymi (the empress's feast) is held to celebrate its successful completion. The moon is addressed as Mama Quilla (Mother Moon). Women take the active role and issue invitations to men to participate. Women's interest in the crops continues to the December solstice, when young boys take over care of the growing crops and the festival of Capac Raymi is held in honour of the sun.

SHARED BELIEFS

Christian missionaries saw elements in Inca belief that convinced them that they were merely 'lost children' of Christ. Indeed, many Andean religious concepts and Christian beliefs are superficially similar. The Andean concept of dualism – oneness within two – is not unlike the Judeo-Christian trinitarian belief of one within three.

The ultimate creator god Viracocha was a rather remote, overarching deity whose omnipresence was similar to the concept of God the Father. Viracocha's pervading presence throughout the universe was an omnipresent force, not an idol (although, like Christ, he was represented on Earth). Inca stories of a flood and of a single man and woman as progenitors of the human race could be perceived as the essence of Christian truth, if slightly corrupted by the passage of time and errors in record.

The biblical story of creation, in which humans began on earth with a man and a woman created by the supreme deity, resembled Andean belief, which also included a flood that destroyed everything that went before. Plagues and divine retribution were familiar, and sacrifices and gifts to the gods – for example the mass sacrifice at Huaca de la Luna at

Below: In this version of Father Valverde's attempt to convert Atahualpa, Pizarro is depicted kneeling – an unlikely occurrence.

Cerro Blanco to alleviate the effects of an El Niño event – were familiar pleas to the supreme being for help in bearing life's daily burdens.

Similarly, the legend of the wandering beggar Viracocha – as Christ, Son of God, who walked upon the earth and taught the people – was reconciled and incorporated. The ability of Viracocha to walk on water convinced many that Jesus must have come to the New World, perhaps after his resurrection or in a second visitation.

Sacred places of worship were also a familiar idea, including wells, springs and the importance of water. The concept of pilgrimage to sacred sites had been an Andean practice from at least the Early Horizon Chavin Cult. Sacred places as repositories for relics were everywhere in the Andean countryside and in villages, towns and cities. Christian worship and attribution of miraculous powers to saints' bones and pieces of the cross was recognizable.

FAMILIAR BELIEFS

Saints' feast days are celebrated with dances, the performers wearing masks to impersonate saints, much as the ancient Moche blood-sacrifice figures wore deity masks. A stone statue of Viracocha made by the Canas peoples of Cacha in the image of a Spanish priest in long white robes, and Viracocha's calling out of the ancestors, were attributed to the Titicaca Basin deity Tunapa, whom the native chronicler Pachacuti Yamqui believed to be Saint Thomas. Another native chronicler, Guamon Poma, believed Viracocha was Saint Bartholomew.

SHARED SYMBOLS

Ancient Andeans were also comfortable with much of Christian symbolism. Worship involved sacred objects: the cross, the chalice, candles and sacred vestments. The creed was 'kept' and recorded in the Bible. God was the creator and his

son was Jesus, who walked the earth and taught. Drugs were used: incense and wine in ceremony and sacred acts. And there was sacrifice, the crucifixion of Jesus Christ, a concept definitely familiar to ancient Andeans.

FINDING COMMON GROUND

Like the Incas, Christian preachers were willing to 'bend' a little in their efforts to convince themselves that their New World

Above: Ancient Andeans would have recognized the concept of human sacrifice but have had difficulty with the victim being described as the god himself.

converts' beliefs proved that Christian religion had been witnessed throughout the world – that things were always as they were in their Christian world. However, the recorders were the Spaniards themselves, and they were inclined to alter the stories they were told to fit preconceived ideas. For example, the three Viracochas (Con Tici, Imaymana and Tocapo) were a perfect triad that could be equated with the Holy Trinity, but what sixteenth-century Spanish priests did not know was that triadism is a concept in many cultures in the world.

In Andean triadism the kin-relationship of father and two sons, or three brothers, is less important than the structure of one principal and two helpers. This form is present in cult histories throughout the Andes. In some versions there is a fourth figure, Taguapaca, who disobeyed the father's instructions and was thrown into the River Desaguadero for his disobedience – the perfect foil of evil destroyed to leave the three principals of the narrative.

One of the ways in which Andean belief has survived is by being combined with Christianity. Some combinations were

Below: This puma devouring sinners was an attempt to seduce Native Americans into Christian belief using an Andean symbol.

deliberate, as Spanish priests tried to ease the acceptance of Christianity. Much else was a natural blending of the Andeans' own beliefs with Christian ones: for example the sun is merged with Jesus, the Virgin Mary with Pacha Mama (the earth goddess) and Saint James of Santiago with Illapa.

IMPORTANT DIFFERENCES

Belief in an afterlife is a universal religious concept, though the idea that one's conduct on Earth was partly responsible for the nature of the afterlife was less entrenched in Andean belief. The difference was the Andean concept of *pachacuti*: a great cycle that repeated endlessly through time. Suffering was here on Earth, and the final journey of the spirit after physical death was allied to the Andean concept of essence, and the idea that death was the ultimate stage in life's cycle, with no thought of rebirth.

The concept of a second coming was embraced in Inkarrí, but is fundamentally more concerned with the return of the Incas to their rightful place in the scheme of things, their ingrained belief in *pachacuti* and a destiny to rule, rather than the Christian concept of Christ's return.

Spanish priests were unable to suppress the Inca solar cult: it survived in the central highlands and to the coast at Pachacamac. The sun continued to be a principal deity superior to mountain protector-guardian deities, and two aspects were recognized as daytime-sun, in the sky, and night-time sun, which travelled through the earth overnight. Throughout the highlands, the cults of Inti and Punchao (daytime sun) survived into colonial times and were associated with maize and the potato. In the 1560s a messianic movement called Taqui Onqoy (dancing sickness) revived the ancient *huacas* of Titicaca, Pachacamac and others,

Right: The Virgin Mary here remarkably resembles an Inca mummy bundle, and even has a staff-holding Inca depicted on her gown.

perhaps eschewing the sun as associated with the Inca elite, who had been overpowered by the Spaniards.

Ultimately, ancient Andean beliefs could not be reconciled with Christian ones. The connections and parallels were too vague, and there were too many variations in Andean belief. Although there are undoubtedly similarities, they are merely superficial, for the concept of one god was fundamentally alien to ancient Andeans. However, Andeans were happy to keep their ancient religious ideas alongside Christianity, as long as they didn't have to give them up entirely. Thus, the Incas remained true to their belief in an established cycle of life in which they were at the cusp, destined to rule in the name of Inti. They were following the path that was ordained, fulfilling their destiny. Of course, the Spanish conquistadors held a similar belief, but they were conquering in the name of *their* god.

SACRED LOCATIONS

Reverence for sacred locations has never abated in Andean belief. From the powers of mountain gods and Pacha Mama to household deities such as Ekkeko, Andeans believe that offerings to such 'gods' can bring good fortune.

Spanish priests and administrators, focusing on conversion and on the elimination of ancestor cults, only slowly realized the tenacity with which Andean peoples stuck to their essential belief in the sacredness of the local landscape. Such beliefs go back to the foundations of the earliest cultures of the Andes and the first architectural ceremonial centres that mimicked the shapes of the landscape. The destruction of cult objects could not weaken such beliefs.

Andeans continue to regard identifiable stones or rock outcrops near their towns as characters from legendary scenes who have been turned to stone.

The ancient site of Pachacamac is perhaps the most ancient pilgrimage site in use. It persisted in colonial times as a

Below: Tens of thousands of people participate annually in the El Calvario ritual, merging Christian belief and sacred places.

sacred place. The Señor de los Milagros, or Crito Morado, here filled the place of the pre-Hispanic cult. Modern Peruvians visit Pachacamac to make offerings, especially to Pacha Mama.

HOUSEHOLD DEITIES

Ekkeko is a case in point. An Aymara deity dating from the Middle Horizon Tiwanaku culture, he was incorporated into Inca religion. Ekkeko household deity figures persisted through colonial times and are kept in households today to bring good luck. They are offered everything from coca leaves to Coca Cola in asking them to bring the household good fortune. The presence of Ekkeko makes every household a 'sacred place'. The use of such deity figures spread in the 1970s to many countries well beyond the Bolivian Altiplano.

Similarly, Inca stone and metal sculptures of plants and animals were considered repositories of health and powers for well-being. They were placed at *huacas* throughout the land. Today, Andeans keep small stones that either resemble animals or plants or have been carved to do so. Known as *inqa, inqaychu,*

Above: Shrines remained sacred to the Inca. The seated-puma-shaped rock at Qenqo continued to remind the Incas of Viracocha.

conopa or *illa*, they are believed to be gifts from mountain *apus*. Some have been passed down through many generations. Modern versions can be miniature plastic trucks, rubber sandals, cans of drink, money or even passports, and they can be bought at pilgrimage sites before being offered to local deities or saints.

Taking an object that belonged to a deceased important person in one's *ayllu* kinship group to that person's favourite place would invoke the person's memory among his descendants and also enhance the power of the sacred place. The act was not merely repetitious, but was meant to build the kin-group's history and link it through time to the present.

HUACA SHRINES

The royal *panaca* and sacred *huacas* of the Inca emperors were especially important to kin-group history. As part of the cult of the Sapa Inca as Inti's representative on earth, when Tupa Yupanqui died, his son Huana Capac visited the places

Above: The Qoyllur Rit'i ritual, begun after an alleged 18th-century miracle, revives the ancient Andean concept of ritual procession.

his father liked best, especially in Cajamarca, and built shrines at them. One tradition in the history of Inca origins describes Mount Huanacauri as the 'father' of the three founding ancestors, who were turned into stone around Cuzco. Even today, some Andeans regard local *huacas* in their region 'like parents'. Such places were believed to have given rise to their ancestors, and local caves were often where Andeans stored the mummified remains of ancestors until they were destroyed in colonial times by the Spaniards. Substantial evidence for

Below: This Qoyllur Rit'i procession is to the sacred Mt Sinakara, where Mariano herded his llamas and met the mestizo boy.

provincial shrine systems like those around Cuzco – for example colonial records – is sparse, however, and probably awaits discovery by ethnohistorians.

QOYLLUR RIT'I

One of the most celebrated 'modern' festivals involving place is Qoyllur Rit'i in the southern Andes, attended annually by tens of thousands of people. Held during the three weeks leading to the feast of Corpus Christi, the ritual is focused on several sanctuaries around Ocongate. Costumed dancers perform in honour of 'El Señor'.

The ritual is a typical mixture of ancient and Christian beliefs. The object of devotion is an image of Christ that miraculously appeared on a rock: El Señor de Qoyllur Rit'i (Lord of the Snow Star). The ritual began in the late 18th century, when the Catholic authorities replaced an indigenous cult with a Christian shrine. The Catholic Church officially accepted the miraculous appearance of Christ's image.

The ancient cult associated Ocongate as a venue of worship at the transition and regeneration of the new year. The blending of Christian and ancient belief revolves around the miracle in which a young llama herder, Mariano, encountered a mestizo boy on Mount Sinakara. Mariano was cold and hungry and the other boy shared his food. Mariano's herd increased and his father offered him new clothes as a reward. Mariano asked for new clothes for his friend too. He took the mestizo boy's

poncho to market to have it duplicated. The Bishop of Cuzco noted the old poncho's fine material and asked Mariano about the mestizo. Church officials sent to meet him encountered him wearing a white tunic, surrounded by a blinding radiance emanating from a silhouette When one official tried to touch it, he grasped a *tayanka* bush, above which, on a rock, appeared the image of Christ crucified. Mariano fell dead and was buried at the foot of the rock where the image appeared. A chapel was built to house the Tanyaka Cross and Mariano's sepulchre. Christ Tanyaka is believed to have been transformed into the rock, and the Catholic Church later had Christ's image painted on the rock-face.

Below: Husband and wife believers burn incense and make an offering to Pacha Mama in a ceremony in the La Paz Valley.

PROCESSIONS, FESTIVALS AND RITES

Architectural forms and sculptures in mud plaster and stone show that processions, ritual festivals and sacred rites were a part of ancient Andean culture.

ANCIENT PROCESSIONS

Ancient Andeans were intimately familiar with the concept of sacred routes. Cuzco alone had more than 300 sacred shrines along sacred *ceque* routes, ranging from monumental buildings to natural features. So important were processional routes to the Incas that archaeologists project their use to as far back as the Initial Period, suggesting that processions through U-shaped ceremonial precincts proceeded down into and through sunken courts, back out of them, and up on to temple platforms mimicking mountains, to honour earth and sky deities.

The established purpose of the famous Nazca desert lines – geoglyphs – was for ritual processions that followed the course of the lines. Geoglyphs of animals, birds or geometric patterns consist of a single line that never crosses itself. There are also nodes from which lines radiate.

The tradition of *ceque* routes made Christian processional routes, such as the Stations of the Cross, easy to comprehend.

Below: The 'festival' of Inti Raymi, the Inca June/winter solstice, attracts large crowds and is taken seriously to revive ancient Inca pageantry at the shrine of Sacsahuaman.

Left: The Nazca even made clay models of ancient processions, including a central shaman.

Pilgrimage to holy shrines was also a common ancient Andean practice. Similarly, ancient Andean sacrificial practices made recognition of the apparent ritual execution of Christ a familiar concept.

The Qoyllur Rit'i ritual involves processions by two groups representing the warm lands of the north-west (from Paucartambo town) and the colder pasture land of the south-east (from Quispicanchis town). The procession represents ancient Andean regional opposition and mutual exchange, and even linguistic dualism, for the Paucartambos are Quechua speakers while the Quispicanchis speak Aymara.

FEAST DAYS

Just as early Christians in a pagan Europe adapted and combined many feast days and ceremonies into the Christian calendar as their religion spread, so Christian Andeans have equated many ancient Andean ceremonial days to established Christian dates.

The recitation of the myth-histories of founding ancestors in provincial communities was made at annual high points such as planting (Pocoymita) and harvesting (Caruaymita), both of

which became associated with Christian holy days. Ancient Andeans began to harvest their various crops in mid-April, and finished the collection and storage of produce by early June. These activities coincided with the disappearance of the Pleiades constellation in the night sky in April and its June reappearance above the horizon. The Pleiades were called *collca* ('storehouse') by the Incas, and ancient Andeans regarded it as the celestial container of the essence of all agricultural produce. With the arrival of Christianity, the movable feast of Corpus Christi soon became equated with the rising of the Pleiades at the same time as the rising of the sun.

Festivals mixing ancient Andean ritual with Christian practice and dates are those of Capac Raymi (December summer solstice) and Inti Raymi (June winter solstice), and the revival of the ritual re-enactment of the founding of Cuzco by Manco Capac, celebrated annually.

Such rituals can be regarded as a rejuvenation of ancient belief and power, which would have been understandable

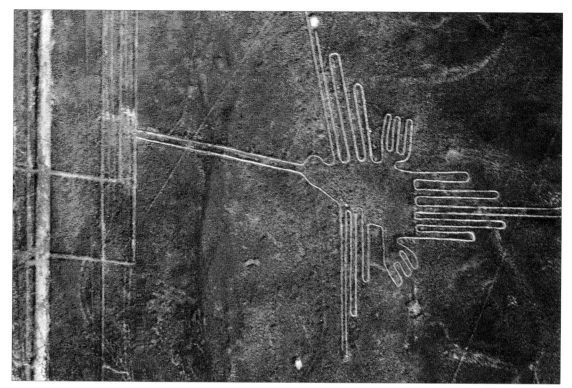

Above: Humming bird in the Nazca desert. Geoglyph lines were thought of as processional pathways, perhaps 'owned' by kin groups.

in an atmosphere and perception of powerlessness against hundreds of years of colonial oppression.

DEEDS OF THE ANCESTORS

When the first Spaniards entered Cuzco they witnessed the arrangement of the mummified Inca emperors in the main plaza. The keepers of Inca history, the *amautas* and *harahuicus*, were responsible for collating the histories and deeds of the emperors. On ritual occasions, it was their task to recite these histories in the forms of short stories by the former and poems by the latter, incorporating stylistic devices such as set speeches, repeated metaphor and refrains intentionally reshaped and elaborated from one performance to the next.

Occasions for such performances included the initiation rites of teenage boys as adults during the month leading

up to Capac Raymi (late November–December), the summer solstice. The boys visited the peaks in the southern Cuzco Valley where the Inca ancestors stopped on their route to Cuzco. Other occasions were at the celebration of military victories, royal successions and, of course, royal funerals.

It was Inca Pahcacuti, religious reformer and initiator of the cult of Inti, who ordered that 'songs' (*cantares* in the Spanish chronicles) were sung by the attendants of the imperial 'statues' (ancestor mummies and *huauques*) at 'fiestas'. The performance began with the deeds of Manco Capac, the founder ancestor, and proceeded through the emperors up to the reigning Sapa Inca. Colonial records describe such performances of myth-histories in provincial centres as well.

STAMPING OUT IDOLATRY

Priests and Spanish administrators fought a continuing battle against what they regarded as idolatry, as manifested in the cults and virtual worship of the

mummified remains of *ayllu* founders and ancestors. They ruthlessly hunted down and tried the perpetrators of ancestor cults and burned their mummified ancestors, until by the end of the 16th century all were destroyed.

In the eyes of the Incas, the Spaniards were equally wicked in their treatment of Inti. The great golden sun disc that hung in the Coricancha had been awarded to one of the conquistadors, who promptly gambled it away in a late-night card game – thus the Andean expression 'to gamble the sun before dawn'.

REVIVALS

Many Inca rites and processions have been revived, especially in the late 20th century. Based, as were their ancestors, primarily on an agricultural way of life, Native South American descendants and mestizos seek to alleviate the hardships of life by continuing to honour traditional belief in the sacredness of the land of their forefathers and to reconcile this with modern life.

ANIMISM AND COCA

Animism was fundamental in ancient Andean religion: the forces of nature were and are believed to be 'living beings' that affect life. Humans were only one group of beings among animals and plants. The images of supernatural beings based on living animals, such as the jaguar, snakes, predatory birds and spiders, and the depiction of transformation, reveal such belief. Animals were thought to possess powers and wisdom that could benefit humans, and certain humans, the shamans, were capable of shape-shifting to become, temporarily, the animal in question and take on the animal's nature.

Below: This Moche spouted vessel displays an intoxicated shaman, holding his wooden stick and coca container to make coca balls.

THE LIVING EARTH

Agriculture was fundamental to ancient Andean civilization and still forms the basis of most of Andean society. Agricultural fertility is therefore deeply ingrained in the Andean psyche, and with it worship of Pacha Mama – the living earth – and the natural elements. Ceremonial rites to Pacha Mama, the matrix for all life, continue to be performed regularly throughout the year, highlighted on important dates in agriculture, and also when visiting sacred places and at the start of a long journey. At harvest cere-monies, young women impersonate Pacha Mama Suyrumama by wearing long red dresses ('mother earth of the long dress that drags along the ground').

The field called Ayllipampa, near Cuzco, is dedicated to Pacha Mama. Bernabé Cobo described how farmers worshipped her at stone altars containing miniature women's clothing in the middle of the field. Other deities associated with Pachcmama are Mama Oca, Mama Coca and Mama Sara (Maize Mother). Central Andeans continue to maintain that the Inca ancestress Mama Huaco, who sowed the first maize field, and others sustain the agricultural well-being of the community. The field of Sausero outside Cuzco was dedicated to her.

Agricultural ferility is also believed to be affected by mountain *apu* deities and celestial gods, including Illapa (lightning and thunder), Cuichu (rainbow) and Ccoa (a supernatural feline who causes destructive hail).

THE POWER OF *CHICHA*

Today, rural *ayllus* continue to plough and plant communal fields at festivals. There are contests to see who can work fastest at ploughing and planting the largest amount of land. Festive meals are served, accompanied by plenty of *chicha* or maize beer. There are *chicha* libations and offerings of coca to Pacha Mama, the community ancestors and the local

Above: Continuing ancient practice, a modern Peruvian makes an offering of coca leaves to a local deity or saint.

sacred places, alongside Christian prayers to the community's patron saints, who seem to have taken the place of the ancestors.

Llamas are ritually honoured in August. They are force-fed a *chicha*, barley and herbal mash to intoxicate them before being released on to the Altiplano, fol-lowed by their equally intoxicated herders singing and playing flutes. Such ritual drunkenness is believed to enhance fer-tility. Libations are poured to invite Pacha Mama and the *apus* to the celebrations. Intoxication also blurs the distinction between humans, animals and the landscape as they all 'dance together'.

SACRIFICE BEHIND THE ALTAR

Ancient sacrifices and offerings continued in secrecy well into Spanish colonial times. Although known as the 'sacrifice behind the altar' syndrome, this is not to be taken literally, as the sacrifices and offerings simply occurred in remote places away from churches. Animal sacrifices, together with offerings of agricultural produce and coca, and the burning of incense with prayers are still practised, often alongside offerings of modern 'western' products such as cigarettes and Coca Cola, and also often in connection with Christian ceremonies.

Mountains (especially volcanoes), caves and springs remain particularly sacred. Mountains continue to be regarded as the dwelling places of the ancestral dead.

The fundamental Andean cosmological frame remains an anchor to Andean society: the sun rises over the sacred mountains in the east, brings life, and sets in the west, the final resting place of the dead.

SHAMANS
Local shamanism also still has an important place in local communities. For everyday illnesses, many Andeans consult their local *curandero*, a person skilled in the use of herbs and potions, harking back to the 5th-century AD Wari cave burial of a herbalist. Shaman-curers were frequently depicted in Moche and other effigy vessels.

Cures include the use of water and perfume exhaled over a (looted) skull from a pre-Hispanic burial, in the belief that the spirit of the deceased person will protect the afflicted as well as the curer from evil interventions. Potent hallucinogenic mescaline brews are still made from the San Pedro cactus. Chants and prayers used in such cures are a mixture

Above: Native South Americans and cholos *(people of Spanish descent) in a Christian-native ceremony at El Calvario, Bolivia.*

of pre-Hispanic and Christian practices. Sticks, which represent swords, are used to fight with the spirits of 'the other world' and keep them from harming the patient. As in ancient times, the shaman acts as an intermediary between the human and spirit worlds.

COCA
The regular chewing of coca leaves continues as a stimulant and aid in coping with the harsh climate and high Andean altitudes. The Spaniards quickly learned its properties of keeping otherwise exhausted labourers and miners energized, and exploited its perceived sacred symbolic power as, once again, their Christian convictions were compromised by practical needs. Coca cultivation increased under Spanish rule. Coca leaves are a frequent offering to Pacha Mama especially, and there is irony in their 'integration' from ancient use to modern times, for the leaf is referred to as Hostia (the Host) and its ritual consumption compared to Holy Communion.

Coca remains a major part of the Andean indigenous economy and is, of course, exploited internationally in its refinement for the drug trade.

Left: A silver figurine depicts a woman with puffed cheeks, chewing a coca wad, which induces stamina and suppresses hunger.

THE RETURN OF THE INCAS

Twentieth-century social studies of Andean culture have discovered an underlying theme that represents a source of post-Conquest cross-Andean unity: the theme of the dying and reviving Inca, as encapsulated in the legend of Inkarrí.

THE FIVE AGES

A late Inca cosmology comprised a five-age sequence of the creation of the Inca world. The First Age was ruled by Viracocha and the other gods, and death was unknown. The Second Age was that of the giants created by Viracocha, who worshipped him but who displeased him and were destroyed by a flood. The Third Age was inhabited by the first humans, again created by Viracocha, but they lived on a primitive level and lacked even the rudiments of civilization. The Fourth Age was that of the *Auca Runa* ('the warriors'), to whom Viracocha presumably imparted the arts of civilization, for these were the creators of the early civilizations such as the Moche and the Tiwanaku.

Below: After unsuccessful revolts against Spanish rule, the legend grew that the Incas retreated east into the rainforest to Paititi.

The Fifth Age was that of the Incas themselves, who spread civilization far and wide through conquest. The Fifth Age ended with the coming of the Spaniards and with the downfall of the Inca Empire, but upon their arrival the Spaniards were hailed as the returning emissaries of the creator and were referred to as *viracocha*s – a term still used as one of respect.

THE STORY OF INKARRÍ

Inkarrí is the central character in a post-Spanish Conquest Inca millenarian belief in the 'dying and reviving Inca'. The derivation of the name itself is a combination of the Quechua word *Inca* and the Spanish word *rey*, both meaning 'king' or 'ruler'. The legend foretells a time when the current sufferings of the original peoples of the Andes will be ended in a cataclysmic transformation of the world, in which the Spanish overlords will be destroyed. The true Inca will be resurrected and reinstated in his rightful place as supreme ruler, and prosperity and justice will be returned to the world.

A typical example of one of the versions of the Inkarrí myth recounts how Inkarrí was the son of a savage woman

Above: A modern Peruvian impersonates the Sapa Inca at the festival of Inti Raymi. It is believed that the emperor will one day return.

and Father Sun. Inkarrí was powerful. He harnessed the sun, his father, and the very wind itself. He drove stones with a whip, ordered them around, and founded a city called K'ellk'ata, probably Cuzco. Then he threw a golden rod from a mountaintop, but found that the city did not fit on the plain where it landed, so he moved the city to its present location. When the Spaniards arrived, however, they imprisoned Inkarrí in a secret place, and his head is all that remains. However, Inkarrí is growing a new body and will return when he is whole again.

PACHACUTI

Belief in the return of Inkarrí is clearly in keeping with the Andean concept of *pachacuti*, the revolution or reversal of time and space. It arose from the native populations' sense that the Spaniards had created oppression and injustice. It may hark back to events of the first few

*Right: Tupac Amaru, the 'last Inca emperor',
was beheaded in Cuzco's central plaza. His
head was spirited away and secretly buried.*

decades after the Spanish Conquest, in
which the last Inca emperor, Atahualpa,
was believed to have been beheaded by
Francisco Pizarro shortly after his defeat,
and to the beheading of Tupac Amaru, a
claimant to the Inca throne, who led an
unsuccessful revolt against Spanish rule
in the 1560s and 1570s. In different
accounts, the two heads were taken to
Lima or to Cuzco, but in both cases the
belief is that, once buried in the ground,
the head becomes a seed that rejoins its
body in anticipation of return.

THE RETURN TO CUZCO
Another belief concerns the removal of
Inca power to a hidden land. The legend
records that upon being expelled from
Cuzco the Incas travelled east through
the mountains. They built bridges as they
went, but they placed enchantments on

*Below: The retreating Incas built enchanted
bridges as they went, so that their route
could not be followed.*

their route so that no one could follow.
If they did, the enchantment caused them
to fall asleep on the spot for ever.

The Incas travelled across the mountains
into the jungle and established a hidden city
called Paititi. Here they remain in hiding.
'Foreigners' who seek Paititi can never find
it. One found a talking bridge; when he
tried to cross it, he was chased away by
huge felines and *amarus* (mythical
serpent-dragons) guarding the bridge.

According to the legend, *pachacuti* will
turn and the Inca will return, following
the route they used when they left Cuzco.
There will be tremendous hail and
lightning, wind and earthquakes. *Amarus*
will roar from mountains and mestizos will
be chased away. When the Incas return
they will recognize only their *runakuna*
descendants, who wear traditional llama-
wool clothing, and the Incas will assume
their rightful place and rule again.

PART TWO

THE INCA WORLD

This fascinating account of the social life of the many peoples of ancient South America reveals the everyday world of men, women and children. It shows how society developed from the first Preceramic villages through to sophisticated towns and social systems in the empires of the Moche, Wari, Chimú and Inca. This history traces the growth of architecture, examining the mysterious Nazca lines in the desert and the temples at Kotosh, La Galgada and Aspero. It shows how, in the absence of contemporary written records, archaeological excavations, preserved architecture and discovered art and artefacts have supplied the evidence that helps us follow the lives of ordinary people from the cradle to the grave. As well as examining the society in which these people lived, it reveals its beautiful fine and applied art from breathtakingly complex textiles to stone, plaster and clay sculptures. In this section you will find out how this magnificent heritage is seen today in the ruins of vast cities and pyramids, and delicate fragments of shining goldwork.

Above: Revolt of the Objects, a mythological theme.
Left: A circular structure in the fortress of Sacsayhuaman.

INTRODUCTION

The Inca Empire was the culmination of thousands of years of cultural evolution, the end product of gradual developments from small farming villages to cities with large populations and sophisticated political, economic and religious organization.

THE ANDEAN AREA

The vast continent of South America, nearly separate geologically and geographically, never formed a single cultural unit. Its inhabitants developed at different paces, although cultures in large areas were aware of and interactive with each other through trade, political alliance, conquest and the diffusion of ideas.

The ancient cultures that archaeologists call 'civilizations' (urban-based societies with centralized political organization and advanced technology) were confined to the Andes mountains and adjacent western coastal valleys and deserts. Sophisticated societies and beliefs were also developed by other South American peoples, but they did not build monumental ceremonial centres or cities, or, for the most part, develop technology of the same complexity or variety as Andean cultures, or establish kingdoms and empires.

Below: Andean foothills, typical upland valley terrain and Mount Illimani, Bolivia.

This book concentrates on the 'Andean Area', where civilizations evolved in the sierras and adjacent foothills and coastal regions, north to south from the present-day Colombian–Ecuadorian border to the northern half of Chile and east to west from the Amazonian Rainforest to the Pacific.

CIVILIZED CONTACTS

The Andean Area is a nuclear region where civilization emerged independently. Other nuclear regions were Mesopotamia, Egypt, north-western India, China, Southeast Asia and Mesoamerica. Ancient Andeans had no direct knowledge of or contact with the peoples of any of these other regions. There is no substantiated confirmation in written records, or any unequivocal archaeological evidence, to prove that sustained contact existed between the Old World and the New before 1492.

There is equally no evidence to suggest the Incas were aware of the Aztec Empire or Maya city-states in Mesoamerica.

By the 1520s, Inca traders were travelling up the north-west coast, making contact and trading with sophisticated metallurgy-producing 'chiefdoms' in north-western South America. Likewise, in the early 16th century, Aztecs traded at the international emporium of Xicalango in the Yucatán Peninsula, and were on the

*Above: Inca maize planting in August (*yupuy quilla, *soil turning) depicted in Poma de Ayala's* Nueva Corónica, *c.1615.*

verge of invading the Maya city-states. The two empires might eventually have met, and the consequences would undoubtedly have been interesting.

WHAT IS CIVILIZATION?

Civilization is an elusive term. Much has been written in an attempt to define it, to list its essential characteristics. Standard dictionary definitions help little, for they tend to state that civilization is the 'opposite of barbarism', and that it involves the arts and refinement of culture. The end product – cultures with cities and a high level of sophisticated technology – seems obvious. Civilization is recognizable when full-blown. But it is the point at which civilization can be said to arrive that is so difficult to perceive and define.

'Laundry lists' of criteria by which civilization can be defined have been made. They include: size, rulership, cities, domesticated animals and plants, irrigation agriculture, social organization (which includes individuals who do not participate in or contribute directly to subsistence), writing, a monetary system, a state army,

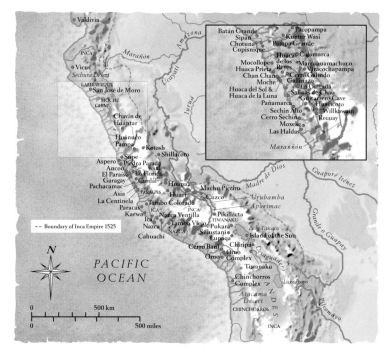

Above: Map of the Andean Area, showing sites, of all periods, discussed in the text.

a road system and a certain level of technological sophistication with specialized craftspeople. Yet every nuclear area listed above lacked one or more of these criteria.

ANDEAN CIVILIZATION

The Andean Area is vast. Within it, long-distance communication was a major feature of its civilization. Communication was also long-lived, for as each successive culture developed, it was based on the developments that preceded it.

Pre-Inca Andean city-states, kingdoms and empires evolved, based on maize and potato agriculture and on the herding of camelids (llamas, alpacas and vicuñas). The range of contrasting landscapes was immense in the Andean Area – from coastal plains and deserts, to inland valleys, to sierra basins and plateaux, to high pampas grasslands, to eastern mountain slopes descending to Amazonian rainforests.

A key factor in Andean cultural development and endurance was access to and control of water, which became important not only functionally, but also religiously. Geographical contrast fostered and nurtured the development of sophisticated agriculture based on complex irrigation technologies and a wide variety of crops, both within and between lowland and highland regions. These developments fostered economic specialization, enabling cultures to develop social hierarchies and complex divisions and distributions of labour and rulership. They also developed trading contacts across long distances, and religious beliefs and structures, both theoretical and architectural.

LEGACY

The sophisticated technologies developed in Andean civilization came to be sponsored by the state. Rulers and the religious hierarchy required large-scale production of exquisite ceramics, textiles and jewellery as statements of social status, state power and religious devotion.

Sadly, these precious archaeological objects attract the interest and greed of modern collectors as much as they do scholars seeking the knowledge such objects can reveal. Since the Spanish Conquest, a legacy of illicit digging for monetary gain and exclusive ownership has fostered trade in antiquities fed by looting on a grand scale.

Undisturbed archaeological evidence, from the humblest building to the elite tombs of Sipán, provides the best source of information about everyday culture and conspicuous consumption of precious objects in their social and ritual contexts. Robbed from the ground by looters, and of its cultural context, it is lost forever.

Below: Highland plateau among the Cordillera de los Frailes, Bolivia.

Above: Totora-reed boats on Lake Titicaca. Design has changed little since ancient times, but modern cloth sails mean less labour.

THE SOURCES

Scholars have three sources of information about the Incas and their predecessors: historical documents, archaeological evidence, and anthropological or ethnological information about Andean peoples.

Written sources are particularly relevant for our picture of Inca society, but the principal sources of knowledge for pre-Inca civilization come from archaeology and anthropology. Artefacts and structures are direct evidence of what ancient Andeans made and used. But the manner of their use and what social, political, economic and religious meanings they have must be interpreted.

For pre-Inca cultures there is almost no historical evidence. Inca records of the peoples they conquered (for example the Chimú Kingdom that began before the Inca Empire and was contemporary to the early Inca), written down after the Spanish Conquest, are subject to Inca imperial views. However, comparison of pre-Inca archaeological evidence with Inca materials and history can reveal similarities that enable scholars to suggest that Inca social, political, economic and religious practices and beliefs were the end results of much earlier developments of these themes.

ARCHAEOLOGICAL PROJECTIONS

In combination with archaeology, much of what we gain from written sources about the Incas and their contemporaries can be 'projected' into the past, as a way of interpreting and understanding pre-Inca civilization and cultures.

Archaeology comprises methods of recovery, analytical procedures and reasoning to reconstruct as much as possible about the nature of people's lives in past cultures. Archaeological evidence is viable wherever and whenever historical evidence does not exist, or does not document groups or aspects of a people or culture. In addition to excavating and collecting artefacts (any object or remains made by humans or left as the result of their activities), archaeologists carefully record their contexts – the positions and relationships between artefacts and the soil in which they are found.

Contexts enable archaeologists to date objects and structures in relationship to each other, to see similarities and differences between types of artefacts, and thus deduce their uses, technology, and social and economic relationships between peoples and cultures. Artefacts, contexts and relationships also enable archaeologists to offer explanations of how cultures functioned, from straightforward deductions about manufacturing technology, to conclusions about trade and reasoned speculation about political relationships and religious beliefs.

DATING

Historical sources normally give dates for the events being recorded, although these are not always accurate. Until 1949 archaeological evidence, unless it could be linked to a historical source, could not be given calendar dates, only dates relative to other archaeological evidence (before, after or at the same time as). Such relative dating was determined by association in the same stratigraphic layer of earth, or in a layer above (later than) or below (earlier than) another artefact. This is true whether the artefact concerned is something small, such as a hand tool, or large, such as the foundation walls of a temple.

Below: Inca farmers tending maize seedlings in irrigated fields in January when the rain came, or qhapaq raymi quilla – the month of feasting, depicted in Poma de Ayala's Nueva Corónica, c.1615.

Above: Professor John Howland Rowe of the University of California at Berkeley at the ruins of the Palace of Emperor Huyana Capac at Quisphuanca, Peru.

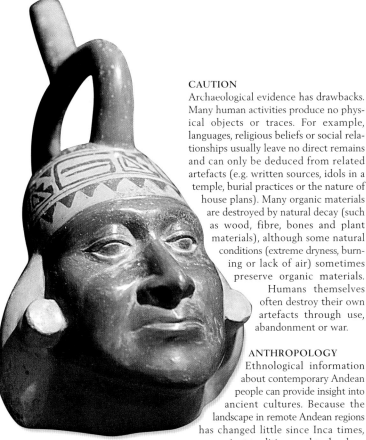

Above: A Moche stirrup-spout effigy bottle modelled as the head of an apparently blind man.

Science has discovered several radiometric ways to determine absolute dates for archaeological materials. Two principal methods are radiocarbon dating and dendrochronology (tree-ring dating). The former is the main method for Andean ancient history because its limits (back to about 50,000 years ago) are well within the range of human occupation of the Andean Area. The latter was developed from the early decades of the 20th century but is of no use in Andean cultures because most of the wood used in Andean architecture has not survived, and a tree-ring sequence is not available for the region.

CAUTION

Archaeological evidence has drawbacks. Many human activities produce no physical objects or traces. For example, languages, religious beliefs or social relationships usually leave no direct remains and can only be deduced from related artefacts (e.g. written sources, idols in a temple, burial practices or the nature of house plans). Many organic materials are destroyed by natural decay (such as wood, fibre, bones and plant materials), although some natural conditions (extreme dryness, burning or lack of air) sometimes preserve organic materials. Humans themselves often destroy their own artefacts through use, abandonment or war.

ANTHROPOLOGY

Ethnological information about contemporary Andean people can provide insight into ancient cultures. Because the landscape in remote Andean regions has changed little since Inca times, some ancient traditions and technology have survived, particularly agricultural methods. Observations of contemporary society can help in the interpretation of otherwise puzzling archaeological remains or historical descriptions, through direct parallels or as models for comparison.

One of the major characteristics of Andean civilization appears to be longevity of technology, cultural practices, social organization and religious belief, which are recognizably different in detail to distinguish diverse peoples and nations through time.

The direct observations of Felipe Guaman Poma de Ayala and the sources used by Bernabé Cobo were the first ethnographies. Later explorers and travellers added to and confirmed many 16th-century records when they recorded native practices. Joining a French expedition to

South America in the late 1730s, Antonio Juan de Ulloa recorded contemporary Andean practices.

Later, Alexander von Humboldt travelled throughout the Americas and recorded his observations on natural history and geology, ethnology and archaeology. His *Political Essay on the Kingdom of New Spain* (1811) and *Researches Concerning the Institutions and Monuments of the Ancient Inhabitants of America* (1814) were monumental works, and his lectures back in Europe brought South America and its peoples into public awareness.

Below: An alpaca herd grazing in the highland Valle de Coloa, Bolivia.

TIMELINE OF THE INCAS AND THEIR ANCESTORS

The chronology of the Andean Area is complex. Archaeologists have developed a scheme based on technological achievements and on changing political organization through time, from the first arrival of humans in the area (15,000–3500BC) to the conquest of the Inca Empire by Francisco Pizarro in 1532. The pace of technological development varied in different regions within the Andean Area, especially in early periods in its history. The development of lasting and strong contact between regions, however, spread both technology and ideas and led to regions depending on each other to some degree. Sometimes this interdependence was due to large areas being under the control of one 'authority', while at other times the unifying link was religious or based on trade/technology.

The principal chronological scheme for the Andean Area comprises a sequence of eight time units: five Periods and three Horizons. Periods are defined as times when political unity across regions was less consolidated. Smaller areas were controlled by city-states, sometimes in loose groupings,

Above: The walled royal compounds of the Chimú capital Chan Chan.

perhaps sharing religious beliefs despite having different political views. The Horizons, by contrast, were times when much larger political units were formed. These units exercised political, economic and religious control over extended areas, usually including different types of terrain rather than being confined to coastal valley groups or sierra city-states.

Different scholars give various dates for the beginnings and endings of the Periods and Horizons, and no two books on Andean civilization give exactly the same dates. The durations of Periods and

Horizons also vary from one region to another within the Andean Area, and the charts have increased in complexity as authors have divided the Andean Area into coastal, sierra and Altiplano regions, or even into north, central and southern coastal regions and north, central and southern highland regions. The dates given here are a compilation from several sources, thus avoiding any anomalies in any specific sources.

CHRONOLOGICAL PERIOD	DATES	PRINCIPAL CULTURES
Lithic / Archaic Period	15,000–3500BC	spread of peoples into the Andean Area hunter-gatherer cultures
Preceramic / Formative Period (Cotton Preceramic)	3500–1800BC	early agriculture and first ceremonial centres
Initial Period	1800–750BC	U-shaped ceremonial centres, platform mounds and sunken courts
Early Horizon	750–200BC	Chavín, Paracas, Pukará (Yaya-Mama) cults
Early Intermediate Period	200BC–AD600	Moche, Nazca and Titicaca Basin confederacies
Middle Horizon	AD600–1000	Wari and Tiwanaku empires
Late Intermediate Period	AD1000–1400	Chimú and Inca empires
Late Horizon	AD1400–1532	Inca Empire and Spanish Conquest

LITHIC / ARCHAIC PERIOD (15,000–3500BC)

Above: View from the Cuz del Condor showing the mountains and valleys of Peru.

Ice-free corridors open up across the Bering Strait *c*.40,000 to *c*.20,000 years ago, but there is no evidence that humans entered the New World until the late stages of this time period.

c.20,000BC Migrating hunter-gatherers, using stone-, bone-, wood- and shell-tool technologies, probably entered the New World from north-east Asia.

from *c*.15,000 years ago Palaeoindians migrated south and east to populate North and South America, reaching Monte Verde in southern Chile *c*.14,850 years ago.

c.8500–5000BC Andean and Altiplano hunter-gatherers occupy cave and rock shelter sites in the Andes (e.g. Pachamachay, Guitarrero, Tres Ventanas and Toquepala caves). Evidence of tending of hemp-like fibre, medicinal plants, herbs and wild tubers.

c.6000BC–*c*.5500BC The first true monumental structures, two long parallel mounds, are built at Nanchoc, a late Archaic Period valley in the Zana Valley, north-west Peru.

by 5000BC plant domestication, as opposed to tending wild plants, is truly underway in the highlands.

c.5000BC The Chinchorros peoples make the first deliberately mummified burials in the Atacama Desert.

PRECERAMIC / FORMATIVE PERIOD (3500–1800BC)

Above: Alpaca grazing in the Valle de Coloa. Camelids were herded c.*3500–1800BC.*

This period is sometimes also called the Cotton Preceramic.

c.3500–1800BC True plant domestication of cotton, squashes, gourds, beans, maize, potatoes, sweet potatoes and chillies. Llamas and other camelids herded on the Altiplano.

c.3500BC Valdivians found Real Alto.

c.3200BC First ceramics made by Valdivian farmers in coastal Ecuador.

by 3000BC the full range of major food plants is grown in the highlands and the guinea pig is bred for meat.

c.3000BC Coastal villages such as Huaca Prieta flourish, producing early textiles.

c.2700BC Early northern coastal civic-ceremonial centres at Aspero – Huaca de los Idolos and Huaca de los Sacrificios.

by 2500BC the llama and alpaca have been truly domesticated.

c.2500BC Clay figurines at Huaca de los Idolos, Aspero.

c.2500–2000BC Large raised mound platforms constructed at El Paraíso, La Galagada and Kotosh.

c.2000BC Carved gourds at Huaca Prieta. Earliest coastal and highland pottery. Loom and heddle weaving begins.

INITIAL PERIOD (1800–750BC)

Above: The U-shaped ceremonial centre of Chavín de Huántar began c.*900BC.*

Spread of pottery, irrigation agriculture, monumental architecture, religious processions and ritual decapitation.

from *c*.1800BC Sophisticated irrigation systems developed in coastal oases, valleys, the highlands and Altiplano.

c.1800BC Construction at Moxeke includes colossal adobe heads.

c.1750BC Builders at La Florida bring the first pottery to this region.

c.1500BC Cerro Sechín flourishes as a major highland town.

c.1500BC Earliest Andean gold foil made at Waywaka, Peruvian highlands.

c.1459–1150BC Hammered gold and copper foil at Mina Perdida, coastal Peru.

c.1400–1200BC Sechín Alto becomes the largest U-shaped civic-ceremonial centre in the New World.

c.1300BC The five platform mounds at Cardál are erected.

c.1200BC Carved lines of warriors at Cerro Sechín show regional conflict.

c.1000BC The El Paraíso Tradition flourishes in the Rimac Valley.

c.900BC Earliest U-shaped ceremonial complex at Chavín de Huántar begins.

EARLY HORIZON
(750–200BC)

Above: The Paracas Peninsula, which was a necropolis site for several settlements.

Religious cults develop around Chavín de Huántar and Pukará. Decapitation, hallucinogenic drug use and ancestor worship become widespread.

*c.*800BC Sechín Alto abandoned as a ceremonial centre.

from *c.*750BC The Old Temple at Chavín established as a cult centre. Influence of the Lanzón deity and the Staff Deity spreads. The Paracas Peninsula serves as a necropolis site, and the Oculate Being is depicted on textiles and ceramics.

*c.*500BC Construction of the New Temple at Chavín de Huántar begins.

*c.*500BC Earliest known fired-clay discs for pottery vessel making, Paracas.

*c.*400–200BC The Old Temple at Chavín enlarged to create the New Temple. The Chavín Cult spreads, especially at Kuntur Wasi and Karwa (Paracas).

*c.*400BC Annual rainfall levels fall in the Titicaca Basin. Pukará becomes centre of the Yaya-Mama Cult.

*c.*350 to 200BC Highland regional conflict evident in fortress-building in the Santa, Casma and Nepeña valleys.

*c.*250BC Beginning of the first settlement at Tiwanaku in the Titicaca Basin.

*c.*200BC Influence of Chavín Cult wanes.

EARLY INTERMEDIATE PERIOD
(200BC–AD600)

Above: Construction of the Moche Huaca del Sol began c.AD100.

Cohesion of the Chavín Cult disintegrates, and several regional chiefdoms develop in the coastal and mountain valleys.

*c.*100BC Rise of the Nazca in the southern Peruvian coastal valleys and Cahuachi founded.

*c.*AD100 Burial of the Old Lord of Sipán in Lambayeque Valley.

*c.*AD100 Sacred ceremonial centre of Cahuachi dominates the Nazca area.

*c.*1st century AD Moche dynasty founded in the northern coastal valleys.

*c.*AD100 Construction of first temple platforms at Huaca del Sol and Huaca de la Luna at Moche begins.

*c.*AD250 Construction of first temple at Pachacamac and start of the Pachacamac Cult. Major construction of temple platforms at Tiwanaku begins.

*c.*AD300 Burial of the Lord of Sipán in Lambayeque Valley.

AD300–550 Several Moche regional cities founded at Huancaco, Pamapa de los Incas, Pañamarca and Mocollope.

*c.*AD500 The Moche ceremonial platforms of the Huacas del Sol and de la Luna were the largest in the area.

*c.*AD700 Moche/Nazca power wanes.

MIDDLE HORIZON
(AD600–1000)

Above: View of wall and monolithic stelae, Semi-Subterranean Court, Tiwanaku.

Much of the Andean Area unified in two empires: Tiwanaku in the south and Wari in the north.

*c.*AD200 Major phase of monumental construction begins at Tiwanaku.

*c.*AD250 Settlement at Huari founded.

*c.*AD300 Major construction of central ceremonial plaza at Tiwanaku begins.

*c.*AD400–750 Elite residential quarters at Tiwanaku built. Tiwanaku colonies established at San Pedro Atacama, Omo and in the Cochabamba Valley.

*c.*AD500 Major construction at Huari and beginning of domination of the central highlands by the Wari Empire.

*c.*AD550 Pampa Grande flourishes, ruled by Sicán Lords.

by *c.*AD600 the cities of Huari and Tiwanaku dominate the highlands, building empires in the central and highlands Altiplano, respectively.

*c.*AD650 Wari city of Pikillacta founded, and Wari colonies established at Jincamocco, Azángaro, Viracochapampa and Marca Huamachuco.

*c.*AD750–1000 Third major phase of palace building begins at Tiwanaku.

*c.*AD850–900 Pikillacta abandoned.

LATE INTERMEDIATE PERIOD
(AD1000–1400)

Above: View of present-day Cuzco and the Cuzco Valley where the Incas settled.

An era of political break-up is charac-terized by the rise of new city-states, including Lambayeque, Chimú and Pachacamac, the Colla and Lupaka king-doms, and numerous city-states in the central and southern Andean valleys.

*c.*AD900–950 Rise of the Lambayeque-Sicán state in northern coastal Peru. Burial of the Sicán Lords at Lambayeque. Sicán capital city at Batán Grande.

*c.*AD950 Sediments of Lake Titicaca show evidence of decreased rainfall and start of a long period of drought lead-ing to the eventual demise of Tiwanaku.

*c.*AD900 Chan Chan, capital of the Chimú, founded in the Moche Valley.

*c.*AD1000 Tiwanaku and Wari empires wane as regional political rivalry reasserts itself.

*c.*AD1000 Huari city-state abandoned.

*c.*1100 The Incas under Manco Capac, migrate into the Cuzco Valley, found Cuzco and establish the Inca dynasty.

*c.*1250 City of Tiwanaku abandoned, perhaps because of changes in climate.

*c.*1300 Sinchi Roca becomes the first emperor to use the title Sapa Inca.

*c.*1350 The Chimú conquer the Lambayeque-Sicán peoples.

LATE HORIZON
(AD1400–1532)

Above: Inca stonework is distinctive in style and among the finest in the world.

In little more than 130 years the Incas build a huge empire, from Colombia to mid-Chile and from the rainforest to the Pacific and establish an imperial cult centred on Inti, the sun god, whose representative on Earth was the Sapa Inca.

*c.*1425 Viracocha, the eighth ruler, begins the Inca conquests and domination of the Cuzco Valley.

1438 Pachacuti Inca Yupanqui defeats the Chancas to dominate the Cuzco Valley and begin the expansion of the Inca Empire both within and outside the valley.

1438–71 Pachacuti begins his rebuild-ing of Cuzco as the imperial capital to the plan of a crouching puma, with the fortress and sun temple of Sacsahuaman forming the puma's head.

*c.*1450 Pachacuti establishes the city of Machu Picchu.

c.1462 Pachacuti begins the conquest of the Kingdom of Chimú.

1471 The Incas conquer the Kingdom of Chimú.

1471–93 Inca Tupac Yupanqui expands the empire west and south, doubling its size – north as far as the present-day Ecuador–Colombia border and south into the Titicaca Basin.

Above: The city of Machu Picchu, founded by Pachacuti c.1450.

1493–1526 Huayna Capac consolidates the empire, building fortresses, road systems, storage redistribution and religious precincts throughout the provinces. The provincial city of Qenqo is founded.

1526 Huayna Capac dies of smallpox without an agreed successor.

1526–32 Huayna Capac's son Huáscar seizes the throne but is challenged by his brother Atahualpa. A six-year civil war ends in the capture of Huáscar.

1530 Inca Empire at its greatest extent, and the largest territory in the world.

1532 Francisco Pizarro lands with a small Spanish army on the north coast of the Inca Empire and marches to meet Atahualpa at Cajamarca. He exploits the disruption of the civil war to play one claimant against the other.

1532 The Spaniards defeat the Incas at the Battle of Cajamarca and capture Atahualpa, holding him for ransom.

1533 Atahualpa condemned in a rigged Spanish trial and executed for adultery and idolatry.

1535 Francisco Pizarro founds Lima as his capital in Spanish Peru.

1541 Pizarro assassinated in his palace at Lima by Almagro and his associates.

IN SEARCH OF THE INCAS

Awareness of ancient civilizations in the New World began to increase in the late 18th and 19th centuries as excavations and the collecting of antiquities developed. Primitive excavations were undertaken in Europe and the Americas. Scholars began to re-examine colonial records, old maps and the objects taken back to Europe by the conquistadors and surviving in ancient graves. Sadly, then and now, the antiquities black market encourages looting, and the ancient sites of South America are riddled with *huaqueros'* (tomb robbers') pits.

The archaeologists and anthropologists of the time began to ask serious questions about the past, and when the ancient historians failed them, or, in the New World, simply did not exist, they began to use archaeology and ethnology to seek their own answers. Their early efforts went little beyond recognition, recording and description of ancient objects and sites. Gradually, however, their growing knowledge led to fieldwork designed to answer specific questions about the rise of civilization in the ancient Andes, and to address the 'problem' of the very presence of white people in the New World prior to the arrival of Europeans.

The early 20th century was a time of discovery, large-scale excavation and the development of scientific archaeology. Modern archaeologists and anthropologists developed all kinds of sophisticated techniques and reasoning during the 20th century to explore Andean civilizations, and they continue their quest into the 21st century.

Left: Archaeologists cleaning the base of one of the many temple tombs at Sipán in the Lambayeque Valley, Peru.

NATIVE AND SPANISH SOURCES

Much of European knowledge about native Andeans was biased according to the viewpoint and nationality of the author of any written source. Early sources are mostly limited to information about the Incas, and authors throughout the later 16th and 17th centuries often copied from earlier writers, so reinforcing their views.

NATIVE RECORD-KEEPING

Neither the Incas nor any earlier Andean civilization developed writing. The Incas did, however, invent a system of record keeping called the *quipu*. This was a system of knot tying and colour coding, kept by trained court officials called *quipucamayoqs*. Records were kept as bundles of llama wool threads, suspended from a main thread or rod. The types, colours and sequences of knots, the directions of tying and other details served as tabulations of the numbers and types of goods collected as imperial taxes, and also as statistics on peoples of the empire, their populations, movements and tax quotas.

Below: The Incas and Spaniards were curious about each other. Asked what the Spaniard eats, the reply is 'gold' (Poma de Ayala, Nueva Corónica, c.1615).

Much information in early Spanish sources comes from consultations with *quipucamayoqs*. For example, in the 1560s and 1570s Sarmiento de Gamboa interviewed more than 100 *quipucamayoqs* to compile an Inca history for the viceroy of Peru; and in 1608 Melchior Carlos Inca, a claimant of the Inca throne, compiled the *Relación de los Quipucamayoqs* using the testimonies of four elderly *quipucamayoqs* recorded in 1542.

A second group of record-keepers, called *amautas*, were court historians who memorized the deeds of the emperors, ancient legends and religious information, which they passed down through generations of *amautas*. They, too, provided information for Spanish sources.

Finally, Inca priests had a detailed knowledge of the gods and their relationships, and of ceremony and ritual. They knew the sacred sites and pathways (*ceques*), and the movements of the sun, moon, Venus, Pleiades and Milky Way. Local priests knew their sacred sites (*huacas*), of which there were thousands throughout the empire.

SPANISH RECORDS

The only written records, therefore, date from after the Spanish Conquest. They include: Spanish conquistador accounts; records of the Catholic clergy as they converted native Andeans to Christianity; records of Spanish administrative officials as they organized their conquered subjects for labour and taxation; legal documents of colonial court actions; and personal letters and histories written by native and Spanish individuals to describe their own lives and views, or to summarize Inca religion and history. These sources reveal much information about Inca daily life, social and political organization and religious beliefs.

First-hand accounts based on direct observation at the time of writing are known as primary sources. Chief among these is the native Felipe Guaman Poma

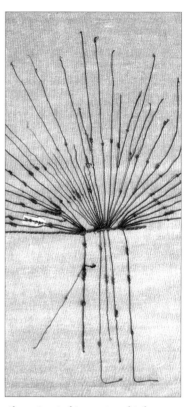

Above: A typical Inca quipu *of tied and dyed knotting, used as a record and memory aid by Inca record-keepers.*

de Ayala's *El Premier Nueva Corónica y Buen Gobierno*, written 1584–1615. He describes Inca life in great detail, protests to the king of Spain about the treatment of the Incas and graphically represents Inca life and religion in 398 drawings.

By contrast, works written by authors using the information in primary sources are known as secondary sources. A principal secondary source is Father Bernabé Cobo's *Historia del Nuevo Mundo* (1653), which includes *Inca Religion and Customs*. Cobo used the works of, among others, Juan Polo de Ondegardo (1560s and 70s), from which he completed the list of Cuzco shrines and *ceques*, and Garcilasco de la Vega ('El Inca'), son of a conquistador and Inca princess, who wrote a commentary on the Inca imperial household and a general history of the Spanish Conquest. Cobo's monumental 20-year work is considered the most balanced and comprehensive early account of Inca history and religion.

APPROACH WITH CAUTION

Such records must be used with caution, however. Each writer, native or Spaniard, was writing from his own cultural point of view and did not fully understand the institutions and social structure of the other. Each inevitably interpreted information about the other from his own viewpoint.

For example, however comprehensive Poma de Ayala's nearly 1,200-page compilation is, his family, originally from

Below: After Pizarro's treachery and capture of Atahualpa at Cajamarca there followed many fierce battles between Inca armies and the Spaniards, here against Francisco Hernández Girón (Poma de Ayala, c.1615).

Huanuco in the Central Highlands, had been forcibly relocated by the Incas to Huamango (Ayacucho). In addition, members of his family served as *quipu-camayoqs* and he himself converted to Christianity and became an interpreter for Spanish administrative and ecclesiastical inspectors. He therefore bore a grudge against the Incas, abhorred the persistence of Andean religious practices, and at the same time protested about the brutality of Spanish treatment of his fellow natives (frequently shown in his depictions).

Incas and Spaniards both had ulterior motives for their conquests and considered themselves a superior race. As a result, they sometimes deliberately falsified their accounts to justify their actions. In particular, the main source for Spanish chroniclers was the Incas themselves, more specifically the Inca ruling class. So information about ordinary Incas and their contemporaries (both elite and common citizens), and about pre-Inca cultures were doubly filtered: first through the

Above: A 16th-century Spanish caravel sailing for the New World. The caravel was a fast and easily manoeuvrable ship with a gently sloping bow and a single stern castle.

Inca elite's preconceptions (in the primary source) and later through Spanish opinions (in the secondary source).

Another note of caution that must be added is the vagueness that pervades places and names in Inca and Spanish writings. Provinces, towns and peoples listed by one traveller differ from those listed by another travelling the same route. There were also widespread movements of peoples over the centuries and by the Incas themselves.

Despite these drawbacks, scholars generally think that the basic events in Inca history were more accurately recorded the closer they occurred to the Spanish Conquest. Also that, by comparing and contrasting several sources describing the same events or information about Inca society, truthful information can be extracted.

EXPLORERS AND THE FIRST ARCHAEOLOGISTS

Early Spanish writings primarily concern the Incas, which leaves our principal source of information about pre-Inca Andean civilization to be archaeology. Until the material remains of ancient sites were explored and excavated there was much speculation but little substance to writings about ancient Andean cultures.

ARCHAEOLOGICAL EXPLORERS
Alexander von Humboldt was the first scholar seriously to consider reasons for the presence of humans in the New World and to attempt to make a record of the ancient ruins he saw in the Andes. He was a pioneer, struggling to separate observation and description from speculation and interpretation.

The first dedicated report on ancient Andean antiquities was that of Mariano Edward de Rivero and John James von Tschudi in 1841. Inspired by antiquarian activities and publications in Europe and North America, Rivero had been appointed director of Peru's national museum in Lima, where antiquities from all over Peru were collected. The two made a systematic record of what was known.

William Prescott's *History of the Conquest of Peru* (1847) did much to inspire enthusiasm for ancient Andean civilization, but by and large did not consider archaeological material. Johann Tschudi's five-volume *Reisen durch Süd Amerika* (1869) and Ephraim G. Squier's *Peru: Incidents of Travel and Exploration in the Land of the Incas* (1877) echo the travels of John Stephens and Frederick Catherwood in Mesoamerica.

These and other early attempts to write about ancient Andean civilization lacked a methodological approach to relate the archaeological materials and ruins to contexts. It was soon realized that the ruins themselves must be explored beyond mere descriptions of their surface remains, and that study of ancient Andean artefacts must go further than collection from looted tombs and description.

THE FIRST EXCAVATORS
One of the earliest deliberate excavations was undertaken by Alphons Stübel and Wilhelm Reiss. At the ancient cemetery of Ancón, north of Lima, they excavated unlooted tombs containing mummy

Above: An early 20th-century photograph of the 'Sun Gate' at Tiwanaku shows it cracked and collapsing. The entire gateway is actually a single monolithic carved block, now repaired.

bundles, thus gaining primary information on burial practices and their contents in context. They published their finds and interpretations in three volumes in *The Necropolis of Ancón in Peru* between 1880 and 1887.

Similarly, Adolph Bandelier carried out excavations of Tiwanaku sites on the islands in the Titicaca Basin, which he published in 1910, and at Tiwanaku itself in 1911. On the Island of the Sun in Titicaca, at the site of Chucaripupata, he found gold, silver, bronze and copper artefacts, including a golden mask, near the sacred rock of Titikala.

The work of Stübel and Reiss inspired a young fellow German, Max Uhle. After studying philology, Uhle switched to archaeology and ethnography and became curator at the Dresden Museum. He met Stübel and collaborated with him to publish *Die Ruinenstätte von Tiahuanaco* in 1892, based on the records and photographs Stübel had made at Tiwanaku. Uhle began his own fieldwork in Peru in the same year and continued until 1912. He was the first to apply the archaeological principles of stratigraphy (assessing

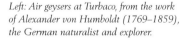

Left: Air geysers at Turbaco, from the work of Alexander von Humboldt (1769–1859), the German naturalist and explorer.

Above: A fanciful engraving of Cuzco, the Inca capital, by the German cartographer Georg Braun, 1594. Pizarro called it "the most noble and great city" when he entered it on 23 March 1534.

the chronology of finds from their positions in the earth) in his excavations. With his knowledge of Inca and Tiwanaku pottery types, his excavations at Pachacamac on the Peruvian coast enabled him to construct the first pre-Inca chronology of ancient Andean ceramics. Knowing that Inca pottery was dated to the 15th and 16th centuries, and that the Incas revered the monuments of ancient Tiwanaku, he reasoned that Tiwanaku ceramics pre-dated the Incas. The pottery he excavated at Pachacamac was often found in the same layers as Inca pottery, but showed no stylistic influence from Tiwanaku. He reasoned that it must be intermediate in date between the two. This was the beginning of 30 years of excavation and analysis in Peru, Bolivia, Ecuador and Chile, during which he used the relative dating method of seriation to provide a chronology of ancient Andean ceramic styles that basically remains valid today.

A 20TH-CENTURY EXPLORER
Adventurous exploration, however, had not ended. Prescott had inspired many, including Hiram Bingham. Young Bingham had gone to Peru in 1911 on a romantic dream. "Archaeology lies

outside my field and I know very little about the Incas, except the fascinating story told by Prescott in his famous *Conquest of Peru*", he declared to the Peruvian Prefect whose *Departamento* he wanted to explore.

Inca imperial Machu Picchu became 'lost' after the Spanish Conquest only because of its remote location. (Colonial records refer to the site and local people knew it well.) Although Bingham always claimed that he wandered by chance up the newly opened road from Cuzco to the north-west towards the Amazon, in fact, Melchor Artega, a local farmer, described the site to Bingham when he and his team arrived in the Urubamba Valley. Artega, Sergeant Carrasco, Bingham's Quechua translator, and a boy even acted as guides. Nevertheless it was Bingham who brought the spectacular find to the attention of the Western world and solved the 'mystery' of the famous site. To his credit, he did not stop there,

Below: A classic view of the Machu Picchu ruins, the Inca imperial retreat and sacred city in the remote Andes north-west of Cuzco.

Above: Alexander von Humboldt, explorer, geographer, naturalist and lecturer, the first person to make a thorough scientific exploration of the Andes, including its archaeological ruins.

but continued to explore, and in his single summer season made several more discoveries of remote Inca sites.

Bingham's 'discovery' of Machu Picchu, for better or worse, will remain one of the most important events in the annals of Andean archaeology, and it made him a celebrity: he became an Ivy League professor, an Air Force hero and was elected to the US Senate.

20TH-CENTURY ARCHAEOLOGY
AND BEYOND

The early 20th century was an age of discovery, large-scale excavation and development of scientific archaeology. Grand multi-disciplinary research programmes were undertaken in the Andes, and Alfred Kroeber and John Rowe of the University of California, Berkeley, refined and expanded Max Uhle's chronological scheme, defining the Periods and Horizons of Andean prehistory. The discovery of radiocarbon dating by Willard Libby enabled calendar dates to be fixed at many sites.

GRAND PROJECTS
Universities, museums and research organizations with enormous resources funded large-scale survey projects and excavations through multiple field seasons. Archaeologists began to ask specific questions about Andean civilization and to undertake work designed to answer them. They went beyond exploration and description to analysis and interpretation,

Below: An adobe brick-lined Nazca shaft tomb, used for the repeated deposition of honoured elite – part of the cult of ancestor worship.

not only of the detailed prehistoric Andean events but also of mechanisms and explanations of why domestication occurred, and why cities arose.

Increasing collections of pottery, metalwork, textiles and other materials prompted the development of methods for conserving and restoring them. This work provided increasingly sophisticated information, making possible complex interpretations that went beyond technology to provide explanations about ancient religion, politics and social structure.

Julio Tello, a native Peruvian, studied archaeology and anthropology at Harvard University, followed by a lifelong career, beginning in the 1920s, investigating the origins of Andean civilization through excavations at the Paracas cemeteries, Sechín Alto and Chavín de Huántar. With Kroeber, he established the Institute of Andean Research in Lima in 1939.

The Second World War only briefly interrupted such studies. Scholars in the 1950s and 1960s extended the reach of projects to all periods of Andean prehistory, until the huge amount of discovery and interpretation required collation and

Above: Moche Huaca del Sol, made of millions of adobe mud bricks. In plan it formed a thick-armed cross, largely destroyed by Spaniards looking for buried treasure.

systemization. In 1969 the Peruvian archaeologist Luis Lumbreras produced the first great synthesis of Peruvian prehistory, *The Peoples and Cultures of Ancient Peru* (translated into English by Betty Meggers in 1974); and in 1971 Gordon Willey published the second volume of his monumental *An Introduction to American Archaeology: South America*.

The increasing fieldwork and accelerating pace of analysis and interpretation during the later 20th and 21st centuries required renewed synthesis. Most notable is Michael Moseley's *The Incas and their Ancestors: The Archaeology of Peru*, published in 1992, then revised in 2001.

REVOLUTION?
A 'revolution' dubbed 'New Archaeology' in the 1960s and 70s applied wider theoretical concepts to archaeological data. Scholars increasingly questioned the system of methods and principles that were used in archaeology and posed deeper questions about alleged cultural universals. This healthy internal analysis happily did not deter fieldwork and data accumulation through excavations and field surveys continued. Archaeologists continue to ask wide questions as well as conduct detailed analysis and interpretation

in specific areas and specialized topics, so expanding our overall understanding of Andean prehistory.

LINES OF ENQUIRY

The Nazca lines have fascinated generations. In the 1940s, Paul and Rose Kosok expounded their theory that the lines were astronomically motivated. Maria Reiche, inspired by the Kosoks, became 'queen of the pampa' and devoted her life to the astronomical cause. Her particular contribution was the extensive mapping of lines, especially the figures. Neither the Kosoks nor Reiche, however, could prove their astronomical theories with convincing statistical evidence.

In the 1970s and 80s, the archaeo-astronomer Frank Aveni conducted the most extensive survey and study of Nazca geoglyphs yet made. He found no statistically significant correlations or directional correlations. Instead, he found 62 nodes from which lines radiated, and discovered there are many generations of lines, earlier ones crossing older ones, concluding that they were for ritual processions, made over generations for specific occasions.

SHAKEN REVELATIONS

In 1950, an earthquake flattened much of Cuzco, including the Dominican church and monastery. Reconstruction of the monastery provided an opportunity to investigate the Coricancha temple beneath, so priority was given to exposing the Inca remains.

Above: Archaeologists of the Instituto Nacional de Cultura uncover the skeleton of one of 72 Inca battle victims in a mass burial at Puruchuco, a suburb of Lima.

Excavations in the monastery plaza revealed an Inca cobblestone floor and wall foundations on the southern and northern sides. With John Rowe's map based on colonial documents, excavators Oscar Ladrón de Guevera and Raymundo Béjar Navarro, together with architectural historians Graziano Gasparini and Luise Margolies, were able to plan and illustrate the appearance of the sacred temple. Much of the monastery ruins were removed and the Coricancha complex was reconstructed, as seen today.

CONTINUED DISCOVERIES

Despite the wealth of Andean metalwork, ceramics and textiles in museums, there is no greater treasure than a collection of such artefacts found *in situ*. The discovery of unlooted Moche tombs at Sipán in the Lambayeque Valley in the late 1980s by Walter Alva and Susana Meneses was just that. Having heard about a *huaquero* raid on the Sipán pyramid, the police in turn raided the robbers' house and recovered artefacts the robbers had taken. The

Left: Ruins of part of the Kalasasaya sacred temple compound at Tiwanaku, Bolivia. They have since been re-erected and the compound partly reconstructed.

police chief then phoned Alva, and under armed guard he and Meneses excavated the low platform at the foot of the pyramid, where they discovered six burial levels, including the fabulously rich tombs of the Lord of Sipán, a Moche priest and the Old Lord of Sipán.

In 2002, the ironically named shanty-town of Tupac Amaru (last 'Inca' emperor, 1571–2) on Lima's outskirts was being cleared for redevelopment. Following modern practice, archaeological investigations preceded, during which an Inca cemetery of up to 10,000 burials was discovered. Some 2,000 burials of men, women and children were recovered, together with 60,000 artefacts, including 40 elite mummy bundles with 'false heads', some with wigs! These finds – everyday items, utensils and food, personal valuables – are being analysed. Their value for the reconstruction of Inca burial practices and everyday life are incalculable.

Even more recently, in 2007, a remarkable discovery was made in the Puruchuco suburb of Lima: a mass grave of 72 bodies killed in battle in 1536. The skull of one drew immediate attention: it was of a young Inca warrior, and it had two round holes in it. Near it was a small plug of bone with musket-ball markings, and electron microscopy detected traces of lead in the skull! It was the first time that evidence of death by gunshot – an Inca shot by a Spaniard – had ever been found in the Americas.

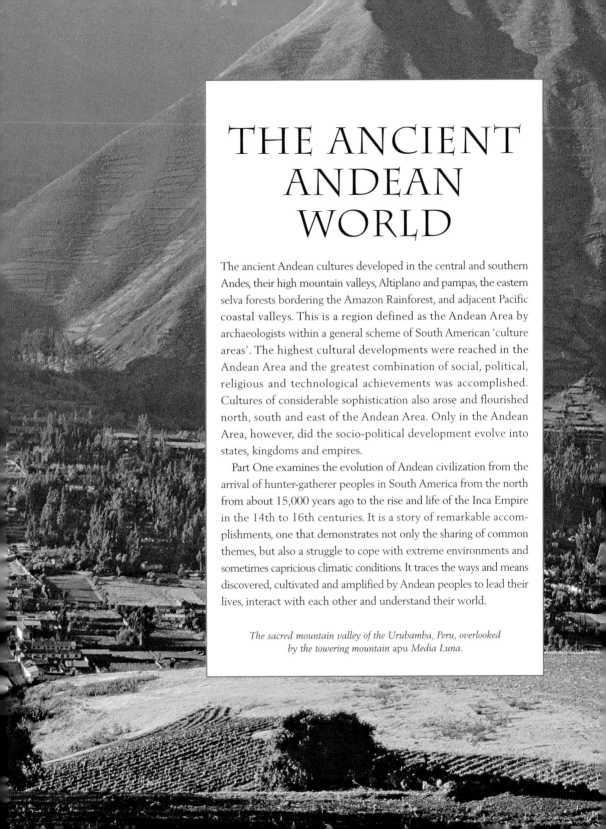

THE ANCIENT ANDEAN WORLD

The ancient Andean cultures developed in the central and southern Andes, their high mountain valleys, Altiplano and pampas, the eastern selva forests bordering the Amazon Rainforest, and adjacent Pacific coastal valleys. This is a region defined as the Andean Area by archaeologists within a general scheme of South American 'culture areas'. The highest cultural developments were reached in the Andean Area and the greatest combination of social, political, religious and technological achievements was accomplished. Cultures of considerable sophistication also arose and flourished north, south and east of the Andean Area. Only in the Andean Area, however, did the socio-political development evolve into states, kingdoms and empires.

Part One examines the evolution of Andean civilization from the arrival of hunter-gatherer peoples in South America from the north from about 15,000 years ago to the rise and life of the Inca Empire in the 14th to 16th centuries. It is a story of remarkable accomplishments, one that demonstrates not only the sharing of common themes, but also a struggle to cope with extreme environments and sometimes capricious climatic conditions. It traces the ways and means discovered, cultivated and amplified by Andean peoples to lead their lives, interact with each other and understand their world.

The sacred mountain valley of the Urubamba, Peru, overlooked by the towering mountain apu Media Luna.

CHAPTER THIRTEEN

LIVING IN THE LANDSCAPE

The diverse landscapes of South America were created by geological processes, and the varied fauna and flora developed as a result of biological evolution. South America includes multiple environmental and ecological zones. Its fauna and flora evolved independently from about 175 million years ago in the middle Jurassic Period, after the super-continent of Pangaea (Antarctica, Australia, India, Africa, Eurasia, and North and South America) began to divide into today's continents. Through remote periods of physical isolation from North America, the flora and fauna of the continent evolved into unique groups and species, which were later mutually exchanged with North America when the landmasses were ultimately reconnected. This combination of events created the landscapes and plant and animal life encountered by the first human migrants into South America as the great Ice Ages of the northern hemisphere ended.

Social evolution created the ultimate sophistication of Andean civilization, which enabled the Incas to create an empire that controlled the largest territory in the world at the time of the Spanish arrival in the New World.

This chapter describes both these worlds – the physical and the socio-political – as they were when an intrepid and determined group of men from the Old World reached the New World of the South American continent in a second episode of migration. This time, it was a clash of urban empires.

Left: The upper Urubamba–Vilcanote River, Peru, a sacred mountain valley whose rich soils are especially productive.

LANDSCAPES OF THE ANDEAN AREA

South America has evolved animal and plant species unique to its regions owing to long periods of physical isolation from North America. Towards the end of the Pliocene Epoch, *c.*3 million years ago, the Central American ridge re-emerged above sea level to reunite North and South America, creating a land bridge for their long-separated mammals.

GEOGRAPHICAL REGIONS
South America includes several major ecological and environmental regions that merge into each other across the breadth and length of the continent: the great western coastal deserts, pierced by scores of oases valleys and their rivers flowing into the Pacific Ocean; the Andean mountain range, winding the entire length of the continent, 7,500km (4,660 miles) from the Caribbean to Tierra del Fuego; the more gradual descent of the eastern Andes; the high Altiplano between the two Andean cordilleras and pampas to the south and east; and the huge Amazon Basin. There are also the rich maritime seascapes of the Pacific, Atlantic and Caribbean coastal waters.

Prehistorians subdivide the continent into zones of cultural development, each characterized by distinct archaeological

Above: South America and the Magellan Straits from the Hydrographic Atlas *of 1571 by Fernan Vaz Dourado.*

evidence and levels of technological and socio-political achievement. None of these zones was culturally isolated, and inter-relationships between zones were never static, but changed through time. The zone with which this book is concerned is the Andean Area. It comprises, west to east, the Pacific coast to the Amazonian Rainforest, and, north to south, roughly the modern Colombian–Ecuadorian border to the northern half of Chile.

THE ANDEAN AREA
The Andean Area is remarkable for its contrasting landscapes, both geographical and cultural. It includes the world's driest deserts, such as the Sechura in northern Peru–Ecuador, the Nazca in central Peru and the Atacama in northern Chile; some of the world's highest mountains, with peaks of more than 7,000m (23,000ft); and some of the lushest rainforests along the eastern edge of the Amazon Basin.

Climatic conditions vary greatly within the zone. El Niño events disrupt weather patterns and marine cycles about every four to ten years, reversing normal patterns by creating floods in coastal regions and drought in the mountains and Altiplano. Throughout Andean history there were

intermittent periods of prolonged drought, coinciding with the cultural periods defined by archaeologists. Evidence from glacial ice cores and lake sediments show sustained drought periods occurring *c.*2200–1900BC, 900–800BC, 400–200BC, AD1–300, AD562–95 and

Below: An Andean mountain peak, Mount Huayna Potosi, Bolivia, with abundant snow most of the year, from which flow waters to make mountain valleys fertile.

Below: The Atacama Desert, northern Chile, is one of the driest places on Earth – high and dry, with sparse, tough vegetation.

Above: Lush Amazonian rainforests flank the eastern Andes. The Incas considered their inhabitants to be subhuman.

AD1100–1450; and intervening wetter periods *c.*AD400–500, AD900–1000 and 1500–1700.

There was also great cultural variation. People developed distinct responses to different landscapes and environments, and distinct cultures. They evolved from wandering hunter-gatherers to early village farming communities as they selected and nurtured certain plants and animals into domestication. Finally, as they developed and mastered increasingly sophisticated socio-political and techno-logical techniques, they evolved into civilizations with spreading towns and cities, kingdoms and even empires.

CIVILIZATION

Archaeologists are involved in never-ending examination and discussion of what defines civilization and what stimulates its devel-opment. Civilization of the highest calibre was attained in the Andean Area, and it evolved in part in response to the chal-lenges presented by its varied landscapes.

Its Pacific coasts are the world's rich-est fishing grounds, the consequence of the cold Humboldt Current that sweeps up from Antarctica and brings huge fish shoals and migrating sea mammals, as well as nurturing rich coastal shellfish and bird populations. There is such abundance that the earliest inhabitants could support large village populations mostly reliant

Right: A high Andean lake valley, the Laguna Colorado, Bolivia, provided abundant flamingos to be hunted.

on the foreshore and near offshore waters for their livings. The river valleys descend-ing from the western Andean foothills to the coastal plains have rich soils on which early peoples learned to practise increas-ingly intense and sophisticated irrigation agriculture. Similarly, in high Andean val-leys and the Altiplano, people graduated from simple rainfall agriculture to increas-ingly intense cultivation using raised fields, hillside terracing and irrigation systems. On the rich grasslands of the southern Andean plateaux, people devel-oped pastoralism with the domestication of the llama and alpaca.

INTERREGIONAL RELATIONS

These developments in agriculture, which led to trading between different regions, and the technological and socio-political advances they stimulated, enabled pop-ulations to increase, so that larger towns and cities came into being. Remarkable throughout Andean prehistory is the con-tinuity of contact between the different regions, beginning from the earliest times, as proved by the discovery of products and raw materials from different regions in the others.

There was exchange between the high-lands and lowlands in both physical objects and ideas. For example, coastal

Above: Vast high grasslands of the southern Andean Altiplano provided an ideal environment for llama and alpaca herding.

products, such as oyster shells, were regarded as exotic treasures among moun-tain cultures. Reciprocally, early coastal textiles were made of the cotton grown locally, and of llama wool traded from Altiplano herders. People also borrowed and exchanged artistic expressions and symbolism between regions. This is demonstrated by the spread of the Chavín Staff Deity from the central highlands to southern desert coasts and the Altiplano; by the recognition by coastal peoples of the sacredness of the mountains, no doubt fostered by a realization that mountains were the ultimate source of their water, and their construction of man-made 'mountains' in the form of huge pyrami-dal platforms; and by the representation of rainforest animals such as monkeys and caymans in Nazca lines and in Chavín stone sculpture.

PLANTS IN THE ANDEAN AREA

Tens of thousands of plant species evolved in South America: grasses and reeds; tropical and western forest trees; cacti; fungi; herbal plants and flowers; and a variety of wild edible fruits and vegetables. Different environments within the Andean Area provided a rich diversity and potential cultigens. Microclimates created by altitude change and latitude provided pockets and refuges for different species.

VEGETATION REGIONS
The Pacific coastal environment is one of the world's richest. Oxygen- and nutrient-rich cold currents support the trillions of phytoplankton that form the base of the coastal food chain. Small fishes feed on these microscopic plants, and are fed upon by predatory fishes, and so on up the food chain. Inland, the coastal plain from Ecuador to northern Chile includes vast expanses of almost barren desert.

The Andes include four vegetation zones: tropical, subtropical, south temperate

and *paramo* (between high *puna* grassland and the snowline). Vegetation in the coastal valleys that punctuate the coastal plain changes up-valley as altitude increases.

The western Andean slopes are characterized by temperate forests, found from near sea level to the tree-line. The lower altitudes have broadleaf evergreen trees, while higher up conifers dominate. Species include the algarrobo, lengas, podocarps, the monkey puzzle and cypresses. Dry forests of the southern Bolivian and northern Argentinian Altiplano feature trees of the pea family, together with vast grasslands, known as *puna*, and a large number of cacti species.

As the eastern Andes, known as selva or *montaña*, descend to the Amazon Basin, they are forested by evergreen trees from *c.*3,000m (10,000ft) and lower, to merge with the tropical rainforest. A host of herbal and medicinal plants include the coca (*Erythroxylon coca*), which became so important in Andean religion and in general use to combat high-altitude fatigue and increase stamina.

CULTIVATED PLANTS
Of the vast number of native species, less than 1 per cent was domesticated by ancient Andeans. Discussions of Andean plants important to civilization ultimately focus on this small percentage of cultigens.

The 23 principal pre-Hispanic cultivated species became domesticated through selective tending. Early agriculture relied on run-off water (especially in coastal valleys) and rainfall (especially in the Andes), until irrigation, terracing and raised-field agriculture were developed as means of increasing yields and areas under cultivation.

Left: The interdependence of highland and lowland, east and west, are exemplified in this Chancay carved wooden club – a rainforest monkey holding a maize cob, an essential early domesticated food plant.

Above: Tambopata Reserve, Peru – misty, forested regions of the eastern Andes, known as selva or montaña *– provided valuable herbs and medicinal plants.*

Altitudinal growing ranges of the domestic plants vary, and their distribution across environmental zones stimulated exchange. It is argued that the wild ranges of most cultigens were extended as humans nurtured those species that seemed most promising and able to provide sustainable yields.

Altitude and latitude (and thus temperature and rainfall) affect both cultivation and distribution. Andean

Below: Quinoa (Chanopodium quinoa) was, alongside the potato and maize, one of the earliest and essential domesticated Andean food plants.

domesticated plants can be grouped by their altitudinal ranges – see the fact box below. An extreme example is the ulluco (an edible tuber), which grows at 3,700–3,830m (12,180–12,560ft).

Less than 20 per cent of these crops grow well at altitudes above 3,000m (10,000ft), while 90 per cent thrive up to 1,000m (3,300ft). It is significant that the mainstays of the ancient Andean diet – maize, potatoes and common beans – can be cultivated at the widest possible range of altitudes. The many cultigens of lower altitude, which formed a complementary role to the classic trio in daily lowland and highland diet, were thus an important part of lowland–highland exchange. The staple diet was supplemented by gathering wild and semi-domesticated fruits and nuts, including cashews, pumpkins, palmettos, pineapples, sour cherries, custard apples, cactus fruits, elderberries and an ancient variety of banana. Wild herbs were gathered for seasoning.

DRUGS, TOOLS AND BUILDINGS
In addition to edible plants, medicinal and hallucinogenic plants played an important role in curing illness and for shamanistic trance inducement. Coca was cultivated, but the hallucinogenic mescaline of the San Pedro cactus and many hallucinogenic mushrooms from the tropical forests were also gathered and traded widely. Maize was used for the fermentation of *chicha* beer, the common drink in weak form and used in stronger form in religious ceremony.

Andean trees provided wood for weapons and tools, such as arrow and spear shafts, the *atl-atl* (spear-thrower) and hardwood war clubs. Tools included the foot-plough, sod-breaking club and hoe handle. Coca snuff pallets and drinking cups (*keros*) were also of wood. Algarrobo tree trunks provided pillars and rafters in early Spanish Colonial buildings, preserving an architectural style depicted in numerous Moche ceramic models.

Cane and totora reeds from riverbanks and the shores of Lake Titicaca and other lakes were extensively used for thatching and for fishing craft. Reeds were also used to make flutes and panpipes.

Most textiles for clothing and llama packs were made of cotton and wool. Cotton was indispensable among coastal peoples for fishing gear (nets, line and bindings), while wild fibrous plants

Above: Cacti in Salar de Uyuruni Isla Pescado, Bolivia, one of many micro-habitats in the southern Andean Altiplano.

provided the rough twine and cordage needed for rope, baskets and containers, sandals and sleeping mats. The cultivated gourd, which preceded pottery for containers, continued to be used throughout pre-Hispanic times for fishing floats as well.

ANDEAN DOMESTICATED PLANTS BY ALTITUDINAL RANGES

Up to 1,000m (3,300ft)
• arracachas (a tuberous root plant) (850–956m/2,790–3,140ft)
• bottle gourds (850–956m/2,790–3,140ft)
• two varieties of chilli peppers (2–1,000m/6.56–3,300ft and 385–1,000m/1,263–3,300ft)
• guavas (28–1,000m/92–3,300ft)
• lima beans (28–1,000m/92–3,300ft)
• peanuts (46–1,000m/151–3,300ft)
• three varieties of squash (850–969m/2,790–3,179ft, 385–1,000m/1,263–3,300ft and 28–1,000m/92–3,300ft)
• sweet potatoes (28–1,000m/92–3,300ft)
• tobacco (57–1,000m/187–3,300ft)

Just over 1,000m (3,300ft)
• cotton (329–1,006m/1,079–3,300ft)
• manioc (46–1,006m/150–3,300ft)

Middle range
• avocados (320–1,750m/1,049–5,741ft)
• coca (450–1,200m/1,476–3,937ft)
• oca (850–1,700m/2,790–5,577ft)

Very wide range
• beans (2–3,700m/6½–12,140ft)
• maize (2–3,350m/6½–10,990ft)
• potatoes (2–3,830m/6½–12,565ft)
• quinoa (28–3,878m/92–12,720ft)
• mashwa (an edible tuber) (850–3,700m/2,788–12,140ft)
• ulluco (an edible tuber) (3,700–3,830m/12,180–12,560ft)

ANIMALS IN THE ANDEAN AREA

The differing environments within the Andean Area supported a large variety of animal species. As with plants, micro-environments fostered the development of species native to different regions. Remarkable traits of Andean Area fauna are their adaptations to the rarefied air of the mountains and their survival in barren desert environments. Ancient Andean peoples also knew of and revered animals from outside the Andean Area.

FOOD SUPPLIES
The earliest Andean hunter-gatherers would still have had mastodons (the larger mammoths had never reached South America), wild horse and ground sloths to hunt. When these became extinct c.8,000BC, large game animals such as deer (white-tailed, brocket and heumul), the llama and other camelids (vicuña and guanaco) were supplemented

Below: The camelid llama, originally a migrant from the north into temperate South America, once domesticated, provided wool and meat. It was a beast of burden and a sacred symbol to ancient Andeans.

by smaller game such as guinea pigs, viscachas (large burrowing rodents), skunk and fowl.

In contrast, coastal peoples hunted sea mammals (sea lions, seals and whales), supplemented by large and small fish, sea birds and a host of foreshore invertebrates, from molluscs to lobsters and crabs to clams and other shellfish. The principal sources of animal protein after the Lithic and Preceramic periods was provided by coastal fishing and sea mammal hunting, and by fishing in Lake Titicaca and similar high lakes. Fish are scarce in Andean highland rivers.

FOOD CHAINS
The marine animal food chain starts with the smaller fish – especially anchovies and sardines – that feed on phytoplankton, and moves up through ocean birds to sea mammals and, ultimately, humans. There are also shallow-water and foreshore invertebrate herbivores and their attendant predators, from mussels and shellfish to crabs, shorebirds, sea mammals and man.

Inland and in the mountains the ultimate predator is the mountain lion or puma, and in the rainforest and lowlands the jaguar; other top predators are raptors. The chain descends down through increasingly smaller animals to the invertebrates that feed on soil and other detritus.

MIGRATION
There are about 600 mammalian species in South America, dominated by rodents and bats, most of which live in the rain-forests. Likewise with birds: the overwhelming variety are tropical; a second group are the western sea and coastal birds; and a third the temperate forest avians and the Andean species, including condors, hawks and the harpy eagle.

The emergence of the Central American land bridge at the end of Pliocene epoch enabled the migration of mammals in both directions between South and North America.

Above: Native burdens were exemplified in Poma de Ayala's Nueva Corónica, c.1615 by symbolic characterization. The royal administrator is a serpent, the itinerant Spaniard a jaguar, the encomendero labour and land-holder a (non-native) lion, the parish priest a fox, the notary a cat, and the native governor a rodent.

Into temperate South America came smilodons (sabretooth cats), wild horses, spectacled bears, tapirs, llamas, peccaries, foxes, rats and mice. Into the tropics came hctcromyid rodents, squirrels and shrews.

From south to north temperate environments went giant ground sloths, armadillos, glyptodons (armadillo-like but larger), porcupines and didelphis rodents; and to tropical areas went cebid monkeys, tree sloths, anteaters, and agouti and paca rodents.

North–south migrants added to these existing native mammals, including a wealth of rodents (including the guinea pig), monkeys, bats and the jaguar, as well as a huge number of bird species, reptiles, amphibians and invertebrates. The greatest varieties of all groups are native to the Amazonian Basin, outside the Andean Area.

Right: The revered jaguar (and its mountain cousin the puma) provided a symbol of strength and cunning to Andean warriors and priests.

DOMESTICATED ANIMALS

As with plants, only a few animals were domesticated: llamas, alpacas, guinea pigs, ducks and dogs. The domestication process was gradual, beginning with the deliberate selection and concentrated tending of these species. The main highland sources of meat were guinea pigs and ducks, although llama and deer were also eaten. Hunting, however, had become the pursuit of the elite in a culture whose staple diet was provided by cultivated plant foods.

The llama is one of three South American camelids: llamas, guanacos and vicuñas. The llama is the domesticated variety of the guanaco, which remained wild and was sometimes hunted for its meat, as was the vicuña. A fourth camelid, the alpaca, was also domesticated or semi-domesticated, but it is uncertain if the breed is the result of descent from the guanaco, or a guanaco/vicuña hybrid. Llamas and alpacas, fully domesticated by c.2500BC, were herded in great flocks, principally for their wool and as pack animals, but also for ritual sacrifice, divination and meat. Their bones were valuable for tool-making and their dung for fertilizer.

Below: An 18th-century watercolour of the guinea pig, an early Andean domesticated rodent, which provided a readily available meat source and still does today.

Guinea pigs were domesticated as early as the late Preceramic Period, but this is evident less from anatomical differences to wild relatives than from what appear to be hutches. Hunting of wild guinea pigs for meat no doubt continued. In later pre-Hispanic times the guinea pig was also used in religious ceremony, divination and curing. Ducks were raised for food and eggs; dogs as hunting companions and food.

REVERED ANIMALS

As well as llamas and guinea pigs, several other native Andean and non-native animals were highly revered and used in ritual and prophecy. The flights and habits of condors, hawks and eagles were carefully observed for divination. Indeed, observation of the mobbing and killing of an eagle by buzzards during ceremonies to honour the sun god Inti were regarded by Inca priests as foretelling the coming fall of the empire. The early twined cloth from Preceramic Huaca Prieta features an eagle with outspread wings and a snake inside its stomach.

The puma and its lowland cousin the jaguar also feature in the earliest Andean art. Use of the jaguar in monumental stone sculpture and portable objects in the Chavín Cult right through to the plan of Inca Cuzco in the form of a crouching puma demonstrate its enduring importance.

As well as the jaguar, monkeys, the cayman (South American freshwater alligator), serpents and a great variety of colourful rainforest birds were especially revered for their powers, cleverness and (in the case of the birds) feathers. All feature repeatedly in Andean art in religious contexts and demonstrate long-distance communication between highlands and lowlands.

THE INCA EMPIRE AT PIZARRO'S ARRIVAL

From humble beginnings as one tribe among several in the Cuzco Valley, the Incas rapidly expanded the territory in their control. Their conquests were few in the first few centuries after the founding ruler Manco Capac had established rule in Cuzco. Even by about 1400, Inca territory comprised only the valleys adjacent to the Cuzco Valley in the Urubamba and Apurimac river drainages.

GREAT EXPANSION
From the reign of Pachacuti Inca Yupanqui (tenth emperor, 1438–71) and his successors, however, the Inca emperors embarked on continuous campaigns to subdue the known world. Inca belief taught them that they were destined to rule, and in fewer than 100 years they ruled the largest empire ever created in

Below: Chan Chan, the capital of the Kingdom of the Chimú, was a serious rival to the late 15th-century expanding Inca Empire until it fell to Inca Pachacuti and his son and heir Tupac Yupanqui in 1471.

the Americas. It stretched from the modern borders of Ecuador and Colombia to more than halfway down the coast of modern Chile (4,200km/2,600 miles; equivalent in distance of roughly Spain to Moscow).

Their empire was long and narrow, however (only *c.*650km/400 miles at its greatest east–west width), and confined to regions familiar to them. The Incas were among a long line of cultures that had spread their control of economic resources in the Andes and western coastal lowlands. Their armies were well equipped and disciplined, and were trained to fight on such terrain in pitched battles, during which two armies were amassed and thrown at each other to 'slug it out' until one force broke ranks and fled or laid down their arms in defeat. Indeed, in many cases, as Inca reputation for fighting skills and fierceness, and the seeming inevitability of conquest, spread, many nations (kingdoms and city-states) did not resist, but surrendered without battle and proceeded to negotiate the best deal they could make.

Above: An Inca post-runner or messenger (chasqui) *depicted in Poma de Ayala's* Nueva Corónica, c.1615.

AMAZONIAN FAILURE
The Incas attempted to expand east into the Amazon Rainforest. Their armies, however, were in unfamiliar terrain and

faced an enemy who fought unconventionally. In the Amazon, the Incas were not confronting organized states, ruled in a manner similar to the long-developed structures in the Andes. Instead, Amazonian peoples lived in small groups with local chiefs; rather than fight, they simply disappeared into the forest and remained illusive.

The products of the rainforest were obtainable by barter, so there was no reason for the Incas to conquer the land except for the motive of dominating the known world. But they ruled almost all the people whom they considered civilized, and the Amazonians could easily be dismissed as subhuman and therefore incapable of participating in the imperial state structure.

ADMINISTRATIVE GENIUS
A large factor in Inca success was the way in which they treated conquered peoples. Inca provincial governors were placed in charge of the four great divisions of the empire – the four quarters of Tahuantinsuyu – conceived to mimic the four world directions: Antisuyu (north-east), Chinchaysuyu (north-west), Cuntisuyu (south-west) and Collasuyu (south-east). But local rulers and chiefs were normally treated with courtesy and kept in place,

Below: Manco Capac, legendary leader of the Inca people and 'founder' of the empire, depicted in an 18th-century genealogy.

where they were allowed to maintain local control. Their sons were taken as house captives to Cuzco, where they were indoctrinated with Inca values; and their daughters were also taken and indoctrinated – some would be offered as pawns for marriages of alliance with other rulers, though others would be sacrificed.

The genius of the Inca Empire was its administrative organization. Inca civil and economic control was simple in concept and followed developments that had evolved over the past 3,000 years of pre-Hispanic Andean civilization. There was an incremental structure of civic control based on decimal multiples of households, with each higher-ranking official being in charge of ten times more households. Like their concept of the cosmos as a series of layers, this structure presented everyone with a clear line of responsibility from one level to the next.

SOCIAL ORGANIZATION
The Incas intensified and formalized social practices that were ingrained in Andean peoples from early times – the idea of reciprocal obligations and of co-operation with one's kin group of relatives, both blood and by marriage, known as the *ayllu*.

While there was no monetary system, there were taxes and obligations to the state, called the *mit'a*, that amounted to the same thing. Every individual owed labour to the Inca state, which through the *mit'a* was fulfilled by the household rather than by each individual. This left

Above: Huánuca Pampa was typical of Inca regional cities and a great storehouse for the redistribution of imperial tax goods.

the household intact and able to fulfil its obligation at home while some member fulfilled *mit'a* service. Quotas of produce (agricultural or textile) were collected into storehouses for redistribution according to need. In this way the Incas ensured that all their subjects had the necessities of life and so largely forestalled rebellion.

Some rebellions did occur, however, and these were dealt with swiftly. Rebellious groups were moved wholesale to distant provinces, where, in unfamiliar territory and among strangers, they were isolated from their secure social structure. In addition, loyal groups were moved into potentially rebellious areas to keep control. The Inca administrators' skill was in indoctrinating people into a system against which it was futile to resist, and which was in most cases familiar.

All land theoretically belonged to the Inca emperor. It was divided into three parts, the produce of which was given to: the emperor and his household, the Inca state religion and the people themselves. The Incas expanded the land under production, rejuvenating old and constructing new terraces and raised fields. They built provincial storehouse capitals, linked by a road system that made it easy to move goods, and armies, throughout the empire. And they created a messenger service to keep the emperor and his governors informed. This was the empire 'discovered' by Francisco Pizarro.

CIVIL WAR: FALL OF THE INCA EMPIRE

By the early 16th century, the Incas ruled almost all the civilized peoples of South America. The twelfth emperor, Huayna Capac (1493–1526), ruled a stable empire, which he was still expanding. He had gone on campaign to the northern provinces to quell an outbreak of rebellion in the recently subdued Quito province.

STILL EXPANDING

The Incas were aware of the wealth of the gold- and silver-working cultures to the north of the empire. Though not quite the urban civilizations of the Andean Area – many lacked the tradition of stone architecture and conurbation – Colombian metalworking cultures were sophisticated chiefdoms with loose confederations of political power. Whether they would have been easily incorporated into the Inca imperial structure will never be known, however, for in the very year (1526) of Francisco Pizarro's second expedition to the north-west coast of South America,

Below: Hatun Rumiyoc Street, Cuzco, showing the wall of the royal palaces of Inca Roca.

Huayna Capac died of a mysterious disease, as did his chosen heir, Ninancuyuchi. The illness was smallpox, which had been introduced by the Spaniards into Mesoamerica and spread south, ravaging the native populations as it did so because they had no resistance to it.

Huayna Capac's and his heir's deaths were a significant blow to the stability of the empire, which was functioning smoothly despite the very recent acquisition of some territories. Huayna Capac had, in fact, inherited most of the empire he ruled intact and had spent most of his campaign consolidating his inheritance and strengthening the infrastructure. He was particularly engaged in building Inca towns in the northern part of the empire.

DISARRAY AND DISRUPTION

The smooth inheritance that had previously been the case was in disarray. Without a living designated heir, the imperial household was in confusion. Huayna Capac had more than a score of sons, one of whom, Atahualpa, was on campaign with him, while another, Huáscar, he had left in Cuzco as one of four governors. Members of the

Above: The Inca civil war was breaking up the empire when the Spaniards arrived. Camac Inca leads his Inca troops (from Poma de Ayala's Nueva Corónica, *c.1615).*

imperial household quickly divided into factions, each with its own interpretation of what Huayna Capac's intentions had been. They questioned whether Huayna Capac had in fact truly or properly anointed Ninancuyuchi. Huáscar's faction naturally claimed that Huayna Capac intended him to inherit, while Atahualpa's faction claimed that Huayna Capac would have wanted Atahualpa to use his control of the army to take control and maintain the security of the empire in its time of crisis over the succession.

In such unprecedented circumstances, Huáscar seized the throne. At first Atahualpa acknowledged him, but when a local chief spread a rumour that Atahualpa was plotting against Huáscar, the latter declared his half-brother an enemy and traitor and civil war ensued.

The war lasted six years before Atahualpa was finally victorious and had captured and imprisoned Huáscar.

Above: Inca emperor Huayna Capac, 12th Sapa Inca, who died of smallpox, setting off the Inca civil war. From an 18th-century 'Cuzco School' Inca genealogy.

EFFECTS ON THE PEOPLE

The effects of these events on the structure of the empire must have been immense, and the speed of the expansion of the empire would now take its toll. With the imperial armies engaged in fighting each other, recently conquered peoples, especially those far from Cuzco, could cease to acknowledge imperial rule and take back local power.

Soldiers in the army of one or other faction, or people who lived where the fighting between the brothers occurred, would have been directly affected by the war, but most ordinary subjects would have simply carried on making a living. The social structure was, at their level, intact and their households and kinship obligations still operative.

While the events of the civil war were unfolding, there is no evidence of widespread rebellion, just as there was no such outbreak after Atahualpa was executed in 1533. Clearly there was an ingrained inertia in ordinary Andean lives to simply get on with daily routine and lie low. The burdens imposed on them by the Incas – such as the labour tax, textile quotas, the Quechua language and the precedence of the imperial state religion on Inti over local gods – were temporarily relieved, but so too was the structure of the redistribution of goods.

External factors also had an effect, and the spread of smallpox was undoubtedly of more immediate concern. It devastated the peoples in the area that had been the northern Kingdom of Chimú shortly after the outbreak that had killed Huayna Capac and Ninancuyuchi.

At the same time, the disruption of the world into which many had been born must have been psychologically devastating. General religious belief among Andean peoples acknowledged the arbitrary power of the gods, and the death of their emperor by such a mysterious disease must have been regarded as divine retribution for something he and they had done.

A PLANNED BREAK-UP?

Some sources indicate that Huayna Capac had planned to divide the empire among several sons. He was disturbed by a prophecy that the empire was ending and that he was the last of the Inca dynasty. He told his sons that Inti had informed him that the demise of the Inca would come with the arrival of powerful foreigners and that the priests had foretold all: a new moon had appeared with three halos, which they said represented the death of Inti, war among his descendants and the break-up of the empire. Some scholars even think that the Inca Empire was over-extended and would not have been able to sustain its unwieldy size – that it was effectively self-dividing by 1526.

Below: Sapa Inca Atahualpa, who challenged the heir designate, Huáscar, when their father Huayna Capac died. From an 18th-century 'Cuzco School' Inca genealogy.

PIZARRO'S CONQUEST

Pizarro's three expeditions (1524–5, 1526–7 and 1531–3) to north-west South America seemed to be the fulfilment of the priests' prophecy. He made his first contact with Inca subjects in 1526, when he encountered a balsa trading raft with two traders from the Inca subject port of Tumbes, laden with gold and silver objects and textiles. The traders described the cities and wealth of the empire to Pizarro.

CLASH OF CULTURES

When Francisco Pizarro began his final expedition, he carried in his head visions of the fabulous civilizations and riches of Mesoamerica. He also projected the confidence and superior attitude of Europeans of the 16th century towards other cultures. Although he undoubtedly appreciated the sophistication of the Inca

Below: Rebellious uprisings were dealt with severely by the Spaniards, shown in an execution scene by the Flemish Theodore de Bry in his Historia Americae *(1602).*

Empire when he saw it himself – how else could it have built the great cities and amassed the riches he saw? – he also held in contempt foreign peoples whose religious beliefs were regarded as heathen and whose political and military abilities were regarded as inferior. The irony is that the Incas, in many respects, felt the same about the peoples they had themselves only recently conquered. Both the Spaniards and the Incas held their peoples and cultures as the pinnacle of social, political and technological achievement. Their abiding philosophy was that they were destined and entitled to rule the known world.

MULTIPLE FACTORS

Despite the obvious disruption of the civil war, what really brought the Inca Empire to its knees? By the time Pizarro arrived on the borders of the empire, Atahualpa had won and was in the process of reconsolidating Inca administrative structure and institutions. The

Above: Francisco Pizarro (1475–1541), Spanish foundling, illiterate pig herder, adventurer and conqueror of the Inca Empire.

empire was weakened, but Atahualpa still had his army, which was vastly superior in numbers to Pizarro's force.

The factors that ensured Pizarro's victory over the Inca are varied.

Despite their seemingly perfect world, in which everyone got what he or she needed, the imperial household was clearly becoming overburdened and demanding a large proportion of the empire's resources. There were also problems with the imperial succession: with so many potential heirs from multiple wives, there were bound to be court intrigues and contestations of legitimacy.

The empire was still expanding north when the Spaniards arrived, and their huge southern acquisitions beyond the Titicaca Basin were very recent. The peoples of many provinces simply bided their time through the civil war. Many must have resented their recent subjugation but were still in awe of Inca power and in fear of the strange events taking place.

The succession to the throne was not fully decided. Many Inca nobility still opposed Atahualpa even though he had

defeated Huáscar. When he occupied Cuzco, Atahualpa ordered the provincial governors and chief administrators to attend him in the capital. Many were of Huáscar's royal *panaca* lineage. Atahualpa committed acts of sacrilege by ordering them put to death, and, further, by ordering the burning of the mummy of Tupac Yupanqui, Huayna Capac's predecessor and ancestor of the *panaca*. These acts not only effectively eliminated potential claimants to the throne, but also broke the imperial line and contradicted the very concept of the Inca world, so fulfilling Huayna Capac's prophecy.

The coincidence of Huayna Capac's death by smallpox and the ensuing civil war can only be labelled a quirk of historical fate. What Pizarro did to seize the opportunity is, however, down to the audacity and character of the man himself and of his Spanish companions. He took advantage of the Inca's own road

Below: Pizarro demanded a room full of gold as ransom for Sapa Inca Atahualpa. This fanciful depiction includes un-Inca classical columns and a medieval chair.

Above: This modern interpretation of the Sapa Inca Atahualpa meeting Pizarro in 1532 in Cajamarca captures something of his alleged haughty nature and elevated importance.

system to move quickly into the heart of the empire, meeting with little resistance. Realizing the disruptive influence of the civil war, he was quick to exploit Atahualpa's hesitation to confront him. He also declared his intentions to be peaceful, possibly to ally himself with one side. He was astute enough to assess the Inca state of mind and to take advantage of their religious beliefs and the prediction of their demise. And he was simply bold and knew that at his age and at this stage of his 'career' the stakes were high and that he must not lose the opportunity.

He was right in most respects. The atrocious acts by Atahualpa against Inca world concepts left his subjects in a stupor. They had seen Atahualpa's hesitancy to challenge Pizarro and witnessed his weakness when captured and his orders to strip the empire of its wealth to ransom himself. They had underestimated the superiority of Spanish technology, misread Pizarro's motives and were unprepared for the psychological impact of ambush – a most un-Inca act. After the ambush and capture of Atahualpa, many finally rebelled, welcoming and joining the Spaniards to throw off the burdens of Inca rule.

DIVINE FATE

The psychological impact of the small-pox epidemic cannot be underestimated. During Huayna Capac's illness, traders from the northern borders reported to him the appearance of bearded strangers in strange ships and reminded him of his priests' prophecy of the end of the Incas. In the Andean belief in the arbitrary power of the gods, it was unambiguous that the disease was divine wrath. The appearance of people who were immune to it made them ready to accept the prophecy, divine approval of the newcomers and the fate of their civilization. Francisco Pizarro himself died a relatively young, supposedly rich, man, murdered by the hands of his own countrymen.

Finally, it must be said that reverence for their local landscape and many ancient beliefs endure today alongside Christian faith as proof of the quiet resilience of ordinary Andeans.

Below: Post-conquest rivalry among the Spanish conquistadors is exemplified in this unsympathetic caricature of Pizarro by 18th-century artist James Gillray.

CHAPTER FOURTEEN

FROM VILLAGES TO CITIES

The development of Andean civilization is divided by archaeologists into a series of defined time periods. This is for organizational convenience, for in reality such divisions are false because they are too rigid and because Andean ancient societies evolved continuously as they adapted to their times.

Through periods of climatic change, population increases and political upheavals, Andean peoples developed social, economic and technological structures and expertise. They slowly accumulated layers of social and political sophistication and religious complexity, moving from bands of hunter-gatherers through the more sedentary lifestyles of agriculturalists to the complicated lives of urban citizens.

As societies increased their ability to produce the essentials of life, more and more people were able to have jobs that were not linked with food production. In this way, specialists were able to increase in number and skill. True urbanism was achieved when the juxtaposition of political, bureaucratic and economic activities balanced and intervened between religious and domestic life. Technical skills and full-time specialization – in crafts or politics or religion – can be sustained only if the economic structure can support them, and the attainment of this balance is the hallmark of urban civilization. This chapter outlines the sweep of Andean prehistory from the first peopling of the continent to the Inca Empire.

Left: The sun temple ruins at the Inca royal estates at Rosaspata in the Vilcabamba Mountains, Peru.

THE FIRST ARRIVALS

People (modern *Homo sapiens*) migrated into the New World from the far north-eastern reaches of Asia during the final stages of the last great global Ice Age (the end of the Pleistocene Period), from at least 15,000 years ago. The archaeological evidence for this migration is scattered and comes from land sites in North, Central and South America. Geological evidence shows us that the world sea level at this time was lower by about 100m (330ft), because much water was still frozen in ice sheets and glaciers. A huge ice sheet covered most of the northern half of the North American continent, extending south from the Arctic.

MIGRATION ROUTES
The lower sea level created a land bridge across the Bering Strait, and the general chronological and geographical distribution of the evidence for the arrival and spread of hunter-gatherer peoples indicates they took this route into the New World. They followed an ice-free corridor that opened up in the western half of the continent between the Cordilleran and Laurentian (or Laurentide) ice sheets,

Below: A Moche moulded red-ware effigy jar, c.400AD. The face reveals 'typical' features of Andean peoples.

Above: Early migrants into South America encountered harsh environments such as the Atacama Desert of northern Chile.

migrating from the north-west to the south-east. As they found ice-free lands south of the ice fields, they spread east, west and south. They found the continent to have a vast larder of long-established animals and plants, most of them indigenously evolved species, and some large game animals (or their immediate ancestors) that had probably migrated from Asia during earlier breaks (interstadials) in the ice sheets – for example the Columbian mammoth, or American mastodon.

This conventional reconstruction of events has been challenged and modified in recent decades. It seems logical to assume that migration also took place by sea along a western coastal route. Island- and coastal-hopping in pursuit of sea mammals lacks direct evidence, which presumably lies beneath the water off the present coastlines. Another recent theory argues that there was also an earlier migration across the ice floes of the North Atlantic into north-eastern North America. This argument is based on conclusions about similarities between the European Solutrian lithic culture of south-western France, dated 22,000–16,500 years ago,

and the Clovis stone point tradition of North America, dated about 10,000 years ago. This theory is rigorously disputed.

MIGRATION GROUPS
Molecular biology, DNA and blood-group evidence shows that these New World immigrants descend from three or four distinct populations, revealing there were several incidents of migration into North America. Those peoples who continued into South America, however, descend from only one of these biological groups.

Below: An imaginative painting showing how the first migrants into the New World from north-east Asia followed game across the land bridge created across the Bering Strait during lowered sea levels in the late Ice Age.

The rate of migration is also a point of controversy and can only be guessed. Nevertheless, the earliest indisputable date for human occupation in South America comes from Monte Verde, southern Chile, about 14,850 years ago (averaged from more than a dozen radiocarbon dates), showing that the pace was rapid, or that early evidence from farther north remains to be found.

MONTE VERDE

At Monte Verde, a group of people lived for a season or two on the banks of a small creek. Eventually, their settlement was abandoned and covered by a peat layer deposited by the river. Their settlement comprised crude wooden-plank or log-floored pole- and hide-walled rectangular huts. There were at least 12 contiguous rooms or huts arranged in two parallel rows. Within them and around the site were found remains of wild potatoes and other plant remains, animal bones (including mastodon) and wooden and stone tools: wooden spears, digging sticks, three wooden mortars, stone scrapers (including three with wooden handles) and egg-sized pebbles, some grooved, believed to be sling and bolas stones. There were also clay-lined hearths for cooking and one human footprint preserved in the peat.

Separate from the dwellings was a single, 3 x 4m (10 x 13ft), Y-plan structure made of a sand-and-gravel floor, and two rows of wooden poles with hide walls forming the arms. The rear of the hut was

Left: Early hunter-gatherers left examples of their art on rock, as here in a depiction of a snake hunt in Zamora, Ecuador.

raised, and the open area between the arms had several clay-lined braziers and the remains of animal hides, burnt reeds, seeds and medicinal plants, including chewed leaves. Other hearths, piles of wood, artefacts, and plant and animal remains were scattered around the structure. Clearly this was a building for special purposes.

SCARCE EVIDENCE

Such rare preservation demonstrates the scarce nature of the evidence for early lithic cultures in the Andean Area. This Archaic or Lithic Period lasted down to about 7,000–5,000 years ago in different areas of the Andes. Lithic sites and surface artefacts have been found throughout South America, including Brazil, Argentina and Uruguay, and the tip of Tierra del Fuego. Finds of lithic artefacts and occupation remains become more widespread after about 7,000 years ago. The varied terrains occupied gave rise to different artefact styles, including adaptations to the mountain environments, where several fluted projectile point styles were used in hunting horse, sloth and other animals, and to several coastal traditions along the Pacific coast, where bone harpoons were used to hunt maritime mammals.

Below: An essential New World hunting tool – and later weapon in war – was the atl-atl. Two hunters are poised to hurl their spears with atl-atls *at vicuñas on a Nazca pot.*

PRECERAMIC VILLAGES

The persistence of lithic-using hunter-gatherer cultures varied in different regions of the Andean Area, and there are few hard facts about exactly where and how the domestication of plants and animals took place in the Andes and western coastal valleys. Increasing heavy exploitation and reliance on certain species appears to have led to plant tending, which, after many generations – both of human populations and of the plants themselves – led to modifications to enhance the species and its yield.

DOMESTICATION – THE THEORY

There are some tens of thousands of plants and animal species in South America, but less than 1 per cent of these have been domesticated. It is argued that in regions where a species thrives and is abundant in its natural environment there is little reason for humans to tend or otherwise try to manipulate it, since they can simply gather it as needed. However, in marginal areas of a species' habitat, there is a need to nurture it if there is to be

Below: Llamas provided many products for early peoples in South America. As well as hunted quarry, they soon became domesticated as herded flocks in the Altiplano.

sufficient for human use, especially if the population in an area is increasing. Species found outside their known native regions can thus be regarded as 'domesticated'.

There are changes in environmental conditions and climate over short distances within the Andean Area, especially with altitude change. Thus even small movements of a species into a new environment introduced human selection as well as natural selection. It is believed that constant 'experiments' of this nature by an increasing human population brought domestication to selected food crops and fixed human reliance on a small number of species. At first they were able to exploit these crops in naturally watered soils; later, in an extension of the experiment, they grew them in soils to which they could bring water through irrigation schemes.

Significantly, however, the earliest known domesticated plants come from Guitarrero Cave, northern Peru, from *c.*8000BC. Fibre-plant remains dominate the Guitarrero assemblage (used for sandals, clothing, cordage, bedding mats and mesh sacks), but there were also specimens of domesticated beans and chilli pepper, both *not* native to the region and therefore probably cultivated there.

Above: One of the earliest uses of clay was for unfired figurines, such as this model of a woman from the early Valdivian culture in Ecuador, c.3500–1500BC.

The increased reliability of selected cultivated food sources also made it possible for people to congregate in larger settlements and to remain there permanently, rather than having to move through the seasons to exploit food sources in their own native environments. Gradually, both in lowland coastal and highland valleys, the number and sizes of settlements grew.

LATE PRECERAMIC ECONOMICS

Three elements form the foundations of the economic developments that characterize the late Preceramic Period in Andean prehistory. These are: the intensive exploitation of maritime resources at coastal settlements; the use of floodplain irrigation in coastal valleys and rainfall agriculture in highland valleys, for early agriculture; and long-distance trade. The last of these elements established, from the earliest times of

Above: A painting from the Mollopunko caves, northern Peru, c.5000BC appears to show a llama being led or tethered with a rope, an indication of early semi-domestication.

permanent settlement, an Andean tradition of reciprocal exchange between highland and lowland communities.

The richness of maritime resources on the Pacific coast made it possible for coastal peoples to live in large settlements mostly supported by maritime food sources. Sites have deep middens of accumulated shellfish, crustacean, fish and sea mammal remains. Until the late Preceramic and into the Initial Period, grown foods were only a marginal part of the diet, but nevertheless included squash, beans, chillies and two introductions to the coast (potatoes and maize) by c.2000BC. Such is the scene at sites up and down the coast, such as Huaca Prieta and Salinas de Chao on the northern coast, Aspero and Piedra Parada on the central coastal, and El Paraíso and Otuma on the southern coast.

Such intense exploitation of maritime resources, however, would not have been possible without a source of cotton for nets and fishing line and gourds for floats. Both these plants are not native to coast environments, and were introduced from tropical regions to the east and north, where they were domesticated early on.

HIGHLAND CHANGES

Similar changes took place in the highlands. Annual precipitation of 5 to 6 months not only supported a rich natural flora but also appears to have provided hunter-gatherer peoples with several intermontane-valley species that became the staples of their diet: potatoes, maize and beans, and a host of other tubers, grains and legumes. There was also meat, including deer, vicuña and guanaco (which remained wild), and the llama, alpaca and guinea pig, all of which show cultural and anatomical signs of domestication by the end of the Preceramic Period.

Plant domestication was underway by 5000BC in the highlands. By about 3000BC most of the full range of food plants capable of being grown in highland valleys had been adopted. Similarly, the guinea pig was bred as a domestic meat source, although anatomical evidence at this early date is insufficient to determine how far true domestication had proceeded. The domestication of the llama and alpaca, herded on the grasslands of the Altiplano, took place gradually over 2,000 years and was complete by c.25,000BC.

Such was the scene at the beginning of the Initial Period at sites such as La Galgada and Huaricoto in the northern highlands, Kotosh and Shillacoto in the central highlands, and Ondores farther south.

Below: Fishing became another important ancient Andean economy. The Aymara still use traditional totora-reed boats to fish on Lake Titcaca on the border of Bolivia–Peru.

THE INITIAL PERIOD

Beginning *c*.2000BC in the Andean Area, the Initial Period was a time of tremendous technological advancements and accomplishments. First, there was a flowering of textile technique and art when the simpler techniques of fibre twining and looping began to be replaced by cloth woven on heddle looms; second, the first ceramics began to be made in the Andean Area; and third, there was growth in monumental architecture building.

WEAVERS AND POTTERS
The invention of weaving using a heddle loom enabled the mass production of cloth. It went hand in hand with developments

Below: A terracotta figurine (c.2300BC) from the Valdivian culture of coastal Ecuador, some of the earliest pottery in the Andes.

in farming and pastoralism. As the farming of greater areas of land produced increased yields in cotton, and the expansion of llama herding in upland regions increased the availability of wool, so the innovation from simpler techniques meant that more textiles could be produced by specialists.

The first ceramics in South America were made, from *c*.3200BC, in the extreme north of the Andean Area by the early farmers of Valdivia on the coast of Ecuador. Pottery of a slightly later date (*c*.3000BC) was produced outside the Andean Area by people at Puerto Hormiga, on the Caribbean coast of Colombia.

For both weaving and pottery making, labour became more concentrated and specialists became possible. The increase in large building projects also fostered the development of social organization that featured specialists in two fields: those who planned and built them, and those who ran them. As some members of society concentrated their skills in agricultural production, so increasing the agricultural yields achievable by fewer farmers, other people were able to devote more of their time to ceramic production and weaving.

SPECIALISTS
No doubt the bulk of the population was not particularly specialized, and the majority of people probably continued to spend most of their time in agriculture, herding and other subsistence pursuits. But the increasingly greater availability of food for less effort inevitably gave people more time to vary their daily lives and to pursue craft activities beyond the purely useful. As a result, forms and varieties of decoration increased and regional styles developed. Thematic motifs reflecting religious belief became incorporated into ceramics and textiles, and special pieces were made for burials.

Together with an increasingly sophisticated evolution in religious beliefs, these innovations and developments themselves

Above: Irrigation techniques using narrow channels to route water into fields, developed by the earliest farmers, continued to be used until Inca times, as here at Tipon, near Cuzco.

became interwoven, on the basis that ceramic production and decoration, textile styles and decoration, and architectural construction were never separate thematically. Religious motivation and the demonstration of religious themes were always incorporated into Andean technological production and architectural form.

PUBLIC ARCHITECTURE
Perhaps these reconfigurations of social structure and time management are most dramatically represented in the expansion of monumental architecture. The size and planning of monumental architecture mirrors religious concepts in mimicking the sacred landscape and in orientation to the sources of sacred waters. Form also reflects what are assumed to be beliefs in Mother Earth and Father Sky deities.

Two classic forms were developed: the platform mound and the sunken court. Platforms supported single or multiple rooms. Often the two forms, plus subsidiary platforms, were combined in complexes forming a U shape. These forms established the traditions that would prevail through the Initial Period and into the Early Horizon.

INLAND MIGRATION

Settlement patterns also changed. Increases in agricultural production were in part made possible by shifting settlement to areas with greater expanses of better-watered lands. The largest centres of population shifted systematically inland in the central and northern coasts of the

Below: Fertile flatland was at a premium in the mountain valleys, so extensive terracing was used to create thousands of narrow fields, as here in Colca Canyon, Peru.

Andean Area. Settlements along the shoreline were abandoned in favour of richer-soiled valley mouths and lower valleys, where river water was more accessible. Maritime resources were not abandoned, but the dependence on agricultural crops by these coastal populations brought important shifts in emphasis and must have had profound effects on the organization and scheduling of their daily lives. Where formerly they lived on the seafront and brought agricultural produce to their settlements, they now began to live in towns among their fields and to travel to the seaside to collect shellfish or embark on fishing and sea mammal hunts.

The reasons for these changes are debated. From the late Preceramic Period, coastal settlements that were predominantly reliant on maritime resources had also incorporated newly domesticated food crops into their economy. But they had been reliant on small satellite settlements

Above: An Inca farmer tapping an irrigation channel to water the maize crop in November (a dry month), depicted in Poma de Ayala's Nueva Corónica, *c.1615.*

in the lower river valleys for agricultural produce, which might imply at least a rudimentary kind of irrigation.

What began in the Initial Period, and what in fact partly defines the period, is the development of much more substantial irrigation works, tapping the rivers with channels to run water into the fields. One reason might have been population growth and consequent pressure on resources. It is certain, however, that the abundant maritime resources would have been able to support even larger populations than our present archaeological knowledge shows us. We also know that there were small environmental changes in the coastlines that left some settlements more isolated from the sea. But these shifts were gradual and subtle.

What seems the best explanation includes both these factors, plus social and economic relationships that had developed in rudimentary fashion in the late Preceramic Period simultaneously. A combination of changing dietary preferences, increased success in farming, socio-political rivalry to control the best resources, and shifting patterns of work as these agricultural 'discoveries' were made seems to be a more plausible cause for both changing settlement patterns and the artistic, architectural and religious enhancements of the Initial Period.

THE EARLY HORIZON

The Early Horizon is defined as a period of cultural cohesion across large regions of the Andean Area, comprising northern and southern spheres. These spheres were not mutually exclusive: there were relationships, trade and influence between their communities, maintaining already-developed Andean cultural traditions of long-distance trade between highlands and lowlands.

INITIAL PERIOD TRADITIONS
The Initial Period flowering in monumental architecture developed into several regional traditions, both coastal and highland, and served the first Andean religious cults. These developments formed the basis of much more widespread Early Horizon traditions.

The classic form was the U-shaped complex, comprising a central mound, wings forming a U, and sunken courts. Many platforms supported complexes of small adjoining or individual rooms. These forms established the traditions that prevailed throughout the Initial Period and into the Early Horizon.

Sunken courts (called *plazas hundidas*) were one tradition. They were usually part of a complex with platforms mounds, but could be on their own. A second tradition, called Kotosh, featured a one-roomed enclosure for intimate worship.

Two further traditions, Supe and El Paraíso, show a new order of magnitude and organization. Earlier ceremonial complexes are more modest in size and are usually associated with domestic remains, indicating that they were built by their local communities. Complexes of the Supe and El Paraíso traditions, however, are larger, more complex and varied, and lack evidence that they were surrounded by immediate residential populations. They appear to be the earliest complexes that were built and maintained as centres for religious worship for regions of communities. The El Paraíso U-shaped ceremonial centre is a representative example of such a complex, associated with irrigation agriculture and dominating the Rimac Valley on the central southern Peruvian coast. The largest U-shaped complex ever built was Sechín Alto in the Casma Valley.

At the same time, the Chiripa Tradition developed in the Titicaca Basin. This consisted of symmetrical arrangements of one-roomed buildings around a square sunken court atop a low platform. The type-site is Chiripa on the southern Titicaca lakeshore, with 16 buildings around its sunken court.

SOCIAL ORGANIZATION
The strong association of monumental architecture in ceremonial complexes serving regions and irrigation agriculture indicates that kinship relations between communities formed strong links. This was an important Initial Period/Early Horizon development that endured throughout the rest of Andean prehistory.

It seems likely that linked communities and shared religious traditions strengthened social systems of communal labour,

Left: Chavín de Huánta united Andean and coastal people in the name of religion – the flanking columns of the Black and White Portal of the New Temple show an eagle (female) and a hawk (male), early examples of duality.

Above: 20th-century archaeologists at work at Chiripa Pata, a pre-Tiwanaku site with a massive temple.

co-operative administration between communities of irrigation works and water rights, perhaps collective land ownership and entitlement to shared resources. Lineage groups were probably moiety-based (two intermarriageable family groups of a descent lineage) from this early period (defined by the *ayllu* in Inca times).

EARLY HORIZON CULTS

These coastal and southern ceremonial centres waned and were eventually abandoned in the early centuries of the 1st millennium BC. In their places arose even stronger, more widespread religious traditions. Two spheres of development can be identified: a northern sphere dominated by the site of Chavín de Huántar and its religious cult, and a southern sphere, slightly more diversified, but with strong religious cults called Pukará–Yaya-Mama in the Titicaca Basin and the Paracas Oculate Being along the southern coast.

CHAVÍN DE HUÁNTAR

With the abandonment of Sechín Alto and other coastal centres, the beliefs and administrative organization associated with U-shaped and sunken-court complexes endured in the highlands. The small, unimposing site of Chavín de Huántar took up the mantle of regional religious focus. Settlement began *c.*900BC at the confluence of the Mosna and Wacheksa rivers, a site apparently deliberately chosen to take advantage of access to western coasts, mountains and eastern

tropical lowlands. The Castillo temple was a classic U-shaped form, although the platform is not high. It endured about 700 years, including phases with an Old Temple and a New Temple, first with a circular sunken court and later with a square one. The ceremonial core was less than a tenth the size of Sechín Alto.

The Castillo appears to have been a cult centre and pilgrimage site for almost the entire Andean Area. Its success can be attributed to established long-distance trade, the spread of Chavín symbolism on portable objects and the integration of llama-herding with irrigation agriculture. While Yaya-Mama and Oculate Being imagery were confined to their respective southern spheres, Chavín's appeal cut across old social boundaries and regionalism, and its universality is demonstrated by the appearance of the Staff Deity as far south as Karwa on

Below: The Oculate Being in his human form, wearing a Paracas-style golden diadem and holding a trophy-headed snake.

Above: Ancestor worship as seen in a Paracas burial tomb containing mummy bundles wrapped around the elite person's body.

the Paracas Peninsula, and of Chavín symbolism on stone sculptures at Pacopampa and Kuntur Wasi in the northern highlands.

The spread of Chavín religious symbolism was extraordinary. Arising at the end of a drought period that caused abandonment of the coastal centres, it catered to coastal and mountain deities alike. Its religious symbolism embraced general concepts of dualism, and earthly and celestial deities represented on a succession of huge stone idols, as well as smaller objects with representations of the Staff Being as both male and female, a feline-serpentine image and a great cayman idol. It is significant that none of the animals or plants on Chavín's stone carvings is native to its highland location.

PUKARÁ AND PARACAS

As the importance of Chiripa waned, so Pukará, north of Lake Titicaca, and about a dozen other sites north and south of the lake, became centres for the Yaya-Mama Cult. Its symbolism was the duality of male and female figures carved on opposite sides of stone stelae. The cult flourished at the same time as Chavín through the middle centuries of the 1st millennium BC.

On the southern coast, the settlement of Paracas represents a third Early Horizon cult, with its extraordinarily rich cemeteries serving regional communities. The principal deity here was the Oculate Being, colourfully represented on textiles and pottery as a wide-eyed, flying sky deity.

THE EARLY INTERMEDIATE PERIOD

Chavín de Huántar was not the capital of a state, but rather a place of religious focus, and the cultural coherence that defines the Early Horizon was religion. While the inhabitants of other cult centres, such as Karwa, Kotosh, Huaricoto, Pacopampa and Kuntur Wasi, clearly felt religious allegiance to the Castillo temple, there is no evidence of political control at sites with Chavín Cult art. There is no identifiable state administrative architecture or other evidence of other than local regional community government and social arrangements.

THE END OF CHAVÍN
Although the demise of Chavín de Huántar and its cult was sudden, the reasons are obscure. Monumental construction in northern and central Peru came to an abrupt end in the 3rd century BC. The centuries either side of the Early Horizon–Early Intermediate Period were plagued by drought. Scholars attribute Chavín's end to an inability to maintain stability and the redistribution of resources during such stressful times.

Below: The capital of the Moche state featured a huge ceremonial centre, including the Huaca del Sol and, shown here, the Huaca de la Luna temple mounds.

Perhaps the length of its success was due to an acceptance of fate and to a focus on religious faith to counter hard times.

THRESHOLD OF URBANISM
Chavín de Huántar and its influence brought Andean civilization to the brink of urbanism, but lacked a truly urban appearance. Its economic life, including the support of craft specialists, was centred on its religion and ceremony.

The abrupt deflation of such strong cultic and artistic coherence brought social withdrawal. Hard times caused greater competition and many centres were abandoned, while others became impoverished. Squatters, for example, occupied the circular sunken plaza at Chavín de Huántar. There were population shifts to hilltop fortresses on both the coast and in the highlands.

With climatic improvement, the best lands were occupied and population increased. Highland peoples combined terraced and raised-field agriculture with mountain pastoralism, while desert coastal peoples built extensive irrigation systems to water the valley bottoms. But once the easily exploited lands were filled, competition was again inevitable. Intermittent periods of drought again punctuated the first few centuries AD.

Above: The Early Intermediate Period Kingdom of the Moche was the Andean Area's earliest state in northern coastal Peru, established through military conquest, exemplified by this effigy pot of a Moche war leader.

Unlike in the Initial Period and Early Horizon, Early Intermediate residential communities outnumbered purely ceremonial ones, and were larger. Although many settlements were fortified, often on hilltops and ridges, undefended settlements were the norm, and small villages filled the valley bottoms.

POLITICAL AND SOCIAL CHANGE
There was a shift from religious cultism to political rule by powerful elites. The political shift was from the powerful

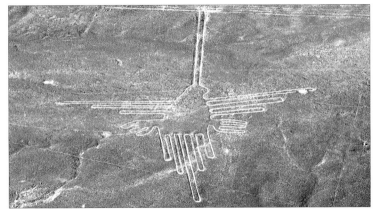

influence of priests to rule by *curacas* (a noble or kingly class distinguished by wealth and power) in the name of the gods. Ceremonial structures were built by the rulers, who marshalled the labour of their 'subjects'.

The civilizations of the Moche in the northern coastal valleys and of the Nazca in the southern coastal deserts demonstrate these changes most clearly. Both developed and flourished from the beginning of the 1st millennium to about AD700. Other nodes of political power were in the Rimac Valley of the central coast (the Lima culture) and several highland states.

INCREASE IN URBANISM

The settlements of these cultures are characterized not only by their greater size but also by the variation of their architecture. Ceremonial centres were still distinct, and sometimes separate, but they were now surrounded by or linked (twinned) with residential areas developed with regular planning. Buildings reflected activities, showing administrative,

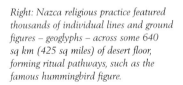

craft specialization and domestic functions. Residence sizes and decoration reveal variations in wealth and status – the birth of socio-economic classes.

Religious overtones in philosophic outlook were still a driving force in people's day-to-day existence, and religious symbolism still dominated art, but the juxtaposition of political, bureaucratic and economic activities, and their intervention between religious and domestic life, form the complexity of parts that define urbanism. These developments were in place throughout the Andes by about AD500.

SPECIALIZATION

Each of these regions produced distinctive ceramics, metalwork and textiles. The renown of Moche craftsmanship rests especially in the quality and quantity of its metallurgists, whereas the potters and weavers of Nazca, where the desiccated conditions of the desert have preserved textiles in particular, possessed an expertise achievable only by specialization. Technical skill and full-time specialization are

Left: Contemporary to the Moche, the Nazca peoples of southern coastal Peru formed a loose confederation of states. Much wealth was represented by their exquisite, colourful textiles, such as this hat, especially associated with ancestor worship and burial.

hallmarks of urbanism. Such practices can be sustained only if the economic structure can support them. There was state sponsorship of crafts, and objects were commissioned by the elite and made specifically for occasions, such as elite burial.

Battle scenes are a frequent Nazca and Moche artistic theme. Particular to Moche culture was a state specialization in ritual combat. Selected boys – the job might even have been hereditary – were trained from an early age to participate in gladiatorial contests with religious overtones. Moche ceramics depict some of these individuals in series of portrait vessels that show them through their lives, revealing those who were successful enough to last until they became the sacrificial victims when their skills waned and they lost their contests.

Particular to Nazca were its ground drawings: animals, plants and geometric shapes outlined on the desert surface were ritual pathways, binding society with religious ceremony.

Representative of these developments are the cities of Moche surrounding the ceremonial mounds of Huaca del Sol and Huaca de la Luna, Gallinazo, Sipán, Pampa Grande and Pañamarca in the northern coastal valleys; Pachacamac and Maranga in the central coast; and the twinned Cahuachi and Ventilla cites in the Nazca Valley. In the northern highlands were Cajamarca, Marca Huamachuco, Recuay and Wilkawain; Huarpa to the south; and in the Altiplano, Omo and the rise of Tiwanaku.

THE MIDDLE HORIZON

The Middle Horizon is defined as a further period of increased unity across regions. Precedents had been set in the later Early Intermediate Period with the evolution of more secular political regimes, albeit of city-states ruling small territories. The difference is in the underlying reasons for cross-regional unity: in the Early Horizon it was religion, while in the Middle Horizon it was politics, economy and military conquest.

MOCHE AND NAZCA
The closest thing to a large area under single rule in the Early Intermediate Period was the Moche Kingdom in the northern coastal valleys. Even this state, however, was characterized by semi-independent rulers from one valley to the next. The Moche were a seafaring people who pursued conquest from one

Below: A kero *drinking cup in the form of an effigy vessel – a puma head – also with a stylized beast and many typical Tiwanaku angular motifs.*

Above: Pikillacta's substantial stone walls formed the regimented town plan of the Wari highland provincial capital near Cuzco.

valley to another by sea invasion, as generations of the sons of kings sought new territories when valleys risked becoming overcrowded. The Moche shifted their centre of power from south to north, from Moche in the Moche Valley to Sipán, and later to Pampa Grande, in the Lambayeque Valley, in the 5th–6th centuries AD. By contrast, the Nazca culture was characterized by what appears to be a loose grouping of city-states.

RISE OF EMPIRES
Moche power collapsed and the Nazca and highland city-states waned with the rise of two civilizations that effectively split the Andean Area between them. They were the Wari and the Tiwanaku. Both expanded through military conquest and colonization. Each had a recognized imperial capital: Huari in a south-central highland intermontane valley between the Huamanga and Huanta basins, and Tiwanku near the southern shores of Lake Titicaca.

From AD650 the political states established by these two civilizations raised the socio-political level of Andean civilization to a new degree of urbanism and state control that in their turn provided models for later powers such as the Chimú and the Inca.

Above: The Wari provincial town near Ayacucho, Peru, shows modular, angular, slab-like stone wall architecture.

SHARED RELIGION, DIFFERENT POLITICS
Wari and Tiwanaku religious symbolism was largely similar. Their rulers and people worshipped the same mountain gods, although they represented them in different media. The focus was on the Staff Deity, represented in imagery similar to that of the Chavín Cult, and which had been so widespread in the Early Horizon. Both Wari and Tiwanaku built in megalithic styles, but large-scale stone statuary was a particular Tiwanaku artistic and religious expression (and one that impressed the Incas centuries later, because it survived, standing silently among the ruins of the ancient city when Inca armies entered the Titicaca Basin).

The differing origins of the two capitals reflect different bases of each empire's power. Tiwanaku had been settled much earlier and had been part of the Early Horizon cult of Pukará–Yaya-Mama. It was thus steeped in religious cult practice. By about AD200 major building was under way and the city soon became the focus of Titicaca Basin religion and power. Tiwanaku representation of the Staff Deity on the Gateway of the Sun can be viewed as taking up the mantle of Chavín de Huántar.

Huari's rise was much later. A small settlement began to expand rapidly at the end of the 5th century AD. Within 100

Above: Tiwanaku, capital of the southern Andean Middle Horizon empire, features numerous enclosed ceremonial compounds at the heart of the city, including the Semi-Subterranean Temple Court, whose walls have sculptured decapitated heads and whose steps lead up to the gateway to the Kalasasaya sacred compound.

Below: The so-called 'monk', one of several colossal stone statues at Tiwanaku, stands in the Kalasasaya sacred compound.

years it was a dominant political power in the south-central highlands and began to expand through military conquest.

ADMINISTRATION AND COLONIZATION
Both empires grew as they took and exercised control of larger areas, each expanding north and south. They met at the La Raya Pass south of Cuzco, and in the upper Moquegua Valley, and there established their borders, under the watchful eyes of Wari garrisons at Pikillacta and Cerro Baúl. There seems to be less evidence of overt militarism at Tiwanaku, while the regimentation of Wari sites appears more martial. Evidence of violence is present in both, however, including stone sculptures of decapitated heads.

In both regimes, their provincial cities and holdings were linked by roads and trade connections, indicating the control of resources. One of Wari's earliest established provincial capitals, Viracochapampa, was 700km (435 miles) north, indicating direct control. This Wari infrastructure was later rejuvenated and improved by the Incas.

Wari expansion appears to have been stimulated by economic tension. To stay in power, Wari rulers needed to secure and control resources. They established deliberate agricultural colonies, such as Jincamocco and Azángaros, and provincial capitals at Viracochapampa and Pikillacta, all in the mid-7th century AD.

Tiwanaku colonization was different. It had a strong agricultural base in the Titicaca Basin, and within this heartland its control was direct. Farther afield control was through trade, for example to San Pedro de Atacama 700km (435 miles) south in northern Chile. Actual colonization by Tiwanaku was closer to home – for example at Omo, west, in the lowland Moquegua Valley, and in the Cochabamba Valley, east, in both cases in sparsely occupied areas – to secure resources they could not grow in the Titicaca Basin.

PATTERNS OF CONTINUITY
These alternative configurations of state organization reflect the path of Andean civilization nicely. The Chavín Cult had introduced widespread religious cohesion despite relative autonomy in local political and social arrangements. Fragmentation of cohesion in the Early Intermediate Period had more to do with the cessation of Chavín influence than with changes in local-level politics or day-to-day life.

The different beginnings and evolutions of these two Middle Horizon empires reflect both elements: imperial state political control from a military base in the case of Wari, similar to Moche expansion, and the centralized cult status and economic basis of Tiwanaku control.

THE LATE INTERMEDIATE PERIOD

Wari and Tiwanaku powers waned swiftly in the final century of the 1st millennium AD. Reasons for the collapse of states are forever debated, but it seems that both empires may have become over-extended. As they colonized areas to secure resources, they no doubt raised resentment among some of their subjects. Abandonment of many of their provincial cities appears to have been sudden.

There is also climatic evidence. Data in cores taken from the Quelccaya icecap and from Lake Titicaca sediments show that rainfall decreased from *c.*AD950 and introduced a new, prolonged period of drought. The lake level dropped several metres (yards) and effectively ended the easy irrigation of raised-field agriculture.

Increased tension, failed crops, social unrest and the breakdown of trade links – all must have contributed to the swift declines of both capitals and their provincial settlements.

FRAGMENTATION AND WARFARE

Once again Andean societies withdrew into their local economies. As had been the case in the Early Intermediate Period, political and macro-social regimes fragmented into city-states, and for roughly the next 400 years local leaders seized power.

Left: A gold and jade repoussé decorated kero *drinking cup, with Staff Being-like imagery of a Sicán Lord, shows the richness of elite north coastal Peru Lambayeque tableware.*

Above: A Chimú finely woven textile exhibits repeated figures wearing elaborate 'ceremonial' headgear and large earrings, plus felines.

With the Late Intermediate Period we come to the threshold of recorded history. Spanish chroniclers, transcribing the histories narrated to them by Inca and other native informants in the early 16th century, describe the period just preceding the rise of the Inca Empire as one of intense warfare between competing 'tribes' or ethnic groups. Strong, warlike leaders were called *sinchis* and they built many hilltop fortifications called *pukarás*, as shown in the archaeological record.

The Inca themselves, in their battles with neighbours in the Cuzco Valley, were participants towards the end of these developments, and indeed their second ruler (12th century) was named Sinchi Roca.

COASTAL STATES

Settlement patterns changed again as people isolated themselves in their local mountain valleys, often living in, or building for retreating to, fortresses overlooking their agricultural lands. Cultural initiatives and the focus of political power returned to the coast with the abandonment of Huari and Tiwanaku.

The traces of Moche culture that lingered in the northern coastal valleys were picked up by leaders living there, perhaps inspired by the visible ruins of the great Moche platform mounds. Following only brief domination by Wari, the Lambayeque-Sicán rulers established a capital at Batán Grande in the La Leche Valley. Like the Moche, they were renowned for their superb metallurgy, known from the royal burials discovered in the capital. Their kingdom was eventually incorporated by the Chimú.

On the central coast, several city-states arose as focuses of local power: the Chancay, Ichma, Cerro Azul and Chincha, all throwing off Wari rule. And the long-established city and pilgrimage oracle of Pachacamac in the Lurin Valley enjoyed a building boom that established it as the premier religious centre along the coast and to the stressed inland communities as well.

Above: A characteristic Chimú polished black effigy vessel or stirrup-spout bottle features a seated priest or elite person seated at a 'throne'.

On the southern coast, the Ica emerged to rule in the Nazca region, while farther south the Chiribaya people emerged from the power vacuum left when the Tiwanaku abandoned the Moquegua Valley.

Highland peoples are less identifiable archaeologically, although many tribal names were recorded from Inca informants. This is partly because they left no substantial legacy of monumental architecture or art, as did their coastal counterparts, before the Incas conquered the highlands.

To combat reduced rainfall and thus a fall in agricultural productivity, people were forced to concentrate on their local

situation and to move to higher, moister elevations and into the wetter, eastern Cordillera. Increased use of terracing was necessary to grow sufficient crops. Competition fostered class separations, as the *chullpa* stone tower burials of the elite show.

Around Lake Titicaca, internecine rivalry resulted in the formation of a loose kingdom of seven confederated capitals or city-states.

CULTURAL DIVERGENCE
Fragmentation was not only political and social. Although art and architecture shared basic technology, approaches and subject matter, inheriting long developments in Andean civilization, the styles became regional: Sicán, Chimú, Chancay, Ica and Chiribaya. Architecture continued to be 'additive', and textiles, ceramics and metalwork mass-produced, standardized and prone to the use of repetitive patterns. Nevertheless, there were distinctive regional styles that can be identified with ethnic groups, both in the highlands and on the coast, the latter

Below: Labyrinthine corridors, compounds and storage rooms are formed within poured-mud, sculpted walls at the Chimú capital of Chan Chan.

Above: The poured-mud walls of Huaca el Dragón, a Chimú temple near the capital Chan Chan has rows of bas-relief warriors surrounding the 'rainbow' sculpture.

area being better documented archaeologically thanks to a return by Andeans, perhaps in their troubled times, to religion. Interestingly, the styles of these coastal peoples are recognized in the offerings they brought to the oracle city of Pachacamac.

Increased emphasis on social hierarchies and the accumulation of wealth by social class and individuals were the result of competition for resources. Elites show a voracious appetite for collecting and hoarding luxury goods. Regimented social control became a hallmark of late Andean social structure.

CHIMÚ
Around AD900 a new city was founded opposite the great Huaca del Sol and de la Luna. This was Chan Chan of the Chimú, which became the capital of the largest kingdom ever seen in the area, subsuming Lambayeque-Sicán culture after invasion *c.*1350. Its rulers, like the Moche, looked to the sea rather than to the highlands for their economic base. They invaded the adjacent valleys and eventually held the peoples of the valleys as far south as Lima in a tightly controlled administrative state. Before their conquest by the Inca, the rulers of Chimú collected huge wealth and created an imperial bureaucracy within their sprawling capital.

THE LATE HORIZON

The conquest of the Chimú Kingdom by the Incas in *c*.1462–70 marks a final episode of the Late Intermediate Period, mainly as a convenient historical date. Other scholars prefer to use 1438, the traditional date for the defeat of the Chancas by Pachacuti, the tenth Inca ruler of Cuzco.

By definition, the Late Horizon was a time of uniformity after a period of diversity. The meteoric rise of the Incas spans the two periods, and a date at which this was achieved to mark the end of the 'period' and the beginning of the 'horizon' is a moot point.

Below: An Inca-style geometric design embellishes this silver dish – tableware for nobles or for ritual offerings – from Ica in the Inca western suyu-quarter of Cuntisuyu.

LEGACY

The legacy of political and social fragmentation in the Late Intermediate Period highland valleys aided the Incas when they began to expand beyond the Cuzco Valley. Their forces frequently met weak or no organized opposition from people in farming communities still recovering from times of drought.

In the central sierra, however, they met stiff resistance from the highland group of city-states called Wanka (or Huanca), in the region of Lake Junin and the Mantaro, Tarma and Chanchamayo rivers. These peoples were primarily llama herders and had not adopted intensive maize agriculture until *c*.AD1000. They built fortified hilltop towns and resisted the Inca armies fiercely, no doubt

Above: Typical Inca close-fitting stonework in a trapezoidal, double-recessed niche with capstone arch in a Cuzco wall.

helped by their knowledge of the terrain. In the end, however, they were defeated by Pachacuti.

The Inca regime was the inheritor of all that came before it. Characteristic of the Inca Empire, above all else, is the Incas' incorporation of the political, social, religious and military cultures of their predecessors. The special talent of the Incas was in their expansion and intensification of these Andean practices.

ACHIEVEMENT

The Incas conquered an empire, albeit fleetingly, that was the largest territory in the world *c*.1530. Over the peoples of their empire they imposed, again only fleetingly, a level of uniformity that had never before existed in the Andean world. The uniformity, however, was less in art and architecture than in the organization of people's activities and social structure. They built extensively, but did not replace existing settlements by rebuilding them, and encouraged local crafts to continue, organizing the produce into their highly controlled economic bureaucracy.

Inca genius lay in their abilities to organize, incorporate and manipulate, and in their engineering. Inca power was expressed especially in their stonework: they rebuilt Cuzco and built provincial administrative capitals with walls of perfectly fitted monolithic blocks.

The Incas rejuvenated, improved and expanded on the roads and way stations built by the Wari and Tiwanaku throughout the central and southern highlands. And they incorporated many Wari outposts. The Incas' own road network comprised more than 33,000km (20,000 miles) of routes linking their capitals and fortresses. Likewise they exploited, extended and increased the terracing and raised-field systems of highland and Altiplano peoples, and expanded irrigation systems, in the never-ending need to increase production for expanding populations.

From the Wari they also copied the practice of relocating people to exploit resources. And they adopted the Wari use

Below: An Inca chicha 'beer' jar with typical geometric decoration.

of the *quipu*, the string and knot system that served as a means of recording administrative essentials and statistics.

THE INCA MESSAGE

The Incas approached politics, social organization and art in terms of standardization and set units. While Inca standard shapes and patterns were imposed, aspects such as different colours marked regional and tribal identities.

In contrast to the intricate technology and exquisite beauty in much of the art and architecture of pre-Inca cultures, Inca art is more geometrically regular and less iconographic. Things Inca seem minimalist and utilitarian by contrast to the art of other Andean cultures. (Sadly, most Inca metalwork and sculpture, and much of their textiles and ceramics, were destroyed by the Spaniards.) Spreading their culture over newly conquered peoples was more to do with giving an impression of imposing power than imposing a new or complex symbolism. The sheer amount and bulk of Inca architecture and its road system, all of which served its bureaucratic organization and social control, was the message.

Even Inca religion was practical. In the late 14th and 15th centuries they increasingly pushed the imperial state cult of Inti, emphasizing that the Sapa Inca was

Above: To feed the huge population of the empire, the Incas made extensive terracing wherever possible to extend agricultural lands, as here at Moray near Cuzco.

the direct descendant of the sun. But they also left local religious belief in place, absorbed local belief into their own and continuously rewrote their history or left it vague with multiple versions and interpretations, to incorporate regional beliefs into the state mythology. The Incas did not challenge the obvious importance and influence of the Pachacamac oracle, but insisted on adding to the importance of the ancient pilgrimage city by building a temple to Inti there to add to the city's importance within the empire.

The imposition of Inca control was total in principal, but practical in application. As long as tribute in produced goods was paid and the labour tax obligation met, the imperial household was satisfied. They reciprocated, albeit non-symmetrically, with the redistribution of their subjects' produce such that all received what they needed.

The Incas generally improved the lives of their subjects and brought peace after their conquests, which was surely better than the continual warfare and competition over resources, both access to them and control over their movements and distribution, that had gone before.

CHAPTER FIFTEEN

BUILDING AN EMPIRE

The Inca Empire was forged in under 100 years, but the cultural development that preceded it took over 2,000 years. The Incas are recognizable archae-ologically by a distinctive artefact assemblage, artistic expressions and architecture by *c.*AD1200.

The widespread exchange of traded items and ideas from the Preceramic and Initial periods coincided with the beginnings of monumental architecture at coastal and highland sites. The occurrence of common com-modities, exotic items and artistic imagery reveals the beginnings of pan-Andean concepts that endured for the rest of Andean prehistory up to Inca times.

The Inca Empire brought a unity never before seen in the Andes over such a large area. Inca unity, however, was not based on imposed cultural uni-formity. The Incas encouraged the regional diversity among their subjects, utilizing their cultural and artistic differences. At the same time, they controlled their movements, regulated the distribution of goods and wealth within an imperial economy, and imposed an all-inclusive religious conformity. They left their subjects in no doubt as to who was in control, and that resisting imperial rule was futile.

Four major concepts underlay the ancient Andean worldview: 'collectivity', 'reciprocity', 'transformation' and 'essence'. The names are words applied by modern anthropologists, but the ideas they represent would have been instantly recog-nizable to ancient Andeans. These ideas underpin everything from the most overarching institutions to the smallest details in ancient Andean art.

Left: When the Incas took over the pilgrimage shrine at Pachacamac, they built their own Temple of the Moon there.

CULTURAL UNITY (COLLECTIVITY)

The concept of collectivity is the idea of corporate thinking. From early times, Andean cultures thought in co-operative terms. People undertook activities that required collective and co-operative efforts, and the organization necessary to achieve agreed goals. Collectivity's underlying basis is that the group is more important than the individual, and in turn that the individual is looked after by the group. The idea involved every member of society in a web of responsibility to contribute to the whole.

Early tools were probably made by most individuals, or within small family groups. As populations increased and lived together in greater numbers, however, those more skilled in different materials or tasks could specialize in them. Specialists could then exchange each other's products or efforts.

By the time of the Inca Empire, and its immediate predecessors, the presence of specialists is known from descriptions of Inca society and its kinship and state structures. Archaeological evidence of similar structures and products in earlier cultures shows Inca culture was the culmination of many earlier developments.

Above and below: Religious themes and economic interdependence spread across vast areas from high lakeland valleys such as the Lake of the Incas (above) to dry landscapes such as the Atacama Desert (below).

This recognition of signs of collective thinking means that the general idea of these cultural features can be projected back to the earliest times. Certainly, many imperial constructs of Wari and Tiwanaku civilization are evident in Inca culture.

COTTON GROWING

The earliest coastal fishing villages reliant on marine resources fostered communities in which each member contributed a part. Fishermen and shore collectors required both intra- and inter-group co-operation, and the collections of both groups were pooled and redistributed within the community.

Cotton fibre was essential for tools for exploiting the marine environment – for nets, line, traps and bags – as well as for clothing and other household items. An increased reliance on cotton, and presumably a growing population needing clothes, led to it eventually being grown as a crop, so securing more control over supply.

Preceramic Period fishing villages dotted along the Pacific coast cultivated fertile flatlands in nearby lower river valleys to grow cotton for use in textiles. Similarly, the domestication of food plants and a few animals also fostered, and must have been achieved originally by, communal effort in highland valleys. Whether common or individual, fields needed watering and tending, and the development of irrigation systems and terracing to exploit more land required collective labour and co-operative use.

Above: This Chancay textile shows several characteristics of unity: figures in a Staff Being-like stance, angular geometric patterns and a monkey figure from the rainforest.

CO-OPERATION IN ADVERSITY

Although marine resources and agricultural production could be abundant, variations in climate and weather could bring cycles of drought or El Niño events, creating times of acute stress. In addition, the general harshness of some Andean Area environments – drought and unproductive years, desert and mountain terrains, each of which had limitations as to what resources were available or could be grown there – caused chronic stress. The people had to adapt socially to meet the demands of these environmental conditions.

The storage and redistribution of food within a community, so evident in Inca society, developed much earlier to supply individual specialists with food and drink, while they supplied artistic, political and religious expertise. Communal co-operation produced sustenance, tools and clothing, and sustained spiritual needs.

MONUMENTAL CO-OPERATION

The construction of monumental architecture in the Preceramic and Initial periods shows corporate effort on another level. It reveals the existence of inequality within the social structure. When large groups of people undertake communal, labour-intensive projects, some individuals need to organize and direct the enterprise. Such leaders need to exercise power among individuals, and thus authority becomes unequally distributed.

Further, the isolated nature of early monumental complexes – for they were not residential places – suggests that they served the towns and villages of the regions around them. Their shapes – pyramidal platforms supporting holy buildings and enclosed spaces clearly meant for crowd assembly – and the artefacts associated with them – figurines and stone sculptures regarded as idols representing deities, the finest ceramics and textiles, and imported items – show that their purpose was for the worship of religious ideas and accepted deities.

Taken together, these features reveal the birth of corporate thinking within and between communities, and of religious concepts that shared widespread acceptance.

ARTISTIC COLLECTIVITY

Collectivity in ancient Andean art can be seen through a certain emphasis on sameness. The limited number of basic ceramic forms, for example, shows conservatism through time, despite details of cultural style that make it possible to identify places and times of manufacture. In all artistic media there is a de-emphasis on portraiture and individual historical detail in favour of an emphasis on common types.

Deities and the general portrayal of them reveals a similar conservatism in the use of Staff Deity figures, and serpentine, feline, severed-head and other imagery. Both real-life and supernatural imagery focuses on roles rather than on individuals, portraying acts and practices rather than specific events linked to known individuals. The detailed decorations on ceramics, textiles and metalwork often concentrate on continuous and repetitive patterning and are often abstract.

Below: The ancient shape of the kero *cup changed little from Nazca to Inca times, and geometric designs perpetuated over millennia.*

TRADE AND MUTUAL OBLIGATION

A second fundamental Andean concept, reciprocity, becomes apparent early in cultures in their long-distance trade and the care taken in burials. It is linked to collectivity in a form of partnership in social structure, economy and art.

OBSIDIAN AND WOOD
Economically, reciprocity involves the exchange of resources. Exotic materials from the highlands were sought by lowland peoples, and vice versa. The exchange of goods is well demonstrated, both archaeologically and in Inca history.

Archaeological evidence shows that reciprocal exchange between lowlands and highlands began in the Preceramic Period, starting an economic pattern that prevailed throughout Andean prehistory. The full range of early highland–lowland exchange is still unknown, but from earliest times it included raw materials, food and finished artefacts. For example, obsidian (a natural volcanic glass used to make cutting blades, scrapers and projectile points) occurs only in highland areas above 4,000m (13,000ft), yet small quantities were found at most Preceramic and Initial Period coastal sites

(e.g. Ancón, Asia, Aspero and Otuma) from at least 3000BC. The closest obsidian source to Aspero is Quispisisa in the south-central Peruvian highlands, 385km (240 miles) to the south-east.

Similarly, wooden thresholds in doorways at coastal Rio Seco were made from trees that grow in the highlands between 1,450m and 3,000m (4,800ft and 10,000ft). The strength of these exchange links is revealed by the fact that neither obsidian nor wood is essential in a coastal economy, yet they were preferred to local materials.

FROM FISH TO FEATHERS
Fish and salt were naturally lacking in the carbohydrate-dominated diet of highland peoples, yet not only are Pacific fish bones and shells found at all Preceramic highland sites with monumental public architecture, but there is also evidence of a trade in salt with coastal sites, where salt-making was carried out in large stone mortars.

Importation of thorny oyster shells both to highland and coastal sites reveals that exotic items from the fringes of the Andean Area were also sought. So, too, does the trade in tropical rainforest bird feathers, imported to highland and coastal sites across the Andes.

Maize, first domesticated in lowland river valleys, was soon found to grow from virtually sea level to 3,350m (more than 10,000ft), and so was added to the highland cuisine. Reciprocally, the discovery of potatoes, oca and ulluco (two other tubers) at some fishing villages reveals that coastal peoples also sought highland foods.

CLOTH AND IDEAS
Manufactured goods were also exchanged. Llama wool from the pampas grasslands was sought by coastal Early Horizon

Left: A Paracas culture wool poncho depicts characteristic Paracas repetitious figures, in wool imported from the llama-herding peoples of the Altiplano.

Paracas and later Nazca weavers to work with alongside cotton for mummy burial wraps. Farther north, cloth at Initial Period Galgada bears designs similar to those on textiles from coastal Huaca Prieta and Asia. And a distinctive stone bead with convex faces on both sides and two parallel drilled holes has been found at both coastal (e.g. Aspero and Bandurria) and highland (e.g. La Galgada and Huaritcoto) sites.

The exchange of objects and commodities also brought the spread of ideas. Similar artistic imagery is the principal sign of this, but the spread of maize and potato growing is another, if more mundane, example. Serpentine, feline, crustacean and avian imagery was used on gourds, ceramics and textiles from the earliest times, spreading among coastal and highland peoples and enduring through time.

KIN AND SOCIAL OBLIGATION

At the same time, the links brought by contact and trade forged personal and communal alliances. Intermarriage was

Below: A Chancay feather headdress exemplifies trade for colourful tropical birds from the eastern rainforests across the Andes to the western coasts.

Above: The early development of weaving led to trade in cotton and llama wool between lowlands and highlands (woman weaving, as depicted by Poma de Ayala, c.1615).

bound to take place, and the resultant blood ties between highland and lowland groups brought reciprocal obligations.

Kinship relations became extremely important in Andean society and are documented for the Late Intermediate Period and Late Horizon as the *ayllu* system. In Inca society the *ayllu* defined a community bound by kinship and territory. The *ayllu* social unit was also defined in political, ritual and economic terms: it could be a band of people or faction, or a state or ethnic group.

The operative force was that each member of the *ayllu* owed other members of the group, and the group as a whole, obligations in labour, food and goods, protection and social ceremony in exchanges to assure the group's cohesion and continuity. These blood relationships extended across generations.

Each *ayllu* could trace its origins back to founding ancestors, and mummified ancestors were honoured and regarded as sacred to the point of including them in community religious ritual and involving them in community decisions. On ceremonial occasions and religious festivals, the mummies were fed and consulted on agricultural and social matters.

Furthermore, there were obligatory relationships between individuals and *ayllus*, on the one

hand, and the state on the other. In Inca times this was demonstrated by the *mit'a* taxation system, a binding agreement of expected produce or labour delivered or performed by *ayllu* members for the state (in the Inca case, for the emperor and imperial household) and for the state religious organization. This dual structure meant that *ayllu* members had to cooperate in selecting some of their members to perform labours for the state, while other members performed tasks within the *ayllu*, including tasks that would have been undertaken by the missing members while on *mit'a* service.

Below: Preservation of the dead by mummification and wrapping in multiple layers of woven textiles, began the practice of ancestor worship that endured from Chinchorros and Paracas to Inca times.

LIVING IN A TRIPARTITE WORLD

Like collectivity and reciprocity, transformation and essence are also related concepts.

LEVELS OF EXISTENCE

Ancient Andeans regarded the universe and existence as consisting of multiple levels. The Inca tripartite realms of living world, world above and world below described by Spanish writers recorded a belief that began in the Preceramic and Initial periods and was shown in temple architecture. Platform mounds, temple rooms and enclosed spaces and sunken courtyards are facsimiles of this conceptual world: sky gods and earth goddesses are symbolized by pyramids and sunken enclosures. The world in which humans encounter and interact with the gods comprises the temples and ceremonial courts and plazas. All levels connected and interacted. Each was vital to the existence of the other two.

TRANSFORMATION

It is thought that processions through temple buildings were symbolic movements from the realm of the womb (the sunken courtyard) to the realm of the sky atop the platform. From the platform, or within an exclusive temple, priests were able to interact with the gods on behalf of the people, transforming the will of the gods to the world of the Earth.

Much Initial Period sculpture appears to show priestly or shamanic transformation in another way, too. As well as being a conduit between the gods and living people, shamanic trance, achieved with the aid of hallucinogenic substances, made priests vehicles between the different levels of the Andean world.

At Preceramic Huaca Prieta, a kind of transformation can be seen in the textile image of two crabs, linked by their tails on one side, and the other halves of whose tails transform into serpents. But it is in the Initial Period that Andean artisans began to

Above: Transformation is implied by the scarification and feline-like nose of this stone trophy head from Chavín de Huántar, and by its presumably drug-induced stare.

show humans in states of transformation. A mud sculpture at Moxeke depicts a caped priest emanating snakes, and painted adobe friezes at Garagay appear to depict transformation from human into insect. Condor markings on the faces of the Mina Perdida fibre figurines provide another example.

JAGUARS AND STONE WARRIORS

One of the most graphic depictions of transformation, however, is at Early Horizon Chavín de Huántar, after which sculptures and ceramic modelling frequently show humans in states of trance or midway between human and beast. At Chavín de Huántar, transformation from human to jaguar is shown in a series of sculptured stone heads on the walls of the New Temple. Other human-to-animal transformations were worked into Paracas and Nazca textiles.

The importance of the concept carried through to Inca times. At the moment of near defeat by the Chanca (traditionally dated 1438), Pachacuti Inca Yupanqui

Left: This clay model of a Moche priest in a state of prayer with joined hands (note the reciprocal hands on his headpiece) appears to be in a state of trance, probably induced by ritual chanting and drugs.

called upon field stones for help, where-upon the stones transformed themselves into warriors to secure Inca victory, then changed back. Ever after, the stones were honoured as a sacred *huaca*.

ESSENCE

Uniting the concepts of collectivity, duality and transformation, essence embodied Andean preference for 'symbolic reality' over appearance. Symbolism represented reality, even if hidden by outward appearance. It was less important for an image to be seen than for it to exist for its own sake. Whether or not it was being seen, an object existed, and, more importantly, what it represented also existed.

This idea was extended to the dismissal of the need for a human audience in some religious rituals. These took place in the

Below: Shamans were important figures in cultures through the Andean Area, depicted here in clay by Bahia culture (c.500BC–AD500), Manabi in Ecuador.

Above: The sunken court of the New Temple at Chavín de Huántar continued the tradition of large enclosures for worshippers in front of temple platforms, on which priests performed religious ceremonies.

intimate confines of exclusive temples or in hidden chambers within temple mounds, enabling priests to control what the mass of people in the plaza witnessed. Thus, what the priests said or interpreted was the essence of what it was necessary for the common populace to know. And such practices simultaneously under-scored religious control and the idea that humans formed only one part in the Andean worldview.

With exceptions in Moche art, there was little recognition of individuals; rather, even where individuals were depicted, the essence of the depiction was the action performed by the person. Individuals were only a part in the whole and were subservient to the theme of the work.

SYMBOLIC CHARACTERIZATION

The paramount importance of symbolism was that it enabled Andean craftsmen to represent the character of a deity or religious concept with features that were commonly recognized. This imagery then spread through different religious cults and endured for great periods of time. So, although cultural styles are distinguishable in different Andean areas, and from different periods of history, many common feline, avian, serpentine, arachnid,

plant and other symbols and features continued to be used from the Early to the Late Horizon.

Essence explains why Andean potters used moulds to make thousands of identical pieces, mostly restricted to a handful of shapes; why metallurgists sometimes painted over the metal, or hid base metals beneath gilding or plate; why elite individuals had their tombs filled with products made primarily for their eventual inhumation; and why weavers executed such elaborate patterns that the subject became illegible but remained true to its supernatural subject matter.

The transformation of procession along Nazca lines, too, retained the essence of its making, for it was not necessary to see the figure in its entirety at once – only to experience the symbolism and meaning of the procession. Essence also explains the seclusion of some idols within hidden chambers while others were on public display. Control of the symbolism was in the hands of the priests.

THE ANDEAN WORLDVIEW

Concepts of universality, continuity through life and death, and a cosmic cycle were all encompassed in the Andean worldview. The development of such views in some ways mirrors the actual evolution of Andean civilization.

BIRTH OF STATES

Changes in Andean society through 'horizons' and 'periods' reflect the nature of these developments through time periods characterized by cycles of greater and less political unity. Periods of political fragmentation were followed by times of political unity, then were replaced in turn by renewed fragmentation. Throughout these periods of waxing and waning political unification and break-up, however, there were certain universal developments that persisted or endured despite the political organization.

Religious concepts that developed in the Initial Period and the Early Horizon continued through centuries and millennia,

Below: Inca religion focused increasingly on the supremacy of the sun, Inti, and Viracocha. When the Incas conquered Pachacamac, they incorporated the shrine into their state religion, but demonstrated their authority by building their own Temple of the Sun there.

and formed a backbone of fundamental and universal concepts for Andean pre-Hispanic cultural development. Social structures involving relations between kinship groups and between highland and lowland peoples continued and provided a stabilizing structure that enabled society to continue at local levels, whoever ruled.

A NATURAL ANALOGUE

Nature itself seemed to comply, and perhaps suggested the idea of cycles to Andean minds. Andean peoples, even as they expanded and refined their levels of social and political organization, remained close to the landscape. This closeness is reflected in the ways in which they moulded the landscape with their irrigation systems and terracing, carved boulders into shapes mimicking the land, and regarded springs, rivers and stone formations as sacred *huacas*.

Life on the land was a repetitious cycle from one generation to another. The germination, growth and death of plants and animals and their coincidence with the seasons formed a backdrop for Andean religious philosophy. The analogy of the cycle of life from an encased, moist plant seed, to a tender young shoot, then a sturdy stem yielding its fruits, to the failing stalk

Above: Coya Mama, representing the moon, married her brother Maco Capac. 18th-century 'Cuzco School' genealogy of Inca emperors.

and, finally, withering plant seems obvious. The seasons and periodic occurrence of drought and floods, as El Niño events altered the Andean weather patterns, provided yet another analogy.

This relationship between ancient Andeans and their philosophical outlook can be called 'ecological'. Because they

Left: The Sillustani chullpas *near Puno, Lake Titicaca, were repeatedly re-opened for new mummy burials by the elite of the 13th-century Collao state.*

The long-lived oracle site of Pachacamac on the Peruvian coast represents another legendary constancy. Named after the worship of the coastal creator god, the pilgrimage centre endured for more than a thousand years, into the Late Horizon, and its ruins remain a sacred site today.

By contrast, in the ancient north coastal kingdom of Lambayeque-Sicán, Fempellec, twelfth in the dynastic succession founded by Naymlap, attempted to remove the sacred idol of Yampalec from its temple to another city. He was thwarted and executed by his priests in order to maintain political and religious continuity.

Below: Lloque Yupanqui, legendary 12th or 13th-century third Inca emperor and direct descendant in the ayllu *kinship founded by Manca Capac, depicted in an 18th-century 'Cuzco School' genealogy of Inca emperors.*

perceived their environment as sacred, they believed they were on Earth not to exploit it, but rather to enjoy its benefits through the grace of the gods. Andeans did not see themselves as the centre or focus of the world, but only as one group among all living things – including animals, plants and the stars. It was through the concessions and indulgence of the gods, who are universal and constant, that people were able to use their fellow living beings in life.

CONSCIOUS CONTINUITY

The cyclical nature and renewal of life represented continuity itself. Conscious political and social actions and decisions by Andean peoples and leaders also reflect this concept.

Ancestor worship, which appears to have begun as early as the Chinchorros and La Paloma peoples some 6,000 years ago, continued in the selection of special individuals and the attempts to bury them in a way that preserved their essence and linked them to the present. By the Late Intermediate Period and Late Horizon, the regular re-opening of *chullpas* in the Titicaca region to bring out the dead, and the special storage and inclusion of *mallquis* mummies in Chimú and Inca ceremony, had brought the association into physical presence.

The *ayllu* kinship structure and requirements of reciprocity strengthen continuity because both giver and receiver know what is required and what can be expected. Based on the worship of *ayllu* ancestors, the Inca imperial succession exemplifies the idea of continuity in being, theoretically, decided according to accepted precedence and formula.

Both the foundation of the Inca state and its succession were grounded in the legendary band of brother and sister founders, premier among whom was Manco Capac, who became first emperor. In theory, each subsequent Inca emperor was a direct descendant of Manco and his sister-wife Mama Ocllo. Significantly, at a crucial moment in Inca history, Yupanqui, son of Viracocha (eighth Inca emperor), defeated the Chanca, who threatened to conquer Cuzco when Viracocha fled the city, and took the name Pachacuti (literally 'revolution' or 'turning over or around'). The Incas themselves thus recognized both continuity of rulership and a cycle of change when Pachacuti began his reign after his father, named after the creator god, had admitted defeat. The god Viracocha, however, remained supreme in the Inca pantheon.

RELIGIOUS CONTINUITY

Perhaps the most obvious indication of Andean continuity is shown in the evolution of its religion, and is prominently visible in its art and architecture.

EARLY TRADITIONS

Early ceremonial centres, and the development of religious traditions at coastal U-shaped structures, and as complex clusters of rooms and temples on platforms in southern highland regions, show prescient Andean religious focus. They also demonstrate the establishment of architectural forms that remained in use throughout pre-Hispanic Andean civilization.

Likewise the serpentine, feline, avian and arachnid imagery so prominent in early ceramics, murals and sculpture continued to flourish regardless of political power structures. It seems that Andean consistency was lodged in its religion and expressed through artistic imagery.

CHAVÍN

The most celebrated and long-lived religious cult of pre-Hispanic Andean civilization was that of Pachacamac. The model of the Pachacamac Cult is used to characterize the Chavín Cult of the Early Horizon.

Chavín de Huántar, a relatively small U-shaped ceremonial centre established in the late Initial Period, appears unprepossessing compared to many much

Below: The long-lived pilgrimage shrine of Pachacamac, centred on the temple mound and oracle of the supreme god Pachacamac.

Above: The New Temple – the deliberately located ceremonial site of Chavín de Huántar – began the Andean tradition of universal religion and pilgrimage shrines.

larger earlier and contemporary U-shaped ceremonial complexes. Its location, however, appears to have been deliberately chosen to command routes between coastal and mountain valleys.

Chavín's success and longevity are indisputably shown by the complexity of its temples and the expense devoted to their enlargement. The New Temple, built from c.500BC, more than doubled the size of the original complex and incorporated the older parts rather than abandoning them. A second temple was built, forming a larger U-shape, and a second sunken court, this time rectangular rather than circular. The complex plazas were capable of holding 1,500 worshippers, and there is evidence that the accommodations for priests and cult artisans increased in number and area.

The spread of the cult was through its religious imagery rather than by imitating its architecture, for no such complex, labyrinthine temple interior was built anywhere else. During the half millennium from c.500BC, Chavín feline imagery spread throughout the northern and central Andes and as far south as Karwa near Paracas in the southern coastal deserts.

Chavín's principal deities formed the core of what must have been a widespread, uniform religion that transcended local political arrangements. The Staff Being became a universal image of divinity and could be either male or female. Jaguar and cayman imagery on Chavín de Huántar's monumental stone architecture and statuary reveal the reach of Chavín interests and influence, for both jaguars and caymans are rainforest animals.

Chavín's sculptural style provides the main signs of the spread of the cult, as shown by portable objects produced by its temple craftsmen and copied locally. It is fundamentally representational, employing conventions that were intentionally mystified. The principal image of the deities was reduced to a series of straight and curved lines and scrolls, and animals were portrayed in formal poses with only essential details – a process termed 'idealization'.

Above: The ritual, sunken enclosure of the Kalasasaya Temple at Tiwanaku provided a large, confined area where worshippers gathered for religious ceremonies.

The intricacy of Chavín temple architecture provided a sense of convention, unity and mystery. There was ritual use of water, an upper platform in the Lanzón idol's chamber that enabled priests to hide and act as the voice of the oracle, and a secret interior passage that permitted priests to emerge suddenly from 'nowhere' on the terrace above the Black and White Portal façade to address the crowds in the plaza.

This combination of idealized imagery and intricate construction presents a series of religious metaphors whose deep meanings were understood only by the initiated. The archaeologist John Rowe likens Chavín's visual metaphors to the literary metaphors used in Old Norse poetry. In both, 'kennings' are direct substitutes whose meaning must be learned. In use they provide mystery and unintelligibility, the understanding of which only priests can provide.

PACHACAMAC

The cult of Pachacamac was so important and powerful that its influence has survived even the colonial conversion to Christianity. Native Andeans to this day travel to the ancient site to make offerings to Pachacamac (the creator) and to Pacha Mama (earth mother). No other Andean site played such a significant role for such a long time.

The widespread influence of the Pachacamac Cult probably dates back to about 1000AD, although the site was founded some time in the 1st century AD and soon became locally influential. Inca and early colonial sources describe it in detail, revealing its longevity and acknowledging its importance and power.

The principal monuments from this period were constructed by the Ichma, who united the Lurín and Rimac valleys of the central coast. Fifteen terraced adobe platforms were raised, with great ramps leading to their summits, along the city's two main streets, running north–south and east–west.

Walls and cell-like rooms surrounded each platform compound, which provided the settings for pilgrim accommodation, public feasting and public ritual preceding consultations of the Pachacamac oracle.

UNIFYING POWERS

We know that Pachacamac was feared because the god was believed to control earthquakes. It is reasoned that Chavín deities' powers lay in control of the weather: rainfall, thunder, lightning, hail, frost and drought.

Both Chavín's and Pachacamc's influence was primarily religious. It was the power of their cults that united people throughout the Andes. The political spin was provided by the Wari and later by the Incas, who each conquered Pachacamac and used its religious prestige to enhance their imperial powers.

Below: The New Temple at Chavín de Huántar hid a labyrinth of inner rooms, and a secret stair used by priests so they could suddenly 'appear' on top of the temple.

SOCIAL AND POLITICAL EVOLUTION

Ancient Andean civilization increased in social and political complexity through time. Bands of hunter-gatherers undoubtedly had leaders, and tasks must have been divided among band members, probably partly along gender lines.

SOCIAL HIERARCHY

From the Preceramic and Initial periods, religious architecture, differential burial treatment and the importation of exotic items reveal important differences in social hierarchy. Possession of special items enhanced social prestige, increasing an individual's power and influence. Two early examples occurred at La Galgada: a single salt crystal was placed beneath the head of the female in an early burial; and a bed of large salt crystals beneath a layer of charcoal formed the base of two later Galgada burials.

Special treatment after death continued throughout Andean prehistory as ancestor worship increased in elaborateness. By the Late Horizon, mummies were regularly included in social occasions and every community had its ancestor mummies.

Below: Burial practices of the Qullasuyus as depicted in Poma de Ayala's Nueva Corónica, *c.1615.*

Above: Establishment of colonies and provincial capitals was an essential part of empire building and control, as exemplified by the regimented streets of the Wari provincial capital at Pikillacta.

CONSTRUCTIVE LEADERSHIP

Monumental architecture requires co-operation among large numbers of people, and directors. The association of differential burial and increasingly complex religious symbolism with ceremonial centres implies the emergence of rulers.

The spread of religious influence throughout large areas, especially from the Early Horizon Chavín Cult, shows the importance of inclusion, though inevitably the power of decision-making became the prerogative of some individuals over others.

In the Early Intermediate Period, coastal state organization was manifested in the Moche state and in the Nazca confederation of city-states. Individual highland city-states flourished, with shifting alliances, until greater unification came in the Middle Horizon with the rise of the Wari and Tiwanaku empires.

RELIGION AND POLITICS

Long-distance trade increased in volume and range through time, bringing tension as well as co-operation and reciprocity.

Tracking the spread of architectural, ceramic and other artefact styles helps us to trace cultural influences. The growth of the Wari and Tiwanaku empires is revealed by the presence of their distinctive ceramics and architecture as they conquered other peoples and built colonizing settlements. Wari outposts included Pikillacta, Viracochapampa, Jincamocco and Azángaros, and Wari pottery appeared at Pachacamac on the coast; a Tiwanaku lowland colony was established at Omo.

Politics and religion were never fully separate. Elaborate Paracas and Nazca burial bundles of important individuals included the cult trappings of trophy heads, while the Moche Sipán Lord burials included the costume of religious ceremonial leaders. The Inca emperor was the representative, perhaps even the incarnation, of Inti, the sun god.

INCLUSION

Organizational structures combined Andean economy, religion, society and politics alongside the unifying cultural and artistic concepts of collectivity, reciprocity, transformation and essence. The goals of Andean social and political arrangements were to secure basic stability and relative prosperity for all, guided by religious belief.

Andean civilization became grounded in state-like institutions (organized groups from across the social divisions working with understood rules of conduct); common beliefs – with powers of interpretation vested in a formal priesthood; state regulation of output; trade and the redistribution of wealth according to accepted social divisions; and state sponsorship of crafts and artistic production.

Inca inclusion of the gods of their subjects reveals the strength of Andean desire for continuity, as does their admiration for and imitation of earlier imperial structures, especially Tiwanaku and Wari. Admiring the ruins of Tiwanaku, they recognized the city and islands of the lake as sacred. They incorporated the ancient city and its beliefs into the imperial state religion, making Tiwanaku and Titicaca the womb of the universe. The official storyline became that the ancestral Inca founders came from there, sanctioned by Viracocha.

Below: The ostentatious regalia of the Moche Lord Sipán burial demonstrates the wealth accumulated by Moche rulers and the skill of their state-controlled craftsmen.

Similarly, Inca inclusiveness adopted Pachacamac, both the deity and the sacred city. Typical of Inca mastery, they acknowledged Pachacamac's antiquity, but took over the shrine, making their supremacy clear by building a temple to Inti next to the ancient temple. To them, it was important to maintain continuity, but also to demonstrate who was in charge.

INCA EXPANSION AND DECLINE

The nature of Inca expansion shows these elements in action. As one tribal state among several in the Cuzco Valley, early Inca expansion required warfare.

As their power grew, however, they employed a variety of strategies. Military conquest continued – for example, the growth of alliances in the Lucre Basin powerful enough to rival their confederation resulted in Inca conquest. In other cases, subjugation was achieved through marriage alliance, or long-established cultural affiliation with the Inca led to gradual political incorporation by the more powerful Inca. Inca interest was in control, not destruction.

An interesting twist is that at the arrival of Spaniards equally resolved on control, sibling rivalry over the imperial succession threatened its continuity internally alongside external threat.

Above: The Spaniards built their Church of Santo Domingo on the shrine of the Inca Temple of the Sun in Cuzco.

A final contributing factor in the demise of the Incas and Andean civilization was biological – the unintentional biological warfare of smallpox. From a population of about nine million in 1533, the native Andean population had been reduced to 500,000 by the early 17th century.

EVERYDAY SURVIVALS

Many fundamental Andean patterns survived the Spanish Conquest. Dietary staples remain maize, potatoes and tubers, as do ways of growing, processing and storing them. Rural markets remain essential. Weaving remains important in Andean economy, both for local consumption and, now, for tourism. Patterns persist, including designs and garments that identify regions. Pottery is still made with coils and moulds, although the art is being slowly eroded by use of plastic containers.

Finally, rural 'vernacular' architecture itself has changed little: cane thatching and adobe mud bricks are still in use, retaining ancient practical solutions to local environments.

STRUCTURE OF EMPIRE

The nature of the Inca Empire was grounded in the slowly evolving principles of earlier imperial states, especially those of Wari, Tiwanaku and Chimú. But although many Inca achievements were based on existing institutions and technologies, it was the scale of their empire that distinguished it.

INCREASE AND ELABORATION

Not only was the Inca Empire the largest in area of any empire in the New World, covering even more territory than the contemporary imperial Aztec state of Mesoamerica, but large size and scale also characterized everything the Incas did. Urban organization, buildings of large, dressed stone blocks without mortar, extensive road building, terracing and landscaping, and their complex administration and organization of textile and ceramic production and metallurgy were all sized and scaled to impress. Inca enterprises often utilized what other states had established or achieved, but they always elaborated, expanded or increased it.

Right: An Inca provincial administrator with his staff of office, depicted in Poma de Ayala's Nueva Corónica, *c.1615.*

The Incas defined their empire through physical structures imposed on the lands of their conquered provinces. The great emperors Pachacuti, Tupac Yupanqui and Huayna Capac – who expanded the empire beyond the confines of the Cuzco Valley – negotiated settlements with their subjects for the right to build roads, way stations and cities. Before embarking on military conquest, they professed friendship along with veiled threats, offering rich gifts to local rulers and the prospect of economic benefits through Inca administration. If such negotiations failed, however, Inca armies could be raised quickly and their well-organized supply systems enabled them to maintain standing armies at great distances from the capital. Inca repute was cumulative – the power and strength of organization in subject territories made the threat of conquest if non-coercive agreements failed all the more persuasive.

DIVERSITY ACCEPTED

While imposing their social regimentation, taxation system, laws and overall rule on conquered peoples, the Incas accepted the diversity of local customs. They incorporated local religious cults and deities into the state pantheon, while insisting on the overarching superiority of Inti and Viracocha. They imposed no dress codes, but allowed regional costumes to distinguish subjects and give them a sense of identity. Although Quechua was the language of administration, and became prestigious to use, they made no attempts to suppress local languages.

EFFECT ON ORDINARY SUBJECTS

The effects of the Inca Empire on ordinary lives were undoubtedly substantial, yet daily routines must have changed little.

Left: Forming the head of the crouching puma in the plan of Inca imperial Cuzco, the Sacsahuaman Temple to Inti, the sun, and fortress-weapons store emphasizes the power of Inca religion and state.

The changes were in emphasis and organization. To an ordinary subject, loyalty must have remained primarily to one's local officials. The systemization of work and the channelling of state quotas into its tripartite application (to the imperial household, the state religious establishment and the people) probably differed little in kind to the burdens of life that existed before incorporation into the empire.

Inca strength was in their brilliant and systematic organization of these matters, and in the powers of their ability to persuade populations to accept this organization, and to see the benefits it could have in times when environmental conditions and drought cycles adversely affected production, but when the state stores could then be drawn upon to redistribute goods.

Below: Inca architecture advertised Inca power, as here at the imperial palace and estate of Huayna Capac at Quispihuanca in the Urubamba Valley near Cuzco.

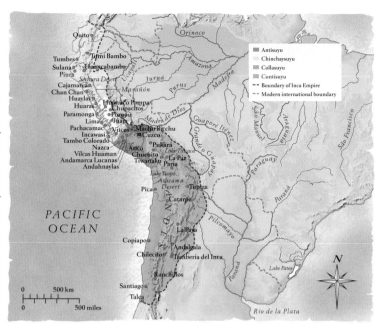

CITIES FOR STABILITY

The Late Intermediate Period was a time of political fragmentation in the highlands, although as Inca expansion began, Chimú continued the Moche and Lambayeque-Sicán succession on the north-west coast. Highland conflict punctuated the centuries from 1100 into the 15th century as El Niño weather events and consequent adverse environmental conditions led to competition for resources. The rise of the Inca Empire and its infrastructure offered resolution to this situation. Inca cities were established in response both to unsettled conditions and to the diversity of landscapes and cultures. The Incas established cities where they did not exist, to lay the foundations for rule, or altered and imposed their cultural stamp on existing cities to achieve the same result.

Their cities established a stage for pageant, spectacle and the display of wealth and power designed to win over their subjects. As ever in Andean civilization, reciprocity underlay this process, for it was a bargain. Not only was it necessary (to avoid military conquest) to gain the hearts and minds of the people, in other words their consent, but it was also

Above: Map of the Inca Empire (Tahuantinsuyu), showing the four quarters (suyus) of the empire and major Inca towns and cities.

an offer to fill their stomachs through an 'equitable' redistribution of life's necessities. People were accustomed to supporting the religious establishment, for it was an integral part of their worldview. They were also used to elite members of society – royal households and local rulers – having more. The Incas, however, offered to add stability and protection to what had been a more unstable arrangement, in return for loyalty and submission to an institutionalized labour tax (the *mit'a*).

The very name of the Inca Empire incorporates a subtlety that reveals the Andean concept of essence. Tahuantinsuyu means 'the four parts'. It was made up of a confederation of alliances, with varying degrees of loyalty, achieved through persuasion, military conquest and kinship ties through arranged marriages. The empire itself was relatively short-lived and, after decades of continuous expansion, had reached a state of civil war when the Spaniards arrived.

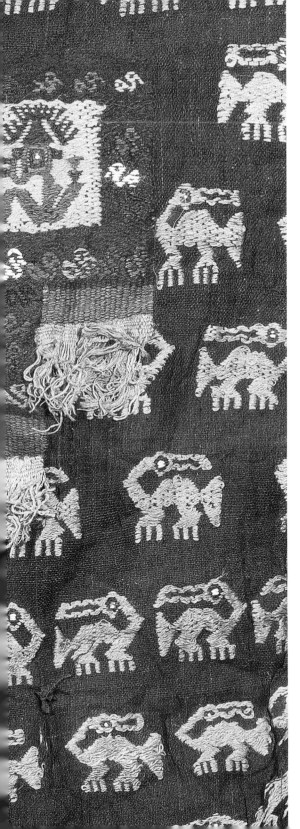

CHAPTER SIXTEEN

THE WORLD OF WORK

Work in general in the ancient Andean world was primarily a continuous routine. Tasks were repetitive and linked to the succession of the seasons.

Much of our information about the economy of the Andean world comes from the ethnohistorical record of the Incas. For pre-Inca times, including the civilizations of the Nazca, Moche, Chimú, Wari, Tiwanaku and Sicán peoples, there is an increasing body of archaeological evidence, which gives us a great amount of detail, particularly about ancient technology. The nature of monumental architecture, and even of domestic architecture, helps to project much of what we know about Inca culture into the past, particularly concerning matters of religious worship. This evidence shows us where pre-Inca cultures differed as well as enabling us to deduce that many practices were similar in pre-Inca societies.

For example, the nature of trade and agriculture in Andean civilization as early as the Initial Period indicates that forms of social organization involving kinship relationships and the divisions of society were developed very early. Similarly, religious concepts and the roles of priests and shamans endured through the centuries.

Inca culture, although distinct, inherited a long legacy of ancient developments. Inca emperors and their administrators adopted and often adapted to local conditions within the confines of their own regimented organization of administration, taxation and social regimentation.

Left: State-supported craftspeople produced exquisite textiles, such as this Chimú nobleman's tunic with its long-billed birds.

CIVIL ADMINISTRATION

We know almost no detail about exactly how pre-Inca states organized society. There were buildings clearly for religious and administrative functions, including the storage and redistribution of goods. Usually the two 'institutions' were inseparable or closely linked, and there were specialists who governed or advised the ruler and others who were priests.

BEFORE THE INCAS
From at least the Early Intermediate Period on there were states, such as the Moche Kingdom of the north-west coastal valleys. The legendary Naymlap, the conquering king following the southern Moche collapse, had a court retinue listing numerous officials: 'Preparer of the Way', 'Blower of the Shell Trumpet', 'Master of the Litter and Throne', 'Royal Cook', 'Royal Cellarer', 'Maker of Feather Garments', 'Steward of Facepaint' and 'Master of the Bath'.

Not until the Chimú Kingdom (Later Intermediate Period) and the Inca Empire (Late Horizon) do we have any records of how states were organized.

SUYUS AND PROVINCES
The Inca Empire was divided into four quarters, called *suyus*, around Cuzco. These were divided into more than 80 provinces, each with a governor. If a conquered population was large,

such as the Chimú, it was designated as a single province, while smaller groups were amalgamated to form provinces. Groups of people were also moved from one province to another to induce loyalty to the empire or as punishment for rebellion.

In theory, each province had about 20,000 households, the basic unit of Andean society (comprising several nuclear families and several generations of related kin). The state bureaucracy was organized from the province downwards, to designate the proportions of land for imperial/state, religious and common use, to collect and distribute tribute, to regulate the *mit'a* tax system, to apply the law and administer justice, and to keep the peace.

THE ADMINISTRATIVE PYRAMID
The Inca emperor was the pinnacle of the administrative pyramid. Immediately below him were four *apos* (officials) in charge of the four *suyus*. *Apos* were close advisers to the emperor, and usually relatives. A governor of each province reported to the *apo* of its *suyu*. Provincial governors were usually Incas, but local chiefs were also used, especially in lower ranks of the administration.

Each province of 20,000 households was divided into administrative units on a decimal system. Two government officials

Above: A richly painted wooden Inca kero *drinking cup showing a house and farmers with foot-ploughs and large storage jars.*

called *curacas*, each in charge of 10,000 households, reported to the governor. Each *curaca* directed five lower-ranking *curacas*, each in charge of 1,000 households; each 1,000-household *curaca* directed two *curacas* of 500 households; and, finally, each 500-household *curaca* governed five 100-household *curacas*.

The *curacas'* main responsibility was to administer the *mit'a* labour tax – to make sure that the correct number of men turned up to work Inca lands, on building projects, serve in the army, work as a craftsman or various other Inca jobs. They also needed to make sure the burden

Left: Luxurious ornaments, such as these Moche gold earrings with lapis lazuli and shell inlay depicting Moche warriors, would have been worn only by rulers and nobles.

was equitably distributed among the household *ayllus* so that none was left with too few male workers. *Curacas* also collected the state tribute and saw to its delivery into state storehouses. They allocated lands to the households (on an annual basis as household constituencies changed). Lastly, *curacas* administered Inca law. Rewards came if all was done well; punishment if not.

SOCIAL CONTROL

Mitimaes (Quechua for 'foreigners') were people brought into a newly conquered territory to replace part of the indigenous population, and conquered subjects moved to the original homeland of the new settlers. They were groups of people forcibly resettled apart from their homelands.

The practice was used in order to exercise demographic and social control, and for economic reorganization. By resettling groups of people within the empire, the Incas could redistribute

Below: A native provincial administrator confiscates a llama as tribute, depicted in Poma de Ayala's Nueva Corónica, *c.1615 – the elderly owner claims that he is not subject to tribute.*

Right: The legendary northern coastal conqueror and ruler Naymlap, who maintained a large entourage of court officials, was depicted on numerous tumi *ceremonial knives, as in this gold Chimú example.*

labour and the commodities grown and produced by different groups, while also mixing together peoples' notions of geographic identity and religious/mythological concepts.

It served two purposes. By shifting people from their place of birth, the Incas exercised control over their destiny. It provided access to new geographical zones and enabled increased production in others. For example, moving a conquered group from a herding zone to a maize-growing zone increased the land available for imperial llama herds and simultaneously provided the workers to enable increased production in the maize-growing zone.

Such a move also helped to maintain control. Rebellious people removed from their homeland weakened both the group moved and their own or neighbouring populations left behind. Equally, moved now to live among loyal subjects, they were less likely to cause trouble. In practice, *mitimaes* moves often involved both purposes, as a loyal group was exchanged for a troublesome one, thus securing the province and continuing its production.

Given Andean reverence for the landscape, removal to an alien place must have had a huge psychological impact. The transplanted group probably had a part of its *ayllu* kinship relations severed from those left behind and was forced to live among strangers whom they could not trust, away from their local deities and sacred *huacas*.

The practice also combined details in the creation myth, such that a pan-Andean/pan-Inca version was propagated.

The result bolstered and legitimized Inca claims of a right to rule – as a 'chosen' people whose divine ruler had sanction by descent from the sun god Inti or from the creator god Viracocha. The term was even used in the creation myth, when Con Tici Viracocha ordered the two survivors of the great flood, thrown up on land at Tiwanaku, to remain there as *mitimaes*.

KINSHIP TIES

The foundation of Inca society rested in kinship relations. The rules and ties of kinship were so well established by Inca times that they appear to represent the result of a long development of social and cultural relationships that began in the earliest Andean cultures. The integration of highland–lowland relationships, and the exchange of products locally and regionally, required that several economic tasks be done simultaneously.

The minimum unit that could accomplish such a balance is, theoretically, a married couple. Yet even with children old enough to help, the requirements of farming, housing, water-collecting, herding, hunting and domestic chores cannot be as efficiently accomplished by a nuclear family as they can be by a larger group. It is arguable that this led to the development of strong kinship ties within larger groups of people to distribute labour better, and to established obligations that each member of the group understood.

Above: A structure of multi-generational kinship obligations developed from early times in ancient Andean culture – Manabí terracotta models of women and children, Ecuador.

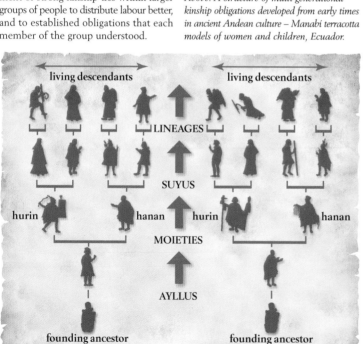

Left: Diagram of the Inca (and earlier) ayllu kinship structure, showing relationships from the founding ancestors through moiety divisions to living descendants of two ayllu collectives. There is a founding ancestor for each of many thousands of ayllus; each lineage group descends from the two moieties of that same ayllu.

AYLLU AND MOIETY

When the Spaniards arrived, Inca society was highly structured and involved a hierarchical arrangement of kinship relationships and obligations called *ayllu*. *Ayllu* comprised both community-bound kinship and territorial 'ownership'. As a social unit, it was defined in terms of economic, political and religious cohesion. As a kinship structure, *ayllu* was based on blood and marital relationships. Each *ayllu* was related back to an accepted common ancestor, a 'founder'. A single *ayllu* could comprise a band, a faction, an ethnic group or even a state.

An idealized extended kinship chart would begin at the *ayllu* level, starting with its founder or founding ancestors. Members of the *ayllu* were grouped into two halves, known by the anthropological term 'moiety'. In the Late Horizon, the Incas called the two moieties *hanan* (upper group) and *hurin* (lower group), and the peoples of each town and province were thus paired.

AN ORGANIZATIONAL CHARTER

The next grouping (or 'tie') was the *suyu*. The *suyu* was the land division assigned to a man and his family (a household), and in Inca times was also used as the fourfold division of the Inca Empire. The lineage of the *suyu* and their descendants comprised the immediate living members of the *ayllu*. In Andean belief, however, physical death was regarded as only one stage or state of being. The dead were equal participants in 'life' through

Below: The family unit was the basis of Andean society – ceramic models of a man, woman and child from the Negativo Carchi people of Ecuador.

ancestor worship, so the mummified remains of ancestors continued to be included in the social structure through ritual.

Ayllu was, therefore, not simply the organization of a group of people, property, and goods and possessions, but rather an organizational charter of relationships and obligations that enabled the tasks and problems of daily work and existence to be shared. Individually it provided a sense of belonging for *each* member and collectively it provided for the security of *all* members.

Ayllu members were not all equal, however. There were individual leaders, although their authority was limited within the obligations of the kinship arrangement. Leadership and greater authority, and indeed nobility, were hereditary. At birth an individual became ranked by his or her genealogical proximity to their *ayllu*, moiety, *suyu* and lineage founders. He or she inherited reciprocal relationships: obligations to and claims upon other members of their *ayllu* for rights, farm and pasture land, water, labour and other collective assets.

EVOLUTION OF *AYLLU*

The argument for the development of *ayllu* at an early date is twofold, based on evidence for social and economic evolution. For economic reasons, the first hunter-gatherer bands entering the Andean Area would have been small groups. Many individuals in a group would be blood-related, but there is no reason to suppose that bands did not meet and intermarry, so establishing kinship relations between groups.

In maritime Andean society, rich marine resources enabled large groups

Above: Both men and women worked in the fields – the Cocha Runa, or First Age peoples, ancestors of the Incas depicted in Poma de Ayala's Nueva Corónica, *c.1615.*

of people to live sedentary lives in seaside villages. Likewise, as plant domestication developed from the selection and tending of, first, wild plants then semi-wild plants and finally domesticated crops, people led more sedentary lives and gathered in large village settlements. Increases in food yield, aided by developments in irrigation, terraces and raised-field agriculture, enabled larger settlements, social specialization and increasingly complex social interactions. Co-operation between individuals and groups involved mutual obligations and, eventually, 'rules' to govern those obligations.

The second part of the argument is that the exchange of products and ideas across geographical zones, as shown in archaeological findings, inevitably included the movement of people from valley to valley and between highlands and lowlands. It seems equally inevitable, therefore, that there would have been intermarriage among people of different zones. These associations were presumably freely entered into in times of peace. Competition for resources, bringing warfare and conquest, would no doubt have resulted in forced unions as well, either by capture and rape or as a result of peace negotiations. Either way, blood relations and kinship ties would be established.

TAXATION AND LABOUR

The fundamental Andean 'capital' was labour. Kinship obligations were enshrined in reciprocity: acceptance that something rendered required a return of equal kind or value, called *mit'a* (Quechua) and *ayni* (Aymara). The concept applied both to *ayllu* relationships and the relationship between the Inca state and its subjects. Like *ayllu*, the concept was of pre-Inca origin; Chimú society was similarly arranged.

Mit'a and *ayni* gave each household access to more labour than it could muster from its own members. *Ayllu* obligations from brothers, sisters, their children, in-laws, nieces and nephews were available for labour exchange under reciprocal obligations, enabling everything from house building to canal construction and maintenance, farming and herding to be achieved. For example, farming tasks were done by *ayllu* teams, plot by household plot. Sometimes repayment was in equal value rather than in kind, such as food for labour. The Incas formalized the *ayllu* social structure into a state institution.

LAND DIVISIONS
Land was divided into three parts: to support the gods, to support the emperor and his household and to support the local community. As the emperor was considered divine, the first two categories were both under his control. Their yields supported

priests, shrine attendants and other religious functionaries, and were stored for use in religious ritual and ancestor veneration on appropriate holy days; produce from imperial land was conspicuously stored against future needs in warehouses at provincial capitals.

Left: Terracing and numerous storehouses represent Inca control, and state produce and redistribution – imperial largesse – at the royal estate of Machu Picchu.

Above: The higher one ranked in Inca society the richer one could afford to dress – an Inca elite tunic depicting intricately woven geometric patterns, felines and plants.

Community land was divided into plots and assigned to *ayllus* and households by local *curacas*. Assignment was done annually, so that the proportions allotted could be changed to meet households' changing needs. A similar threefold division was also applied to Altiplano pastureland.

INCA AND PRE-INCA TAXES

The Incas exploited their subjects' sense of reciprocal obligation for state tax purposes. Tax in labour was extracted from both men and women, but labour tax on the two state-owned land divisions applied only to men. This was an annual draft of labour gangs from the *ayllus* and involved work on divine and imperial lands: agriculture and herding, imperial construction projects, military service, transporting goods from state storehouses, or being a runner in the imperial postal service.

We have no pre-Inca records of *mit'a* labour, but archaeologically recognized responses to periodic drought throughout Andean history indicate that *ayllu* and *mit'a* organization was practised and applied across geographical zones. For example, through centuries of lowland drought, *c*.AD1100–1450, the focus of intensive cultivation was gradually shifted from lower, warmer elevations to higher, cooler ones with sufficient rainfall, and to the better-watered eastern Andean slopes. Similarly, on a site scale, the marked adobe bricks of the Huaca del Sol

Below: An imperial Inca accountant with his quipu *record of produce and goods for redistribution, from Poma de Ayala (c.1615).*

pyramid at Middle Horizon Moche show that individual community labour gangs completed different sections.

Another form of state taxation involved textiles. Like reciprocation in textiles within *ayllu* exchange, the value of textiles, calculated in labour, was in effect also a labour tax. Both men and women rendered tribute in cloth production to local governors and to the imperial state. Specified quantities of fibre, wool and cotton were distributed annually, from which men made cordage and rope, and women made cloth. The former was stored and used for all sorts of containers (for example for llama sacks for imperial trade caravans), and for bridge making. Cloth, also stored, was used for the priesthood and the imperial household, as gifts to conquered rulers turned imperial governors, for army kit and for redistribution among communities according to need.

IMPERIAL OBLIGATIONS

Imperial Inca taxation brought vast revenues into state storehouses. The elite proportion of the population that was permanently subsidized by the system was perhaps 10 per cent. There were the higher-ranking decision makers and the lower-ranking implementers of state institutions and projects. The contribution of the first group was, of course, to govern and to preside over religious ritual. They ranged from local to state priests and other religious persons, to local and higher

Above: A symbol of Inca power – a kancha *storehouse (reconstructed) at the imperial provincial estate and administrative centre of Ollantaytambo in the Urubamba Valley.*

governors and administrators, to conquered royal households, and finally to the imperial household itself.

The second rank comprised individuals who were subsidized because their occupations and technical expertise employed them in non-subsistence jobs. These were the state accountants and historians (the *quipucamayoqs* and *amautas*), agronomists, hydrologists, architects, engineers, surveyors and all the specialist craftspeople employed by the state to produce metalwork, ceramics, masonry, gemstones and woodwork required for the imperial and other ruling households. Some of this production was purely and solely for the cults of the dead.

The distribution of goods from imperial storehouses was not one-directional. The entrenched concept of reciprocity meant that the state also realized and accepted its obligations. The use of state stores was critical to a mutually beneficial relationship between ruler and ruled. Holy days and special days were liberally supplied from the state storehouses with food and drink. Crop failures and other hard times brought by natural disaster could be alleviated through redistribution, according to rank and need, by the state of the goods produced by common labour.

TRADE AND ECONOMY

Neither the Incas nor any pre-Inca culture practised a monetary economy. There was no standard value system with a currency of fixed denominations. There was undoubtedly a sense of value in terms of prized metals, and derived from the efforts to procure commodities, but otherwise value was based on the relative worth of one object or commodity against another, on scarcity, environmental conditions and their effects on annual production, on distance and on the recognized labour involved in production.

ANDEAN VALUES

Even regarding precious metals, it is difficult to understand completely the Inca sense of their value as a contemporary European would have valued them. Metals were mixed, and sometimes the precious metal, say gold, was only a veneer over base metal, making the object appear gold even though it was not pure. This Andean concept of essence – the

Below: These Chimú kero *drinking cups are of gold inlaid with turquoise.*

appearance of an object (what it represented) being more important than the actual substance – is alien to Western ideas of value. Sometimes the precious metal itself was covered in paint.

Moche-Sipán and Lambayeque-Sicán elite burials show that precious objects were lavished on individuals in tombs, showing some sense of the intrinsic worth of precious metal objects on their own merit and as special pieces. Exquisite textiles and ceramics were made by the Nazca and other cultures, not as valued items in this life but as provision, as valued offerings, in the next. Their use was for the deceased in the next phase of their existence. The objects were made specifically for the tomb, and thus not for use until after death. Similarly, the real value of precious metal objects was as offerings to the gods. Their exchange rate was measured in rain to water crops, against a good sea harvest and for protection through appeasement against natural disasters such as earthquakes, flooding or drought, and for the general wellbeing of the people.

Above: Inca state control of textile production and trade can be traced back in Andean history to the earliest times – a Wari tunic of wool and cotton, whose fibres were exchanged between highland and coastal producers.

Textiles were especially valued, and the value of different qualities of textiles was well understood in terms of the labour involved to produce them. In Inca times textiles were the nearest Andean concept to 'coinage', and because their value was understood in terms of labour they were, in effect, reciprocal labour for labour. Because cloth was so highly valued in Andean cultures, it was used by the Incas in a similar way to currency. Regular allocations of cloth were given to army units and it was 'paid' as a reward for government services. Whether textiles were used in this way by any pre-Inca cultures is not known.

STATE-CONTROLLED TRADE

Many commodities were under state control, in terms of control of their production, for example coca growing, or in terms of state redistribution of commodities among the populace. There was also much production under state-commissioned enterprise or industry to provide ceramics, textiles, metal objects and even wooden drinking cups for the extended royal household and government officials and their

households. There were also mass-produced everyday goods, such as eating platters, for feeding *mit'a* labourers.

There was undoubtedly a sense of more highly and less highly regarded objects. No commoner in the Inca Empire used the highly carved and painted *kero* cups that were used by members of the royal household, or wore the sort of precious jewellery worn by elite members of society.

Trade between regions in the Late Horizon was state controlled. How far back into pre-Inca times such state control of trade was practised is hard to ascertain. Yet it seems logical that Inca practices were not late inventions. Rather, the institutionalization of regional trade must have been developed in earlier empires and their societies, such as Tiwanaku and Wari in the Middle Horizon, and by the Early Intermediate Period Moche states and the Kingdom of Chimú in the Late Intermediate Period, in the same area. A major reason for the rise of regional kingdoms was competition for control over resources.

In the Inca state no individual, apart from the emperor, owned land. By imperial decree, all land in the empire

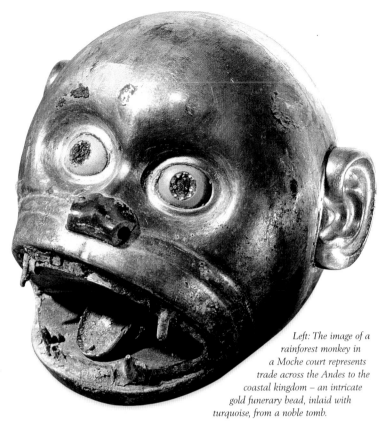

Left: The image of a rainforest monkey in a Moche court represents trade across the Andes to the coastal kingdom – an intricate gold funerary bead, inlaid with turquoise, from a noble tomb.

Below: Transport in ancient Andean cultures was done on the backs of llamas – useless as draught animals, in mountain terrain, carrying side pouches, they were the ideal caravan animals for Andean trade.

belonged to the reigning Sapa Inca. The early development of agriculture throughout the Andean Area shows communal effort for survival.

Irrigation structures had to serve everyone and could not be built piecemeal by individuals. Water, whether it came from rivers whose ultimate source was in the distant mountains or from local rainfall, had to be redistributed from a common source across the landscape to fields, or had to be pooled and moved about among extended terracing and raised fields.

Individuals had rights to work the land but not to sell it. Land was owned by, or its use granted to, the *ayllu* kinship groups.

Individual ownership was limited to personal tools and objects – household tools, ceramics, personal clothing and jewellery – procured through barter or acquired as gifts.

BARTER

Local economies were based on local produce from the communal third land division. Goods were exchanged by barter, redistributed according to need and *ayllu* kinship obligation among households, and exchanged in local markets within and between communities. In bartering between individuals, worth was relative and open to negotiation at the time of exchange.

The ancient use of llama caravans confirms the pre-Inca existence of merchants to move goods between regions. Perhaps the Andean development of such strong *ayllu* kinship reciprocity made the need for a monetary system unnecessary. Where goods from one region to another were available under obligatory exchanges between extended relations, there would have been no need to 'buy' things in the Western sense. Local markets continue to be an endemic part of the Andean economy today.

ANDEAN AND INCA ROADS

Roads and trade routes were part of Andean civilization from early times. The spread of religious ideas and the exchange of highland and lowland commodities obviate the use of established routes. Until the Late Intermediate Period and Late Horizon, however, there is less archaeological evidence.

Water transport was also important. While steep mountain streams were unnavigable, the lower reaches of western coastal rivers were. The sea provided the fastest transport, along the coast between Pacific valleys, and boats criss-crossed Lake Titicaca between cities around its shores. Pizarro's second expedition to South America encountered Inca trading vessels from Tumbes off the north-west coast when he approached the northern border of the empire.

Roads and streets defined city and town plans. Roads from outlying residential areas focused on ceremonial precincts. For example, Nazca settlements were linked by straight routes across intervening desert (for example, from the

Below: The Inca road network was expanded from earlier Middle Horizon roads of the Wari and Tiwanaku empires – spanning seemingly impassable gorges with rope bridges.

ceremonial 'city' of Cahuachi to the 'capital' of Ventilla), and Wari settlements featured regular street grids. Anthony Aveni has described many similarities between the Inca road system and the Nazca lines across long distances.

LIFELINE OF THE EMPIRE
The Inca road system was the lifeline of the empire. Its core was based on earlier established routes. Inca roads connected many former Wari and Tiwanaku Middle Horizon cities and former Wari way stations. The Wari Empire was the first to use its road system for state control. Likewise, the Chimú road system was taken over and improved by the Incas.

Inca roads varied between extremes, from formally constructed, paved roads to narrow paths. John Hyslop has identified and traced more than 23,000km (14,300 miles) of Inca roads, and estimates that the entire Inca system totalled as many as 40,000km (25,000 miles). A main highland route ran along the Andean spine from Cuzco to Quito in northernmost Chinchaysuyu; later, an extension ran into modern Colombia. A second 'trunk' road went south, through north-west Argentina and Chile, from

Above: The Rumicolca route was the entrance to imperial Inca Cuzco, through which royal and noble parties and trader goods entered the city.

Cuzco beyond modern Santiago. Two branches circumnavigated Lake Titicaca and rejoined south of it.

A parallel route ran along the coast, tracing a route from Santiago, across the southern deserts, north-west to the pilgrimage city of Pachacamac, then hugged the mouths of north-west coastal valleys before turning inland to skirt the Sechura Desert. After returning to the coast, it looped back inland to Tumibamba to join the highland route to Quito.

Between trunk routes, roads connected major Inca towns and cities, with as many as 1,000 *tambos* (way stations) along them between cities. Several roads also linked the two major roads at intervals, facilitating highland–lowland trade along ancient routes.

CONSTRUCTION
Difficult terrain was avoided whenever possible. Roads followed the lie of the land, staying below high altitudes by traversing mountain passes and skirting

swamps and deserts. The wheel was unknown in Andean civilization, and the llama is intractable as a draught animal, so apart from litters to carry Inca and other elites, there were no vehicles. Thus road shapes could be adapted to the terrain. Travel was on foot and transport was by load-bearing llama caravans.

Widths of Inca roads varied between *c*.1m and 25m (*c*.3ft and 82ft), sometimes even wider. Mountain roads were narrow, while coastal roads were normally wider and straighter. Although natural contours were followed, the Incas were remarkable for coping when the shorter route was desired or when they encountered what might seem insurmountable obstacles or chasms. Some roads took direct routes, ascending steep slopes, while others used zigzags to lessen the angle of ascent.

Mountain roads often followed cliff faces, and Inca rope suspension bridges spanned deep chasms, anchored at either end with wood or stone superstructures on stone footings. Constant use required frequent repair, yet some Inca bridges were still in use in the 19th century. In a

Below: The Chaka Suyuyuq, *Governor of Bridges, was an important Inca state official, shown here inspecting a rope bridge in Poma de Ayala's* Nueva Corónica, *c.1615.*

few cases, natural stone bridges were used. In other cases, for example at Lake Titicaca, there were reed pontoons across rivers, sections of lake and wet ground, and sometimes travellers were carried across rivers in baskets on cables. There were also river ferries of balsa wood, reed and gourd-float rafts.

Coastal roads were frequently defined by low stone or mud-brick walls, especially to keep desert sands from encroaching, or by rows of wooden posts or stone markers. Side walls lined routes across agricultural lands, and stone pavements formed causeways and canals across wetlands.

TRAVEL

Settlements and *tambos* along the roads served for lodgings and storage. They varied in size according to need, and also often served as seats of local administration. Large *tambos* were located in towns, while smaller ones were sited, theoretically, at intervals of a day's journey apart (in reality they were anywhere from a few hours' walk to a long day's march).

Traders drove llama caravans to transport exotic items between highlands and lowlands and along the coast, but day-to-day necessities were obtained in local barter and by imperial redistribution from provincial stores. General touring was infrequent, except for religious pilgrimage (most likely undertaken by designated representatives, i.e. religious leaders).

Above: The Puyupatamarca way station ruins are one of many along the 'Inca Trail' to Machu Picchu.

Religious processions travelled along the *ceque* system, feeding into the roads to and from the provincial capitals for hostage-holding and sacrificial victims.

IMPERIAL COMMUNICATIONS

Inca roads were a means of control, meant to impress subject peoples with Inca power. They were used to move the army from province to province, to move groups of people (*mitimaes*) among the provinces and for royal pilgrimage. Imperial permission was required to travel on official roads.

Imperial communications between the capital and administrative cities was conducted by a system of runners. Roughly every 1.6km (1 mile) along the major roads, huts were built on either side of the route to shelter a *chasqui* messenger. As a runner approached a hut, he called out and the waiting messenger joined him as he ran. The message was relayed orally and perhaps a *quipu* was passed, after which the fresh messenger ran as fast as possible to the next hut. Messages could be relayed *c*.240km (150 miles) a day in this way; a message could reach Lima on the coast from Cuzco in three days. Each runner served a 15-day rotation and the service was part of the *mit'a* labour obligation.

FARMING, HERDING AND HUNTING

The Andean Area is one of several prime areas in the world where peoples observed and learned to control the cycles of natural plant and animal reproduction, thus domesticating a selection of plants and animals and basing their subsistence on them. Throughout ancient times, subsistence agriculture was supplemented by hunting, fishing and collecting wild animals and plants.

From the Early Horizon the bulk of ancient Andean economy was based on agriculture and llama herding. Hunting, fishing and collecting formed important parts of the economy and were more important in earlier times than later.

Hunting became less important because the staple diet was fixed on the principal food crops, and gradually became the sport of the elite. Fishing on Lake Titicaca remained important for the cultures of the Titicaca Basin and on Lake Poopó to the south. The annual sardine and anchovy runs in the Humboldt Current and the migrations of sea mammals provided important protein sources in the diets of coastal cultures throughout Andean history (and still do).

Below: The other protein and vitamin plant food of ancient Andeans was maize. It was first domesticated in Mesoamerica and its cultivation eventually diffused through to South American ancient cultures.

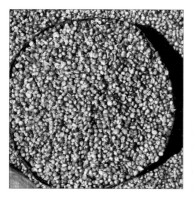

Above: Potatoes were an essential source of carbohydrates and vitamins for Andean peoples, from the collection of wild potato tubers through to their domestication in the Preceramic Period. In winter they were freeze-dried and stored.

Alongside agriculture were the state-organized industries such as textile, ceramic and metal production.

EDIBLE PLANTS

By Inca times a considerable variety of plants and animals was grown, herded and hunted. Principal as a subsistence crop was maize. It was grown both as the staple proportion of dietary intake and for the production of *chicha* beer, used both as a general drink in its weaker form and as an important libation in religious ritual in stronger form.

Other plants were more regional and included potatoes and other tubers (oca and ullucu) in more highland zones, low-altitude tubers such as manioc and yuca, mashwa (a higher-altitude tuber), the high-protein grain quinoa, a variety of beans and also squashes, sweet potatoes, tomatoes, chilli peppers, avocados and peanuts.

Non-edible plants cultivated and/or harvested included coca, cotton, gourds for containers and reeds and fibres for construction and basketry and containers. Tobacco was also grown for medicinal and ritual use. After the earliest phases of domestication, the distribution of these crop plants was primarily altitudinal.

Many plants could be grown in a range roughly from a few metres or yards above sea level to about 1,000m (3,300ft). Others – one variety of chilli pepper, a variety of squash, coca, cotton, gourds, oca, the avocado – were grown in a mid-range zone of about 300–400m (985–1,310ft) above sea level to 1,000–1,500m (3,300–4,920ft). Still others had a much wider range, such as quinoa (28–3,878m/92–12,720ft), the common bean (2–3,700m/6½–12,140ft), potatoes (2–3,830m/6½–12,565ft) and maize (2–3,350m/6½–10,990ft); or a more restricted high-altitude extreme, such as ulluco (an edible tuber, 3,700–3,830m/12,180–12,560ft) and mashwa (850–3,700m /2,788–12,140ft).

Collected plants included wild fruits and many herbs for medicinal and ritual purposes. Eastern forest and tropical hallucinogenic mushrooms were, like

Below: Chilli peppers, first domesticated in the coastal lowlands, added flavour to the staple Andean diet of maize and potatoes.

tropical feathers, traded into the Andean Area. The San Pedro cactus was harvested for its buttons, which are a rich source of hallucinogenic mescaline.

DOMESTICATED ANIMALS

Ancient Andeans domesticated only a few species of animals. The principal herded animals were the llama and the alpaca, both New World camelids. In addition to these, guinea pigs and ducks were bred

Left: So important was maize that it was even rendered in silver by imperial craftsmen. It was both secular, as essential food, and sacred, used to make chicha *beer for consumption in religious festivals.*

in captivity or semi-captivity for meat. Dogs were pets and hunting companions, though were also bred for meat.

Herds of llamas and alpacas were kept throughout the highlands, but formed an especially important part of the Altiplano economy of the Titicaca Basin and to the south of it. Here, vast herds were kept and their needs controlled the rhythm of life. The llama and alpaca were kept principally for their wool and as pack animals, but they also provided meat and sacrificial animals, and their bones were used to make into tools.

HUNTING AND FISHING

Hunted land animals were principally deer and the guanaco (the wild camelid from which the llama was domesticated). The fourth New World camelid, the vicuña, was semi-domesticated – herds were trapped, sheared for their extremely soft wool, and released back into the mountains. Wild birds, both coastal and mountain, were also taken, especially eastern tropical rainforest birds for their colourful feathers, although these were mostly bartered for rather than collected directly.

Fishing and shellfish collection supplemented most coastal people's diets, and surpassed agriculture as the main dietary sources in rich coastal areas in earlier periods. Anchovies and sardines were staples in coastal cultures. Sea mammals, especially seals and sea lions, were also hunted. In addition, there were crabs and a wide variety of shellfish. Shellfish were traded to high altitudes in small amounts, and in Inca times fresh seafood was brought to the emperor in a matter of a day or two by *chasqui* runners. Peoples of the Titicaca Basin made extensive use of freshwater fishing.

Above: Maize planting in September, Quya Raymi Killa *or month of the feast of the moon, depicted in Poma de Ayala's* Nueva Corónica, *c.1615.*

COMMUNAL FARMING

In Inca times, agricultural work was separated into repetitive, modular tasks that could be undertaken in succession in the various plots held by individual households. It seems logical to assume that such practices were pre-Inca, although in the various earliest cultures it is uncertain how communal agricultural practices were.

The evidence for communal activities, revealed in monumental architecture, increases at sites in the later Preceramic Period and especially in the Initial Period. It can be argued, therefore, that if labour forces were marshalled for work on building projects, this must have resulted in a division of labour between farmers and builders by which the latter were fed by the former. Alternatively, building projects might have been undertaken during slacker periods of the agricultural year. Even so, communal efforts in architecture may indicate the same for agriculture.

In Preceramic and Initial Period coastal societies, farming in the valleys was separate from the rich fishing and foreshore shellfish collection. However, the two communities obviously needed to co-operate on a communal basis, especially for the cotton fibre that was essential for fishing nets and other tools.

Above: Fishing, both in lakes and off the western coast provided essential protein in the Andean diet from the earliest times – Moche pot of a man fishing with a line and bait.

IRRIGATION AGRICULTURE

As populations increased, the richest lands for run-off water agriculture in coastal valleys and rainfall agriculture in the sierra were brought into cultivation. The need for more land surface for growing became acute in coastal plains, mountain valleys and in the Titicaca Basin. To bring water to land farther and farther from rivers, or to channel it from hillsides to mountain valley fields, prompted the invention of irrigation systems. The communal labour foundations of farming, of labour division in societies practising mixed farming and herding economies and of monument building were utilized in building and maintaining canals and required the development of strict rules of access, probably including designated 'officials' to regulate quantities and timing of access to water.

Competition for water and land frequently caused conflict, sometimes leading to open warfare, of which there is ample evidence during some periods of ancient Andean history. Prolonged periods of drought were especially stressful, and caused conflict and population movements.

TERRACING AND RAISED FIELDS

Increasing the amount of land available for crops was achieved in two ways: terracing and raised fields. The steep sides of mountain valleys and the slopes of lower river valleys were modified to create elaborate systems of terracing, often to the point where some terrace 'fields' were only about 1m (3ft) wide. The Inca are famous for their extensive

Right: A Moche pot showing two men fishing from a reed raft with a chicha *beer jar placed between them.*

terracing, which was necessary to feed a growing population and to provide food for the storehouses as insurance against drought years. The co-operative effort required to build and maintain terraces, and to collect and channel rainwater to them, shows high levels of communal organization, which, as with most such practices, were intensified and formalized by the Inca in their *mit'a* labour tax structure.

The same co-operative efforts were required in draining marshlands by digging canals using wooden digging sticks and spades between plots of raised fields – raised with the soil from the channels. Extensive systems of raised-field agriculture surrounded cities in the Titicaca Basin especially. In drought times, when the water level fell, raised fields had to be abandoned, causing population shifts and even the abandonment of cities in the basin.

Ancient Andean fields were fertilized from two principal sources, depending on location: llama dung was the main source of rejuvenating soil nutrients in the sierra and Altiplano, while coastal peoples collected huge amounts of seabird guano from offshore islands to bring to their valley fields. Fish fertilizer was also used by coastal and lake peoples.

The tools of agriculture were primarily wood, stone and base metal implements. Andean peoples possessed no draught animals, but the llama was used as a pack animal as well as for its wool and meat. Agricultural fields were prepared and sown using three simple tools: a foot-plough, a wooden club and a slicing-hoe. The foot-plough was used to break the soil's surface and turn the ploughed chunks of earth. The wooden club was used to break up the clods into finer soil. Further soil breaking, weeding and tending the crops after planting was done using the slicing-hoe, which had a blade parallel to the wooden handle.

Planting was by hand, as was harvesting. Both men and women worked the fields, especially in non-Inca cultures.

HUNTING AND FISHING

Ancient Andean hunting was done with spears and the *atl-atl* – a stick with a notched end into which the butt of the spear was rested while the other end was held along with the spear shaft. Use of the *atl-atl* greatly extended the distance and power of the weapon when thrown. The bolas (leather strips with stones tied at the ends) was also used; it was thrown so that it wrapped itself around the prey's legs and brought it down for dispatching with spear, club or knife. Birds were also taken with the bolas, and with slings and snares. The bow and arrow was not an Inca weapon, but was used by semi-tropical and tropical peoples.

Fishing was done primarily with nets thrown from small boats, including single-man reed craft on which a fisherman sat astride. Sea mammals were hunted with spears and harpoons 'riding' such craft. Many Moche ceramic pieces depict seal hunts and sea fishing with nets.

Below: The coast at Quebrada la Vaca, near Chala, where the Incas caught fish.

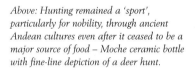

Above: Hunting remained a 'sport', particularly for nobility, through ancient Andean cultures even after it ceased to be a major source of food – Moche ceramic bottle with fine-line depiction of a deer hunt.

INCA FARMING

In Inca agriculture, ploughing, planting and harvesting were done by the assembled workforce plot by plot, but each couple in the force worked designated segments or rows in the plot. This practice of segmentation of labour kept the service rendered and thus the obligational returned service clearly defined. Similarly, if several *ayllu* kinship groups worked on a canal-building project, although each built and maintained a designated section, the entire canal gave benefit to the whole community of fields for which it was built.

CRAFT AND CRAFT WORKERS

Specialized craftsmen and women were among the subsidized people of the Inca Empire. Archaeological evidence that some of the best, finest and most elaborate metalwork, textiles and ceramics were produced especially for burials shows that specialists had been employed by pre-Inca states as well, such as the Moche, Nazca, Wari and Tiwanaku, Lambayeque-Sicán and Chimú. Weaving, ceramic and metalworking compounds have been excavated at sites of these cultures and of the Inca.

Other specialized craftspeople included workers in stone (both masons and gemstone artists), feather workers, and carvers of shell, bone and wood (who made, especially, the decorated *kero* cups for *chicha* beer drinking).

VALUED SPECIALISTS

There was a variety of crafts and a high degree of distinction and expertise within crafts. The fact that craftspeople were

Below: This decorated Moche dish rim depicts a scene of two weavers, possibly a mother teaching her daughter to weave, as well as Moche potters' skill in fine-line decoration.

subsidized highlights their valued places in Inca and pre-Inca societies. Cloth and other crafted goods could be given in exchange within *ayllu* kinship *mit'a* and *ayni* exchange obligations.

WEAVING AND WEAVERS

Weaving was a premier specialized craft from very early times. Textiles preserved in Paracas and Nazca graves reveal the use of intricate patterns, depictions of deities and narrative scenes, and numerous colours, showing the care with which they were made. The numerous layers of mummy bundles demonstrate their importance. Many pieces were included in the mummy wrap before being finished – a clear indication that the pieces were planned specifically for burial and were begun well in advance, most likely when the person was in good health.

Weaving was specifically a female craft, although men worked rougher fibres into cord and rope for more utilitarian uses. In Inca times all women wove, from the common women subjects of the empire, through women of elite households, to the wives of the emperor. For commoners,

Above: From its invention, weaving remained an essential task throughout life – an old woman weaving on a backstrap loom, depicted in Poma de Ayala's Nueva Corónica, *c.1615.*

weaving was a craft and hallmark of femininity in which a woman took pride in clothing her family; to the elite, weaving was a symbolic demonstration of femininity, rather than a necessity. Textile production occupied more people and labour than any other Inca craft, and in intensity of labour was probably surpassed only by agriculture.

CERAMICS AND POTTERS

Pottery, once established and spread among ancient Andean cultures, replaced much of the early roles of rough fibres and gourds for containers, although never completely. Beyond its basic role for practical purposes of storage and cooking (the pots for which were homemade, unspecialized and often plain), ceramics soon became more and more elaborate. Pottery began to serve more than just as containers and took on roles within ritual and burial and as an indication of social rank. Some pots must also have had no purpose other than ornament. At the same time, some pottery simultaneously served, consciously or otherwise, as a record of culture by depicting mythological scenes and scenes of daily life as well as holding liquids and food.

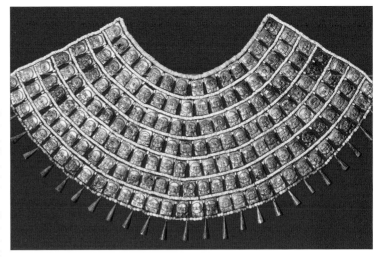

Such increased complexity of design, decoration and use fostered the existence of dedicated potters who could be supplied with food, accommodation and clothing by other members of society. The Incas, and perhaps earlier empires such as Wari and Chimú, established communities of potters specifically to supply uniform vessels. The plates and large, pointed-based, long-necked storage jars used by the Incas in their storehouses to distribute food and drink to *mit'a* workers were uniformly decorated so that there could be no doubt as to the source of the hospitality.

The exquisite craftsmanship of Moche pottery has always stood out among Andean wares. Not only are Moche ceramics a source of narrative information through scene painting on red-on-cream vessels, but also many Moche ceramic

Below: Finely woven Paracas wool textiles in southern coastal Peru reveal trade for Altiplano wool and depict ritual decapitation for the cult of trophy heads. Their complexity and use as mummy wraps involved their preparation through one's lifetime.

pieces are clearly portraiture and depictions of specific rituals, including shamanism, animalistic transformation, healing, combat and sexual acts.

METALLURGY AND METALLURGISTS

A third premier craft in ancient Andean society was metalworking. Exquisite, elite gold, silver, copper and alloy pieces were made from Paracas and Nazca times. Metalworkers flourished in Moche culture and later in the Lambayeque-Sicán and Chimú states – all three successive cultures in the north-west coastal valleys.

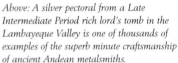

Above: A silver pectoral from a Late Intermediate Period rich lord's tomb in the Lambayeque Valley is one of thousands of examples of the superb minute craftsmanship of ancient Andean metalsmiths.

This is perhaps not surprising, as they are geographically the closest to the areas in modern-day Colombia and Ecuador where the earliest, and most elaborate, metallurgy in the Americas developed.

Gold and silver were used extensively, both by the Incas and pre-Inca peoples. These metals were used exclusively for luxury jewellery and ritual objects. They were used both pure and as gilding and plate, and in some cases were even covered with paint. Many specialist pieces, for example gold and silver llama figurines, were made especially for burial with a sacrificial victim. Among the Incas, gold and silver were restricted to use by the nobility. Commoners could use only copper or bronze (a copper and tin, or arsenic, alloy), but the craftsmanship involved in the manufacture of such base-metal objects was no less skilled.

Copper was made into items of personal adornment, such as pins to fasten clothing, pendants, earrings, bracelets and armlets; also for sheet-copper burial masks and for *tumi*, crescent-shaped sacrificial knives. Copper is too soft for tools, so in addition to jewellery, bronze was used to make axes, knives, chisels, pins and tweezers, and the heads for war clubs.

MILITARY SERVICE AND WARFARE

We know little of the pre-Inca armies, except that they were successful in conquering and controlling large areas. The Moche were particularly warlike; the Naymlap legend may be an Early Intermediate folk memory of the invasion of the Lambayeque Valley, establishing the late Moche dynasty by conquest.

EARLY CONFLICT

Early warfare is depicted in stone and ceramics. The more than 300 carved slabs at Initial Period Cerro Sechín have been interpreted as a war memorial. The large slabs, which constitute about 7 per cent of the total slabs, portray a procession of triumphant warriors wearing pillbox hats and loincloths, and carrying staffs and darts. Other slabs show the disembodied remains of the vanquished, and at least one warrior has a decapitated head dangling from his waist. Two slabs carved with banners flank the compound's central gateway.

Are these sculptures evidence of small-scale, seasonal raiding between towns? Or are they commemorating

a great historical victory, or a symbolic battle, rather than a specific event? Another view argues that the scene is an elaborate hallucinogenic ritual. One slab depicts toad eggs (representing toads known to carry hallucinogens?). Disembodiment is typical of Andean hallucinogenic transformation.

Cerro Sechín dates to the beginnings of Andean civilized society, when towns were becoming cities, and their locations and spacing across the landscape imply conflict and equidistant positioning in competition for resources, especially water. Early Intermediate Period Nazca pots show battle scenes – complex depictions of intertwined warriors in chaotic mêlées.

RITUAL COMBAT

Moche battle scenes usually depict pairs of warriors, both Moche. They are thought to depict ritual combat rather than scenes of conquest. The Huaca de la Luna walls at Moche, however, and at Huaca Cao Viejo near by, are painted with ranks of armed warriors, leaving little

Above: As well as building an empire through conquest, the Moche had a cult of celebrated 'gladiatorial' or ritual combat, as depicted here on a moulded spouted bottle.

doubt that Moche Sipán Lords, buried with war clubs and other war regalia, were military leaders as well as statesmen. Accompanying tombs include warrior burials, and Moche metalwork frequently depicts individual warriors.

Moche city-states saw frequent conflict. Individual combat scenes may represent minimal battles between rival Moche city-states, much as Black Figure paintings did in ancient Greece. This interpretation is in keeping with the ancient Andean concept of 'essence'.

Left: One of the best-known portrayals of ancient Andean warfare is the Cerro Sechín highland temple of sculpted slabs that forms the wall around the temple complex, including both victorious warriors and the severed heads of the defeated.

The Middle Horizon Tiwanaku and Wari empires were built by conquest. Each expanded within its territory, and maintained frontiers with fortresses. Wari expansion was marked by stone forts with regimented barrack-like planning – for example at Cerro Baúl in the Moquegua Valley and Pikillacta, strategically located in the Cuzco Valley roughly halfway between the two imperial capitals of Huari and Tiwanaku.

ARMS, ARMOUR, TACTICS

Andean warfare was conducted in pitched battles of hand-to-hand fighting, until one side broke. A pair of hammered gold and silver Wari figures portrays imposing warriors holding shields and spear-throwers, wearing four-cornered helmets and geometrically patterned rectangular tunics. Their whole composition

Left: A spouted, polished, moulded effigy bottle of a warrior with his spear and feathered war bonnet – Moche, showing earlier Chavin-style influence.

resembles the rectangular, compartment-like nature of Wari military architecture and is not dissimilar to Inca soldiers in their chequered tunics. A Wari vessel depicts heavily armed warriors kneeling in a flotilla of reed boats, apparently on a raid heading towards Tiwanaku across Lake Titicaca.

Late Intermediate and Late Horizon conflict is demonstrated in Inca legendary history. Typical is the tale of the turning point in Inca history – the defeat of the Chanca and the establishment of Pachacuti's reign. The provincial garrisoned town of Huánuco Pampa near Quito includes both identifiable barracks in the north of the city and 700 storage houses for tribute, army rations and civilian stores.

Weapons were similar to those for hunting: clubs, knives, spears and spear-throwers, slings and the bolas. The bow and arrow was known, but was not an Andean weapon – the Incas employed bowmen from the rainforest. The bolas was thrown at an enemy's legs to bring him down, after which he could be speared or clubbed to death. Warriors carried shields (Inca shields were rectangular or trapezoidal) and wore quilted cotton armour. Inca soldiers depicted in Guaman Poma de Ayala's *Nueva Corónica y Buen Gobierno, c.1615*, wear black-and-white chequered tunic uniforms and are shown in ranked squadrons in battle and storming city walls.

INCA CONQUEST

The success of Inca imperial expansion is undoubtedly the result of superior military leadership and organization. As territories were conquered and assimilated into Inca society, the army increasingly comprised recruits

Above: An Inca warrior presenting a severed head, from Poma de Ayala's Nueva Corónica, c.1615.

from conquered peoples. Service in the army was part of the *mita'a* labour tax. Another factor in Inca military success was their catering organization: Inca roads and storehouses for military supplies made deployment in far-flung provinces rapid and efficient.

Some provinces were subdued without battle, the people being persuaded that submission to the Incas was preferable to resistance. Confrontation always ended in defeat, immediately or eventually. Battle against an Inca army resulted in many killed. Inca terms of conquest, either after submission or defeat, were the same – 'fair' but severe. If a city or people submitted without a fight, no one was killed. All land was transferred to state ownership and the Incas gave the conquered people permission to use it. Produce was divided into three parts: for the state (meaning the royal household), for the state religion and for the people. Local leaders were usually retained and incorporated into Inca state structure. Sons of local leaders were taken to Cuzco to be trained in Inca statecraft and policy, and were then made leaders when their fathers died. Similarly, local shrines were left, but idols were often removed to Cuzco as hostages, and could be damaged or destroyed as punishment for rebellion.

CIVIL SERVANTS AND JUSTICE

The division between a royal or imperial household and members of a state civil service is not an easy one. The entourage of the legendary King Naymlap included a number of special court posts whose holders accompanied the king and performed specific duties exclusively for him.

CIVIL SERVICES

Without records, we have no knowledge of pre-Inca civil duties, but can surmise that there must have been some informal or formal organization for urban planning and maintenance. An annual round of religious ceremony must have been in the hands of the priests. Daily secular administration must have been in the hands of citizens appointed by rulers or chosen by the mutual agreement of some members of society (e.g. the 'elders'). As always, these functions in pre-Inca society were obviously fulfilled but until the Incas we have little evidence of how they were organized or performed.

The Incas copied much from those who came before them, as a continuum in Andean civilization's evolution. We can therefore only assume that what little we know of civil administration from the Inca records might also apply in pre-Inca

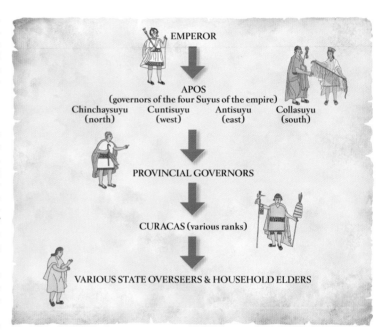

Above: Diagram of the Inca imperial government administrative hierarchy, showing delegation of power from the Sapa Inca *through* apo suyu *and provincial governors, curacas and household elders.*

urban society, such as the kingdoms of the Chimú and the Moche, or the empires of the Wari and Tiwanaku.

Many workers in the Inca state economy and social organization, who would be called civil servants in modern Western society, were either appointees of the emperor or draftees of the *mit'a* labour system such as record-keepers, storehouse administrators, road engineers or messenger runners.

GOVERNMENT APPOINTEES

Government posts comprised appointed individuals in a hierarchy based on heredity and/or ability. The highest ranks, the *apo* appointees of the emperor, governed each of the four *suyu* divisions of the empire. Those below them were also

Left: An imperial Inca prison with prisoner depicted in Poma de Ayala's Nueva Corónica, *c.1615.*

appointees, as governors of provinces and *curacas* of decreasing numbers of households. The day-to-day regulation of labour was in the hands of household elders.

Other administrative roles included the court historians and record-keepers, overseers in state workshops for the production of pottery, metalwork and textiles, clerks to oversee the collection and redistribution of goods in the state storehouses, and engineers and military commanders. Owners of imperial and noble estates chose their own administrators, which were thus private appointments, but the functions they performed were similar to those of civil servants on state lands.

Amautas (historians) and *quipucamayoqs* (record-keepers) were selected from the nobility and their posts became hereditary; army commanders likewise. There was formal training for these jobs. Other civil servants were no doubt selected for their skills and aptitudes for the tasks, having been trained on the job. Many were no doubt also hereditary in practice.

RULES

Performing these jobs in Inca society was according to established 'rules', allegedly established by the ninth emperor, Pachacuti, who also decreed the punishments applicable to each type of crime. There were quotas of agricultural produce, numbers of pots, tools, weapons and jewellery, lengths of cloth, and sections of road, irrigation canals, terracing or buildings set by imperial decree to be fulfilled.

Below: Vilcashuamán was an Inca administrative centre with a large plaza flanked by the Temple of the Sun and with an ushnu *platform.*

Successful fulfilment of quotas, keeping the peace, and efficiency in administering the *mit'a* labour tax was rewarded. Failure was treated by a regime increasing punishment from public humiliation to beatings to execution. There were also prisons for holding suspects and criminals.

ADMINISTRATION OF JUSTICE

Application of Inca law was part of the administrative system and presided over by the *curacas* (officials below Inca provincial governors, in charge of a certain number of households) of the places in which the crimes were committed. Cases involving parties within the same division of 100 households, for example, were ruled on by the appropriate *curaca* of those 100 households; a case that involved individuals from different units of 100 households was presided over by the *curaca* of the 500 households in which the two smaller divisions resided. Trials were normally within five days of being caught; punishment was immediate upon conviction.

Above: Capital punishment by stoning was the ultimate fate of convicted adulterers in Inca society, here depicted in Poma de Ayala's Nueva Corónica, *c.1615.*

Inca *curacas* were given rewards for doing a good job, but if the opposite were the case, they too were punished. Punishment for laziness might be a public and humiliating rebuke by the provincial governor. Gross misconduct and dishonesty, such as abusing the *mit'a* system or embezzling state property, was punishable by execution.

Punishments for violating the laws were strict and could be severe. They included capital punishment. When the crime was one punishable by death, the case was overseen by the provincial governor rather than by a *curaca*. For if a *curaca* executed a person without the permission of his governor, he would have a heavy stone dropped on his back from a height of about 1m (3ft); if he committed the transgression a second time, he was put to death.

There were no formal courthouses as such, although the open, high-walled courtyards called *kanchas* must have included buildings among those surrounding their plazas specifically for hearing criminal cases. The *ushnu* platforms in such courtyards might have been used for this purpose.

The Spanish Colonial administration naturally placed Spaniards in the highest ranks of their new government. But at more local levels, like the Incas before them, they continued to use native leaders.

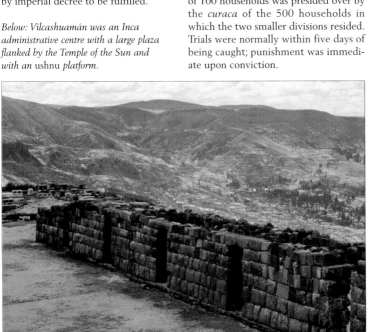

PRIESTS AND SHAMANS

Throughout Andean civilization, priests existed, residing at temples and pilgrimage sites. The oracle above the Lanzón monolith in the Old Temple at Early Horizon Chavín de Huántar must have had priests to act in giving answers to supplicants. Later, the oracle at Pachacamac had similar specialists. From the Initial Period, temple buildings and precincts must have served as places to instruct acolytes into the priesthood by in-service training.

The rich Early Intermediate Period Moche burials, and those of the Late Intermediate Period Sicán-Lambayeque,

Below: A Moche pottery jar representing a shaman holding a wooden stick used to prepare coca balls.

appear to be of priests or lords. Moche ceramics and murals depict several scenes of priests and priestesses administering at ritual ceremonies.

GODS OR PRIESTS?

It is often difficult to tell, however, if the stone sculpture and other depictions in many Andean cultures are of priests or of the gods themselves. For example, the Early Horizon Pukará Decapitator figure depicts a seated male figure, holding an axe and a severed head. His cap is decorated with supernatural faces. He is either a supernatural composite being, or a man wearing a representative mask with a fanged mouth. Similarly, buried at the base of the western staircase of the Akapana temple at Middle Horizon Tiwanaku was a black basalt image of a seated, puma-headed person (a *chachapuma*), also holding a severed head. Another Tiwanaku *chachapuma* sculpture is of a standing figure holding a severed head. Are these representations of the gods or of priests impersonating them?

In early civilizations it seems likely that rulers and priests were the same, or were of the same family. Separate roles were evident in some cultures, however, as shown in the story of Fempellec. This twelfth ruler of the Naymlap Dynasty, sometime in the late Middle Horizon or early Late Intermediate Period, came into conflict with the priests of Chot when he attempted to remove the idol of Yampallec to another city. The story also demonstrates the considerable power of priests in at least this Andean society, for the priests, acting for the gods and in behalf of the people, expelled Fempellec.

RELIGIOUS POWER

The power of religious cults, and thus the influence of priests, is amply shown by the Early Horizon spread of the Chavín Cult. Earlier, the Kotosh Tradition may have been the earliest such regional Andean cult. The cult and priests of

Above: A terracotta model of a shaman with an elaborate headdress from the Jamacoaque culture, Ecuador.

Pachacamac, an oracle and pilgrimage centre that endured more than a millennium on the central Peruvian coast, certainly exercised great power, for they were even recognized and honoured by the Inca emperors. Such was the power of the cult that priests of distant communities solicited the Pachacamac priests for permission to establish branch shrines in their home towns to the creator god Pachacamac. If deemed to have the ability to support cult activities, a priest from Pachacamac was assigned to the new shrine and the community supplied labour and produce from assigned lands to support him and the shrine. Part of the produce was kept for the shrine and

Horizon sunken circular court at Chavín de Huántar. Spiders with human heads were frequently depicted in the Moche and later cultures.

Drug paraphernalia has frequently been found among grave goods, but a unique late 5th-century AD cave burial near Wari is that of a local medicine man, herbalist or shaman. He was accompanied by his tools: a wooden snuff tablet decorated with a Tiwanaku 'attendant angel' figure, a basket with multicoloured, front-facing deity figures and various herbal plants.

PRIESTS AND PRIESTESSES

Inca priests and priestesses were full-time specialists, supported by the state. A third of conquered lands were designated for their upkeep. Such a large portion indicates that there was a correspondent sector in Inca society devoted to state religion.

Inca priests were organized into a hierarchy resembling that of the Inca civil service. Priestly ranking went according to the importance, and thus rank, of the shrine he served. The top priest was a close relative of the emperor, and the high priest of the state cult of Inti (the sun). Each of the chief priests or priestesses of the other five principal Inca deities came next in rank, each housed in a separate *wasi* (chamber) in the Coricancha: Viracocha (creator), Quilla (Moon), Chaska-Qoylor (Venus), Illapa (thunder, lightning) and Cuichu (rainbow). A similar hierarchy existed in each shrine or temple, from the chief shrine priest or priestess down to his or her attendants and trainees.

Above: This elaborate hand-painted French wallpaper dates from 1826 and shows the European fascination with Inca sun worship.

the rest sent back to Pachacamac. Such branches were thought of as the wives, children or brothers and sisters of the main cult city.

SHAMANS AND HEALERS

Temple priests were supplemented in local communities by shamans and healers. The careful preparation and mummification of bodies before burial at Chinchorros as early as 5000BC, and at the Paracas and Nazca cemeteries demonstrate their early existence. Many Moche pots portray men and women healers at work, laying on hands and administering herbs and drugs.

Transformation, in which a priest or shaman changed into another being (part-human, part-beast), is a common Andean religious theme. From the Initial Period onwards, wall sculptures, murals and depictions on pottery and textiles show figures in various states of transformation. Some of the earliest are the Initial Period wall paintings of insects with human heads at Garagay, the wall sculptures of shamanic trance at Moxeke and the staged stone sculpture of jaguar transformation in the Early

Left: A lively terracotta figurine of a shaman wearing a headdress decorated with snake heads and dancing during a ceremony of the Bahia culture, Manabi, Ecuador.

345

CHAPTER SEVENTEEN

DAILY LIFE

Most of what we know about the daily lives of ordinary people in Inca and pre-Inca times comes from archaeological evidence. The private lives and education of Inca subjects is hardly commented on in the early Spanish sources, whose authors were more interested in the lives of the Inca emperors and in the workings of the *mit'a* labour tax system and collection of wealth. Native writers, such as Garcilasco de la Vega and Felipe Guaman Poma de Ayala, give some information on daily life, and the 398 drawings in the latter's book show many aspects of Inca life and culture.

Archaeological work has concentrated on the more monumental and central areas of sites, or on wide aerial studies of sites in their settings. Much work also focuses on the art of Andean civilization and on the most spectacular objects. As a result, we know less about the ordinary ancient Andean. We know little of the daily routines followed by most subjects of the empire, except that they must have been taken up by a regular annual cycle required by an agricultural way of life for most people.

For the ordinary citizen, life in Inca times would have been a repetitive round of routine tasks and mutual obligations within one's *ayllu* kinship group, punctuated or relieved by *mit'a* labour tax duties for the state, and by a regular schedule of religious ceremony and festivity. In earlier times, as civilized state societies increased in territorial control, population and administrative complexity, divisions within societies of different tasks created more varied roles for different groups of citizens.

Left: Inca kero *cup showing a man hunting llamas with bolas, a weapon using cords weighted at the ends.*

COMMUNITY, HOUSEHOLD AND ADULTHOOD

Andean society was based around the family household, and family structure and ritual bound society together.

COMMUNITY

From the early farming villages of the Initial Period and Early Horizon, much larger towns, and eventually cities, developed near or around increasingly large and elaborate ritual centres. The building of such sites required some form of civil control and organization of labour on a formal basis, most likely utilizing the forms of kinship obligations that developed in agricultural communities.

Andean cultures did not formally divide state and religion, although as civilization developed there were specialist leaders, rulers, administrators and priests. In everyday life, civil duties and religion appear always to have been mixed in the daily tasks of making a living, seasonal work routines and an annual cycle of ritual and supplication to the gods for prosperity and wellbeing.

Nevertheless, certain sites were devoted to religious and ritual activities, while other sites were the thriving towns and cities of residents engaged in

Below: Silver Inca figurines of an alpaca, whose long, fine wool was used in the finest textiles, a llama and a female votive figure.

day-to-day agricultural tasks, community and state administration and regulation of the economy.

HOUSEHOLD

The household was the basic unit of most Andean societies. Agricultural families were nuclear, but indications are that the formal kinship ties (*ayllu*) described in the sources for the Incas and their subjects in the Late Horizon were developments from much earlier times. Their formulation and development probably began and operated on some scale to regulate labour and economy from the beginnings of village and town life. In Inca society, both men and women lived in their parent's household until marriage.

Daily tasks were planting, tending and harvesting crops, herding llamas, hunting and fishing, making household items, building and repairing houses, irrigation structures and terracing, and making cloth, clothing, jewellery, and weapons and tools.

While men worked in the fields or were away on

Above: Originally spreading to South America from Mesoamerica via the Central American cultures, maize remained a daily staple of the Andean diet.

mit'a labour service for the emperor, the daily domestic chores of cooking, cleaning and washing were done by women. Before the Inca conquest, gender roles were less differentiated: women helped in agriculture, men span, wove and made pottery as well as women.

As inheritance in Inca society was through both the father's and mother's sides of the family, a noblewoman could own land and llama herds in her own right. Women thus controlled a certain proportion of Inca economic resources, but it is unknown how much.

PUBERTY AND ADULTHOOD

A girl's puberty began with her first menstruation, shortly after which a ceremony was held to recognize this life transition. The girl remained in the house for three days, during which she could eat nothing until the third day, when she was allowed some raw maize. On the fourth day, her mother bathed her and plaited her hair. Relatives assembled at the house. The girl dressed in new clothes made for the occasion, came out

of confinement and served food and drink to the assembly. Her most important uncle pronounced her permanent name and, as at the first-naming ceremony, she received gifts.

Inca boys' puberty was marked by a common ritual, held at age 14 (considered to coincide roughly with the onset of puberty). For commoners, the ceremonies were less elaborate than they were for boys from the Inca royal, noble and elite provincial classes. The principal purpose was to initiate boys as men and warriors, and as proper members of Inca society. The rituals took place over three weeks, requiring preparation during the preceding several months. Mothers made their sons fine garments specifically for the ceremonies.

Below: The popularity of 're-recreating' Inca ceremony and ritual incorporates modern elements (laced shoes and balloons) as well as 'traditional' textiles.

In November, the boys went on pilgrimage to the Inca sacred mountain of Huanacauri, near Cuzco (or a local sacred mountain in the province). Each boy led a llama. He asked the spirit of the mountain for permission to perform the ceremonies of puberty. The llamas were sacrificed by having their throats slit and a priest smeared the blood across each boy's face. Each boy received a sling to signify his warrior status. The boys danced, then performed certain ritual 'chores': collecting

Above: A typical Inca house was open plan with a central hearth and a trapezoidal doorway. Most household activities were performed outdoors.

straw for their relatives to sit on at the final ceremony and chewing maize to ferment *chicha* beer for the ceremonies.

The formal puberty rites took place in December, within the Capac Raymi summer solstice festival. The initiates made a second pilgrimage to Huanacauri, where they sacrificed more llamas. When they returned home, waiting relatives whipped them on their legs to make them strong and brave. The boys performed a sacred dance and drank *chicha*.

After a week's rest, they sacrificed more llamas, were whipped again, and performed a dance atop the hill of Anahuarque near Huanacauri (or other local sacred *huaca*). The boys then raced down the hill's rugged terrain; at the bottom, girls from the same class gave them more *chicha*.

The next task was to walk to several other hills around Cuzco, then receive a loincloth in formal recognition of manhood. The final visit was to the sacred spring of Callispuquio, where initiates were met by relatives who gave them their warrior's weapons: a boy's principal uncle gave him a shield, sling and war mace; other relatives lectured him on the proper male and Inca noble conduct. His ears were pierced for earplugs that marked his status as an Inca noble (or provincial elite) and warrior.

FOOD AND DRINK

The wide variety of early domesticated plants exploited by ancient Andeans provided the basic diet, which was supplemented by hunting and fishing, depending on local availability. Sea fishing and shellfish, for example, were more important at coastal sites, as was fishing at Lake Titicaca and other Altiplano lakes. In the sierra, hunting was mostly for a small number of mammals and rodents after the large game animals of the late Ice Age had become extinct.

FROM HUNTER-GATHERING
TO GROWING
In the Archaic Period, hunting and gathering prevailed and at rock shelters and cave sites such as Pachamachay and Guitarrero almost all faunal and floral remains are of wild varieties hunted and collected. Even in the Preceramic Period the wild components of bone and plant remains at sites such as Kotosh, La Galgada, Huaricoto, Salinas de Chao and

Below: The elaborate channelling and distribution of water was essential for Andean daily household use as well as for agriculture. Fountains at Inca Yupanqui's imperial lodge at Tambo Machay.

others, including caves still occupied in the Ayacucho and Calejón de Huaylas, are high.

Coastal sites were able to rely on hunting and collecting of shellfish well into the late Preceramic Period because the coastal food sources were so abundant. Only from the Initial Period onwards, when the domestic flora and fauna remains at sites predominate, can we see the full range of domesticated plants and animals from the physical changes brought through domestication.

DAILY DIET
We cannot know the daily meal routines of pre-Inca cultures. It may or may not be legitimate to project what we know from Inca records back into pre-Inca times.

The principal foods of Andean peoples were maize, potatoes, oca and ulluca (both tubers), quinoa and tarwi (high-protein grains), and kidney, lima and string beans and squashes. More regional staples included peanuts, manioc and mashwa (a higher-altitude tuber). These were supplemented with a variety of herbs as seasoning, especially chilli peppers and mint, and with fruits and nuts (both

Above: An elaborately decorated Inca kero *cup depicts a puma or jaguar, an ever-present religious image woven into daily use.*

domesticated and wild), including peanuts and cashews, tomatoes, pumpkins, palmettos, pineapples, sour cherries, custard apples, cactus fruits, elderberries, guavas, avocados and an ancient variety of banana. Animal protein, including fish, was available, but the main sources of meat in the highlands were guinea pigs and ducks. Llama and deer meat was also eaten.

Locally, day-to-day meals were fairly staple and monotonous, though redistribution of foodstuffs between highlands and lowlands made it less so. Local markets supplied by traders provided the opportunity to barter for highland and lowland produce. Nevertheless, commerce in the Inca Empire was virtually non-existent because all aspects of the economy were so regulated by the state. Within provinces, people were allowed to have local markets, where they could exchange everyday foods and other items such as tools and common jewellery. Luxury

Above: To the staples of maize and the potato were added numerous gourds and herbal condiments ground in wooden mortars.

items and exotic foods, however, were held in the state's monopoly and were produced, collected and stored by the state.

Apart from water, the main drink was *chicha* – weakly fermented beer made from maize and several other plants. Although it was drunk daily, it also played a significant role in religious ritual and in life-stage ceremonies. Bernabé Cobo claims that water was only drunk when no *chicha* was available!

COOKING AND EATING

The Incas ate only two meals a day: a morning meal (8–9 o'clock) and early evening meal (4–5 o'clock). Meals were taken seated on the ground outdoors, with the women facing the cooking pots and sitting back-to-back with the men.

It is not known whether different foods or combinations of foods were consumed for the different meals. Ordinary people ate off flat pottery plates and drank from wooden or ceramic beakers (*kero* cups). Royals and nobles ate and drank from copper, gold and silver plates and cups.

Cooking was done in ceramic pots set on tripods or pedestals placed directly over the fire. Food was both boiled and roasted in the flames. Mixed foods in soups and stews were common as the main dishes. Maize was prepared in several ways, including roasting on the cob, in stews, as a kind of baked or boiled cornbread, and popped (although popcorn was considered a delicacy eaten mostly by royals and nobles). Potatoes were both baked and boiled.

STORAGE AND FOOD PROCESSING

Foodstuffs and *chicha* were stored in the house in large ceramic jars, usually with pointed bases to stabilize them in the ground. Uncooked household storage was kept in attics and rafter space, or in mud-plastered cornstalk bins, or in mud-lined floor-pits. General harvest and main stores were kept in outdoor adobe brick buildings until needed in the house. Maize, peanuts and other grains and nuts were stored dry.

Right: Inca ceramic figurine of a parrot eating a rather plump maize cob or gourd links western coastal food with a tropical import.

Meat, fish and potatoes were freeze-dried for preservation and storage. Freeze-drying was done in the cold, dry winter. Meat (*charqui*) and fish were cut into thin strips, pounded, then left to dry in the sun during the day and freeze at night. Potatoes were soaked in water to soften them, then left to freeze at night; during the day, thawing evaporated the water. Repeated freezing and thawing eventually left the dried pulp (*chuño*). Freeze-drying enabled the Incas to store large quantities of staples in state storehouses (*collcas*) for imperial use and for redistribution, and made food much easier to transport.

Chicha was made by chewing the maize kernels (or other seeds) to split the pulp, then spitting the mash into jars of warm water. Salivary enzymes broke down the sugars in the pulp and began fermentation. For daily *chicha*, fermentation was allowed for a few days. Longer fermentation produced stronger *chicha* for religious use.

BIRTH, CHILDHOOD AND EDUCATION

Birth in Inca society, like all events through life, was considered part of a great cycle. Death was not an end, rather the continuation of the cycle in a different state of being. Other significant Inca childhood events were the first haircut and recognition of the onset of puberty; later rituals were marriage, then death and burial.

BIRTH

There were no special places for birth to take place, and it was not an especially marked event. Women relatives might assist at the time of birth, in the house. A woman simply delivered the child, then took it to the nearest stream to bathe herself and the baby. The newborn child was carried in a cloth sling for the first four days of its life and was then laid in a cradle. It then spent most of its life in either a sling or a cradle until it could walk. Garcilasco de la Vega

Below: As most daily activities took place outdoors, Inca babies were kept warm and close-by swaddled in layers of textiles (month-old baby from Poma de Ayala's Nueva Corónica, c.1615).

claims that Inca women never picked up their babies to suckle or play with them, lest they became 'cry babies', but it can hardly be the case that women did not regularly suckle their babies until they could take solid food.

More or less immediately after birth, a woman returned to her daily duties in the household. It is likely that elite women had an easier experience, and there were *yanaconas* (servants or personal attendants) to help at birth and in nursing and raising the child.

CHILD-NAMING

In Inca society, the naming of a child was delayed until it was weaned, at about 1 year old. This was known as the 'first-naming' and was associated with the child's first haircut. To mark the event, the parents gave a party to honour the child, to which they invited relatives and friends. The party included much drinking, music-making and dancing, and must have provided welcome relief from daily routines. The party came to an end when the eldest male relative cut a piece of the child's hair and trimmed his/her nails. Then he gave the chosen name. Other relatives cut locks of the child's hair and presented gifts to it.

The name given at this ceremony was used throughout childhood, but was not considered permanent, for a lifelong name was not given until the child reached maturity, marked by puberty ceremonies. The onset of puberty was considered the

Left: Moche potters depicted every scene imaginable, including this scene of a woman giving birth, helped by two 'midwives', on a stirrup-spout bottle.

end of childhood and beginning of adulthood, and the event was marked by special, different, initiation rituals for boys and girls.

PLAY

There is little evidence of toys, but play must have been part of a child's life, perhaps learning to play a flute or drum, making miniature pots and clothing for figurines, and dancing.

Much of childhood was occupied in learning household activities appropriate and achievable as the child grew up. When strong enough, boys began to help with farming tasks and with herding animals. They also began to learn skills with weapons, both for hunting and for eventually serving in the army, and perhaps accompanied adult men when they went hunting and fishing. Girls helped with the numerous household

Above: Andean boys and girls took on daily chores and daily responsibilities at an early age. This Inca boy depicted in Poma de Ayala's Nueva Corónica, *c.1615, hones his hunting and warrior skills with a sling.*

chores of preparing meals, cleaning, spinning and weaving, and minding younger sisters and brothers.

EDUCATION

There was no formal state education in Inca society, or, as far as we know, in any pre-Inca culture, at least not for all boys and girls. No archaeological evidence can be clearly identified as a place of learning or instruction, although from the Initial Period onwards temple buildings and precincts must have served as places to instruct acolytes into the priesthood by in-service training.

Likewise, the skills needed for farming, fishing, hunting, spinning, weaving, potting, metalworking, construction and any other daily tasks and crafts were basically taught in the home by parents or by practising professionals to novices in workshops or on-site in informal apprenticeships. With no writing system in any Andean civilization, all knowledge was obviously passed on verbally and by demonstration.

There are only four exceptions to this picture. The first two are the Inca state accountants and historians (*quipucamayoqs* and *amautas*), whose positions were nevertheless hereditary and therefore taught to sons by their fathers. The only

boys and girls who were taught in a 'school' were the sons of Inca and provincial nobles, and the girls chosen to become *acllas* (or *acllyaconas*), 'chosen women' to serve in the state cult of Inti (the sun), and some as imperial concubines or to become 'gifts' in imperial political alliances.

The sons of the nobility (including provincial *curacas*) received four years of education at a school in Cuzco. Their teachers were the *amautas*, who taught them Quechua (the Inca language) in the first year, Inca religion in the second, *quipu* 'reading' in the third and Inca history in the fourth. Learning was by rote through memorization and repetition, and through practice. Discipline was strict and included beatings, although these were restricted to a single beating per day – striking the soles of the feet 10 times with a cane. The principal purpose of this education of the sons of nobles and provincial *curacas* was to indoctrinate them as loyal subjects for when they took up leadership in local administration.

Girls were chosen to become *acllyaconas* at about 10; they were selected from the daughters of conquered peoples. They were first taken to a provincial capital, where they were taught in the *acllahuasi* (house of the *acllyaconas*) cloisters for four years: learning to spin, weave, cook, make *chicha* (beer), and the elements of Inca religion, especially how to serve Inti (the sun). Then they were taken to Cuzco and presented to the emperor, who decided whether they were to enter the Cuzco *acllahuasi*, become

Right: Face markings, an elaborate hat and earrings, and a poised kero *cup in this Chancay anthropomorphic ceramic vessel possibly indicate that the girl is participating in a libation ritual.*

part of the emperor's court (perhaps one of his concubines) or be given in marriage or concubinage to a provincial governor or nobleman.

The daughters of the imperial court and of provincial nobles were also 'educated', although not so formally in a school, rather in the houses of Cuzco noblewomen.

MARRIAGE AND INHERITANCE

Inca marriage was normally monogamous. Such an arrangement was not, however, a legal or social obligation, rather an economical one. A man could have more than one wife but only if he had sufficient wealth to support them and their children. Nobles often took several wives, and the Inca emperor could have as many wives as he wanted. In a glimpse of pre-Inca practice, the tale of Naymlap, founder of the northern coastal dynasty of the Lambayeque culture, mentions among his 'noble company' his wife, Ceterni, and a harem. The wives of some of his sons are also named.

CHOOSING PARTNERS

Inca emperors had the pick of the *aclla* (or *acllyaconas*) 'chosen women' from the cult of the 'Virgins of the Sun', and could also use the chosen women as favours and in marriage alliances with other rulers.

If a man had more than one wife, there was always a distinction between a principal wife and any secondary wives. The distinction was established in the formal

Below: Terracotta figurines of a couple wearing headdresses and with pectorals and earplugs, holding cups, Chancay culture.

Right: Exemplifying the ancient union of marriage on a brightly painted spouted bottle (known as a huaco) from a Nazca tomb.

ceremony in which a man married his first, and therefore principal, wife. Subsequent wives were simply taken into the household. A secondary wife could not replace the principal wife, even upon the death of the latter – a principle that was meant to alleviate jealousy, and perhaps even murder, of the principal wife.

IMPERIAL BLOODLINES

In the imperial line, because the Incas believed the imperial *ayllu* had ultimately been founded by, and was therefore descended from, Inti (the sun god), the emperor was considered to be divine. To keep the imperial bloodline pure for purposes of ascent to the throne, therefore, the emperor was also required to have one official wife, the *coya*, who was supposed to be his full sister. The heir to the throne, chosen by the reigning emperor, was selected from the children of their union. The children of the emperor's secondary wives formed the *panacas* (royal *ayllus*). Marriages within non-royal *ayllus* were not obliged to be to sisters because no question of divinity or pureness of descent was involved.

Despite these theoretical 'rules' or laws of imperial descent, by the 12th–13th generations of Inca rulers, the succession of the death of Huayna Capac (twelfth emperor) was disputed by two half-brothers, Huáscar and Atahualpa, from different imperial wives.

One other curious Inca elite marriage custom was the pairing of noble couples. One Inca source claimed that marriageable young men and women of the highest nobility lined up annually in the main plaza in Cuzco, whereupon the emperor selected pairs and formally married them. It would seem safe to conjecture that pairs lined up such that pre-arranged or hoped-for matches could be achieved.

WIFELY DUTIES

One of the main duties of the secondary wives in a large household was to act as child-carers for the legitimate sons of their husband, both their own sons and the sons of the principal wife. When these sons reached puberty, one duty of the secondary wife was to teach him about sex, including having intercourse with him, although presumably not with her own sons.

And when such a son married, the secondary wife remained in his household and continued with the duties of a secondary wife.

Such complicated arrangements were not the norm among the bulk of Andean society. Inca marriage was usually within one's *ayllu*, as this practice maintained the existing rights, property and obligations of the collective. Related families usually lived near each other in their *suyu* quarters, divided into their two moieties. A woman normally moved into her husband's *suyu* and moiety, but remained a member of her ancestral moiety and lineage. Inheritance was both through the male and female lines. This 'gender parallelism' represents an aspect of the fundamental Andean concept of duality. Men traced their ancestry and birthrights through their fathers, while women traced theirs through their mothers.

MARRIAGE RITES

The marriage ceremony incorporated and ritualized this gender equality between husband and wife. Marriage agreements and arrangements were made either by a couple's parents or by the couple themselves. The ancestral *mallquis* mummies were often consulted on the suitability of the match, although how their opinion was determined is uncertain. The usual age for marriage was about 25 years for men and between 16 and 20 for women.

The marriage ceremony was simple, if formal. The groom, accompanied by his family, went to the bride's house, where he was greeted and his bride formally presented to him. The groom's family signalled their acceptance of the girl by placing a sandal on her foot – a wool sandal if she was a virgin and a grass sandal if she was not. (Virginity was not a requirement of marriage, although the Spanish sources give no information about how virginity, or otherwise, was determined.)

Left: Chimú polished black bridge-spout bottle showing a domestic scene of a woman with braided hair holding her baby.

Above: Moche potters were not shy of depicting old age, as on this stirrup-spouted bottle of an elderly couple embracing.

Next, both families travelled to the groom's home. His bride presented him with gifts, and the elders of the two families expounded to the couple on the many duties and responsibilities of family life. Once these sober rituals were completed, the wedding was celebrated with a feast and the presentation of gifts to the newlyweds by family members. As a formal acknowledgement of the reciprocal relationship being established in this first stage of marriage, between both the marrying couple and their respective lineages, the bride's parents often signified their agreement by accepting a gift of coca from the groom's parents.

Divorce was not recognized in Inca law, and a man who cast aside his wife was punished and required to take her back.

GENDER ROLES

In the earliest times, we can only surmise and use the example of hunter-gatherer societies of today to reconstruct gender roles. Game-hunting must have been predominantly a male pursuit; gathering while tending children a female role. Coastal cultures, for example, probably combined these occupations seamlessly as men fished and hunted sea mammals from small boats offshore while woman and children gathered shellfish along the foreshore.

However, it is too easy to slip into this apparent 'obvious' division of labour. If children participated in gathering, they would have included both boys and girls, at least up to a certain age. The necessary collection and preparation of materials for building shelters must have been a combined effort by both men and women.

Below: Spinning and weaving were a continuous task for Inca women. As well as the more mobile backstrap loom, large textiles were made on horizontal single-heddle looms.

Similarly, there is no reason to think that spiritual matters – shamanism, divining and soliciting the gods, and medicinal and herbal practices – were the exclusive realm of one gender or the other. In early times of basic survival, roles must have been more mixed, and the group effort as a whole was the most important factor.

Before Inca conquest and their institutionalization of life, gender roles were less fixed. In Inca society, male and female roles became more defined, especially in the primary conception that men were soldiers and women were cloth makers. The elite classes had servants and personal attendants to make life easier, but elite men still served as soldiers in the imperial army and elite women still spun and wove to demonstrate their respective masculinity and femininity.

Spanish sources say more about men's roles than women's, especially about men's obligations under *mit'a* labour, as craftsmen and in the imperial court.

Above: Both men and women performed tasks in the fields. Here men turn the soil with foot-ploughs while women crush the sods into finer soil (depicted in Poma de Ayala's Nueva Corónica, *c.1615).*

MEN'S ROLES

The principal role fulfilled by men in the Inca Empire was their obligation of tax. All taxpaying individuals, that is heads of households, were required to provide someone to work for a certain period of time each year in the state *mit'a* labour system. Inca practice was formalized, but there is every reason to believe that the system was not wholly invented by the Incas.

Evidence from pre-Inca coastal and highland cultures indicates that labour levies were employed for major communal constructions. The makers' marks on the adobe bricks of the Moche Huaca del Sol show that the monument was built by organized gangs of workers using some system of state regimentation of the workforce. Similarly, the regimented nature of Wari architecture indicates that the labour forces that built them were marshalled on a regular basis as and when additions were built at the capital city, provincial cities and fortresses.

The Inca *mit'a* required men to discharge various roles, depending on their individual skills. A man could be drafted into the army, or he could be employed in road and bridge building, or other state constructions. He could serve as an administrator in the state redistribution system, or be a transporter of food and goods to and from them. If he was a skilled craftsman, his services might be employed in the production of metalwork or ceramics for the state. A large proportion of *mit'a* labour was used to work the lands or to tend the llama flocks designated for the support of the imperial and elite households, and of religious cults.

WOMEN'S ROLES

Women were typically in charge of the household. In common households, women performed the principal tasks of child rearing, especially when children were young, and were responsible for preparing meals, cleaning, washing and making cloth and clothing for the family. When old enough, children contributed to household activities. At this time, boys' and girls' roles differentiated and they began to take on traditional gender roles.

A particular role fulfilled by women in Inca and pre-Inca society was spinning and weaving. Cotton was the predominant fibre in the lowlands and wool in the highlands. Spinning was done with a drop spindle and therefore enabled women to spin thread almost anywhere and while otherwise preoccupied. For example, when simply walking between tasks it was possible to keep the spindle whorl in motion while feeding cotton or wool to it from a ball in the hand.

The importance of cloth and the persistent demand for it by the Inca state bureaucracy meant that all women span and wove, from the humblest citizen to the women of the imperial household. Women also played a significant role in religion, one special role being life in the imperial cult of 'chosen women', the *acllas* (or *acllyaconas*). Women also played the principal role tending the temple and in the cult of the Moon.

Left: Service in battle was a principal obligation of Inca men and also in much earlier empires – as shown by this Moche warrior with shield and war club as a stirrup-spouted pot.

Above: Small gardens for growing gourds and herbs and other condiments were tended near the household. The man is offering coca leaves to the woman (note the early adoption of European chickens); depicted in Poma de Ayala's Nueva Corónica, *c.1615.*

COMMUNAL TASKS

On lands designated for the support of commoners, both men and women performed the planting, care and harvest of crops. Hunting and fishing remained men's work, although shellfish collection probably remained a task for women and children.

The nature of *ayllu* kinship ties and obligations shows that much of farm labour and local building activities such as irrigation canals and house-building was accomplished by the combined efforts of men and women, each having roles in the preparation and use of the various materials and tasks involved.

Members of the imperial Inca court and other elite society had an easier life. They could draw upon the resources of private estates and *mit'a* tribute. (They were themselves, of course, exempt from *mit'a* obligations.) Noblemen could also fill command positions in the Inca army or serve as officials in state administrative positions. Priestly positions were also open to them.

CLOTHING AND HAIRSTYLES

People's clothing and hairstyles established their ethnic identity. Among a tribe or nation, differences in style and quality of clothing and jewellery indicated social rank and status. In Andean creation, Viracocha made figurines and painted them with the costumes and hairstyles of different nations. In his wanderings, he assigned distinctive clothing, hairstyles and languages as he called forth peoples and nations from the Earth.

INCA DAILY WEAR
Ordinary Incas wore simple clothing. Women wrapped a large cloth around the body, pinned at the shoulders and tied with a belt at the waist. A mantle was draped over the shoulders and fastened at the front with a large copper pin (*tupu*). Thickened thighs and ankles, considered by Incas a special attribute of feminine beauty, were enhanced by tying string above and below the knees.

Men wore a loincloth wrapped around the waist and groin and a cloth tunic over the body. The tunic comprised a

Below: This tunic of fine alpaca wool, with its elaborate interlocking geometric designs and stylistic feline and crab motifs, would have been worn by a nobleman, and perhaps accompanied him to his tomb.

Above: Elaborate ceremonial hats brought together elements of design and materials from throughout the Inca Empire, as in this wool hat with volutes and stepped-fret designs, and tropical feather adornment.

large cloth folded double and sewn together, leaving slits for the head and arms. Men covered their legs from knee to ankle with wraps of cotton or wool fringes. In the cold, they wore long capes over their shoulders.

Despite its simple design, clothing was usually decorated with symbolic, brightly coloured patterns. Ordinary daywear was decorated with a single band of square designs around the waist and along the lower edge, plus an inverted triangle at the neck. Designs on men's clothing were standardized to signify membership of a particular group – distinct for his *ayllu* or as a member of one of the royal *panacas*.

Footwear for both men and women was sandals, secured with woollen straps tied across the foot. Commoners wore sandals woven from wild plant fibres, or of cotton, llama or alpaca wool. Soles were leather (deer or other animal hide).

HATS
Both men and women wore headdresses, the shapes of which were, in addition to cloth decoration, indicators of ethnic identity. Inca men wore cloth headbands. Hats were conical or flared cloth pieces, with elite versions being decorated with cloth and metalwork tassels and feathers. Nazca burials include elite individuals with tall, feathered headpieces, revealing wealth and long-distance contacts with sources of brightly coloured tropical bird feathers. Nazca figures on pottery and figurines wear tight, rectangular 'hats', perhaps representing the cloth turbans (wrapped around and over the head with the ends tied in front) found on Nazca mummies.

Moche people wore a variety of helmet-like headpieces. Examples of Wari and Tiwanaku hats are blocky, often cube-shaped, and sometimes have cloth horns at the corners. But such headgear is probably the elaborate wear of ritual, for priests and nobles, rather than common wear.

STYLES AND DISTINCTIONS
There was little difference in style between commoner and elite; quality and quantity were the main distinctions – the cut of the cloth and its fineness, the amount of jewellery and other accoutrements, and the decorative elaboration and materials used. Whereas common *tupus* were copper, nobles used silver and gold ones. Inca and other nobles wore feather headdresses and crowns of silver and gold. Nobles

attached gold and silver ornaments to their sandals, and Inca emperors wore non-functional silver or gold sandals; copper and gold sandals were also found in earlier elite Moche and Lambayeque-Sicán burials.

The Inca emperor's headband was long enough to wrap several times around his head and only he could wear a headband decorated with a fringe of tassels that hung over his forehead, and carry a stick with a dangling pompom.

Inca imperial and other heads of state, and priests, wore clothes cut from the finest textiles, dyed with the richest colours. Only they had access to exotic fibres, such as alpaca and vicuña wool, tropical bird feathers and embellishments of gold and silver thread. Inca elites were especially fond of tropical feather decorations: mantles

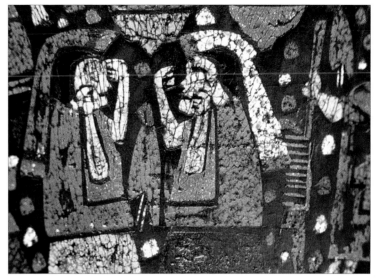

were sometimes covered entirely in feathers, or in gold, silver or copper discs, to emphasize high social status.

PRE-INCA CLOTHING

Inca clothing and jewellery reflects what was worn in earlier cultures. The fine clothes and featherwork of the Lords of Chimór (Chimú) are especially notable. The elaborate wraps of Paracas and Nazca burials and the costumes worn by figures on pottery, murals, metalwork and stone sculpture must be viewed with caution regarding everyday wear. Much of the special cloth and headgear in burials is costume for special occasions – burials, ritual ceremony or battle gear – or is worn by representations of deities. Interestingly, Viracocha (Creator) is described as wearing a simple, rough cloak or even rags!

SPECIAL COSTUME

More elaborate, special costumes, styled on the themes described above, were made for special ritual occasions.

Left: As well as garments, llama wool and elaborate patterns were applied to utilitarian accessories, such as this Inca coca leaf bag with opposing rows of llama figures.

Above: Distinctive ceremonial costumes are also known from decorations on objects, as on this painted kero *cup showing priests or priestesses in ritual dress and headgear.*

Jewellery was worn mostly by nobles. Inca women wore *tupus* and necklaces. Men wore little or no jewellery, but the insignia of Inca nobility was the large earplugs given at puberty. These were round, about 5cm (2in) in diameter and held by a shaft through the earlobe. They were made of copper, silver, gold or metal alloy, or stone. Men also wore metal bracelets.

Men who showed particular bravery in battle were awarded metal discs to wear around the neck. They often donned necklaces of the teeth of their human victims. The Incas also painted their faces in mourning, and Inca warriors wore warpaint into battle.

HAIRSTYLES

Inca hairstyles were simple: men cut their hair short and bound it by a cloth headband, whereas women grew it long with a central parting. A woman cut her hair only in mourning or as a sign of disgrace. An Inca girl grew her hair throughout childhood, for at the onset of puberty it was braided by her mother on the fourth day after her first menstruation, as one of the signs of her transition to adulthood.

CRIME AND PUNISHMENT

Inca life was highly regimented, both because the general necessity to make a living took up most of people's time, and because the state regulated most activity in some way or other. Such must have been the case in pre-Inca cultures as well. There would consequently *seem* to have been little crime as we know it.

THE LAW

There was, however, Inca law, and pre-Inca societies undoubtedly had social rules, the transgression of which, if discovered, entailed punishment of some sort by the state or by one's peers. No archaeological evidence can be definitively ascribed to a crime or punishment. Even the gruesome treatment of the individuals in some Nazca graves seems to be religiously motivated rather than owing to criminal punishment. (At Cahuachi some men, women or children had their mouth pinned by cactus spines or tongue removed and placed in a pouch, or had their eyes blocked, their skull perforated for threading on a cord, or even excrement inserted into the mouth.)

There is a hint of such control, inevitably involving religion, however, in the famous tale of Fempellec, the

Above: Incarceration was one option for crime: the so-called prison buildings at Machu Picchu, possibly also used to hold noble captives for ransom.

ambitious twelfth descendant of the conquering king Naymlap of the northern coastal valleys. Fempellec attempted to remove the greenstone idol of the state dynastic god Yampallec from the capital Chot to another city. The cult priests, however, heartily disapproved of this sacrilegious act. A demon appeared (conjured up by the priests?) in the form of a beautiful woman, who seduced Fempellec – an act that caused 30 days of rain followed by a year of drought and the inevitable crop failures and famine. In retribution the priests seized and bound Fempellec, then threw him into the sea and left him to drown. Such rough justice probably represents a moral tale about what respect is owed to the gods and the consequences

Left: Punishment for crime was scaled not only according to the crime, but also according to social rank – the higher your rank the more severe your punishment. Plucking out an eye was one punishment for treason (from Poma de Ayala's Nueva Corónica, *c.1615).*

that can be expected if they are not honoured. The gods wreaked punishment on the people, and the priests exercised their punishment on the person responsible for the 'crime'.

APPLICATION OF LAW

Inca civil law applied to various social and state activities. Pachacuti Inca Yupanqui (tenth emperor, 1438–71) is credited by Garcilasco de la Vega with having set down basic Inca law, including punishments for blasphemy, patricide, fratricide, homicide, treason, adultery, child-stealing, seduction, theft and arson. Inca law governed tribal rights and obligations to the empire, the division of land and other property, the system of work rotation and the *mit'a* tax system. (The basic laws were few: laziness, lying, stealing, murder and adultery were crimes.) It also applied to

Above: Pachacuti Yupanqui, tenth Sapa Inca, is credited with setting out the basic Inca laws in the 15th century after his successful defence of Cuzco and defeat of the Chancas (oil on canvas, 18th-century 'Peruvian School').

proper conduct as an adult and as a married man or woman and the treatment of others, including the support of the elderly and disabled.

PUNISHMENT
There was a different punishment for every crime; but the punishment meted out to the perpetrator was scaled according to his or her social rank: the higher the status of the individual, the more severe the punishment. For example, although virginity was not a requirement of marriage, adultery by a commoner was punished by torture. But if a noblewoman committed adultery, both parties of the crime were put to death. A common punishment was beating with a stone club, sometimes to death. Other methods of execution were to be thrown off a cliff, or to be hung over a ravine by the hair until the roots gave way. A slovenly housewife was made to eat the household dirt; a husband who did not keep a tidy house had to eat dirt or drink his family's dirty bath water. Laziness was punished by whipping; chronic laziness by death.

CAPITAL PUNISHMENT
In a state that so highly regulated the collection and redistribution of property (the foodstuffs and materials produced under state organization), it was inevitable that a crime against the government was dealt with especially severely. Stealing from fields, whether they were state, religious or commoners' lands, was punishable by death. The same applied to theft from llama herds or from state storehouses.

It was rare for an Inca citizen or subject to be without the basic necessities of life. Therefore maltreatment of the elderly or disabled, to whom one would owe obligations in the *ayllu* kinship system, would be harshly dealt with.

Divorce was not recognized. A husband who cast aside his wife was forced to take her back; doing so again brought public whipping; a third time meant execution by clubbing or being thrown off a cliff.

Treason was punished by imprisonment, which almost always resulted in death. The traitor was thrown into an underground cell filled with venomous snakes and dangerous animals in Cuzco.

In addition to the basic laws of the land, the Inca emperor was entitled to enact new laws to suit his needs and new occasions. For example, Pachacuti is credited with decreeing that only princes and their sons could wear gold, silver and precious stone ornaments, multicoloured feather plumes or vicuña wool.

Below: Adultery was a serious crime: commoners were tortured, as depicted here by Poma de Ayala, c.1615; nobles who committed adultery were put to death.

MUSIC, DANCE AND RECREATION

We do not know what ancient Inca or pre-Inca music sounded like. The Peruvian or Andean panpipe music that became popular in the latter half of the 20th century cannot be taken as representative of pre-Hispanic Andean music for two reasons. First, accompanying guitars, and probably the harp, are post-Spanish Conquest introductions; second, new rhythms, melodies and musical concepts from European and other cultures have inevitably influenced it in the 500 years since the Spanish Conquest.

There is undoubtedly some continuity, however. The so-called Peruvian panpipes have an ancient Andean history and thus at least physical continuity. Andean rhythms are also distinctly different from Western European cadences, and might also reflect continuity. But we have no written examples of Andean music, so cannot be certain.

THE INSTRUMENTS

Archaeologists have found examples of instruments dating from at least the Early Horizon. There are Paracas and Nazca flutes, resembling modern recorders. Flutes were the only instrument in general use throughout the Andes. Panpipes comprise joined pottery or cane flutes of different lengths to produce different notes and tones. Ancient pottery examples differ from modern panpipes in that they have closed ends; thus sound is produced by blowing across the tops rather than through them.

Seashell trumpets were also used, different sizes and shapes producing haunting single tones. Moche pots, for example, depict figures blowing conch trumpets. Among the entourage of the legendary Naymlap is one Fonga Sigde, 'Blower of the Shell Trumpet'. Finally, there was a variety of percussion instruments: drums, tambourines, bells, rattles, and clackers of animal bone and wood.

THE ROLE OF MUSIC

Ancient Andean music and dance appears to have been predominantly for ceremony, played at special occasions for specific purposes, rather than as pure entertainment, although they undoubtedly gave participants and onlookers pleasure. Music formed a central role in Nazca ritual, as depicted on wall paintings at Cahuachi. Ritual processions along Nazca line figures were probably accompanied by flutes, drums, bells and trumpets.

Moche music appears to have been primarily associated with religion, sacrifice and war. Moche pots frequently

Left: A Chimú bottle with a group of musicians around the spout, showing a panpipe player flanked by two percussionists with gourd drums.

Above: Music and dance were frequently portrayed by the Moche in pottery, as here in this flute player effigy stirrup-spout bottle.

depict groups of musicians – principally flute, trumpet and drum players – as part of ritual combat and sacrifice scenes, and shamanism. Copper, gold and silver bells were attached to the metal plates covering the body of the Sipán Lord burial, and the accompanying burial of one of his ritual assistants was evidently a panpipe musician. The Moche associated the peanut with flute-playing.

Moche flutes and rattles in the handles of ritual vessels were for trance-inducement. Drums were used in religious ritual, and may also have been used to set a pace for weaving – a drum was found in the Pampa Grande textile workshop.

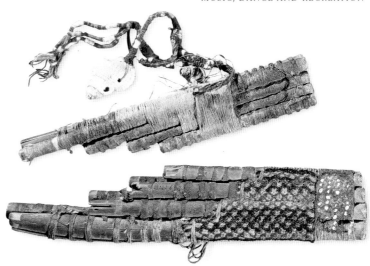

Inca music accompanied dance at festivals and initiation rites. It was also important in 'entertaining' labourers who worked on Inca engineering and agricultural projects. Gifted individuals were also trained as royal court musicians, and it is recorded that some players played several flutes together to extend the sound range. Flutes were also used for love songs, and drums, trumpets and flutes accompanied Inca armies on the march.

STRANGE MUSIC

Curiously, some Late Horizon Chimú double-chambered vessels, the two parts connected by a bridge, produced a whistle. The liquid level in the chambers changes tone, which escapes from a hole at the top of one chamber.

The tonal qualities of water for religious inspiration were also appreciated at Chavín de Huantár. Running gushing water around the interior conduits of the chambers of its labyrinthine temple produced an awesome roar from the door (mouth) of the temple that was heard by the assembled worshippers in the courtyard outside.

THE DANCE

Inca dancing was restricted to ritual occasions: seasonal festivals in the agricultural year, to accompany religious ceremony,

and at life-stage recognition. The idea of social dancing did not exist. Such was undoubtedly the purpose of dance in pre-Inca cultures as well.

Inca dance was formal, with participants performing a series of specific movements in unison. Special dances were performed by men (for example at puberty rites), and women (for example at harvesting rituals); other dances involved both sexes. When *mallquis* mummies were brought out to participate in the ceremony, songs and dances were performed before them, and stories of their exploits recited.

RECREATION

Almost nothing is known about ancient Andean 'leisure' activities, probably because there was little time for anything other than the necessary daily tasks. Even ritual dancing, singing and music were considered essential for life and wellbeing rather than recreation or entertainment. Children began to fulfil daily tasks as soon as they were capable.

Chicha beer drinking on ritual and ceremonial occasions could obviously *de facto* become 'recreational'.

Left: Drums made of wood, pottery, gourds and stretched hide were also common instruments for ritual and dance ceremonies. This Moche stirrup-spout bottle is in the shape of a drummer with his bone or wooden beater, his hat held with a chin strap.

Above: Various pipes and flutes were the most common instruments. Sets of pitched panpipes were made of both pottery and reeds bound with twine or decorated textiles, such as these Nazca examples.

Inca children played with balls and tops and at games using rounded pottery pieces for markers and counters. Adults played a dice game with five, rather than six, numbers. There were also board games that used bean counters. The Incas also gambled, often for high stakes. Inca nobles played a game called *aylloscas*, in which entire estates were wagered. We do not know the rules for any of these games.

Warfare being so important in Inca society, boys were 'trained' in games of skill intended to test them and make them brave and tough. There were races and mock battles that were taken with such seriousness that severe injuries are recorded.

Nothing is known of recreation in pre-Inca cultures, except perhaps the ritual combat of the Moche, in which individuals had lifetime careers. This was a deadly profession, however, for religious purposes and sacrifice.

By Inca times, hunting was mostly recreational. It broke the monotonous routine of agriculture, and also had the outcome of providing meat. Hunting by Inca and provincial noblemen was surely recreation for them.

363

DEATH AND BURIAL

Death in the Andean world was not considered the end of existence: it was the next stage or state of being after life on Earth. Archaeological evidence of elite and common burials shows that elaborate preparations were made, almost throughout life, for this next state of being. Moreover, the Andean worldview applied this belief to all living things – humans, animals and plants – and to the Earth itself as a 'living' entity.

LIKE A PLANT
Anthropologist Frank Salomon describes the Andean outlook on life's cycle as a "pervasive vegetative metaphor". Plants provide a metaphor for human and animal life as they progress from tender shoots through firmer, resilient stems and plants, then mature, rigid, but drier plants, and finally to a desiccated state – just as humans progress from newborns, through infanthood, puberty, young adulthood, old age, and death, though enduring as mummies. The mummified body was likened to a dried pod from which seeds of new life dropped.

ELITE AND COMMON
Burial and afterlife, however, varied throughout Andean civilization. The greatest contrast is in the treatment of elite members of society and common people. The rich burials of nobles and priests in Moche-Sipán and Lambayeque-Sicán tombs and the elaborate burials of some Nazca dead, for example, contrast with simpler interments in common graves with a few tools and pots.

PRESERVING THE BODY
The Initial Period Chinchorros and La Paloma peoples of the Chilean

Above: A Nazca mummy bundle, the final wrapping being a plain woven shroud bound with cord.

coast show attempts to preserve the actual flesh in addition to the soul or essence of 'life'.

In the Early Horizon and Early Intermediate Period, the unfinished states of some Paracas and Nazca mummy textile wraps show that they were being prepared long before, and in anticipation of, physical death. Paracas and Nazca elaborate burial procedures show that considerable care and planning were involved. Nevertheless, burial in tombs removed the bodies from the living. Ancestor worship or honour was evident in these cultures, as demonstrated by the care of burial and by the fact that most tombs were reopened periodically to place other kin members inside

Left: A bulky Paracas mummy bundle with effigy face and feathered cap – the higher your rank, the more elaborate the bundle and textile patterns.

Above: On the southern Peruvian coast, the Nazca are noted for deep, mud-brick-lined tombs, ancestral vaults, which they reopened for successive burials through generations.

them. Late Intermediate Period people in the Titicaca Basin placed their mummies in special burial towers – *chullpas* – as sepulchres meant to be reopened periodically for the deposit of other mummies.

Other cultures, however, treated their mummies differently. Chimú mummies of deceased rulers were housed in their own compounds, within a virtual city of the dead, within a city of the living. Each compound housed a living retinue to look after the dead ruler's remains, perform rituals respecting it, and collect food and other goods for daily life.

Inca mummies were kept very much as a part of the lives of the living. They were visited regularly and brought out on ritual occasions. They were consulted for advice, honoured with recitals of poetry and stories, and even 'fed' on ritual occasions.

PACARINA

Andean cultures believed that the essence of a dead person ultimately went to a final resting. The physical body was only a vessel for this life – the person's 'vital force', or soul, found its way to *pacarina*. *Pacarina* was the place of origin of one's ancestors and the ultimate source of rebirth. It could be a tree, rock, cave, spring or lake – a magical shelter from the world's ravages.

There were different names for *pacarina*. The people of Collasuyu and Cuntisuyu called it Puquina Pampa and Coropuna. Documents from Cajatambo call it Uma Pacha; and the peoples of the Lima region called it Upaymarca. Coastal peoples named the 'Island of Guano' as the final resting place.

Of common belief was a final resting place of farms, where the dead sowed their seeds. The spirit continued to tend the fields and crops, and to experience thirst and hunger as the body does on Earth, and so was fed by the living with offerings of food and drink. Those still living nevertheless also considered the spirits

of the dead to be dangerous. It was thus necessary to help the dead person's soul reach the end of its journey, lest the spirit wander among the living causing violence, sickness and accidents.

SACRIFICE

Death by ritual sacrifice was a special form of death and burial that was practised throughout Andean civilization. Human and animal sacrifices were performed to honour and supplicate the gods, commemorate the building of temples to them and appease the forces of nature. Decapitation, bludgeoning and strangulation were common.

Moche ritual combat was a special form of sacrificial death, as was the Inca practice of sacrifice and burial on remote high mountaintops. Another Inca practice was deliberate exposure to lightning, and if killed by it, burial of the *qhaqha* (lightning victim) at the place of death.

Below: Ancestral sepulchres were common in Andean cultures from early times. The Collao are famous for their stone chullpa *towers, one group of which is at Sillustani near Puno, Lake Titicaca.*

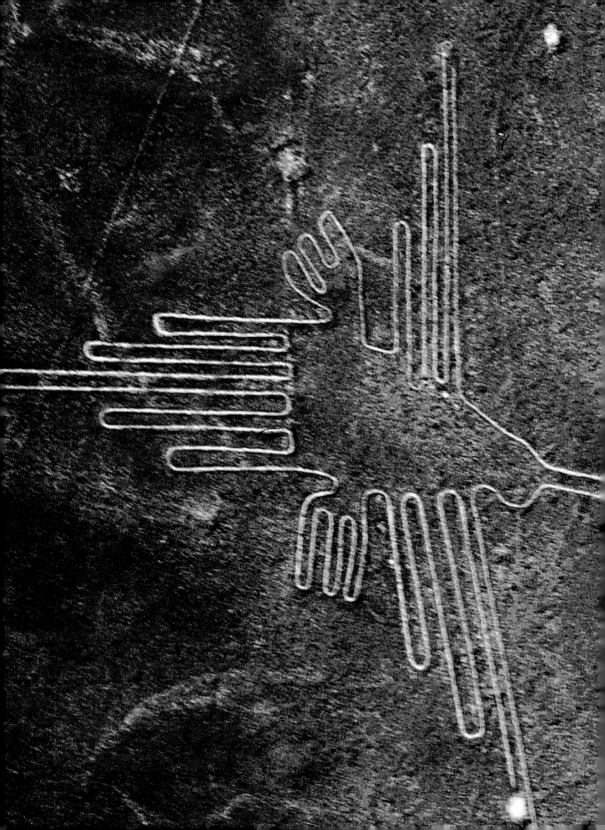

CHAPTER EIGHTEEN

RELIGIOUS BELIEFS

Ancient Andeans' cosmogony and cosmology – their stories of how the world came into being and how it worked – helped them cope with the events of everyday life and with the periodic stress they faced in what was to them a sometimes unpredictable environment. The ancient Greek word *cosmeo* means 'to order or arrange', and incorporates the idea of 'good order'. Not surprisingly, then, ancient Andean mythical explanations of their cosmos and its origins put them in good order.

Astronomical observations, especially of the sun, moon and Milky Way, revealed to ancient Andeans a regular relationship between solar and lunar cycles and the seasons. Their observations enabled them to create a calendar, regulate their religious ceremonies and plan their work. Irregularities, such as natural disasters, were less understood because they appeared to be unpredictable. They were regarded as punishment by the gods for wrongdoing.

The gods created the world and divided it into its parts: the world of the living (the Inca *Kai Pacha*), the world above (*Hanan Pacha*) and the world below (*Uku Pacha*). Overseeing all was a supreme god or being (with various names, the two most common being Viracocha and Pachacamac), and a large pantheon of other deities. This world worked and was in good order because the gods made it so. The reciprocal part to be played by humans, in order to keep the world in good order, was proper deference to and worship of the gods.

Left: Symbolism and ritual pathways were a hallmark of ancient Andean religion, as in this Nazca hummingbird geoglyph.

BELIEF SYSTEMS AND LITERATURE

Without the favour of the gods, life could be difficult. At a daily level, religion permeated every aspect of Andean life. Thought about how the world was created and humans' place within it is evident in early burials, within which everyday items were included, presumably in the belief that the buried person would need them in some sort of afterlife. The careful treatment of bodies, attempting to preserve them, or to clothe and prepare them for burial in other special ways, shows that a belief in an afterlife had developed in Chinchorros, La Paloma, Paracas and other early cultures, and continued into Inca times.

RISE AND INCREASING COMPLEXITY

Religious beliefs became formalized alongside an increasing complexity in social and political organization. Imagery of deities representing the forces of nature and creation increased as religion developed its own organizational status within the state. A separate hierarchy of

Below: The Chincha in coastal Peru, one of many Inca conquests, had a shrine at La Centinella, a characteristic adobe brick temple mound forming the focus of an urban ceremonial centre.

individuals became dedicated to looking after the appeasement of the gods as intermediaries between the deities and the common people. Elaborate histories, now called mythology, developed as accepted explanations of how the world came into being, how humans were created, and what constituted proper conduct towards the gods.

The gods controlled the forces of nature and were believed to be responsible for events that brought benefit and wellbeing to humans, as well as disaster and hardship. It was therefore believed necessary to plead with them and make special efforts to solicit their approval. Specialists with powers and status that enabled them to negotiate with the gods on behalf of humans had to be provided for. Their needs (or demands) became substantial. In the Inca Empire the produce from a third of all lands was given for the upkeep of the state religion.

PRIESTS AS INTERMEDIARIES

Priestly communication with the gods was through trance-like states, even shape shifting (it was believed), to solicit guidance and sacred favour; conducting ritual and sacrificial offerings (animal and human) to the gods; and making images of them in stone, pottery, wood and

Above: Many Andean beliefs in natural deities endure. A 20th-century Aymara couple here prepare offerings at the Huaca of Mount Illimani.

metal, which were housed as idols in special temples. Priests also gave instruction and guidance to individuals and groups at mass ceremonies through omens and oracles.

Ceremonies to honour the gods became increasingly elaborate as Andean civilization evolved. The course of the seasons, regulating daily and seasonal patterns of life and work, together with observations of the heavens and the regular movements of celestial bodies, fostered the development of a cycle of rituals performed on specific dates. These included the solstices and equinoxes, and were co-ordinated with human lifecycles through the stages of birth, childhood, initiation into adulthood and death.

SACRED PLACES AND SPACES

Natural and man-made sacred places were numerous and varied. Mountains, bodies of water, springs and the sky were all sacred in their own right. In them and on them the gods were thought to dwell or be embodied. The term *huaca* (Quechua) was applied to any sacred location – natural, man-made or a

modified natural place – embodying the spirit of a deity, and where offerings were made: caves, islands, springs, outcrops of rock, mountains, a boulder or pile of stones, even a field in which a significant event took place. The term *apu* (literally 'lord' in Quechua) was used for sacred peaks in a land dominated by prominent volcanic cones.

Designating space and building special structures for ceremonial performances began early. A Y-shaped structure was built on one side of the village at Monte Verde some 14,800 years ago. It had a raised, sand and gravel floor and associated artefacts differentiating it from the ordinary houses. These included clay-lined braziers at the rear of the hut,

Below: Diagram of Yana Phuyu (the 'Dark Cloud' constellations): animal shapes seen by Andean peoples in Ch'aska Mayu, *the 'celestial river' of the Milky Way.*

medicinal plants and chewed leaves, seeds, hides, animal bones and apparent burnt offerings.

In time, all Andean cultures built large, elaborate structures and enclosures for ceremony and worship. Different forms were combined in ceremonial complexes within cities, or in the landscapes around them. There were raised mounds, pyramid-platforms for supporting temples; sunken courts (round, square or rectangular); labyrinthine buildings or complexes housing images of the gods; walled sacred compounds; and geoglyphs or designated routes laid out on the ground, such as the Nazca lines and figures, and Inca sacred *ceque* site lines and routes.

SACRED LITERATURE

The only ancient Andean literature known is Inca. However, the recurrence in Chimú and Inca culture of the story of the 'Revolt of the Objects' (graphically

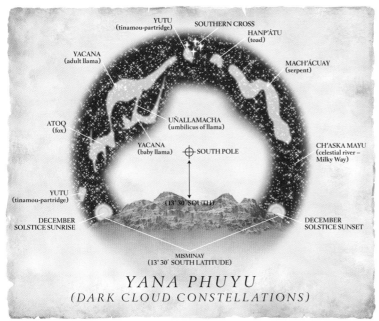

Above: The Ponce Monolith at Tiwanaku, believed to be a petrified member of a former race of giants, is representative of Andean belief systems featuring successive ages of creation.

depicted in Moche murals at the Huaca de la Luna) reveals that this tale had been told for at least a millennium!

Inca literature was oral, and mostly dealt with religion and history. There were stories, legends, songs, poems and doctrines. Being passed down verbally, they were subject to variation and personal interpretation. Few examples survive because so little was recorded or translated by Spanish officials. On the contrary, they resolutely destroyed it as idolatrous.

There were four categories: religious prayers and hymns, dramatic histories or legends, narrative poems, and songs. Prayers and hymns praise the gods and goddesses. Only two dramatic pieces survive, as poor translations. Narrative poems, memorized for recital at public ceremonies, almost all concern religion and histories of the emperors. Dramatic pieces, also emphasizing religious themes, were performed at dances, recited by one or two 'actors' and a chorus. Poetry and song (the former set to music) were mostly love songs.

YUTU
(tinamou-partridge)
SOUTHERN CROSS
HANP'ÁTU
(toad)
YACANA
(adult llama)
MACH'ÁCUAY
(serpent)
ATOQ
(fox)
UÑALLAMACHA
(umbilicus of llama)
YACANA
(baby llama)
SOUTH POLE
CH'ASKA MAYU
(celestial river –
Milky Way)
YUTU
(tinamou-partridge)
(13' 30' SOUTH)
DECEMBER
SOLSTICE SUNRISE
DECEMBER
SOLSTICE SUNSET
MISMINAY
(13' 30' SOUTH LATITUDE)

YANA PHUYU
(DARK CLOUD CONSTELLATIONS)

COMMON THEMES AND CONTINUITY

Religious beliefs about how the world worked were the enduring matrix that bound Andean civilization. Concepts that developed in Preceramic times continued, with cultural distinctiveness and elaboration, through to Inca times.

NATURAL AND RELIGIOUS CONTROLS

Ancient Andeans believed that natural forces were created and controlled by the gods. With so much of daily life and survival bound by the landscape, the ancient Andean worldview reflected the landscape by adhesion to it and through a sympathetic harmony with it.

Andean cities and, before true urbanization, the earliest ceremonial complexes of the Preceramic and Initial periods, maintained their relationship with the natural world not only through their physical configurations and economic viability but also through their religious institutions. Priests and shamans mediated society's ties to nature and relationships with the gods.

URBAN FOCUS

Ceremonial complexes and, later, religious precincts in cities were the focus for religious activities. Cities and buildings

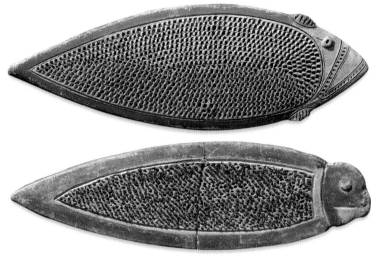

Above: Aquatic themes were common in Andean art, here exemplified by two fish carved from manioc (cassava) husks, La Tolita culture of Ecuador.

were oriented according to sacred concepts. Astronomical orientations sometimes guided routes and alignments. Temples and pyramid-platforms frequently faced sacred mountains, and sometimes even mimicked their contours

or profiles. Canals brought water to cities from holy springs. Even the plan of Cuzco, a crouching puma, honoured a revered animal.

Common architectural forms endured throughout ancient Andean history. The raising of tiered platform mounds began as early as 6000BC at Nanchoc in the Zana Valley. The combination of platforms and sunken courtyards, and the U-shaped configuration of temple complexes begun in Preceramic Period cultures, continued to the Late Horizon. Open plazas hosted large ritual gatherings, while enclosed courts were for more intimate worship. Sacred lines, predetermined pathways in the deserts and walled complexes, including sunken courts, controlled people's movements and directed them into ritual patterns. Windowless chambers and hidden passageways accommodated exclusive ritual and promoted mystery and power.

Left: Mount Parinacota, Chile: the permanence of the landscape was revered in the animism of mountains especially, each of which had its own huaca or spiritual essence, or was dwelt in or on by a deity.

Open ceremonial space was juxtaposed by elements of hiddenness and obscurity: temple interiors and ceremonial compounds could be labyrinthine; oracles were housed in dark inner chambers; some ceremonies were performed by and for specialists only; sunken courtyards restricted numbers and obscured or regulated ritual.

These structures and activities were designed to ensure a proper relationship with the gods and nature. Offerings were made of the most precious objects, including the lives of animals and humans offered in dedication, honour and placation.

SUPREME BEINGS

A distinctive principal deity or creator being is recognizable in most cultures or regions. Mountain deities naturally predominated in highland cultures and sea gods in coastal valleys, yet early widespread contact between highlands, coasts and tropical forests spread more universal themes, even if imagery was culturally distinctive.

Below: Crustaceans were a common symbolic theme on Andean pottery and textiles. Here prawns are featured on a Nazca bridge-spout bottle.

The supreme deity at Chavin de Huántar, represented in the Staff Deity, was widespread in the Early Horizon, and could be male or female. The evolution of this supreme deity through several hundred years of the Chávin Cult incorporates combinations of feline, tropical cayman, serpentine and avian imagery.

Sky deities or attributes are common, and in addition to deities embodied in terrestrial features such as mountains or springs, the sun and the moon were commonly worshipped. The Moche supreme deity, often known as the Decapitator, features a rayed head, like the sun, and feline fangs. The Paracas–Nazca Oculate Being is distinctly celestial, depicted most frequently horizontally and with streaming appendages as if flying. Pachacamac, from his centre of worship in the city of Pachacamac, represented a supreme being with whom lesser deities throughout the Andean Area sought alliance through their priests. Official Inca religion simultaneously worshipped the supreme being Viracocha, the Creator, and promoted a state cult of the Sun (Inti), as well as worshipping other deities.

Above: The great Inti temple of Sacsahuaman was the ultimate sun temple and ceremonial precinct of Inca worship.

RELIGIOUS CEREMONY

People came to ancient Andean cities not for markets, as in other ancient civilizations, but for ritual. Special quarters housed craft workers who produced only luxury items and purpose-made ritual vessels destined for the elite, for offerings to the gods, and for burial. Annual cycles of ceremonies brought people into the cities in huge crowds during certain seasons. Elite goods, stored by the priestly and noble classes, were bestowed upon the celebrants on these occasions.

Regular ceremonies throughout the year were portrayed in art. Common animals and themes were depicted in all media and there was colour everywhere: in murals on temples and compound walls; on stone and wood sculptures; in polychrome ceramics and textiles for daily, ceremonial and funerary use; and in shimmering metalwork. Such imagery was a perpetual reminder to people of their religious obligations and need to solicit the favour of the gods.

371

Above: The great mud-brick temple mound at Moche, the Huaca de la Luna, forms a pair with the Huaca del Sol to honour two ancient fundamental Andean deities.

COMMON IMAGERY AND DUALITY

Ceremonial centre planning and common imagery developed in the Preceramic and Initial periods and became entrenched in the Early Horizon.

Widespread connections between coastal, highland and tropical forest cultures for exotic materials spread ideas and knowledge of plants and animals. Thus feline, serpentine and avian imagery became universal in the earliest textiles and later on in pottery and architectural sculptures. Insects, spiders, fish, and crustaceans and shellfish were also common themes. Composite beings, part-human/part-beast, were frequently portrayed as manifestations of deities, humans taking divine parts in ritual or humans in transformation under the influence of hallucinogenic substances.

Duality, with juxtaposed imagery and two-headed creatures, was commonly used in all media. From the Huaca Prieta twined double-headed crab and serpent cloth of *c.*2500BC, via the hawk and eagle images on the Black and White Portal columns at Chavín de Huántar's

New Temple *c.*500BC, the male-female Yaya-Mama sculptures of the Titicaca Basin, the paired Tiwanaku, Wari and Inca gold figurines, and the two-faced Pachacamac idol to the twinned facing birds on a Chimú spondylus shell ornament, duality was a vital artery in Andean belief.

The use of hallucinogenic substances – another common religious practice – was believed to induce transformation, and is frequently depicted. Priests or shamans under the influence were believed to be able to gain insight regarding the cosmos and divine intentions, to take on the characteristics of revered animals such as a jaguar or raptor, and to heal the sick. Hallucinogenic trance was a means of temporarily departing this world and entering the 'other side' – yet another manifestation of duality.

Even economic and social structure reflect this concept, in the reciprocal trade relationships between highlands and lowlands and the division of kinship groups into two moiety groups: *hanan* (upper) and *hurin* (lower).

Right: The majestic condor, symbolic of the Andes, was sacred. Here a condor soars with extended talons on a Nazca bridge-spout bottle.

SACRIFICE

Sacrificial offerings to the gods solicited good weather and productive harvests, herding and fishing. They were also atonement to angry gods who caused natural disasters and El Niño weather cycles.

Human sacrifice frequently accompanied temple dedications and elite burials. From the sacrificed adult buried near the infant at Huaca de los Sacrificios at Preceramic Aspero, through the blood groove in the Lanzón Stela at Chavín de Huántar, the Moche and Tiwanaku decapitator deities, the mass grave behind the Huaca de la Luna at Moche and the 17 sacrificial victims in a Sicán tomb at Batán Grande, to Inca *capacocha* sacrifices, the taking of human (and animal) life pervaded Andean religion.

There was also a special cult of severed heads. At Preceramic Asia on the Peruvian central coast, eight severed heads were wrapped in a mat and ritually interred, while Nazca collectors perforated trophy head skulls and strung them on cords. Chavín de Huántar and Tiwanaku temple builders mounted stone-carved severed heads on plaza walls, and Inca warriors drank victory toasts from the skulls of slain opponents.

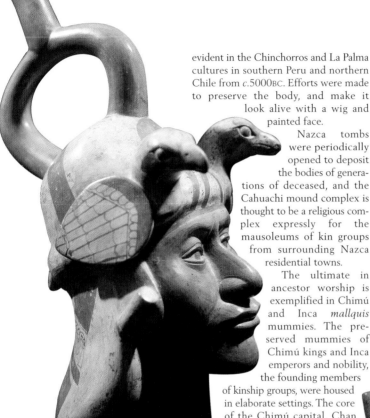

Above: A Moche portrait vessel, one of hundreds of individual portrait stirrup-spout bottle, shows a 'chief' – possibly a successful 'gladiator' – wearing a winged bird helmet.

ANCESTOR WORSHIP

Ancient Andean religious beliefs regarded 'being' as a perpetual cycle or revolution (*pachacuti* in Quechua). Death was considered a different state of being, in which the dead person entered another world and in some respects carried on in a life not dissimilar to the one departed on Earth.

Thus it was important to maintain links with the 'other side' through ancestor worship. Special preparation before burial is evident in the Chinchorros and La Palma cultures in southern Peru and northern Chile from *c.*5000BC. Efforts were made to preserve the body, and make it look alive with a wig and painted face.

Nazca tombs were periodically opened to deposit the bodies of generations of deceased, and the Cahuachi mound complex is thought to be a religious complex expressly for the mausoleums of kin groups from surrounding Nazca residential towns.

The ultimate in ancestor worship is exemplified in Chimú and Inca *mallquis* mummies. The preserved mummies of Chimú kings and Inca emperors and nobility, the founding members of kinship groups, were housed in elaborate settings. The core of the Chimú capital, Chan Chan, comprised vast walled compounds to house the dead rulers' mummies and their living retainers. Inca imperial *mallquis* were kept in special rooms in the sacred Coricancha temple. Virtually every Andean community in the Late Horizon had its *ayllu* ancestor mummies, stored in temples or in nearby sacred caves, to be brought out at religious rituals and consulted on communal and personal matters.

RELIGIOUS TRADITIONS, PILGRIMAGE AND ORACLES

Religious continuity was secured in ancient Andean civilization through the early development of recognizable 'traditions'. The earliest of these are perhaps the Kotosh Religious Tradition, exemplified by the successive Temple of the Crossed Hands and Temple of the Niches at Kotosh, and the Plazas Hundidas Tradition (hidden courts), both prevailing in the Preceramic and Initial periods.

Continuity and coherence in the Early Horizon was through religious belief rather than political unification. Two spheres, although not exclusive, focused on the Chavín Cult and Staff Deity in the northern and central Andes, and in the Pukará Yaya-Mama Cult of the Titicaca Basin.

Many early U-shaped ceremonial centres and Kotosh Tradition sites were centres for local communities. Whether their religious influence was more widespread because they were cult centres is open to debate. Later sites, such as Chavín de Huántar, Moche, Tiwanaku and Pachacamac, and imperial Inca Cuzco itself, were certainly cult and pilgrimage centres, recognized as such through analogy with the pilgrimage and oracle city of Pachacamac, which endured despite Wari, Inca and Spanish conquest and is thus described in chronicles.

Below: A whistle-spout/bridge-spout bottle of the Early Intermediate Period Vicus culture features crayfish on gourd bases and a feeding bird.

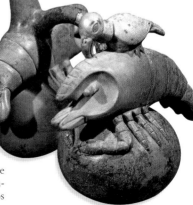

CREATION AND COSMOLOGY

Andean cosmological belief was 'organic'. The universe was regarded as an animate being, a living entity, rather than as a mechanical object. Celestial motions, the seasons and the ways the natural world functioned were ordered, and could be relied on. They believed that the universe was ordered, and thus showed design. But at the same time, it was believed to have been created by the gods and so was controlled by them.

CREATION AND CREATORS
Beliefs stemming from the forces of nature provided a common base from which later Andean cultures constructed elaborate stories of creation. Most included a great flood and the survival of

a single man and woman. Variations explain several stages of creation, in which the gods made the universe, the sun and moon, and perfected their design of humankind to make beings capable of worshipping them properly.

The two most important creator gods were Viracocha and Pachacamac. They were almost interchangeable as all-powerful gods, somewhat aloof and removed from day-to-day affairs, although Pachacamac was predominantly a coastal and lowland deity, while Viracocha predominated in the highlands.

VIRACOCHA AND THE BASIC STORY
The creation of the universe was thought to have taken place in the Titicaca Basin. Viracocha emerged from Lake Titicaca and made a dark world, without sun, moon or stars, and a race of giants. This race was to live peacefully and worship Viracocha, but instead it defied him. He turned some of the giants into stone; others were swallowed by the earth and sea. A great flood (*unu pachacuti*) swamped the land, drowning everything but one man and one woman, who landed at Tiwanaku.

Left: One of the many stone stelae at Tiwanaku, believed to be the petrified bodies of a former race of giants.

Above: To many Andean cultures Tiwanaku and Lake Titicaca were the place of the origin of the world and of humans. Tiwanaku's Akapana temple mound and stellae, depicted here in 1845 by Alcides D'Obigny, was long a site of religious pilgrimage.

Next Viracocha created the sun, moon and stars, and set them in motion from the Island of the Sun and Island of the Moon in the lake. He made a second, normal-sized human race from stone and clay, named them and painted them with their national costumes and hairstyles, then dispersed them underground in their future homelands. With two or three helpers he then travelled through the land, calling forth the nations to re-emerge through caves, and also from hills and lakes, as he went, until he reached the north-west coast and disappeared across the sea – in one version on a cloak raft, in another walking on the water.

THE FIVE AGES
An Inca version of creation, retold by Guaman Poma de Ayala, was of five ages of creation.

The first age was darkness. Its inhabitants, the *Wari Wiracocharuna*, were primitive, wore leaf clothing and ate 'unprocessed vegetal matter'. They worshipped Viracocha and Pachacamac, but they were later destroyed in an unspecified manner.

The second age had the more advanced race of the *Wari Runa* as its inhabitants. They wore animal skins, practised primitive agriculture and lived in peace, believing Viracocha to be their creator. Nevertheless, a great flood ended their existence.

The third age, inhabited by the *Purun Runa*, was civilized. People practised irrigation agriculture, span and dyed wool and cotton, made pottery and mined for metal to make jewellery. Each town had a ruler, but there was increased warfare as the population increased. Pachacamac was worshipped as the creator.

The *Auca Runa* inhabited the fourth age. Civilization and technology were more sophisticated in every regard. Conflict had increased to the point where people lived in fortified towns on hilltops. The social arrangements of *ayllu* kinship divisions and decimal administration came into being. It is not specified how this age ended.

The fifth age was that of the Incas and all they brought and created: imperial rule, *ayllus* and bipartite 'moiety' divisions of *hanan* (upper) and *hurin* (lower), and decimal bureaucracy. There were six principal gods, the most important being Viracocha, the Creator, and Inti, the Sun.

These creation stories, and many permutations of them, were meant to explain how the world came to be, why the gods were important and should be honoured, and how the technology and craftsmanship came into being. Guaman Poma de Ayala's version amounts to a potted history. The Incas became a repository for religious developments going back to the Preceramic Period. They embraced the multitudes of local deities and creation stories.

COSMOLOGY AND CALENDARS

The regularities of the seasons, the cycles of the sun, the phases of the moon and the progression of the Milky Way across the night sky were evidence of a plan, of a supreme intelligence who had created them and set them in motion – a being

Above The Wari Runa *were the second race of people in the Inca creation myth of successive 'ages', depicted in Poma de Ayala's* Nueva Corónica, c.1615.

or deity who afterwards took an overarching position but left daily issues to lesser, local deities.

The Incas tracked the movements of the sun and moon and created two calendars: a solar ('day-time'), 365-day year and a lunar ('night-time'), 328-day year. They do not seem to have been overly concerned with the 37-day discrepancy, possibly due to the fact that Inca calendrical observations were not essentially for the purpose of timekeeping. More important was to determine the correct times for religious rituals and festivals, to mark the beginning of important agricultural tasks, and to worship the sun and moon as deities.

The rotation of the Milky Way was important, but only the Pleiades, possibly the Southern Cross, and the summer and winter solstices were especially noted. More importantly, the voids between the stars, called 'dark cloud constellations', were envisaged as beasts known on Earth, and named after adult and baby llamas, the fox, the partridge, the toad and the snake and other animals.

Left: Believing Lake Titicaca to be the origin of the world, including the sun and the moon, the Incas built a temple to Inti on the Island of the Sun in the lake, to which Inca emperors made annual pilgrimages.

PILGRIMAGE, ORACLES AND SHRINES

Religious power and the ascendancy of priests in Andean civilization is evident in the monumentality of religious architecture. Ceremonial centres of terraced platforms, temples and ritual courtyards were focuses for communities of the surrounding regions. With true urbanism, from *c.*500BC, cities were dominated by their central ceremonial precincts.

RELIGIOUS TRADITIONS

Construction of common elements in ceremonial centres suggests widespread similarities in belief. Archaeologists recognize several early 'religious traditions', two of which flourished in the late Preceramic and Initial periods: the Kotosh Religious Tradition and the Plazas Hundidas Tradition. Significant in each is the division of space into forms that reflected religious belief, and that classified space horizontally and vertically, and as open and closed.

No ceremonial centre, however, appears to be dominant, although U-shaped ceremonial centres did serve local regions. The association of platform mounds and sunken courts nevertheless suggests the early link between a celestial deity and an earth mother.

Below: The fanged jaguar deity was one of several major themes in Chavín religious ritual, featured here in bas-relief on stone at Chavín de Huántar.

CHAVÍN DE HUÁNTAR

This settlement, which appears to have been deliberately located between the highlands and the coast, with access to exotic materials from deserts and tropical forests as well as locally, emerged in the Early Horizon as a unifying centre.

It was not a residential city. Rather it perpetuated the U-shaped temple tradition. A restricted residential complex was sufficient only for priests and attendants, and a limited number of craftspeople to produce portable objects with Chavín Cult imagery.

Celestial and earth deity association is evident in the embracing of a sunken court between the arms of U-shaped platform mounds. The Old Temple enclosed a circular sunken court and the New Temple a rectangular one. Projecting back the known importance of earth and sky association in Inca creation mythology, the Lanzón Stela in the central chamber of the Old Temple provides a metaphor of transition from earth to sky in its perforation of the upper gallery floor. So, too, the pairing, skyward gaze and invertibility of the Tello Stone caymans, the eagle and hawk of the Black and White Portal columns, and the Raimondi Stela in the New Temple.

Above: As well as animal figures, Nazca geoglyphs depicted sacred plants, here a cactus, on the desert floor. It forms a continuous line that never crosses itself, to form a ritual pathway.

The widespread distribution of Chavín symbolism in the north and central Andes, even as far as Paracas in the southern coastal desert, strengthens the argument that it was the earliest Andean 'international' pilgrimage site. The enlargement of the temple to a size that could accommodate 1,500 people in its courtyards and plazas reveals a growing importance over several hundred years of existence.

PACHACAMAC

The idea of a truly international pilgrimage site, a 'cathedral' for Andean religious worship, is well attested archaeologically and in Spanish documents for Pachacamac on the central Peruvian coast. Established in the early first millennium AD, its platform mound and windowless temple housing a wooden Pachacamac idol soon became a destination for pilgrims throughout the Andes.

Right: The pilgrimage temple and cult at Pachacamac endured for more than a millennium, a longevity and sacredness that the Incas could not ignore, but rather honoured and joined by building additional temples, including the so-called Temple of the Virgins.

Spanish eyewitness accounts in 1534 record that the city thronged with pilgrims, whose dress showed them to have come from throughout the Inca Empire. Priests, nobles and pilgrims were admitted and given accommodation in the vast complex of courts and rooms surrounding the temple. To enter the lower plaza of the temple, the supplicant had to 'fast' for 20 days. To enter the upper plaza meant a year-long 'fast'. ('Fasting' in this context required abstinence from salt, chilli peppers and sexual intercourse.)

ORACLE AT PACHACAMAC

The Pachacamac idol was veiled and only priests were allowed into the temple room itself. Questions put to the Pachacamac oracle concerned the weather, harvests, health matters and warfare. A priest relayed the god's answers to the supplicant, followed by hefty demands

for tribute and donations. So powerful was the oracle that failure to comply with his mandates was believed to bring earthquakes and other natural disasters. Tupac Yupanqui, eleventh Inca Emperor and conqueror of the region, was made to fast for 40 days before he was allowed to consult the god; and, like other pilgrims, he was allowed to do so only through a cult priest. Even the mighty Inca had to recognize the importance of Pachacamac!

Lesser cults and their priests from all over the Andes sought alliance with the cult. Branch shrines were established only if they could assign lands and produce sufficient food to support a Pachacamac

priest on site. Allied shrines were considered the 'wives', 'children' or 'brothers and sisters' of the Pachacamac Cult.

TIWANAKU

The power and well-documented status and longevity of Pachacamac provides archaeologists with powerful arguments for interpreting other sites as pilgrimage cities and oracles. As well as Chavín de Huántar, the Titicaca Basin appears to have been the focus of an early cult called the Yaya-Mama (male-female) Tradition, one of whose ceremonial centres was Early Horizon Pukará, north of the lake.

The region was soon dominated by Tiwanaku, however, whose empire flourished in the Middle Horizon. The size and complexity of Tiwanaku's platforms, sacrificial burials, sunken courtyards and symbolic statuary clearly reveal it to have been another pilgrimage and cathedral city. Recent research shows that in addition to its Akapana, Kalasasaya and Semi-Subterranean Court complex in the city centre, the Pumapunku complex almost 1 km (½ mile) to the south-west served as both a ritual gateway into the sacred city and a ceremonial theatre for worshipping pilgrims.

Left: Tiwanaku, pilgrimage centre and religious capital of an empire, had several large, stone-built temples and sacred compounds, including the Pumapunku – ritual gateway to the sacred city.

SACRIFICE, SLAUGHTER AND RITUAL

Human and animal sacrifices played an important role in ancient Andean civilization. They were widespread and very ancient. Sacrificial rituals accompanied religious worship and were often an aftermath of warfare, presumably also with religious motives.

The earliest example of human sacrifice is from late Preceramic Period Aspero. At the summit of the Huaca de los Sacrificios platform there were two burials, apparently dedicatory offerings to the gods to inaugurate the temple. One was an infant, specially adorned in a cap of 500 shell, plant and clay beads,

Below: On a Moche effigy stirrup-spouted red-line painted bottle, a transformed skeletal priest sacrifices a deer.

accompanied by a gourd vessel, wrapped in layers of cotton cloth and a cane mat and placed in a basket, then covered by a sculptured four-legged stone basin. The second was a sacrificed adult, whose body was so tightly flexed that that limbs had had to be cut to force the body into a small pit.

HUMAN SLAUGHTER
The great wall of carved stone slabs at Cerro Sechín is an early example of war-related sacrifice. Stacks of smaller slabs between tall slabs depicting triumphant warriors are carved with mutilated, contorted victims. The wall appears to be a war memorial. Agonized victims are shown nude, their torsos sliced with incised slashes, their eyes bulging with pain. Some bodies are headless, others limbless, some upside down. Blood and entrails spill out. There are disembodied legs, arms, rows of eyes, stacked vertebrae and heads with closed eyes. One victorious warrior carries a severed head dangling from his waistband.

Parallel themes occur on north coastal Cupisnique stone vessels and pottery. Carved steatite (soapstone) bowls depict spiders with exaggerated pincers, surrounded by severed heads. Ceramic effigy vessels show captives with bound hands, and stirrup-spout bottles are incised with severed heads, linked by cords or in net bags.

Farther north, at the late Valdivian Real Alto site, a stone-lined tomb on the summit of the low platform called the Charnal Mound contained a female burial. Next to the tomb was a dismembered male sacrificial victim surrounded by seven chert knives. Seven other male skeletons were in a common grave near by.

Two of the three high-relief adobe sculptures at Moxeke are of headless torsos, probably deliberately

Above: A principal Moche deity, and ritual sacrificer, imitated by priests was the Fanged God, depicted here in polychrome murals at the Huaca de la Luna at the Moche capital. He holds a sacrificial copper blade in his left hand.

decapitated, and the third is a colossal head, also probably a decapitation. The latest temple at Kotosh, towards the end of the Initial Period, included three headless bodies beneath the floor, presumably ritually decapitated to dedicate the temple.

SEVERED HEADS AND SACRIFICES
The tradition of severed heads was widespread and long-lived. Following these Initial Period examples, Early Horizon examples include more than 40 stone heads with tenons for mounting on the wall of the New Temple façade at highland Chavín de Huántar.

Within the central chamber of the Old Temple, the top of the Lanzón Stela comprises a spike from the deity's head, leaving a flat surface on top of the head. A groove carved from the tip of the spike down to the flat surface becomes shaped like a cross with a central depression, mirroring the plan of the Lanzón Gallery and the circular plaza. It is thought that blood from sacrificial victims was poured down the groove into the cross, eventually spilling over the stone itself. An engraved human finger bone was found in the gallery above the Lanzón.

Above: Ritual decapitation, probably combined in warfare and religious belief, began in the pre-Chavín Initial Period, as shown here by a warrior and decapitated victim on one of the temple wall slabs at Cerro Sechín.

In Paracas and Nazca on the south Peruvian coast, many burials include decapitated skulls and mutilated bodies, often with a cord around the neck or perforations in the skull meant for stringing them on a cord as a collection of trophy heads. Severed heads also adorn many Paracas and Nazca ceramics and textiles, especially in association with the Oculate Being – a flying deity figure shown trailing severed heads on streamers. Many Paracas and Nazca textiles are bordered with miniature woven severed heads.

THE MOCHE DECAPITATOR

Decapitator deities and imagery are known throughout Andean civilization.

Some of the most dramatic evidence of human sacrifice is that from the Moche. From the walls of Platform 1 of the Great Plaza of the Huaca de la Luna stares the grim face of the Decapitator God, with glaring white eyes, black hair and beard, and snarling mouth containing both human teeth and feline fangs. On Moche artefacts throughout the northern kingdom – ceramics, metalwork and textiles as well as architectural decoration – the Decapitator reminded Moche citizens daily of his grim presence.

As well as his face, he was depicted full-figured, holding a crescent-shaped *tumi* (ceremonial knife) and a severed human head. Intricate metalwork also shows spiders brandishing *tumi* knives and severed heads.

At Cao Viejo–El Brujo, the top terrace of a platform mound shows the segmented legs of a spider or crab Decapitator God brandishing a *tumi* sacrificial knife. (Before its destruction by looters, its fanged mouth was also visible.) Such imagery harks back to Cupisnique depictions in the same region.

SACRIFICE RITUAL

The Sacrifice Ritual depicted in Moche murals and in fine-line drawings on pottery involves four principal protagonists: the Warrior Priest, the Bird Priest, a Priestess and a feline-masked figure wearing a headdress with long, jagged-ended streamers. The ritual scene includes figures slitting the throats of naked sacrificial victims, then presenting the priests with goblets filled with the victims' blood. The now-destroyed Moche murals at Pañamarca showed the Priestess leading such a presentation procession: she carries a goblet and is followed by smaller figures presenting goblets and by a crawling, fanged serpent.

Moche sacrifice was intimately related to ritual combat. Warriors in Moche armour are depicted on pottery and as effigy vessels, pitted in single combat. The scenery appears to be the

Right: Sacred mountains were scenes of ritual sacrifice right up to Inca times. Here a Moche potter has depicted a ritual sacrifice on a mountain-shaped spouted bottle.

margins of fields. Successive scenes show the losing warrior stripped naked and with a rope around his neck, to be led away for sacrifice.

THE DECAPITATOR

Equally prominent among southern cultures was the Decapitator. Nazca portrayal of the Oculate Being with streaming severed heads has been mentioned. In the Pukará culture of the Titicaca Basin and its successor, Tiwanaku, the Decapitator and severed heads feature incessantly in stone sculpture, on pottery and textiles, in metalwork, and in wood and bone carving.

Scores of carved stone severed heads are mounted on

At San José Moro were found two graves with women buried in them. Both women wore and were accompanied by items identifying them as representatives of the Priestess in the mural at Pañamarca.

MASS GRAVES

Discoveries behind Moche's Huaca de la Luna platform, at Tiwanaku's Akapana platform and at Late Intermediate Period Batán Grande exemplify scenes of mass sacrifice that are reminiscent of the victory mutilations at Cerro Sechín.

At Moche an enclosure contained a mass grave of 40 men, aged 15 to 30. They appear to have been pushed into the grave from a stone outcrop after having been mutilated, then killed. Skulls,

Below: A Moche effigy jug in the form of a priest, partly transformed with feline fanged mouth and drug-glazed eyes, sacrificing two animals symbolic of Andean religious belief – a bird and a snake.

the walls of the Semi-Subterranean Courtyard. A special group of Tiwanaku stone sculptures known as *chachapumas* are puma-headed warriors holding a severed head and *tumi* knife.

Cut and polished human skulls found at Tiwanaku are evidence of the taking of trophy heads in battle – an Inca practice documented by Spanish chroniclers. (Inca warriors celebrated victory using drinking cups made from the skulls of important vanquished leaders.)

UNLOOTED TOMBS

Direct evidence of the reality of Moche sacrificial scenes was found in unlooted tombs discovered at Sipán in the Lambayeque Valley (dated *c.*AD300) and at San José Moro in the Jequetepeque Valley (*c.*AD600), showing that the practice was both widespread and of long duration. One Sipán tomb contained the burial of a figure that was dressed and

Above: The so-called prison quarter at Machu Picchu features a tomb-like cavern and sacrificial stone block carved as a condor (foreground).

accompanied by regalia identical to that of the Warrior Priest: back-flap, crescent-shaped rattles, ear-spools, a gold, crescent-shaped headdress, two *tumi* knives and a gold sceptre.

Not far from his tomb, a second tomb contained a body wearing an owl-adorned headdress, with grave goods, including a copper goblet and other items identifying him as the Bird Priest. Approximately 10m (33ft) west of the Bird Priest's tomb were sealed chambers filled with hundreds of pots, miniature copper war clubs, shields, headdresses and goblets. Scattered among these offerings were the skeletal remains of severed human hands and feet – presumably collected from sacrificial victims and stored.

Above: The Early Intermediate Period Nazca continued a long-practised tradition of ritual beheading, shown on this brightly painted bridge-spout bottle of a warrior holding his trophy head.

ribs and finger, arm and leg bones show cut marks. Some skeletons were splayed out as if tied to stakes; some had their femurs torn from the pelvis; and several skulls had their jaws torn away. The thick layer of rain-deposited sediment that covered the grave suggests that the sacrifice was performed in response to an El Niño weather event that disrupted the kingdom's economic stability, and that the offering was made to supplicate the wrath of the gods.

On the north-west corner of the first terrace of the Tiwanaku Akapana platform, excavators found 21 human burials mingled with llama bones and elegant pottery (dated *c.*AD600–800). Cut marks and compression fractures on the human bones reveal hacking with knives and heavy blows from clubs. Some skeletons had selected bones removed; other burials were only of skulls or torsos. Many belonged to adult males aged 17–30; others were children.

Another Akapana 'burial' (dated *c.*AD600) was a destroyed chamber containing deliberately smashed pots, over which were splayed the skeleton of an adult male and the skull fragments of a juvenile. It has been suggested that these Akapana burials were sacrifices associated with a single momentous event, such as the dedication of the temple.

At the Sicán-Lambayeque city of Batán Grande, another mass grave contained 17 sacrificial victims accompanied by Ecuadorian conch shells, lapis lazuli, precious metal artefacts and 500kg (1,200lb) of copper artefacts.

CAPACOCHAS

Almost all Inca rituals included sacrifice, usually of llamas or guinea pigs. Brown llamas were sacrificed to Viracocha (the Creator), white to Inti (the Sun God) and dappled to Illapa (the Thunder). Animal sacrifices were performed by throat-slitting.

Coronations, war and natural catastrophes involved human sacrifice to solicit or supplicate the gods. The victims were provincial (non-Inca) children aged 10–15 years old. They needed to be physically perfect. After the victim had been feasted, so as to offer him or her to Viracocha well satisfied, he/she was clubbed or strangled, and had the throat slit or the heart cut out and offered to Viracocha still beating.

A special child sacrifice – the *capacocha* – was preceded by a ritual procession along a straight sacred *ceque* line in Cuzco. The child's parents participated and considered the choice of their child to be an honour. *Capacocha* victims were sanctified in the Coricancha temple in Cuzco before walking back to be sacrificed in their province.

All of the ancient Andean cultures worshipped mountain gods. Only the Incas, however, ventured onto high peaks to kill and bury sacrificial victims there. Special sacrifices were made of children, who were marched barefoot to the mountain-top, where they were clubbed or strangled – or even buried alive – and interred with miniature dressed human figurines, miniature gold or silver llama figurines, and pouches containing their baby teeth and nail parings. Such sacrifices have been discovered on Cerro el Pomo and Mount Aconcagua in northern Chile, and on Ampato in Peru and Llullaillaco in northern Argentina.

Right: The ritual sacrifice of a black llama, depicted in Poma de Ayala's Nueva Corónica, *c.1615.*

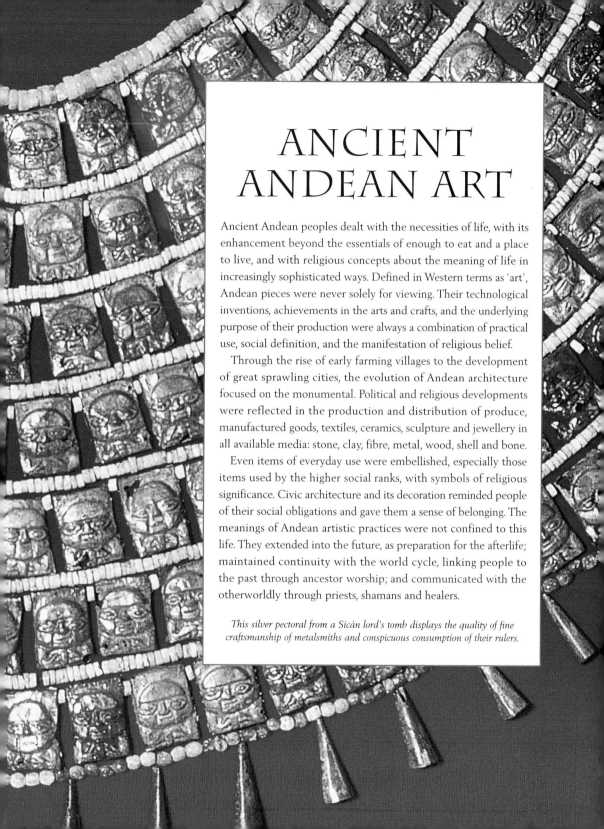

ANCIENT ANDEAN ART

Ancient Andean peoples dealt with the necessities of life, with its enhancement beyond the essentials of enough to eat and a place to live, and with religious concepts about the meaning of life in increasingly sophisticated ways. Defined in Western terms as 'art', Andean pieces were never solely for viewing. Their technological inventions, achievements in the arts and crafts, and the underlying purpose of their production were always a combination of practical use, social definition, and the manifestation of religious belief.

Through the rise of early farming villages to the development of great sprawling cities, the evolution of Andean architecture focused on the monumental. Political and religious developments were reflected in the production and distribution of produce, manufactured goods, textiles, ceramics, sculpture and jewellery in all available media: stone, clay, fibre, metal, wood, shell and bone.

Even items of everyday use were embellished, especially those items used by the higher social ranks, with symbols of religious significance. Civic architecture and its decoration reminded people of their social obligations and gave them a sense of belonging. The meanings of Andean artistic practices were not confined to this life. They extended into the future, as preparation for the afterlife; maintained continuity with the world cycle, linking people to the past through ancestor worship; and communicated with the otherworldly through priests, shamans and healers.

This silver pectoral from a Sicán lord's tomb displays the quality of fine craftsmanship of metalsmiths and conspicuous consumption of their rulers.

CHAPTER NINETEEN

ARCHITECTURE

Ancient Andean builders tended to use materials as close to hand as possible. Thus, coastal peoples regularly built with mud – or adobe – bricks, while highland peoples favoured stone. Cobbles and rough field stones were also used, often plastered with mud or clay. Little is known of quarrying techniques until Inca sources, but quarrying consisted mostly of collecting from convenient sources rather than actually cutting the stone from outcrops.

Monumental architecture emphasized power and authority. The use of materials that had to be imported also enhanced prestige and indicated superior social standing. So, too, did elaborate decoration on buildings and walls. Monumental architecture, both in size and complexity of form, appeared at around 2700BC in the Andean Area and developed early traditions that lasted through to Inca times. Each successive culture copied and borrowed from predecessors, but also developed its own distinctive innovations.

From the beginning, much Andean architecture was devoted to religious purposes and themes. It was used to worship the gods, reflect the sacred landscape and impress human populations. There were cults, annual religious rituals, pilgrimage and oracle sites. Open and restricted spaces controlled participation in ritual, creating uniformity and mystery, through form and layout.

The architecture involved a variety of decorative techniques and styles: plastering, stone facing, stone carving, plaster carving, mud moulding and mural painting, as well as the combination of several techniques together.

Left: The stone architecture of the circular Temple to Inti, sun god of the Incas, forms the head in Cuzco's crouching puma.

STONE QUARRYING AND WORKING

One of the most recognizable Inca skills was their mastery of stoneworking. Their use of large, dressed stone blocks follows a 4,000-year history of the use of stone architecture, beginning with the first stone-clad platform mounds of the Preceramic Period.

QUARRIES
The Inca, and presumably pre-Inca, builders did not quarry building stone in the modern sense: they did not cut blocks from rock faces or detach sections of bedrock by undercutting. Instead, quarries were established at scree faces or prised loose from fragmented rock faces.

Blocks weighing 5 tons (tonnes) or more were roughly dressed at quarries by being hammered with river cobbles (hammerstones) before being transported to construction sites. Smaller blocks were dressed on five of their six faces, then transported for refined dressing and fitting at building sites. Quarry sites are littered with whole and shattered hammerstones, which were brought from riverbeds and were selected for their shape and hardness.

Most stone for building construction was obtained locally, or from as near as possible. By contrast, stone for sculpture was imported from greater distances when special stone was wanted, because it was precious, or because it was a desired colour or texture, or exotic or valuable in some other way. For example, as early as the Preceramic Period, coastal peoples imported small amounts of obsidian (a natural volcanic glass) from highland sources hundreds of kilometres (miles) away for superior or more prestigious knives and other tools. The Late Horizon Inca central plaza of Haucaypata–Cusipata in Cuzco was covered with a layer of sand imported from the coast.

Several Inca quarries are known, for example at Kachiqhata near Ollantaytambo, for that site and perhaps earlier constructions, and at outcrops just north of Sacsahuaman.

TRANSPORT
Ancient Andean transport was on human and animal backs. There were no transport vehicles, as the wheel was unknown and llamas are notoriously adverse to pulling. Transporting goods through mountains in vehicles would also have required an extensive road system – not just trunk roads connecting major cities, but more than just pathways within and between local communities.

Above: Inca stonemasons fitting blocks on a wall, depicted in Poma de Ayala's Nueva Corónica, c.1615.

These methods were unsuitable for transporting stone blocks. Instead, gangs of men dragged the blocks with ropes, on the ground or possibly on log rollers or sledges. Earth and cobble ramps were built at quarries to drag stone blocks down; other ramps at construction sites enabled blocks to be hauled into position. Ramps at Sacsahuaman were levelled after construction, but some ramps were left at Sillustani near Lake Titicaca.

STONEWORKING
Inca stonework is remarkable for its huge stone building blocks, which were carefully and painstakingly fitted together by matching angle for angle at the points of contact between blocks, so that no mortar was needed to hold them together. The oft-repeated phrase that not even a knife blade can be slid between blocks

Left: Closely fitted block stonework at Tambo Machay hunting lodge. Multiple trapezoidal niches and steep staircased passages form solid blocks that 'sympathize' with the landscape.

describes their precision. Withstanding 500 years of earthquakes also shows the strength of their construction. Earthquakes often destroy most modern houses, leaving only Inca buildings and foundations standing.

Precise fitting was used only on the most important buildings: temples, administrative offices and palaces. For other buildings techniques were less recognizably Inca, but continued methods developed for millennia and used local, undressed stone or adobe blocks (mud bricks).

Such strength is also true of Inca terracing and irrigation systems. Despite being in an active volcanic region, Inca terraced fields and irrigation conduits continue to be used.

As with almost everything else in Andean civilization, construction was related to and intimate with the landscape.

SHAPING TECHNIQUES
The careful fitting of Inca fine masonry walls was achieved by laboriously pecking the surfaces with harder stone 'hammers' and chiselling with bronze tools. The rock surface was more shattered and ground away than cut, but

unwanted stone could also be sheared away by hitting the face with glancing blows. Grinding with smooth stones and perhaps wet sand (although there is no evidence of smooth polishing) achieved final fitting. Inca blocks retain the small pitting left by these methods.

Blocks were usually of various shapes, but for the most important buildings uniform rectangular prism or cube blocks were fitted in courses like bricks. Varyingly shaped blocks were dressed along their edges to fit snugly, and used especially when very large blocks were fitted, such as on massive walls for terracing or stabilizing riverbanks. The final grinding and fitting of stone blocks on refined buildings were done *in situ*, and therefore blocks must have had to be lifted and taken down repeatedly to

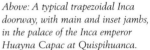

Above: A typical trapezoidal Inca doorway, with main and inset jambs, in the palace of the Inca emperor Huayna Capac at Quispihuanca.

achieve their exact fit. Corners were made strong by interlocking header and stretcher construction.

Inca engineers used plumb-bobs and two-stick slide rules for positioning and possibly for transcribing the shape of one face to another as a template. Bronze and wooden levers and crowbars were used to manoeuvre blocks.

LABOUR
These tedious and time-consuming methods suggest the massive labour forces needed to complete masonry work. Specialist engineers and skilled stonemasons did the fine work, but the tasks of quarrying or collecting, hauling and rough shaping involved large gangs, as did the making of earthen ramps for raising stones up to higher courses. Construction was one of the tasks that could be assigned to workers in the *mit'a* tax draft. The chronicler Pedro de Ondegardo recorded that as many as 20 men could work for an entire year on dressing and fitting some of the largest stone blocks.

Left: The most famous Inca stone – the 12-cornered, carefully fitted block in a monolithic wall on Hatun Rumiyoc Street, Cuzco. The base is a single side, the right and left sides have three angles each, and the top no fewer than five.

MONUMENTAL ARCHITECTURE

The size and monumental nature of ancient Andean architecture is undoubtedly impressive, and this is true even when most of the features are flattened and only the foundations survive.

FIRST MONUMENTAL STRUCTURES

Large-scale monumental architecture began as early as 2700BC, in the Preceramic Period. In the Initial Period, from c.2000BC, at a time when the use of ceramics and other technological innovations (including irrigation canals) was beginning, ceremonial centres were built throughout coastal and highland river valleys. It was the beginning of large-scale public architecture, including huge individual monuments, and extensive and complex ceremonial compounds. These were some of the largest structures ever built in the Americas.

These centres were monuments to the gods and their purpose was for religious gatherings. They were not cities, for there were few associated dwellings and they lacked the density of buildings and area coverage characteristic of cities, but as focuses of public labour and worship they provided the core idea that later became

Above: Huaca de la Luna, Moche. Whatever the building materials – adobe bricks or colossal stone blocks – Andean architects aspired to imposing, monumental structures for their ceremonial centres.

Below: Machu Picchu. Inca architecture followed a long tradition of 'fitting' the landscape. In mountainous terrain, ridges were levelled for enclosures and buildings, while steep slopes were terraced with stone bulwarks.

a feature of Andean cities. The few dwellings were those of resident attendants of the cults. Each ceremonial centre served groups of scattered towns and villages.

ASPERO

The earliest such ceremonial centre was Aspero (c.2700BC), on the northern Peruvian coast. Covering more than 12ha (30 acres) along the north bluff of the Supe River, Aspero comprised six or seven large platform mounds (4m/13ft or more high), eleven smaller mounds (1–2m/3¼–6½ft high), plus interspersed plazas and terraces. The outer walls of the mounds were faced with locally quarried stone set in mud mortar. The bulks of the mounds were built up using loose mesh bags of sedge fibre filled with rubble, cobbles and quarried stone.

EL PARAÍSO

Construction at El Paraíso, near the central Peruvian coast on the south bank and plain of the Chillón River, began c.2000BC. El Paraíso initiated two significant trends: settlements were established inland, a short distance from the coast, and their general plans took the shape of a U. El Paraíso covered 50ha (125 acres) or more and its builders used about

100,000 tons (tonnes) of quarried stone to make platform mounds and other buildings. The two largest mounds are each about 50m (165ft) wide and run parallel for 400m (¼ mile) to form the sides of the U-plan, enclosing a 7ha (17 acre) plaza. The base of the U was formed by a building of 50sq m (540sq ft), 8m (25ft) high, with two stairways.

KOTOSH AND LA GALGADA

In the highlands, at about the same time, monumental architecture was not so grand in scale, but provided the same function of public focus. At Kotosh, the Temple of the Crossed Hands was a square chamber on a raised platform, one of two mounds at the site. At La Galgada there were also two temple mounds, flanking a circular court.

THE BIG ONES

The heyday of U-shaped ceremonial structures began c.1500BC, and it is estimated that these centres had about 1,000

residents each. Up to the beginning of the Early Horizon and the ascendancy of Chavín de Huántar, three monumental architectural traditions developed at coastal sites, representing culturally related regions of independent ceremonial centres and their communities. These were the U-shaped ceremonial centres of the south-central Peruvian coast, the rectangular mound and circular forecourt complexes of the north-central coast, and the low-platform complexes of the northern coast.

Sites include La Florída, Cardál, Sechín Alto, Pampa de las Llamas–Moxeke, Las Haldas, Cerro Sechín, Caballo Muerto, Cupisnique and many others. Sechín Alto and Moxeke were the largest U-shaped complexes ever built in the Andean Area: nearly 1.5km (just under 1 mile) and 1km (just over ½ mile) long, respectively. By comparison, the Las Haldas U-shaped complex was c.440m (less than ½ mile) long.

MONUMENTALITY WITHIN CITIES

The monumental tradition started in the late Preceramic and Initial periods continued through the remainder of Andean prehistory. Early Horizon people continued to build ceremonial centres of platforms and plazas, exemplified by Chavín de Huántar and the Nazca centre of Cahuachi.

From about the middle of the Early Horizon (c.500BC), the complexity of sites began to include the variation in structures, craft specialization, social hierarchy and population densities characteristic of cities. Early Intermediate Period architecture included the huge platforms of the Moche, which were seemingly attempts to build miniature mountains on the coast in honour of the gods of the distant inland peaks.

Monumental architecture in the Middle Horizon, exemplified by Tiwanaku and Huari, show this continuity in large, high platforms in combination with rectangular ceremonial plazas. Tiwanaku featured huge monolithic gateways, and introduced the innovations of standard units of measurements, blocks prepared ready to fit, and grooves for using ropes to manoeuvre them into

Above: Wall of the Tschudi ciudadela, Chan Chan of the Chimú. Fine river-laid silts in the western coastal valleys provided abundant material for poured-mud walls to create huge compounds, elaborately moulded and carved.

position and hold them with T- or I-shaped metal clamps. Wari architecture developed a military-like precision of grid planning, built with huge cut-stone blocks.

Late Intermediate Period cities, such as Pachacamac, Chan Chan, Batán Grande and La Centinela, to name but a few, were huge complexes of compounds, plazas and administrative buildings surrounded by dense populations in suburban housing.

Late Horizon Inca monumental architecture is self-evident. From the city of Cuzco and its temple-fortress of Sacsahuaman through the mountain retreat of Machu Picchu to the numerous Inca provincial capitals, monumental and ceremonial architecture was built to impose and advertise Inca power. Huge blocks of stone were shaped to fit together without mortar and to build massive walls for temples and other public buildings, and for agricultural terracing and the encasement of rivers in Cuzco.

Left: Sacsahuaman, Cuzco. Inca architects frequently used the base rock itself to shape monumental structures, almost seamlessly integrating such stonework into the parts constructed from colossal cut and shaped stones.

RITUAL FOCUS

The organized nature of Inca cities and their focus on religious ritual did not develop suddenly, but began with the first Preceramic monumental architecture. Organization of space as a perception of the universe and as a reflection of the landscape was endemic in Andean architectural form.

The development of U-shaped ceremonial centres, pyramidal platforms, sunken courtyards and clustered temple chambers around courts were fundamental Andean architectural forms. People in different regions developed different forms, singly or in combinations. Such forms reflected the essence of religious belief and how religious ritual was conducted, and the shape of the landscape in which the beliefs developed. The forms endured throughout Andean ancient history.

THE U-SHAPED PLAN
During the Initial Period, the U-shaped plan developed in in the northern coastal cultures, spread into the adjacent mountainous regions, and might be regarded as reaching its fullest expression at Chavín de Huántar, where the holy city seems to have been located deliberately between

Below: Worshippers' attention in Moche's ritual enclosures was directed to lurid murals. Here the Decapitator God stares menacingly from a wall of the Huaca de la Luna, Moche.

Above: The Nazca lines of Peru's southern coastal deserts reveal the early development of ancient Andean ritual focus in architecture.

coast and high sierra. Combined with sunken courtyards and labyrinthine interiors, the temple fulfilled a third religious function: that of a pilgrimage centre.

The U-shaped form endured into the Late Horizon. It was used in miniature at Chan Chan, within the *ciudadela* compounds of the Chimú rulers.

CONTROL
The focus on ritual in ceremonial centres and urban ceremonial precincts included public and private architectural elements. The key was an emphasis on control.

Religious ritual became highly structured. The nature and layout of structures at ceremonial centres and city precincts suggest that they guided public processions along designated routes. Inca Cuzco had a radiating set of sacred pathways, called *ceque* lines, for religious observation. They were the routes followed by priests in leading religious processions, by initiates in coming-of-age rituals, and by sacrificial victims on their way out of the city.

Similarly, of more ancient date, the Nazca lines in the deserts of southern coastal Peru were pathways for religious procession. It has been suggested that they were even sometimes purpose-built

for a single event, and that the pathways along individual figures and geometric shapes belonged to specific kinship groups.

VARIOUS STRUCTURES
Elements of ceremonial complexes reveal different aspects of religious ceremony. There were specific areas for large gatherings, in which the general public was clearly meant to congregate and in which their level of participation was accommodated. Other areas were equally clearly built to restrict participation in religious worship to a privileged few.

PLAZAS
Huge areas, plazas and courts, enclosed by large platforms or walls, characterized Initial Period U-shaped ceremonial centres and platform mound complexes in the Early Horizon and Early Intermediate Period. Chavín de Huántar's two succeeding temples each wrapped themselves around an open-ended courtyard for crowds. The ceremonial cores of Moche cities and the pilgrimage city

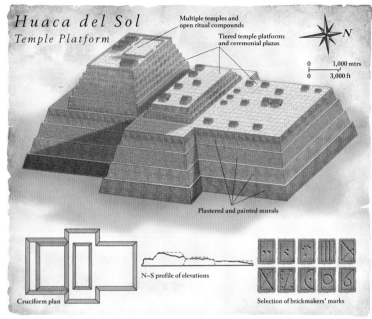

Huaca del Sol
Temple Platform

Multiple temples and open ritual compounds

Tiered temple platforms and ceremonial plazas

N

Plastered and painted murals

N–S profile of elevations

Cruciform plan

Selection of brickmakers' marks

of Pachacamac on the central Peruvian coast were formed of intricate collections of large and small courtyards for large and small gatherings.

The Middle Horizon Moche successors at Pampa Grande surrounded the dominant platform mound of Huaca Fortaleza with a complex of large walled courts and more open plazas beyond them. The singular walled enclosure at Galindo comprised a large court with a sunken rectangular court within it. In Wari cities large public plazas were enclosed within grid-planned walls and streets. At Tiwanaku the Akapana temple platform fronted a large, open plaza.

Late Intermediate Period cities continued the tradition. Sicán Batán Grande's ceremonial precinct comprised large open plazas defined by clusters of platform mounds and other buildings, reminiscent of Pampa Grande. Each *ciudadela* compound at the Chimú capital Chan Chan included a large courtyard within high walls, separated from the highly subdivided area beyond. There were similar courts at Tucume Viejo, where the compounds were anchored around the Huaca Larga platform and the huge, artificially stepped peak

Below: The Kalasasaya and Semi-Subterranean Court at Tiwanaku, where rulers and priests performed their rituals.

of La Raya. The ceremonial precinct at Chincha La Centinela comprised walled courts and low platforms clustered around a dominant higher platform mound.

Inca cities included large plazas with *ushnu* platforms for observing and addressing gathered crowds.

RESTRICTIONS

The counterparts to public areas were smaller courts, sunken courts and enclosed rooms. These were an equally long-lived tradition. They began in the subdivided buildings atop platforms at

Above: Reconstruction of Huaca del Sol temple, Moche, showing ground plan, north–south elevations and brickmakers' marks.

sites such as Kotosh, La Galgada, Huaca de los Reyes, Cerro Sechín and many others in northern and central Peru. Farther south, Chiripa in the Titicaca Basin exemplifies a tradition of single-roomed buildings surrounding a courtyard atop a low platform.

In later periods the intricately subdivided temples of Chavín de Huántar and Pachacamac, through to the complexes of rooms at Chan Chan and the Coricancha temple of Inca Cuzco, were meant to restrict the performance and observance of religious ritual to a select few.

Between these two extremes, combinations of plazas containing sunken courtyards, fronted by platform mounds supporting temples, reveal the controlled nature of ancient Andean religious ceremony. Participants were gathered, then led in managed processions along prescribed routes into and through sunken courts or other restricted areas, before priests and selected individuals mounted the platforms to perform special rites within private temples.

LABYRINTHINE SECRETS

Restriction of intimate religious ritual to selected individuals formed the counterpart to great public extravaganzas. The Incas impressed their subjects with glittering spectacles and public addresses to advertise and emphasize their power. As in other spheres, they were following Wari and Tiwanaku practice in a long-lived tradition of public ceremony.

PUBLIC AND PRIVATE RITUAL

From the Initial Period onwards the importance of religion as a driving force in the development of cities nurtured the growing power of the priesthood. Religious influence in everyday life was exemplified in the development and spread of cults, three of the most famous being those of Chavín, Pachacamac and Inca Inti.

Priestly power and control were revealed in the secretive nature of some elements of worship and the restriction of some rituals to selected individuals or as private events.

PRIVATE ROOMS

Constructions of platforms supporting subdivided temples began towards the end of the Preceramic Period and flourished in the Initial Period. The Temple of the Crossed Hands at Kotosh, the round-cornered chambers at La Galgada, the

Above: New Temple gateway, Chavín de Huántar. Not all ritual was witnessed by crowds of worshippers, as much took place within inner chambers whose passages were known only to the priests.

chambered compounds atop the Huaca de los Idolos and Huaca de los Sacrificios at Aspero, and the complex of interconnected rooms at El Paraíso all typify the development of intricate temple interiors.

The importance of religious figures, whether priest-kings or separate from the rulers, developed early and grew in strength through Andean civilization. The extent of cults was relatively localized until the Chavín Cult spread an unprecedented religious unity in the Early Horizon. Chavín de Huántar became a pilgrimage centre to which people came from great distances to consult the oracle of its chief deity.

Intimate religious practice is suggested by the labyrinthine nature of Chavín de Huántar's temples, Old and New. While the platform arms of each temple embrace a circular (Old Temple) and square (New Temple) sunken court, the

Left: The Lanzón carved stone monolith, Chavín de Huántar. Hidden deep within the multi-storeyed chambers at the back of the Old Temple, it served as an oracle chamber and place of ritual bloodletting, channelled and pooled by grooves and a dish carved in the notched stone.

Right: Entrance to the Semi-Subterranean Court, Tiwanaku. The central ceremonial core formed a complex of temple mounds and enclosed courts for more intimate rituals.

temple interiors comprise mysterious dark corridors connecting inner rooms and chambers, water conduits and niches. Its courts and plazas could hold 1,500 worshippers, while its inner chambers had room for a mere fraction as many.

ORACLES AND ROARING TEMPLES

A staircase rises from the Old Temple plaza in alignment with steps into and out of the sunken circular court. Crowds could participate in ritual and processions in the plaza and circular court, but could hardly do so inside the temple's constricted spaces. A corridor leads to an inner two-storey chamber within which stood the Lanzón Stela, the chief idol. The floor of the chamber above its base is holed to accommodate the notched upper portion of the stela, and it is suggested that a priest could conceal himself in the upper chamber to act as the voice of the deity to pronounce oracles.

The increasing status of the Chavín Cult was shown by more than doubling the temple's size with the addition of the New Temple c.500BC. Further secrecy was

incorporated because no staircase leads to the top of the New Temple terraces. Stairs led only to a platform and square court before the Black and White Portal on the first terrace. Instead, priests could appear mysteriously on the top terrace, or at two rectangular 'reverse balconies' above the Black and White Portal via interior stairs.

The Old and New temples were used together, maintaining the continuity of the deities and cult, and the elaborate interior chambers were multipurpose. Ritual paraphernalia and stores of manufactured and exotic goods were probably kept in niches and smaller chambers. It has also been suggested that some chambers were hermit-like cells for priests and temple attendants. It is also thought that the winding conduits and shafts served the dual purpose both of ventilation and as conduits through which to flush water and cause a roaring noise to echo through the empty corridors – a noise that could have its pitch modulated by the opening and closing of ventilation ducts.

Such measures, together with oracular status, certainly would have enhanced and perpetuated Chavín as a centre of supernatural power and authority.

Left: Temple of the Moon. For more than a millennium Pachacamac was a centre of pilgrimage and worship, focused on its oracle temple, and replete with additions of new temples, courts and accommodations for pilgrims.

PATIOS AND COMPOUNDS

The tradition of controlled worship was obvious at Tiwanaku as well. At Tiwanaku, instead of enclosed chambers, worship was regulated by a complex of open-air plazas, platforms with sunken courts and semi-subterranean courtyards. The elements were linked by monumental gateways marking the boundaries of sacred spaces and isolation atop the Akapana temple platform, thus restricting who entered and how many could participate.

At the sacred oracle site of Pachacamac (from the 1st century AD) the Pachacamac idol and oracle was housed in a small temple atop a platform mound. Its isolation and size restricted it to worship by a few people at a time. North and west of the oracle temple were ramped platforms and an elaborate complex of room suites, passages and small patios around larger courtyards. These were quarters, halls and sacred spaces in which pilgrims could worship in small groups.

Finally, in the imperial compounds of Chimú kings at Chan Chan, walled off from large courtyards, were the intricate complexes of miniature U-shaped ceremonial precincts and seeming mazes of large and small rooms, niches, store blocks and palaces of the dead rulers, each an inner city within greater Chan Chan.

ARCHITECTURAL DECORATION

Ancient Andean stone and mud-brick constructions were often highly embellished. Decorations included stone facing, mud plaster, adobe-brick friezes, sculpting in poured mud and mural-painting on walls.

Traces of paint on walls have been found at some of the earliest coastal and highland sites. Common Inca practice was to plaster cobble- and fieldstone walls with mud and then paint them. Tambo Colorado, a typical example, has traces of red and yellow ochre paint surviving on its adobe walls.

According to Spanish chroniclers, the Incas covered the interior walls of the Coricancha temple with sheets of gold!

PAINTED WALLS

The earliest evidence of wall painting and sculpting was discovered at Aspero, on the central Peruvian coast. The platform mound of Huaca de los Idolos supported a series of room complexes, one replacing the other through continuous use. The rough stone walls were mud-plastered and some were painted red or yellow. Passageways lead from a main court to more private chambers behind it, one of which is decorated with a white clay frieze of five parallel horizontal bands, clapboard-like. There are also plastered benches and cubical niches around some walls.

Below: Huaca de la Luna, Moche. Worshippers were constantly reminded of the gods in vivid murals of the Decapitator God.

Above: Huaca de la Luna, Moche. Colourful murals on the courtyard walls included rows of figures holding hands.

Paint was also found on the walls of the Temple of the Crossed Hands at highland Kotosh. A stylized white serpent was painted on the stairway leading to the temple, and the entryway was painted red. Inside, two sets of crossed hands were sculpted into the yellow-brown mud-plaster below cubical niches. It is thought that they represent a male and female pair, characteristically exemplifying Andean duality.

EARLY MURALS

The Initial Period U-shaped ceremonial complex of Garagay, on the central Peruvian coast, has one of the most remarkable early wall friezes in its Middle Temple. Running the length and height of the walls, low-relief mud-brick sculpturing shows a fanged face with a whorl (an arachnid pedipalp or mucus secretion?) within spider web-like cross-hatching; a long-bodied insect with a human head; and two facing fanged faces. Stylized geometric motifs separate each figure, and traces of bright red, blue, yellow and white paint were found on the various elements. The insect probably represents shamanistic transformation.

Early murals were also found on the walls of the earliest (*c.*1800BC) building phases at Cerro Sechín. Exterior walls were painted pink, interior walls blue, and the entryway to the main chamber had a mural of large black felines with red-orange

paws and white claws on a yellow background. The main façade of the second-phase temple had clay friezes and multicoloured incised line figures, including an upside-down human with closed eyes and blood streaming from the head.

MOCHE MURALS

Early Intermediate Period Moche sites are famous for their murals. A mural on Huaca de la Luna's Platform III walls

Below: The massive poured-mud walls at Chan Chan of the Chimú were elaborately moulded and carved with repetitious motifs.

Right: Cerro Sechín commemorated a military victory or a ritual battle in low-relief on slabs forming a wall around the temple complex.

shows the story of the 'Revolt of the Objects', in which inanimate objects counter depictions of ordinary humans: a warrior with a fox's head, a boat with legs, a ceremonial staff with legs and arms chasing a fallen warrior. It appears to be a mythological portrayal of chaos, a story that was told to Spanish chroniclers at the time of the conquest.

Walls in the Great Patio of Platform I feature a grimacing, fanged face with bulging red-and-black-rimmed eyes and curling black hair and beard. The face is of a sea god or the Decapitator, set within a diamond frame and surrounded by stepped-motif figures with red-and-white-circle eyes. Another wall depicts a line of Moche warriors.

Now-destroyed murals at Pañamarca (Mural E), south of Moche, showed part of 'The Sacrifice Ceremony', led by a priestess holding a goblet and followed by a procession of smaller figures presenting goblets, plus a crawling, fanged and forked-tongued serpent. It represents the conclusion of Moche ritual combat by sacrifice of the loser and 'The Presentation Ceremony'.

PACHACAMAC AND CHANCAY

Mud-plastered walls at coastal sites were the ideal medium for mural-painting. The Middle Horizon and Late Intermediate Period temple mound terrace walls of Pachacamac were once covered in bright murals, repainted up to 16 times. Plants and animals were depicted in bright reds, blues, greens, yellows and whites, emphasizing the natural abundance of the long-lived pilgrimage city in its fertile river valley. Reed and human-hair brushes were found near one of the terraces.

At Cerro Trinidad, one long adobe wall was painted in four colours with interlaced fish – a design used on Chancay pottery.

STONE WARRIORS

The carving of stone friezes along walls was another characteristic form of Andean architectural decoration. One of the earliest and most famous is the great wall surrounding the temple complex at Initial Period Cerro Sechín. A wall of more than 300 upright slabs comprises alternating tall single slabs and shorter stacks of small slabs. Each is carved in low relief with incised lines. The tall slabs show triumphant warriors wearing pillbox hats and brandishing war clubs or staffs of authority. Stacks of smaller slabs between them display their mutilated victims. Some lack legs, or are twisted in painful contortions; others are mere decapitated heads with streaming hair; one shows his intestines spilling out. The figures appear to be in procession, marching around the temple to converge at the front staircase, where two tall flanking slabs depict banners. Flanking the rear stairway are two warriors holding a club and staff.

Below: Artist's reconstruction of Huaca de la Luna, Moche, and plan of the ceremonial precinct showing the relationship between the Huaca del Sol and de la Luna.

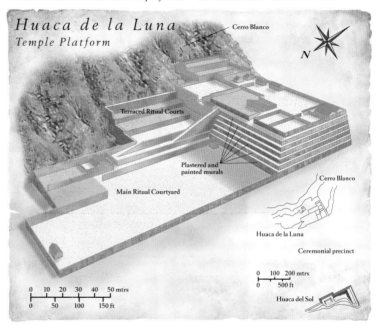

Huaca de la Luna
Temple Platform

Cerro Blanco

N

Terraced Ritual Courts

Plastered and painted murals

Main Ritual Courtyard

Cerro Blanco

Huaca de la Luna

Ceremonial precinct

| 0 | 10 | 20 | 30 | 40 | 50 mtrs |
| 0 | | 50 | | 100 | 150 ft |

| 0 | 100 | 200 mtrs |
| 0 | | 500 ft |

Huaca del Sol

Not far away, and of similar date, at Moxeke a single, rectangular stone slab was found, carved on two adjacent sides. One side has a naturalistic human hand carved inside a hand-shaped depression, and the other face has a central, forked-tongue snake head with two bodies curling back on themselves in incised lines on either side of the head.

CHAVÍN TRANSFORMATIONS

The highland, Initial Period cult site of Chavín de Huántar features rows of carved stone friezes at its Old and New Temples. Portraying religious themes of shamanistic transformation, a procession of figures marches around the walls of the Old Temple's circular sunken court. An upper register of slabs has a low-relief procession of side-facing humanoid figures with fanged mouths and streaming, snake-headed hair. They wear serpentine belts, tunics and trousers. Their finger- and toenails curl in harpy eagle-like claws. One carries a San Pedro cactus branch and another a conch-shell trumpet. The register below them, separated by two rows of plain slabs, is a row of prowling jaguars on rectangular slabs.

The seven or more paired humanoid and jaguar sets depict a scene of shamans displaying the hallucinogenic cactus used for mystic ritual, and to induce transformation from human to jaguar.

Similar themes and imagery were continued in the New Temple, which more than doubled the size of the complex.

Above: Murals at Garagay depict a human-feline-serpentine face within a cross-hatched spider's web on the Middle Temple wall.

The façade forming the lowest tier of the New Temple's main platform was decorated with fully sculpted heads, mounted on the wall with tenons. Although only one was found in place, more than 40 were found during excavations.

The heads display a succession of 'states' in human transformation into beast. The mouths show successive alteration of the lips and teeth from human to feline fangs and curling sides; snouts become projected; noses become progressively flatter, with frontal nostrils; almond-shaped human eyes change to bulging round ones, weeping mucus (a characteristic reaction to drug-taking); cheeks become scarified to represent whiskers.

The heads flanked the Black and White Portal, the columns of its entrance themselves carved in low-relief with two avian figures, heads tilted back to peer straight up, and wings outspread in typical raptor hunting flight. The pair represents Andean religious duality in two ways: the north column, supporting the white (female) granite half-lintel, depicts an eagle – identifiable by an eagle's pronounced cere (nostril hole in the beak), and as female by the 'vagina dentata' between its legs; the south column, supporting the black (male) limestone half-lintel, is a hawk – identifiable as a

hawk by the band running through the eye and as male by his central frontal fang 'penis metaphor'.

TIWANAKU STONE FRIEZES

Highland Tiwanaku, whose citizens built their stone temples, platform mounds and sunken courts through the late Early Intermediate Period and Middle Horizon, also features sculptured stone decorations. Around the walls of the Semi-Subterranean Court were mounted scores of severed heads, tenoned into the walls at various heights.

Tiwanaku's builders also carved the monumental Gateway of the Sun. Made from a single huge slab measuring 3.8m (12½ft) wide and 2.8m (9ft) high, with a 1.4m (4½ft) opening, above its rebate jambs is a frieze in low- and high-relief depicting the Staff Being flanked by running 'angels'. The high-relief, central, front-facing, staff-bearing figure is the ray-headed Sun God/Staff Deity, standing on a stepped platform. Running (or flying?) towards him are three flanking rows of 48 bird-like figures, with feathered heads and wings, each holding a single staff. Beneath the whole runs a strip of geometric shapes, and flanking the entryway are two rectangular niches.

Below: Faint traces of rich temple murals at Cerro Sechin – crabs flanking the entrance to a chamber – are some of the earliest Andean murals.

Above: Moche El Brujo includes courtyard murals with a 'dancing' figure linking hands with others.

Many other Tiwanaku monolithic wall slabs are decorated with rows of inset stepped-diamond shapes – sometimes called the 'Andean Cross' – a shape first used in the Middle Horizon and also used on textiles and by the Incas.

FORMS IN MUD AND PLASTER

The characteristic coastal use of mud-bricks and thick plastering lent itself to carving and moulding. The mud-brick painted friezes at Garagay are described above, and atop Mound A two clay sculptures of humans with circular shields were set into the terrace wall.

To announce elite power and authority, huge carved adobe sculptures adorned the faces of terraces and sunken courtyards. At Moxeke, three sculptures depicted a caped figure, a central shaman with snakes, and a grinning face. At the Huaca de los Reyes mound of Caballo Muerto, four huge adobe heads decorate the summit. Almost 2m (6ft) high, they portray human-like faces with clenched teeth, but also feline fangs, flared nostrils and gaping eyes. They were probably once painted.

Middle Horizon Moche Cao Viejo–El Brujo, in the Chicama Valley, has, on a base terrace, a frieze of 10 life-size naked prisoners, ropes around their necks, led by a warrior. The top terrace shows the legs of a spider or crab Decapitator God brandishing a *tumi* sacrificial knife. (Before its destruction by looters, its fanged mouth and double ear spools were also visible.)

POURED-MUD MOULDING

The ultimate expression in decorated mud walls are those at Chan Chan and other Chimú and Chincha cities, such as Huaca del Dragón and La Centinela.

In a riot of variations, in disciplined and regularly uniform applied forms, Chimú poured-mud walls depict all manner of creatures and geometric shapes. There are rows of identical fish, birds and other creatures, and stacked staff-bearing humanoids with animal heads. There are diamond-lattice patterns and parallel horizontal lines of moulding creating a shutter-effect. Stylized, stepped-fret fish, birds and other animals add an abstract dimension.

Huaca del Dragón features walls with rainbow-like arcs topped with curled solar flares (or waves?) framed by moulded rectangular borders. Mythical creatures support the ends of the arcs, together flanking and framing twinned, facing mythical creatures with sinuous bodies and web-like tails. Long-tailed mythical figures holding axe-bladed staffs march in a frieze above them.

Contemporary Chincha La Centinela's builders painted most of its walls brilliant white and carved them with similar high-relief friezes of birds, fish and geometric patterns.

Below: The great 'Gateway of the Sun' at Tiwanaku is perhaps the most famous single shaped and carved stone in ancient Andean civilization. It depicts a central Staff Deity flanked by numerous 'running' attendants.

INCA STRUCTURES

Inca buildings, with rare exceptions, were rectangular in plan, regardless of size, purpose or quality. Most were a single room, with one door in a long wall, or several if the building was exceptionally long. Most were single-storey, although often had a second level when built against a hillside, but in Cuzco there were two-storey and occasionally three-storey buildings. More rarely, U-shaped and round structures were built.

The standardization of form simultaneously fulfilled the goals of practicality, aesthetics, a perverse sense of 'equality' among official Inca citizens, and political power. Fineness of stonework, décor and size reinforced social hierarchy. Even the sacred Coricancha temple was a standard form – although one elevated to a higher status with sheet-gold-plated walls.

MATERIALS
Fine, fitted masonry was used only for the most important structures. Most walls were of unshaped stone set in mud mortar, using materials collected from nearby fields. Coastal buildings were of adobe blocks (mud bricks), though in the rainier highlands adobe was less practical. Both fieldstone and adobe walls were smoothed with poured mud or clay plaster, then painted.

Below: Careful interlocking precluded the need for mortar in Inca stonework; and the use of huge blocks and inclining the walls of structures made them resistant to earthquakes.

Above: Sacsahuaman. The close-fitting shaped stone blocks of the Inca Sun Temple integrate with the shape of the hill of which they form a 'natural' extension.

Roofs were of thatch, supported by wooden or cane poles, steeply sloped at an angle of about 60 degrees in highland regions to shed rain. Highland builders used *ichu* grass. Nails were unknown; the pole frames were lashed together with rope, and secured to the walls on stone pegs built into the walls. Some Inca walls also have stone rings at the gable crown.

The Incas are renowned for the fineness of their masonry dressing and for the precision of fitting. Huge blocks in the most important temples and administrative buildings were laboriously pecked, tested, removed and adjusted, then refitted until not even a knife blade could be slid into the joins. One famous block, on Hatun Rumiyoc Street, Cuzco, has 12 angled sides!

INCA FEATURES
Three notable Inca features are: battered (inclined) walls, a lack of interior room divisions (with rare exceptions) and the use of trapezoidal (narrower at top than at base) doorways, windows and wall niches.

Inca walls are inclined at an angle of 4–6 degrees from base to top, being thicker at the base. Reasons for this are uncertain. At a practical level, the incline counters the outward thrust of the roof structure, and so the walls may be more earthquake resistant. Undoubtedly, however, part of the reason was aesthetic. The visual effect, called entasis, is an appearance of greater height and refinement, making Inca walls look more imposing and so impressing and displaying power.

The significance of trapezoids is equally uncertain, but they were probably also chosen for earthquake stability and aesthetics. Many trapezoidal entrances, especially gateways to compounds, have double jambs; windows and niches are

Below: The most careful sizing, shaping and dressing was used on temples and imperial buildings, as here in the Temple of Inti at Ollantaytambo, north of Cuzco.

Right: At the country palace at Pisac, the contrast in the quality of stonework for the Intihuatana quarter (Place of the Sun) and a more ordinary building is evident.

often double-framed. Trapezoids are a central and northern feature; rectangular forms were used south of Lake Titicaca.

Dressed stone walls often have protruding stone pegs on gables and inside. Pegs are dressed stone cylinders imbedded into the masonry, or, in more important buildings, carved from single ashlar building blocks. Some are square in section. Exterior pegs were anchors for roof ties; interior pegs presumably for hanging things on them, as Inca buildings had little furniture except for wall niche repositories.

BUILDING TYPES

A *kancha* was a group of three or more rectangular buildings around an open courtyard, the whole enclosed by a wall. *Kanchas* varied in size and purpose: dwellings, temples, factories, administrative buildings, sometimes combined in the same compound. Residential *kanchas* probably housed extended families.

Kallankas were large, long buildings, often with several doorways opening into a plaza. Their size and public nature

Below: The temples of the Coricancha have some of the finest examples of dressed-stone walls and trapezoidal windows and doorways.

suggests that they were for ceremony and for housing Inca officials touring the imperial provinces.

The *ushnu* is a platform at the centre or one side of the main plaza of state settlements. It was used for state occasions as a viewing stand for rituals, reviewing troops and receiving subject leaders. Built only in Cuzco and imperial provincial cities, it was a symbol of Inca domination.

Inca public buildings – administrative *kanchas* and temples – are normally identified by their size and fine masonry, and by the use of trapezoidal doorways. These features are more readily identifiable in the Cuzco area and in the provincial capitals of the central and northern provinces, but are rare in the western and southern provinces. It seems that impressive buildings were felt important as symbols of power and dominance, either to demonstrate conquest in areas without imperial traditions or to emphasize Inca superiority in kingdoms with them.

INCA HOUSES

Houses were similar for all social ranks: a single-roomed rectangular building with one door, often no windows and a pitched thatch roof. Walls were mortar-fitted fieldstones, mud-plastered and painted for commoners, while of finer masonry and larger for royalty, nobles and high officials.

Outside the core area around Cuzco, provincial housing was often different, of local shapes and materials (for example adobe bricks in desert and coastal regions; or round in plan and with flat, woven reed roofs). Inca policy was to leave local customs in place so long as they did not conflict with the state system. Often the only way to tell if an area was under Inca control was the presence of an Inca official *kancha* or *kallanka* among local buildings and the presence of Inca pottery.

Below: A trapezoidal doorway at imperial Ollantaytambo has the remnants of projecting stone pegs flanking the entry.

CHAPTER TWENTY

ANCIENT ANDEAN CITIES

Ancient Andean urbanism developed from about 500BC. Before this time, huge ceremonial centres were built to serve the religious needs of collected communities. The sheer size of many early ceremonial centres reveals the rise of leadership and the power of religious beliefs. Co-operative labour had to be organized to gather huge amounts of stone, mud for adobe bricks and mortar, wood and other perishable materials for superstructures, and fibre baskets and ropes for containing rubble core material and for hauling stone blocks into place.

The monumental architectural traditions of ancient Andean civilization preceded true cities. Once class systems had developed and cities housed rulers, priests, craftspeople and commoners, structures reflected these developments in both the elaborate palaces built near urban ritual precincts and the smaller, more squalid and irregular clusters of suburban housing in urban sprawl. Domestic architecture mostly used local materials in rough-and-ready structures, while more elite architecture brought materials from farther afield.

As petty states, kingdoms and empires waxed and waned, administrative compounds and cities incorporated vast storage structures for the collection and redistribution of wealth. Times of conflict brought social movements and the construction of hilltop forts as competition increased over valuable lands and commodities, culminating in the vast Inca Empire briefly uniting the Andean peoples.

Left: Imperial Machu Picchu in its remote mountain fastness provides an enduring image of ancient Inca civilization.

URBAN CIVILIZATION

In the Andes, urban centres evolved around early monumental architecture built as focuses of religious devotion, from about the middle of the 3rd millennium BC. Urban civilizations evolved independently in Mesopotamia, Egypt, the Indus Valley, China, Mesoamerica and the Andes. General reasons for initial urban developments are similar, but in detail the shapes of their evolution are specific to the cultural and environmental circumstances in each area.

PRE-INDUSTRIAL CITIES

The first ceremonial complexes appeared in coastal and adjacent highland valleys in the central and southern Andes by 2500BC. The earliest pattern, not truly urban, comprised stone-faced platforms with ceremonial buildings on top,

Below: Imperial Inca Pisac. Urban compounds in mountain landscapes are a constant feature of Andean urbanism.

surrounded by scattered farming and fishing villages, whose inhabitants organized the communal labour to raise the monumental structures. Their construction obviates central political powers capable of organizing and regulating the work.

None of these early sites had dense, permanent populations. They were focuses for religious devotion by the people of the surrounding communities, and had only limited residential accommodation.

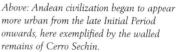

Above: Andean civilization began to appear more urban from the late Initial Period onwards, here exemplified by the walled remains of Cerro Sechin.

Structures were temples and ritual courtyards, lacking the variety in shapes and sizes that indicates the social hierarchy and occupational variety characteristic of a city.

Pre-industrial urbanism is difficult to define. Scholars agree, however, that, in addition to large populations in densely concentrated residential buildings (say, more than 5,000), there must be monumental architecture, and other buildings, large and small, that serve other purposes (administration, craft production and various civic functions).

From early ceremonial complexes and surrounding towns and villages, Andean cities became large, dense urban environments. They remained the focus of religious observance, but also regulated the economy, were the centres of state manufacture and housed the political rulers. After several thousand years of evolution, Andean cities had become urban networks linked by roads, and embodied state institutions to rule empires, the ultimate culmination of which was the Inca Empire.

Public architecture represents a huge communal commitment. Even in a non-monetary economy it demands considerable resources and powers in organization and redistribution. Builders

of public architecture must be motivated and fed. At the end of 4,000 years of development, the Incas were masters at this process.

RELIGION AND ECONOMY

Two institutions governed Andean urban growth and purpose: religion and economy. These settlements were not market places (although there is some evidence of a market in Inca Cuzco); rather, they were repositories for produce, collected into storehouses by the state for communal redistribution. Supplying religious celebrants with food and drink at ceremonies linked religion and economy for a common purpose. At times of agricultural stress, stores were also used to help people through lean times.

Cities were also locations for state 'factories' – compounds in which craftspeople, supported by the state, produced elite ceramics, metalwork and textiles for royal and noble consumption.

In these ways, Andean cities fulfilled economic functions – exchange through redistribution and gift-giving – and were places of religious focus, hospitality and entertainment. Giving was reciprocal: cities were sources of gifts but also places to which to bring tax, tribute and religious offerings. Andean cities were sources of innovation and influence

Below: At royal Chan Chan, capital of Chimú, the vast city was made up of a grid plan of streets and compounds.

through these combined roles, which in turn enhanced and perpetuated their importance and power.

A specific trait of ancient Andean cities was that much of the population lived in them only part-time: urban populations rose and fell in conjunction with the ceremonial calendar. From surrounding agricultural towns and villages, and suburbs around ceremonial centres, people flocked into the great plazas for religious observances. At other times, city centres may have been largely vacant except for rulers, priests, their service personnel and elite craftspeople, watching over hundreds of empty halls and plazas.

FITTING INTO THE LANDSCAPE

Cities were part of the landscape, both physically and metaphorically. Their plans often conformed to contours – built against hillsides, terraced, set in grid plans, or sprawled across the flat desert plain incorporating natural mounds in their constructions. Principal ceremonial centres were often oriented towards specific mountains, and their profiles sometimes mimicked distant horizons. Most famously, the plan of imperial Inca Cuzco formed the shape of a crouching puma, while 4,000 years earlier, U-shaped ceremonial complexes stretched their 'arms' out to the distant rainy mountains.

The Incas often combined a dual statement – carving rooms into rocky outcrops and thus embedding their architecture in

Above: Reconstruction of the temple tomb of the imperial Lords of Moche Sipán in the Lambayeque Valley.

nature, modifying but following the landscape, at the same time emphasizing their domination of it. For example, rooms around a plaza at Chinchero mimic and complement the valley's terrace fields. At Machu Picchu, the profile of the Sacred Rock at the northern end follows that of a peak in the distance.

Tiwanaku also had a distinct imagery: it reflected Lake Titicaca, making the ceremonial core an artificial 'island' within a moat, and the Akapana platform mound simulated, in essence, the distant peak of Mount Illimani.

URBAN CONTROL

The layout of Andean cities, especially in the imperial cultures of the Wari, Tiwanaku, Chimú and Incas, controlled people's movements. Inca officials regulated access to and movement within and through public areas. Inca city plans dictated the areas and buildings to which people had access and the people with whom they interacted. Just as the land was regulated and controlled by designating different parts for the upkeep of the populace and state institutions, so cityscapes comprised buildings, streets and plazas that reflected both imperial political power and control, and also religious ideology.

CEREMONIAL CENTRES AND ENCLOSURES

Ancient Andean ceremonial architecture began with mound-building. Elevated architecture gave a structure special status, segregating it from ordinary construction: height gave spatial separation and conferred sacredness. Even the 'special' building at Archaic Period Monte Verde had a raised floor.

Mounds emulated mountains, and mound summits provided ritual spaces and platforms for sacred buildings. Ascending them was a ceremonial act, approaching the sky gods. In association with enclosed spaces, mounds were the characteristic duo of Andean ceremonial architecture.

MONTE VERDE AND NANCHOC

Andean ceremonial architecture began more than 14,000 years ago at Monte Verde in south-central Chile. Here, hunter-gatherers built a village with two groups of structures: dwellings and a special, Y-shaped building separated from them. In the latter's floor were clay-lined braziers and remains of medicinal plants, chewed leaves, seeds, hides, animal bones and apparent burnt offerings.

Truly monumental structures came several thousand years later at Nanchoc, a late Archaic Period village in the Zana Valley of north-western Peru. Between 6000 and 5500BC the inhabitants erected

Below: Interior of the Temple of Inti, Cuzco, whose niches held gold and silver figures and whose walls were allegedly lined with sheet gold.

two long parallel mounds – lozenge-shaped, c.35m (114ft) long, c.1.5m (5ft) high and 15m (49ft) apart. Each had three tiers, built over a period of time, enlarged with layers of rubble between flat tops and faced with stones.

Nanchoc's mounds established several enduring Andean architectural and religious patterns: twinned terraced platforms indicate that mound-building and the concept of duality evolved simultaneously. There was periodic construction between periods of use. Each renewal involved 'temple interment', and enlargement as the old mound became the core of the new one.

Unique among nearly 50 Archaic sites in the valley, Nanchoc was probably built by and to serve these communities. It required organized community labour. Episodic construction reveals not only sacred continuity but also enduring leadership. It was a means of reaffirming corporate identity, and twin mounds suggest early social division of kinship groups into two 'moieties'.

SETTING THE STAGE

With the stage thus set, the Preceramic and Initial periods became the platform for Andean ceremonial architecture.

Above: The Semi-Subterranean Court at Tiwanaku, a sunken enclosure adjacent to the Kalasasaya and Akapana temple mounds, is lined with carved stone trophy heads.

Ceremonial complexes became the focus of Andean architecture for the next 5,000 years throughout the western coastal valleys and Andean highlands. Some were huge; some were raised above the flat valley floors; others were terraced against hillsides. They embodied a wealth of styles and structural combinations, but always involved the formal organization of space in order to accommodate ritual and to control worshippers' access and movements.

Early ceremonial centres were nodes of religious focus among settlements, with little domestic settlement immediately around them. The same elements – platforms and enclosed spaces – became the religious precincts of later cities, surrounded by sprawling urban complexes.

Vast complexes of temple mounds and sunken court enclosures were built at Sechín Alto, Las Haldas, Huaca de los Reyes and dozens of other sites. Sechín Alto exemplifies a long, linear arrangement with a principal platform from the summit of which is a view down a succession of huge open plazas and circular sunken courts flanked by mounds. In contrast, Huaca de los Reyes comprises a large, but compact block of smaller U-shaped temple-mound groups, each embracing a rectangular sunken court, the whole itself forming a U-shaped complex with a large rectangular sunken court, beyond which is an even larger one.

THE EARLY HORIZON
AND BEYOND

The multitude of U-shaped ceremonial centres that dominated the Initial Period gave way to urban centres in later periods, as political powers unified larger areas. A handful of cities began to dominate. They became the 'cathedral cities' of Andean religion and places of pilgrimage among a host of lesser sites and deities.

First Chavín de Huántar, Chiripa and Pukará introduced a new level of religious coherence in the spread of cults. Chavín feline, Staff Deity and reptilian imagery became widespread in portable and statuary art throughout the north and central Andes. The temples at Chavín de Huántar replicated the U-shaped temple formula, and introduced elements of complexity and secrecy in temple interiors previously unseen.

Below: The Pumapunku sunken court at imperial Tiwanaku, the gateway and first port of call for pilgrims to the sacred city.

Chiripa and Pukará, in the Titicaca Basin, developed a tradition of low mounds to support symmetrically arranged groups of single-room buildings around a sunken rectangular court. Pukará exemplifies a cult centre for double-sided Yaya-Mama (male-female) statuary that spread throughout the southern Andean Altiplano.

URBAN PRECINCTS

Cities incorporated the patterns established in these early periods. In the Early Intermediate Period, Moche and Tiwanaku brought the beginnings of state formation, with satellite administrative towns. In the southern coastal deserts, Cahuachi and Ventilla represent two aspects of administrative city and religious centre, among several forming a loose confederation.

Middle Horizon Huari and Tiwanaku were simultaneously imperial capitals and religious cities. Late Intermediate Period

Above: One of the monumental gateways into the Sun Temple and fortress of Sacsahuaman, on the promontory northwest of imperial Cuzco.

Chan Chan, capital of the Chimú Kingdom, was the ultimate combination of extensive urbanism surrounding a complex of ceremonial enclosures – the enclosed cities of the dead Chimú rulers.

By the 15th and 16th centuries, Andean cities had become the focus for ceremony that symbolized the nature and existence of the state in a close alliance of religion and imperial government. Cities hosted ceremonies that were deeply imbued with meaning, ostentatious mass gatherings for festivals and the redistribution of wealth through imperial gift-giving. Precinct plans and ceremonial enclosures became imperial tools for control of both ritual and people.

RITUAL AND FUNERARY COMPOUNDS

Two ancient Andean traditions were the association of burials with temples and the establishment of cemeteries separate from residential areas. For example, Early Horizon Paracas and Early Intermediate Period Nazca cemeteries were dedicated ceremonial sites and necropolises. By contrast, Late Intermediate Period Chan Chan had cemeteries interspersed within the vast urban complex among the residential districts.

Funeral monuments were seen as a way of maintaining contact between the living and the dead. A common practice in many cultures was the periodic re-opening of tombs for the deposit of more bodies.

CEMETERIES
The most famous cemeteries are those of the Paracas and Nazca in the deserts of the southern coast. Paracas tombs show not only the characteristic Andean tradition of preserving the interred person as a mummy bundle, but also the established

tradition of kinship mausoleums that became common in Andean civilization. Tombs were regularly entered to insert new burials through the generations, and the existing mummies often rearranged to honour the new occupant. There were two 'types': bottle-shaped 'Cavernas' shaft tombs, which formed a round burial chamber at the base of a shaft, with a stone-lined entrance at the top, and 'Necropolis' underground vaults of stone-walled, rectangular, upper-entry chambers, with steps leading down to stone-walled, rectangular crypts.

DEDICATORY BURIALS
Sacrifices often accompanied temple dedications. The Preceramic infant burial and sacrificed adult at Huaca de los Sacrificios at Aspero is perhaps the earliest example.

Many later temple platforms were also so honoured. Phase III at Moche Huaca del Sol, Cerro Blanco, included sacrificial burials within adobe-brick tombs, the

victims laid on fibre mats within the tombs. The Phase IV mound included the burial of a man, woman and llama in a grave atop the second tier.

At Tiwanaku, headless burials were found beneath the first terrace of the Akapana temple platform. Attendants were sacrificed and interred to accompany the royal Moche burials, and one Sicán tomb at Batán Grande was accompanied by 17 sacrificial victims.

PILGRIMAGE BURIALS
The powerful oracle shrine of Pachacamac near modern Lima operated for more than 1,000 years. Its pronouncements were so honoured that even the Incas recognized its authority and sought its advice. In the Late Intermediate Period Pachacamac Ichma Kingdom, the city witnessed the establishment of numerous foreign compounds, which expanded the city.

Terraced adobe-brick platforms with ramps were surrounded within walled compounds dedicated to foreign deities. Built as elite residential compounds and sanctuaries, they included forecourts, cell-like rooms and cemeteries for pilgrims.

LINKING LIVING AND DEAD
Anticipating later Chimú practice, one mound at late Moche Galindo lies within a large, walled enclosure. With platform, storage compartments and burial mound, it may have been the residence of the city's ruling elite.

At Middle Horizon Huari, the Vegachayoq Moqo sector was first a royal palace, then 'converted' into a mortuary monument and cemetery for the deceased ruler. Parts of the royal palace were ritually interred or 'retired' – an Andean treatment of buildings as alive and needing burial.

Left: A pre-Inca burial tower or chullpa *of the Lupaka people situated at Paucartambos, near Cuzco.*

In the Monjahayoq sector, a royal tomb comprised a complex of four superimposed stone-slab burial chambers, creating a subterranean funerary 'palace'. Four rooms in the top level overlay a 21-chamber second level, then the royal tomb – a shaft and chamber forming a llama profile in plan, the entrance through the mouth and the tail forming the fourth-level tomb.

CHULLPAS AND CIUDADELAS

These practices entrenched the tradition of continuous contact between living and dead. In the late periods, burial chambers became true funerary monuments or compounds.

The Late Intermediate Period and Late Horizon Collas in the Titicaca Basin built fitted-stone towers called *chullpas*. Of volcanic masonry, circular or square in plan, one to three storeys tall, they are dressed on the exterior but left rough on the interior to form a rubble wall with beaten earth. Their interior vaults have domed tops of corbel arching, with an exterior rim projection. Access is through a small, rectangular entry at the base, facing the sunrise. Burials within are flexed and placed in a series of superimposed niches in the walls.

Erected near towns or in separated groups, the *chullpas* were family mausoleums, containing generations of burials, the bodies wrapped in rich textiles. They were regularly entered to deposit new burials or alternatively to take the mummies out to be honoured at ceremonies.

Groups of *chullpas* were erected at Sillustani and several other sites around Lake Titicaca. They are associated with standing stone circles, whose entrances also face the sunrise.

The ultimate funerary monuments are the *ciudadelas* of Chan Chan, the Chimú capital. Each high-walled enclosure was a separate 'dead' city within greater Chan Chan, and, like the palace at Huari, had progressed from existence as an imperial palace enclosure housing the royal court, to a funerary compound to house the deceased king and his retainers. Each enclosed a large plaza for ceremony,

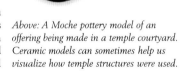

Above: A Moche pottery model of an offering being made in a temple courtyard. Ceramic models can sometimes help us visualize how temple structures were used.

smaller interior courts and patios, housing for the king's retainers, lines of storage niches to hold royal tribute and wealth, and the royal tomb within a platform mound forming a miniature U-shaped structure. Similar Chimú enclosures were built at Tucume Viejo and Chincha La Centinela.

The Chachapoyas in the northeastern Andes built numerous cylindrical tombs at Los Pinchudos containing multiple burials.

The Inca Coricancha temple in Cuzco included special chambers to house the deceased Inca *mallquis* mummies of deceased rulers.

Left: The chullpa *burial towers of Chusaqueri, Oruro on the Bolivian Altiplano form a funerary complex for ancestor burial through generations.*

ADMINISTRATIVE ARCHITECTURE

Administrative structures are difficult to identify, but the close relationship between rulers and religious leaders suggests that some structures at early ceremonial centres were administrative.

As social hierarchy developed, higher classes gained control over disproportionate amounts of wealth, and so administrative mechanisms were needed to redistribute it. In Inca times, religious festivals provided the venue for redistribution and we can conjecture that this practice was ancient.

MOXEKE AND STORAGE
Before they could be given away, or redistributed in elite burials, goods had to be collected and stored. Rows and groups of smaller buildings around the principal religious platforms, plazas and temples were probably storehouses.

For example, the Huaca A complex at Moxeke (Pampa de los Llamas, in the Casma Valley of northern coastal Peru)

Below: Within Chan Chan's compounds were vast complexes of administrative and storage buildings around inner courtyards.

was a well-planned, symmetrical arrangement. Long corridors connected large and small rooms with wall niches, the whole forming a large walled compound – the very image of a bureaucratic structure.

Two large halls occupied the centre of the low platform, each fronted by a court reached by steps. Between the halls was an inner courtyard. To either side there were smaller rooms along corridors. In groups and lining the outer compound sides there were even smaller rooms, some with intercommunicating doorways, opening onto long corridors running the length of the compound. The complex clearly accommodated storage and public ceremony, perhaps even banquets.

Huaca A sits on one side of a large rectangular public plaza. On the other side stood a tiered pyramidal structure, with round-cornered, tower-like mounds at the rear, backing an open terrace plaza reached by a monumental staircase. The tier faces were decorated with painted clay sculptures – clearly a temple.

Similarly, the massive complex at Huaca de los Reyes, also on the north coast, comprises a principal temple platform

Above: Fine stone shaping and fitting was reserved for imperial and state architecture, as here at one of Machu Picchu's many administrative kallankas.

and plaza, plus numerous smaller groups of platforms and rows of small, single-room buildings. The vast complexes of Sechín Alto and scores of other U-shaped ceremonial centres also include numerous smaller structures around them. At these and scores of other Initial Period and Early Horizon sites, the different groups of buildings are inseparably intertwined with bureaucratic and religious activities.

It is suggested that some of the small interior rooms at Chavín de Huántar were also for storage.

DIFFERENT APPROACHES
Moche and Nazca cities represent different administrative approaches. The Moche capital at Cerro Blanco provided a model at the apex of a hierarchy of administrative structures. The two great pyramid platforms of the Huaca del Sol and the Huaca de la Luna were religious

*Above: The vast mud-walled enclosed
ciudadela compounds of Chan Chan of the
Chimú formed imperial cities within the
city. Their carved walls shielded complexes
of administrative buildings.*

monuments surrounded by smaller complexes of administrative units. Like the
capital, the Moche administrative centre
at Pañamarca copied many of the capital's
features. A principal adobe brick pyramid
platform dominated the centre of a complex of spacious courts and buildings to
administer the religious and economic
affairs of the region.

The Nazca confederation of states in the
southern coastal deserts separated religious
centres and working cities. Ventilla, a sprawling residential city whose habitation
terraces and walled compounds of mounds
and administrative structures covered at
least 2sq km (495 acres), was linked by a
road to Cahuachi, a place of religious ritual and complex of family mausoleums.

IMPERIAL ADMINISTRATION

Middle Horizon Wari developed an
administrative structure that became the
hallmark of the Chimú and Incas.

The modular regimentation and additive nature of Wari architecture, with
rows of walled precincts and multi-storey
buildings at the capital, Huari, was
repeated in several provincial centres. The
well-preserved grid plan of Pikillacta on
Wari's southern border is perhaps the best

known. Other Wari centres were at
Jincamocco, Wari's 'gateway' to the south
coast, Azángaro in the centre, and
Viracochapampa and Marca Huamachuco
on the northern frontier.

A fundamental factor in Wari administration was a compulsion to gather and
control resources – to produce, collect
and store them.

Tiwanaku, Wari's rival to the south, was
primarily a ceremonial centre of ritual pyramids, sunken courts and plazas, surrounded
by residential areas. Unlike at Wari cities,
archaeologists have found no rows of
storehouses or obvious bureaucratic structures. Tiwanaku has been described as a
'patrician city', in which residency near
the centre may have been restricted to
aristocracy and their retainers.

CHIMÚ AND INCA

At Chan Chan, the Chimú introduced an
administrative twist. Its vast compounds
housed row upon row of storage rooms
and niches along corridors, within high-
walled compounds called *ciudadelas*.
These housed the accumulated wealth of
successive dead emperors. Bureaucracies
of retainers continued to collect, admin-
istrate and redistribute this wealth
alongside the administration of the living
emperor and population.

The Incas imposed distinct administrative architecture at their provincial cities
– such as Huánuco Pampa and Tambo
Colorado – built to impress conquered

subjects with Inca power and authority.
Although not replicas of Cuzco, they
contained similar elements: a main plaza
for public ceremonies (and subsidiary
plazas); an *ushnu* platform in the plaza
for viewing, public hearings and the
administration of justice; surrounding
kallanka compounds of buildings for
bureaucratic residency and official functions; and blocks of *collca* storehouses. In
addition there were temples to Viracocha
and/or Inti the sun god (and sometimes
to other principal Inca gods) and an
acllahuasi compound (for the chosen
women weavers and *chicha* beer makers).

*Below: Tambo Colorado, so-called for its red
adobe mud-brick walls, was typical of Inca
provincial administrative cities, with
complexes of kanchas and storehouses.*

ELITE AND ROYAL RESIDENCES

Building monumental architecture involved different layers of command. There had to be leaders to marshal the labour forces, and labourers and craftspeople to do the work.

EARLY DISTINCTIONS
There is evidence of differences in residential quality as early as the Initial Period. Moxeke dwellings include some with plastered and painted interior walls and storage niches, aligned with the ceremonial centre. Most Initial Period and Early Horizon commoners, however, lived in scattered villages and farmsteads.

In Early Horizon Chavín de Huántar, only priests and special craftspeople were allowed to live near the temple.

URBAN DISTINCTIONS
This pattern prevailed into the Early Intermediate Period. With the development of cities by c.500BC, the pattern became

Below: Machu Picchu, perched above the Urubamba River north-west of Cuzco, is the best-known imperial retreat of Inca Pachacuti.

one of elite residences sited near the monumental religious precincts, with common dwellings farther out, intermixed with lesser elite residences and workshops.

At the Moche capital, Cerro Blanco, finer houses were near the base of the Huaca del Sol and south-west of the Huaca de la Luna. They were built of shaped stone and mud-plastered walls and were often painted. They had larger rooms and storage structures than the jostled, simple housing farther from the religious precinct, and their owners used finer ceramics.

Moche Galindo elite residents lived in large, bench-lined rooms, and had separate kitchens and storage rooms. Their neighbourhood was segregated from common housing by a wall and ditch. Similarly, Pampa Grande (c.AD550 to the Late Intermediate Period) had elite residences with large rooms and plastered stone walls at Huaca Forteleza, the principal pyramid, and north of it. The rich burial of the Sicán Lord with hoards of specially crafted gold, silver and other jewellery and objects reveals the existence of an affluent social class.

Above: A recessed ('double-jam') doorway at the imperial Palace of Huayna Capac at Quispihuanca in the Urubamba Valley.

TIWANAKU PALACES
Unlike earlier cities, or contemporary Wari cities, there is no evidence of blocks of storehouses at Middle Horizon Tiwanaku, or any obvious 'administrative' structures. However, from c.AD400 there were elite residential *barrios* around the ceremonial precinct. High adobe walls on cobblestone foundations surrounded elite compounds. By c.AD750 these were razed to provide space for the Putuni ritual mound–palace complex.

The Putuni ritual mound occupied a raised platform 50m (165ft) each side, with a sunken court and an eastern entrance. Adjacent, on its north-west corner, the north and west palaces were two of four palace residences surrounding a central courtyard. Each had foundations of finely cut stone and adobe walls, smoothly plastered.

The 'Palace of Multicoloured Rooms' walls were painted with blue, green, red, orange and yellow mineral pigments. Up to 15 coats of the same colour on some wall fragments reveal numerous redecorations. It had a carved stone lintel (with strutting, ray-headed feline figures), stone-paved inner patios, canals supplying it with spring water, sewage drains into the city's main drains, and a large kitchen (suitable for preparing feasts). Rooms had their own hearths and storage niches.

Right: The imperial Inca provincial capital at Huánuco Pampa in Chinchaysuyu quarter included an imperial palace entered through a wide gateway leading to a complex of kancha *compounds.*

There were dedicatory human burials at its entrance and four corners, plus a llama foetus burial. All included rich burial offerings: gold, silver, copper and stone ornaments, including a turquoise-bead necklace, gold mask or pectoral with repoussé face and other jewellery, a silver tube filled with blue pigment, a carved marine shell and finely carved bone utensils, and fine ceramics.

Other residences near the Putuni complex were also made of fine, cut-stone buildings, making the whole area west of the Akapana–Kalasasaya ceremonial precinct an elite neighbourhood.

CHIMÚ AND INCA PALACES
The compounds known as *ciudadelas* at Chan Chan were the royal residences of Chimú kings and their courts. Each comprised an elaborate complex of hundreds of large and smaller rooms, rows of storerooms and miniature U-shaped temples.

Below: The Tschudi audiencia *compound: The centre of the Chimú capital Chan Chan comprised walled royal compounds (*ciudadelas*), one for the ruling king and one for each deceased king and an attendant court and administrative staff.*

When a king died, the compound became a 'dead' palace and his tomb was bureaucratically maintained. Their massive mud-brick walls and interior walls were embellished with moulded friezes of religious imagery and geometric patterns.

Cuzco and other Inca cities, following ancient precedent, had distinct districts: *hanan* (upper) and *hurin* (lower). Although described by Spanish chroniclers as having palaces and temples around spacious plazas, it is mostly impossible to identify individual Inca structures according to function, the Coricancha temple being an obvious exception.

Inca houses were similar for all social ranks: single-roomed rectangular buildings with one door, no windows and pitched thatch roofs. Those for royalty, nobles and high officials were larger and of fine masonry.

Spanish chroniclers describe a number of palaces around the Haucaypata and Cusipata plazas in *hanan* Cuzco. The Casana compound, north-west of the plazas, comprised several large halls encircled by a fine masonry wall. Garcilasco de la Vega says that its largest hall could hold 3,000 people. Two round towers flanked the compound's main entrance.

One palace of Huáscar (thirteenth Inca emperor) was east of Cusipata, but there are no details except that it was claimed by Diego de Almagro (Pizarro's second in command), and was therefore presumably an impressive residence.

Similarly, chroniclers name other palaces at Amarucancha (Serpent Enclosure), south-east of Haucaypata, facing the Casana, which was built by Huascar and awarded to Hernando de Soto. There was also the Hatuncancha compound at the eastern corner of Haucaypata and two compounds of fine masonry halls at Pucamarca and Cusicancha, south-east of Amarucancha.

All these compounds basically comprised large halls with single entrances, built of fine-dressed masonry. It is primarily their sizes, stonework and mention by Spanish chroniclers that identifies them as 'palaces'. (Even at Machu Picchu, clearly an imperial retreat, we do not know the actual use of most of the buildings.)

Below: Fine Inca masonry is preserved in many Peruvian buildings. At Andahuaylillas, the doorway of an elite residence has a lintel carved with two facing pumas.

DOMESTIC ARCHITECTURE

Evidence of ancient Andean housing is abundant but less explored then elite and royal residences. Materials varied through time and due to local resources.

EARLY HOUSES

Hunter-gatherers used rock shelters and caves, while coastal peoples, such as the La Paloma of Chile, built reed round-houses.

Materials and styles varied considerably among Preceramic coastal villages. Huaca Prieta houses were square, semi-subterranean buildings of river cobbles, with wooden and whalebone roof beams, while houses at Asia were of fieldstones and adobe set in clay mortar. Other coastal peoples used beach cobbles, basalt and granite fieldstones, adobe or coral blocks. Many had central hearths and most had storage pits.

Highland populations lived in small, scattered hamlets and farmsteads. La Galgada is one of the few sites where houses have been excavated. They were

Below: A black polished-ware Chimú bottle shows the steep roof pitch and rectangular form changed little in the Late Intermediate Period and Late Horizon.

oval, up to 14sq m (150sq ft), with unpainted walls of fieldstones in clay mortar, earthen floors and built-in firepits.

INITIAL PERIOD HOUSES

Residential hamlets occupied hill-sides and the margins of cultivable land around U-shaped ceremonial centres. Houses at Ancón and Cardál formed quadrangular groups of dwellings measuring *c*.2.5m (8–9ft) on each side. They had stone footings, but the upper walls were of perishable materials: cobbles set in seaweed and marsh grass at coastal Ancón, and field-stones and hemispherical adobe bricks in clay mortar at inland Cardál.

Storage pits were outside dwellings, sometimes as separate buildings. Cooking was done in separate buildings or outdoors. Associated artefacts suggest that there were separate buildings for 'industry', including stone and bone working, and fibre and cotton textiles making. Early pottery serving vessels remained the same sizes throughout the Initial Period, while cooking pots became larger, suggesting increasing prosperity.

Moxeke had two dwelling groups. One, behind and aligned with the ceremonial platforms and central plaza, had houses of quarried-stone walls covered with mud plaster (sometimes painted red inside), with interior wall niches and small store-rooms behind them. The other group comprised irregularly aligned dwellings of cobblestone footings and perishable upper walls. Such differences, and associated artefacts, suggest distinct elite and common inhabitants.

At Montegrande, one of about 50 Initial Period sites in the Jequetepeque Valley, houses formed clusters around patios (inner courtyards), and were

Above: A bridge-spout bottle provides clues to ancient Inca house styles showing typical rectangular kallankas *with thatched roofs.*

built of cane and mud plaster. Alignment with the ceremonial platforms indicates agreed planning.

CHAVÍN AND MOCHE HOUSING

Although Chavín de Huántar was not a city, a residential section was built in flat areas around the temple (estimated population, 2–3,000). House groups comprised fieldstone dwellings, storage buildings and workshops. Associated artefacts show that different residential clusters produced different Chavín portable objects.

Contemporary Paracas housing continued coastal traditions of single-room residences of cobbles and adobe bricks set in mortar.

From *c*.500BC Andean cities comprised central ceremonial and administrative buildings surrounded by increasingly larger suburban residential areas. As at Moxeke, social differentiation was found at Moche Cerro Blanco. Dwellings at the

base of Huaca del Sol and south-west of Huaca de la Luna range from simple dwellings of river-cobble foundations and walls of perishable materials, to finer houses of shaped-stone, mud-plastered walls. The latter had larger rooms and storage structures and their occupants used finer ceramics, which were made in dedicated workshops.

Moche Galindo had four zones of residential structures, exemplifying the nature of Andean urban suburbs. Anticipating the dedicated storage blocks of Inca times, stone-lined bins were built on hillside terraces. As at Cerro Blanco there were well-built elite residences, with large, bench-lined rooms, storage rooms and kitchens, while the common, smaller houses were crowded together on the hillside overlooking the ceremonial centre, and segregated by a wall and ditch.

A similar pattern – ceremonial mound and precinct, surrounded by residential *barrios* – evolved at Pampa Grande, established *c.*AD550 and occupied into the Late Intermediate Period. There were elite residences at and north of Huaca Forteleza; high-level citizens, who oversaw the workshops, in compounds; low-level administrators in smaller compounds; and craftsmen and farmers in irregular groups of single-room residences.

Below: Rows of domestic houses formed attached 'terraces' on a regular grid plan of streets at Middle Horizon Wari Pikillacta.

WARI, TIWANAKU

Great cities of the Wari and Tiwanaku included large, suburban residential populations around their ceremonial precincts, incorporating workshops for pottery, metalwork and textiles, and *chicha* beer breweries. Wari citizens lived in rows of houses along narrow streets within large rectangular compounds. Subdividing the compounds were groups of patios (inner courtyards) with low benches and stone-lined canals, and surrounded by one-, two- or even three-storey houses (probably housing extended families), and workshops, as found, for example, at Huari, Viracochapampa, Pikillacta and other sites.

Tiwanaku citizens lived in similar housing. Distinct elite residential *barrios* at Tiwanaku were near the ceremonial plaza, while common citizens lived farther out, in cobblestone- and adobe-walled houses with thatched roofs.

CHIMÚ AND INCA

These patterns continued into the Late Intermediate Period and Late Horizon. Chan Chan's vast urban population of

Above: The ruins of a kallanka *at Machu Picchu and the evidence from clay models enable accurate reconstruction, with a thatched roof – note the exterior stone 'pegs' on the gables, for securing the roof structure.*

commoners lived around and beyond the elite residences, in *barrio* complexes of small, irregular rooms with common walls, mostly in the south, west and south-west city. Walls were mud-plastered cane or *quincha* (wattle-and-daub).

These were self-contained neighbourhoods with winding streets, common wells and cemeteries. Patio areas comprised house, kitchen, storage areas and workshops.

The typical Inca house was a single-roomed, usually single-storey rectangular structure with stone walls and a pitched thatch roof. The house was the realm of women and children (until boys were old enough to help in the fields). Inca houses were primarily shelters; most activities were done outdoors. They had only open doorways and windows. Families slept huddled together on straw or twined fibre pallets.

FORTRESSES AND WARFARE

Most ancient Andean warfare involved pitched battles on open land. Early warfare is depicted in stone sculpture and on painted ceramics. However, as periods of political cohesion interchanged with periods of fragmentation, there was need for fortifications as places of safe refuge during times of competition between city-states and in times of imperial conquest.

EARLY WARFARE
Plant and animal domestication and development of irrigation agriculture in early times entailed co-operation within communities, but as the best lands were occupied, disputes arose between communities.

The 300 carved slabs at Initial Period Cerro Sechín are a procession of triumphant warriors and their victims. Whether a war memorial for a specific victory or representing a symbolic battle,

Below: Sacsahuaman, built by Inca Pachacuti atop the hill north-west of Cuzco, had both a sacred and military function – at its core was the Temple to Inti (the Sun), while its stout stone walls and terraces formed a defensive position and its rooms were used to store military equipment.

Above: The Chimú fortress at Paramonga guarded the kingdom's borders at a mountain pass and presented a formidable obstacle to Inca conquest.

they are evidence of conflict by *c.*1200BC, probably small-scale, seasonal raiding between towns.

Although the Early Horizon brought religious coherence and less conflict under the influence of the Chavín and Yaya-Mama cults, sacrifice and trophy-head collection continued.

The breakdown of these cults in the Early Intermediate Period brought social withdrawal, increased competition and the abandonment of many settlements. Populations moved to hilltop fortresses

both on coasts and in highlands. Periods of drought in the early centuries AD brought hard times.

HILLFORTS
The Santa Valley and its tributaries of northern coastal Peru has been intensively surveyed, locating 54 Early Horizon sites. Most were towns – groups of small 'polities' – but 21 were hilltop forts built in remote positions to enhance defensibility. They are best interpreted as citadels, as permanent occupation would have been difficult so far away from water and agriculture. Each features one or more massive 1–2m (3–6ft) high stone enclosure walls, from which slingers could repulse enemies, plus bastions, buttresses and narrow, baffled entrances. A few have dry trenches on vulnerable sides.

Similar forts were also built in the Casma and Nepeña valleys. Chanquillo (mid-4th–2nd centuries BC), in Casma, typifies these refuges: two outer subcircular walls with steep entrances and bastions follow the contours, encircling a lozenge-shaped inner wall. Within this are two circular towers within circular walls and a multi-roomed rectangular structure for temporary occupation.

Citadels proliferated outside the north-central coast in post-Chavín times, for example in the Viru, Moche and Chicama valleys.

MOCHE AND WARI FORTS
A typical Moche fortified site was Galindo in the Moche Valley. It began as a fortress, strategically located at the valley neck, with stout rectangular walls and parapets with piles of slingstones. It changed to a hinterland site and elite burial enclosure in the early Middle Horizon as the Moche power base shifted from south to north – abandoning Cerro Blanco for a capital at Pampa Grande, in Lambayeque.

Cerro Chepén in the northern coastal mountains is perhaps one of a chain of Moche fortresses. It sprawls across a 450m

Left: A projecting tower at the Chimú fortress of Paramonga provides a superb view of the valley below, and of any approaching enemies.

(1,500ft) high ridge and contained a central palace with hundreds of rooms and barracks for about 5,000.

Middle Horizon Wari and Tiwanaku imperial coherence put an end to regional conflict and fortifications. Tiwanaku cities were focused on ceremony and ritual, and although the Wari conquered the central and northern Andean states, there seems to have been a guarded peace between the two empires.

The only recorded Wari fortress, Cerro Baúl (c.AD600–700), represents a brief encounter and Wari retreat within Tiwanaku territory in the Moquegua Valley. It occupies a sheer-sided mountain top of 600m (1,970ft) with 10ha (25 acres) of circular, D-shaped and rectangular single- and multi-storey structures grouped around patios.

WARRING STATES

Political fragmentation and endemic regional conflict returned in the Late Intermediate Period. Inca records transcribed by Spanish chroniclers describe intense warfare between competing 'tribes' or ethnic groups broken up into numerous petty states. Strong, warlike leaders called *sinchis*

Right: Resembling the terraced monolithic stone 'walls' at Sacsahuaman, Cuzco, the imperial Inca city and fortress at Ollantaytambo, north-west of Cuzco, could be easily defended.

built hilltop fortifications that are called *pukarás*, as is shown in the archaeological record.

The Wanka of central Peru's Mantaro Valley, for example, were typical of the Inca Fourth Age. Regional warfare caused them to build their towns on high ridges and hilltops, fortified with stout walls.

The Chimú of the north-west coast carved out the largest state. Its southern limits were guarded by the mountaintop fortress of Paramonga in the Fortaleza Valley. Massive adobe brick walls rise in several tiers to a final, central citadel-palace, with characteristic trapezoidal doorways.

As the Inca Empire expanded, it incorporated existing cities, including the Chimú Kingdom. New Inca cities served

as anchors for regional stability, rallying points, and staging points for future campaigns. These Inca administrative centres were capable of defence, but were less fortresses than imperial provincial capitals, for Inca warfare involved large armies and pitched battles. The Incas conquered by force and negotiation. Once hilltop fortresses were taken and razed they ruled through intimidation and power rather than from garrisoned citadels.

Nevertheless, Ollantaytambo in the Urubamba Valley was a combined Inca imperial retreat, temple and fortress. Built on a mountain shoulder above a strategic pass on the Inca road north of Cuzco, it was one place where the Inca court made a last-ditch stand against the Spaniards.

The fortress-temple of Sacsahuaman formed the 'head' of puma-shaped imperial Cuzco. Its circular tower was a temple to the sun god Inti and its rooms were used to store weapons and armour for the imperial troops. Its massive stone walls would have presented a formidable citadel for the capital.

U-SHAPED CEREMONIAL COMPLEXES

Sechín Alto and Moxeke-Pampa de las Llamas are two fine examples of U-shaped ceremonial centres.

SECHÍN ALTO

One of the premier examples of a coastal valley U-shaped ceremonial centre, Sechín Alto is representative of early Andean coastal religious traditions. Built and occupied from about the middle of the second millennium BC, it represents a huge investment of labour and therefore demonstrates that tremendous political power must have been used to marshal and organize the workforces needed to complete it. Its sheer size is a mark of distinction, for it dwarfs almost all other U-shaped ceremonial centres built before it or contemporary to it. Its final form

Below: Artist's reconstruction of Sechín Alto, the largest U-shaped ceremonial centre ever built, comprising a succession of plazas and temple mounds stretching c.1.5km (1 mile).

covered more than 200ha (495 acres), making it 15 times larger than the later, highland ceremonial complex of Chavín de Huántar.

The site was located and excavated by the native Peruvian archaeologist Julio C. Tello in the 1930s, and its structures were further explored and analyzed by Sheila and Thomas Pozorski in the 1980s.

Sechín Alto was built in the Sechín branch of the Casma Valley of north-central coastal Peru, south-east of the Sechín River, and was one of many U-shaped ceremonial complexes of the Initial Period and Early Horizon. The huge complex is oriented roughly north-east–south-west. Forming the base of the U shape at its western end is a truncated mound measuring 300 × 250m (984 × 820ft), rising 44m (144ft) above the floor of the valley. Huge granite stone blocks were quarried and roughly dressed to face the platform, with the blocks set in a mortar of silty clay. Later, 20th-century looters

dug a pit 20m (66ft) into the platform, revealing an inner mound made of conical adobe 'bricks' – a preceding construction of 1500BC or earlier.

Running north-east of the core mound are four large plazas: three of them are roughly rectangular and the largest is square. The three rectangular plazas each has a round sunken courtyard, aligned along the axis of the ceremonial platform. The largest circular sunken court, in the farthest plaza north-east of the base platform, is c.80m (c.265ft) in diameter. From the base platform to the most easterly plaza it is some 1,100m (3,639ft); including the base monument, the entire central complex stretches nearly 1.5km (1 mile).

Subsidiary mounds and other constructions flank the plazas along their northern and southern edges. Some are long, narrow platforms, while others are groups of aligned small square and rectangular platforms, some of which are on the tops of the long platforms. Still others appear to be complexes of rooms on the small mounds.

Farther north-west and south-east of these main structures there are scattered remains of other square and rectangular mounds, but most of the evidence for any surrounding domestic structures has been destroyed by modern agricultural activities.

Sechín Alto functioned for some 800 years, from before 1500BC to c.800BC. Its size and complexity show that it must have represented a considerable political power in the valley, which probably extended to the surrounding region, although there were four similar contemporary ceremonial centres in the Casma Valley, and five others just before the rise of Chavín de Huántar in the north-central highlands, towards the end of the Initial Period. Adjacent coastal valleys also had dozens of contemporary U-shaped ceremonial complexes.

Architecturally and religiously, Sechín Alto is considered part of a tradition called El Paraíso. It stands at the height of the U-shaped ceremonial religious creed.

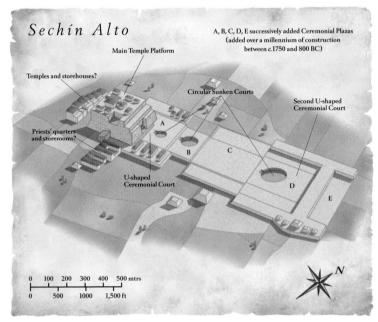

Sechín Alto

A, B, C, D, E successively added Ceremonial Plazas (added over a millennium of construction between c.1750 and 800 BC)

Main Temple Platform

Temples and storehouses?

Circular Sunken Courts

Second U-shaped Ceremonial Court

Priests' quarters and storerooms?

A

B   C

U-shaped Ceremonial Court

D

E

N

| 0 | 100 | 200 | 300 | 400 | 500 mtrs |

| 0 | 500 | 1000 | 1,500 ft |

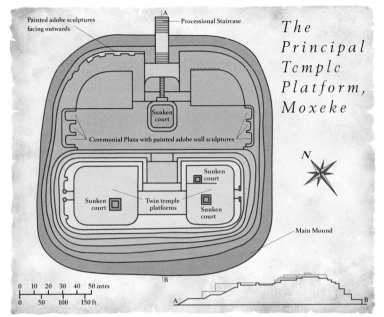

*The
Principal
Temple
Platform,
Moxeke*

Huaca A supports a central walled compound comprising scores of small chambers, possibly for the storage of religious paraphernalia and food. Along this central plaza more than 70 rectangular stone platforms, some never completed, were erected in lines flanking the north-west and south-east sides. In some cases domestic structures appear to have been destroyed to build them, but their function remains uncertain.

The Moxeke-Pampa de las Llamas complex was built and occupied for about 400 years. Like Sechín Alto, taking the Moxeke mound as the principal platform and base of the U-shape, the open arms of the U formed by the plazas and other platforms face the north-east, to the mountains and source of life-giving waters.

Above: Plan of the principal temple mound at Moxeke, a rival centre to Sechín Alto; it formed the base of a U-shaped ceremonial complex (profile in lower right shows platform elevations from north to south).

As well as the huge base platform and wings flanking the aligned plazas, there are five 'attendant' platforms – three behind (south-west) of the main platform and two south-east of it – each forming the base of a much smaller U-shaped structure. As in all complexes of the creed of the El Paraíso tradition, the arms of the U are open to the ultimate source of the waters that make the valley fertile: the distant mountains.

MOXEKE

The contemporary complex at Moxeke-Pampa de las Llamas, south of Sechín Alto, was undoubtedly a rival. It is the second largest such centre in the valley in the later Initial Period, also occupying about 200ha (495 acres). Moxeke was first excavated by Tello in 1937.

Like Sechín Alto, it was a linear complex. At Moxeke-Pampa de las Llamas, however, there were two monumental mounds – called Moxeke and Huaca A –

separated by a kilometre of aligned plazas, the largest of which is 350m (1,150ft) long. The Moxeke tiered platform was roughly square, but with rounded corners. Atop it were several chambers, and a central staircase ascends its north-east face.

Below: View of Chanquillo in the Casma Valley, once an Early Horizon fortress and probable ceremonial centre, looking towards the mountains faced by many U-shaped ceremonial structures.

PARACAS AND NAZCA CITIES

The abundance of exquisitely preserved Paracas mummy burials and their textiles has overshadowed the fact that the site was the residence of a living population as well. Archaeologists at first concentrated their efforts on what have been revealed as the dedicated cemeteries for the settlements of an entire region.

CENTRAL PARACAS
The central settlement of the Paracas people was on the Paracas Peninsula, on and around the hill of Cerro Colorado. An area of about 4,000sq m (1 acre) was occupied by habitations, known as the Cavernas phase. Square and rectangular structures of adobe walls with stone foundations were separated by narrower passageways, and compounds of such residences were scattered across the plain below Cerro Colorado. Later, the northern slope of Cerro Colorado became the new cemetery, known as the Necropolis (or Topará) phase.

Together with the deliberately separated cemeteries, the town was occupied *c.*300BC–*c.*AD200. From about 300BC

Below: The Paracas Peninsula, where three cemeteries contained generations of elite and common burials of mummified remains in multiple-layered textile bundles.

Paracas peoples were weaving not only with cotton but also with llama wool, revealing long-distance contacts with mountain herders and lending a metropolitan aspect to their culture.

TRIPARTITE 'URBANISM'
The area of the Pisco Valley and Paracas Bay is a rich environment for marine life, both on- and off-shore. Around the bay, numerous smaller, contemporary fishing hamlets were settled, whose inhabitants would have used the cemeteries as well. Similarly, in the adjacent Pisco Valley, other settlements were established for agriculture.

Altogether, domestic structures and refuse sprawl across some 54ha (133 acres). The central Paracas town was served by a spring for water, but the population relied on the settlements of the adjacent valleys for their agricultural produce.

Thus Paracas 'urban planning' appears to have comprised a tripartite pattern. Seacoast hamlets exploited the foreshore and sea, inland valley settlements irrigated and farmed the fertile lands for produce, and a central sacred town, perhaps regarded as the holiest shrine, maintained and administered sacred rites at dedicated cemeteries for the burial of the region's dead.

Above: An embroidered Paracas tunic showing a probable deity that seems to combine the Oculate Being and a Chavín-style Staff Deity, plus serpent and feline imagery.

NAZCA CONTINUITY
The partly contemporary and subsequent Nazca culture followed this pattern in the same areas of the Peruvian south coast. Nazca civilization, flourishing between *c.*100BC and *c.*AD700, was spread over a wider region of coastal valleys, making up the watersheds of the Ica and Río Grande de Nazca rivers and the Ayacucho highlands to the east.

However, in this coastal desert region many rivers never reach the sea, and in their narrow valleys support only limited irrigation networks. It has been estimated that the Nazca drainage, for example, would have been capable of supporting perhaps 15,000–22,000 people in scattered settlements.

A DELIBERATE SETTLEMENT
One of the best-known Nazca settlements is Cahuachi in the Nazca Valley, west of modern Nazca. Settlement began as a small village in the 1st century BC, and by about AD100 it had become the dominant regional centre.

Right: On the desert floor outside their cities the Nazca made and maintained hundreds of geoglyphs – ritual pathways of geometric shapes and ground images.

Its location was not accidental. For geological reasons the Nazca River flows on the surface up-valley from the site, then in mid-valley becomes subterranean, to re-surface down-valley. Cahuachi faces the Nazca Desert to the north-east, upon which the famous Nazca lines, or geoglyphs, are scattered – ritual pathways in the forms of animal and plant outlines and geometric patterns and lines.

In an area prone to drought, a need to exploit the nature of the water resource led the ancient Nazcans to develop an ingenious subterranean water-channelling system to tap the river and run-off water. Using river cobbles, they built underground aqueducts and filtering galleries, which led to reservoirs that minimized surface evaporation and fed irrigation canals. Thus the centre exploited an area of surrounding agricultural settlements and sacred landscape use.

Cahuachi comprised a core of about 40 low hills, enhanced with platforms of adobe bricks. The largest, called the Great Temple, rises *c.*30m (*c.*98ft) high in six or seven terraces. Surrounding the platforms are plazas and adobe-walled

Below: Some Nazca geoglyphs combine ritual pathways with aligned areas of large 'designated space', possibly for the gathering of crowds of worshippers.

compounds. There are no workshops or storage structures, or domestic refuse. These features support the interpretation of Cahuachi as a sacred centre, a religious city for worship and burial, which served the population in the settlements of the surrounding region. The entire settlement covers about 11.5sq km (2,841 acres).

In contrast, a nearly straight road leads north from Cahuachi to Ventilla. Here, covering at least 2sq km (495 acres; much of the site has been destroyed beneath modern agriculture), sprawled a residential city of habitation terraces, walled compounds and mounds. It is the largest Nazca settlement known, and believed to be the urban counterpart to Cahuachi.

Major construction at Cahuachi ceased *c.*AD550 as Nazca civilization began to wane.

Thus Nazca civilization, like Paracas, appears to have comprised a tripartite configuration. Dispersed settlements exploited the available coastal and valley environments, expanding on the Paracas pattern as regional population increased. Their inhabitants exchanged produce and marine resources among themselves (as well as trading with more distant cultures), and were served by specialized towns for civil administration and for sacred rites and burial. In addition, the adjacent desert floor became a canvas upon which ritual pathways supplemented the sacred purposes of the shrine and cemetery capital.

ROYAL MOCHE

The Moche people built several large man-made structures in their capital, including the alleged temples to the Sun and Moon.

SUN AND MOON PYRAMIDS
The Huacas del Sol and de la Luna formed the core of the most important ceremonial centre of the Early Intermediate Period Moche Kingdom. Construction of the two monumental platforms was begun c.AD100. By c.AD450 Moche was the capital of the southern Moche realm. Between c.AD300 and 550 several ceremonial centres were built to administer the southern Moche valleys: Huancaco in the Virú Valley, the misnamed Pampa de los Incas in the Santa, Pañamarca in the Nepeña, and Mocollope in the Chicama. Dominating them all was the capital at Moche in the Moche Valley.

The names 'Sol' and 'Luna' are modern. We are uncertain of the site's ancient name, but an early Spanish Colonial document refers to the site as 'Capuxaida'.

Below: Murals at Moche Huaca de la Luna include a rich array of creatures important to religious ritual and economic wellbeing – for a coastal civilization, sea fish were important.

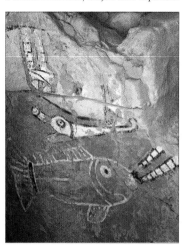

The Moche complex follows planning traditions dating back to earlier periods in the northern and central coastal Peruvian valleys, with dominant ceremonial platforms within a working city. The two platforms stand 500m (1,650ft) apart across a now open area. The pyramids are constructed of millions of unbaked adobe bricks.

MAN-MADE MOUNTAINS
The Huaca del Sol, rising 40m (130ft) above the Moche Valley floor, is the largest single man-made structure ever built in the ancient Andes. In Andean religious tradition it appears that the Moche were attempting to create symbolic mountains on the river plain, perhaps to honour the sky gods, and in recognition that the ultimate source of the waters of their rivers came from the distant mountains to the east. Spanish treasure-seekers used those very waters in 1602 when they attempted to wash away Huaca del Sol by diverting the River Moche, obliterating about two-thirds of it. Enough of two wings remain to show the cross-shaped plan of the monumental platform.

Huaca del Sol formed a cross of thick arms on the long axis (345m/1,130ft) and stubby arms across the short axis (160m/525ft). Built in four tiers, the summit is reached by a monumental ramp up its north side.

Huaca de la Luna sits at the base of a small hill called Cerro Blanco. It was raised in three tiers against the western side of the hill to form a platform 290m (950ft) wide (north–south) and 210m

Above: San José de Moro, Jequetepeque Valley, Peru, where rich Moche tombs were found containing the remains of priestesses dressed like those in the Moche Pañamarca murals.

(690ft) deep (east–west) for the support of three smaller platform-mounds, four plazas and several roofed enclosures. It rises 32m (105ft) above the valley floor.

Below: A Moche ceramic effigy of a warrior with a war club from the Atacama Desert in northern Chile reveals Moche influence from northern coastal Peru.

Above: The huge Moche Huaca del Sol was built of an estimated 143 million adobe mud bricks. Its construction was apparently done by gangs of workmen.

Many exterior walls were whitewashed, or were painted with red or yellow ochre. The faces of many of the courtyard walls are decorated with a varied array of friezes in moulded mud-plaster and murals of religious themes. As with the Huaca del Sol, Spanish looters destroyed more than two-thirds of the uppermost tier when they dug a huge pit in the belief that the foundations contained treasure.

Archaeologists have identified eight stages in the construction of Huaca del Sol, as it was modified and enhanced over the centuries, most of them finished before AD450. At least six phases of construction are recognized for Huaca de la Luna.

NEARLY 200 MILLION BRICKS!
The millions of adobe bricks of the two pyramids themselves reveal something of the immense organizational effort necessary to build them, and the political power the monuments must represent. Archaeologists estimate that Huaca del Sol required some 143 million bricks and Huaca de la Luna 50 million. Many bricks were needed simply to bury earlier structures and make levelled platforms for new construction. The rectangular, moulded bricks are stacked in tall, column-like segments. Groups of bricks are impressed with distinct 'maker's marks', of which more than 100 marks and patterns have been found. Marks include single or multiple dots, placed at different positions on the brick faces, sometimes

even in patterns resembling animal paw marks. Other marks are lines running across, down or diagonally on the brick faces. Still others are curved lines, or combinations of lines and dots. Some are miniature symbols: a dot and circle, or dot and curve; a crook-like line; an S-shape; a U-shape; a human footprint; a duck-like footprint; a dot with radiating arms; and a pottery jar profile.

A WORKING CITY
In its heyday, the ancient city covered about 3sq km (740 acres). Archaeological evidence shows that the expanse between the two platforms, and beyond them, was occupied by hundreds of workshops and houses, incorporating the religious structures within the city, much like a medieval European cathedral city. Most of the ancient city is buried beneath up to 2m (6½ft) of washed-in alluvium.

Excavations have revealed houses; pottery, metalworking and textile workshops of cobblestone foundations, with superstructures of perishable materials (presumably cane, thatch and wood); and more well-built housing of stone, with plastered adobe walls. The latter had larger rooms and finer ceramics associated with them.

Within workshops the excavators found large ceramic water-storage jars, stores of ground clay and finished vessels, and also the kilns and tools for pottery making, including scores of moulds. Finished products included containers, many of them painted with combat and deer-hunting scenes, and figurines, portrait heads, rattles, weavers' spindle whorls and crucibles for holding molten metal. Other shops had *tuyères* (ceramic tips of blow-tubes used in metalworking) and metal slag.

Excavators also discovered a winding canal especially dug to bring water into the workshops and residential areas.

Below: A mural at Moche Huaca de la Luna shows colourful ritual imagery of Andean creatures, including humans, fish, tropical birds and monkeys, and a jaguar.

IMPERIAL TIWANAKU

The capital of the Tiwanaku Empire was the world's highest ancient city, seated on the plain south of Lake Titicaca in modern Bolivia at 3,850m (12,600ft) above sea level.

EARLY BEGINNINGS
Tiwanaku was founded as early as *c.*250BC, one of several centres of the Yaya-Mama religious cult, based at the cities of Pukará and Taraco at the north end of the lake, and succeeding earlier architectural traditions at Chiripa, on the south lakeshore. Monumental construction had begun by *c.*AD200, in the middle of the Early Intermediate Period and by AD500 Tiwanaku was the capital of a substantial empire ruling the southern Andean region through the Middle Horizon until *c.*AD1000. In this period of political and religious unification, Tiwanku rivalled the central Andean Wari Empire. By the Late Horizon the city lay in ruins, but was recognized as a sacred city by the Incas.

Below: A carved stone alignment atop the Akapana ceremonial mound at Tiwanaku, showing slots, shelves and holes.

At its height, the capital covered some 6sq km (1,485 acres). Notice of the ancient ruins began with Cieza de León in the 16th century. Studies of the standing monuments were undertaken by Ephraim G. Squier, Alphons Stübel and Max Uhle in the 19th century and were continued by Adolph Bandelier, who excavated several parts of the site in 1911. Wendell C. Bennett did excavations in the 1940s, as did Alan Kolata in the 1980s along with surveys of the entire region.

Excavations concentrated on the main civic-ceremonial monuments, stone gateways, ceremonial platforms and stone sculptures of the city centre, and their art. Evidence of the surrounding residential city is substantial, but much lies beneath agricultural fields. The ancient city was surrounded by raised fields created by draining the wetlands of the southern lakeshore plain with canals – a technology lost during the Spanish Colonial period but revived in the late 20th century.

THE CIVIC-CEREMONIAL CORE
Among the high Andean peaks of the Titicaca Basin, Tiwanaku was believed to be the home of mountain deities and the

Above: The so-called Gateway of the Moon at Tiwanaku, like the Gateway of the Sun, is made from a single stone block. Its lintel is carved with typical Tiwanaku geometric patterns.

ultimate origin of the Supreme Being, Viracocha. The nearby Islands of the Sun and the Moon in the southern lake were believed to be the places of the origin of celestial bodies. The ceremonial core of the city appears to have been deliberately planned as an artificial 'island', surrounded by a moat, its monuments mimicking the surrounding landscape as symbolic 'mountains' and 'valleys'.

The shape of the carefully planned ceremonial centre was conceived by *c.*AD300. The principal monuments are aligned east–west, and are laid out in a grid pattern. A system of stone-lined and covered drains channelled rainwater from the monuments and plazas into the moat.

Assigning exact functions to the various structures is difficult. Undoubtedly some were sacred temples and others served more civic functions, including palaces for Tiwanaku's rulers. Several monumental stone gateways into open plazas, together with standing colossal statuary, show that the core area was public and provided large spaces for ceremonial gatherings – religious and civic.

Above: The Kalasasaya walled compound and Semi-Subterranean Court in Tiwanaku's ceremonial centre reveal a huge enclosure for large numbers of worshippers and a smaller sunken court for more intimate ritual.

TEMPLES AND SUNKEN COURTS

The most sacred structure was the Akapana Temple. Standing 17m (56ft) above the city plaza, it covered an area of 50sq m (540sq ft), in the shape of a 'stepped' cross. At its summit stood a sunken court, drained by covered water channels. Its core was built up of rough fill and clay when the moat was excavated. The top is reached by staircases up the east and west ends, continuing as staircases descending into the sunken court, itself in the plan of a quadrilateral stepped cross.

North of Akapana, the Semi-Subterranean Temple (a sunken court measuring 28.5 × 26m/94 × 85ft) is entered by a staircase on its south side. From the court walls protrude carved stone heads, and in the centre stand several carved stone stelae, originally including the 'Bennett Stela' (7.3m/24ft high) of a richly dressed human, possibly a monument to one of Tiwanaku's ancient rulers. North of Akapana and west of the Semi-Subterranean Temple, the Kalasasaya is a low-lying rectangular platform (130 × 120m/427 × 394ft), which forms a large precinct for public ritual. It is reached by a stairway between two gigantic stone pillars and its walls are made up of alternating sandstone pillars and ashlar blocks.

In the north-west corner of the Kalasasaya stands the Gateway of the Sun, comprising a single huge andesite block, carved with the 'Gateway God' – a deity reminiscent of the Chavín Staff Being, standing on a stepped platform and flanked by three rows of winged figures. Within the precinct stands the Ponce Stela (3.5m/11½ft), perhaps of another of the city's rulers.

Other nearby ceremonial precincts include the Putuni and Kheri Kala compounds, aligned west of Kalasasaya, and the Chunchukala off the north-west corner. South-east of Akapana the T-shaped Pumapunku temple mound comprised three sandstone slab-covered tiers (5m/16ft high and covering 150sq m/1,615sq ft). Its sunken summit court-yard might have been an earlier location of the Gateway of the Sun.

SUBURBS OF TIWANAKU

The surrounding residential city comprised dense concentrations of adobe-walled houses on cobblestone foundations. There were also distinct elite *barrios* of high, adobe-walled compounds on river-cobble platforms. Estimates of the ancient city's population range from 20,000 to 40,000 inhabitants.

Alan Kolata describes Tiwanaku as a 'patrician city', in which residence was restricted to those who served imperial functions – a precursor of Inca Cuzco.

Below: From within the Semi-Subterranean Court the Kalasasaya's entry gate frames the Ponce Stela, one of several monolithic 'gods' standing in Tiwanaku's ceremonial centre.

IMPERIAL HUARI

Huari, the ancient Middle Horizon capital of the Wari Empire, sits in a central Andean highland plateau about 2,800m (9,180ft) above sea level. The imperial rival of Tiwanaku, together the two empires ruled the central and southern Andes, sharing much in religious heritage but differing in artistic and architectural expression, and apparently in their imperial modes of expansion and operation.

NEGLECTED RUINS

Huari's ruins were neglected in comparison to those of Tiwanaku, for they lack the obvious monumentality of singular, outstanding structures and colossal statuary. Huari's principal 20th-century surveyors and excavators are Wendell C. Bennett and Luis Lumbreras in the 1940s and 1950s, and William Isbell through the 1970s and 1980s. The ruins were noticed

Below: Cacti and agave line ancient fields near the Wari city of Ayacucho.

Above: Ruins of the hillfort on top of Cerro Baúl in the Moquegua Valley, the only valley to house both early Wari and Tiwanaku colonies.

by Cieza de León, who travelled through the area in the 1540s, though he commented only that there were 'some large and very old buildings' there 'in a state of ruin and decay'. The site has been much looted, its sculptures mostly found in nearby farmhouses and many of its walls robbed from Spanish Colonial times for building stone.

Huari did not have the ancient pedigree steeped in local cultural development that Tiwanaku did, and seems to have arisen rapidly in a region that earlier had only scattered small towns. It was a city planned according to what appear to be strict rules of modular units, incrementally expanded as need arose, but seemingly at random, without the deliberate and preconceived planning of Tiwanaku. Ancient Huari's heyday as an imperial capital was from *c.*AD600 to 800, when it covered as much as 5.5sq km (1,360 acres).

GRID PLAN

Huari is laid out across undulating terrain, disregarding local topography in favour of a uniformity of structural planning. Its architectural forms have no local or regional forerunners. It comprised a grid

pattern of high-walled compounds made of roughly dressed megalithic ashlar blocks, a pattern that is the hallmark of Huari itself and of Wari provincial cities, which were built as the empire expanded.

From regional settlement, possibly as early as the 3rd century AD, the city began its rapid growth towards the end of the 5th century AD, and within 100 years had become the leading regional ceremonial and residential centre. The city grew quickly, from 1 to 2sq km (250–490 acres), until the core of ancient Huari covered up to 3sq km (740 acres), with suburban residential additions of up to another 2.5sq km (620 acres). Population estimates vary widely between 10,000 and 70,000 inhabitants.

The early city was built around several large ceremonial enclosures of dressed stone: the Cheqo Wasi enclosure, and temple complexes called Vegachayoq Moqo and Moraduchayoq. Moraduchayoq was semi-subterranean and made of finely dressed volcanic tuff blocks reminiscent

Above: This magnificent gold mask and mummy bundle from the Wari culture dates from c.AD800.

of the type of construction used at Tiwanaku, perhaps by design. Most other compound and structure walls at Huari are built of rougher, quarried stone blocks set in mud mortar.

The Moraduchayoq Temple was short-lived, however, for it was dismantled c.AD650, while more residential structures were built to fill the areas around the ceremonial enclosures. These urban and suburban dwellings were distinct rectangular and trapezoidal compounds separated by narrow streets forming a grid-like urban plan. In the northern sector of the city the compounds typically measured 150–300m (490–985ft) each side.

Within the high walls of the compounds were numerous square and rectangular courtyard groups surrounded by long, narrow, domestic rooms, some multi-storey, with narrow doorways into the courtyards and between rooms. Some compound and house walls still stand as high as 12m (40ft), indicating perhaps three storeys. Some compound walls are

massive, being several metres or yards wide. Projecting corbels supported the upper floors; roofs were probably thatched. Courtyards often had stone benches along their sides, numerous wall niches and stone-lined drains beneath their floors.

In addition to the domestic compounds, excavations revealed what must have been pottery workshops in the northern sector called Ushpa Qoto. These compounds had storage areas containing pottery moulds for producing multiple, uniform vessels and unformed lumps of clay and other pottery-making equipment.

INSTANT COLLAPSE
Much of this rapid civic expansion in Huari appears to have been unfinished. The long, massive walls, which appear to date from the city's final decades, surround compounds that were never filled in with domestic divisions, but rather reflect an ambitious urban renewal that

came to nothing. Political crisis appears to have caused the rapid collapse of the empire, for the city was abandoned shortly after the walls were erected.

Endemic of the rapid development of the capital, the Wari founded a provincial city, Pikillacta, near Cuzco, c.AD650. It comprised a huge, single rectangular enclosure 630 × 745m (2,067 × 2,444ft), enclosing nearly 0.5 sq km (124 acres). The compound was subdivided into four sectors, nearly all of which were further divided into regimented, cell-like rooms, and a few with long, peripheral galleries and halls lined with niches. There is only one larger and a few smaller open areas. Pikillacta was abandoned later than the capital, c.AD850–900. Some of the doorways were sealed and there is evidence of fire in the central sector of the city.

Below: Eroded hills tower over the stone ruins of Pikillacta, the provincial city founded by the Wari c.AD650.

CHAN CHAN OF THE CHIMÚ

The imperial capital of the Chimú Empire was founded between AD900 and 1000, and flourished until its conquest by the Incas in the 1470s. Chimú rulers were the inheritors of the north-west coast traditions of ancient Moche and Lambayeque-Sicán. Their capital, Chan Chan, was north of the river, not far from the ancient ruins of the Huacas del Sol and de la Luna in the Moche Valley.

LIVING AND DEAD CITIZENRY
Chan Chan was a city of both the living and the dead. Its centre covers 6sq km (1,480 acres), while greater ancient Chan Chan covered a total area of *c.*20sq km (4,940 acres). Not all of the city was occupied at the same time, and it is conjectured that city architects earmarked

Below: The central precinct of the vast city of Chan Chan, the Chimú capital, housed the compounds of the living and dead (former) rulers, and was a rich prize to the Incas.

areas of open land for future development. Nevertheless, Chan Chan at its height was the largest city ever known in the ancient Andes (and rivals the size of ancient Teotihuacán in Mesoamerica). A great wall marks the northern city limits, through which a long avenue runs north–south towards the imperial residential core of the city.

Chan Chan's most famous structures, and the ruins most examined, are its great rectangular walled compounds, called *ciudadelas* (a modern name meaning 'citadel'), enclosed within monumental mud-plastered walls. There are 10 named compounds and possibly several others recognizable in plans of the central city. Those named are: Chayhuac, Uhle, Tello, Laberinto (Labyrinth), Grán Chimú, Squier, Velarde, Bandelier, Tschudi and Rivero. All are oriented with their long axes north–south. North and east of them there are several larger structures, known as *huacas* (Huacas Obispo, las Conchas, Toledo,

Above: The Tschudi and other ciudadela *compounds at Chan Chan have hundreds of* audiencia *courtyards lined with sculpted poured-mud walls and storage niches.*

las Avispas and el Higo) – huge, presumably ceremonial, platforms, one of which (Obispo) is 20m (66ft) above the valley floor – that might have supported temples. (Treasure-seekers have so severely destroyed them with pits that we cannot be certain.)

The *ciudadela* walls are made of tapia (poured adobe or mud) on stone foundations. Most are well preserved, and stand as high as 9m (30ft). Each compound is believed to have housed the reigning Chimú emperor, along with his court retainers and civil servants to administer the affairs of state – perhaps much like the Forbidden City of imperial Chinese Beijing.

INTERIOR DIVISIONS
Most *ciudadelas* have a single entrance on the north side, through a doorway flanked by niches in which stand carved and painted wooden statues. Within, each compound is subdivided north to south, although internal organization varies in the earlier *ciudadelas*. There is first a large entry courtyard with walls decorated with mud-brick friezes, then miniature U-shaped temple structures called *audiencias* – reminiscent of the ancient U-shaped complexes of the Initial Period and Early Horizon more than 1,000 years earlier – and finally the burial platform

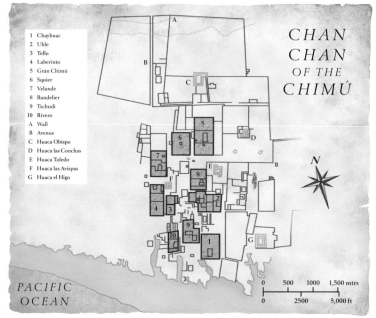

1 Chayhuac
2 Uhle
3 Tello
4 Laberinto
5 Grán Chimú
6 Squier
7 Velarde
8 Bandelier
9 Tschudi
10 Rivero
A Wall
B Avenue
C Huaca Obispo
D Huaca las Conchas
E Huaca Toledo
F Huaca las Avispas
G Huaca el Higo

CHAN
CHAN
OF THE
CHIMÚ

N

PACIFIC
OCEAN

| 0 | 500 | 1000 | 1,500 mtrs |
| 0 | | 2500 | 5,000 ft |

Right: The remains of a massive poured-mud wall at Chan Chan reveals the huge bulk of the royal compounds.

of the deceased ruler. Nine *ciudadelas* include a truncated pyramid in the southeast corner, concealing rooms entered from the top of the platform and a main room to house the mummified body of the deceased ruler.

Other inner courts, connected to the *audiencias*, are lined with rows of storerooms. Adjoining wings of patios and rooms contain walk-in wells and are thought to be the residences for retainers and servants to maintain the compounds.

A CONFUSING HISTORY

The named *ciudadelas* provide a tantalizing parallel with Chimú legend. Depending on how they are designated, scholars count between 9 and 12 palace compounds. An *Anonymous History of Trujillo* of 1604 records the legendary founder of the Chimú dynasty as Chimu

Below: The poured-mud walls of every royal compound at Chan Chan are covered with sculpted geometric patterns and imagery.

Capac or Taycanamu, followed by 11 more rulers. Inca sources, however, record only ten Chimú rulers.

The sequence of *ciudadela* history is uncertain. It is argued that *ciudadela* Chayhuac, the most southerly, is the earliest, and that the capital first expanded northwards, including Uhle. Gran Chimú and the great wall demarked the northern limit of the imperial centre. Further expansion filled in the western core, including Tello and Laberinto. After that the central city was filled in with *ciudadelas* Squier, Velarde, Bandelier, Tschudi and Rivero, with room being made for the last two by razing parts of the old southern core.

Some scholars reason that the rectangular plans and tripartite internal divisions of the *ciudadelas* were inspired by the walled compounds and cell-like divisions of Wari cities. Others argue that they reflect a pattern begun in the preceding civil government of the late Moche city of Galindo, a physically much closer model.

URBAN SPRAWL

The urban sprawl of Chan Chan comprised emulative compounds of elite citizens among and around the *ciudadelas*, and compact *barrios* of small-roomed residences of the ordinary citizenry, estimated at about 26,000, in the south and west of the city. Common citizens comprised a main group of farmers, and the personal retainers of elite households, skilled artisans and craftspeople such as potters, weavers, carvers and metalworkers, traders and labourers – about half in each group.

Whereas the *ciudadelas* contained as many as 200 storerooms, no elite residence had more than 10. Ordinary citizens lived in cane-walled and plastered (called *quincha* or wattle-and-daub) houses. These had common walls and were organized into distinct *barrios* (neighbourhoods) lining winding streets. Scattered among them were a few better houses of minor elites.

Among the southern suburbs were also several cemeteries and garden plots dug into the valley floor to tap the water table (some still in use today).

THE IMPERIAL INCA CAPITAL AND ITS CITIES

The Incas established provincial administrative cities at strategic locations throughout the empire. Sometimes Inca administrative buildings, temples and ceremonial plazas with *ushnu* platforms were built within existing cities, as in the Chimú Kingdom or at Pachacamac. In other cases they built new cities, colonizing unoccupied areas by moving whole populations of conquered subjects.

CUZCO

The imperial capital, the 'navel of the world', was mostly built by Pachacuti and his successors. It had a unique plan – that of a crouching puma. Other Inca cities followed more conventional grid plans. Wedged into the confluences of the Chunchullmayo, Tullumayo and Huatanay rivers, the river courses were channelled within conduits of stone walls.

The core of the city comprised two ceremonial plazas, around which were arranged numerous *kancha* compounds of large, thatch-roofed *kallanka* halls. Some were the residences of living Inca emperors; others housed the mummies (*mallquis*) of deceased rulers.

Cuzco's most sacred building, southeast of the plazas, was the Coricancha (the 'Golden Enclosure'), the temple of the

principal Inca deities: Viracocha (Creator), Inti (Sun), Quilla (Moon), Chaska-Qoylor (Venus), Illapa (Thunder and the weather) and Cuichu (Rainbow). Its masonry exemplifies Inca stone fitting and now supports the Church of Santo Domingo. From the Coricancha radiated 41 sacred *ceque* routes and lines to shrines and holy sites.

North-west of the city, the sacred temple of Sacsahuaman sat on a hill looming over the plazas and formed the head of the puma. Made of closely fitted masonry blocks and planned with regular angles to mimic the peaks and valleys of the distant mountains, its revetments terraced the summit, on which stood a rare circular Inca Sun temple. Simultaneously sacred and military, Sacsahuaman was the venue for religious ritual and the storehouse for Inca army weapons and armour.

The four main imperial trunk roads emanated from the city, leading through planned agricultural settlements, terraced fields, canals and state storehouses.

HUÁNUCO PAMPA

This imperial administrative centre was built on the highland trunk road heading north from Cuzco to Quito via Cajamarca. It sat at an elevation of 3,800m (12,500ft) in Chinchaysuyu

Above: Special niches were built into the Coricancha temple to Inti, the sun, at Cuzco, for mounting plate-gold sheets on the walls.

quarter. It was one of the largest Inca settlements, covering some 2sq km (495 acres). Construction began in the middle of the 15th century and was still underway when Pizarro invaded the empire. By then, it comprised some 4,000 structures.

Its two-tiered *ushnu* platform, symbol of Inca domination, was the largest in the empire. It measured 32 x 48m (105 x 157ft) at the base, and overlooked a ceremonial plaza of 550 x 350m (1,800 x 1,150ft).

The city contained elements similar to those at Cuzco, and fit for a major administrative capital. There was an *acllahuasi* (house of the virgins – devotees to Inti), a *kallanka* (administrative building for imperial officials) and several *kancha* compounds of administrative buildings.

Left: The rocky outcrops of Sacsahuaman to the north-west of the imperial capital were formed into the temple to the sun god Inti.

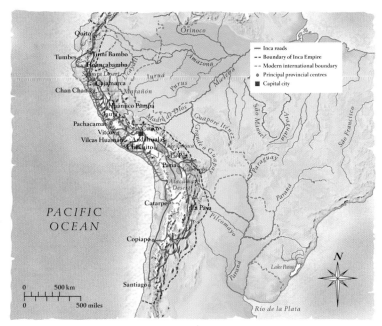

Right: Throughout their empire, along with the imperial roads system, the Incas established provincial administrative cities.

On the hillside south of the city the Incas built rows of hundreds of storehouses for goods collected by imperial tax officials.

OLLANTAYTAMBO

Like Machu Picchu, Ollantaytambo was an imperial estate and retreat north of the capital, at the confluence of the Urubamba and Patakancha rivers, in Antisuyu quarter.

The eastern part was residential, as distinct from the western side, which had a temple to Viracocha and Inti and its associated structures. Just north of Cuzco, on a spur road to Machu Picchu, it was a small city for about 1,000 permanent residents.

So close to the capital, Ollantaytambo was probably an imperial household residence, and an administrative and ceremonial centre for the empire. It was a late Inca foundation, and its Temple to Inti was still being built when the Spaniards invaded. Unused building stones, quarried from nearby Kachiqhata, litter the site.

Stone shrines at carved rock faces lie below and north of the temple hill, which is surrounded by elaborate waterworks.

Below: Huánuco Pampa, an Inca provincial administrative city, was built with mortarless, fitted stone blocks.

TAMBO COLORADO

At the end of a trunk road running west, this city linked Cuzco to the coast, near the Chinchaysuyu–Cuntisuyu border. It is the best-preserved Inca coastal foundation, deliberately planned and built in local style using adobe brick construction. Traces of red, yellow and white paint survive on the plastered walls of its *kallanka* and other administrative and residential buildings.

The city's trapezoidal-shaped ceremonial plaza has a low-lying *ushnu* at its western end.

TAMBO VIEJO

In Cuntisuyu quarter, south-west of Cuzco in the Acari Valley, Tambo Viejo was established on an ancient Nazca site. The coastal trunk road ran into its ceremonial plaza and led north to Tambo Colorado.

The rectangular plaza, built by a bluff of the river, has an *ushnu* platform of river cobbles, and overlooks the river as well as the plaza.

VILCAS HUAMÁN

As Inca imperial aspirations in the early 15th century expanded beyond the Cuzco Valley, Vilcas, 80km (50 miles) south-east of

Ayacucho in Cuntisuyu quarter, was one of the first regions conquered. The modern city covers most of the Inca buildings, but the Spanish Colonial plaza corresponds to the Inca ceremonial one. Its *ushnu* platform, on one side of the plaza, is constructed of classic Inca fine-fitted, block masonry, and is one of the most elaborate ever built. A stone staircase led to the summit through a double-jambed entryway.

Facing the plaza, the Temple to Inti sits on a triple-terraced platform with trapezoidal doorways and niches, and is approached by a dual stairway.

Below: Tambo Colorado utilized scarce local stone and the fine silts of the coastal plain to build its mud-brick walls.

MACHU PICCHU AND THE INCA TRAIL

Machu Picchu is probably the best-known and most-photographed Andean site. North of the Inca capital at Cuzco, it is perched dramatically in the high Andes above the Urubamba River, profiles of its structures framed by distant snow-capped peaks. Machu Picchu has been variously described as a remote Inca fortress, an imperial sanctuary, and a citadel – a last place of retreat and refuge of the Inca imperial household.

AN IMPERIAL ESTATE

In fact it was originally none of these things, but to some extent it effectively served in all of these capacities and more.

The site was chosen and established by the emperor Pachacuti Inca Yupanqui, the reigning Sapa Inca in the mid-15th century. Imperial and early Spanish Colonial records show that the site and area were an imperial estate of Pachacuti, subsequently inherited by his successors. Another imperial estate established by Pachacuti was at Ollantaytambo, farther upstream in the Urubamba Valley.

LOST AND FOUND

After the Spanish Conquest the site was effectively 'lost' because of its remote location. Although referred to in colonial records, its location remained a mystery and intrigued 19th-century explorers and archaeologists. It was re-discovered by

Above: Winding roads leading to Machu Picchu, probably the most evocative of all ancient Andean cities.

Hiram Bingham in 1911 on a general exploring expedition in which Bingham's own tale makes it seem as if he stumbled upon the ancient ruins by chance. In fact, locals had known of the site since colonial times, and a local farmer had described the site to Bingham when he and his team arrived in the valley.

Bingham brought the spectacular find to the attention of the Western world and claimed that he had discovered the last Inca capital. Subsequent systematic survey of the Urubamba Valley, however, has shown that the final Inca capital was established at Vilcabamba, much farther downstream.

Machu Picchu's inaccessible position, apparent defensive walls and surrounding dry moat led to its label as a fortress and retreat. However, its architecture is predominantly religious and these defensive

Left: The Torreón at Machu Picchu incorporates a stone outcrop with a rare Inca curved wall of fitted stones.

features appear to have been more for restricting access than for repelling attackers. A mountain road linked the site to a series of minor settlements strung up the Urubamba Valley along the forested slopes of high forest.

SACRED ARCHITECTURE

Its impressive architecture was certainly carefully built to special requirements. The granite building material was quarried locally on-site. The quality of the stone finishing and fitting is of the highest Inca standards, especially in the structures known as the Temple of the Three Windows and the Torreón (Tower; sometimes also referred to as the Observatorio). The latter was most likely actually a temple to Inti, the sun god, and indeed is perhaps the primary function of the entire site.

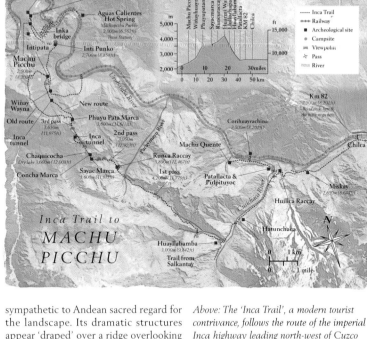

Inca Trail to
MACHU PICCHU

But we will probably never fully know the meaning of Machu Picchu. It is likely that the site's purpose altered through time, even though its rapid establishment and construction were planned. The Inca emperors developed a tradition of building commemorative monuments and establishing settlements to mark their conquests. Early in his reign, Pachacuti had subdued the area, in conquests that more than doubled the size of the empire ruled by his predecessor. Machu Picchu itself, together with the smaller sites and road to it (the 'Inca Trail'), are typical of such memorialization. Sixteenth-century Spanish Colonial documents of land-tenure suggest that the settlement was the headquarters of an estate founded by Pachacuti and managed through the later 15th and early 16th centuries by his lineage.

'CITY' OR MANOR?

Machu Picchu's architects integrated the structures and compounds into the lie of the land. The architecture is deliberately

Below: Machu Picchu, imperial city, estate and mountain retreat of the Incas built by Pachacuti Inca Yupanqui (1438–71).

sympathetic to Andean sacred regard for the landscape. Its dramatic structures appear 'draped' over a ridge overlooking the river. A chain of 16 spring-fed, stone-lined water channels lead into catchments to supply the site. Doorways and windows were positioned to frame views of nearby peaks of the Urubamba and Vilcabamba ranges, and natural outcrops were carved to imitate mountain shapes.

Above: The 'Inca Trail', a modern tourist contrivance, follows the route of the imperial Inca highway leading north-west of Cuzco up the Urubamba Valley to Machu Picchu.

The quality of the construction and the obvious religious purposes of many of its structures show that it was more than a remote outpost in the eastern Inca provinces, however. The residential remains at Machu Picchu indicate that about 1,000 people lived there. Together with administrative compounds and workshops it formed a functioning imperial source of income as well as a religious retreat – in fact, like many other estates, a sort of miniature city reflecting the capital at Cuzco.

BYPASSED

Machu Picchu was abandoned in the second decade of the 16th century, shortly before the Spanish invasion. It thus could never have been a last redoubt of the beleaguered Inca imperial household. The Spaniards, pursuing a rebel Inca force that had retreated to Vilcabamba, followed a route through the adjacent Amaybamba Valley to the north-east of Ollantaytambo, thus missing Machu Picchu entirely.

CHAPTER TWENTY-ONE

STONE AND CLAY SCULPTURE

Ancient Andeans sculptured in all materials – stone, clay, wood, metals and textiles. This chapter covers stone and clay sculpture.

Mountain peoples tended to sculpt in stone, while coastal peoples worked with mud and clay.

The range of styles and subjects is extraordinary. Much of the purpose of monumental stone sculpture, plaster wall carving and small clay figurines was connected with religious ritual. Whether they were made from adobe or stone, these colossal statues, sculpted walls, statuary and all kinds of imagery were carved to portray fearsome human-beast figures to awe ceremonial audiences and constantly remind them of their duties to the gods. Alternatively, statuary and imagery were buried as offerings in caches or human burials associated with temples.

Effigy vessels were especially popular from the Early Intermediate Period onwards. Almost every kind of animal and bird was sculpted. Bottles were made in the shapes of gourds. Humans are portrayed with almost every imaginable condition or doing everyday and ritual tasks.

And there are even models of buildings – curious, functional vessels in the shapes of houses and temples, which help archaeologists to understand aspects of ancient Andean life that are otherwise undocumented.

Left: Huaca del Dragón near the Chimú capital of Chan Chan – detail of rainbow and solar flare wall sculpture.

CARVING IN STONE

Stone sculpturing began in, or was brought to, the New World by the earliest hunter-gatherers. These were the carefully crafted stone tools used for hunting and food processing. Finely shaped projectile points demonstrate the developed skills of their makers as surely as do the artistic sculpted stone figures of deities, animals and plants of ancient Andean civilizations.

STONE WARRIORS

The earliest large stone sculptures of the Andean Area are the provocative incised figures on the flat stone stelae forming the wall of Cerro Sechín at the junction of the Sechín and Moxeke rivers in the Casma Valley. No other Peruvian Initial Period or Early Horizon site has more individual sculptures – nearly 400 in all.

Granite blocks quarried from the hill behind the site were carefully dressed by pecking and abrasion with sand and water to make flat-sided slabs of two sizes: *c*.3 × 1m (*c*.10 × 3ft) and *c*.85cm × 70cm (*c*.2½ft × 2⅓ft).

These were incised with fine lines *c*.7mm (⅓in) deep and *c*.11mm (½in) wide, depicting victorious warriors and their victims, plus two banners on tall stelae flanking the main platform's central staircase. Victims and their body parts – including numerous severed heads – have closed eyes and agonized mouths and are contorted in postures of torture and pain, some with spilled entrails. Marching victorious warriors carry war clubs, and severed heads dangle from their belts or hands. Two slabs with similar warriors flank the temple compound's back entrance.

The gruesome accuracy of these sculptures initiated an Andean tradition of realism in sculpture, as well as the glorification of beheading and collecting trophy heads. Similar stone slabs have also been found at Sechín Alto and Chupacoto.

Of similar date, a single, rectangular stone slab at Moxeke has two incised faces: a naturalistic human hand and a double-bodied snake.

Above: Some of the earliest Andean stone carving was monumental and commemorative, including this head from Cerro Sechín.

MORTARS, BOWLS AND A MOSAIC

In a completely different style, angular mythical humanoid figures, facing full frontal (anticipating Chavín staff-bearing figures), with one arm outstretched and a corresponding motif covering one eye, adorn the outsides of large stone mortars from Santa and Nepeña valley sites.

Initial Period Cupisnique steatite stone bowls continued the trophy head motif and anticipate the complex imagery of later sculpture. Their interiors have elaborate carved spiders – an imagery anticipating Moche spider art. With bulbous bodies, exaggerated pincer-jaws, pedipalps (male reproductive organs) or spinnerets (female silk-spinning organs), they bear human faces and frequently grasp trophy heads or net bags of severed heads. They are frequently surrounded by lush plant growth, from which sprout human heads, hands and other body parts.

Left: A wall of stone slabs at Cerro Sechín shows a procession of warriors and their defeated enemies, including many body parts.

A more bizarre form of stone sculpture is the geoglyph (65 × 23m/*c*.215 × 76ft) at Pampa de Caña Cruz in the Zaña Valley. Much earlier than the Nazca lines, thousands of small rock fragments (*c*.10cm/4in in diameter) make up a rectangular face framed with 'hair', with round eyes and nose, fanged mouth and squared jaw – resembling figures on Cupisnique pottery. Two long 'legs' form a simplified body. Contrasting with the surrounding soil, dark stones outline the white stone face and body and rose-coloured stone 'hair' piece.

This 'mosaic' has no known parallel in Peru. However, large-scale religious imagery became widespread in Early Intermediate Period and later geoglyphs formed by stone outlines, especially on the Nazca desert floor.

'LIVING' STONE

The Incas are known for their precisely fitted stone walls. They regarded stone as 'alive' – indeed the Quechua word for 'boulder' also means 'to begin'.

Whereas earlier cultures carved detached monolithic and smaller stone, the Incas literally carved and modelled the landscape itself. The Observatorio or Torreón at Machu Picchu, for example, begins with the huge boulder that forms

Below: Beneath the Torreón at Machu Picchu Inca masons enlarged a natural cleft in the stone outcrop into a temple room to Inti, the sun.

its foundation, and the cleft in the base of the boulder is itself carved into a semi-hidden temple room.

Also at Machu Picchu, the Intihuatana Stone (the 'Hitching Post of the Sun') is a stone outcrop carved into angles, recesses and a central square pillar. This and other *intihuatanas*, possibly used in astronomical observations, connect the sky to the Earth in characteristic Andean duality and cosmological wholeness and containment.

The Sacred Rock at the northern end of Machu Picchu has been carefully modified into a platform 'supporting' the natural outcrop shaped to mimic the outline of the distant mountain skyline – again linking earth and sky.

The rocky outcrop at Qenqo provides another example. A semicircular enclosure forms a ritual space around a natural outcrop left untouched, as its profile resembles a seated puma. A nearby outcrop is carved into steps and water channels, while a cleft beneath them, as at Machu Picchu, is carved into a room.

The very structure of the walls at Sacsahuaman forms a sculpture in stone and space as its angles change direction to 'sculpt' the sky into light and shadow, like the distant mountains and gorges that form its backdrop. And the vast outcrop of Rodadero opposite the walls has been carved into a huge stepped 'throne'.

Above: At Sayhuite, Peru, Inca sculptors modelled a huge glacial boulder sitting on the valley floor into a miniature urban model including houses, streets, temple platforms, platforms, channels and terraced garden plots.

THREE MODELS

Among the most remarkable Andean stone sculptures are three large-scale models of Andean architecture itself.

At Tiwanaku, the Kantatayita mound east of the Akapana includes a huge boulder carved into a maquette (roughly scaled 1 to 10) of a platform and ceremonial plaza. It is complete with staircases ascending to the flat-topped platform with sunken courts, just like those of the Tiwanaku central precinct itself.

The Incas, not content to carve stone outcrops into human-scale works, carved a large glacial boulder at Sayhuite into an entire town and landscape model. In cascading terraces there are miniature buildings, patios, platforms and water channels.

Finally, above the Chinchero Valley, Inca masons carved an entire outcrop into a miniature system of terraces and enclosures, echoing the actual terraces of the valley sides. The sculpture seems both to embed the work in nature and emphasize Inca domination of the land.

STONE AND CLAY SCULPTURE

STONEWORK OF THE CHAVÍN

The body of stone sculpture at Chavín de Huántar dominated the religious imagery of the Early Horizon. It comprises three huge deity idols, carved stone slabs decorating the walls of the Old and New Temple courtyards, and many smaller pieces.

STONE IDOLS
The Old Temple housed the Lanzón Stela, or Great Image, a lance-shaped granite monolith (4.5m/15ft high) carved with human, feline and serpent attributes. Its monster visage is thick-lipped, drawn in a hideous snarl and punctuated by long, outward-curving canines. Its eyebrows and hair end in serpent heads. Its right hand is raised, its left lowered, towards sky and earth deities respectively, 'embracing' the universe; its feet and hands end in claws. Its tunic, waistband and headdress are decorated with feline heads, and snakes dangle from its waist. Its notched head has a carved, cross-shaped receptacle thought to be for channelling the blood of sacrifices.

Below: The Chavín Cult's Lanzón Stela had a notch for ritual blood sacrifice and was carved with the image of the jaguar-mouthed, taloned supreme deity and serpent imagery.

In the New Temple's courtyard, or perhaps in an inner gallery, stood the Tello Obelisk (2.5m/8ft high), also of granite. Its faces are carved with two jungle caymans. Notched like the Lanzón, additional carvings on and around the caymans depict plants and animals, including peanuts and manioc from the tropical lowlands, and *Strombus* and *Spondylus* shells of species native to the Ecuadorian coast, jaguars, serpents and raptors.

The Raimondi Stela, the third, and latest-dating, monolithic idol, is carved in extremely low relief on a highly polished granite slab (1.98m/6ft × 0.74m/2⅖ft × 0.17m/6⅖in). It depicts the supreme Chavín Cult god, the Staff Deity. Its stylistic similarity to the avian creatures on the columns of the Black and White Portal suggests that it once stood within one of the New Temple's chambers.

The Raimondi Staff Deity has clawed hands and feet, a mouth with huge curved fangs and ears bedecked with ornaments. Outstretched arms clutch elaborate plumed staffs. Unlike many other portrayals of the Staff Deity, its

Above: Stone blocks at the entry stairway of the rectangular plaza at Chavín de Huántar embellished it with sacred cayman imagery, with rows of teeth and clawed feet, and serpents.

genitalia are non-specific, as if to embrace male and female duality and opposites at the same time, thereby balancing the Andean worldview. Further, when inverted, the image shows a new set of faces. The image appears to be rising and the eyes gaze skywards; the inverted figure's eyes look down and it appears to plunge from the sky – more duality.

In similar low relief, columns flanking the Black and White Portal depict two avian figures, heads tilted back to peer straight up, wings outspread in characteristic raptor hunting flight. The north column supports a white granite half-lintel and depicts a female eagle (identifiable by its beak cere – nostril hole – and 'vagina dentata'); the south column supports a black limestone half-lintel and depicts a hawk (identifiable by the band through its eye and a central frontal fang 'penis metaphor').

Above: The Raimondi monolith from Chavín de Huántar's New Temple was the final expression of the Chavín supreme Staff Deity.

SHAMANS AND JAGUARS

The stone walls of the sunken circular courtyard are carved with a scene of shamanic transformation. In low relief on an upper register marches a procession of profiled humanoid figures with fanged mouths and streaming, snake-headed hair. They wear serpentine belts, tunics and trousers. Their finger- and toenails are raptor claws. One carries a San Pedro cactus branch and another a conch-shell trumpet.

A lower register depicts a row of prowling jaguars on rectangular slabs. At least seven paired humanoid and jaguar sets depict a shaman in transformation from human to jaguar, using the hallucinogenic cactus in a mystic ritual.

A similar transformation is represented by fully sculpted heads on the New Temple façade. Of the 40 found, one was tenoned into the wall, revealing that the mounted set displayed a succession of 'states' in human transformation into beast. Faces alter as lips and teeth curl from human to feline fangs, snouts project, noses flatten, cheeks become scarified with whiskers and almond-shaped human eyes change to bulging round ones, weeping mucus – a reaction to drug-taking.

DUALITY IN STONE

In the Titicaca Basin, the Pukará–Yaya-Mama Cult style was contemporary with later Chavín. The hallmarks of its imagery were the depiction of yaya (male) and mama (female) figures or symbols on opposite sides of slab monoliths erected at Pukará Taraco, Tambo Cusi and other sites around the lake, and the Pukará Decapitator God. Other Pukará stone carving includes characteristic Andean feline, serpentine and fish imagery.

Writhing skyward- and earthward-facing snakes enhance the duality of the Yaya-Mama imagery. The Decapitator is a seated figure holding a sacrificial axe and severed head. With bulging eyes and feline snout and fangs, this sculpture represents the god himself or a priest wearing his mask. Many smaller Pukará figures bear female symbols of earth and water.

Portable Pukará stone sculpture included rectangular, twinned boxes, the sides depicting faces or masks surrounded with serpent and plant-like rays, anticipating the rayed heads of Tiwanaku sculpture and textiles.

Below: More than 40 jaguar-mouthed stone heads adorned the upper walls around the New Temple at Chavín de Huántar.

MONUMENTAL STONEWORK AT TIWANAKU

As an imperial capital and religious centre, everything about Tiwanaku was monumental and colossal. Titicaca was the birthplace of the world. Its city reflected the landscape; the city itself was a sculpture or model mimicking the mountains and valleys in its terraced platforms and plazas, and the rivers, lake and islands in its water channels, drains and moat.

Its statuary constantly reminded citizens and pilgrims who flocked to its temples and ceremonies of their duty to honour the gods. The Incas believed the great statues to be the ancient race of giants turned to stone by Viracocha as a flawed race.

Tiwanaku lacks Pukará occupation but inherited its sacred imagery. At least seven Yaya-Mama monoliths were found around the site, including Stela 15 (*c*.2m/*c*.7ft tall), which stood in the Semi-Subterranean Temple beside the much taller Bennett Stela. And the lower portion (the Thunderbolt) of the 2.5-tonne (ton), *c*.5.75m (*c*.19ft) Arapa Pukará monolith, which was removed 212km (132 miles) from Arapa at the north end of the lake to Tiwanaku Putuni palace.

Tiwanaku sculptors also inherited the Decapitator Cult. The black basalt image of a seated, puma-headed person (*chachapuma*) holding a severed head in his lap stood at the base of the western staircase of the Akapana platform. Another, standing, *chachapuma* also holds a severed head.

The walls of the Semi-Subterranean Temple are adorned with scores of tenoned severed heads. Unlike those at Chavín de Huántar, they do not depict shamanic transformation, but suggest that the courtyard was a place of sacrificial rituals.

SOUTHERN GIANTS

Tiwanaku sculptors carved colossal stone monoliths whose scale was unsurpassed until Inca times. The two most famous are the Bennett Stela (7.3m/24ft high) and the Ponce Stela (3.5m/11½ft high).

The Bennett Stela, the tallest Andean statue ever carved, represents a richly dressed human thought to be one of Tiahuanaco's rulers or a divine ruler. He/she holds a *kero* beaker and a staff-like object, perhaps a snuff tablet. Low-relief features portray large, sub-rectangular eyes, weeping, long, geometric-patterned streams

Above: One of several colossal monolithic stone statues in the Kalasasaya enclosed court at Tiwanaku, with hands motif.

down the cheeks, a pursed sub-rectangular mouth, and chunky fingers and toes. The massive, angular head, turban-like headpiece, belt band and short legs are reminiscent of Pukará sculpture.

Scores of small, incised figures and symbols adorn the giant's body. There are rayed faces, llamas, birds, and feline creatures and mythical beasts, snakes and panels of flowering plants – in all, some 30 figures facing frontally but with 'running' legs. The complex imagery is thought to encode Tiwanaku's state ideology and cosmology. The central rayed faces and front-facing, ray-headed figure with up-raised arms – resembling the central figure on the Gateway of the Sun – no doubt represent the creator deity Viracocha.

Left: The walls of the Semi-Subterranean Temple at Tiwanaku are lined with carved stone 'trophy' heads tenoned into the walls, possibly indicating that the sunken court was a place of ritual beheading.

Left: The Gateway of the Sun, standing at the north-west corner of the Kalasasaya enclosure at Tiwanaku has a central Staff Deity image thought by some to represent the supreme deity Viracocha.

Below: The Bennett Stela, the tallest Andean statue ever carved, is decorated with rich clothing and coca-snuff accoutrements.

Within the Kalasasaya precinct stands the Ponce Stela, perhaps another of the city's rulers, framed by the main gateway into the Semi-Subterranean Temple. Like the Bennett Stela, it portrays a richly clothed figure holding a *kero* beaker and staff or snuff tablet.

Numerous smaller stone sculptures, known as 'ancestor figures', mimic the Bennett Stela and Ponce Stela in their features and stance.

THE GREAT GATEWAY

At the north-west corner of the Kalasasaya stands the famous Gateway of the Sun. A large crack on its right side suggests that it was moved, and it is thought that it originally formed one of a series of gateways leading worshippers into the city. Several similar gateways found in the Pumapunku compound suggest that the Gateway of the Sun may once have stood there.

It is an extraordinary monolith. It appears to comprise two stone slabs supporting a carved lintel, but is in fact a single huge andesite block (3.8m/12½ft wide, 2.8m/9ft high, with a 1.4m/4½ft opening). The lintel is completely carved above its rebated jambs. The central figure portrays, in high-relief, the 'Gateway God', thought to be Viracocha the creator or Thunapa, god of thunder, a humanoid figure standing on a stepped platform that resembles the tiered mounds of the sacred precinct itself. Like other Tiwanaku imagery, he has 'weeping' eyes, an over-sized, rayed head and short legs below a serpentine belt band. Four head rays end in feline heads and the top, central ray is a front-facing feline. His outstretched arms hold staffs with raptor-headed ends. The resemblance to the Chavin Staff Deity is undeniable, but the style is definitely southern Andean. One interpretation is that the staffs are a spear-thrower and quiver of darts.

Flanking the god, in low relief, are 48 winged figures in profile (called the Tiwanaku 'angels'), in three rows of eight, running towards him. Some have human faces, others avian faces, and each holds a staff resembling one or the other of the god's staffs.

Flanking the entryway below are two rectangular niches. And the rear of the gateway has a band of three rebates to form a multiple jamb with false, blind doorways on either side and four upper niches.

Many Tiwanaku monolithic wall slabs are decorated with rows of inset stepped-diamond shapes – sometimes called the 'Andean Cross' – a shape first used in the Middle Horizon and also used on textiles and by the Incas. Numerous lintels are adorned with rows of ray-headed mythical beasts arrayed in facing lines.

PLASTER AND MUD WALL SCULPTURES

Sculptors in arid environments frequently worked in clay and mud, which did not perish as they would in the rainy highlands. This was especially true along the northern Peruvian coast in the Initial Period.

CROSSED HANDS
Kotosh, on the arid, rain-shadowed slopes of the eastern Andes, was occupied c.2500–c.2000BC. Two rubble-filled mounds supporting temples of field cobbles plastered with mud were enlarged several times. The Kotosh Tradition, probably the earliest Andean religious cult, not surprisingly also has the earliest plaster wall sculptures.

By c.2000BC the larger mound had reached a height of 13.7m (45ft), rising in three tiers and supporting groups of up to 100 successive, superimposed chambers, including seven successive temples on the lowest tier. On the middle platform, however, sat the most famous temple, the Temple of the Crossed Hands.

Below: One of the carved poured-mud walls at Huaca del Dragón near Chan Chan, showing creatures supporting a rainbow serpent and solar crescent.

Roughly square in plan (9.5 x 9.3m/31½ x 31ft), its upper walls were recessed to support a log-beam and clay-plaster roof. A painted white serpent adorns its stairway, and its entrance is red. The interior floor is split-level, with a stone-lined ritual fire pit in the centre.

The northern wall, facing the entrance, has five equal-spaced niches. The two flanking the larger central niche have low-relief sculpted clay friezes of crossed hands and forearms, one set smaller than the other. The symmetrical arrangement of niches and crossed hands are clearly early Andean expressions of duality. The different-sized hands are thought to be man and woman, signifying unity between otherwise opposing forces.

The sacredness of the temple is revealed by the fact that the friezes were carefully covered with sand before the temple was abandoned and filled with rubble.

SPIDER, INSECT AND MONSTER
Garagay, a coastal U-shaped ceremonial centre, was occupied from the mid-2nd to mid-1st millennium BC. Its Middle Temple had an entire wall carved and painted with a low-relief plaster frieze. Panels between stylized plant-like figures and geometric motifs there show three mythical creatures – humanized animals.

A face with thick-lipped, fanged mouth and languid, sinister-looking eye peers from a web-like ring. An arachnid pedipalp curls from its human nose. Farther along, a huge human-headed insect crawls along the wall, with detailed head, thorax and tail. On a third panel, an enormous split face has drooping, half-crescent eyes, thick lips and six long fangs. Traces of red, blue, yellow and white mineral paints were found on the friezes, and as many as 10 layers of clay and paint repairs.

Another wall, on the summit of Mound A, has two low-relief plaster sculptures of humans carrying round shields. The modelling of their hands and feet are especially realistic, including their nails.

Above: The Temple of the Crossed Hands at Kotosh is one of the earliest plaster wall sculptures in ancient Andean civilization. The smaller of the two pairs, crossed left over right, is thought to be female; the larger, crossed right over left, male; and together representing duality.

GODS, SHAMANS, RULERS?
The 30m (100ft), tiered rectangular platform at Moxeke was built of large conical adobe blocks and enlarged many times. The final rebuilding included massive stone revetment walls. On the third platform, large white and pink niches (3.9m/13ft wide; 1.7m/5¾ft deep), puncture the wall 10m (31½ft) above the plaza. Inside them stand colossal, high-relief unbaked clay sculptures.

Two are cloaked torsos, their heads destroyed – possibly in deliberate ritual beheadings. One holds the corners of its cape; the other wears a more elaborate cloak and twisted cord sash, and holds double-headed snakes in raised hands. Both wear short, pleated skirts. One is painted entirely black.

A third is an enormous, emerald green head with a grinning, thick-lipped mouth and rows of straight teeth. Pink vertical lines run from its squinting, half-crescent, black-pupil eyes, either side of flaring black nostrils, giving it a menacing appearance.

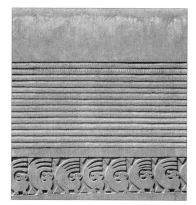

Above: Chan Chan surfaces were moulded like panelling and sculpted with rows of repeated animals and birds.

Another head has an expressionless face with closed mouth and eyes resembling the Cerro Sechín severed heads.

The scale, positions and appearance of these sculptures reveal a major role in ritual worship. Peering from their niches flanking the staircase, with several terraces rising behind them to a ritual platform summit, provides a dramatic, overpowering presence to worshippers crowded in the plaza below.

The Caballo Muerto mound at Huaca de los Reyes has four colossal adobe heads on its summit. Like the Moxeke sculptures, they dominate the ritual platform and the plaza below. Almost 2m (6ft) high, they portray humanoid faces with feline features: thick-lipped mouths in the same style as at Moxeke, clenched teeth, but also feline fangs, flaring, cat-like noses and huge staring, sub-rectangular eyes with deep round pupils. Like the Moxeke sculptures, they were probably once painted.

THE PUNKURÍ FRIEZES
Several successive tiers at coastal Punkurí have carved plaster friezes. The oldest one depicts a supernatural avian figure with fish and monkeys on its body.

The second platform is famous for its larger-than-life painted and carved frieze of a snarling feline on the middle of the staircase. With its green face, blue pupils, red gums, crossed white fangs and clawed

paws, it presented a startling, iconic image to priests ascending to the summit of the temple platform! Later tiers have stylized geometric forms.

A WARRIOR AND HIS CAPTIVES
The Middle Horizon Moche site Cao Viejo–El Brujo has a carved mud frieze showing continuity with the Initial Period themes described above.

Along one terrace trots a life-size warrior leading 10 naked prisoners by a rope around their necks. Like the figures of Mound A at Garagay, they show a studied realism in their movement and limb shaping. Sadly now destroyed, the top platform terrace showed the segmented

Below: The plastered walls of Moche sites, as here at the Huaca de la Luna temple, were brightly painted with geometric frames, symbols and sacred imagery.

Above: The tall, thick poured-mud walls and platforms of the Huaca del Dragón (Pyramid of the Dragon), Chan Chan.

legs of a spider or crab sculpture. One claw held a sacrificial *tumi* knife, an arachnid representation of the Moche Decapitator God.

The walls at Moche Huaca de la Luna depicting the Decapitator are also sculpted low-relief plaster, but are usually described as murals because of their vibrant colours.

The ultimate and most vibrant expression of mud-clay sculpting is that of the Chimú in the Late Intermediate Period. Continuing early traditions of wall decorations, the Chimú covered almost every bit of wall surface in their elite residences and temples with sculptured friezes. Like Inca carving of natural stone outcrops to modify the living landscape, Chimú mud structures themselves were sculptures in their totalities.

The Kingdom of the Chimú began in the 10th century AD with the founding of their capital at Chan Chan. They were the inheritors of the Moche and conquerors of the Sicán-Lambayeque, but both continued and broke earlier traditions.

ADOBE 'MOUNTAINS'

Chan Chan was built near the mouth of the Moche River, on the north banks. The vast bulks of the ancient Moche capital's pyramids of Huaca del Sol and Huaca de la Luna, by then having stood silent for several hundred years, were only a short distance away on the south banks. They must have been regarded by the Chimú with similar awe to that of the Incas for the ruins of Tiwanaku. Like their Moche ancestors, the Chimú raised huge platforms to create 'mountains' on the flat coastal plains. Forming a crescent north-east of the city centre are four great adobe mounds supporting the city's temples: Huaca del Obispo, Huaca de las Conchas, Tres Huacas and Huaca del Higo. A fifth temple, Huaca del Olvido, lies to the south.

The most celebrated structures at Chan Chan form the vast central civic and ceremonial city core. Tall, thick walls enclose between nine and twelve huge compounds, each a city within the city, housing first the living king and then his burial mound and morbid city. The Spaniards called these compounds *ciudadelas* (citadels) because of their formidable walls and the complexity of their interior arrangements.

Above: Chan Chan of the Chimú comprises a huge ceremonial urban centre in which every surface was sculpted in mud – walls, benches, niches and pilasters.

The *ciudadela* walls are made of *tapia* (poured adobe or mud) on stone foundations. Most are well preserved, and stand as high as 9m (28¼ft). The smooth, sheer wall surfaces were rarely left unadorned, especially the walls of the huge public plazas forming the first element in each *ciudadela*.

BUILT TO IMPRESS

Perhaps inspired by the ruins of the Moche, Chimú rulers sought to impress their subjects and foreign visitors with their power. They embellished their compounds with the labours of thousands of artisans, creating a city centre that rivals the exuberance, complexity and scale of the Alhambra of Moorish Granada and the mosques of western African cities such as Djenne.

Left: Long walls at Chan Chan were moulded into panels, with sculpted channels of swimming fish and rows of part bird, part four-legged creatures.

Right: The rainbow and solar flare theme sculpted in repetitious panels at Huaca del Dragón near Chan Chan cover the entire surface of the main platform.

The chronological sequence of the *ciudadelas* has several exponents, but it is generally undisputed that they were built as each ruler died and a new ruler ascended the throne. There is some evidence that they were built in pairs. As the kingdom grew, the compounds became larger and more elaborate.

The first was probably Chayhuac, possibly that of Chimú's legendary founder King Taycanamo; then Tello and Uhle together; next were Laberinto and Grán Chimú. The late-phase *ciudadelas* – Bandelier, Valarde, Rivero and Tschudi – were built in rapid succession, the last possibly being the palace compound of Minchançaman, the Chimú king conquered by the Incas. The Squier *ciudadela* appears to be unfinished.

Below: In detail the rainbow and solar flare arch scenes differ. The enclosed figures are always the twinned mythical creatures, but the supporting figures and serpent heads vary.

PATTERN MOULDING

Using wooden moulds, the *tapia* was poured onto the walls. The clay appears to have been applied in two layers, first the poured mud wall itself, then a 2cm (¾ in) or thicker layer, which was moulded or carved while drying. There was a limited range of motifs, the Chimú preference being for repetition on a vast scale.

Repetition and angularity are used to the extreme at Chan Chan in its late phases, but at other Chimú cities, such as Huaca del Dragón, there are more rounded forms. Although there are mythical animals, in contrast to earlier traditions there is less religious imagery in preference for secular themes.

At Huaca del Dragón, a platform mound north-west of Chan Chan sometimes called the 'Temple of the Rainbow', a repeated motif features rainbow-like arcs topped with curled solar flares or wave patterns framed within moulded rectangular borders. Mythical creatures support the arc ends, themselves flanking twinned, face-to-face mythical creatures with sinuous bodies and web-like tails. Long-tailed mythical figures holding axe-bladed staffs march in a frieze above.

At Chan Chan there are panels and bands forming row upon row of repetitious geometric patterns and marching animals, birds and fishes. Vast expanses of wall are covered with diamond lattices and stepped-fret patterning. Upon closer examination of some of the latter, they are seen to be curious flying seabirds or fish. Solid bands of moulding form lines upon which march long rows of curious half-bird, half-quadruped creatures.

Huge expanses of horizontal moulded bands resemble louvred panels, bordered by rows of creatures or rows of large circular 'buttons'. The walls of many of the vast storage compounds within *ciudadelas* are formed of deep, diamond-shaped niches, almost like stacked, square-sectioned cylinders, resembling giant wine racks.

At contemporary Chincha La Centinela, the walls are carved with similar friezes of birds, fish and geometric patterns, and painted brilliant white.

CERAMIC SCULPTURE

Andean figurines were made both as solid clay objects and as functional pottery.

LITTLE IDOLS

Late Preceramic Period Aspero produced some of the earliest unbaked clay figurines, dated earlier than 2500BC. Between two floors of a temple atop Huaca de Los Idolos archaeologists found a cache of fragments representing at least 13 figurines (5–15cm/2–6in).

Eleven are women, of which four appear to be pregnant. They are seated, legs crossed, arms against their sides and forearms across their chests. Eyes and mouths are mere slits. They wear thigh-length skirts, flat hats and necklaces. A male figurine was found near by.

Below: A Nazca effigy, spouted bottle of a panpipe player, whose wide eyes and odd costume with apparently exposed genitalia indicate a religious, drug-induced trance.

Like most such items, they were produced for the public domain rather than for individual use. Similar figurines have also been found at Bandurria, El Paraíso, Kotosh and Río Seco.

TEMPLE OFFERINGS

Baked and unbaked figurines were found at Kotosh. Two crude, baked human-animal figures were associated with the Temple of the Crossed Hands, and an unbaked figure wearing a conical hat, plus three other unbaked objects, were associated with the succeeding Templo Blanco.

At Initial Period Garagay, offerings of baked and painted figures were associated with the Middle Temple and its plaster friezes. Some are dressed in minute textiles and one has fangs. Again, the public nature of these offerings and the human-beast forms of some confirm their religious connotations.

HOUSEHOLD FIGURES

In contrast, Initial Period coastal villagers produced numerous small baked solid and hollow figures of nude women, always in domestic contexts. Particular attention was given to realistic modelling of hair, facial features, breasts and navels. A larger example from Curayacu has a headband, hair falling over the shoulders, delicately fingered hands on stomach, and disproportionately short legs. The strands of hair, eyebrows, lidded eyes with pupils, triangular nose, ears and full-lipped mouth are especially finely rendered. They are thought to be associated with household curing rituals, or perhaps childbirth.

Also in domestic contexts, solid clay figurines were found exclusively in the 'elite' residences at Moxeke, suggesting the development of social hierarchy.

Ceramic figurines were relatively rare in southern cultures. One example from a Paracas burial portrays a rotund

Above: A Paracas male figurine dressed in a short tunic and mantle resembling the patterns on Paracas textiles, and a headband that appears to hold a flute.

figure with puny arms and hands on hips. A thick-necked head has a stylized face with eyes, mouth and chin rendered merely as incised lines. He wears a curious headband with circles and a tube ornament. Incised lines and cream paint indicate clothing and a bib or collar similar to actual shell and stone ones. The slit eyes may possibly indicate death, and the piece might be an ancestor idol.

Above: A mould-made Moche spouted bottle depicting a man playing panpipes, apparently very much engrossed in his music.

SEALS, ANIMALS AND TUNICS

Cupisnique peoples of the northern coast made numerous baked clay figurines and seals, both rollers and stamps (presumably for decorating pottery vessels), found in houses and graves. Examples from late occupation at Huaca Prieta include a bird stamp with a long curved beak, and a seated figurine with curious oversized hands and feet, big ears and a gnome-like hat.

Highland Pacopampa potters also made ceramic seals. One example shows a stylized feline of thick, angular, slab-like lines; there were also numerous crude animal figurines, including felines, dogs, bears and viscachas (a burrowing rodent).

In contrast, an ovoid structure, possibly a priest's residence, on El Mirador hill west of the Pacopampa temple, contained the broken remains of several fine hollow figurines. Originally *c.*48cm (19in) high, they portray tall, elegant male figures with shoulder-length hair, sideburns, unusually large ears, long, straight noses (with nostril holes) arching into eyebrows, pupil-less eyes, open, rectangular mouths, and ground-length, sleeveless tunics, but bare feet.

FUNCTIONAL FIGURINES

Later cultures made fewer clay figurines as such. The Moche and later cultures, however, excelled in making ceramic effigy vessels. Functional stirrup-spout and bridge-spout bottles, bowls and jars of all sizes and styles were made in the shapes of animals, birds and objects. There are human figurine vessels, monkey jars, jaguar bowls and deer bottles, bird vessels, vessels in the shapes of gourds, *kero* drinking cups with sculpted human faces on them, and ceramic panpipes.

A quite extraordinary Early Intermediate Period Recuay piece is of a warrior-priest in an elaborate disc and serpent headdress who is leading a sacrificial llama.

Highly polished, painted Nazca figurines of men and women are often naked except for a loin-cloth, and have tattoos or show full Nazca costume as effigy vessels.

The range of subjects depicted by Moche potters is legendary. Hundreds of Moche stirrup-spout bottles were shaped as animals and birds, and hundreds more portray human occupations and activities – everything from hunting with a

Right: A Chimú polished black-ware stirrup-spouted bottle of a dog nursing her four pups.

blowgun, warriors, flute-playing, shamans treating patients, childbirth and sexual acts of all kinds, as well as a huge range of human portrait vessels depicting all manner of human conditions and ages.

Tiwanaku and Wari, Chimú and Inca potters made jars and bowls with bird heads, humans holding oyster shells or catching lobsters, or drinking cups whose bases are shaped as human hands and feet, complete with nails.

CERAMIC MODELS

Finally, there are building models. Recuay and Moche potters, especially, made bottles shaped as houses: a Moche house with roof combs and a miniature human occupant; a Recuay court with small storehouses; a Recuay double-chambered pot with a house and man peering from beneath his gabled roof; a Lambayeque bridge-spout bottle replete with simulated stepped-fret plaster decorations and entryway flanked by two tiny human guards.

CHAPTER TWENTY-TWO

CERAMICS

Most ancient Andeans used no pottery for the first 10,000 years after humans entered South America. Once ceramics were invented, however, differences in style developed rapidly among coastal and high-land peoples, dictated by available materials and by cultural preferences in expression.

Fired clay, being one of the most durable materials, survives in abundance in archaeological sites. It thus forms a large proportion of the finds from excavations both as whole vessels and in fragments. It provides archaeologists with the means to recognize differences in vessel forms and decorative styles over wide areas, and through time, and thus enables them to identify cultures through their characteristic ceramics, and to determine broad themes in economic and social change and contact through trade.

Andean potters were prolific and exuberant in their output, both in quantity and in the variety of what they portrayed in natural shapes and narrative scenes painted on their pottery. These features enable scholars to surmise meanings for the repeated themes and imagery they observe, as well as to deduce the power and influence of cultures spatially and through time.

Although ancient Andeans used flat, circular potting discs from early times, they never mechanized these in any way to create a potter's wheel. Instead, they continued to make pots by the coil method, building up the vessel walls and turning the potting disc by hand merely to position the part being worked on. Other pots were mould-made.

Left: A Nazca polychrome jar, possibly for chicha *beer, depicting a warrior or entranced shaman.*

THE FIRST CONTAINERS

From the time that humans entered the South American continent, about 15,000 years ago, for more than 10,000 years they used no pottery, neither for containers nor for figurines or other artefacts. Hunter-gatherer peoples travelled light.

EARLY BEGINNINGS
Even in areas where an abundance of food and other materials allowed denser concentrations of people, ceramics came into use only thousands of years later, in the Initial Period. In these places, where the inhabitants concentrated on marine hunting and gathering, pottery would have been less useful than cotton and other fibres from gathered, and eventually domesticated, plants. Cotton was essential for nets, lines and containers for fishing.

For millennia, until knowledge of potting spread geographically, fibres and gourds were used for containers of all kinds. No doubt animal hides and wood were also used.

Examples are very few, for preservation of organic materials requires special conditions (severe desiccation or oxygen-free environments such as waterlogging), and these occur rarely in archaeological sites. However, the regular twisting,

looping and knotting techniques used to make these early artefacts indicate that before the Preceramic Period (*c*.3500–1800BC) there had been a long development in techniques through the Lithic or Archaic Period. No early examples include patterning or other decoration.

BASKETS AND STONE MORTARS
For the Preceramic Period there is more evidence. Sites show the gradual evolution from relatively egalitarian societies living in small villages exploiting rich resources by the sea or in mountain valleys, to the beginnings of social status divisions and the marshalling of labour for the erection of monumental architecture in complex ceremonial centres.

Excavators found twined baskets and looped reed and sedge satchels at La Galgada, in the upper Tablachaca-Santa Valley, and at Huaca Prieta in the Chicama Valley near the northern Peruvian coast, and at other highland and coastal sites. Evidence of highland–lowland trade includes bivalve shells, used as small containers for pigments.

Above: Basketry from plant fibre was also used in early containers, decorated with vegetable dyes and sometimes preserved in dry sites such as the Atacama Desert.

Stone mortars were another late Preceramic non-ceramic container found at several sites. At Salinas de Chao excavators found a large number of stone mortars used to evaporate seawater into salt crystals, for trade with highland peoples.

GOURDS
Plain and carved gourd containers, including bottles, bowls and ladles, come from a few Preceramic sites. Plain gourds were also used as fishing-net floats, and appear to have been domesticated, along with cotton, at an early date, perhaps by 5000BC. A large twined cotton fishing net with attached gourd floats was found at Huaca Prieta.

After the inner vegetable matter was removed, gourds were decorated either by excising or scraping off the gourd's outer skin when it was still soft or by incising fine lines on the surface of the gourd once it had been left to dry and harden. In a few examples a technique

Left: The earliest containers were gourds – later pottery vessels sometimes mimicked gourd shapes, as in this Chavin Early Horizon spouted bottle in the shape of linked gourds with black plant-like motifs.

Above: This ceramic sculpture of a Valdivian mother and child is surely indicative of fertility.

However, the introduction of pottery at Peruvian coastal and highland sites was only one part of a wider range of cultural changes identifiable, for example at late Preceramic El Paraíso. Populations at coastal sites began to shift inland, abandoning some of the U-shaped ceremonial complexes of the Preceramic Period to build new complexes in the fertile lower river valleys. As well as making pots, economics had begun to shift from marine economies to agricultural crops. La Galgada, El Paraíso, Piedra Parada and other sites show the beginning of the use of small-scale irrigation works.

There seems to be a combination of reasons for these shifts, and for the increased importance of highland sites. Population

Below: An early Chavín stirrup-spouted bottle, one of the earliest container shapes, with highly stylized feline imagery.

Above: A bizarre two-headed Valdivian female ceramic figurine, possibly representing fertility, duality, or mythological transformation.

lowlands to their east, as well as imitating some coastal features. Surface decoration on highland pots is common, especially groups of incised parallel lines and hatching, filled with red, white and yellow mineral pigments after firing. Sherds of Kotosh- and Shillacoto-style ceramics have been found at the Cave of Owls in the eastern rainforest, while tropical forest trade sherds have been found at Kotosh and Shillacoto.

NOT JUST POTS

The beginning of ceramic production is one criterion used to define the Initial Period, particularly because pottery forms an important part of the archaeological records from that point onwards, is well preserved and provides archaeologists with varieties in styles that enable them to define different cultures.

increases may be one reason, although there is no convincing evidence that coastal agriculture or marine resources were being depleted. The coincident geographic coastal uplift and ocean shelf subduction did force fish shoals farther offshore into deeper waters, and also lowered coastal water tables. Non-environmental reasons may have included competition between groups for the richest, most easily worked farmlands and simply changes in dietary and work preferences. If production of crops could be increased by moving inland to fertile lower valleys rather than risking the open sea, people may have simply made that choice from one generation to the next. The coincidence of increasingly efficient farming and the use of ceramics in which to store and cook that produce cannot be by pure chance.

451

THE SHAPES OF POTS

The earliest Andean ceramics were limited to a few shapes and mostly imitated the familiar forms of gourd containers. From the simple shapes of the Initial Period, however, variety soon developed into regional styles. Distinctive forms were made that became hallmarks of pre-Hispanic Andean civilization.

MAKING POTS

Ancient Andeans never invented the wheel, either for transport or for pottery making. However, fired-clay discs were used as platforms to turn vessels as they were made, the earliest known being from Paracas c.500BC. Interestingly, although the use of drop spindles to spin fibres was an obvious example of horizontal rotary motion, it never occurred to ancient Andeans to apply this to a spinning disc on which pots could be formed.

Andean potting used three techniques: coiling, paddle and anvil, and moulding. Coiling and hand-modelling were the principal techniques until the Early Intermediate Period, when moulding became an added method, particularly on the north-west Peruvian coast.

Coiled ceramics were made by forming long coils of clay, building up the shape of the vessels by placing the rings one on top the other, then smoothing the ridges out to form smooth sides using maize cobs, bone or wooden paddles, pebbles or shells. Cloth or hide was used to achieve a final smoothness.

The paddle and anvil technique was begun by forming the base of the vessel from a lump of clay, using the hands, or by moulding it over an existing vessel or other shape, then adding more clay to build up the sides. The sides were formed and smoothed by patting the outside with a wooden paddle, against a smooth stone held inside the vessel wall as an anvil.

Moulding involved both forming the clay over an existing form and by pressing the clay into a prepared mould (a method used particularly by the Early Intermediate Period Moche, for example). The process for smoothing the clay pot was the same as for coiled vessels.

Different cultures preferred one or other of these methods, but all three methods were employed, depending on the style and purpose of the pottery. Simple wares for everyday use were

Above: A realistic ceramic hand pottery stamp from the Early Intermediate Period Jamacoaque culture of Ecuador.

most easily made quickly by coiling, or by paddle and anvil. Such wares needed little decoration and were primarily utilitarian.

PROFESSIONAL POTTERS

Apart from such utilitarian containers, made by the users, especially in earlier periods, potting soon became a specialist's art, particularly to produce complex forms and ceramics intended for special purposes. This development coincided with specializations within society and as agricultural production became efficient enough for fewer farmers to grow enough to support full-time specialists of many kinds.

Left: Despite their zoomorphic rodent shapes, these Early Horizon Chorrera culture 'whistle' spout bottles were utilitarian.

Left: This Nazca parrot-shaped bridge-spouted bottle reveals long-distance cultural contacts.

For the mass-production of vessels, an employment that became institutionalized in the great states of later periods (especially in the imperial states of the Moche, Wari, Tiwanaku, Sicán, Chimú and Inca), the use of moulds could speed up production. Nevertheless, professional potters, working full-time for the state, could also produce masses of coil-made vessels. Buildings and compounds that were pottery factories have been excavated at Wari, Chimú and Inca sites in particular. For example, Inca state potters produced uniform plates and pointed storage jars for feeding *mit'a* state workers.

TWO DISTINCT ANDEAN FORMS

Plates, shallow and spherical bowls, beakers or vases, bottle-necked jars (imitating gourds), globular jars and large storage jars were used across all Andean cultures from the later Initial Period and Early Horizon. Vessel sides and rims were straight, flared, incurved and rolled; bases were flat, rounded and in some cases had stout 'legs'.

Two distinct Andean forms were the stirrup-spout bottle and the double-spout-and-bridge bottle. The

Below: Another Nazca painted bridge-spouted bottle, of more 'conventional' container shape, depicts strange humanoid figures seemingly participating in drug-induced trances or transformation ceremonies.

first was a bottle with a single spout rising from a stirrup-shaped loop on the top of the vessel. The latter, as its name implies, had two spouts, between which was a handle-like bridge made from a flattened strap of plain or decorated clay. Both forms were made in a huge variety of shapes and decorations by different cultures in different periods.

Cultural styles were primarily the product of details in shape and in decoration using this range of forms.

USING POTS

The uses of pottery also quickly transcended mere utilitarian use, although that remained a principal function of form. Vessels were used for specific ceremonial roles as offerings and in the performance of ritual. Especially fine vessels were deposited in burials. And, both in life and in burial, the fineness and production quality of vessels reflected social status.

Within the range of utilitarian forms – bottles, plates, cups and jars, for pouring, eating, drinking and storage – shapes could be elaborate and even bizarre. Some pots were

undoubtedly purely ornamental – perhaps a household prized possession, or made specifically for burial.

EFFIGIES AND BIZARRE FORMS

Many ceramic pieces, especially stirrup-spout and double-spout-and-bridge bottles, and beakers/vases, were made as effigy vessels. They depicted either individuals as types within society (for example a shaman) or an actual individual (a practice possibly unique among the Moche). Bottles and other containers were made in the shapes of animals (for example for incense burning in a bowl forming the animal's body). Others imitated vegetable shapes, such as gourds, tubers and cactuses. Some bottle bodies were even rectangular-sided and stepped.

Still other vessels, perfectly functional, depicted whole scenes, such as a shaman healing a patient, priestly animalistic transformation, coca snuffing, combat and sexual acts. Moche ceramics are especially notable for such moulded imagery, while Nazca and other styles are especially notable for depicting such themes as painted decoration.

Fired ceramics were also used for other artefacts. Figurines were produced in abundance probably as votive offerings at temples and to represent deities. There were also ceramic masks depicting deities. Models of temples, houses and storehouses were made, and even fired clay panpipes.

CERAMIC DECORATION

Just as there was great variation in the details of shapes among the primary ceramic vessel forms in Andean civilization, so also were there a number of decorative techniques. Variation in the use of these techniques produced distinctive styles among cultures and through time. The imagery and geometric or abstract decoration of Andean pots was done using all these methods, and by combinations of them.

POLISHING
Glazing was unknown in pre-Hispanic America, but a fine shine could be achieved by polishing the surface with a fine, hard stone, and by rubbing the partially dried pot with the hands or a cloth before firing. Moche potters polished the painted areas of their pots, while Nazca potters carefully polished the whole design area, sometimes smudging the paint colours. Early Horizon Chavín and Late Intermediate Period Chimú potters produced distinctive, highly polished, shiny black wares.

MODELLING, TWO-PART MOULDS AND CUT DECORATION
Modelling was accomplished by making the desired shape by hand moulding, building up the object, animal, plant or person in bits. Wooden and bone sticks and punches, and metal tools and knives were also used to achieve finer shaping. From the Early Intermediate Period onwards the use of fired-clay moulds in two halves became widespread, especially among north-west coast cultures.

If the vessel was not moulded, decorative techniques applied to the smoothed surface included punching, incising, excising, stamping and painting. Punched and incised decorations were some of the earliest techniques. Rows of punched dots, incised lines (cutting into the surface with a sharp tool) and shapes were used extensively on Initial Period ceramics among the coastal and inland cultures whose

peoples built U-shaped ceremonial centres. Excision (cutting out fine sections of clay from the pot's surface, leaving a recessed area) was also was used to make symbolic images and geometric designs.

SLIPS AND PAINTING
Pigments derived from vegetables and ground minerals were used to make paints and thick pastes to rub into incised and excised decorations. Runny 'paint' (a suspension of fine clay in water) was also used as slips to cover a vessel surface or chosen areas.

The earliest paints were used in the 2nd millennium BC in pottery from Kotosh, Shillacoto and other highland sites, whose potters applied red, white and yellow paint to rows of incised lines

Above: An Early Intermediate Period Tuncahuan bowl from Ecuador with geometric decoration.

and patterns. In the 1st millennium BC, potters in southern Peru began to apply mineral pigments mixed with plant resins into incised designs, after firing, to form a lacquer-like coating. Such post-firing painting and use of resin became a distinctive practice among Paracas potters.

Slips were usually applied by dipping the vessel in the paint. Areas that a potter wanted to remain free of colour were protected by the use of wax. After dipping, the wax was melted away to reveal the, usually lighter, clay colour, creating a negative painted effect. Paracas and Nazca potters were particularly fond of this method.

Paint colours included white, black, brown, red, yellow, purple and blue; variations in shades and intensity produced grey, orange, pink and violet. The Nazca used up to 15 distinct colours. Pigment sources probably included haematite (iron ore) for red, limonite (hydrated haematite) for yellow and possibly manganese and pyrolusite (magnesium dioxide) as sources of black.

In contrast, Moche potters used mainly red and white slips, both made from fine white and red clay, the latter being the same clay from which the Moche made their pots. Black and red were also used for fine-line drawing of narrative scenes, depicting everything from ceremonial sacrifice and ritual combat to hunting scenes. Often, both unpainted and painted areas were polished to create different shades of red and white to cream.

As well as rubbing paints and pastes into incised and excised areas, and negative painting techniques, paints were probably applied with fine animal-hair or vegetable-fibre brushes.

STAMPING

Another method of decoration was the use of stamps and pressing a negative moulded figure on to the vessel surface (as opposed to moulding the entire vessel using two half moulds). Combinations of lines and geometric patterns were made by pressing a wooden paddle stamp on to the wet pot to raise the design above the vessel's wall. Fired-clay stamps were also used to raise geometric, floral and animal designs and figures.

Left: A terracotta model of a house from the Cupisnique culture, c.700–300BC. Many such pieces were highly polished.

Above: A double-bodied, spouted Chancay bottle from the Late Intermediate Period possibly implies duality by its half-and-half painted body.

COMBINING TECHNIQUES

Nazca, Moche, Wari and Tiwanaku potters, in particular, excelled in combinations of all sorts of moulded and modelled, then painted, effigy vessels.

The potters made and depicted many kinds of people, deities, animals and plants. There are vessels showing single figures and groups of figures, young and old, performing all manner of daily tasks, from hunting, combat, sacrifice and ceremony, to washing one's hair, expressing the pain of a backache, giving birth or having sex.

Occasionally, shell and stone (e.g. turquoise) inlays were also applied to decorate pottery, for example as eyes.

CULTURAL STYLES

Cultural styles were mainly distinct in details of shape within a range of vessel forms, and in their methods and types of decorations applied to them.

INITIAL COASTAL AND HIGHLAND

After introduction *c.*2000BC, Andean ceramic styles began differentiating within coastal and highland cultures. North and central coastal potters used simple designs of incised lines and geometric shapes. Virú and Moche valley potters, by contrast, made thick-walled, dark red and black bowls and necked jars, mainly plain, but also with simple finger impressions, punched and incised patterns.

The central coastal Ancón style featured similar forms with incised and punched decoration, sometimes painted. Pottery making had reached south coastal sites by *c.*1300BC, where its most distinguishing characteristic

was the use of negative painting (masking areas before dipping the pot into slip paint).

The highland Wairajirca style – at Kotosh, Shillacoto and other sites – developed from *c.*1800BC. The most common forms were cups, bowls and vases, but the first stirrup-spout bottles were also made. Decoration comprised bands of incised lines and circles filled with red, white and yellow paints after firing. Raised patterns were created by excision. Highland styles show similarities to contemporary eastern tropical lowland Tutishcainyo ceramics.

EARLY HORIZON STYLES

Three distinctive Early Horizon styles were Chavín culture in the highlands, Cupisnique on the north-west coast and Paracas on the south coast. Chavín potters made distinctive polished grey-black ware – open bowls, globular and stirrup-spout bottles. Decoration was mostly incising, but also stamping and punching. Contrasting areas were defined by polishing and texturing with depressions by shells or combs and also by applying dark red and graphite grey paints. More complex geometric patterns and symbolic serpent, feline and bird imagery came later.

Cupisnique-style bottles and globular vessels are typically black or grey. Stirrup-spout bottles feature a trapezoidal-shaped stirrup, including effigy vessels of marine and terrestrial animals and people. Irregular incised lines were sometimes filled with red paint after firing.

Early Paracas potters produced Chavín-inspired stirrup-spout bottles and forms with fine-line incised feline imagery. In

Left: An Inca effigy jar portraying a man carrying a jug and kero *cups, probably for* chicha *beer for ritual drinking, and wearing a half-moon pendant.*

Above: An Early Intermediate Period Virú bridge-spouted, double-bodied bottle, possibly a whistle vessel, with a parrot head.

the later 1st millennium BC, the Paracas style developed distinctive, highly colourful ceramics using incised patterns and imagery filled with red, orange, yellow, blue, green and brown paints and resin after firing. Circle, dot and line patterns were used to create a negative painted effect in lighter slip-colour under a dark over-colour.

EARLY INTERMEDIATE PERIOD

Prominent styles in the Early Intermediate Period were dominated by north-west coastal Salinar, Gallinazo, Recuay and Moche wares and by south coastal Nazca and early Tiwanaku pottery. The quality and quantity of production indicates that potters had become full-time specialists, perhaps supported by the state. Mould-made ceramics became dominant in the north, while coil-made and highly colourful pottery characterized southern styles.

Salinar potters introduced the double-spout-and-bridge bottle. Use of Chavín-Cupisnique feline motifs waned, while human and animal effigy vessels proliferated, including erotic imagery. Gallinazo ceramics shared and continued these features with highly naturalistic modelling and introduced negative painting techniques on geometric and feline imagery.

Contemporary Moche coastal and adjacent highland Recuay styles introduced an exuberance of modelled and moulded effigy forms representing all manner of life scenes from the exotic to the mundane, including human portraiture. Utilitarian forms included bowls, bottles, jars, dippers and spoons. Moche pottery is distinctive for its highly polished, bright red colour, and for its depiction of narrative scenes in fine red or black line drawings. It has been intensely studied and is divided into five phases of development.

Recuay potters were the first to depict 'the common man'. Recuay ware is distinguished by its white paste, and by human and animal (most frequently feline) imagery, in white, black and red.

Nazca and early Tiwanku ceramics are highly polychrome styles. Nazca wares spread throughout the Nazca, Ica, Chincha, Pisco and Acari valleys. Modelling is infrequent (almost always of humans), while painting predominated, in up to 15 colours or shades of white, black, brown, red, yellow, purple and blue, as well as violet, orange, pink and grey. Complex scenes of intertwined geometric patterns, deities, humans and animals cover whole pot surfaces, continuing the Paracas tradition.

Later Nazca potters changed from pre-firing painting to post-firing negative painting, using slips and wax to keep areas unpainted, paint resins delimited by incised lines to create a lacquer-like finish, and high polishing. Through several phases it evolved from more naturalistic to more abstract forms of decoration and imagery.

MIDDLE HORIZON MASS PRODUCTION

Growing political unity under the Tiwanaku and Wari empires spread their ceramics far and wide. Production was simplified and mass production in state-sponsored factories was introduced. Tiwanaku pottery is multicoloured on a distinctive orange base. Decoration is predominantly religious, depicting feline, serpentine and deity imagery (especially a figure holding staffs in outstretched hands), as on stone sculpture and textiles. Use of slips and colour range were similar to Nazca wares. A distinctive Tiwanakoid form is the tall *kero* drinking beaker; there were also huge, thick-walled, multicoloured storage urns set in pits.

In contrast, Wari pottery, also polychrome, is mostly secular. Geometric patterns and effigy vessels (both painted and moulded) predominate, and emphasis is on the world of humans. Towards the end of the Middle Horizon, decoration became more geometric and abstract, and quality declined.

CHIMÚ, CHANCAY AND INCA

The Chimú continued the Moche and Wari tradition of mass production using moulds, and decorating in several colours, but quality declined in favour of quantity. Plain polished black and red wares

Above: An Early Horizon north-west coastal Peru Cupisnique stirrup-spouted effigy bottle of a man carrying a llama, and presumably wearing regional headgear.

were also made. Plates and ring-based bowls were introduced for the first time, and tripod bowls also became common; stirrup-spout bottles declined.

Central-coastal Chancay ware was another main style. Using crude, gritty clay, forms include oblong, narrow-necked bottles and jars with handles. Human faces were painted in grey-black on white slip backgrounds; there were also nude female effigies with outstretched arms.

Inca ceramics are characterized by painted decoration in black and white on red. Designs are geometric, especially fern motifs, triangles and rhomboids. Bird and animal imagery is stylized to the point of being abstract. Characteristic shapes are flat, round plates, *kero* cups and pointed-base, globular bottles with flared necks and handles.

Below: A south-west coastal Peru Paracas drinking cup with typical geometric decoration reminiscent of textile patterns.

INTERPRETING THE POTS

Two categories of ceramics co-existed in Andean civilization: utilitarian and special. The groups were not exclusive – the same forms were used for both – but wares for daily use were not necessarily made by specialists. Special wares, although functional, were meant for ceremonial and ritual uses, and some forms, such as animal-shaped incense burners, were clearly purpose made. Despite changing decorative styles and predominant techniques of manufacture in different areas, there were several common symbolic motifs and imagery that reflected pan-Andean religious beliefs.

CULTURAL RECORDS
Even highly decorated utilitarian wares, produced for social elites, served simultaneously, consciously or otherwise, as a record of culture by depicting mythological scenes and scenes of daily life as well as holding liquids and food.

Below: An Early Intermediate Period Pashash lidded jar with geometric, textile-like decoration and the image of a double-headed serpent, probably representing duality.

Right: Vivid subjects and delicate images decorate many Nazca pots, such as this bridge-spouted bottle depicting hummingbirds sipping nectar from a flower.

Spanish documents make almost no mention of pottery, so it is only through archaeology and comparison of the imagery on ceramics with our knowledge of Inca and earlier religion that we can surmise what the decoration meant.

The effort taken, especially by potters up to the Late Intermediate Period, to decorate pottery obviates its importance to convey messages to those making and using it. As well as being purely aesthetic, the ritual use of pottery shows that it was made for specific purposes. Making pieces especially for burial with the dead emphasizes the importance of the afterlife and the need to prepare for it.

Pottery models of houses and temples give us a rare insight of how reconstructions of the archaeological excavations of their foundations might look.

RELIGIOUS MEANINGS
In the Early Horizon, Chavín religious influence became widespread through symbolism, especially of feline, serpentine and cayman imagery, on portable artefacts – pottery, textiles and metalwork. The snarling feline with bared teeth and long canines, and serpent heads and bodies are thought to symbolize the power of these creatures and admiration of them. They were depicted through all the techniques – painted, incised in outline and moulded – showing their universal application across styles.

The snarling feline motif all but disappeared in the Early Intermediate Period, to reappear in Moche and later ceramics, again both as incised and painted imagery. The mouth is often wide open, and feline features are often combined with human features to represent transformation by shamans or priests. Bird and other animal transformation is also represented.

Imagery in different regions hints at predominant economic strengths, such as marine creatures on coastal wares. But the appearance of tropical animals (jaguars, caymans and tropical birds) on highland wares also shows the strength of highland–lowland contacts and the supernatural regard for those creatures by highland peoples.

Other deity imagery includes the Staff Deity, which characterizes Chavín, Tiwanaku and Chimú art, including on ceramics. Other local deities are also represented, such as the Oculate Being, which was so important in south coastal Paracas and Nazca culture.

THEMES

A ritual theme in Moche ceramics is the 'presentation scene', a simpler form of which also appears on Chancay pottery. In it, one figure, dressed in a shirt, short kilt and conical helmet, proffers a goblet to a seated or more prominent figure. There are also scenes showing cloth being offered.

A prominent theme in Paracas and Nazca pottery shows a deity or masked semi-human holding a severed head – trophy heads also being an important image in other media.

Below: Painted ceramic vessel with a snake-shaped handle from the Tiwanaku culture.

Above: A ceramic vessel from the Recuay culture (c.300–600AD) showing a snake with a feline head.

REMINDERS OF LIFE

The apparent exuberance of Nazca and Moche ceramics reveals the importance of the images and scenes as reminders to people of what was important. The portrayal of everyday narrative scenes, as well as more exotic events, from healing, to sex, to architectural models, and the care and time taken to mould and paint them, reveals the richness of life.

In Moche art, the ritual combat scene is often repeated, and Moche potters are the only ones known who definitely portrayed actual living people. One Moche man was portrayed 45 times, documenting much of his life. But whether depicting a living person or a type, Moche potters covered the range of human conditions from youth to old age and from health to sickness in effigy vessels showing backache, birth, healing and death.

The complex battle scenes on Nazca pottery contrast with ritual single-combat scenes on Moche pottery. Both, however, reveal an importance in conflict and in the ultimate outcome of sacrifice and death.

CONVENTIONS

Certain 'rules' of execution can also be detected in the uniformity and the stylization with Nazca and Moche pottery. Slip colours are only white or red. Background colours, on which detailed Nazca scenes were painted, are only painted in black, white or shades of red. Mythical beings on Paracas and Nazca pots are always shown frontal, and they are usually associated with severed heads.

Moche potters used conventions in the poses and actions of their animal, human and semi-human figures. The space between the feet indicated whether the figure was standing, walking, running or dancing. The angle of the torso and positions of the limbs showed speed, falling over or death. Despite such conventions, it is thought that the nuances of style in finishing and depicting facial features in the repetitious mould-made and painted forms sometimes reveals the hand of the same artist.

POWER AND CONTROL

The mass production of repetitious forms by the Wari, Tiwanaku, Chimú and Inca empires was a statement of power. It served to remind subjects of state control of production and provision of employment, alongside regulation of the economy.

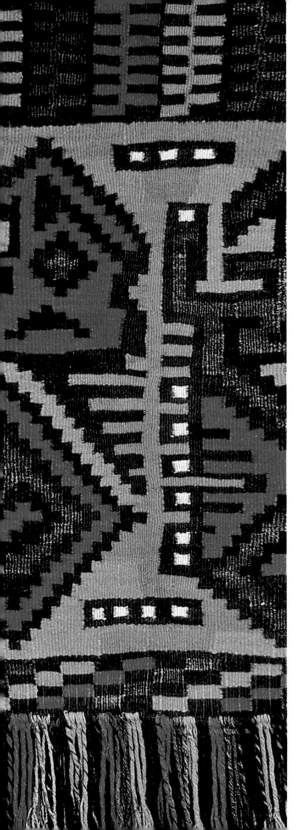

CHAPTER TWENTY-THREE

FIBREWORK, COSTUME AND FEATHERWORK

The importance of cloth and fibre arts in Andean civilization cannot be underestimated. Fibrous plants were among the earliest domesticated plants. Mostly utilitarian at first, in time cloth became the most important exchange commodity other than food, and in Inca times served, in value, as a sort of 'coinage' of the realm.

Preceramic peoples worked plant fibres by simple twisting, twining and looping, making twine and bindings for spear, arrow and drill points, bolas stones and for slings. Sleeping mats, sandals and simple clothing were made with simple looping, as were nets, bags and carriers. These were the first steps towards the sophisticated weaving that became a hallmark of Andean civilization.

All women wove. In pre-Inca times textile production may not have been so exclusive to women, but in Inca society spinning and weaving were symbolic demonstrations of womanhood and they were done by all women, from the most common subject, through the noblewomen of the imperial household to the Sapa Inca's principal wife.

The importance of textiles to the Inca is epitomized in a statement attributed to Atahualpa, last Inca emperor, upon meeting Pizarro in Cajamarca: "I know what you have done along this road. You have taken the cloth from the temples, and I shall not leave until it has been returned to me." This, despite the Inca wealth in gold and silver!

Left: A late Early Intermediate Period Nazca or early Middle Horizon Wari poncho with stylized bird and animal imagery.

TWINING, SPINNING AND WEAVING

The variety and quantity of Andean textiles that have survived are phenomenal. Whereas ancient Mesoamerican textile studies are greatly reliant on pictures in ancient manuscripts (*códices*), Andean preservation has provided thousands of examples to study directly.

USEFUL *AND* SYMBOLIC
Late Archaic and Preceramic peoples twisted and twined wild plant fibres primarily for utilitarian objects. Twine and cordage provided binding for spear, arrow and drill points, and for bolas stones and slings. Looped cordage enabled them to make a variety of basic 'textiles' such as simple clothing, and various nets, bags

Below: A Moche red-line ceramic dish showing an old woman (left, with wrinkles) allegedly instructing a younger woman in the art of weaving, and talking, or possibly chanting or singing.

and carriers. Containers were fibre sacks, as well as animal skins, dried gourds and wooden vessels, before the discovery or invention of fired ceramics.

Utilitarian uses never ceased, however (footwear, mats, tools and bags required constant quantities of twine and cordage, and ordinary daywear required plain woven cloth), and remained important right through to Inca times. For example, quotas of cordage were required of male Inca subjects for the many bridges and army weapons needed. Cords dyed and knotted into *quipus* provided a means of keeping imperial accounts.

Soon, however, alongside developments in irrigation agriculture, monumental architecture and sophisticated religious beliefs, cloth became more symbolically utilitarian, as a medium for conveying religious concepts, for social and regional differentiation in clothing styles, and for preserving the dead.

Above: Llama wool spinning and weaving in the Andes was developed simultaneously with coastal cotton fibre use from the 1st millennium BC.

TEXTILE PRODUCTION
Plant fibres were simply shredded, dried and twisted into twine and cord, then knotted and looped (weft twisted around weft) into bags, baskets, sandals and other items. The earliest items are of hemp-like brome and agave plant fibres from Guitarrero Cave, dated *c*.8000BC. Cotton was one of the first Andean domesticated plants. It was grown in the coastal valleys of Peru and Ecuador from *c*.3000BC, although its wild ancestor must have been collected and tended earlier, before it was actively cropped.

By the 3rd millennium BC (Initial Period), cotton textiles were being made from Ecuador, through Peru to northern Chile. The llama and alpaca were domesticated in the Altiplano around the Titicaca Basin during the Preceramic Period. Evidence is lacking, but it is assumed that llama and alpaca wool spinning and weaving developed during this period and through the Initial Period, for there is ample evidence in the Early Horizon of wool used in Paracas embroidery on the south coast. Some wool use was found at Preceramic Aspero, but it was not until the Early Intermediate Period that wool was used extensively by central and north coastal peoples.

Above: A Chancay Late Intermediate Period wool and cotton tapestry cloth demonstrates the constant contact and interchange between coastal plains and mountains.

Nearly three-quarters of the early cotton textiles from Huaca Prieta are twined; the remainder are woven, or looped as netting. Twining does not involve a loom. The vertical warp threads are diverted slightly right and left and held by twisted horizontal weft threads – thus the weft turn around the warp rather than interweaving with it. The process is manual. Using different coloured threads enables the maker to produce patterns and pictures by trading the warp threads from the front to the back of the cloth, creating zigzag designs and images.

Loom weaving began in the Initial Period, from *c.*2000BC, with the invention of heddles – flat sticks to raise groups of threads in order to weave between them quickly – and the backstrap loom. Twining died out, but looping and sprang (interlinking sets of cloth elements) continued to be used for bags and hats.

Cotton was spun by beating the fibres out, rolling them into a cylinder and attaching it to a post, then drawing out the thread while twisting the cylinder. Wool was spun with the drop spindle.

LOOMS

All the techniques used by ancient Andeans for textile production were known by the end of the Early Horizon (*c.*200BC). In addition to knotting, looping and twining, these were: the plying of several strands (of wool) together;

Below: The continuous need for wool and cotton thread and yarn for weaving required daily drop spinning by women of all ranks in the Inca Empire and earlier (depicted in Poma de Ayala's Nueva Corónica, *c.1615).*

braiding; the use of discontinuous warp and weft to create imagery and patterns, also of supplementary warp and weft threads and complementary sets of warp or weft; warp wrapping (creating the design on the warp by wrapping it in coloured yarn before weaving); embroidery and tapestry; textile painting; tie-dying; and the use of double and triple cloth (interconnected layering).

Most ancient Andean weaving was done on backstrap looms, although other types were known, especially the vertical (suspended) loom. Warp threads were wound in a figure of eight around two posts. The warp ends are tied to wooden bars, one of which is fixed to a post or wall peg and the other to a backstrap around the weaver's waist. Warp tension is adjustable by leaning back or easing up.

Warp sheds are created, first, by the figure of eight of the preparation, then by lifting alternate warps on loops of thread called leaches, attached to a heddle stick. Weft threads are passed through the sheds, as they are lifted and lowered, with thread on a bobbin, then beat down against the earlier wefts. By lifting different sets of warps in sheds less than the entire width of the cloth, and/or by passing the weft through less than the full-width shed, patterns and images can be created within the warp and weft.

EARLY COTTON TEXTILES

Wild cotton relatives grow in northern Peruvian coastal valleys. Evidence of fibre use at Archaic Guitarrero Cave, and widespread production of cotton textiles from Ecuador to northern Chile at late Initial Period coastal sites, indicates millennia of wild cotton collection and tending before planting and extension of its cultivable range. Truly domesticated cotton (*Gossypium barbadense*) grows at 320–1,000m (1,050–3,280ft) above sea level.

COTTON DESIGNS

Lowland textiles are dominated by cotton, although llama wool, as it became more available through highland–lowland trade from the late Initial Period, was increasingly combined with cotton, especially at Paracas. Cotton takes dyes less easily than wool, so use of wool increased

Below: A Middle Horizon Wari woven poncho of wool and cotton fibre, with characteristic geometric patterns (some are possibly highly stylized faces), reveals trade for fibre between coastal cotton growers and Altiplano llama herders.

the colour range through the Early Horizon. Textile painting was also developed on the coast, perhaps for this reason.

Preceramic coastal fishing peoples relied heavily on cotton for knotted nets and line, found at most sites, including nets up to 30m (98ft) long.

Preceramic Huaca Prieta produced some of the earliest cotton fabrics, of which more than 9,000 fragments were found. Their designs show the earliest Andean concerns with visual messages, including multiple meaning and composite imagery. Complex patterns and imagery were created using twining with spaced wefts and exposed warps of different colours (red, yellow, blue, black dyed, and natural white and brown cotton), plus looping and knotting, in characteristic zigzag contours.

Human, bird, serpent, crab, fish and other animal imagery was used singly and in repetitive interlocking patterns. Multiple meanings are conveyed in double-headed birds and snakes, crabs that transform into snakes, and other creatures with multiple attributes. One famous piece portrays

Above: A painted, cotton Paracas, southern coastal Peruvian burial wrap depicts Staff Deity figures within diamond panels, revealing the influence of the Chavín Cult from farther north.

a raptor with spread wings, and a snake inside its stomach. Similar imagery is found on textiles from Asia and La Galgada.

CHAVÍN TEXTILES

Early Horizon Chavin textiles include more than 200 pieces from Karwa and other southern coastal sites, where they have survived. They include the earliest painted Andean textiles. It is assumed that highland Chavin sites used similar textiles. Northern coastal Cupisnique weavers also painted cotton textiles.

Karwa textiles were a medium for the spread of the Chavín Staff Deity. Female Staff Deity imagery was painted in brown and rose on plain woven cotton cloth. Sometimes several pieces were sewn together, for example a circle of jaguars

reminiscent of the circular sunken court jaguar sculptures at Chavín de Huántar. Cloth belts resemble that on the Lanzón Stela and many painted figures carry staffs or San Pedro cacti.

Karwa textiles always portray supernatural beings as female. Eyes substitute for breasts; fanged mouths for vaginas; and they carry plant staffs, often intertwined, or as animated cotton plants and bolls. Profiled attendants are either male or genderless. Like the Raimondi Stela at Chavín de Huántar, the female images present a second image when inverted. It is thought that she portrays an Earth goddess, and that the pieces are hangings, canopies and altar covers. Other fragments are clothing or mummy wraps. Braiding around textile edges is thought to be a symbol of continuity.

PARACAS TEXTILES

Contemporary Paracas weavers developed embroidery, using imported alpaca wool from the Altiplano on cotton backing cloths, sometimes also incorporating tropical bird feathers. They also invented discontinuous warp and weft techniques. By not passing the whole lengths of weft or warp threads across or down the loom, they could make highly complex woven imagery and patterns.

Hundreds of mummy bundles in the Paracas Cerro Colorado, Arena Blanca and Wari Kayan cemeteries include rich textile wraps. Bundles range widely from rough cotton mantles to elaborate multiple-bundle wraps of plain and highly decorated textiles, holding gold, feather, animal-skin and imported shell offerings. (Incorporating grave goods was a means of maintaining an individual's integrity and possession.) The largest bundles are up to 2m (6½ft) tall, and the largest cloths are 3.4 x 26m (11ft x 85ft)!

Paracas embroidery covers the whole of the ground cloth in vibrant colours, patterns and images. Motifs and imagery are usually applied at borders, neck-slits and in columns in the centres of mantles

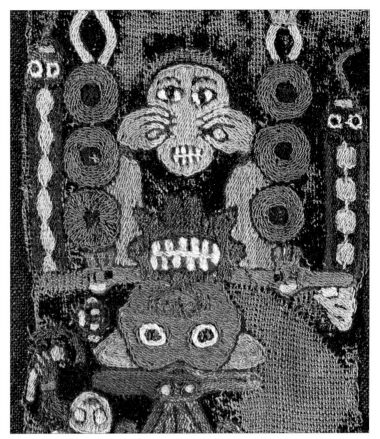

or wraps. The textiles include the work of masters and apprentices – many cloths have a central panel of perfectly formed figures flanked by panels less well executed, attempting to copy the master's panel. Some cloths appear to be practice pieces; some are unfinished before burial. Calculations of the hours taken to make these complex pieces and multiple mummy wraps indicate that they occupied lifetimes, suggesting that preparation was specifically for burial.

LINEAR AND BLOCK COLOUR

The linear style comprises stitches sewn in and out of the ground cloth, always moving forwards and leaving visible lines of thread. In contrast, Block Colour style covers the thread by stitching forwards, then half backwards, then forwards again with slightly overlapping diagonal stitches. Linear textiles are more restrictive than

Above: A complex Initial Period Paracas embroidered burial shroud, made of fine alpaca wool, with dual central figures. The figure with the golden diadem is probably the Oculate Being and the other a shaman in a drug-induced trance, plus serpent and trophy head imagery.

Block Colour ones, being limited to straight lines of thin colour in red, green, gold or blue, while more expansive Block Colour textiles have blocks of solid colours and outlined, curved figures and patterns, and a colour palette of 19 colours and shades. Linear designs accommodate the shape of the long, flying Oculate Being. Motifs and imagery are not restricted to borders but often occur in cloth centres and as symmetrical arrangements.

Moche and Nazca textiles continued Early Horizon techniques and themes into the Early Intermediate Period.

WOOL FROM THE HIGHLANDS

Camelid llamas and alpacas were fully domesticated by *c.*2500BC. The process lasted several thousand years in the grass-lands of south-central Peru around Lake Junin and the Altiplano around the Lake Titicaca Basin. Their domestication is evident from the steady decline in deer remains and the increase in camelid bones at late Archaic and Preceramic Period sites.

THE IMPORTANCE OF WOOL
Llamas were bred for three reasons: their meat, their carrying capacity and their wool. Llama wool, heavier and greasier than alpaca wool, was woven primarily for coarse cloth used for heavy-duty articles such as mats, sacks, saddlebags and cordage. Softer, longer alpaca wool was spun and woven for clothing and other fabric. Still finer, softer, wild vicuña wool was highly prized, especially by the Incas, who captured vicuñas for shearing in special hunts.

Alpacas and llamas were shorn between December and March and their wool spun simply by pulling and arrang-ing the fibres to lie parallel, then winding the resulting 'roving' around the forearm or on a wooden distaff, and spinning it with a wooden drop spindle.

Below: Llamas herded for wool also served as pack animals in caravans, carrying goods between the highlands and lowlands.

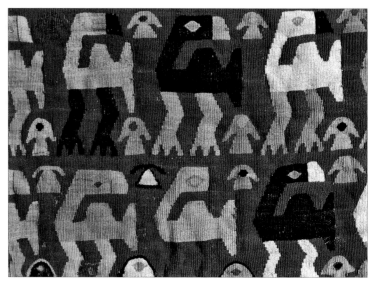

Wool has two advantages over cotton: its staple is a longer fibre, which spins and adheres more readily, and it will take dyes more easily, thus increasing the range of colours and shades available for design. In Chimú weaving, cotton was almost always spun and used as single strands, whereas llama and alpaca wool threads were almost always plied: spun, then, two strands plied together. Spinning and ply-ing were usually in the same direction.

WOOL EMBROIDERY AND DWW
Spun alpaca wool became prominent in Paracas embroidery, which provides some of the earliest combinations of cotton and wool (the wool embroidery being done on plain cotton cloth).

Paracas and Nazca weavers made huge quantities of wool and cotton cloth for everyday use and for burial clothing and wraps. With a wide colour palette, the hours required to produce large cloth wraps, both as wool embroidery on cot-ton backing and as discontinuous warp and weft (DWW) designs, shows that it was a major occupation.

Above: A Late Intermediate Period Chancay woollen tunic with 'pink' flamingos, native to the Peruvian coast. Such finely woven cloth was worn by individuals of high rank.

Religious imagery was especially impor-tant. The principal Paracas and Nazca creator, the Oculate Being, was portrayed in many forms. A wide-eyed being, he is associated with water and the sky. Usually shown horizontal, as if flying, he faces front with large, circular, staring eyes and long, streaming appendages, an attribute easily achieved both with line stitching and DWW. Such streamers often end in tro-phy heads or small woven figures. In some cases he wears a headband like the gold headbands found on buried mummies.

Other themes are birds, serpents and shamans with streaming hair, frequently as scores of small, twinned and repeated figures. In the Linear embroidery style, Oculate Beings or serpentine figures are often interlocking in a continuous border around the cloth edge and in strips across its width.

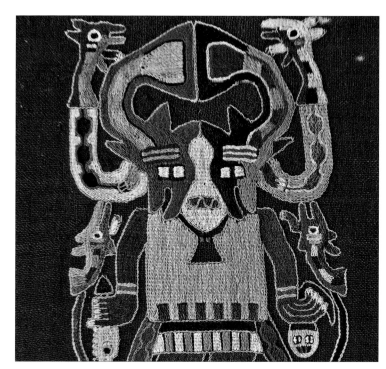

Left: A woollen Paracas burial shroud features a main central figure wearing a horned headpiece, probably the Oculate Being, but revealing Chavin Cult influence.

usually in repetitive, interlocking patterns. The work was mostly in cotton, with wool worked in as superstructual patterns. Humans or deities wear large headdresses or have rayed heads. Some tapestries feature repeated small human figures with crescent-shaped headgear, surrounded by raptors holding trophy heads. Central coastal Chancay weavers began to make 'gauze' cloth – open weaving in which the image is almost invisible in the net-like fabric unless held against a dark background.

The Incas honoured local weaving traditions, but introduced standardization in cloth production. In organized textile workshops at provincial capitals and principal towns, specialist weavers produced regular quotas of cloth, mostly of interlocking tapestry with geometric patterns.

Below: A Nazca–Wari woollen bag with stylized animal motifs and fur fringes. Woollen bags served for personal possessions and as panniers for llama caravans transporting produce between regions.

TAPESTRY

Early Intermediate Period and Middle Horizon coastal weavers developed tapestry. As a convenient use of small lengths of wool of various colours, tapestry designs became extremely colourful and complex.

On the south coast, tapestry replaced embroidery in importance, depicting the same imagery as before, especially geometric designs. Painting on cotton cloth also became more important. On the central and northern coasts, cotton and wool tapestry continued side by side through the Early Intermediate Period. Imagery favoured double- and multi-headed snakes, fish and supernatural composite beings – humanoid snakes, birds and fish. Interlocking, stepped-fret geometric designs were also popular.

TIWANAKU-WARI TAPESTRY

New styles in wool weaving reached the coast in the Middle Horizon, originating in the highlands among Tiwanaku and Wari weavers. Environmental conditions in the highlands, however, preclude most preservation of fabrics from these sites, from which only poor examples survive.

Tunics and hangings depict the imagery seen on Tiwanaku pottery and stone sculpture. The central, staff-bearing, ray-headed deity on the Gateway of the Sun is frequently portrayed, sometimes as a central figurehead surrounded or flanked by smaller staff-bearing figures. Winged figures known as 'angels' copy the 'attendant messenger' figures on the same monument. Mountain pumas and condors also came into more prominence as images.

LATE INTERMEDIATE AND LATE HORIZON CLOTH

Coastal weavers continued split-woven and DWW tapestry, combining cotton and wool. Feline, serpentine, avian and fish imagery became extremely complex as interlocking patterns of figures, similar to imagery on ceramics and mud wall sculpture; there were also dignitaries, shamans or deities with elaborate headdresses. The use of brocade – using extra wefts – was introduced as well.

Chimú and other north coastal weavers specialized in complicated geometric motifs in endless repetitions, plus jaguars and pumas, raptors and condors, fish and snakes,

GRASSES AND FIBRES

Grasses were an early and essential part of Andean economy. From Archaic times they continued to play an important role throughout Andean prehistory. Grass fibres were made into the earliest basketry and net bag containers before ceramics were discovered. Alongside gourds and wooden containers, baskets were used for the collection, storage and transport of wild plant foods.

EARLY CORDS
Few examples survive, but the regular twisting, looping and knotting techniques used by hunter-gatherers to make these articles suggest that there was a long period of development in techniques throughout the Lithic Period. None of the earliest examples shows patterning or decoration.

Below: One of the principal uses for totora reed by coastal peoples was for one-man fishing boats (today called caballitos *– 'little horses'), combining a local product to catch locally abundant fish. Depicted on Moche pottery, such boats are still used today.*

The earliest Andean fibrework comes from Guitarrero Cave in the north-central Andes. The dry cave deposits contained the earliest evidence of domesticated plants in South America, plants collected, then tended and deliberately planted, not for their food value but for 'industrial' and medicinal use, including hemp-like plants of the *Fuscraea*, *Tillandsia* and *Puya* species. These plants and fragments of the containers and other articles made from them predominate over plant foods and wood.

Containers, rough clothing, sandals and sleeping mats were made of simply twisted cordage. An open-mesh net bag from the lower cave deposits was made with simple knotting and looping. Other fragments of fabric show twining, with each weft strand manually twisted around the warp threads. A chert stone scraper from Guitarerro Cave, dated *c*.5500BC, has its butt wrapped in deer hide secured with twisted cord binding.

Use of plant fibres at Lithic Period sites is the beginning of the long association of fibre wrapping and important objects.

Above: A Late Intermediate Period Chancay ceramic effigy bottle, showing a man holding a small dog on a fibre rope, perched on his shoulder.

BODY SUPPORTS AND STUFFING
Another early use of 'fibres' was of sacred significance. The world's earliest mummies, dated *c*.5000BC, at Chinchorros in northern Chile were supported and bound with cane sticks and cords. After allowing the body to decompose, the bones were reassembled and supported by thin cane bundles tied with twine. Then the 'body' was remade by stuffing its cavities with fibre and feathers before sewing the dried skin over the body and applying a clay coating or mask. It is assumed that these practices were attempts to honour the spirit of the dead in the beginnings of ancestor cults.

CONTAINERS, BOATS AND BURIAL
Twined cord satchels, and reed and sedge baskets formed prominent parts of the assemblages at Huaca Prieta, La Galgada and other coastal villages. Some of the earliest ancient Andean textiles are also of

rough fibre, mostly from the cactus *Furcraea occidentalis* (an agave-like plant). Its sharp, pointed leaves can be crushed and shredded to produce fibres up 50cm (20in) long, which can then be twisted together to make cordage. The bast from a milkweed plant (*Asclepias*) was also used to make fibre. The leaves needed to be soaked for a long time before they could be beaten to release their fibres, then crudely 'spun' by rolling them between the palms or with the palm on the thigh.

Fishing peoples often combined (plied) fibre bast with cotton, especially when stronger cordage or netting was required. The strongest nets and basketry were made from grasses alone.

Cotton, wild and later domestic, was essential for Preceramic coastal fishing villagers for lines and nets. In their fishing and foreshore shellfish-collecting economy, however, they also needed basketry for

Below: Rope making was a labour tax in the Inca Empire. Every man was required to produce a specified quota of cordage for rope, especially to make and repair bridges.

collection and storage, and reeds for their fishing boats. They grew totora bulrush reeds specifically for boat making, as did peoples around the lakeshores of Titicaca and other mountain lakes. Reeds were also used for sails by Late Intermediate Period coastal fishers and traders. These water-craft traditions continue today.

Preceramic burials usually included at least a mat and plain cloth wrapping, if not more elaborate clothing. For example, the infant burial bundle at Huaca de los Sacrificios at Aspero was placed in a reed basket before being wrapped in textiles. Women were often buried with their weaving baskets, which were reed or sedge containers for spindles, threads and loom tools.

ARCHITECTURAL SUPPORT

Plant materials and rough fibre cordage played important parts in early housing and even in the earliest monumental architecture. For example, La Paloma coastal peoples lived in cane and reed huts with grass roofs. Thatch roofing was used by coastal and highland peoples right through to Inca times.

Above: Traditional use of totora reeds for roofing endures in these houses on a totora-reed 'floating island' near the shoreline on Lake Titicaca.

Plant chaff was an important element in mud-plaster architecture, providing a binding both for smooth plaster coverings on stone walls and in adobe brick walls.

The earliest platform mounds were built up with rubble before being finished off with impressive adobe brick or stone facings. Open-mesh satchels, called *shicra* in Inca times, made of split reeds and capable of holding as much as 36kg (80lb), were used to haul stone rubble. The baskets were not emptied, but were deposited *en masse* on the mound. The *shicras* found intact at late Preceramic El Paraíso each held 17.6–36kg (40–80lb).

In Inca times, men's role in the imperial textile taxation was to produce required quotas of cordage. Without strong cordage, Inca quarrying (rope for haulage), house building (cordage for roof binding) and bridge building (for suspension bridge cables) would not have existed.

CLOTHING STYLES

In ancient Andean society, cloth was wealth: it was exchanged between rulers, given as rewards for good service, and used to fulfil reciprocal obligations between members of kinship *ayllus*. It was important in the relationship between state and subject, and was presented at public ceremonies as items in the redistribution of wealth. Special clothing marked changes in life cycles, both as costume for initiation ceremonies and as a mark of age, social status and distinction. Specific people wore specific clothes for specific occasions. Cloth was offered to the gods in burnt offerings, used to dress and preserve mummies, and offered in burials. Finally, cloth provided a medium for representing the gods and religious imagery reflecting cosmological concepts.

INCA CLOTH
The Incas defined two grades of cloth: fine cloth, called *qompi*, was divided into two sub-grades, for tribute fabrics and 'best' cloth for royal and religious use; and *awasca* cloth – a plain, coarser fabric – was for ordinary use.

Below: This llama wool hat with geometric designs from the Atacama Desert shows Tiwanaku influence.

Above: Intricately woven textiles such as this Paracas poncho burial wrap with flying Oculate Beings were the preserve of the rich.

The Incas encouraged diversity among their subjects, not least in maintaining local textile traditions and clothing styles. Regional patterns and imagery, costumes and headdresses were badges of ethnic identity, for these were regarded as having been designated by Viracocha the Creator himself.

Ephraim G. Squier described the importance of clothing diversity in his 1877 book, *Peru: Incidents of Travel and Exploration in the Land of the Incas*: "If they were Yungas, they went muffled like gypsies; if Collas, they wore caps shaped like mortars, of wool; if Canas, they wore larger caps … The Cañari wore a kind of narrow wooden crown like the rim of a sieve; the Huancas, strands that fell below their chin, and their hair braided; the Canchis, broad black or red bands over their forehead."

STYLE
Andean clothing was mostly un-tailored. Tunics or shirts were made from two rectangular panels of cloth, woven at the maximum width of the loom,

then sewn together along one edge, folded in half, and sewn down the sides, leaving openings for the head and arms. Capes or cloaks were made from two or more cloths stitched together.

Because clothing is often found in graves, it is sometimes difficult to determine what was daily wear, ritual costume or clothing specifically for burial. The mummy bundles of Paracas and Nazca vary in their richness and in the number of layers of cloth. Elaborate mummy bundles, presumably of rich, higher-status individuals, wore a loincloth, embroidered cloth belt, tunic or short poncho, shoulder mantle and turban.

Much Andean clothing is depicted on pottery and stone sculpture. For example, 13 late Preceramic figurines from Huaca de los Idolos at Aspero portray 11 women wearing thigh-length skirts, but no sandals. Some wear flat-topped hats and square-beaded red necklaces (two such beads were actually found). The capes worn by the Initial Period mud-sculptured figures at Moxeke are not dissimilar to those on the later

Below: Distinctive regional textile decoration and headgear is revealed on painted pottery, as on this Nazca jar.

Paracas mummies. And the elegant male figurines from Initial Period El Mirador wear full-length, sleeveless tunics, but also have bare feet.

Nazca effigy pots wear ponchos and tunics like those on mummies, with decorated neck and sleeve borders. A figurine vessel of a panpipe player wears a plain tunic with star-shaped neck decoration; other Nazca vessels depict a man's tunic and a woman's shawl-like mantle with circular designs; and a Nazca double-spout, stepped-fret bottle shows warriors wearing tunics with fringed borders and lampshade-shaped hats.

Another Nazca double-spout vessel portrays a stout fellow in a plain loincloth, brown and white chequered shirt and a matching, tightly wrapped turban around his head.

Below: This Middle Horizon Tiwanaku woollen unku *tunic shows a more unusual diagonal pattern of different coloured rows of flowers, requiring an extremely complex weaving technique.*

HEADGEAR

Moche ceramics are especially revealing, featuring an astonishing variety of geometric decorations on tight-fitting headdresses. Some are long strips of cloth wrapped twice around the head and tied at the back.

Others are bandanna-style cloths fitted over the head, with the front end wrapped around to the back and tied. Some Moche figures wear tight-fitting short-sleeved shirts.

Equally distinctive are Tiwanaku-Wari box-shaped wool hats. Made up of five tapestry woven panels sewn together to form sides and top, their vibrant colours, geometric patterns, and rows of winged beasts, birds and abstract human figures resemble the imagery on ceramics. Some sport little points or tassels at the top corners.

Tiwanaku-Wari hangings and clothing were made with interlocking DWW weaving rather than the slit-weaving tapestry of the earlier coastal traditions. Imagery and patterns are elongated and compressed. Faces are frequently split up into small rectangular elements.

Tiwanaku-style tunics were made so that the warp threads lie horizontally across the chest rather than vertically (as in earlier coastal tunics). They were made of two rectangular cloths sewn down the warp edges, leaving an unsewn mid-section for the head of the wearer. Some Tiwanaku tunics were made of a single

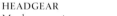

Above: This Middle Horizon Wari mummy bundle reveals the wealth of the buried person by the sheer number of wraps to create the bulky mummy, including an outer unku *tunic, woven wool and fibre scarf and 'hair'.*

cloth, the head slit being made by a long section of discontinuous warp from each side. Likewise, Tiwanaku and Wari effigy pots show figures wearing just such hats and bordered tunics.

Inca 'factory-produced' cloth was primarily of interlocking tapestry tunics, also with the warp running horizontally across the chest of the wearer and mostly decorated with geometric patterns. Vicuña wool, and cloth embellished with gold, silver or feathers, was restricted to imperial and noble use.

RITUAL COSTUME

Much of the cloth created in the Early Horizon was for ritual purposes. The complex imagery and geometric patterns on rectangular lengths of cloth bore religious significance, reflecting Andean cosmological concepts. They were hangings, canopies and altar covers for the temples, and burial wraps.

PRIESTLY GARB

The figurines from the highland Initial Period site of El Mirador were found in an unusual ovoid building separated from, but close to, the main temple site of Pacopampa. The sculptures were especially finely made and other finds included Pacific shells, foreign ceramics and exotic figurines of felines, dogs, bears and chinchilla-like rodents. The temple included an elaborate drainage system, anticipating that at Chavín de Huántar. This evidence and context suggest association with the temple. The figures are thought to represent priests and the ovoid building a priestly residence. If this is correct, then their long tunics are presumably ritual dress, for their length would make them impractical for daily work. Similarly, the mud sculptures at Moxeke, in niches atop the main public platform, were clearly

religious figures. Two cloaked torsos are either priests or gods, whose missing heads may represent ritual beheadings. Although the capes are 'typically' Andean, one figure also wears a twisted cord sash and holds double-headed snakes, which might be part of the costume. Both wear short, pleated skirts.

These Initial Period finds suggest both that some clothing was special to the priestly function, while other garb, although essentially the same as daily wear, was more elaborate in its decoration and of finer quality. An effigy bottle from a looted tomb in the Jequetepeque Valley is exemplary. The small spouted bottle (26.8cm/10½in) portrays an elegantly attired man playing an ocarina. His tunic, like those made throughout Andean history, drapes over his body, but is especially richly decorated with stylized feline and avian figures, whose details are picked out in many colours.

SNAKE MEN

The wall sculptures in Chavín de Huántar's circular sunken court also depict priests in ritual costumes. They are composite creatures, representing gods, shamanistic transformation or priests

Above: A Chimú wooden figure with a mud mask, carrying a kero cup. The mask, earrings and headpiece are probably ritual costume.

acting out these roles. They wear collared, long-sleeve shirts, trousers (or perhaps just anklets?), elaborate, braided-snake headdresses and snake belts. They have strange, stepped-fret 'wings' on their backs, decorated with feline mouths. Their own mouths have huge canines and their feet and hands are talons. The whole scene is one of ritual procession and transformation, and the elaborate costumes of the priests can only have been made especially for such occasions.

The richly adorned mummy bundles of Paracas and Nazca are also difficult to interpret. The care and time involved in making the textiles, and the labour of preparing the burials, can be attributed only to ritual beliefs. Despite variation in the quality and quantity of textiles,

Left: The Inti Raymi winter solstice, revived in 20th-century Peru, brings out latter-day Incas in 'ancient' ritual costume.

these burials reveal social hierarchy, although it is uncertain whether the clothing was specifically for burial or also represents daily wear, according to rank. The records of elaborate, rich clothing worn by certain classes in later periods by Chimú and Inca nobility, however, suggests that the standard loincloth, tunic, mantle and turban were 'normal' wear, although there were perhaps pieces specially made for burial. Perhaps Paracas and Nazca priests enacted ritual myth dressed in the mantles so richly decorated with mythical imagery.

PRIESTS AND PRIESTESSES AS GODS

There is no doubt that the elaborate costumes worn by the priests and priestesses depicted in Moche murals and on pottery are ritual costume. The Sacrifice and Presentation ceremonies show them

Left: An Early Horizon Chavin effigy pot portrays a shaman or priest with facial scarification, wearing a jaguar headdress and playing a flute, probably using ritual music to induce hallucinations.

dressed in colourful tunics with decorated neck borders, belts, a pleated skirt on the priestess, and various extraordinary head-dresses with tassels, crescent-knife shapes or bandanna styles.

There is little doubt, too, that the extremely rich burials at Sipán and San José de Moro represent individuals whose tasks were to impersonate these deities in the ritual. Their burial costumes are exactly those of the murals, showing the Warrior Priest, Owl Priest, and Priestess in feathered tunic. In addition to his gold and other jewellery, and gilded copper adorned capes, the Warrior Priest even wore ceremonial copper sandals.

Similarly, the gear worn by Moche warriors on pottery and murals, although undoubtedly the same as that used in battle, also represents ritual weapons and armour. It was a sort of gladiatorial combat, performed for religious purposes, the ultimate outcome of which was the sacrifice of the loser.

Equally revealing is the burial at Dos Cabezas of a tall Moche priest wearing a bat-motif hat. His tomb also included 18 other headdresses, assumed to be for the performance of his many ritual roles.

GOLDEN CAPES

Gold ornament was often applied to mantles, and it seems reasonable to assume that such clothing was not for everyday wear, with the exception of kings and emperors. Chimú weavers specialized in ritual garments incorporating

Above: From the earliest times Andean ritual costume required materials and dye colours from far-flung regions. This Nazca headdress from southern Peru has tropical bird feathers, traded in from the rainforest.

rich patterns of coloured tropical feathers, gold and silver spangles, beads and tasselled edges.

Inca dress was of standard type for all, the difference being in the richness of the wool, the elaboration of decoration and colour, and the embellishment with gold, silver and feathers.

New clothing was made for boys and girls for their initiation rites. The rather elaborate costumes donned today in re-enactments of Inca rituals bear resemblance to ancient costume, but inevitably have been elaborated in combinations of colonial influence and modern imagination. Nevertheless, such re-enactments represent a statement of independence and resistance.

FEATHERS AND FEATHERWORK

Coastal and tropical rainforest bird feathers were important in Andean cultures from the Initial Period. Exotic tropical feathers were traded right across the Andes from the eastern lowlands and rainforests by coastal cultures.

Making feather costumes demanded great labour and conferred considerable importance to the wearer, advertising one's high status in society.

FEATHER OFFERINGS

In early periods, feathers were included in burials and caches as offerings. Ritual offerings on platform summits at late Preceramic Aspero included a buried offering of red and yellow feather arrangements. Loose green, pink, blue and yellow feathers and down were found beneath a floor at El Paraíso; a carved stick at Río Seco was covered with white feathers; and there were red and orange macaw feathers in burials at La Galgada.

Below: This Late Intermediate Period Chancay ceremonial headdress shows a characteristic chequered pattern and brilliant yellow tropical parrot feather decoration.

Below: Remarkable preservation in the Paracas Desert necropolis in southern Peru has left unspoiled a feather and rope-fibre fan and woven cotton bag decorated with tropical parrot feathers for holding personal burial items.

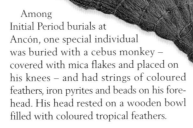

Among Initial Period burials at Ancón, one special individual was buried with a cebus monkey – covered with mica flakes and placed on his knees – and had strings of coloured feathers, iron pyrites and beads on his forehead. His head rested on a wooden bowl filled with coloured tropical feathers.

FEATHERED TEXTILES

Tropical feathers were also imported by Paracas and Nazca weavers. Feather decorations were inserted among embroidered patterns, and braided strips of cloth held long feathers to create a sort of tall bonnet. Feathers were also cached with gold, animal skins and exotic shells in burials.

By the Early Intermediate Period, elaborate ritual clothing included entire mantles of feathers. An unusual Nazca tunic is made of a cotton back-cloth covered in bright yellow tropical feathers, highlighting a turquoise 'running' monkey with yellow eyes, also of feathers. The monkey constitutes another connection between coastal peoples and rainforest tribes.

The Priestess in Mural E at Moche Pañamarca wears a distinctive feathered mantle in the Presentation Ceremony.

Middle Horizon cultures extended the use of feather garments as status items. A Wari mantle comprises intricately combined cream, orange, black and blue feathers to make two orange eight-pointed stars with faces, above an orange double-headed snake. The three elements are thought to represent duality and the four directions.

As well as actual feathers, Pukará, Tiwanaku, Wari and Lambayeque-Sicán Middle Horizon art features heads with rayed feathers. The most superb example is perhaps the gold mask from Huaca Loro Tomb 1 at Batán Grande: its human visage wears a tall headdress with a central vampire bat face and 90 delicate golden feathers.

CHIMÚ FEATHERWORK

Late Intermediate Period Chimú weavers were especially adept at incorporating feathers into costumes. On plain-weave

white cotton back-cloths, they sewed rows of tiny, bright red, pink, orange, yellow, green and blue tropical bird feathers, creating garments as brilliant and shimmering as those covered in thousands of tiny gold squares.

Feathers were attached by bending their quill ends over a thread of the back-cloth and fixing it with a second thread, which was knotted around the bend of each quill. Each feather-holding thread was stitched down to the fabric so that the feathers overlapped, hiding the cloth.

Bird feathers included: tinamou, cormorant, great and snowy egret, Chilean flamingo, Muscovy duck, Salvin's curassow, macaws (blue-and-yellow, Scarlet, red and green), parakeet, trogon, purple honeycreeper, and various Amazonian parrots and tanagers.

One Chimú poncho bears images of light blue pelicans made up of feathers, with red feather eye circles and beaks. Two large pelicans are borne on litters of red and green feathers, carried by smaller, blue-feather pelicans along a blue-feather road. An exemplary Chimú piece, a ceremonial headdress, combines white, yellow, black, grey, turquoise and pink feathers from flamingos, macaws, razor-billed curassows and parrots. Its main body includes two human figures wearing axe-crescent hats, below a flared crown of long white macaw feathers and stepped-fret decoration in pink, yellow and black. Even the eyes, mouths, fingers and toes are intricately rendered in different coloured feathers.

The expense of importing enough tropical bird feathers to cover entire tunics meant that only Chimú kings and nobles wore such clothing. They were ostentatious declarations of their power and wealth. The making of such garments required thousands of retained artists, supported by commoners through taxation.

INCA FEATHERWORK
Likewise, only Inca emperors and nobility wore feathered cloaks, and Atahualpa commissioned a mantle made from bat skins. The Chachapoyas of the north-eastern Andes, in Inca Chinchaysuyu, were specialist traders with Amazonian tribes for their tropical products, including feathers, to the Incas and the Chimú before them.

It is significant in this context that the roster of court officials in the legendary Naymlap's entourage includes one

Left: Detail from a Late Intermediate Period tunic of brilliant tropical macaw feathers from the Amazon, probably depicting a shaman in ritual trance.

Above: A Chimú ritual featherwork poncho, depicting a Staff Deity-like figure and different coastal birds and fish, reflecting the Chimú reliance on the sea.

Llapchillulli, 'Purveyor of Feathercloth Garments'. Clearly, valuable trade links for tropical feathers between the northern Peruvian coast and the eastern Andes and Amazonia were perpetuated for hundreds of years by Lambayeque-Sicán lords and their Chimú successors.

Inca featherwork was as important as, or even more valuable than, metalwork and cloth, because of its relative rarity. As well as being sewn on back-cloth for human garments, featherwork features in headdresses of great complexity, and also on miniature figurines. Some Inca ceremonial headdresses feature great crescents of long-tail raptor and condor feathers, as well as tropical bird feathers.

In addition to feather mantles and cloaks, Inca emperors, borne on litters, were shaded with macaw-feather parasols.

DRESSED FIGURINES

Andean peoples frequently used figurines as ritual offerings and in burials. Clay, metal and cloth figurines were 'dressed', mirroring their makers' clothing styles.

PAINTED AND ACTUAL CLOTHING
While some early figurines are naked, others wear clothing similar to cotton and woollen cloth found in excavations. There are, for example, late Preceramic figurines from Huaca de los Idolos of women wearing thigh-length skirts, flat-topped hats and square-beaded red necklaces; a rotund

Below: A Middle Horizon dated Chancay figurine of dyed cotton forming a face and body, plus garment wraps around cane and straw body and limbs.

Paracas burial figurine with a curious headband of circles and tube ornament, and incised-line and cream-painted clothing and 'shells' collar; tall Pacopampa figurines in long, sleeveless tunics; and numerous Nazca and Moche effigy vessels of people 'dressed' in typical garments.

At Initial Period Mina Perdida (2nd millennium BC), however, a fibre human effigy figure is made of a jointed, thread-wrapped gourd dressed in a cotton mantle. It was found face down on a platform terrace, and possibly represents a shaman in transformation, for it has condor markings on its face.

WOVEN FIGURE FRINGES
Many Paracas and Nazca cotton textiles feature fringes comprising rows of severed heads. Several, however, have rows of small woven human figures, c.30mm (1¼in) tall. One such Nazca burial wrap shows a line of musicians, standing with arms in the air, or across their bodies, their hands holding tiny woven rattles or bells. Each wears a tunic with a decorated band at the hips.

MINUSCULE GOLD AND STONE CLOTHES
One of three earspools in Tomb I of the Moche Lord of Sipán depicts a tiny figure of Lord Sipán himself of astonishingly intricate workmanship. The tiny figure is dressed in a tunic made of polished turquoise chips, a gold mask (complete with miniature, movable, gold crescent-shaped nosepiece), a necklace of minuscule golden owl heads, minute gold belt bells, two minute circular gold and turquoise earspools, and a headdress of turquoise chips and gold *tumi*-knife crescent and stepped, golden 'horns'. He holds a round gold shield and a removable golden war club.

This figure is flanked by two even smaller warriors made of turquoise chips, each wearing a turquoise-chip tunic, necklace and multi-layered helmet with gold

Above: Two woollen textile figurines used as Late Intermediate Period Chancay funerary offerings, a female (left with longer tunic) and male (right), representing duality.

tumi-knife crescent. They also have gold and turquoise earspools and carry circular gold and turquoise shields.

At Wari Pikillacta, 40 tiny figurines, each about 25mm (1in) high, were made of tiny precious stones, and are 'dressed' in tunics, mantles and hats of gold foil, and belts of precious stone chips and shell.

THE WEAVING LESSON
An astonishing Late Intermediate Period cotton cloth 'sculpture', Chancay or Chimú, depicts a mother teaching her daughter to weave. The two tiny figures sit on a woven, stuffed 'pillow' with stripy white, black, red, orange and yellow decorations. The mother works a miniature backstrap loom fixed to a wooden 'post' stuck into the pillow. The loom is complete with warp and weft threads, wooden warp beam and shed sticks. She holds a heddle rod poised to insert into the miniature shed. She is inclined

towards her daughter as if explaining her work, and a head cloth of loose-weave, orange and yellow chequered pattern that resembles Chancay open-work weaving covers her long, dark brown hair.

Below: An Inca gold figurine, richly dressed in woollen clothing held with a miniature gold tupu *pin. Such figures represented* mamaconas *or* acllas, *the chosen women of the imperial court, and were sometimes deposited in child sacrifice burials.*

Her daughter sits beside the loom, her own long hair arranged in a minute topknot, spilling from a close-fitting hat with stripes and minute animal-heads decoration.

Both mother and daughter wear robes with stripy patterns and fringed bottoms. Details of their eyes, including pupils, noses and mouths are rendered in minute stitches.

Not only is this piece astonishing for its detail, but it is also one of the few actual images showing us ancient Andean weaving.

CLOTH 'DOLLS' AND DRESSED METAL

Many Late Intermediate Period Chancay burials contain offerings of cloth 'dolls'. Reminiscent of earlier Nazca fringe figures, they are of wrapped yarn and embroidered fabrics. Facial features and hair, stick-like arms and fingers, and decorated clothing are all of woven and stitched threads.

Inca gold and silver figurines of nude men and women have been looted from and found in undisturbed sacrificial child burials, often on remote mountaintops. Some are dressed, and miniature clothing has been found separately elsewhere, indicating that all such figurines were dressed. Their clothing was possibly removed for some sacred moment in the sacrifice ritual or burial ceremony.

The silver Cerro del Plomo figurine from Chile wears a brown and white mantle over a similar tunic. Both have strips and edges of red and yellow decoration. The mantle is tied

Above: A Late Intermediate Period Chancay reed figurine with cotton textile features, hair and clothing – probably a funerary offering.

with a tiny, decorated cord with rectangular shell toggles, and held with a miniature silver *tupu* pin. A magnificent, brilliant, red feather semicircular headdress crowns the head.

Two gold figurines from a burial of three sacrificed children on Mount Llullaillaco, Argentina, were equally magnificently dressed. Both wear white wool mantles, with red, yellow and black, and red and black borders. One is female, with gold and silver *tupus* pinning her mantle. Her long, tightly bound hair is moulded in gold, and a headdress of red and orange feathers frames her face.

The male figure has large, looped earpieces and a close-fitting cap, both moulded in gold. His mostly white mantel covers a red, yellow and black tunic, and he wears a grey turban with a sheet-gold ornament fixed to the front with a red and gold-headed pin, and an array of yellow feathers at the back.

CHAPTER TWENTY-FOUR

METAL, WOOD, STONE, SHELL AND BONE

Apart from ceramics and stone sculpture, few ancient Andean items are of a single material. Most metal artefacts are alloys of gold and silver, gold and copper or silver and copper. Many stone, wood and metal objects are embellished with stone and shell inlay.

With these materials and media, Andean craftsmen created exquisite objects as well as utilitarian tools. Even some of the most common objects were highly carved, shaped or decorated. Most techniques were known from the earliest times. Shells and exotic stones were made into beads in the Preceramic Period if not earlier, and the first gold foil dates from *c*.1500BC.

Exotic materials were sought throughout the Andean Area and beyond, including turquoise, lapis lazuli and spondylus, or thorny oyster, shell. Working with gold and silver was highly controlled.

These materials advertised an individual's social status, and yet their value was primarily in the objects they were used to create and in the religious symbolism they represented. Ancient Andeans had no defined monetary values or currency. Only the copper *naipes* found in bundles in Sicán-Lambayeque tombs at Batán Grande (but rare elsewhere) possibly had an agreed exchange value. Spanish chronicles report that "6,000 seafaring Chincha merchants" used copper as a medium of exchange with Ecuadorian peoples.

Left: A Lambayeque sheet gold burial mask with Sicán 'comma-shaped' copper inlay eyes and nose beads.

MINING AND METAL TECHNOLOGY

We know little about Inca or pre-Inca mining. The Spaniards, primarily interested in gold and silver, quickly took over these areas and imposed their own techniques in the first century after the conquest.

Abundant sources of gold, silver and copper in Peru and Bolivia are found pure (gold and copper) and in ores (silver and copper). Most prehistoric Andean gold was retrieved from streams by washing the gravel in wooden trays. Sometimes streams were diverted to expose gold-bearing gravels. Lesser amounts were excavated from one-man trenches.

Mine shafts for silver and copper ores were 1m (1 yard) or so to perhaps 70m (230ft) long. Vertical shafts were only as deep as the dirt could be thrown up to the surface, then another hole was started near by. Wooden, bronze and antler tools were used to dig, and stone and deer antler hammers and picks were used to break up veins of ore, and to crush it. Excavated material was brought out in hide sacks and fibre baskets.

Spanish chroniclers record that Inca mines were worked only in the summer, from noon to sunset. Mining, like so many other tasks, was carried out as part of the Inca *mit'a* labour tax.

Crushed silver and copper ores were heated in clay crucibles to melt the metal and drain it from the ore. Relatively pure veins of copper yielded pieces that could be worked cold, as copper is relatively soft.

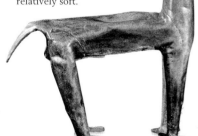

Above: Moche gold and turquoise necklace. Moche goldsmiths often combined gold beads with semi-precious imported stones.

Gold-bearing streams and ore deposits were considered sacred places. Ceremonies were held at them to honour their holy spirits and solicit ease of extraction. Gold and silver collection and mining were restricted under state control in the Inca Empire (and, as they were regarded as precious, probably under elite control in pre-Inca cultures as well). Copper extraction and use was widespread and less regulated.

METAL TECHNOLOGY

Andean metalsmiths were superbly skilled, and undertook extremely delicate work as well as large-scale pieces. They were specialized craftsmen, employed by the state or maintained as retainers of the elite to produce tools and exquisite items for elite consumption.

Left: Small figurines, such as this sheet-gold, sculpted llama, were made in abundance by the Incas, and often placed in the tombs of sacrificed children.

Objects were produced in small compounds, partly residential, partly workshop, where the metals were heated, hammered, bonded and formed into all manner of utilitarian and sumptuary objects.

Techniques included hammering into sheets to make the metal pliable, annealing, repoussé, incised and cut-out designs, joining and soldering, mould and lost-wax casting, gilding, burnishing and over-painting.

All of these methods were known in the Andean Area, although central Andean, Ecuadorian and southern Colombian metalsmiths preferred working with sheet metals and metal strands to create sculpture and jewellery, using sheet metal rolled, hammered and formed into objects and jewellery. Metalsmiths in northern Colombia and Central America favoured casting (including lost-wax casting, in which the figure is made of wax, then covered with clay, leaving a channel for molten metal to be poured in, which melts and drains away the wax; once the clay covering is broken, the object remains).

Utilitarian objects were made of copper and bronze, including knives, war club heads, agricultural hoes and digging implements, tweezers and beads. Gold and silver were used to make exquisite elite objects, including all sorts of jewellery, masks and figurines.

HAMMERING

Before being hammered, ingots of workable size were made from smaller pieces melted together. Hammering was done with hard, fine-grained stones (usually of magnetite, haematite or fine-grained basalt), formed into flat, round or cylindrical anvils and unshafted hammerstones, held in the hand. As hammering proceeded, the flattened sheet was annealed (reheated until it glowed red, then quenched with water) to prevent it from becoming brittle and cracking.

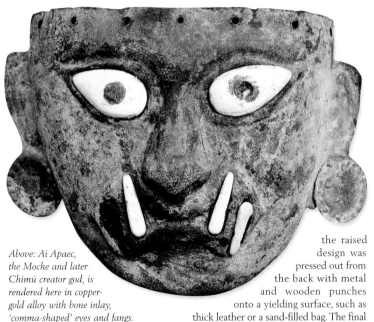

*Above: Ai Apaec,
the Moche and later
Chimú creator god, is
rendered here in copper-
gold alloy with bone inlay,
'comma-shaped' eyes and fangs.*

REPOUSSÉ AND INCISION

The process of repoussé – the creation
of relief designs from behind – began with
cutting out the shape with a thin-bladed
chisel. The pattern was scribed onto the
metal, sometimes using templates, then

*Below: Using the lost-wax technique,
the Muisca people made exquisite gold
necklaces of identical tiny figurine 'beads'.*

the raised
design was
pressed out from
the back with metal
and wooden punches
onto a yielding surface, such as
thick leather or a sand-filled bag. The final
design was refined and sharpened from
the front with fine tools.

Incised designs were also scored into
metal figures, and areas of metal were
sometimes cut out.

JOINING AND BONDING

Multi-piece objects, sometimes of different metals, were combined by several
techniques. Edges were overlapped and
hammer-welded, with annealing, sometimes including the clinching of the edges
by folding them over on each other.
Soldering and brazing were accomplished
with melted bits of metal alloy. Moche
spot-welding was second to none, with
some pieces including hundreds of individual spot-solderings. Granulation, or
diffusion bonding, was used for very fine
work, such as tiny beads or fine wire.
Copper compound and organic glue were
applied at the joins of gold or silver parts,
then heated to burn away the glue and
form a copper-alloy brazed bonding.

Mechanical joins were formed in a
variety of ways, including stapling, lacing
with a metal strip, pinning and clinching.

*Right: Inca metalsmiths made numerous
solid silver (as here, with copper hairpiece)
and gold male and female figurines.*

MOULDING

Cast moulding was rare, as few pieces
were solid. Chisels and axes were made
in simple, open moulds of stone or clay,
into which molten metal was poured.

FINISHING

Objects were highly polished, burnished
with dried animal dung, wood, metal,
leather and cloth. Sometimes the actual
metal was over-painted. Many objects
were gilded, using extremely thin gold foil.

PRECIOUS METALS AND EARLY METALWORK

All Andean metal that glittered was not gold, for Andeans were more interested in the essence of appearance. Most 'gold' objects were in fact alloys with a gilded surface. Alloys included tin and copper bronze, gold and silver, silver and copper or gold and copper (tumbaga). Different metals were also combined individually in pieces of work, as well as inlaid with stone, lapis lazuli from Chile and shell. Masks were often painted over, so hiding the metal!

VALUE AND SYMBOLISM

The production and exchange of sumptuary goods of all kinds was controlled by the elite in cities. Rather than a market economy, however, precious metal artefacts were used as items of prestige and as gifts and hospitality. Their value was in the political alliances they helped to seal and in the religious continuity and enforcement they secured. Most exchange was in the context of religious or political ceremony.

Below: The Chimú, successors of the Moche-Sipán and Lambayeque-Sicán north-west coast goldworking tradition, shod their buried kings with exquisitely fine leather sandals with sheet-gold clasp ornaments with turquoise inlays.

Above: Moche paired gold half-discs were embossed with solar flares or wave motifs – and may have been used as earrings or clothing ornaments.

Gold and silver objects were widely traded, yet neither had a market value. What was important was the symbolism of the objects. Apart from tools, metalwork was devoted to elite objects meant to be used and worn by upper classes and as funerary offerings. Thus, commoners ate from pottery plates while Inca nobles used identical plates but made from gold or silver. Decoration always involved religious symbolism, either as images of the gods, sacrifice and sacred animals, or the symbolic representation of life (for example in exquisitely modelled animals, birds and agricultural plants). Cuzco even had a zoo–garden of gold and silver replicas.

The ultimate symbolism is expressed in the Inca concept of gold as 'the sweat of the Sun' and silver as 'the tears of the Moon'.

EARLY METALWORK

The earliest known New World metalwork is gold. It comes from Waywaka, in the Andahuaylas Valley of the central Peruvian highlands. Here, a stone bowl contained a metalworker's tools, and a burial contained pieces of thin, beaten gold foil (nine pieces in the hand, with lapis lazuli beads, and one in the mouth), dated *c.*1500BC. The tools comprised a cylindrical, flared-top stone anvil and three stone hammers for beating the gold into foil.

Roughly contemporary, at Mina Perdida, on the central Peruvian coast, small pieces of hammered gold and copper foil

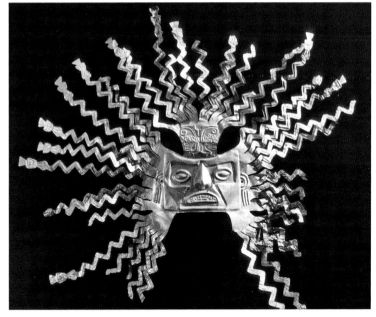

Right: La Tolita goldsmiths, in the far northern corner of Inca Chinchaysuyu quarter, were part of a northern tradition of smithing producing fine sheet-metal ritual objects, such as this Sun God mask with repoussé face and cut sheet-gold rays.

were found on its platform, dated *c.*1450–1150BC. Some pieces are gilded copper, and they appear to have been thrown from the ceremonial summit.

Slightly later, villagers of the Wankarani culture near Lake Poopó (south of Lake Titicaca) developed copper technology, as shown by pieces of smelted slag dated *c.*1200–800BC.

These mid- to late Initial Period finds are scant evidence of the prolific metallurgical technology subsequently practised in later periods throughout Andean civilization. Nevertheless, they demonstrate the early beginning of combining metals, 'essence' in representation through gilding, and the association of metal offerings both with burials and with religious ceremony.

EARLY HORIZON METALWORK

Metallurgy techniques in the Early Horizon period appear fully developed in comparison to the earliest finds, revealing that much intervening development must have taken place. Forged and annealed gold and silver figurines with Chavín motifs have been found at Chavín de Huántar and other Chavín sites. Soldering and repoussé were employed, as were alloys of gold, silver and copper. Chavín–Chongoyape goldsmiths used sheet metal to make objects to inter or store in caches. Gold sheets were decorated in repoussé and rolled into tall cylinders, thought to be crowns, face masks, pectorals and smaller pieces for application to clothing. Their imagery is typically Chavín and Cupisnique: the Staff Being and feline faces. Characteristic Chavín obscurity or illegibility is achieved in complex, busy designs bordering on the abstract. Whole images are obscured in the curvatures, and sometimes the work is so complex that symbols are revealed only in the play of light and shadow.

Gold, 'wholly other' and immutable, incorporates a sacred message, and is the reflection of the sun. Gold on the outside, as gilding or on clothing, reflected the inner quality of the elite wearer.

A gold alloy pectoral disc from Chavín de Huántar depicts a central feline fanged face, while around the edge an interlaced braid represents continuity and unity of the cult. A cylindrical crown from Chongoyape depicts in repoussé the full figure of the Staff Deity, with highly stylized staffs, snake-like swirls from its head and a flared-nostril feline face on the torso. Although it resembles the Staff Deity image on the Raimondi Stela at Chavín de Huántar, both pieces reflect the range of interpretation allowed within Chavín imagery as the cult spread north and south from the cult site.

PARACAS AND NAZCA METALWORK

Spanning the Early Horizon and Early Intermediate Period, Paracas, Nazca and Moche metalwork preserved many Chavín elements but also developed their own unique styles.

Gold objects placed in Paracas and Nazca graves of distinguished individuals reveal the growing differentiation in social hierarchy. Thin sheets of nearly pure gold were cut into elaborate silhouettes and decorated with sparse repoussé details, but highly polished to achieve maximum glitter. Mummy bundles include noserings, mouth and whole face masks, forehead ornaments, headdress plumes with sea animals, clothing discs and gold staffs.

Left: A Chavín gold jaguar figurine with embossed pelt markings.

MOCHE LORDS OF SIPÁN

The true glory of ancient Andean gold, silver and copper artistry comes to life in the rich tombs of the north-west Peruvian coast. Moche artisans were capable of the tiniest attention to detail, such as the kneecaps of a figure adorning an earring or a bead on the body of a spider. Moche metalsmiths also developed the use of shell and stone inlay, and combinations of gold and silver, to maximize colour contrasts between gold, silver, orange-red shell or turquoise lapis lazuli.

Moche gilding also merits special mention. Instead of applying gold to the surface, bathing gold-alloy objects in natural acids depleted the outermost layer of silver or copper to leave a thin layer of pure gold – thus gilding from within.

LORD OF SIPÁN

The greatest single collection of Moche gold, silver and copper objects comes from 12 elite, unlooted burials at Sipán in the Lambayeque Valley. Spanning roughly 200 years from AD100 to 300, and including the burials of several lords and retainers, the tombs contained hundreds of gold, silver, copper, turquoise and shell objects and textiles.

Tomb I, of the Lord of Sipán (identified as the Warrior Priest of the Moche Sacrifice and Presentation ceremonies depicted in murals and on pottery), contained some 451 objects. His solid gold head crescent spanned 60cm (2ft). Gold and silver backflaps lay beneath him. Above and below the body were textiles

adorned with gilded-copper platelets forming full-on human figures with turquoise bracelets, also a gilded-copper headdress with the same figure. His face is covered with a sheet-gold mask, his forehead with a gold strip, and gold, silver and copper nose-crescents and other jewellery adorn his face. He wears three pairs of gold and turquoise earspools (one depicts the lord himself, with a miniature detachable war club, swinging nosepiece and necklace), a gold and silver necklace of peanuts, and turquoise

Left: An exquisitely fine Moche gold and turquoise inlay 'supernatural' toucan, made of cut sheet gold, rolled, with repoussé, moulded and etched details, and revealing long-distance contacts between Pacific coast and tropical rainforest.

Above: The Sipán Lord 'royal' Moche tombs, among the few unlooted ancient Andean elite burials, produced prodigious amounts of gold and copper metalwork.

and gold bead bracelets. He holds gold and copper ingots and a gold rattle sceptre of war victims. Several gold and silver crescent-shaped bells depict the Decapitator.

OWL PRIEST

Tomb 2 contained the Owl Priest, wearing a gilded-copper headdress decorated with an owl with outspread wings, and a gilded-copper double necklace. Each strand comprised nine grimacing faces, the upper group with up-turned mouths, the lower group with down-turned mouths.

THE OLD LORD

Tomb 3 contained the body of the Old Lord of Sipán, buried 200 years earlier. He was buried with gold and silver sceptres and six necklaces (three gold and three silver). One of these was a necklace of 10 round gold beads depicting spiders perched on webs, a human face adorning each spider body. The delicate legs, webs, bodies and bead backing each required more than 100 solder points.

The Old Lord wore a gold nosepiece, and four gold and silver earspools. A miniature gold warrior (only centimetres/inches tall) holds a war club and round shield. His tiny nose-crescent moves, his turquoise eyes have tiny black stone pupils, and he wears a square-beaded turquoise necklace, turquoise earspools and a proportionately enormous thin, sheet-gold headdress of flaring bands and gold discs that dangle, plus a central owl.

Beneath the funerary mask of the Old Lord excavators found the astounding 'Ulluchu Man', at nearly 60cm (2ft) tall the opposite of the miniature warrior masterpiece. The sheet-metal figure was originally fixed to a textile banner, itself covered with gilded metal platelets and on which were found samples of ulluchu (papaya-like) fruit.

He is a human crab of gilded copper, with inlaid shell ornaments as eyes and on his abdomen and crab legs. He has a human face and legs, plus large, upheld

Below: A Moche moulded sheet-gold and gold and turquoise bead necklace worthy of a princess, probably representing the creator god Viracocha, or the founder Lord Naymlap.

crab claws and six crab legs. His headdress has curled ends and an owl face, plus a crescent *tumi*-knife-bladed top. He wears a necklace of round-eyed owl heads. Such imagery is associated with war prisoners and sacrifice, and the fruit may have contributed anticoagulant properties to the goblets of blood drunk in the Sacrifice and Presentation ceremony.

LOOTED TREASURES
Many more Moche gold, silver and alloy objects have been recovered. Sadly, most are known only out of context and identified as Moche by their style. For example, from the looted tombs of Loma

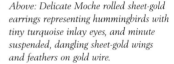

Above: Delicate Moche rolled sheet-gold earrings representing hummingbirds with tiny turquoise inlay eyes, and minute suspended, dangling sheet-gold wings and feathers on gold wire.

Negra in the Piura Valley come 14 hammered gold and silver nosepieces, pectorals and textile adornments. One is a simple, plain crescent. Others depict a face wearing a flaring crown; rows of crawling spiders; a row of seabirds; a double-headed, braided snake; facing crayfish; facing iguanas; the Decapitator holding a *tumi* knife and a severed head by the hair; a row of snails; and a row of alternating snake heads and human skulls.

Such rich finds display the gamut of Moche imagery: human sacrifice and religious ceremony, closeness to the sea, and long-distant trade (for the inlaid stones).

A fine example of the continuing illegal trade in precious antiquities is the recovery in London in 2006 of a large sheet-gold mask of the Moche Decapitator, presumed to have been looted 20 years ago from a tomb. The god's grimacing, fanged face is surrounded by curling head rays, intricately cut out with triangular, denticulate edges and ending in stylized, round-eyed creatures – the very image of the Decapitator so vividly depicted on the walls of Moche Huaca de la Luna in the Lambayeque Valley.

SICÁN LORDS AND METALSMITHS

The succeeding Sicán culture of the late Middle Horizon and first half of the Late Intermediate Period in the Lambayeque Valley has produced equally rich burials at Batán Grande. One grave of a lesser individual had more than 100kg (220lb) of copper alloy objects; richer graves held hundreds of gold and silver ornaments and vessels. Analyses of more than 1,000 artefacts has shown them to be 12- to 18-carat gold-silver-copper alloy – about the same as much gold jewellery made today. Other pieces, and most of the waste scrap metal, are tumbaga – a gold-silver-copper alloy of less than 10 carats.

MORE LOOTED TREASURES
Sadly, between the 1930s and 1970s the Lambayeque and adjacent valleys of the now Poma National Historical Sanctuary were desecrated by looters. Generations of *huaqueros* excavated more than

Below: An elite Sicán burial skull adorned with a cloth headdress topped with feathers and rows of attached gold discs.

100,000 pits, seeking ancient tombs and their precious artefacts to satisfy the demands of greedy collectors. Thousands of objects have been purchased and thus saved by museums for the enjoyment of all, but the evidence of their cultural contexts has been destroyed.

TREASURE IN THE TOMB
The Sicán Lord in Tomb I in the Huaca Loro temple mound, dated *c*.1000AD, contained a man about 40–50 years old, entombed seated, his body inverted, and his head turned 180 degrees to be right-side up. He wore a gold mask (46 × 29cm/*c*.18 × 12in) and his body was painted deep red with cinnabar (mercuric sulphide), possibly to represent blood. His burial was accompanied by the sacrifices of two women and two children.

His *c*.9sq m (96sq ft) grave at the bottom of an 11m (36ft) shaft contained 1.2 tons (tonnes) of gold, silver and alloy objects arranged around him and in caches and containers.

His cloth mantle (now decayed away), placed beneath his body, was sewn with nearly 2,000 gold foil squares. Objects immediately around or on him included a wooden staff with gold decoration, a gold *tumi* knife, a gold headdress, gold

Above: An elite necklace of rolled and moulded sheet gold and moulded gold beads representing a Sicán Lord or possibly Viracocha the creator god.

shin covers, some tumbaga gloves measuring 2m (6½ft) long, (one grasping a gold *kero* cup with a silver rattle base), and gold earspools. He was covered in a thick layer of stone, amber, shell and metal beads. Near by were *c*.500kg (*c*.1,100lb) of tumbaga scraps and *c*.250kg (*c*.550lb) of copper-arsenic tools.

There were caches of objects in niches dug into the tomb walls. A box lined with woven mats contained 60 objects, including 5 gold and silver crowns, 4 headbands, 12 *tumi*-knife-shaped head pieces, 6 head ornaments set with delicate gold feathers, three 3 fans, 14 discs (staff attachments or headdress backings), and 4 parabolic headpiece attachments.

One niche contained 1,500 bundles of small, uniformly sized *naipes* (copper-arsenic I-shaped bars – each bundle containing 12 or 13 pieces), which were possibly a form of 'currency'. Also two silver-alloy *tumi* knives, thousands of gold foil squares and up to 24 tumbaga miniature masks identical to the one worn by the lord.

A LORDLY VISAGE

One tall head ornament comprised a gilded copper mask, painted red, and decorated with the face of the Sicán Lord, including inset precious stones. The forehead panel features a protruding vampire bat face and the tall crescent above it has etched geometric shapes, bulbous gold discs and an array of delicate golden feathers. There were several other similar pieces, the masks painted green or white.

The Sicán Lord image occurs on hundreds of objects, as a full figure or head only. He has a definitive half-circle face (the upper circle half being a crescent headdress) and eyes shaped like horizontal commas. His full figure often holds staffs. One Sicán grave contained more than 200 gold beakers with his image.

THE SICÁN METAL INDUSTRY

These objects come from the workshops of specialists. The placement even of the leftover scraps and inferior objects in tombs reveals their value, and emphasizes the prestige of the elite occupant.

Right: A Lambayeque-Sicán ceremonial bronze tumi *knife, topped with the delicate gold figure of a Sicán Lord or the Decapitator God, wearing a sun-flare or wave motif headdress.*

Batán Grande included mounds (the north platform of Huaca Loro and the north-east platform of Huaca Las Ventanas) supporting complexes of multi-roomed adobe buildings. They have split-level floors and integral adobe benches along their walls. In them excavators found copper slag and droplets of copper alloys from melting metal ore in bowl furnaces, no doubt using the locally abundant algarrobo (carob) trees as charcoal fuel.

Sicán-Lambayeque metalsmiths also ushered in the 'bronze age' of northern Peru. While gold-alloyed pieces advertise the social prestige of the owner, Sicán discovery and extensive use of arsenical-copper for making bronze enabled them to make sturdier blades and tools, the use of which was perpetuated by the Chimú and Incas after them.

Moreover, objects found in the Sicán Lord's caches reveal the existence of sophisticated metalworking training. Some of these pieces are of inferior quality and workmanship, as if made by lesser-skilled smiths or as practice pieces. The various stages of preparing the alloys, making the sheet metal, inscribing designs and cutting them out, and the artistry of forming and bonding the sheets, and producing

Left: Continuing the Moche tradition of fine sheet-gold work, Lambayeque-Sicán metalsmiths applied their skills to utilitarian objects such as this embossed copper-gold alloy kero *drinking cup, probably used for rituals.*

repoussé decorations and fine finishing, could be designated to apprentices and more skilled craftsmen as the work proceeded. For example, one gold cup with a Sicán Lord face has a raggedly chiselled chin, its silver base is pitted and traces of silver on the cup indicate that the silver was overheated and melted during bonding.

CHIMÚ AND INCA METALWORK

The spectacular Sipán and Batán Grande finds help to place ancient Andean metalwork into context and reveal details of metalworking techniques and 'industrial' output. Elite members of society, in control of the redistribution of wealth, dominated production and use. Spanish chronicles record thriving metallurgical industries in the Late Intermediate Kingdom of Chimú and among the Incas. The Incas forcibly resettled whole communities of metalsmiths in Cuzco to produce thousands of gold and silver objects in dedicated workshops.

MOCHE–SICÁN INHERITANCE
The Chimú subsumed and continued Sicán-Lambayeque smithing traditions, and much of their production is almost indistinguishable. They continued the Lambayeque introduction of making metal copies of ceramic shapes, particularly stirrup-spout bottles. Moche-Lambayeque fine metalwork traditions are exemplified by a Chimú silver stirrup-spout bottle and a pair of golden earspools, both with delicate repoussé decoration.

Below: A fine Chimú rolled sheet-gold, cone-shaped and turquoise bead necklace with gold face bead.

The Chimú silver stirrup-spout bottle is a miniature *audiencia* compound, part of a Chan Chan *ciudadela*. The curiously shaped piece is more like a sealed box surmounted by a stirrup spout. Intricately folded tiny sheet-silver figures decorate the bevelled ends of the bottle: an important official sits in a niche, while attendants stand at the vessel's corners. The flat sides and lower ends are decorated in repoussé, showing designs almost identical to those on the mud-sculpted walls of Chan Chan *ciudadelas*.

The surfaces of the pair of gold-silver Chimú earspools are covered in a story-like vignette in repoussé. At the tops are curious balconied structures, each surmounted by two tiny birds. Below the structure, a crinkled surface represents the sea, within which floats a rectangular raft. Two men on the raft stand back to back and bend over to receive spiny oyster shells from divers. Other divers collect more shells from the seabed. This charming picture must have made these earspools the pride and joy of some Chimú lord or lady!

INCA METALWORKING
Central highland cultures also had long-standing metalworking traditions. Some of the earliest copper working is from the Altiplano. Tiwanaku and Wari metalworkers produced distinctive styles in sheet metals, and their traditions were inherited by the Incas. Innovatively, Tiwanaku architects secured stone blocks with bronze staple-shaped clamps.

Two superlative examples exemplify Middle Horizon metallurgy. A Tiwanaku plaque of hammered sheet gold depicts a block-like face reminiscent of their stone sculptures. The hollowed eyes and mouth probably held stone insets. Fine incised lines around the face mimic the angular patterns of Tiwanaku textiles.

Above: This cast silver Inca male figurine represents an idealized Inca noble, identifiable by earlobes stretched from wearing ear discs. Note inlay gold bands on the hat, face and ankles, and inlay purple stone and orange-pink shell plaques.

A hammered sheet-silver Wari figure represents a warrior. The square-bodied, square-headed fighter wears a four-cornered hat, carries a shield and spear-thrower, and, like the Tiwanaku piece, is incised with fine lines representing his cloth tunic. He was one of a pair, the other being of gold, in characteristic Andean duality.

The great bulk of Inca gold and silver work was destroyed by the Spaniards. The chronicles report that they carried off and melted down 700 loads of gold sheathing from the Coricancha walls! The famous Cuzco garden of life-sized gold and silver plants and animals can only be imagined from remnant examples, such as a gold and silver maize stalk.

Other Inca gold and silver work has been found in provincial and mountaintop *capacocha* burials undiscovered by the Spaniards, such as votive llama figurines and cast-silver human figures. The Incas were fond of pairs of figures in gold and silver. Fortunately, many such figurines have survived, depicting males and females typically holding their hands to their breasts.

Below: Chimú lords, kings and priests used rolled and beaten sheet-gold gauntlets such as these, intricately decorated with embossed patterns and figures of lords or gods, probably in rituals and/or burials.

THE FIRST LOOTERS

Although the Incas honoured the Chan Chan *ciudadela* burial compounds of the Chimú dynasty, after the Spanish Conquest, they were systematically looted by the Spaniards, whose Castilian king established a royal smelter in the Moche valley to insure receipt of the crown's 20 per cent tax.

And there is the sad story of Atahualpa's ransom. Imprisoned in a palace room after his capture by Pizarro, Atahualpa realized that Spanish regard for gold and silver was different from Inca perceptions. He offered to fill his 5 × 6.75m (17 × 22ft) prison room with gold as high as he could reach. Pizarro, exploiting his advantage, also demanded that an adjoining small room be filled twice with silver. Atahualpa agreed, asked for two months for the task, and ordered the collection of gold and silver objects from all over the empire.

This singular episode highlights the different Andean and European perceptions of wealth. As religious symbols, Andean

Above: In conspicuous displays of wealth and power, Chimú and Inca nobles wore ceremonial tunics of fine alpaca wool with thousands of sheet-gold plaques or discs sewn onto them. This Inca example from southern Peru probably formed part of a mummy bundle.

gold and silver represented the essence of the sun and moon, but individual objects could be replaced. Their importance lay in the prestige they brought and in the imagery of the gods they displayed. Spanish interest was purely monetary. They cared neither for the artistry nor for any religious value the pieces held. In Spanish eyes, Inca gold and silver meant wealth and the destruction of idolatrous images.

This sad legacy continues. The unlooted tombs at Sipán and Batán Grande are rare examples of ancient Andean conspicuous consumption of precious metals in their social and ritual contexts.

CARVING AND BUILDING IN WOOD

Wood is rarely preserved in archaeological sites, except under special conditions. Enough has survived from Andean sites, however, to show that it was used in a variety of ways.

PRECERAMIC AND INITIAL PERIOD USES
Early migrants into the New World used wood for spear shafts and *atl-atl* spear-throwers (for big game), and throwing sticks (for small game), and also for stone-tool handles, digging sticks, mortars and fire drills, and for butchering, food collecting and processing.

Below: An Inca wooden coca snuff scoop, with a hand-forearm handle holding a disc scoop intricately carved with mythological figures, presumably representing drug-induced transformation.

Wooden earplugs are known from Preceramic sites. Burial offerings at the Initial Period coastal site of Ancón included a wooden bowl containing feathers, set beneath the head, and a tropical forest *chonta* wood figurine with inlaid shell eyes and articulated arms from a female burial. At Moxeke, a wooden figurine was found in one of the Huaca A platform rooms.

SNUFF TABLETS AND *KEROS*
Tiwanaku and Wari shamans used flat wooden snuff tablets for preparing coca and other hallucinogenic substances. Carved and highly polished, their handles depict animals, beast-headed men and geometric designs, inlaid with stone ornament. Other portable wooden artefacts depicted the Staff Deity.

Elaborately carved wooden *kero* drinking cups were a Middle Horizon speciality, continued by the Incas and into Spanish Colonial times. Many are painted. One carved Tiwanaku example depicts the Staff Deity dressed almost identically to the central figure on the Gateway of the Sun at the Kalasasaya compound.

An exquisite Chimú wooden *kero* comprises a cup, painted with a simple red and black design and black rim, on top of which was a carved figure inlaid with gold, turquoise and shell, standing on a mushroom-shaped pedestal. The grinning figure has a row of rectangular shell teeth, round, red shell eyes and a pillbox hat with shell-inlaid earflaps, and holds a golden cross at chest height.

WOODEN LITTERS
The celebrated Lambayeque-Chimú ceremonial litter is an elaborate frame sheathed with sheet gold. Six main panels and two smaller ones represent small 'houses'. The main houses have central doorways, sloping roofs and dangling gold crescent-shaped eave decorations. Inside stand three Sicán Lord warriors, with characteristic horizontal-comma eyes.

Above: A carved wooden post showing a stylized face, probably part of a thatched roof support, demonstrates Inca carving skill.

Single figures stand in the end houses and between the upper row of houses. Holes indicate that the litter was originally studded with feathers. Such a rich item must have transported a ruler.

The frame of a carved wooden litter was also found in the Lord Sicán tomb at Batán Grande.

IDOLS AND COFFINS
A small, windowless temple atop the main platform at the pilgrimage city of Pachacamac housed a carved wooden idol. It was kept behind a veil, and only priests were allowed to ascend the platform and enter the temple. The figure was carved with human faces on both sides, to represent duality. This idol was destroyed by Hernando Pizarro, whereupon the oracle 'fell silent', but several similar figures, presumed from Pachacamac, are in museums.

Above: Kero *drinking cups were for everyday use and for ritual drinking. Made of wood, pottery and precious metals, this Inca wooden example, depicting an Inca warrior, was probably used by a noble.*

The entryways of Chimú royal *ciudadelas* at Chan Chan were guarded by carved wooden figures standing in niches.

The Chachapoyas stood a row of upright wooden coffins on a rocky ledge at Karajia, on the north-western Inca tropical mountain borders. The 'heads' are carved with full, round beards and wear cylindrical hats, some with human skulls on top. The bodies are painted as clothing. At Los Pinchudos, they built round burial structures with stone mosaic exteriors, above which they placed rows of wooden, highly phallic male figures.

The Moche Sipán Lord was laid to rest on a wooden-slat support and placed in a wooden plank coffin, sewn with cords.

WOOD IN ARCHITECTURE

Rafters of wood supported the thatch roofs of stone and adobe walls. Highland and tropical wood was imported to coastal and desert areas for this purpose, and many adobe walls have insets for beams (for example at Sipán).

Wood began to be imported in the late Preceramic Period. Wooden thresholds at coastal Río Seco are made from trees that grow at 1,450–3,000m (4,785–10,000ft). The importance of these exchange links is revealed by the fact that neither wood nor highland obsidian was essential in the coastal economy, yet they were sought in preference to local materials. At Initial Period Garagay, wooden posts set into lined circular pits supported the roof of the Middle Temple.

The Chimú used wooden moulds to decorate their Late Intermediate Period mud walls.

COMMON TOOLS

A number of Late Intermediate Period Chancay wooden burial masks were found in non-elite graves. With basic features, shell inlays for eyes and often painted red, they appear to be a widespread extension of ancestor cults among citizens.

The Ica-Chincha and other central Peruvian coastal peoples made long, paddle-like objects with delicately carved openwork on the paddle top and along the shaft. One example has a row of long-beaked seabirds and a larger seabird on top of the shaft 'pommel'. Such artefacts are variously identified as ceremonial digging sticks, boat paddles or raft-steering paddles.

Balsa-wood rafts were the standard coastal trading vessels, such as the raft encountered by Pizarro's captain, Bartholomew Ruíz, in 1527 on his second voyage down the north-west South American coast. Laden with Inca gold and silver objects and textiles, the traders were from the Inca port of Tumbes.

Wood was essential in textile weaving for weaving tools and parts. Spindle whorls were ceramic or wood. Backstrap looms required wooden warp beams, shed sticks, heddle rods, bobbins and beating paddles.

Humblest of all, farmers' digging and planting sticks, and handles for agricultural implements, were essential items in planting, tending and harvesting the produce of villages, towns, city-states, kingdoms and empires throughout ancient Andean history.

Below: One of the finest surviving pieces of ancient Andean woodwork is this Lambayeque-Chimú royal litter or palanquin.

STONE, SHELL AND BONE

Ancient Andeans used semi-precious stones, bone and shell for small items of jewellery, on their own or as inlaid work.

OBSIDIAN
The earliest Andean hunter-gatherers used local stone for tools. Obsidian (natural volcanic glass), only available from specific highland locations, soon became preferred and was imported by coastal fishing and farming villages from Preceramic times.

TURQUOISE AND LAPIS LAZULI
Sources of turquoise and lapis lazuli (lazurite) were also rare – turquoise coming from the highlands, lapis lazuli

Below: A Chimú wooden bowl, with inlaid mother-of-pearl, turquoise and spondylus shell representing a wide-eyed sun-god-like face-skull.

from northern Chile. Tiny lapis lazuli beads were found in the hand of the highland Waywaka burial, which also contained the earliest gold foil, *c.*1500BC. Cupisnique burials include shell, turquoise, lapis lazuli and quartz crystal necklaces, and Chavín craftsmen also used exotic stones.

Moche jewellers used stone appliqué extensively, especially finely shaped turquoise chips. Sicán-Lambayeque craftsmen introduced techniques of inlaying shaped and polished turquoise and shell in gold and silver work, and in wood.

One of three gold and turquoise earspools in the Moche Sipán Lord's tomb depicts the lord himself, with two attendants flanking him. All three figures wear headdresses made up of minute turquoise chips. Another earspool has a running

Above: A shell container for lime, used with coca-leaf chewing, whose shape the artisan used to form into a stylized bird, from the Capuli culture of Ecuador.

deer made of shaped turquoise chips and tiny dark stone cloven hoofs, within a gold-bead and turquoise-chip circle.

Wari and Tiwanaku royalty imported turquoise, lapis lazuli, chrysacola minerals and greenstones from distant sources. An elaborate wooden Tiwanaku *kero* cup comprises a cup and 'stem' in the shape of a figure holding a gold cross. His clothing has numerous shell and gold inlays and a turquoise stone in the middle of the headdress. Forty intricately carved, 25mm (1in) figurines of tiny stone and shell chips and gold foil were found at Wari Pikillacta.

The body of the Sicán Lord at Batán Grande was covered in a 10cm- (4in-) thick layer of amber, shell, gold and silver alloy and stone beads (sodalite, amethyst, quartz crystal, turquoise, fluorite and calcite).

Emeralds were imported from Colombia. They were inlaid in Sicán-Lambayeque, Chimú and Inca jewellery.

Quartz crystals were especially coveted by shamans for ritual divinations.

SHELL
Jewellery was made from Preceramic times, mostly as shell necklaces. Shells were abundant at Preceramic coastal villages, and they were exchanged for wood and obsidian with people in the highland regions.

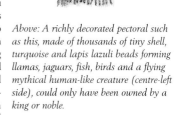

Strombus (conch) and spondylus (thorny oyster; *Spondylus princeps*) shells were especially sought. Shell trumpets were used in religious ritual. One sculptured figure in Chavín de Huántar's circular sunken court, for example, blows a conch trumpet. The dynastic founder Naymlap's royal entourage included Fonga Sigde, 'Blower of the Shell Trumpet', and Pitz Zofi 'Preparer of the Way', who ground and spread shell dust before his ruler.

Spondylus shells were particularly prestigious. They are found only in the warmer waters off the Ecuadorian coast and farther north, and therefore are exotic imports. Preceramic and Initial Period coastal

Below: These five finely carved bone figurines of the Early Intermediate Period Narrio culture of Ecuador might have had shell or stone inlay eyes and were probably temple pieces, possibly fertility figurines.

peoples imported them, and Cupisnique people made thousands of shell beads and pendants from local shells and spondylus. They sewed shells to their garments and even made bead skirts.

In the Early Horizon, as well as at Chavín de Huántar and other highland sites, spondylus shells were traded as far south as Paracas in southern coastal Peru. Elite individuals in rich mummy bundle burials wear necklaces of tubular and spondylus shells, thus declaring their high social status.

Sicán-Lambayeque lords and Chimú kings imported thousands of spondylus shells for their craftsmen to shape into jewellery and inlay in gold objects. Fonga Sigde was responsible for importing spondylus shells to Naymlap's court and may have worn earplugs such as the gold pair depicting divers collecting spondylus shells and handing them to men on rafts. Thorny oysters are even depicted and sculpted on Chimú ceramics and sculpted mud walls.

A particularly fine Chimú spondylus shell piece exemplifies the quality of their craftsmanship. Having removed the spines and smoothed the edge of an orange spondylus, the jeweller inlaid dark purple *Spondylus calcifer* into the top portion, to frame two exquisite, darker orange *S. princeps* birds and diamonds. Facing each other in characteristic, symbolic Andean duality, each bird pecks a fish, a typical Chimú motif. The birds and fish have tiny inlaid turquoise eyes, and the whole is highly finished to a uniform smoothness.

Inca craftsmen (or Chimú craftsmen resettled in Cuzco) also worked spondylus. For example, an especially fine necklace of 13 rectangular spondylus plaques was found on the Inca *capacocha* burial of a boy at Llullaillaco. Chachapoyas people included spondylus shell offerings in their round, stone mosaic burial structures.

Above: A richly decorated pectoral such as this, made of thousands of tiny shell, turquoise and lapis lazuli beads forming llamas, jaguars, fish, birds and a flying mythical human-like creature (centre-left side), could only have been owned by a king or noble.

CARVING IN BONE

Bone was also carved from early times. There are bone pins inlaid with turquoise from La Galgada burials, and an amber pendant. Four bone figurines with round staring eyes were found at Cerro Narrio in southern Ecuador.

Carved Chavín pieces include a human finger bone with incised bird motifs, found in the gallery above the Lanzón Stela, a hallucinogenic snuff spatula incised with a snarling feline motif (with traces of red paint) and two carved objects from Shillacoto (rubbed with charcoal).

A pair of highly polished, naked whalebone figurines from a Nazca grave have square shell headdresses and painted eyes.

A Moche bone spatula is carved as a clenched fist and forearm, incised with intertwined figures and inlaid with turquoise chips.

Incas soldiers used skulls of enemy slain as gruesome victory cups from which to drink *chicha* beer!

FUNERARY ART

Ancient Andean production of ceramics, textiles, metal objects and metal, stone, shell and bone jewellery served multiple purposes. Andean 'art' was not produced for its own sake. Craftsmanship, artistry and aesthetic aspects were important, but the two primary purposes for its production were religious and economic.

POWER, CONTROL AND ARTISTRY
High-quality craftsmanship and artistry were important in producing sumptuary items, to enable individuals of high social status to advertise and emphasize their position. As with other aspects of Andean civilization, much was aimed at demonstrating power and control, and with impressing others with these issues. Much had to do with essence. Dressing in the most elaborate and exquisite garments, wearing the best jewellery and using the best-quality pottery were outward signs that the person wearing and using these items was also of superior quality.

Although the craftsmen and those people for whom the objects were produced cannot have been oblivious to the pure aesthetics of the pieces, they were striving to represent a mindset constantly influenced by religious considerations.

Below: Elite burial masks are thought to represent transformation of the deceased into a deity. This late Moche or Lambayeque gold example represents another 'transformation' and the concept of 'essence', as the gold bears traces of covering paint!

The social evolution of Andean civilization produced a class of citizens – royalty, nobility and religious leaders – whose purpose was to rule, administer the economy and intervene with the gods on the public's behalf. The entire worldview was governed by the need to maintain balance with divine powers for the welfare of humans and their life on Earth.

RELIGIOUS SYMBOLISM AND ECONOMIC BALANCE
Production of luxury items was to honour the deities and to provide for the redistribution of wealth, however unequally, within Andean society. The deposition of so much sumptuary production in royal and elite graves reveals that the value of the precious metals and other high-quality objects came not from their financial value, but

Above: The earliest funerary 'art' is represented in Chinchorros burials (northern Chile from c.6000BC), in which bodies were preserved with salt after removing the viscera and stuffing with straw, then shaped in clay and given facial features.

from their worth as demonstrations of power, control, rank and an ability to consume conspicuously. Placing such tremendous wealth in tombs effectively removed it from circulation among humans, but it enhanced the prestige of the tomb's occupant and secured favour from the gods.

Death in the ancient Andean world was only the end of one stage in a cycle of being. Entombment was not necessarily permanent. In many cultures, the mummies (Inca *mallquis*) were regularly 'worshipped', kept in accessible tombs, or in special caves or temples, and brought out on ritual occasions to be consulted,

Above: The burial of an Inca noble, possibly a southern lord, as the text is Aymara of the Titicaca region and the mummy is being placed in a stone chullpa *tower in which an earlier skeleton sits (depicted in Poma de Ayala's* Nueva Corónica, *c.1615).*

entertained and given food and drink. Nazca tombs and *chullpa* burial towers were kinship mausoleums regularly reopened for the deposit of descendants through generations.

The removal of luxury goods from circulation also perpetuated the need for their production and supported continued elite conspicuous consumption, and therefore royal, elite and religious control. The effect was to keep the economy active and healthy. The bulk of the population, engaged in agriculture, supported elite and religious leaders, and the craftspeople necessary to produce sumptuary goods. The exclusivity of Chimú royal compounds at Chan Chan and their massive storage rooms are exemplary in this regard.

The situation can be regarded as an unconscious perpetuation of the Andean cyclical worldview.

CONFIRMING CEREMONY

Funerary art brings together all forms of Andean craft production. Although much of what has been found in burials and tombs was probably worn and used in life, it was also ultimately made in preparation for burial. Religious symbolism was paramount, both in the subject matter portrayed on the objects and in its presentation in the tombs.

Confirmation of the religious rituals depicted on Moche murals, for example, has been found in the Sipán and other elite burials. The principal bodies were dressed in identical regalia to that worn by the priests and priestesses of Moche Sacrifice and Presentation ceremonies shown on walls and ceramics. Their attendants in the tombs were their retainers for the next state of being, and were sacrificial victims, part of Andean religious practice from the earliest Initial Period tombs at U-shaped ceremonial centres.

In Sicán-Lambayeque elite burials at Batán Grande one tomb contained 17 sacrificial victims. And the caches of copper *naipes* suggest both that Batán Grande was the centre for their production and that their value was not only an exchange mechanism in life.

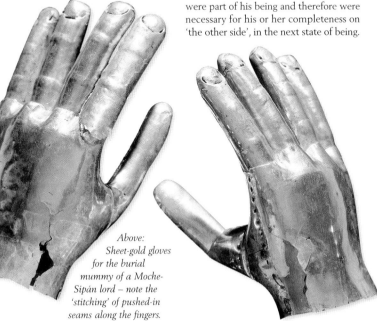

Above: Sheet-gold gloves for the burial mummy of a Moche-Sipán lord – note the 'stitching' of pushed-in seams along the fingers.

JUST FOR BURIAL

The preparation of items specifically for burial is suggested by Paracas and Nazca mummy bundles. Some of the textiles, whose intricate weaving and complex symbolism necessitated great labour over long time periods (sometimes perhaps even a lifetime), are unfinished. This indicates that the individual died before the item could be finished by the maker. Other possible explanations are that the items were being made expressly for the eventuality of burial with the deceased, but that it was also necessary to include them unfinished because they 'belonged' to that person in every sense. Alternatively, some items might have been deliberately left unfinished so that they could be completed by the individual in the next life.

The concept that a set of possessions was specific to an individual may also be the explanation of the deposition of inferior goods in the Sicán Lord's tomb. All items made for and possessed by that person were part of his being and therefore were necessary for his or her completeness on 'the other side', in the next state of being.

497

GLOSSARY AND FURTHER READING

aclla (or acllyacona) a chosen woman, selected to serve in the imperial cult of Inti
acllahuasi special compounds in which to house *acllas*
adobe mud brick
Altiplano high plateaus regions, especially in southern Andes
amaru mythical serpent-dragon figure
amautas Inca court officials responsible for memorizing Inca history and religion
'Andean Area' sierras and adjacent foothills and Pacific coastal valleys, east to the *montañas* of the eastern Andes and edge of the Amazonian Rainforest, north to south from the present-day Colombian–Ecuadorian border to the northern half of Chile
apacheta special type of *huaca* – a stone cairn at a mountain pass or crossroads
apo Inca official in charge of a *suyu*
apu type of *huaca* – sacred mountain deity
atl-atl spear-thrower used by hunter-gatherers and in warfare
Auca Runa people of the fourth age in Inca creation
audiencia miniature U-shaped temple, sacred compound in a *ciudadela* at Chan Chan
awasca Inca plain, coarser fabric, for ordinary wear
ayar legendary Inca ancestor
aylloscas Inca gambling game played by nobles
ayllu community bound in kinship both by blood and marriage, and with territory held in common
Aymara principal Inca language of the southern Andes
ayni Aymara term for *mit'a*

camelids New World descendants of Camedilae family. In the Andean Area these are the llama, guanaco, vicuña and alpaca
capacocha specially selected Inca sacrificial victim, usually noble, often a child
cayman South American freshwater alligator
ceque sacred pathway or sight line in Andean religion, especially from Inca Cuzco. Walked in religious ceremonies and by sacrificial victims
chachapuma puma-headed person/statuary
charqui strips of sun-dried and freeze-dried meat or fish
chasqui Inca imperial messenger/road runner
chicha beer made from fermented maize
chullpa Late Intermediate Period and Late Horizon stone burial towers
chuño the dried pulp left by repeatedly freeze-drying and thawing potatoes
ciudadela huge walled compound of ruling or dead Chimú king at Chan Chan
collcas Inca state storehouses for large quantities of such staples as *charqui* and *chuño*
collectivity Andean idea of corporate thinking:

people undertook activities as co-operative efforts, and considered the group more important than the individual, while the groups looked after the individual
coya official wife of the Inca emperor
curacas local leader or chief, or one of several levels of Inca officials
DWW discontinuous warp and weft
essence Andean concept, related to *transformation*, that the basic nature of an object and its appearance are more important than its actual substance. Applied in art to symbolism and decoration
geoglyph geometric shape or figure from the Nazca Desert and other Andean Area places
hanan upper: applied to one *moiety* of a lineage group (*ayllu*) and to a subdivision of a town or province
Hanan Pacha the Inca world of above
huaca sacred place: natural, man-made, or a modified natural feature
huaqueros in South American archaeology, tomb robbers, looters of archaeological sites; and the pits they left
hunter-gatherers people who live by hunting game, fishing, and gathering wild plants
hurin lower: applied to one *moiety* of a lineage group (*ayllu*) and to a subdivision of a town or province
Inti the sun god; also the Inca emperor
intihuatana 'hitching post of the sun' – Inca rock platform used as a sort of altar for sun observation and worship

Kai Pacha the Inca world of the living
kallanka large rectangular Inca hall used for public purposes
kancha walled enclosure of residential and storage buildings
kero Andean drinking cup, especially for drinking *chicha*
mallquis mummified remains of Inca rulers and nobility
mama female part of the Early Horizon Yaya-Mama cult around Lake Titicaca
manioc low-altitude tropical vegetable tuber
mashwa low-altitude Andean vegetable tuber
mit'a 'tax' obligation to do periodic labour for the state
mitimaes peoples redistributed within the Inca Empire
moiety half division of a lineage group (e.g. *ayllus*). The two intermarriageable family groups of a descent lineage
montaña the forested slopes of the eastern Andes
oca high-altitude Andean vegetable tuber
pacarina a place of origin, the place from which one's ancestors emerged
pachacuti turning over, revolution, a cycle of world events or states of being
pampas extensive temperate, upland grasslands in the south Andean Area
panacas Cuzco imperial *ayllus* comprising the descendants of each Inca emperor
plazas hundidas 'hidden' open courts, semi-subterranean
pukarás Late Intermediate and Late Horizon hilltop fortresses
puna Andean sierra basin or valley, a high, cold plateau
Purun Runa people of the third age in Inca creation

qompi Inca fine cloth for royal and religious use
Quechua principal Inca language of the central and northern Andes
quincha mud-plastered cane used in Andean house walls
quinoa high-protein grain
quipucamayoqs literally 'knot makers'. Inca court officials responsible for *quipus*
quipus Inca system of knotting wool and cotton strings to record basic economic and historical information
reciprocity Andean concept, linked to *collectivity*, of reciprocal trade over long distances and an acceptance of mutual obligations within social co-operation
Sapa the Inca emperor
selva see *montaña*
shaman ceremonial leader, healer or priest

sinchis warrior leaders of the Later Intermediate Period and Late Horizon who built hilltop fortifications called *pukarás*
stela carved stone ritual monument or statuary
suyu division of the Inca Empire, which comprised four *suyus*, or 'quarters', of unequal size
Tahuantinsuyu 'The four parts' – Inca name for their empire
tambos way-stations on Inca, Wari and Tiwanaku roads to accommodate officials, pilgrims and postal runners
tapia poured adobe or mud on stone foundations, which was carved after it dried
tarwi high-protein Andean grain
transformation Andean concept of alternative or even a procession of states of being.

Applied to humans in their life and death, to altered states and other worlds entered by shamans in drug-induced trance, to objects such as the creation of a textile from the cotton plant, in art as the transformation of imagery from one creature to another, and in religious processions enacting such transformations
tumbaga amalgamation of copper and gold (or sometimes silver)
tumi copper or bronze crescent-shaped knife used for ritual decapitation; ceremonial *tumis* were made of precious metals
tupu large copper pin used by Inca women to secure a mantle. Nobles used *tupus* of precious metals
Uku Pacha the Inca world of below

ulluco Highland vegetable tuber
U-shaped complex Andean and coastal western valley temples comprising a main end platform mound with subsidiary long platform mounds extending from its front corners to form a U shape enclosing a plaza
ushnu Inca stone platform in Cuzco and provincial capitals used for imperial observation and address
Wari Runa people of the second age in Inca creation
Wari Wiracocharuna people of the first age in Inca creation
yanacona selected Inca court retainer or servant
yaya male part of the Early Horizon Yaya-Mama Cult around Lake Titicaca
yuca high-altitude Andean vegetable tuber

FURTHER READING

Bowden, Garth, *The Moche* (Blackwell, Cambridge, MA and Oxford, 1999)
Bruhns, Karen Olson, *Ancient South America* (Cambridge University Press, Cambridge, 1994)
Burger, Richard L., *Chavín and the Origins of Andean Civilization* (Thames and Hudson, London, 1995)
Hemming, John, *The Conquest of the Incas* (Penguin Books, London, 1983)
Janusek, John Wayne, *Ancient Tiwanaku* (Cambridge University Press, 2008)
Jones, David M., *The Illustrated Encyclopedia of the Incas* (Lorenz Books, London, 2007)

Malpass, Michael A., *Daily Life in the Inca Empire* (Greenwood Press, Westport, CT and London, 1996)
Minelli, Laura Laurencich (ed.), *et al., The Inca World: the Development of Pre-Columbian Peru, A.D. 1000–1534* (translated by Andrew Ellis, James Bishop and Angelica Mercurio Ciampi, University of Oklahoma Press, Norman, 1999)
Moseley, Michael E., *The Incas and their Ancestors* (2nd edition, Thames and Hudson, London, 2001)

Quilter, Jeffrey, *Treasures of the Andes: the Glories of Inca and Pre-Columbian South America* (Duncan Baird, London, 2005)
Shimada, Izumi, *Pampa Grande and the Mochica Culture* (University of Texas Press, Austin, 1994)
Steele, Paul R., *Handbook of Inca Mythology* (ABC Clio, Santa Barbara, CA, 2004)
Stone-Miller, Rebecca, *Art of the Andes from Chavín to Inca* (2nd edition, Thames and Hudson, London, 2002)
von Hagen, Adriana, and Morris, Craig, *The Cities of the Ancient Andes* (Thames and Hudson, London, 1998)

Young-Sánchez, Margaret, *et al., Tiwanaku, Ancestors of the Inca* (Denver Art Museum, Denver and University of Nebraska Press, Lincoln and London, 2004)

INDEX

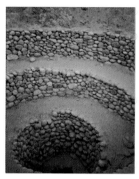

Pañamarca 262, 299, 379, 395, 409, 420, 476
Paracas 29, 89, 115, 143, 168, 170, 191, 203, 222, 225, 228, 229, 260, 262, 297, 368, 371, 379, 412, 418, 444, 495
  art 146, 187
  burials 232, 234, 262, 297, 318, 345, 359, 364, 406, 418, 444, 467, 468, 469, 474–5, 476, 478
  cemeteries 169, 187, 236
  ceramics 452, 454, 456, 457, 459
  culture 114, 186, 224, 234
  fabrics 239
  metalwork 339, 485
  mummies 88–9, 225, 234
  necropolis 90
  pottery 89
  textiles 297, 310, 311, 312, 338, 339, 359, 364, 418, 464, 466–9, 472, 474–5, 476, 478
Paracas Peninsula 88, 185, 222, 234
Paracas-Nazca Oculate 131
Paraíso Tradition 85
Paramonga 414, 415
Paria 37
Pariacaca 63
Pashash 458
pastoralism 72, 106
Paucarcollas 111
Paucartambos 248, 406
Piedra Parada 100–1, 148, 166, 293, 451
Pifos 111
Pikillacta 93, 94, 120–1, 262, 300, 301, 318, 341, 409, 413, 425, 478
Pikimachay Cave 80
pilgrimage 66, 135, 164, 297, 302, 316, 333, 344, 349, 373, 374, 376–7, 392, 405, 438
  burials 406
Pilillacta 16

Pinahua Capac 110, 209
Pisac 181, 199
Piura Valley 116
Pizarro, Francisco 20–1, 34, 42–3, 44–5, 96–7, 177, 242–3, 253, 263, 284, 286–7, 463
Pizarro, Hernando 43, 44–5, 196
place names 25
plants 25
platform mounds 102, 106, 148, 166, 185
platforms 135, 160, 170, 171
  pyramidal 93, 139
Plazas Hundidas Tradition 373, 376
Pleiades (collca) 77, 135, 221, 248
Poma de Ayala, Felipe Guaman 266–7
Ponce Stela 119, 204
Pongmassa 208
pottery 24, 84, 90
Preceramic Period 15, 82–3, 260, 261, 292–3
priesthood 171, 189, 226–7, 229, 230, 238–9, 262, 312, 313, 342, 344–5, 357, 359, 368, 370, 372, 376, 378, 379, 380, 392, 458, 474–5, 476
mit'a tax system 328

processional routes 70, 248
provinces 324
Pucamarca 411
Pucca Pukará 38
Puerto Hormiga 294, 450
Pukará 88-9, 118, 149, 164, 170, 192–3, 194, 229, 260, 262, 297, 344, 373, 377, 379, 405, 422, 437, 476
  ceramics 89, 228
  cult 89
  culture 89
  Decapitator 193, 229
Pumapunku 119
pumas 171, 280, 281, 370, 371
Puná 111
Punkurí 441
Puquina Pampa 221
Puruchuco 25
Pururaucas 62, 63, 238
Putuni 192, 410, 411
pyramid-platforms 295, 312, 369, 370, 390, 408–9

Q

Qenqo 62, 134, 147, 151, 263, 435
Qoyllur Rit'i 247–8
Quechua 285, 320, 353
Quecuamaran 24
Quilla 150, 174, 176, 181, 345

Quingan 116
quipu 22, 24, 25, 163, 266, 305, 353, 464
quipucamayoqs 22, 23, 124, 212, 215
quipus 124, 128
Quispihuanca 321, 387, 410
Quito 34, 39, 45, 111

R

Raimondi Stela 87, 109, 149, 151, 165, 184–5
rainfall 56, 59, 82, 107
raised platforms 154, 180
Raua 212
Real Alto 261, 378
reciprocity, concept of 138, 140, 142, 144, 158, 307, 310–11
record-keepers 73
Recuay 299, 445, 456–7, 459
redistribution of goods 73, 283, 285, 309, 321, 324, 328, 329, 351, 371, 403, 409, 472
religion 262, 283, 285, 301, 305, 312–19, 344–5, 367–81, 388, 394
  sacred sites see huacas
  and the state 348
  tripartite world 312
  see also ancestor worship; gods; pilgrimage; priesthood; sacrifice; shamans; temples

ACKNOWLEDGEMENTS

The Ancient Art and Architecture Collection: 5.5, 8bl, 12bl, 15tl, 15br, 41bl, 69bl, 851, 86bl, 94bl, 97bm, 115tl, 123tr, 157tr, 164bl, 165bl, 167tl, 195tr, 218-219, 220tr, 227bl, 223tr; /C.M. Dixon: 379b ; /Prisma: 267r; /J.Sparshatt: 297tl.

The Art Archive: 339t, 320b, 340t, 365t, 382–3, 408b, 409t, 441tl; /Album/J. Enrique Molina: 208, 223t, 228bl, 237tr, 339t, 320b, 340t, 365t, 382–3, 408b, 409t, 441tl; /Alcazar, Seville/Dagli Orti: 20tr, /Amano Museum, Lima/Album /J. Enrique Molina: 238bl, /Amano Museum, Lima/Dagli Orti: 5br, 149tm, /Amano Museum, Lima/Mireille Vautier: 145bl, 228tr, /Archaeological Museum, Lima/Album/J. Enrique Molina: 224bl, /Archaeological Museum, Lima/Dagli Orti: 29tm, 82, 88, 89tm, 130–1, 136bl, 140bl, 146bl, 146tr, 151bm, 158bl, 183tr, 183bm, 184, 192bl, 221br, 233, 234bl, 248tr, /Archaeological Museum, Lima/Mireille Vautier: 139bl, 163bl, 207tr, 238tr, 250bl, /Archbishops Palace Museum, Cuzco/ Mireille Vautier: 214tl, /Arteaga Collection, Peru/Mireille Vautier: 155br, 214br, /Biblioteca Nazionale Marciana, Venice/Dagli Orti: 43tl, /Bibliotheque des Arts Decoratifs, Paris/Dagli Orti: 242bl, /Stephanie Colasanti: 164tr, 169tr, 173t, 215tm, 215br, 243tl, 248bl, /Dagli Orti: 4.4, 4.5, 5.1, 16tr, 48tr, 64bl, 78–9, 84bl, 92, 98-9, 106bl,

109tr, 118bl, 132-3, 137bl, 138tr, 139tr, 148tr, 154, 166bl, 166br, 170bl, 170tr, 173br, 174bl, 175bl, 176tr, 180tr, 181t, 182bl, 194, 196bl, 197bl, 199t, 204tr, 217br, 224tr, 246tr, /Chavez Ballon Collection, Lima/Mireille Vautier: 198tr, /Gold Museum, Lima/Mireille Vautier: 189, /La Gringa Collection /Mireille Vautier: 141br, /Money Museum, Potosi, Bolivia/Mireille Vautier: 245tr, /Musee du Chateau de Versailles/Dagli Orti: 21tr, /Museo Banco de Guayaquil, Ecuador/Dagli Orti: 5.3, 178–9, /Museo Ciudad, Mexico/Dagli Orti: 26r, /Museo de Arte Colonial de Santa Catalina, Cuzco/Dagli Orti: 244, /Museo de Arte Municipal, Lima/Dagli Orti: 235, /Museo del Banco Central de Reserva, Lima/Dagli Orti: 239bl, /Museo del Oro, Lima/Dagli Orti: 117bm, 138bl, 141tr, 225, 231br, 232bl, /Museo Nacional de Historica, Lima/Mireille Vautier: 253tr, /Museo Nacional Tiahuanacu, La Paz, Bolivia/Dagli Orti: 14ml, 124tr, /Museo Pedro de Osma, Lima/Dagli Orti: 5.6, 240–1, /Museo Pedro de Osma, Lima/Mireille Vautier: 31tr, 39tr, 110tr, 212tr, 213bl, /Museo Regional de Ica, Peru/Dagli Orti: 187, /Museum Larco Herra, Lima/Album/J. Enrique Molina: 182tm, /Navy Historical Service, Vincennes, France /Dagli Orti: 16bl, /Science Academy, Lisbon/ Dagli Orti: 23, /University Museum, Cuzco/Mireille Vautier: 40tr, 125br, 162bl, 163tr, 180bl, /Mireille Vautier: 231tl, 242tr, 251bl.

The Bridgeman Art Library: /Collection of the New-York Historical Society: 361t. /Museo del Oro, Lima: 325r; /Private Collection: 6.4, 287br, 322–3.

Corbis: /© Brian A. Vikander: 7.1, 254–5, 384–5, 425b; /© Mike Theiss/National Geographic Society 10–11; /© Paolo Aguilar/ epa: 271t; /Academy of Natural Sciences of

Philadelphia: 281b; /Atlantide Phototravel: 395t; /Blaine Harrington III: 290t; /Charles and Josette Lenars: 436t and b; /Francesco Venturi: 449b; /Gian Berto Vanni: 349b; /Nathan Benn: 290bl; /Richard List: 437b; /The Gallery Collection: 348b; /Yann Arthus-Bertrand: 371t.

Andrew McLeod: 6br, 8tr, 15bl, 16tm, 17bm, 17br, 144tm, 165tr, 256bm, 257bm, 259tr, 269b, 263r, 398t, 410b, 430t, 435b, 504t, 504b, 511t, 512br, 512tl.

Sally Phillips: 9bl, 15bm, 16br, 106tr, 162tr, 464t, 500t, 502b, 503b, 509ll, 510bl.

Frances Reynolds: 7tr, 15tr, 16bl, 17tm, 17bl, 50tr, 51tl, 72tr, 111tr, 129br, 259br, 261m, 263m, 293t, 398bl, 399bl, 399br, 414b, 261l, 263l, 498, 505b, 506br, 507tr 511b.

Nick Saunders: 16bm, 17tl, 29tr, 39bl, 42bl, 62bl, 651bl, 66tr, 69tr, 74tr, 93tr, 121tl, 125t, 151tr, 160tr, 166tr, 168bl, 175tr, 177br, 190, 198bl, 202bl, 212bl, 226t, 229, 239tl, 491bl, 495.

South American Pictures: 21bl, 21bl, 22bl, 24bl, 35bl, 38tr, 40bl, 41tr, 42br, 44bl, 44tr, 45tr, 73tl, 76tr, 97tr, 111bl, 126bl, 128tr, 141tl, 196tr, 202tr, 203bl, 209bl, 223br, 230tr, 234tr, 237bl, 243br, 374t, 500bl, 507br, 508tl, 509tr, 510tm; /Ann Bailetti: 120tr; /Anna McVittie: 278t, 300tr, 368b, 424b;

ACKNOWLEDGEMENTS

/Archaeological Museum Lima/Gianni Dagli Orti: 472t; /Bill Leimbach: 474b; /Britt Dyer: 66bl, 270b, 334bl, 394bl, 397t, 440b; /Chris Sharp: 13br, 68tr, 81br, 103, 198t, 222tr & bl, 246t, 370b, 420br; /Danny Aeberhard: 57tr; /Gianni Dagli Orti: 427b; /Hilary Bradt: 77; /Jason P Howe: 252tr, 269; /Joseph Martin: 42tr; /Karen Ward: 59tr, 67tl; /Kathy Jarvis: 4.2, 4.3, 16tl, 28tr, 30–1, 37, 46–7, 48bl, 49tl, 60–1, 67br, 86tm, 86br, 87tl, 87br, 109bl, 143tr, 149br, 283t, 316t, 343b, 406, 407b, 411t, 429bl; /Kim Richardson: 294t, 424t, 493t, 493bl; /Kimball Morrison: 181br, 256b, 276br, 333t, 397b, 468b; /Luke Peters: 364t; /Marion Morrison: 64tr, 105br, 204bl; /Peter Ryley: 71bl; /Philippe Bowles: 63t, 431b; /Robert Francis: 52tr, 91bl, 95bm, 116tr, 260, 298b, 303b, 389t, 390b, 394t, 420bl, 421b, 427t, 442t; /Steve Harrison: 59bl; /Tony Morrison: 2, 4br, 4.1, 5.4, 6.1, 6.2, 7.2, 7.4, 12tr, 13tl, 18-19, 22tr, 27bl, 27tr, 28bl, 29bl, 32–3, 34bl, 34tr, 36bl, 36tr, 38bl, 45b, 50bl, 51br, 51tr, 52bl, 53bl, 53tr, 54tr, 55bl, 56bl, 56tr, 57bl, 58bl, 62tr, 63br, 65tr, 69bl, 70tr, 71tr, 75, 89bl, 89br, 90bl, 91tr, 93bl, 94tr, 95t, 96bl, 100, 102tr, 104tr, 105tl, 107br, 110b, 114tr, 115br, 117t, 118tr, 119br, 120bl, 121br, 122bl, 123bl, 127, 128bl, 134bl, 134tr, 135tr, 136tr, 142, 144b, 148bl, 150bl, 160bl, 161tl, 161br, 167br, 168tr, 169bl, 171tr, 171bl, 174tr, 177tl, 182br, 185b, 186bl, 188bl, 192tr, 195bl, 199bm, 200–1, 203tr, 205t, 206bl, 206tr, 207bl, 209tr, 210bl, 210tr, 211bl, 211tr, 216bl, 217tl, 220bl, 221tl, 226bm, 257b, 258tl, 259tl and tr, 266r, 268r, 271b, 272–3, 262l

and m, 274–5, 276bl, 277tl, tr and b, 278br, 280b, 281t, 288–9, 292b, 293b, 295b, 299t and b, 300tm and b, 301t and b, 302b, 304t, 305b, 308b, 311br, 317t, 318t, 319t and b, 321b, 331b, 332t and b, 337b, 340b, 3500t and b, 359t, 350t, 365b, 368t, 369t, 372t, 375b, 377t, 386b, 387t and b, 388b, 389b, 390t, 391b, 400–1, 402t, 404b, 405b, 410t, 411bl, 413b, 418t and b, 419t, 421t, 422b, 423t, 425t, 428t, 429tr, 430b, 434b, 438t and b, 439t, 441b, 445t, 446–7, 450tl, tr and b, 471tr and b, 474t, 478b, 479t, 487b, 488b, 489b, 492t &bl, 493br, 496tr, 497tr, 498bl, 499bl.

Werner Forman Archive: 14tr, 126tr, 137tr, 143tl; /Art Institute of Chicago: 355t; /British Museum, London: 24tr, 72bl, 116bl, 143br, 158tr, 338b, 464b; /Dallas Museum of Art, Dallas: 3, 7.5, 7.6, 90tr, 91tl, 135bl, 227tr, 462–3, 477t, 480–1, 491t, 496b; /David Bernstein Collection, New York: 4.6, 112–13, 114bl, 122tr, 140tr, 150r, 156tr, 186tr, 297b, 331t, 358t, 467, 475b, 483br, 484t, 494t; /Guggenheim Museum, New York: 58tr; /Maxwell Museum of Anthropology, Albuquerque, NM: 80bl, 81tl; /Museum fur Volkerkunde, Berlin: 25, 73br, 83tr, 104bl, 129tl, 157bl, 191bl, 193tl, 193br, 205bl, 222bl, 230bl, 236, 239br, 328t, 335b, 336b, 358b, 479b, 489t, 490t, 492b; /N.J. Saunders: 6.6, 264–5, 262r, 328b, 329t, 356b, 366–7, 374b, 376t, 377b, 378t, 403t, 404t, 408t, 417b, 419b, 420t, 422t, 423b, 428b, 443t, 470b, 486t; /National Museum of Denmark, Copenhagen: 304b; /Private Collection: 5.2, 83bl, 152–3, 157br, 159bl, 460b, 486b; /Rassiga Collection: 465t; /Royal Museum of Art & History, Brussels: 188tr.

p.1 Lambeyeque–Sicán gold burial mask. p.2 Winay Wayna. p.3 Moche effigy jar. 511t: Sacsayhuaman. 511b: Runkuaqay. Above: Machu Picchu. Below: Cuzco.

This edition is published by Lorenz Books an imprint of Anness Publishing Ltd Blaby Road, Wigston, Leicestershire LE18 4SE info@anness.com

www.lorenzbooks.com; ww.annesspublishing.com

Anness Publishing has a new picture agency outlet for images for publishing, promotions or advertising. Please visit our website www.practicalpictures.com for more information.

ETHICAL TRADING POLICY: Because of our ongoing ecological investment programme, you have the reassurance of knowing that a tree is being cultivated to replace the materials used to make the book you are holding. For further information, go to www.annesspublishing.com/trees

Publisher: Joanna Lorenz
Editor: Joy Wotton
Designer: Nigel Partridge
Illustrators: Vanessa Card, Anthony Duke and Rob Highton
Production Controller: Christine Ni

© Anness Publishing Ltd 2012

Previously published in two separate volume, *The Illustrated Encyclopedia of the Incas* and *The Inca World*

PUBLISHER'S NOTE: Although the information in this book is believed to be accurate at the time of going to press, neither the authors nor the publisher can accept any legal responsibility or liability for any errors or omissions that may be made.